Steel Centurions

Italian Armoured Formations of the Second World War 1940-43

Paolo Morisi

Helion & Company

Helion & Company Limited
Unit 8 Amherst Business Centre
Budbrooke Road
Warwick
CV34 5WE
England
Tel. 01926 499 619
Email: info@helion.co.uk
Website: www.helion.co.uk
Twitter: @helionbooks
Visit our blog at blog.helion.co.uk

Published by Helion & Company 2023
Designed and typeset by Mach 3 Solutions (www.mach3solutions.co.uk)
Cover designed by Paul Hewitt, Battlefield Design (www.battlefield-design.co.uk)

Text © Paolo Morisi 2023
Images © Ufficio Storico, Rome
Maps drawn by Paul Hewitt, Battlefield Design (www.battlefield-design.co.uk)
© Helion & Company Ltd 2023

Every reasonable effort has been made to trace copyright holders and to obtain their permission for the use of copyright material. The author and publisher apologize for any errors or omissions in this work and would be grateful if notified of any corrections that should be incorporated in future reprints or editions of this book.

ISBN 9-7-81911628-81-1

British Library Cataloguing-in-Publication Data.
A catalogue record for this book is available from the British Library.

All rights reserved. No part of this publication may be reproduced, stored in a retrieval system, or transmitted, in any form, or by any means, electronic, mechanical, photocopying, recording or otherwise, without the express written consent of Helion & Company Limited.

For details of other military history titles published by Helion & Company Limited contact the above address or visit our website: http://www.helion.co.uk.

We always welcome receipt of book proposals from prospective authors.

Contents

List of Photographs		iv
List of Maps		vii
Introduction		viii
1	Birth of the Italian Armoured Units and Their Development	14
2	Minor Armoured Campaign	78
3	North Africa	109
4	Further Advance	219
5	Gazala and Tobruk	224
6	El Alamein	265
7	Tunisia	337
8	Sicily	373
9	M Armoured Division and Ariete II	396
Conclusion		406

Appendices

I	Rommel Communication to Axis Troops after the Tobruk Battle of Early May 1941	422
II	Rommel Communication to Axis Troops on 21 January 1942	424
III	Italian Armoured Vehicle Production 1940-1945	425
IV	Medaglia d'oro Awarded to Armoured Officers and Men	426
V	American Assessments of Italian Weapons	429
Bibliography		433

List of Photographs

General Francesco Saverio Grazioli. The commander of the arditi army corps in the First World War. In the 1920s and 30s Grazioli became the main advocate of the progressives within the Italian Army who advocated for the formation of mechanized divisions.   i

General Ettore Bastico awards a medal of bravery to a *Giovane Fascista*. Born in Bologna, Bastico had the tough assignment during the North African campaign of tempering Rommel's desire to always go on the offensive as well resposibilities for supplying the frontline troops with weapons, fuel, water and food.   i

Victory parade at the end of the Spanish Civil War. The Italian trucks are towing 37/45 and 47/32 guns.   i

Fiat 2000 tank. This is the first tank designed in Italy immediately after the end of the First World War.   ii

Renault FT-17 tank in the service of the Italian Army.   ii

Blackshirts at a parade. These were volunteer units separate from the Royal Army. In 1943 these units would form an armored division equipped with German tanks and motorized artillery.   ii

Blackshirts at a parade.   iii

Fiat 3000 tank testing anti-tank defenses. The first Fiat 3000s were designated as the *carro d'assalto Fiat 3000*, Mod. 21 and their armament, consisted of two 6.5 mm machine guns. Later some tanks adopted a 37 mm gun as main armament.   iii

Fiat 3000 tank testing anti-tank defenses.   iii

Italian soldier and anti-tank defenses somewhere in Sicily.   iv

Breda 20/65 anti-aircraft gun mounted on SPA-38 truck. The Breda 20/65 was developed during the 1930s to be deployed as a dual-function weapon. It could be used both in an anti-aircraft role and against ground targets. It was similarly effective against lightly armoured vehicles such as trucks, armoured cars and light tanks. The *Breda's* ammunition could penetrate armour up to 30mm thick.   iv

Cannone da 75/32 being pulled by a light tractor TL-37.   iv

Bersaglieri strongpoint in North Africa. These were the elite infantry units of the Army in North Africa. Most units were motorized.   v

Italian M 13/40 tank testing anti-tank defenses.   v

M13/40 tank in Greece in 1941.   v

Carristi during the Greek campaign.   vi

47/32 gun manned by *Bersaglieri*. It was effective against armored vehicles and British Cruiser and Crusader tanks but it became obsolete, lacking firepower, when facing Lee, Grant and Sherman tanks in 1942. It had a particularly difficult time against Matilda II tanks during Operation Compass.   vi

Anti-aircraft position in North Africa.	vi
Autocannone da 90/53 abandoned in the desert. It proved an excellent anti-tank weapon thanks to the powerful 90 mm gun during the North African campaign. During the Allied landing on the shores of Sicily some *Autocannoni* da 90/53 on *Breda* 52 were used in the indirect fire role against Allied vessels.	vii
Howitzer 100/17 mounted on a *Lancia* 3-Ro. The weapon played a key role during Operation Crusader. It was originally designed by Skoda and several batteries were given to the Italians at the end of the First World War.	vii
Medium tank fighting in Greece.	viii
Carristi during the Greek campaign.	viii
Bersaglieri on the march in North Africa.	viii
Bersaglieri handling enemy soldiers. During the Second World War the *Bersaglieri* regiments were organized in armoured, motorized and fast divisions. They fought on all fronts, showing their capabilities and dedication. The Field Marshal Rommel, the Italian-German Army Commander in Northern Africa, is believed to have said: " the German soldier has astonished the world, the Italian Bersagliere soldier has astonished the German one…"	ix
Italian tank perforated by enemy shell.	ix
Captured *autocannone* da 102/35 captured by the British.	ix
M13/40 on the move.	x
Semovente da 75/18 a successful weapon introduced by the Italians in early 1942. It belonged to a family of Italians self-propelled guns based on the chassis of the Italian medium M13/40, M14/41, and later M15/42 tanks armed with a 75 mm Ansaldo cannon in the casemate. It is the most widely produced self-propelled gun in the Kingdom of Italy during the Second World War, capable of fighting against almost all opposing armored vehicles. It was used in various roles by the Regio Esercito for infantry support and as a tank destroyer.	x
Semoventi da 105/25 at Ansaldo factory in Genoa ready to be shipped out to the Army. More than 600 *semoventi* vehicles representing different models were produced in total by the Italian industry during the war. It was also appreciated by the Wehrmacht, which captured several of them and put them back into service in its armored divisions in 1943.	x
Prototype of *semovente* da 90/53 on a Breda 501. This was an early prototype built by Ansaldo with colaboration from Breda factories.	xi
M3 Lee tank captured by the Italians.	xi
Bottom:*Semovente* with extra protection. The use of more protection made the vehicle more impervious to enemy fire but it made it also slower. The vehicles main advantage point was its low silohuette but it was hampered by its underpowered engine.	xi
Giovani Fascisti at Bir el Gobi. These were volunteer units primarily comprised of university students. The photo depicts them in their slit trenches as an armored vehicle burns in front of their position.	xii
Italian armored unit on the move.	xii
Giovani Fascisti with anti-tank gun.	xii
Captured A15 Crusader.	xiii
Tank hunting training.	xiii
Semovente da 75/34 on the chassis of a M42.	xiv
Captured self-propelled gun.	xiv
Tank shooting practice.	xiv
Ariete parade in Tripoli.	xv

Semoventi training somewhere in Tunisia.	xv
British tank immobilized by the *medaglia d'Oro* Ippolito Nicolini at Bir el Gobi.	xv
Italian artillerymen with a German 88/56 gun battery in Egypt.	xvi
Bersaglieri strongpoint in North Africa.	xvi
Anti-tank hunters training.	xvi
Captured 25-pdr gun used by the Italians.	xvii
Arditi mortorized unit in Tunisia. These soldiers fough well at the Battle of Primosole in Sicily in July 1943. They used their armored vehicles to counter-attack the British near the important bridge.	xvii
Arditi mortorized unit in Tunisia.	xvii
Officers of the *Arditi* motorized units.	xviii
Officers of the *Arditi* motorized units.	xviii
Officers of the *Arditi* motorized units.	xix
Italian artillerymen with a German 88/56 gun battery in Egypt.	xix
Bottom:Italian anti-aircraft position in North Africa.	xix
Captured Pak-40 gun in Sicily.	xx
Giovani Fascisti position at Bir el Gobi.	xx
Skoda da 47 captured by the Americans in Sicily.	xx
Captured 6-pdr British gun.	xxi
Semovente da 47/32 in Tunisia. The *Semovente* L40 da 47/32 was developed by Ansaldo and built by FIAT between 1942 and 1944. It was designed to support assault infantry units of the *Regio Esercito* in the form of direct fire support from the *Cannone da* 47/32 *modello* 1935 medium support gun.	xxi
Italian *cannone* da 75/34 *modello* 97/38 in the defense of Sicily.	xxi
Batterie Volanti unit. In order to provide anti-tank support against the technically superior British armored forces, the availability of captured British vehicles from spring of 1941 on led to mount on them 20mm and 65mm guns.	xxii
Autoblinbo AB41. The AB41 was the standard reconnaissance armored car of the Royal Italian Army which used it with excellent results in the African Campaign, the Russian Front and the Balkans from mid-1941 to September 8th, 1943.	xxii
Blackshirt M division.	xxii
Italian officer during the defense of Sicily.	xxiii
Italian *cannone* da 75/34 *modello* 97/38 in the defense of Sicily.	xxiii
Italian artillery piece in Greece.	xxiv
Anti-aircraft crew in Greece.	xxiv
Renault R 35 knocked out in Sicily. These captured vehicles equipped a battalion of Italian armored personnel.	xxiv
Cannone da 75/34 *modello* 97 in the defense of Sicily.	xxv
Cannone da 105/25 in position in Sicily.	xxv
British officer inspectes Italian anti-aircraft position.	xxv
Autocannone da 75/27 modello 11. Along with the modello 6 this was the standard gun of the artillery regiments of the mechanized divisions during the war.	xxvi
Credits for all photos: Ufficio Storico in Rome.	xxvi

List of Maps

1 The Greek Campaign: Italian Plan of Attack, 28 October 1940.   89
2 The Battle of Bir el Gobi, 18–20 November 1941.   181
3 Kasserine Pass, February 1943.   348
4 The Battle of Gela, 10–11 July 1943.   383

Introduction

> Declaration of war. First I received Poncet, who tried not to betray his emotion. I told him, "you probably understood the reason for your being called." He answered with a fleeting smile. "Although I am not very intelligent I have understood this time." After having listened to the declaration of war, he replied, "it's a dagger blow to a man who has already fallen. I thank you nonetheless for using the velvet glove," he continued saying that he had foreseen all this for two years, and that he no longer hoped that he could avoid it after the signing of the Pact of Steel. He was not able to resign himself to considering me an enemy, nor could he consider any Italian. However, as for the future it was necessary to find some formula for European life, he hoped that an unbridgeable chasm could not be created between Italy and France.

So wrote Count Galeazzo Ciano, Italy's foreign minister for most of the Second World War, in his diary on the day, 10 June 1940, the fascist regime entered the conflict. The war began for Italy in a very slow and uneventful fashion. There were no immediate plans to take Malta or to launch an offensive in Africa as the Army found itself at war more for political rather than military reasons. At the time, with France on the brink of total collapse under the hammer blows of the German Panzer divisions, Italy's leader Mussolini and his military entourage believed that the war would last just a few weeks or at the most two months. It was expected that once the German forces had defeated the French army, Britain would sue for peace and Italy would reap the benefits of being on the winning side of the war.

Italy's declaration of war was thus based almost exclusively on a political calculus that the conflict would be brief and would require little expenditure of equipment and fuel. In fact, a few days prior to the declaration of war against France and Britain the Italian High Command (*Comando Supremo*) had informed Mussolini that the Army was bereft of major equipment and that according to long term procurement plans it could only be ready for war by mid-1943. Just to give an example, at the time Italy's armoured divisions were few (three) and under strength and most tanks units were equipped with light tanks that were largely obsolete by 1940 standards. Britain, Germany and France, for instance, by that time were already able to field armoured divisions primarily equipped with a combination of light and medium tanks and with truck mounted artillery guns. Some like the French and the British could even deploy infantry tanks that were more robust than the standard medium tank and were much more powerful than the Italian light tanks. The British Infantry Tank Mark II (known as the Matilda II), for instance, being a good example of a heavy armoured unit that was impervious to the clear majority of Italian anti-tank guns in 1940-41. In addition to better equipment the major powers could also field more armoured divisions and had greater stockpiles of fuel to allow the divisions to fight for prolonged periods of time. Italy was very dependent upon Germany for coal and fuel supply after the Munich Agreement of 1938 since the Allies had blocked access to key North African markets and the nation was a net importer of energy commodities. Thus, despite the nation being unprepared for a long war of attrition, Mussolini had nonetheless entered the war believing that it would be brief. But after France collapsed, Britain chose to stand fast and to carry on. Britain was then the target of a large-scale aerial bombing campaign by the *Luftwaffe* which ultimately led to a standstill and the cancellation of Operation Sealion, the seaborne invasion of Britain. The decision by Hitler not to invade Britain in 1940 represented a major shock to the Italians, which as a result of the cancellation or postponement of Operation Sealion, began to fear of a major concentration of British forces in North Africa. Britain was then attacked in a preemptive strike by the Italians in North Africa in September 1940, but after resisting the initial onslaught, the Commonwealth forces counter-attacked in December 1940-January 1941 and achieved a major success against the retreating Italian infantry units. After Britain fought off the German aerial onslaught, Hitler eventually, after briefly considering German participation to the naval war in the Mediterranean, opened a second front by invading the Soviet Union in June 1941. Because of this action the Axis was now forced to face a multi-front war much like what Germany and Austria-Hungary experienced during the First World War. Shortly thereafter, the United States also entered the war on the side of the Allies and the Axis nations were then forced to wage war against opponents such as the Soviet Union and the United States that could wield overwhelming economic and industrial power. In fact, the combined German and Italian economic power could never match the output, especially with regards to tanks and anti-tank units, of the Allies and thus their chances of winning the war by mid-1942 became smaller and smaller. Historian MacGregor Knox, for example, asserts that Germany's decision-making led to a slippery slope toward global war by the end of 1941 that "would have destroyed the Fascist regime of Italy regardless of their level of military or economic effectiveness."[1]

The history of Italy's armoured units is primarily one centered on industrial performance and output and technological advancement together with the quality of the manpower that was made available to them. These were the key determining factors, along with logistic and supply concerns, that undercut the Army's war effort and specifically its armoured arm in North Africa. One of the main factors that led to the defeat of the Axis forces was their weaker economic position versus the Allied powers, especially after 1941. The campaign in North Africa is a prime example of the lack of economic power necessary to wage a modern war. The combined German and Italian armoured divisions under the leadership of General Erwin Rommel, which never exceed a total force of five armoured or partially mechanized divisions at any one time, achieved some degree of successes in North Africa between 1941-42 often displaying cohesive armoured tactics. Even by 1943, when the Axis powers were about to be evicted from North Africa, their armoured units, which by then were all severely understrength, displayed again above average tactical maneuvers against the American infantry and armoured forces at the Battle of Kasserine Pass. By then Italy had also dispatched to North Africa its last remaining armoured division since all the others had been destroyed at the final battle of El Alamein. But even though the Axis still held a small tactical edge in armoured warfare, their armoured divisions were vastly

---

1   Macgregor Knox, *Hitler's Italian Allies* (Cambridge: Cambridge University Press, 2002), p. x.

outnumbered and the firepower and performance of their tanks (especially Italian tanks) was not keeping up with those of the Allies. Italy, for instance, still fought with the M.13/40 and M.14/41 medium tanks that were no match for the American Sherman or the British Valentine tanks, while newer, more effective equipment only came in small numbers. In addition, as the Allies armoured units overcame the Axis defenses at El Alamein first and on the Mareth Line in Tunisia later their confidence and morale grew pushing them on to final victory.

When the Axis Tunisian bridgehead capitulated in the spring of 1943 Italy lost all its armoured units and most motorized units and by then the Fascist regime began to tremble and by July of 1943 it collapsed paving the way for the Armistice of Cassibile and the final surrender. Before the armistice was signed the remnants of the Italian armoured units, mostly some hastily put together tactical mobile groups armed with *semoventi* self-propelled guns and captured French Renault R35 tanks, executed several counter-attacks to push back the Allied forces that had landed in Sicily. Most counters failed and resulted in the destruction of the few armoured reserves that Italy possessed. The last remaining armoured units, that at the time were still training, were the Blackshirt M Armoured Division which was equipped exclusively with German self-propelled guns, artillery pieces and tanks and the *Ariete II*. Because of the downfall of the regime and the armistice of 1943 the first unit was never deployed in battle. The other unit, also still being constituted in mid-1943, was undergoing training and was not fully equipped or combat ready when Italy surrendered.

This book aims to reconstruct the history of Italy's armoured units during the Second World War with a focus upon the North African campaign which was Italy's major theater of operation during the war and where it fielded its major armoured divisions. The book will first detail the development of Italy's armoured units during the pre-war period, including the evolution of the tactical and strategic thinking of the Italian Army as related to tanks and armoured vehicles. It will then detail Italian armoured weapons as related to its mechanized and motorized units, including the typical makeup of the standard Italian armoured division, its main weapons and its organization. This chapter will also compare the strength of the standard Italian armoured unit versus those of the Allies and of the Germans. The second chapter will focus upon the campaigns of the war that saw limited participation by Italy's armoured units such as those waged against France, Greece, East Africa, Yugoslavia and the Soviet Union. The third, fourth, fifth and sixth chapters will focus upon the North African campaign fought in Libya and Egypt, while the seventh chapter will focus upon the Tunisian campaign. The eight chapter will deal with the Battle for Sicily while the ninth chapter will focus upon the M armoured division, perhaps Italy's most advanced effort to develop a modern armoured formation during the Second World War.

The final chapter will provide an overall assessment of Italy's armoured units during the Second World War by analyzing their performance with regards to the concept of military effectiveness. The latter is a concept developed to capture, measure and compare how nations wage war. Specifically, its defined as a "process by which armed forces convert resources into fighting power. A fully effective military is one that derives maximum combat power from the resources physically and politically available. Effectiveness thus incorporates some notion of efficiency."[2] The concept can be readily applied to the North African campaign because it was a

---

2   Allan R. Millet, Williamson Murray and Kenneth H. Watman, 'The Effectiveness of Military Organizations' in Allan R. Millet and Williamson Murray (eds.), *Military Effectiveness*, vol 2, (Cambridge: Cambridge Univ. Press, 2020), pp. 1-30.

campaign that was dominated by machines at the expense of the number of infantry soldiers. A lean and well equipped war machine was much more vital than one that was more numerous but less well equipped and with low levels of motorization and mechanization. The North African campaign being a machine intensive conflict landed itself well to a war of movement where armies deployed resources to move forces and material quickly across large sections of territory. As Bastian Matteo Scianna asserts regarding the Second World War in general but that aptly applies specifically to the North African campaign: "One benchmark was arguably the ability to wage combined arms maneuver warfare (with artillery, armour and aircraft) on the divisional and corps levels. This included the capability to command, control, supply and maintain these forces in the field."[3] The Germans were particularly adept at waging this type of warfare having already implemented successful all arms offensives against Poland and France between 1939-40. The Commonwealth forces had prior to the start of the war gained valuable experience in training in desert environments, while they had not conducted large scale armoured offensives in such challenging conditions. The Italians had made the shift to mechanized warfare in 1938 but they too lacked experience moving large numbers of mechanized and motorized troops in the North African desert. There the climate was an issue but the overall logistics challenge of moving troops, material and equipment from Italy to North Africa to sustain the campaign and replenish losses was an even bigger problem. This analysis will thus focus upon the evolution of the combined arms concept as it relates to the Italian Army during the Second World War but specifically in relation to Italy's biggest wartime theater, the North African Libyan and Egyptian territories where it faced the Commonwealth units. Indicators of military effectiveness in the conduct of combined arms warfare will be considered throughout such as an army's tactics, its capabilities (including equipment and personnel) and its level of training. In addition other relevant factors such as leadership, military planning and innovation and lastly supply. To assess the performance of the Italian Army and specifically its armoured units during the war, we must first detail the current scholarly debate and review the relevant military literature surrounding Italy's performance during the war. MacGregor Knox's[4] study 'Hitler's Italian Allies' is not only one of the first scholarly works to examine Italian military effectiveness under Fascism, but it's a starting point for any serious evaluation of Italy's performance in the war. Knox concluded that substandard weapons, airplanes and armoured vehicles above all, was one of the factors that impinged upon Italian combat effectiveness but he also pointed to Italy's short-lived military history, and primarily its lack of an entrenched military culture and tradition, to explain its failings during the Second World War. Knox focused his evaluation of the Italian Army performance primarily on the first year of the war when Italy fought its parallel war in France, North Africa and in the Balkans and concluded that it's not too stellar performance was the result of a weak organization whose senior and middle level officers were conservative, poorly trained and unable to implement combined arms tactics. His focus was thus on substandard equipment but also on poor planning and equally poor execution of war plans by the Italian military hierarchy. Although Knox's work was pioneering it has received criticism. A first set of critics has focused on Knox's time bound analysis between 1940-41 when the Italian Army was still ramping up production for the war, while he neglected, they argue, to deeply evaluate the 1942-43 period

---

3   Bastian Matteo Scianna, *The Italian War on the Eastern Front 1941-1943* (London: Palgrave, 2019), p. 17.
4   Macgregor Knox, *Hitler's Italian Allies* (Cambridge: Cambridge University Press, 2002).

when the Army improved its performance markedly. A second set of critics has focused upon Knox's almost exclusive focus on military culture to explain military performance and effectiveness. They list other factors such as economic power, size of the manufacturing sector and other economic and political variables as being more important than military culture in explaining the pitfalls of the Italian Army during the first year of the war. Despite the critics, Knox's analysis has been pervasive in the military literature and it has influenced several scholars that have written extensively on the Italian Army.[5]

One of the first military scholars whose work has taken a different view from Knox's analysis of the Italian Army is John Gooch, who in the introduction to a classic study on military strategy and tactics titled 'Decisive Campaigns of the Second World War' writes with regards to the North African campaign that "The denigration of the Italian performance owes some of its virulence to Rommel, who was not above claiming for the Afrika Korps victories which had been in fact won by his ally." Further, he adds that the section of the book written by Lucio Ceva and dedicated to the North African campaign sheds a new light on the Axis effort and that "the careful study of the organizational aspects of the campaign and his evidence of the improvement of the fighting quality of the Italian troops by the end of 1941 will do much to redress this balance."[6] Referring to historian Lucio Ceva's contribution to 'Decisive Campaigns' John Gooch argues that the Italian campaign must be evaluated in a different light from the standard scholarship of the campaign such as the works of Basil Liddell Hart and many others.

The work of historian James Sadkovich has argued that Knox in his major works such as 'Common Destiny: Dictatorship, Foreign Policy,' and 'War in Fascist Italy and Nazi Germany,' and 'Hitler's Italian Allies' has seized "every opportunity to criticize the Italian Army even when there was little reason to do so."[7]

Sadkovich maintains that factors such as wartime Allied propaganda, post war studies of the North African campaign based on the 'Rommel Myth' and primarily on Rommel's reconstruction of events, and a general lack of balance in the use of selected primary sources used in historical reconstructions of the war as three of the main factors that have influenced the way in which the performance of the Italian Army has been incorrectly assessed or simply neglected.

Sadkovich is not the only historian that has taken this position. Another historian Lucio Ceva, for instance, has provided a reappraisal of the Italian Army and especially of its armoured and artillery units during the North African campaign.[8] In a similar vein Jack Greene and Alessandro Massignani in their pivotal 'Rommel's North Africa Campaign' have argued that the military effectiveness of the Italian Army in North Africa was greater than what has been generally been assumed in many studies of the campaign which have typically exaggerated Rommel's and his Afrika Korps' role in the fighting while downplaying that of the Italians.

---

5 Emanuele Sica, *Mussolini's Army in the French Riviera* (Chicago: Univ. of Illinois Press, 2016) and Domenico Petracarro, 'The Italian Army in Africa: An Attempt at Historical Perspective', *War and Society*, vol. 9, n. 2 (1991), pp. 103-127 are two of the many works on the Second World War and the Italian Army that are highly influenced by Knox's works.
6 John Gooch (ed.) *Decisive Campaigns of the Second World War* (London: Frank Cass, 2004), p. 6.
7 James J. Sadkovich, 'Anglo-American Bias and the Italo-Greek War of 1940-41', *The Journal of Military History*, vol. 58, n. 4 (1994), pp. 617-42.
8 Lucio Ceva, 'The North African Campaign 1940-43: A Reconsideration', *Journal of Strategic Studies*, vol. 13, n. 1, 1990, pp. 84-104.

Similarly, Ian Walker's 'Iron Hulls, Iron Hearts,' provides a very exhaustive study of the Italian armoured units arguing that their crews fought effectively despite their modest equipment.

Richard Carrier has shown through his research based on evidence gathered from the military archives how the Italian Army and especially the standard infantry soldier's performance in the anti-tank defense improved over the course of the North African campaign. He argues that the infantry units became more effective against Allied tanks thanks to more training, German assistance and greater combat experience.[9]

Finally, Scianna whilst analyzing the Eastern Front campaign, has provided a very different assessment of the combat performance of the Italian troops against the Soviet army that specifically underlines the fierceness of the fighting along the Don river. His work also goes a long way in debunking the myth of the Italian soldier passively resisting the Axis Anti-Soviet campaign.[10]

---

9 Richard Carrier, 'Some Reflections on the Fighting Power of the Italian Army in North Africa, 1940–1943', *War in History*, 2015, Vol. 22, N.4, pp. 503–528.
10 Bastian Matteo Scianna, *The Italian War on the Eastern Front*, pp. 1-25.

1

Birth of the Italian Armoured Units and Their Development

Early Developments

The Italian Army initially began to consider tanks as a new weapon to support the infantry in 1917 when an officer, *Capitano* Alfredo Bennicelli, dispatched by the War Minister Vittorio Zupelli to France and acting as an attaché with the French Army, witnessed their deployment on the Western Front. *Capitano* Bennicelli outlined in a detailed report to the Italian *Comando Supremo* how the French Army had impressively used tanks to overcome barbed wire defenses and machine gun positions and had ultimately used armour to allow the infantry to advance past the German trench lines.[1] Because of this report, the High Command decided to import a French Schneider CA-1 tank that was to be used exclusively for tests and technical evaluations.[2] The machine was successfully tested at Tricesimo giving very good results to the point that the Italian army obtained four more Renault tanks from the French. Then in 1918 General Francesco Saverio Grazioli, one of the 'fathers' of the *arditi* units, introduced the concept of merging up to forty French Renault FT tanks within the newly formed assault division of *arditi*, *bersaglieri* and cavalry units. These units, comprised of the fastest and most offensive minded troops within the Italian Army, were to act in unison to spearhead an attack to breech the Austro-Hungarian defenses with a concentrated push along the Isonzo front. Tanks and other motor vehicles such as armoured cars were to not only be deployed to overcome the defensive lines but also to chase after the retreating enemy soldiers and cut them off once the offensive thrust had achieved its preliminary objectives. Unfortunately, the idea, although highly innovative for its time, was not embraced by the General Armando Diaz and General Pietro Badoglio and during the last offensive (Vittorio Veneto of October 1918) against Austria-Hungary no tanks were utilized in the battle.

---

1   Many of these tanks were first employed in the Nivelle Offensive on 16 April 1917 but their deployment and the results of the operation were not encouraging. Later, in late 1917 and early 1918 Schneider tanks were used again in other offensives. The tank weight was 13.6 tons and the main armament was a Schneider 75mm gun.

2   A few months later the Italian Army also ordered three Renault FT tanks.

As historian Filippo Cappellano asserts the Italians fielded no tanks in the battle but they did deploy a new unit that would influence the constitution of both the *celeri* (fast motorized units) and armoured divisions in the post-war period:

> In the final battle of Vittorio Veneto, an important role was played by the Assault Army Corps, which constituted the main Italian tactical-systematic innovation of the conflict. Based on two divisions of assault infantrymen (arditi) and a rifle regiment (bersaglieri), they lacked a logistic component and were equipped with small pieces of light artillery, transportable by pack animals. They were reinforced by cavalry regiments, motorcycle units, autocannon groups and light-armoured car squadrons, which played a major part in the pursuit of the routed Austro-Hungarian units. Extensively equipped with mechanical means for transporting troops, the Assault Army Corps was conceived for both rapid, wide-ranging maneuvers, and for break-through operations with the support of medium and heavy artillery.[3]

The rejection of Grazioli's idea of incorporating forty tanks in the *arditi* assault army corps, however, had not prevented the army from creating an embryonic tank unit on 1 September 1918. A specialized tank section called *Reparto Speciale di Marcia Carri Armati d'Assalto (*fast tank special assault unit*)* was formed and led by Maggiore Corsale, but it had no tanks and thus it remained in an experimental phase for the remaining months of the war. Along with this unit the first armoured training center was also founded. It was named "Scuola carri d'assalto" (assault tank school) which was instituted at the *Reparto di Marcia Trattrici d'Artiglieria* (tractor towed artillery unit) based in Verona with an initial force of 200 soldiers. The first batch of soldiers that joined the unit were all volunteers coming from all branches of the army and most had some prior experience either in operating a car or agricultural motorized equipment.

The first tanks that were commissioned by the army, except a preliminary and limited batch, were very light tanks that were designed for combat in the pre or high mountain areas of Italy. The first Italian tank was the Fiat 2000 which was designed during the First World War by two engineers Carlo Cavalli and Giulio Cesare Cappa and produced in limited numbers in 1918.[4] The Fiat *modello* 18 mounted a Fiat A12 engine and travelled at a speed of 7.5 kph and had a fuel autonomy of approximately 75 kilometers. Its armament was based on one 67/17 gun in the turret and seven Fiat-Revelli mod. 1914 machine guns. The armour was 15-20 mm thick. It was a tank that was to be used in a Western Front, entrenched warfare type scenario and it was to be used to break down enemy defenses. In December of 1918 the *1. Batteria Autonoma Carri Armati* (1st Autonomous Tank Battery or Unit) was constituted in Turin and was originally based upon two sections. The first section was equipped with two Fiat 2000 tanks while

---

3   Encyclopedia-1914-1918 <https://encyclopedia.1914-1918-online.net/article/warfare_1914-1918_italy> (accessed 2 May 2020). See also Cappellano, Filippo/Di Martino, Basilio, *Un esercito forgiato nelle trincee. L'evoluzione tattica dell'esercito Italiano nella grande guerra* (Udine: Gaspari, 2008), pp. 174-182.
4   The Fiat 2000 was shown to the public on 2 April 1919 when Bennicelli organized a training exercise that was conducted in Rome and purposely organized to bring attention to the new discipline. The training session was attended by the King and his entourage as well as a large mass of people. It saw the deployment of one Fiat 2000, one Renault FT17 and a modified FT17 with a 105mm howitzer in place of the gun. This was the first Italian self-propelled gun prototype.

the second was equipped with three French Renault FT17 tanks. The latter was placed at the disposal of the *Batteria Autonoma Carri Armati* and in contrast to the Fiat 2000 it could be more readily deployed in a mountainous environment. This unit was created within the artillery branch and it was also based on volunteers.[5] The *1. Batteria Autonoma* was first deployed in combat in 1919 when Italy put down a rebellion in Libya. The deployment of the Fiat 2000 in North Africa demonstrated that the tank was poorly designed and that it was too slow and not suited to operate during offensive operations. In fact, a report issued in 1923 outlined how the tank was under powered and traveled at a slower speed than the Libyan cavalry units. It was reputed to be "not useful for combat deployments given its large size and excessive weight."[6] During the Libyan conflict two Fiat 2000 tanks were put out of action by the enemy which even though lacking any heavy guns was still able to immobilize the bulky and exceedingly slow moving tank. Thus, given the limited number of Fiat 2000 tanks produced and its negative performance in Libya the Italian Army decided to discontinue its production and to focus the manufacturing effort upon the Fiat 3000.[7]

In 1923 the Italian manufacturer Fiat received a contract from the Army to produce several tanks using a license from Renault. The result was the design and manufacture of the Fiat 21-3000, styled on the Renault FT17 tank. This was a two-man vehicle, with two turreted machine guns, weighting six tons and capable of 20.9 kph or 13 mph. It is estimated that only 100 of these tanks were built because of the limited contract between Fiat and the Army. For many years, this was the only tank fielded by the Italian Army and it was used during its periodic field exercises. It was designated as *carro di rottura* (assault tank) and it was to be deployed by dedicated tank units supporting the infantry in breaking through the enemy defensive line.

In 1925 tanks were used in large scale army maneuvers in which for the first time it was decided to modify a few Fiat 3000 by taking away the machine gun and instead mounting on the turret a gun (*Cannone da* 37/40).

The machine gun version of the tank first saw deployment in 1926 in Libya when the Italian Army was called to put down a local insurgency. There the Fiat 3000 performed very poorly as its slow speed prevented the mechanized units from maintaining the speed of the cavalry and the armoured cars units when they charged against an enemy position at Jarabub. Subsequently after the insurrection was put down fifty Fiat 3000 were deployed in Libya mainly to carry out reconnaissance functions, while others were used for the annual training exercises in Italy. Up until the mid-1930s the Fiat 3000 was the only tank utilized by the Army, but by the late 1930s, however, as the Fiat 3000 fleet was poorly maintained and obsolete, the Army stopped using them altogether. In the Spanish Civil War, for instance, the Fiat 3000 was considered obsolete and was not deployed. By then it was used primarily to equip and train reserve units.

In 1927 further progress toward the consolidation of an armoured force was made when the *Reggimento Carri Armati* (armoured regiment) was created with the strength of 100 tanks and five battalions, each of which had two companies with nine tanks per company. It was based in

---

5   The coat of arms of the armoured units derives from a French design and was sewn on the right sleeve of the uniform. The badge, which was first used by the 1. Batteria Autonoma, depicts a helmet surmounted by two crossed cannons. It was later modified when a machine gun replaced one of the two cannons and a flame replaced the helmet.
6   Bruno Benvenuti, 'Regio Esercito carro armato FIAT 2000', *Storia Militare*, N.12, 1994, pp. 43-48.
7   Ibid.

Rome at Forte Tiburtino, an old roman fort that was large enough to allow the tanks crews to exercise and maneuver within its confines. This was the first armoured regiment of the Italian Army, but its full development was retarded because it lacked trained drivers and officers. Although such a unit had been created, the tanks "remained those that had been designed twelve years before. The lack of new and better tanks would be one of the weakest parts of Italian policy in this period."[8] In fact, the regiment was still equipped with the Fiat 3000 which until 1933 was the only available tank to the Italian Army. In March 1929, the tank regiment formed four Lancia-Ansaldo 1ZM armoured squadrons, that were to be assigned to the tank battalions for surveillance and reconnaissance duties. These units were later merged into a battalion of armoured vehicles and put under the command of *Tenente Colonnello* Valentino Babini, an officer that would tie his career to the armoured units.

Motorization vs Mechanization

While the first tank unit was being constituted, *Comando Supremo,* the upper military circles, the military academies, and the specialized military publications began to consider the tank as a new combat weapon. Much of the debate was centered on critically evaluating the ideas and concepts expounded by the more progressive military theorists in vogue in Britain, France and Germany. In Europe, the debate centered on the role of new technologies such as vehicles (tanks and armoured cars) and airplanes in warfare. As the debate intensified, two schools of thought emerged in most countries that expounded very different and competing theories. On the one hand, there were the supporters of motorization and on the other, those of mechanization. The first group maintained that vehicles had to be integrated into the large standing armies of the nineteenth century essentially as a support weapon to infantry. Motorization was a way to improve battlefield performance by moving artillery forward, supplies and combat units to the front and increasing reconnaissance capabilities, while also fielding tanks to support the infantry. The second group argued for a radical reorganization of traditional armies into smaller, but better armed and specialized units where tanks and armoured vehicles provided mobility, firepower, and cutting edge assaults against fortified enemy positions. The thought was that these highly mobile artillery units could punch through holes in enemy defenses and overcome the positional warfare of the First World War and achieve this objective without causing as many casualties as during the great offensives of 1917-18. In short, a mechanized army could overcome entrenched positions as it did at Cambrai, Soissons, and Amiens during the First World War and with improved engines and designs it could do so in a faster and more agile way.

Originally as historian John Sweet asserts in Italy the motorization advocates prevailed:

> Italian policy on the use of tanks remained unchanged in the 1920s. Originally formulated in 1918, when the first decision to produce tanks was made, tanks were simply support weapons for the infantry. The armour and firepower of the tank would deal with those obstacles, such as machine gun positions, that held up the infantry.[9]

---

8 John Timothy Sweet, *Iron Arm: The Mechanization of Mussolini's Army, 1920–40* (New York: Stackpole, 2016), p. 63.
9 Ibid., p. 49.

In the early days, especially after the First World War, tanks were not seen as having an autonomous combat role and were to be used solely to support infantry attacks. Moreover, at the time there was no discussion regarding the size or makeup of the standing army or regarding the constitution of specialized armoured units having an independent role vis a vis the infantry. Italy was coming out of the war virtually bankrupt and the financial constraints called for stark choices: either to keep a large standing army or to break up the standing army and devolve resources to construct modern and autonomous tank regiments and to support the fledgling Italian air force. The traditionalists also had greater representation at the highest echelon of the army, including the head of *Comando Supremo*. As the Italian Chief of General Staff, Badoglio, summarized in 1926 for Mussolini, armour was not a priority for the Army: "The nature of our terrain limits considerably the use of tanks, and thus the lack, and even the total absence of them, does not have the same consequences which it would have for other nations, for example France and Germany. We can thus wait calmly."[10]

Although, the traditionalists prevailed also because their thesis of a large standing army was useful to the regime and its policies (i.e., a large standing army provided jobs for many while the resources to build tanks and fighter planes did less so), the progressives began to keenly make their case for a more innovative and modern army.

In the 1920s Italy had two major progressive thinkers, Giulio Douhet and Francesco Saverio Grazioli. Douhet's most noted book *Il dominio dell'aria* (1921) argued two main points: First, that Italy's First World War effort had been completely flawed because it had been focused upon a large standing army centered on obsolete tactics that saw the infantry hopelessly taking on concentrated uphill enemy defenses. This strategy, in Douhet's view, was not only highly costly in terms of casualties but it also did not lead to success in the battlefield. Second, future warfare was to be based on modern offensives which were to take the form of mechanized land forces assisted above by the important role performed by aerial forces. The latter were to effectuate strategic bombing operations aimed at disorganizing and annihilating the enemy's defenses ahead of a major offensive. In such machine based offensives the number of infantry units required was smaller than during the First World War and the soldiers of these units were to be more specialized in such tasks as trench busting, cutting wires, eliminating pockets of stubborn defense with new weapons such as machine guns, flamethrowers and small mortars. Their role would have been to open a path for the armoured units to advance thus Douhet completely turned on its head the early theories which saw the machines as a mere support weapon and the infantry as the primary offensive unit.

Douhet was considered a radical by his peers and few understood or had the political wherewithal to support his ideas. Given Italy's depleted military budget following the First World War, Dohuet's ideas, if implemented, would have caused a large-scaleand largely unwanted reorganization of the military. This would have entailed a considerable scale down of the infantry divisions and a consequent shift of resources to the air force and the armoured units. The standing army would have been shrunk considerably to free up funds for tanks and airplanes. Such an option, especially in the volatile economic climate of the late 1920s, would have thrown many people into unemployment or force them into early retirement from the army. While it would have created additional jobs with the Italian manufacturers such as Fiat, Ansaldo and

---

10 Macgregor Knox, *Mussolini Unleashed* (Cambridge; Cambridge University Press, 1999), p. 26.

the airplane plants and some job creation within the air force and the more specialized branches of the army, it would have devastated the infantry and the concept of the large standing army. Moreover, at this point most Italian military theorists still maintained that a future war would most likely look like the First World War with Italy fighting a defensive battle in the Alps. At the time, no one foresaw a conflict outside of Europe and in terrain that was not mountainous such as in North Africa.

General Grazioli was probably one of the most innovative thinkers within the highest circle of the Italian military elite and he expounded ideas that were more progressive than those of Badoglio and other leading traditionalists. After the First World War Badoglio was promoted to Army Chief of Staff on 4 May 1925, thus assuming the position that had been held by General Armando Diaz during the First World War. This position was attained by Badoglio after he had become the de facto number two to Diaz during the last year of the war. Badoglio right after the war in 1922 was marginalized temporarily by the rise of Mussolini and his party. But after a brief hiatus he was back at the top of the military leadership presumably because he was considered as the most experienced senior officer. But Mussolini did not fully trust him and placed General Grazioli has the number two within *Comando Supremo* by nominating him in 1925 as *sottocapo di Stato Maggiore dell'Esercito*. Thus, for a few years an uneasy partnership was established between the more traditional Badoglio against the military theorist Grazioli. While Badoglio was a fairly conservative in running the Army, Grazioli was the proponent of a much slimmer but better equipped Army. He was inspired by the principles that had guided him during the First World War such as a military strategy that favored a war of movement in which tanks and airplanes were to play a more central role. Unfortunately, his tenure within the High Command was brief (he left in 1927) after several of his ideas had been opposed by the traditionalist Badoglio. He continued to hold positions of prominence but after 1927 he was outside of the inner circle of the military elite and thus unable to directly influence the military's organizational structure and its objectives.

In contrast to Douhet, General Grazioli on the other hand, focused his studies upon the infantry and his main thesis was that future wars were going to be won by technology rather than by the numbers of bayonets and that Italy necessitated to develop eight armoured divisions which would be the primary offensive weapons to breech enemy lines. As historian Paolo Battistelli argues: "The need to overcome the stalemate situation characteristic of the First World War battlefields was acknowledged in the early 1930s by General Francesco Saverio Grazioli, who had emphasized the need to use machines on the battlefield while demanding quality before quantity."[11]

In the 1920 and early 1930s Grazioli was often assigned to inspect the training exercises of other European armies on behalf of the Italian *Comando Supremo*. In this capacity, he observed the latest continental military equipment and strategy developments and he was also able to compare the state of readiness of the Italian Army versus these major powers. During his tours, General Grazioli was struck particularly by the Soviet Army of the early 1930s and its deployment of large tank regiments and paratroopers which were deployed in deep penetration maneuvers. Grazioli's recommendations to *Comando Supremo* focused on bringing in more

---

11 Andrew Sangster, and Pier Paolo Battistelli, *Myths, Amnesia and Reality in Military Conflicts, 1935-1945* (Cambridge: Scholars Publishing, 2017), p. 66.

tanks, anti-tank guns, self-propelled guns, paratroopers and highly specialized infantry units etc. rather than bayonets. This view envisioned the politically dangerous idea of scaling back the number of infantry battalions at the expense of the growth of the armoured divisions. Another role that was carried out by Grazioli in the 1930s was to organize and oversee the annual training maneuvers of the Italian Army. In this capacity he sought to introduce a degree of mobility to the Army with exercises that focused on a dynamic defense and long range offensive operations that made extensive use of tanks, motorized artillery units and airplanes. According to historian Basilio di Martino General Grazioli was the key architect of the highly important August 1934 training maneuvers which "were organized to give a demonstration of the level of efficiency achieved in just over a decade by the armed forces of fascist Italy."[12] They took place in the Apennine hills and saw the deployment in large numbers of both armour and truck mounted artillery units. The proposed theme of the training exercise was the conflict between two states divided by the Apennine ridge and the overall goal was to put in practice the new tactics of the army which were, as Grazioli asserted, "inspired by movement and maneuvering."[13] Both sides based their action on these principles, aiming to resume the initiative as soon as possible and meanwhile conducting a dynamic and mobile defense.

Grazioli was also a collaborator to several newspapers and magazines where he used the printed word bully pulpit to report on the latest military continental developments. In a letter dated 10 November 1930 Grazioli wrote to Mussolini criticizing General Gazzera, who was then the Minister of War, for his lack of innovative ideas and urging Mussolini to hasten "the pace of modernization of the armed forces and that despite the advances much more needs to be done."[14] A year later Grazioli doubled down this time in public by writing an article that detailed the training and equipment shortcomings of the Italian military in the famous Florentine magazine *Nuova Antologia*. In the article, which was written for the general public and not primarily for the consumption of the military elite, Grazioli agreed with Douhet arguing that a "sudden and unexpected heavy blow, by air and by land, to surprise and jolt the enemy was a precondition for a successful operation." Moreover, Italy required to transform its military into a less bureaucratic organization since a "small army perfected and ready for war in every feature, vibrant with combative vigor in every fiber, oriented towards the practical needs of modern war and animated with the impatient desire to fight it using the dynamic character of decisive maneuver warfare."[15] At the time, his opinions caused an uproar because they were perceived as very critical of the Army in general and this reflected poorly on the regime that had made the rebuilding of the military as one of its main goals since 1924. The article did not spell the end of Grazioli's career within the armed forces, but they did make him a figure that had to be kept away from the military's levers of power. His articles and letters indirectly implicated the work of Pietro Gazzera, Minister of War between 1929 to 1933 who led the Italian Army to develop along a traditional path centered primarily on infantry and artillery since it was an instrument that was to operate primarily in the mountainous regions of northern Italy.

---

12   Basilio Di Martino, 'Giulio Douhet and the Doctrine of Air Power in Italy'. *Nacelles*, N. 9, Fall 2020, p. 77.
13   Ufficio Storico, 'Commento alle grandi manovre pronunziato da S.E. il Generale Grazioli al gran rapporto finale', August 1934, Rep. L-13, Fondo Grazioli.
14   Renzo De Felice, *Mussolini, il Duce, Vol, III* (Turin: Einaudi, 1999), p. 44.
15   Francesco Saverio Grazioli, 'L'esercito e la guerra', *Nuova Antologia*, July 1931.

At the time Italian military planners were facing the two front war scenario (facing France and Yugoslavia) where artillery and number of infantry divisions counted more than more modern equipment such as tanks and aircraft.

Gazzera also argued that under his leadership the army was slowly modernizing itself with the implementation of some major transformations regarding the role of the cavalry and the creation of new *celeri* units. He still considered armoured and mobile divisions to not be a priority since both were deemed unsuitable to operate in the mountainous areas and also because of a lack of funding.[16] According to historian John Gooch, "This was the stance of a conservative and probably also a calculated staking out of that position against reformists such as Grazioli and Canevari who were arguing for an offensive army resting on quality and not a defensive one founded on quantity."[17]

General Emilio Canevari was also one of the most influential innovators that echoed in his writings many of the concerns expressed by Grazioli. In a number of essays published in *Il Regime Fascista* in September 1931 Canevari expressed opinions that were highly critical of the handling of the military forces by the duo Gazzera and Badoglio.[18] He argued that the strength of the army should not be measured by the number of infantry divisions but by "tactical advancements which consist in an increase in firepower and mobility. Without them it is impossible to make progress. A modern division necessitates mechanized and motorized elements and a large expenditure of fuel."[19] In addition, to being somewhat sidelined in the public debate arena, the innovators had to face off with several advocates of a more traditional military approach and despite their best efforts Grazioli, Douhet and Canevari remained in the minority in terms of military opinion and thinking throughout the 1920s and early 1930s. While Douhet died in February 1930 and therefore could no longer contribute to the debate during the critical decade before the start of the Second World War, Grazioli was ultimately sidelined within the Italian military elite circles and ultimately retired from the military becoming a Senator. Meanwhile Canevari would go on to assume positions of prominence within the Navy despite his interest in infantry and armoured tactics. Thus, despite the innovators' best efforts the traditionalist largely won the intellectual argument during that time also because their logic was functional to the stability of the regime.

Planning for Mountain Warfare and Light Tanks

Throughout the early 1930s the Italian Army continued to plan for a war against other European countries along the alpine border, most specifically against Yugoslavia. In such a campaign the armoured units were not expected to play an important role given the inability of the tanks to maneuver and operate effectively in a mountainous environment.

Thus, building an armoured component to the Army was not considered to be one of the primary missions for the Italian military which instead continued to focus its limited budget on rebuilding

---

16 Ufficio Storico: Intervento del ministro P. Gazzera, 'Note sull'efficienza complessiva dell'esercito', 28 January 1933.
17 John Gooch, *Mussolini and his Generals*, p. 208.
18 Emilio Canevari, *La guerra italiana*, Vol. I (Rome: Studi Politici, 1948), p. 246.
19 Ibid.

the infantry and the artillery branches. Moreover, none of the major officers or military planners at the time, despite the Fascist regime's slow conversion toward Germany and against France and Britain on the major foreign policy issues, envisioned a war outside Europe. The strategic planning documents of the Italian military of 1932 and 1933 envisioned a two front war beginning with an offense against Yugoslavia and then an attack against France, since the latter was an ally of the former and it was feared that it would intervene. The military budget was limited compared to Italy's requirements for a two front war scenario and the funding had to be split up amongst the three main branches. As a result armour was still not part of a revitalized army since there were few vehicles and the ones that were available were not technically advanced.

Although the 1934 training maneuvers represented a break with the past and were carried in the mountainous terrain of the Apennines to simulate battlefield conditions along the eastern border, they still revealed that the Army lacked certain types of modern weapons. The main goal of the training was to implement new offensive tactics that involved the initial breakthrough of the enemy positions and then the exploitation of the initial success by penetrating deeply into the enemy rear. Tanks were used alongside the infantry in the simulated attacks. Overall, the tanks performed well but a few problems related to the coordination of the assault also emerged as the tanks were not equipped with radios. At this point the tank was still viewed by the Traditionalists primarily as an infantry support tool to be used to knock out machine guns and mortar positions that stood in the way of the infantry attack. Although Italy lacked a heavy infantry 'breakthrough' tank, the tactical outlook maintained a preference for light tanks that could travel through narrow mountain bridges. The Italian L.3 light tank designed to be able to operate in the mountainous terrain found in Northern Italy, thus became the tank of choice of the army. This tank would be deployed in the Italy-Ethiopian war, then the Spanish Civil War and would even see combat during the Second World War, although at that stage it was largely obsolete.

The basic design of the L.3 tank consisted of only three tons of steel, with machine guns as the main weapons, with steel tracks and 9mm of armour protection. Its design development dated back to 1927 when the Army acquired a single British Carden Loyd Mark VI tank that was used for testing. Then in 1929, with the acquisition of twenty-five British Carden Loyd Mark VI tanks, Fiat bought the license for the tankette and began domestic production of the L.3 tank series. The first prototype was ready in the same year, called CV-29, which stood for "*Carro Veloce modello 1929*". *Carro Veloce* means 'fast tank,' which was the main feature of the vehicle. At the time, with the *Comando Supremo* envisioning a war against Yugoslavia along the alpine border, the light tank fit the purpose because it was small and agile enough to travel through the narrow bridges and roads of the northern border. Fiat together with the Army decided to build the L.3 tank series based on domestic specifications but these were highly influenced by the design of the British light tank. Fiat/Ansaldo's modification of the Mark VI, armed with a Fiat *modello* 14 water-cooled 6.5mm machine gun was approved by the Italian military and production began in 1930 with a design that was intended to influence future Italian tank development. Based on the CV-29, Ansaldo in 1933 began production of the CV-33, a 3-ton tank named *Carro Veloce 33* (also known as the L.3 Tank) which became the basis of all Italian tank units up until 1939.[20] A second variant was also built with the flame thrower instead of the

---

20 General Ugo Cavallero, who left the army just after the Great War, became general director of Pirelli tires. Then with Mussolini's backing, he was appointed president of Ansaldo, the heavy industry Genoa based company specializing in steel, construction and military equipment (armour, guns, and

machine gun. Development of the L.3 Lf (Lf for *lancia fiamme*, "flamethrower") flame tank, based on the L.3 tankette design, began in 1935.

According to military planners the CV-33 offered several advantages to the Italian Army mainly a fast (25 mph) and agile vehicle that could also travel well on mountain roads and bridges given its small size. Moreover, it would allow the Army to create effective mechanized divisions combining fast tanks and trucks carrying infantry. It main downside was that the tank had no turret and was only equipped with machine guns. Another shortcoming of Italian tank design of the time was that it did not yet envision tank against tank battle encounters which would later become dominating factors of several Second World War campaigns. The light tank was the basis of a limited armoured doctrine were tanks were seen primarily to take on infantry defenses rather than enemy tank units or exploit breeches in enemy defenses to make long drives into the enemy's rear. As historians Battistelli and Cappellano correctly point out: "The fact that these assessments did not take account of tank-versus-tank combat reveals how inadequate Italian tank design and doctrine were, particularly on the eve of World War II."[21]

The armoured personnel up to the start of the Second World War appreciated the L.3 tank for its speed and maneuverability but not its light skinned armour which offered very little protection. Moreover, "the tracks come out of the rollers all the time and the Fiat 14/15 machine guns jam after four or five shots. When operating this tank the crew must always be ready to stop the tank and take apart some of the components of the machine gun. Even at times the engine will stop working all of a sudden and the crew will have to leave the tank and get it to work again. This is very challenging especially during a running battle when shots are whizzing all around and shells exploding."[22] During most of the 1930s the proponents of the more conservative motorization theory continued to prevail within *Comando Supremo* and the most relevant military circles. Their strong support for light tanks ensued that for many years Italy would not develop a medium tank.

> Although debated, thanks also to a widespread distribution of Fuller's and Liddell Hart's books and articles (partly published in the Rivista Militare, the army's official journal), armoured and mechanized warfare were not seriously considered by the army staff, inclined only to consider a partial motorization of the army, focused on infantry and artillery and in particular on mountain warfare.[23]

One of the most prominent Traditionalists was Gazzera arguing that horses still had a central role in the battlefield. Gazzera was not opposed to the tank per se but was other priorities as more important. Other main representatives of the motorization approach, for instance, argued for the need of more trucks and armoured cars but not necessarily more tanks.

---

tanks). Through Cavallero's extensive contacts in the military, Ansaldo became an even greater key supplier to the armed forces. In 1933 Ansaldo began producing L.3 tanks and Cavallero signed a ten-year contract between the military and Ansaldo and Fiat to build tanks. In late 1933 an "armour scandal" broke out in which newspaper reports revealed that Ansaldo/Fiat made tanks with inferior steel resulting in vehicles that were less resistant. Cavallero was ultimately acquitted.

21 Pier Paolo Battistelli and Filippo Cappellano, *Italian Light Tanks: 1919-45*, p. 11.
22 Rinaldo Panetta, *Il ponte di Klisura* (Milan: Mursia, 1974), p. 9.
23 Ibid., p. 16.

Tanks and War: Early Experiments

In October 1935 Italy began the Second Italo-Ethiopian War and tanks were used during the campaign especially during phases in which the Italian Army was on the offensive. During the final phase of the campaign in February of 1936 the Italian Army launched a series of large scale attacks where the tanks played a key role in overcoming enemy resistance. Throughout the offensive, *Comando Supremo* began to appreciate more the role that both tanks and motor vehicles could play in supporting the infantry offensive since large distances had to be covered. Mechanized and motorized army units were one of the keys to not only break down enemy resistance but also to exploit any initial success by transporting troops and equipment on faster moving vehicles rather than horses or packed mules. The light tanks, however, were not invulnerable to enemy fire. At one battle, for example, at Dembeguina Pass in December 1935, the Italians lost five tanks due to the extremely narrow and obstacle ridden road on which the tanks were forced to advance. Thus, the slow-moving column attracted considerable enemy fire that debilitated the tanks. Although overall the campaign highlighted a positive role for the armour, the specific experience at Dembeguina Pass led many military planners to stress the need for a tighter coordination between tanks and infantry and that the former should be protected while fighting in conjunction with the infantry. These considerations, meant to protect the light tanks from enemy fire, were sound and could work well when the infantry was motorized or was equipped with self-propelled artillery.

General Badoglio, who had substituted Emilio De Bono on 17 December 1935 to lead the Italian forces in Ethiopia, did not fully embrace the potential of the new weapon. In the campaign, the Italian tank units deployed had overall performed satisfactorily but in certain instances their attacking potential had been stalemated by the rough roads and the wild terrain. Thus, in Badoglio's evaluation of the campaign, armoured cars, motorized infantry and fast moving motorized and non-motorized machine gun units had proved more useful services than tanks during the offensive operations. Largely based on this unique experience in Africa, Badoglio, who would later lead the *Comando Supremo* in 1940, never became a full-fledged supporter of maneuver warfare and his focus and doctrinal approach was more grounded on infantry, artillery and machine guns rather than armour. He used the experiences of the campaign in Africa to develop a European strategy which was predicated on winning a swift campaign with overwhelming manpower during offensive operations. Reinforcing an offensive with more bayonets and guns was the way to achieve a breakthrough. As Battistelli points out: "Inter-service cooperation between the Army and the air force was essential, and as he remarked cooperation was necessary because neither of the services were in a condition to achieve victory alone. Firepower was another factor, artillery and machine guns for the infantry, while he believed tanks would fail because of the unsuitability of the roads and the conditions of the terrain."[24] Most of the tactics and strategies associated with armoured warfare were alien to him even by 1940:

> In late May of 1940, while German columns were still chasing the disorganized remnants of the French and British armies across northeastern France, Efisio Marras, Italy's military

---

24 Andrew Sangster, and Pier Paolo Battistelli, *Myths, Amnesia and Reality in Military Conflicts, 1935-1945*, p. 67.

attaché in Berlin, submitted a report on German operations to SIM. More detailed reports followed in late July. By then, Italy was at war with France and Britain, and the Chief of Italy's General Staff, Pietro Badoglio, shelved the reports with the comment that, "We will study it when the war is over." (Studieremo a guerra finita.)……. In the fall and winter of 1939-40, Badoglio's immediate concern was not armoured doctrine, but how Italy could "close the doors of the house," create an effective defense against air attacks, and stockpile enough raw materials and fuel oil to wage war for more than a few months.[25]

As several historians have pointed out the performance of tanks in Ethiopia delayed both technical and doctrinal armoured innovation as the tanks performed satisfactorily but against an enemy that was very weak.[26] Thus the light tanks that were deployed were not matched up against European enemy forces that were in any way representative of the mechanized or motorized forces that the Army would face in the Second World War.

By the close of the conflict the *Reggimento Carri Armati* was expanded considerably despite Badoglio's reservations with the creation of twelve armoured battalions consecutively numbered 1 to 12. In addition, seven *battaglioni carri d'assalto coloniali* were also constituted alongside several reconnaissance units.

Spanish Civil War

Italy was also involved in the Spanish Civil War which came on the heels of the Ethiopian campaign, a factor which limited the Army planners' ability to assess the needs of the armed forces and conduct a full review of the armoured vehicles used in Africa. In 1936 the conflict between Nationalists and Republicans erupted in Spain and it soon became an important international affair to the point that Italy was one of the countries drawn into it. In the Spanish Civil War the Italian Army deployed the *Corpo delle Truppe Volontarie*, (volunteer corps) which brought together Fascist militia and regular Army personnel and also comprised motorized units, a tank unit, artillery units and air forces. Its total force was approximately 78,500 soldiers, 300 artillery pieces, and about 700 planes. This force initially also included an armoured unit of 150 soldiers and thirty-one tanks. A few weeks later an additional thirty tanks were also dispatched. In 1937 building upon the first nucleus of armoured units the *Raggruppamento Carristi* and led by *Colonnello Carrista* Valentino Babini a tank battalion was constituted and it became the main Italian armoured combat unit during the campaign in Spain.

The Italian units were involved in the first major battle of the campaign with a victory at Malaga where the armour fought well alongside the infantry. The operation began on 5 February 1937 and the Italian units were deployed into three columns with the first two columns driving directly toward Malaga's enemy defenses, while the third against its flank. During the battle, Italian tanks were engaged in a frontal attack against Russian-made tanks for the first time and came out on top after a brief engagement. While the Soviet tanks were heavier, the Republicans did not know how to operate them effectively and suffered against the Italian crews' greater

---

25 James J. Sadkovich, 'Some Considerations Regarding Italian Armoured Doctrine Prior to June 1940', *Global War Studies*, vol. 9, n.1, 2012, p. 64.
26 John Sweet, *Iron Arm*, pp. 109-125.

ability at maneuvering at their flanks. Both the armour and the infantry were then able to break through the poorly equipped Republican defenses which lacked anti-tank guns and heavy artillery. The tank unit was then involved in the Battle of Guadalajara between 8-24 March 1937 and the subsequent Republican Army counterattack. The Italian troops attacked the enemy positions but the bad weather and the consequent lack of air force support derailed the initial plan of attack and the troops were forced to make a frontal attack without the full support of the artillery whose arrival was in part delayed by the muddy terrain. With 30,000 infantry soldiers, a tank battalion from *Littorio*, eight armoured cars, and a motorcycle company, the Italians advanced thirty-five kilometers by the third day of battle. But the enemy, now better equipped with heavy guns, blocked any further advance. Thus, the operation soon stalemated rebuffed by the enemy anti-tank screen and Italian casualties mounted. Afterwards, the Republicans counter-attacked forcing the 1st MVSN (*Milizia Volontaria per la Sicurezza Nazionale*) Division to withdraw. In the meantime, *Littorio* Division, which successfully repulsed and broke through the positions of the XI International Brigade and the 2nd Republican Brigade, found itself isolated as a result of the militia's withdrawal. Ultimately, it was also forced to withdraw its tanks and artillery in order to avoid being cut-off from the enemy counter. Despite being checked, the Italians had inflicted heavy casualties and its tank battalion had fought as one cohesive unit, while the heavier Soviet tanks had been deployed in a piecemeal fashion. Despite fighting well together, the light tanks in several combat encounters revealed their ineffectiveness, i.e., their light skin amour which could be penetrated even by enemy machine guns and the lack of firepower since the tanks were armed with machine guns instead of cannons. Moreover, they were a poor match in terms of their lack of firepower and soft-skinned armour for the Soviet medium tanks operated by the Republicans.

As Sadkovich asserts:

> The Italians had already learned in Ethiopia that the CV 33 could not be employed successfully without the protection of infantry and anti-tank guns, but in Spain the question of whether it should be employed at all arose, owing to the presence of heavier Soviet tanks (but not to competition from German tanks, which, like the CV were thin skinned and carried only two machine guns).[27]

After being checked at Guadalajara the Italian force, utilizing both a motorized and a smaller armoured component, recovered to win an important victory at Santander and then deployed its armoured component to achieve other key victories. On 14 July 1938, the Italian force played a key part in the siege of Valencia by barraging the enemy defenses. The enemy stubbornly defended its positions, but on 16 July an audacious maneuver by the *carri veloci* bypassed several enemy positions forcing the Republicans to pull back and abandon their defensive line. This breakthrough paved the way for *Littorio* along with the *XXIII Marzo* and the *Fiamme Azzurre* Divisions to advance over fifty miles in enemy territory with the tanks leading the infantry troops, while the artillery paved their way with a heavy barrage against the enemy lines. On 25 July, the important enemy position of Viver was seized and the tanks played another important

---

27 James J, Sadkovich, 'Some Considerations Regarding Italian Armoured Doctrine Prior to June 1940', p. 54.

role in that attack. The brilliant maneuver by the light tanks was ultimately checked by a diversionary Republican attack that began on the same day fifty miles north. Thus, the Italian tanks and the artillery were diverted to parry the enemy blow. Finally, the Italian troops would then go to participate in the final offensive of the campaign at Toledo on 27 March 1939.

Like the Ethiopian campaign, the involvement of the Italian Army in Spain proved that the light tanks were fast but also vulnerable to enemy fire and they were also prone to mechanical breakdown during long hauls. The campaign nevertheless was very important for Italy's armoured units because it allowed them to gain valuable experience and for the commanders to determine the strengths and weaknesses of Italian armour. Specifically, they understood that the Army needed to modernize its tanks by making a move toward more heavy tanks. One of the tactical innovations, for example, which were made during the campaign was to carry the anti-tank guns forward into battle along with the tanks to better protect them. Trucks were used by both the armoured units and the motorized infantry units to carry behind them anti-tank guns or in portee' so that they could be readily deployed in battle alongside tanks and other units. Although the guns were used to compensate for the light Italian tanks, this move ultimately led to the development of larger guns on portee' and the self-propelled gun, the *semovente*, which proved very useful during the Second World War.[28] Another lesson learned was the defense in depth approach against enemy armour. This was achieved by "using anti-tank guns in mass, calling in support from divisional artillery and attacking tanks with flamethrowers, grenades and artillery at close range to destroy the threads and suspensions."[29] Thus, an important anti-tank doctrine was developed and successfully adopted which enabled the infantry to better deal with enemy tanks.

Another important lesson was that the army's future needs were for three types of tanks including a medium and a heavy tank whose need was keenly felt especially when facing Soviet tanks.[30] Unfortunately, even though the campaign was very valuable from the point of view of learning and adaptation to modern armoured warfare, it ended too close to the start of the Second World War therefore all the improvements that could have been made were not implemented due to a lack of funds and the suddenness with which the new conflict began. Moreover, many of the key lessons from the Spanish Civil War were embraced by the leaders of the Italian contingent in Spain but not necessarily by the upper echelons of the Army including Badoglio and his inner circle. Ultimately, historians Lucio Ceva and Andrea Curami have argued that Italy's campaign in Ethiopia, but especially its participation to the Spanish Civil War, had also some negative repercussions on the Army's overall modernization. They argue specifically that both conflicts, by tying down resources, delayed the development of a medium tank and the introduction of much needed mechanized tactics and capabilities.[31] One of the positive aspects of the conflict was that the Spanish campaign led to the slow conversion toward mechaniza-

---

28 A tank officer of Littorio Division Dino Campini after the war wrote that he never understood why the Army and Ansaldo respectively continued to demand for and to produce the M.13 tanks. It would have been more beneficial, in his view, for the war effort to produce more semoventi.
29 James J. Sadkovich, "Some Considerations Regarding Italian Armoured Doctrine Prior to June 1940," pp. 45-46.
30 Alberto Rovighi and Filippo Stefani, *La partecipazione italiana alla guerra civile spagnola*, vol. I (Rome: Ufficio Storico, 1993).
31 Lucio Ceva and Andrea Curami, *La meccanizzazione dell'esercito italiano dalle origini al 1943*, vol. I (Rome: Ufficio Storico, 1994), pp. 194-209.

tion and ultimately to a more autonomous combat role for tanks and mobile anti-tank weapons. But this came at the expense of more immediate technological developments with regard to armoured warfare and fighter aircraft.

At the end of 1937 (November) an important meeting sanctioned by *Comando Supremo* and involving many generals took place to discuss the state of readiness of the military considering the early experiences in the Spanish Civil War.

Much of the discussion revolved around the fact that a future war would most likely take a similar form to the highly mobile Spanish Civil War rather than to the entrenched positional warfare of the Alps during the First World War. In fact, it was the experience of the Spanish campaign that forced the military planners to begin to envision military campaigns conducted in non-mountainous terrain and away from Italy's northern border. With regard to armoured warfare the discussion centered on which type of tanks should the army commission? How many tanks divisions were needed? What type of weapon was better suited for the tanks? Etc....

At that stage, tank production was centered primarily on the L.3 light tanks, the so-called *carro veloce* originally designed for mountain warfare, even though its performance up to that point in the Spanish Civil War had been substandard. As discussed previously, by 1933 the original design of the CV-29 had been improved with the CV-33 which was a slightly heavier, two-man turretless, machine gun armed tankette. Then a few years later the CV-38 was introduced. Cheap to build, the L tank series design gave the Italian military a steady flow of new tanks which were readily put into service. The Chief of the General Staff of the Army and Undersecretary of War, General Alberto Pariani, between 7 October 1936 till 3 November 1939, reiterated the established policy that Italy's armoured units were to be grounded upon machine gun armed light tanks which were to be used in mass during offensive operations.

The *carro veloce* he argued, "acts more with its mass than with its machine gun, like a horse."[32] His only concession to the critics of the *carro veloce* was that the army would begin to fund several hundred tanks armed with a 20mm cannon in addition to the ones armed with machine guns. The opinions put forth by the critics of the *carro veloce* were centered on its lack of firepower and its weak armour. General Ettore Bastico, who had commanded Italian forces in Spain, stressed that the *carro veloce* was obsolete lacking firepower and for being much too vulnerable. Bastico argued for the development of a medium tank and that 150 of these vehicles should become the back bone of new tank divisions. Another interesting proposal was put forth by General Visconti Prasca that stressed that armoured units should be equipped with their own mobile artillery to increase firepower. This was a very useful suggestion not only to increase the punch of the armoured divisions but also to provide them with the defensive backbone against enemy armour. Lastly, another interesting proposal was put forth by several generals stressing the need to equip the armoured divisions with 75mm self-propelled guns for the anti-tank defense. On the other hand, the experiences of the Spanish Civil War where several tanks were lost to enemy forces induced many generals to think that armour was not critical for winning future wars. In fact, General Emilio Canevari drew from the Spanish Civil War the following conclusions: "Tanks could not spearhead an assault, given their need to be constantly protected by the infantry."[33]

---

32 John Gooch, *Mussolini and His Generals: The Armed Forces and Fascist Foreign Policy* (Cambridge: Cambridge University Press, 2002), p. 363.
33 Andrew Sangster, and Pier Paolo Battistelli, *Myths, Amnesia and Reality in Military Conflicts*, p. 68.

Some others such as *Tenente Colonnello* Augusto D'Amico, who had participated to the Spanish campaign, stressed that the army had learned valuable lessons in Spain which would be useful for Italian troops deployed in faraway war fronts:

> He proposed that at least half of a unit's guns be "packed" (someggiati), because these had arrived in a timely fashion while both "horse-drawn" (ippotrainata) and guns towed by motor vehicles tended to lag during advances. He also advised putting artillery under brigade command to avoid the "pyrotechnic displays" that had proven ineffective and occasionally hindered their own infantry in Spain.[34]

Historian Brian Sullivan argues that even though conservatives were well represented within the upper echelons of the Italian military, some progressive thinkers had by 1937 perceived the flaws of the light tanks considering the experience of the Spanish campaign. The problem for Sullivan was not that the army was ruled by conservatives, but that its plans were hampered by limited budgets and fiscal constraints that prevented the development of new weapons.

The light tanks, Sullivan argues, were strongly criticized by the progressives after the Spanish campaign for being too vulnerable to enemy fire even small arms fire which in some cases had penetrated its amour. It was also noted that the tank lacked firepower and that a proper cannon should be installed instead of the machine guns.

As Sullivan asserts:

> However, the fundamental lessons of the ground war the need for combined arms maneuver warfare, the requirements for vastly improved tanks, for tracked cross country vehicles of all kinds, for mobile and modern artillery, for effective radio equipment, for air support of mechanized operations — were understood and disseminated in 1939-40. The problem was that the Italian Army lacked the financial resources to apply these lessons, the vast mobilization of 1939-40 overwhelmed the training organization and the Italian armaments industry resisted the heavy cost of supplying the necessary new arms and equipment.[35]

The same point was made in the British Official History of the Second World War: "Italy, however, was engaged in a struggle against difficult economic conditions for which her government's foreign policy was largely responsible. She had been living on a war basis since 1935. Her adverse trading balance was very large and the Budget for 1939-40 forecast a heavy deficit. It was difficult to see how she could be in any condition for war; a further armaments race at this juncture was likely to be disastrous."[36] Historian Lucio Ceva has made a similar argument. During the Spanish campaign the Army wasted large amounts of equipment and other resources and put further pressure on its limited budget. The war also delayed the development of medium tanks because financial resources had to

---

34 James J. Sadkovich, 'Some Considerations Regarding Italian Armoured Doctrine Prior to June 1940', *Global War Studies*, pp. 49-50.
35 Brian R. Sullivan, 'The Consequences of Italian Intervention in the Spanish Civil War', Conference Paper.
36 I.S.O. Playfair, *The Mediterranean and Middle East, Volume I: The Early Successes against Italy to May 1941* (London: Her Majesty's Stationary Office, 1954), p. 38.

be used to replace lost equipment rather than be devoted to the design and construction of new weapons.[37] Thus, it can be argued that some valuable lessons had been learned by Italy's participation to the Spanish Civil War, but it is also right to point out that many of these lessons either could not be readily put into practice such as a swift shift toward medium tank production, or were not readily transmitted to the Army through enhanced training. Infantry troops deployed in 1940 in North Africa, for instance, greatly feared British tank units because they were unable to deal with them lacking a proper anti-tank gun. In contrast, the Italian units deployed in Spain a few years earlier using a combined arms approach could deal with Soviet armour much more effectively. Thus, lack of field experience and of proper training inhibited the Italian infantry's performance in 1940, especially when facing the British heavy infantry tanks. The most positive result arising from the Spanish experience was the realization of the weakness of the light tanks and the need for a newer medium tank for the armoured units. In 1936 design work began on the M.11/39 tank, Italy's first medium tank. But it would take three years to supply the Army which such units, albeit in very limited numbers.

Guerra di Rapido Corso

Meanwhile, in the second half of the 1930s a new breed of military theorists had emerged that continued to put forth the arguments originally developed by Grazioli and Douhet. One of the main military theorists to write a pamphlet containing innovative ideas about tanks and military strategy was Ottavio Zoppi, another general that like Grazioli was closely associated with the *arditi*, who had been nominated inspector general of the infantry. In 1935 he published *I Celeri*, a text stressing how a combined unit comprised of *bersaglieri*, cavalry and tank units, should be trained for maneuver warfare to spearhead infantry attacks in the mountainous regions of Italy. Since the book did not envision Italy fighting anywhere else than in the mountainous regions there was a focus exclusively on light tank units that could travel along the narrow lanes of Italy's borders with France or Yugoslavia. Its biggest merit was that its core concepts became part of the tactical and strategic underpinnings of the Italian military, which began to adopt maneuver warfare during this period, while its biggest limitation was not envisioning a war of maneuver in other theaters of operation such as North Africa that necessitated other types of tanks and self-propelled artillery.

Zoppi's work and advocacy on behalf of the armoured units led first to the creation on 1 June 1936 of the first motorized brigade (*1° Brigata Motorizzata*) of the Italian Army comprised of the: 1st Tank Battalion based on two companies with L.3 tanks, a *Bersaglieri* regiment, a motorized artillery group, and a sapper platoon. Although this represented a step in the right direction especially because it comprised artillery and armour into one brigade, these *celeri* units (fast assault units) were too weak especially because as Sweet asserts they were still founded on the obsolete light tanks. However, flawed by their obsolete equipment, this experimental tank unit with its basic three pillar structure became the basis of all future mechanized Italian units

---

37 Lucio Ceva, 'The North African Campaign 1940-43: A Reconsideration', *Journal of Strategic Studies*, vol. 13, n. 1, 1990, p. 90.

since it included special assault and engineer infantry units, artillery to defend against enemy tank attacks and armoured units.

Then, in 1937 two armoured brigades were formed: 1° and 2° *Brigata Corazzata*. The 1st Armoured Brigade (*1° Brigata Corazzata*), for instance, was comprised of the 31st tank Regiment and the 5th *Bersaglieri Regiment*, supported by a company of 47mm guns, a battery of 20mm guns, and an engineering unit. The *cannone da 47/32 modello 1935* was the standard anti-tank gun of the Italian infantry and it would be used extensively during the war. It was originally designed by an Austrian company (Böhler) in 1935. In 1937 the Italian manufacturer Breda through a license deal began to manufacture it in Italy primarily in two plants (Piacenza and Torino). The gun could fire both armour piercing and high explosive projectiles and it was effective against light to medium armoured tanks. It became less effective in 1942 when the Allied forces introduced heavier and more powerful medium tanks. Breda also manufactured the *Cannone-Mitragliera da 20/65 modello 35* which was 20mm anti-aircraft gun. The infantry and the armoured troops used it in a dual role; as an anti-aircraft weapon with high explosive projectiles, and as an anti-tank or armoured vehicles weapon using armour-piercing shells.

Another progressive thinker of the 1930s was *Colonnello* Adolfo Infante who penned in 1934 an important study on the role of armoured warfare and whose ideas were strongly influenced by the leading British theorists of the time such as Liddell Hart and Fuller. In a famous passage of his work he asserted:

> While the air force carries out the first great bombing actions against the vital centers of enemy war potential, an armoured brigade composed of some 200 tanks and capable of covering three hundred kilometers in twenty-four hours will be able to execute surprise penetrations, reach some of these centers and complete the destruction begun by the air force.[38]

His work was of relevance because it envisioned the constitution of large, armoured units (mainly brigades) capable of autonomous combat in the form of long distance sweeps against the enemy positions and aiming at not only overcoming frontline defenses but also lunging forward to disrupt rear artillery, logistics and storage operations and centers. It was also innovative because it envisioned Italy fighting with armoured units in the African theater or in other non-mountainous theaters of operations.

General Amerigo Coppi was another of the leading modernizers during the late 1930s. In the *Rivista di Fanteria* Coppi in 1939 observed:

> That even though our mountainous frontier is an obstacle to the proper operation of mechanized units, we cannot discount the possibility that a future war will be waged far away from Italy where the terrain is favorable to armoured maneuver.... Therefore, I am favorable to the constitution of autonomous mechanized units to implement maneuver warfare by agile, fast, fully equipped and completely armed armoured brigades. To carry out such task, the mechanized units should be equipped with the following: motor cycle and armoured vehicles units for reconnaissance, large scale tank brigades capable of breaking through

---

38 John Gooch, *Mussolini and His Generals*, p. 236.

enemy defenses, ample artillery batteries to enact preparatory fires for the tanks and equipment with self-propelled guns. They should also be comprised of assault troops capable of infiltrating and occupying enemy positions, antitank units capable of fighting off enemy tanks, anti-aircraft units and chemical and special sapper's sections capable of effectuating smoke screens and destroy bridges or enemy trenches. In addition, such units should also be equipped with their own aircraft to reconnaissance enemy movements and most importantly their own mobile fuel units so that tanks can be supplied far away from their depots.[39]

According to historian John Sweet it was after the Spanish Civil War that the Italian *Comando Supremo* made a clear turn toward mechanization of the Army. Spurred in part by this new wave of military theorists Sweet argues that:

> Italy changed from a policy of motorization to mechanization in 1938. Italian perceptions about the next war had changed radically because of the Ethiopian war, the Spanish Civil War, and the changing alliances that resulted. Italy could no longer depend on Britain. The embargo over Ethiopia had shown that. France, an ally since 1859, also opposed Italian aggression. Together these countries had protected the Mediterranean and colonial areas so that Italy could concentrate on Europe. Now Italy had to think of a war against a European power in Africa as well as worry about the Mediterranean shores that England now protected.[40]

The key individuals behind this new course were Generals Federico Baistrocchi and Alberto Pariani, who aimed to combine the strength of armour with that of the infantry to implement a lightning war, or a decisive offensive campaign that would resolve a conflict quickly and avoid the positional warfare of the First World War. Baistrocchi argued that not only was an attritional conflict obsolete but also unsuitable for a country like Italy: "a war of position that seeks, and even achieves, victory through the opponent's slow and progressive crumbling, would both in materiel and in moral prostrate a nation like ours, rich in men but poor in raw materials."[41]

Baistrocchi wanted to be a modernizer focused on maneuver warfare with an army built on new foundations, favoring quality over quantity, with a highly mechanized core. He had had been nominated on 1 October 1934 *Capo di Stato Maggiore del Regio Esercito* (Chief of the Army General Staff), a post that he held until 1936 after having been the number two in the Ministry of War. He had already demonstrated his intent to modernize the army when as undersecretary of state for the Ministry he had selected Grazioli in August 1934 has the officer in charge of the summer maneuvers which for the first time saw a tight collaboration between the army, the armoured units and the air force. In 1935 Baistrocchi issued new measures in the form of a pamphlet that directed the operations of large offensive units. These were to be trained to be deployed in a rapid war of movement and equipped with offensive weapons such as mortars, machine guns and other crew served weapons. In addition, they were to be strengthened with

---

39 James J. Sadkovich, 'Some Considerations Regarding Italian Armoured Doctrine Prior to June 1940', p. 64.
40 John Timothy Sweet, *Iron Arm*, p. 113.
41 Oreste Bovio, *In alto la bandiera. Storia del Regio Esercito* (Foggia: Bastogi Editrice Italiana, 1999), pp. 141-143.

the provision of new artillery pieces, trucks and tanks. With regard to armour the new directive stated that: "Based on terrain and our type of war we need light and fast tanks."[42] General Pariani took over for Baistrocchi on 7 October 1936, as the latter was opposed to Italian intervention in Spain, becoming *Capo di Stato Maggiore del Regio Esercito* and also holding the deputy position in the Ministry of War. Both recognized that Italy did not have the resources to wage a lengthy war and sought to introduce the new concept of la *guerra di rapido corso*[43] (lightning war) to improve the combat tactics of the Army. Pariani's policy updated the 1935 tactical documents on the deployment of army corps and infantry divisions. The pointless, highly attritional direct attacks of the First World War were to be replaced with flanking operations aimed at delivering a fatal blow to the enemy. If deep maneuvers against the enemy flanks were not practicable given the terrain, then the attack was to be undertaken by a concentration of forces whereby a massive artillery bombardment was to support an attack by infantry and armoured vehicles. The experience of war in the 1930s campaigns, for example, had set in motion a different vision regarding the deployment of tanks and mobile artillery in battle. Both were to assume much more autonomous combat roles bringing about the shift from motorization to mechanization.[44]

The new Army policy not only called for an increase in the mechanization in the *Regio Esercito* but also a new armoured tactical disposition entitled "Impiego delle unita' carriste"[45] (on the Employment of Armoured Units) which was issued simultaneously. In this new tactical disposition the armoured division (*divisione corazzata*) was originally given a secondary role of a mobile reserve. It would intervene once the infantry in cooperation with the artillery had struck a decisive blow against the enemy line. The armour would be then thrown into the fight by relying upon the speed of the *carro veloce* to exploit the initial success and conduct deep flanking maneuvers to arrive at the enemy's rear. In addition, armoured units could also be deployed to conduct attacks against poorly constructed or under siege enemy positions as well as to conduct reconnaissance with other units.

The 1938 policy change also envisioned other main roles for the armoured units. The first role was an infantry support role where the armour would be used to knock out stubborn centers of enemy resistance in conjunction with the infantry. Second, within the *celeri* divisions the armoured units were to act in unison in a speedy maneuver with the attacking infantry to obtain a key breakthrough against the enemy. Third, armoured divisions would maneuver against the flanks of the enemy line to conduct a wide sweep to encircle the enemy and arrive at his rear. The new *guerra di rapido corso*, however, had not yet addressed the potential for a tank versus tank battle mainly because of the light construction of the *carro veloce*. During the Spanish Civil War, for instance, the *carro veloce*, was seldom used against the heavier Soviet tanks and the few times that it had been deployed in such manner, the Italian tank crews had suffered casualties. Also, the light tanks were too weak to take on entrenched enemy defenses endowed with an anti-tank screen. Clearly lacking heavier tanks the new policy could not be readily adopted. In fact, to implement the new policy on 29 July 1938 the *Regio Esercito* launched a long term rearmament

---

42 Ufficio Storico, Comando Supremo, 'Direttive generali per una guerra di movimento', 23 Settembre 1935.
43 Ufficio Storico, Comando Supremo, 'Per una guerra di rapido corso', 27 Novembre 1938.
44 Ibid.
45 Nicola Pignato, *Gli Autoveicoli da combattimento dell'Esercito Italiano, vol. 2* (Rome: Ufficio Storico, 2002), p. 17.

program that was intended to enable Italy to be ready for a major war in 1943. This project not only required an extended period of peace for Italy to build up its mechanized force and its air force but also lead to the gradual expansion of its strategic industrial plants.

The major problem at the time was that while the military's thinking was evolving the government and the Army had failed to put enough pressure on the national military industry to push it to develop newer and larger tanks. Hence there had been no progress to wean off the local industry from producing light tanks as the army was still equipped with the *carro veloce* that had proved itself highly unreliable during the Spanish conflict. The lack of medium tanks, trucked and motorized infantry and effective anti-tank guns retarded the tactical implementation of the policy change toward mechanization. For historian James Sadkovich, the delays in modernizing the army along with the limited industrial base are the two factors that accounted for Italy's not stellar performance in the first year of the war and what ultimately consigned it to defeat.[46]

Armata del Po'

The *Ordinamento Pariani* (taking its name from General Pariani) of 1938 enacted a complete reorganization of the Italian armed forces. *Capo di Stato Maggiore dell'esercito* Pariani favored the conversion of the standard division from a triangular to a binary regiment structure, with two instead of three infantry regiments, three artillery groups, and support services and vehicles. Despite critics which argued that a binary division was weak compared to standard triangular divisions that were common to most European armies, the change took place with little opposition. The new structure based on two regiments would not prove successful during the first year in the Second World War due to the high attrition rate and the stalemate in Greece and in other fronts: "This Italian hope, based mainly on the fact that the Italian resources are insufficient for a long war, has not been fulfilled, and in practice the system has been found to have the serious defect that it leaves the divisional commander no reserve. Particularly in the hard-fought Albanian campaign was it noted that after a division had been involved in active operations for any time, and sometimes even after only a week, it had to be withdrawn from the line to refit."[47] But nonetheless it served the interests of Pariani and the reformers because a scaled down infantry division was easier to motorize having less men and equipment. Also given the dearth of certain types of equipment it gave the Army the possibility to concentrate its resources.

What made the standard Italian infantry division weak was also its overall lack of artillery guns, the ratio of guns to division was much lower compared to a French or British division, and it also had more outdated field guns many of which dated to before or during the First World War.

With regard to armoured warfare the new order authorized in November 1938 the formation of a field mechanized and motorized unit based upon two army corps under the command of General Ettore Bastico. In total the *6a Armata* (6th Army) or *Armata del Po'* was to be constituted

---

46　James J. Sadkovich, 'Of Myths and Men: Rommel and the Italians in North Africa, 1940–1942', *The International History Review*, vol. 13, Issue 2, 1991.
47　'Notes on Italian Organization in War Department Military Intelligence Service', *Tactical and Technical Trends*, Number 26, 3 June 1943.

by seven divisions (three *celeri*, two armoured and two motorized) and was to become the strategic reserve, the deep maneuver and breakthrough unit of the Italian Army. Its two armoured divisions at the time were still in an embryonic state and would later take the name of *Ariete* and *Centauro*. Each *Regio Esercito* armoured division was initially to be constituted by one tank regiment of four battalions, one *Bersaglieri* regiment of three battalions: one on motorcycles, and the other two on trucks.[48] Each division would also have one anti-tank company with six 47mm guns, one artillery regiment with twenty-four motorized 75mm artillery guns and twelve 20mm anti-aircraft guns, plus an engineer company, and supporting services. Three of the four armoured battalions were to be equipped with a total of 184 M (medium) tanks, while the fourth battalion was to have P tanks (heavy tanks). It was recognized at the time that the new combat arm was a work in progress and that two areas required special attention. First, each mechanized division was to be complemented with mobile reconnaissance units and that therefore industry was tasked with designing armoured cars. Second, it was recognized that there was a lack of mobile artillery within the mechanized divisions and especially of self-propelled guns. An important document issued by *Comando Supremo* reported that: "It is opportune to constitute special patrol units to conduct the reconnaissance of the terrain of operation of the armoured units…The existing mobile artillery (75/27 guns) will in the future have to be substituted by new equipment such as the cannone da 75/34 that better responds to the needs of the mechanized artillery. These guns will likely be mounted on the chassis of medium tanks to constitute semoventi units."[49]

The role of this new unit was to act as a strategic reserve and intervene in any area of Italy's northern frontier that was under threat. While on the border with France the *6a Armata* was to play a defensive role that encompassed the intervention of the unit to counter-attack only after the enemy had broken through the defensive line and had already been weakened by the Italian infantry, in the border with Yugoslavia the unit was to be deployed for purely offensive minded operations. Its main role there was to attack from bases near Trieste and Udine with the objective of capturing Ljubljana. Thus, army planners did not initially envision that the unit would be deployed in areas away from the Alpine frontier and no thought had been paid to deploying it in North or East Africa. The plan to constitute such a unit was ambitious given Italy's financial constraints and limited industrial output. For instance, at the outbreak of the war, there were no heavy infantry tanks available to break through the enemy positions, nor medium tanks or self-propelled guns or armoured cars. Thus, due to budget constraints, difficulties in getting the national industry to change its focus from building light tanks and the lack of adequate stocks of fuel and raw materials for industry, the *Armata del Po'* remained a concept rather than a fully equipped combat unit until 1940. This remained the reality of this armoured unit even though it was led by an experienced commander such as General Bastico and its officer staff was comprised of capable individuals, most which came from the Spanish Civil War experience.

The delays in fully bringing up to full staff the new combat unit were caused not only by the absence of modern medium and heavy tanks but also by the lack of trained drivers and artillery

---

48 *Bersaglieri* (Sharpshooters) comprised the elite light infantry of the Italian army. Some of the most advanced units of Bersaglieri were fully motorized and attached to armoured and motorized divisions.
49 Ufficio Storico, 'Relazione del Comando del Corpo d'Armato Corazzato', Ufficio di Stato Maggiore sulle grandi esercitazioni, 9 Settembre 1939.

personnel. The rate of motorization of Italian society in 1938 was very low, much lower than in Britain and France as less than ten percent of the population drove a car. This meant that it was not an easy task to recruit experienced tank and vehicle drivers. Most of these personnel had to be recruited and then extensively trained. Another problem was the fuel which had to be imported and was not abundant to begin with, a factor which limited the number of training exercises. In 1936, for instance, Italy imported 94.9% of its crude oil supply needs and became heavily dependent on Germany after the Ethiopian crisis. Thus, the need to stockpile oil reserves became very important and it led to the curtailment of several training exercises. Italy's financial constraints in 1939, which severely limited the military budget, even forced the cancellation of a major order for medium tanks. In fact, in 1939, after realizing that the L.3 tank had major limitations, the Army commissioned Ansaldo/Fiat to build a medium tank that was not only heavier than the *carro veloce* but also faster and with a more powerful gun. Italian authorities initially planned to produce 268 medium tanks, 697 new L tanks (armed with 20mm cannon), and 48 armoured cars in 1939. Ultimately, the financial constraints limited this massive order to a much more limited procurement plan of 100 medium tanks, 250 L tanks and 30 armoured vehicles.

Notwithstanding the financial constraints historian John Sweet argues that with the formation of the armoured divisions: "Italy moved ahead of most other nations. Although Britain and France had more experience in tanks and a larger proportion of their army motorized, they did not have an armoured striking force that the Italians now possessed."[50]

Sweet makes an interesting point regarding the *guerra di rapido corso* and the *Armata del Po'* specifically but overlooks that unfortunately Italy had embraced the concept of armoured warfare but its domestic industry lacked the adequate number of tanks to equip the army corps and its tank fleet was not up to par to heavier and more potent British and especially French tanks of 1940. Thus, there was a strategy for mechanized warfare, but there was little or no material to implement it and the industrial capacity was clearly also lacking.

Italy's Armoured Units 1939-40

During the latter part of 1939 (August) the Army conducted its last major peacetime training. Here the armoured and motorized *Armata del Po'* was deployed almost in its entirety to conduct rehearsed maneuvers along the north-west border. While training was conducted almost in its entirety with the light tanks, it was also the first time that the first batch of M.11/39 medium tanks was also utilized and on the occasion, they were driven by technicians from the Ansaldo factory. "The most drastic lesson learned from these maneuvers was to reaffirm that the L.3 battle tank was inadequate. The tank battalion, the striking force of the division had inadequate power."[51] The great maneuvers of 1939 had clearly outlined other deficiencies that hampered the coordination of the *Armata del Po'* during a campaign of maneuver warfare such as the absence of armoured vehicles used for reconnaissance and of truck borne anti-tank guns. Because of these observations several priorities were identified such as the constitution of mobile reconnaissance

---

50   John Timothy Sweet, *Iron Arm*, p. 131.
51   Major Howard Christie, *Fallen Eagles: The Italian 10th Army in the Opening Campaign in the Western Desert* (New York: Pickle Partners, 2012), p. 23.

patrols and the reinforcement of the infantry units with more anti-tank weapons that could be carried or towed to the front by trucks.[52]

The first issue, the lack of medium tanks, was underlined particularly by *Colonnello* Livio Negro, who had commanded the 132nd Armoured Brigade which in a detailed report summarized the capabilities of Italian armoured units versus its main competitors. He argued that most European armies had transitioned toward mechanization and the introduction of medium tanks and mobile self-propelled artillery. Negro recommended the creation of new combat units which would relegate the *carro veloce* to reconnaissance duties, while using medium tanks and self-propelled artillery as the key combat arms.

The problems raised by Negro were long standing and the solutions could not be implemented immediately. Thus, in 1940 the mechanized units were assembled again under the *Armata del Po'* to be deployed in wide sweeping type maneuvers but they still lacked key equipment and capabilities to implement such tactics. Radio equipment, for instance, was nonexistent, there was still a lack of medium tanks and of reconnaissance armed vehicles and trucks to transport the mechanized/motorized infantry to the field of battle.

As Cappellano and Pignato assert: "In 1940 the mechanization of the Italian Army was still in an experimental phase and the tools of deployment of large tank units in the battle were still primitive. The potential of the mechanized units and for the fruitful collaboration between tanks, infantry and artillery units had not been fully understood or adopted by most of the ranks of the army."[53]

Italy was clearly the weakest armoured force amongst the major contenders at the outbreak of the war. It lacked the industrial scale of the major European powers and it still manufactured tanks with outdated production methods that were devoid of modern welding techniques. Italy also had less tanks at the beginning of the war than any of the major powers and its major deficiency was the lack of a proven armoured strategy in non-mountainous environments. In the 1930s the Italian military elites had prepared the army for a likely future war against France or Yugoslavia that was to be waged across the mountain ranges. For this reason alone, Italian tank production privileged for a long time small, armoured units that were suited for the mountainous terrain. Unfortunately, such units were not suited for North Africa or for other non-mountainous terrains of operation that developed as a result of the Second World War. In early 1939, as Germany was aggressively threatening Poland and building up for war, Italy belatedly kick started the formation of its armoured and motorized divisions. The first unit was formed on 1 February 1939 and named *132ª Divisione Corazzata Ariete* (Ram armoured division). Then on 20 April 1939 the *131ª Divisione Corazzata Centauro* (Centaur) was constituted. The third armoured division, the *133ª Divisione Corazzata Littorio,* was formed in November 1939.

In addition to the armoured regiments of the armoured divisions, at the time the Italian Army also possessed four armoured regiments that were independent: 1°, 2°, 3°, and 4° *Reggimenti Fanteria Carrista*. These units would be deployed in a piecemeal fashion during the war. Worthy of note is the 3° *Reggimento Fanteria Carrista* which evolved from the *Reggimento Carri Armati*, the first Italian armoured regiment formed in 1927. At the same time, two infantry motorized divisions were also created and were constituted primarily by infantry troops (two regiments of

---

52 *Rivista di Cultura Militare*, vol IV, August and September 1939.
53 Filippo Cappellano and Nicola Pignato, *Andare contro i carri armati* (Gorizia: LEG, 2007) p. 61.

motorized infantry and one artillery regiment) but they also included one small tank battalion. These were the *102ᵃ Divisione Motorizzata Trento* which was announced on 2 February and the *101ᵃ Divisione Motorizzata Trieste* announced on 4 April 1939. Their role was to conduct rapid maneuvers, perform combat engineer type roles and exploit any initial breech made by the armoured units. These units were based upon existing armoured brigades and infantry battalions.

The *Ariete* was assembled by unifying under a single organization many of the tank units that had been formed in the 1920s and 1930s. Divisional origins date to 1937 when the 2° *Brigata Corazzata* (2nd Armoured Brigade) was formed in Milan. This unit was initially comprised only by the 3° *Reggimento Bersaglieri*. But a year later 8° *Reggimento Bersaglieri* and the 32° *Reggimento Carristi* were added in November 1938. On 1 February 1939, the Brigade was enlarged to a full armoured division and was renamed *132ᵃ Divisione Corazzata Ariete* and incorporating three regiments: the 8th *Bersaglieri*, the 32nd *Reggimento Carristi* and the 132nd *Reggimento Artiglieria Corazzata*, as well as other divisional units.

Its 1939 organization included:

- *32° Reggimento Carristi* based on the I, II and III *Battaglioni*. The first two battalions were equipped shortly thereafter with the M.11/39 medium tanks while the third was equipped initially with the light tanks and then with the heavier M.13/40 tanks by July 1940.
- *8° Reggimento Bersaglieri* which was comprised of the motorized (one on motorcycles and two with trucks) infantry battalions (III, V and XII) and the 132ᵃ *Compagnia Controcarri* equipped with truck mounted 47mm antitank guns.
- *132° Reggimento Artiglieria Corazzata* was the artillery arm of the division and was based on I and II *Battaglioni* with twenty-four 75/27mm guns, some of which were also truck mounted.
- *132ᵃ Compagnia Mista Genio* was mainly comprised of sappers and combat engineers.
- *Centauro*'s origins relate back to the 1° *Brigata Motorizzata* (1st Motorized Brigade) founded in Siena in June 1936. A year later it became the 1° *Brigata Corazzata* (1st Armoured Brigade).
- *Centauro* also had a similar organization to *Ariete* with:
- *31° Reggimento Carristi* with the I, II, III, IV armoured *battaglioni* equipped exclusively with the L.3 tanks.
- *5° Reggimento Bersaglieri* with the XXII motorcycles *Battaglione* and the XIV and XXIV mobile *Battaglioni*.
- *131° Reggimento artiglieria Corazzata* with the I, II, III *Gruppi* (75/27 truck mounted guns).
- The *Littorio* Division was the last armoured unit formed in 1939 but it was the first to be deployed during the war.
- The *Littorio* had originally fought during the Spanish civil war but in 1939 primarily as an infantry motorized unit, similarly to *Ariete* and *Centauro*, it was organized on three major components: a tank regiment, an artillery regiment, and a motorized *Bersaglieri* regiment.
- *33° Reggimento Carristi* (with I, II, III and IV *Battaglioni*), equipped with L.3 tanks.
- *12° Reggimento Bersaglieri* with three battalions (XXI, XXIII, XXXVI).
- *133° Reggimento Artiglieria Corazzata* with two groups (I, II) with 75/27 guns.

A standard armoured division would have, at least on paper, the following strength: 273 officers, 484 ncos, 6,612 soldiers, 76 gun rifles, 410 machine guns, sixteen 20mm guns, 184 M tanks, eight 47/32 anti-tank guns, twenty-four 75/27 guns, 581 trucks, 1,170 motorcycles, and 48 tractors. In mid-1940, when Italy entered the war, the armoured force consisted of approximately 2,000 light tanks of the *carro veloce* variety, a few hundred Fiat 3000 post-First World war vintage tanks and approximately seventy M.11/39 medium tanks. While the first M.13/40 tanks entered service in July 1940. Thus, it was a very weak force which clearly lacked an adequate number of armoured divisions and medium tanks and self-propelled guns. In 1940, for instance, *Littorio* was still equipped with light obsolete CV-35 tanks. Its commander, General Gervasio Bitossi, who led *Littorio* during the Spanish Civil War, accepted to resume its command "only after being promised medium tanks." [54]

On the eve of the war (25 May 1940) General Rodolfo Graziani was tasked with assessing the state of readiness of the armoured forces on behalf of *Comando Supremo* and his conclusions were not very positive: "The two armoured divisions Ariete and Littorio are divisions in name only since they only have light tanks and only 70 medium tanks. They have no armoured vehicles nor heavy tanks."[55]

A pessimistic Graziani argued that the best policy for Italy was to buy time and delay any major offensive operation involving the armoured units.

Italian Armour Compared to Other European Armoured Forces

Despite the strategic turn toward mechanization, in 1940 the Army was still heavily infantry centered with seventy-three divisions of which only three were armoured and two were motorized. How did the standard Italian armoured division compare to similar British, German or French units? What were its strengths and how well balanced was it? For example the *Ariete* Division, which was by 1940 or early 1941, the only Italian armoured division that was close to full rank, for comparison purposes with other European armoured divisions.

Together with the standard headquarters and support services, *Ariete's* major units included the 32° *Reggimento Carrista* (32nd Armoured Regiment) on three tank battalions, the 8° *Reggimento Bersaglieri* (8th *Bersaglieri* Regiment) constituted on two truck borne special infantry battalions and one on motorcycles and finally the 132° *Reggimento Artiglieria Corazzata* (132nd Artillery Regiment) with two groups of 75/27 guns and two batteries of 20mm anti-aircraft guns. Each of the units had a different role to play in the field of battle. The armoured regiment was assigned the following tasks: "In addition to being employed in small units for reconnaissance and flank security, the armoured regiment was to be used as a compact mass of 250 tanks to generate shock (urto), penetrate enemy positions and, exploit and pressure the enemy after his defenses had been breached."[56] In 1940 when Italy was mostly equipped with light tanks, the

---

54 James J. Sadkovich, 'Some Considerations Regarding Italian Armoured Doctrine Prior to June 1940', p. 59.
55 Lucio Ceva and Andrea Curami, *La meccanizzazione dell'esercito dale origini fino al 1943*, vol. 2 pp. 284.
56 James J. Sadkovich, '[Some Considerations Regarding Italian Armoured Doctrine Prior to June 1940', *Global War Studies*, vol. 9, n.1, 2012, p. 54.

tactical dispositions did not yet envision tank versus tank battle deployments. At the time, light tanks were effective against lightly armed infantry positions or they were to be deployed once the enemy (both its tanks and infantry) was retreating and its heavy anti-tank equipment was being loaded on trucks. It would only be later in 1941 when the tactical dispositions for armour were changed that Italian tank units were expected to be also engaged against enemy tank formations. This came only after the medium tanks were introduced into service.

The second pillar of the armoured division was comprised by its motorized *Bersaglieri* infantry units. "These units had a wide variety of tasks, from reconnaissance, flank security, infiltration, the occupation of key points, and envelopment (aggiramenti) to exploitation and pursuit."[57] The *Bersaglieri* had generally received more training than the standard infantry units prior to the war and were particularly skilled in shooting and advancing on foot for long distances. They were the elite infantry troops of the Italian Army and could count upon effective infantry crew served weapons for 1940 standards such as the 81mm mortars modello 1935 and the 47mm anti-tank gun. Lastly, the third pillar was the mobile artillery regiment. "The artillery was to provide direct support, batter enemy artillery, engage enemy tanks, and fend off hostile aircraft. Services and a company of engineers completed the division, which lacked only a chemical arm and its own air support."[58]

Its main artillery weapon the 75/27 gun, although reliable was considered to be only moderately effective by the Allies: "The standard light field piece of the Italian army is the 75/27 weapon (caliber 75-mm., length of bore 27 calibers) of which there are three models, 06, 11, and 12. British users consider it satisfactory equipment, and find that it gives good results in spite of constant use. Its disadvantages are: (a) light hitting-power; (b) at ranges above 6,600 yards, it is necessary to use a false angle of sight, slope the platform and dig a hole for the trail; (c) poor fragmentation effect."[59] It was pointed out that in contrast to the Italian divisions that were equipped with the 75mm gun, the French or British divisions were equipped with guns of 100mm or more. In contrast the performance of the Breda 20/65 anti-aircraft gun was appreciated by the Allies. Whenever the Allies were able to capture these guns they were distributed amongst the infantry divisions which used them extensively throughout the campaign.

By mid-1941, for example, when *Ariete* arrived to North Africa it had 113 light and 91 medium tanks and a total strength of approximately 7,500 soldiers, twenty-four 75mm guns, twelve 20mm guns and twelve 47mm anti-tank guns.

As Walker asserts:

> The Italian armoured division of 1940 represented a well-balanced force of all arms, designed to operate together under a single command. It had the potential to operate in an extremely flexible way using its combination of armour, infantry and artillery. It was still weak in armour, with its inferior light tanks and this would remain the case until 1941; and it was also weaker than it might have been in artillery and antitank guns, although these deficiencies would be remedied through wartime experience. It is important, however, to

---

57   Ibid.
58   Ibid.
59   'Italian 75-mm Field Gun – Models 06, 11 and 12', War Department Military Intelligence Service *Tactical and Technical Trends*, Number 7, 10 September, 1942.

be clear that it remained, even at full strength, smaller than its British and German equivalents, a point seldom made clear in wartime accounts.[60]

Its primary strength was that it was a true combined arms unit comprised of both armour and motorized infantry and mobile artillery which were all necessary elements to take down entrenched enemy defenses as well as to fight off enemy tank attacks. Its main weakness was the initial lack of medium tanks, which was partly rectified in 1941, and the lack of heavy infantry tanks and self-propelled guns. Its other main weakness was the range and firepower of its artillery. Its 75/27 and 47mm guns were effective in penetrating light enemy tanks, but were less effective against heavy infantry tanks. This defect was also rectified later in the conflict with the introduction in late 1941 and 1942 of more powerful anti-tank guns. But for the first part of the campaign the 75mm remained the main field gun, while the 47mm remained the main anti-tank weapon. The lack of dedicated reconnaissance units was also a major issue during the first year of the war and it would take some time for the Italian armoured units to introduce proper units equipped with armoured vehicles and comprised of experienced personnel especially at the NCO and officer level. Another major problem for *Ariete* in the early stages of the conflict was the absence of a recovery and repair dedicated tank unit. It also did not have great amounts of spare parts for the tanks forcing the crews to often scrounge around for parts from debilitated tanks or from enemy armour. Lastly, it had very antiquated communication systems and this issue would plague the division for the remaining of the war. The lack of radios on tanks was extremely detrimental to a war of movement typical of the North African front.

The standard German armoured division such as for example the 15th Panzer Division, which fought in the desert beginning in the spring of 1941, was organized as follows: an armoured regiment (8th Panzer Regiment) with two battalions (1st and 2nd). At full strength, each battalion had four companies with twenty-one tanks apiece. In total the armoured regiment including the command and the signal tanks had approximately 194 tanks, none of which were light by Italian standards. A motorized infantry regiment of three battalions (115th *Schützen* Regiment). An artillery regiment (33rd Panzer Artillery Regiment) with two light and one heavy guns battalions where each battalion had three batteries and each battery had four guns. Two of these battalions were armed with 105mm gun-howitzers, and one with 150mm howitzers. Its anti-tank battalion (33rd *Panzerjäger* Battalion) was comprised of three companies, each of which had twelve anti-tank guns which were mostly Pak 50mm units and some 88mm Flak 36 units. An armoured reconnaissance battalion (33rd Panzer Reconnaissance Battalion) with thirty armoured cars. The division also had a combat engineer unit (33rd Pioneer Battalion) and a signal communications battalion with a radio and a telephone communications company (33rd Signals Battalion) and finally some supply units. Even though in 1941 the German armoured divisions were still equipped with medium tanks such as the *Panzerkampfwagen* I, and II with 30mm of armour they also possessed the *Panzerkampfwagen* III with a 50mm short barrel gun which could debilitate a Matilda II tank at 350 yards. They also possessed a smaller number of very effective equipment in the form of the *Panzerkampfwagen* IV which carried a short barrel 75mm gun which had a penetrative power capable of damaging 45mm of armour at a distance of

---

60 Ian Walker, *Iron Hulls, Iron Hearts* (Ramsbury: Crowood Press, 2003), p. 51.

600 yards.⁶¹ A major strength of the German armoured division was its anti-tank battalion. This unit typically accompanied the tank battalions in the attack, covering their flank and supporting them by picking out and neutralizing enemy tank and antitank defenses. It also possessed slower moving antitank units that would follow the armoured battalions to purposely engage enemy tanks directed at the flanks and rear of the German tanks. The anti-tank battalion was primarily equipped beginning in the spring of 1941 with a 50mm antitank gun. This replaced the 37mm antitank gun, which had been the main German antitank weapon between 1939-40. The 50mm could fire both high-explosive and armour-piercing projectiles which could pierce the armour of British infantry tanks and Cruiser tanks, and of certain medium American tanks. Also, no other army in 1941 could match the German 88mm Flak 36 gun which was also furnished in limited numbers to the armoured units and that could be used as a very effective anti-tank weapon and was first deployed in this fashion in France. It could penetrate a Matilda II tank at a distance of 2,000 yards. An American intelligence report noted that the 88mm was equally effective against the ground targets and especially for targeting armoured vehicles with a special armoured piercing shell: "The 88mm is basically a gun for firing on moving targets. The crew is also specially trained for firing on highly rapid moving targets, primarily on airplanes. The whole control apparatus is designed for fast moving targets with a very rapid rate of fire: 25 rounds per minute. The gun is capable of great volume fire and extreme accuracy against moving targets of any type. It is equally efficient on targets on the ground as well as in the air. For attacks on armoured vehicles, it is provided with a special armour-piercing shell."⁶²

The combination use of the anti-tank weapons was another distinctive feature of the German armoured units which led to a very effective anti-tank defense based on different ranging tactics: "To increase the element of surprise, all antitank weapons should open fire only when they are certain of success. Even after 88mm antiaircraft guns have already opened effective fire, the 37mm and 50mm antitank guns must remain silent so as not to be observed by enemy tanks. Only at a distance of a few hundred meters are they to open fire on the heaviest English tanks with the antitank shell No. 40."⁶³

The standard armoured division, with a total of well over 10,000 soldiers, also had greater availability of support services such as reconnaissance vehicles and numerous types of explosive and standard shells and could rely on its superior training. Each tank battalion had qualified mechanics that could be readily deployed to make repairs. The armoured regiment had a repair shop, with a truck carrying spare parts, which followed the fighting units. A percentage of tank repairs could be made on the battlefield and for more significant repairs there was a support unit equipped with recovery vehicles. The great variety of anti-tank ammunition, for example, was unmatched. The 50mm antitank gun, for example, could fire armour-piercing shells,

---

61   The German medium tanks were very much improved during the war, meanwhile the pace of technical innovation of the Italian tanks was much slower hampered by lack of effective motors and other problems. The German *Panzerkampfwagen III*, for example, was a light medium tank of 20 tons. Originally it was armed with one 37mm gun and two light machine guns, but in most cases the 37mm was replaced by a 50mm gun and in some cases a 75mm gun. Its maximum speed was 28 mph.
62   'A Tactical Study of the Effectiveness of the German 88 mm Anti-Aircraft Gun as an Anti-Tank Weapon in the Libyan Battle', Military Intelligence Service, War Department, *Tactical and Technical Trends*, Number 1, 18 June 1942.
63   'German Methods of Warfare in the Libyan Desert', Military Intelligence Service, *Information Bulletin*, Number 20, July 1942.

high-explosive shells, and armour-piercing Panzergarnate 40. According to Allied estimates the latter furnished good armour-piercing performance at 500 yards. Most importantly the German Panzer divisions possessed a higher degree of motorization (much higher than the Italian units) that allowed the infantry units, for example, to maintain a similar pace with the tank units. Moreover, radio sets had been installed in all tanks to coordinate combat action more precisely. Another key feature of the German armoured units was its superior ability to conduct reconnaissance. The division in fact would deploy its motorized reconnaissance battalion, equipped with armoured vehicles and numerous automatic weapons, well in advance of the tank attack. The motorized reconnaissance battalion was something the Italian armoured units had not fully developed at the start of the campaign and that would be introduced incrementally overtime first with the *Corpo Armato di Manovra* (CAM) and then with the introduction of the AB armoured vehicles series which entered service late into the game. Meanwhile the German armoured unit could deploy its reconnaissance vehicles to cover distances up to 60 miles to locate and estimate the strength of the enemy while also spotting its field and mobile gun positions.

The British armoured division was somewhere in the middle. It was generally stronger than the Italian division because of its more effective medium tanks and its ability to field heavy infantry tanks, but weaker and less well trained than the German Division. It also typically had less infantry and anti-tank guns than the standard Italian division. The standard British armoured division had 11,000 soldiers, 340 tanks, and sixteen 25-pdr guns. It consisted of two armoured brigades, each of three battalions of medium and light tanks; a support unit comprised of two motorized infantry battalions and field artillery and anti-tank regiments. In early 1941, for example, the 7th Armoured Division had 200 light and medium tanks with the 4th Armoured Brigade and the 7th Armoured Brigade but it could also count upon forty-five Matilda II infantry tanks of the 7th Royal Tank Regiment. The majority of its tanks were the A9, A10 and A13 Cruiser tanks with a 2-pdr gun. Later the A15 Crusader, which was equipped with a 7.92mm BESA machine gun and a 2-pdr gun (which was eventually upgraded to a 6-pdr), was also introduced. Some of the first Crusaders made their appearance in the spring of 1941 during Operation Battleaxe and then later they were deployed in much larger numbers during Operation Crusader. Its artillery consisted of the following units: the 3rd Royal Horse Artillery equipped with 25-pdr field guns and with 37mm Bofors anti-tank guns, while 4th Royal Horse Artillery was equipped with 25-pdr guns. The 106th Royal Horse Artillery was primarily equipped with 37mm Bofors anti-tank guns on portees as well as captured Italian 20mm guns. Its infantry was comprised of two battalions and its cavalry/reconnaissance unit was the 11th Hussars equipped initially with Rolls Royce and Morris armoured cars. Thus, in general it had more tanks, and a greater diversity of tanks, but less artillery than the standard Italian armoured division. It also was lighter in terms of the infantry units it could deploy. As Ian Walker asserts: "It was a powerful force when its brigades operated together, although it was deficient in infantry and artillery, especially when its brigades operated independently, as was frequent the case. In comparison to the typical British armoured division, the Italian equivalent had more infantry and artillery, but had fewer tanks. An Italian armoured division was broadly equivalent to a British armoured brigade in tank strength but had the advantage of integrated infantry and artillery."[64]

64 Ian Walker, *Iron Hulls, Iron Hearts*, p. 50.

The comparison between a French and an Italian armoured division also demonstrates that the former was better equipped than the latter. According to Italian intelligence services estimates a standard French armoured division in 1940 had more tanks and guns and had also greater firepower. It had 255 tanks that were constructed of thicker armour and albeit slower than Italian tanks they were also more heavily armed. At the outbreak of the Second World War the main weapon of the French armoured divisions was the Char B1 bis, built by Renault and it was equipped with a 75mm howitzer and a 7.5mm machine gun mounted in the hull as well as a 47mm anti-tank cannon and a second 7.5mm machine gun. Its armour was 60mm thick on its front and turret, 55mm on its sides. The French tank was slower than the standard Italian light tank and could travel at much shorter distances, but in a tank to tank encounter the light or even the standard medium Italian tank would have had no chance. Moreover, the standard French division had fifty-two anti-tank guns and twenty-five artillery batteries. The standard Italian 47mm anti-tank gun was comparable to the French gun, but the French also possessed fifty-two guns per division against the Italians with twelve guns. The standard French division also had more soldiers, up to 10,000. Thus, the disparity in strength between the two standard divisions was evident and the French artillery especially could penetrate the armour of any Italian tank. In short, the French division on paper was superior to the Italian armoured division in both armour and anti-tank weaponry.

This comparison with the French led an Italian general, Fidenzio Dall'Ora, to argue that the Italian armoured units, given its limited firepower, should only go head to head against a French reinforced infantry division or an armoured division during "the final phase of an action" when the French division was retreating and in considerable disarray.[65] His assessment was also based on the fact that since the early days during the inception and early design of the M.11/39 tank in 1936 even this medium tank was intended to be used as a 'breakthrough tank' for assaulting enemy infantry or motorized formations. It was not envisioned that the medium tank be used for tank against tank encounters or deployed against a potent anti-tank screen.

Ultimately, the combat worth of an armoured force cannot be assessed by only comparing the numbers of tanks and guns with those of the enemy. The variety and types of tanks such as light, medium and heavy, is of critical importance as well as their mechanical reliability. Another factor was the firepower of the armoured division which was not only assessed in terms of the number, size and range of the guns of the tank battalions but also its anti-tank capabilities. Efficiency of intercommunication and the versatility of the command structure were two other key features. While the Italian armoured division had greater artillery support, the British counterpart had more efficient and diverse armoured forces including heavy tanks. It also had better divisional intercommunication systems as well as more advanced reconnaissance capabilities. The French had antiquated communication systems like the Italians but they compensated for such a weakness by having more powerful guns and tanks.

---

65   James J. Sadkovich, 'Some Considerations Regarding Italian Armoured Doctrine Prior to June 1940', p. 68.

Armoured Doctrine in Europe in 1940

Just prior to the start of the Second World War the balance of power amongst the nations of Europe as it related to armoured forces and tactics presented a very uneven scenario, but it clearly showed that Italy was at a disadvantage to when compared to other major powers.

In France, Colonel Charles de Gaulle was one of the main critics of General Petain's entrenched focus on fixed defenses such as the Maginot Line and held by large numbers of infantry troops. In the inter-war years, he had written the book titled *Ver Armee de Metier* which advocated the use of tanks and infantry during offensive operations. In the post First World war period the French Army continued to hold the lead that it held during the war by producing large quantities of top rated tanks. The Somua S35 tank with its 45mm cannon, for instance, was faster and more powerful than the standard German panzer tanks of 1940. In 1939, the French armoured force was the leading Allied tank force with 5,800 tanks. Moreover, French tanks were considered generally to be more durable than their German opponents.

As de Gaulle argued the major problem with the French army was that at the start of the war it lacked a coherent armoured strategy and tactics that could mirror or rival Germany's offensive tactical predispositions. According to French infantry tactics the tanks were not considered as independent units and were to be deployed in a piecemeal fashion providing close support to infantry on the battlefield. The tanks were to be used to break the stalemate of trench warfare by dealing with the concrete pillboxes or bunkers that held up the infantry advance. For this reason, thick armour and potent guns were of capital importance to French tank design. Although, generally endowed with increased firepower, French tanks were generally slower than their German counterparts. They also lacked the training in fighting in a uniform fashion and their radio equipment was generally inferior to the Germans. Regarding the brief German campaign against France in the early stages of the Second World War tank historian Kenneth Macksey asserts that the French armoured force lacked an armoured tactical plan that could rival their German counterpart:

> The French tanks rarely maneuvered, seeing it in the nature of their role (encouraged by thick armour) to fight from static positions and engage in the kind of duels which honor demanded and which Fuller had deprecated in 1917. In any case the tactics of immobility were forced upon them by lack of radio communication at the lower levels. Battle plans were issued verbally in advance of action; subunits had to congregate and stop to receive fresh detailed orders; and most commands in battle were relayed by flag signal – which frequently were invisible among dispersed positions and through mist of battle smoke.[66]

This largely explains why the French armoured units suffered tremendously in the confrontations with their German counterparts during the campaign in 1940 and why only in a few exceptions (such as the tank battalions led by de Gaulle) did they properly match up with the Panzers. In 1939-40 not only was de Gaulle considered at best an upstart and a nuisance by the French military hierarchy, but his writings on armoured warfare had not been adopted by the French Army. The latter still deployed the tanks in a piecemeal fashion in 1940 and in many

---

66 Kenneth Macksey, *Tank Versus Tank* (London: Grub Street, 1999), p. 65.

battle encounters with the *Wehrmacht* it failed to ward off its opponents' deep sweep maneuvers or to even be able to harass the German Panzer formations as they ultimately advanced deep into French territory. Indeed, some of the key factors, amongst many others, behind the French defeat was the army's focus on fixed defenses and the doctrine of using armoured units as a mere support function to the infantry.

In the inter-war period Britain had several worthy advocates for modern armoured warfare and J.F.C. Fuller was probably the most ardent tank supporter. As chief of staff of the British tank corps during the First World War, he was the architect of the surprise tank attack during the Battle of Cambrai on 20 November 1917 where the British forces put forth the first massed tank assault in the history of warfare. Just before the end of the First World War Fuller had written Plan 1919 that combined the use of storm and commando infantry in the vanguard supported by mechanized forces and aerial power. "Fuller had envisaged in his famous Plan 1919 the concept of the fast tanks breaking through the enemy lines and, supported by mobile infantry and artillery and by air power, ranging far, wide and disruptively deep in the enemy rear while heavy tanks broke down and bypassed enemy main defenses."[67]

After the war, Fuller continued to advocate for the transformation of Britain's military forces from an infantry centered army to one based upon mechanized divisions. Fuller wrote many works such as Tanks in the Great War (1920), The Reformation of War (1923), On Future Warfare (1928), and Memoirs of an Unconventional Soldier (1936) in which he argued on behalf of the centrality of tanks for modern warfare. In the mid-twenties, another British officer, Basil Liddell Hart also wrote several works on military theory in which he criticized the tactics of frontal infantry assaults used by Britain during the First World War. Instead Liddell Hart first proposed that infantry should attack accompanied by tanks and primarily with the soldiers riding on or advancing behind armoured vehicles. He proposed that while the tanks would advance while firing upon enemy defenses, the infantry would be carried to the frontline by motorized assets to knock out concentrated enemy defenses that held up the armoured units. Liddell Hart then later foresaw the need for a combined arms force with armoured units and mobile infantry and artillery.[68]

In 1927, Great Britain constituted its first mechanized force, albeit it was not homogeneous as it was based upon a different number and types of armoured vehicles and tanks. Then shortly thereafter its tanks were fitted with radios enabling the coordination of the various units during training exercises. In the 1930s the military continued to build up its armoured force but there were huge disagreements between planners that wanted to build a force of infantry, 'heavy' tanks versus those that wanted a fast and agile force predicated on light and medium tanks.

Unfortunately, Fuller's theories were not fully embraced in Britain and by 1939 the British Expeditionary Force was still mainly formed by infantry divisions and it had only a more limited armoured force. It also lacked a coherent tactical deployment for the armoured units that could rival German armoured tactical supremacy: "The tank was a British invention of the First World War, but the urge for economy in the inter-war years resulted in the British losing their lead. Very few tanks were built, and work on design and research was severely restricted. The result

---

67 Kenneth Macksey, *Tank Versus Tank*, p. 42.
68 Brian Bond, *Liddell Hart: A Study of his Military Thought* (London: Cassell, 1977).

was that in 1939 the armoured arm was in a very backward state. The latest tanks naturally went to France."[69]

Germany was the main beneficiary of these British and French innovative theories which had been translated into German and were used widely during the officer training courses of the Wehrmacht in the 1930s. The German Army had more outdated, lighter tanks than either France or Britain, while it was also less motorized as the horse was still the main means of transportation for the infantry soldiers and their provisions. In 1939 it had only six armoured divisions and 2,400 tanks, or half the strength of the French Army. Despite these disadvantages, the army was well trained for a war of movement utilizing the combined power of air and land based forces. General Heinz Guderian was the main architect of the German blitzkrieg tactics. In 1937 he published *Achtung! Panzer!* a work that was not original in nature but had the benefit of incorporating the theories of the British Major-General J.F.C. Fuller and Colonel Charles de Gaulle and adapting them to the German reality. Both advocated the creation of independent tank brigades that were to attack enemy lines in conjunction with aerial and specialized infantry forces to effectuate deep flanking maneuvers aimed at trapping frontline troops and then reaching rear defenses. Luckily for Germany Guderian, despite opposition from more conservative elements within the army, enjoyed the support of most of the army and of the top political leaders. The army also for the most part embraced armoured warfare. Thus, tanks in the German army were used not in a piecemeal fashion but in massed formations in conjunction with truck mounted artillery units to punch holes in the enemy line and to isolate segments of the enemy, which were then surrounded and captured by motorized German infantry divisions while the tanks ranged forward to repeat the process. Time after time deep drives into enemy territory by Panzer divisions in Poland and France were thus followed by motorized infantry and foot soldiers which cleared and mopped up enemy trenches. These tactics were supported by dive bombers that attacked and disrupted the enemy's supply and communications lines and spread panic and confusion in its rear, thus further paralyzing enemy defensive capabilities. Mechanization was the key to the German fast moving offensives, or "lightning war," so named because of the unprecedented speed and mobility that were its salient characteristics. With tested and well-trained maneuvers adopted against Poland, the German Panzer divisions constituted a force with no equal in Europe. Thus, the German army, at least in 1939-41 held a tactical superiority versus the Allied forces and especially versus the French that allowed it to win the campaign in the West.

During the North African campaign, German, tactical armed superiority would achieve relevant victories while deploying comparatively very few resources. In the desert, German doctrine focused on the Sturmtruppen tactics of the Great War adopted and updated to mechanized warfare. The focus was to concentrate armour, mobile artillery and infantry against the critical point of decision where the enemy defenses were weak or in a disorganized state. Time and time again the German armoured units would engage the British tanks and then make believe that they were about to flee as if they were on the losing end of the confrontation.

As British tanks commenced pursuit of their adversary, they were met by an advanced screen of mobile anti-gun units armed primarily with 88mm Flak 36 guns. These very powerful guns

---

69 I.S.O. Playfair, *The Mediterranean and Middle East, Volume I: The Early Successes against Italy to May 1941* (London: Her Majesty's Stationary Office, 1954), p. 104.

would then typically knock out several enemy tanks. In the words of a British commander: "He (Rommel's) handling of armour, antitank guns and mechanized formations in cooperation was, with the Shwerpunkt principle, much better than our dispersed idea of fighting."[70] The same tactic was repeatedly employed throughout the desert campaign leading to several successful encounters against the Allies. Even in 1943 at the battle of the Kasserine Pass the Germans obtained a critical victory against the green Americans which were pitted against a screen of 88mm units and several tank battalions. According to the authoritative West Point History of the war "Rommel benefited from the use of the 88mm anti-aircraft gun as an effective tank killer and from the higher quality of German tanks compared to those of the British. He was a master of the battle of maneuver, taking risks and surprising his enemy."[71]

The British on the other hand failed in their counteroffensives in 1941 "because of a lack of effective air support and the unsophisticated use of armour in frontal assaults against well defended positions."[72] According to historian Niall Barr the German Panzer divisions possessed several attributes and capabilities that made them dominant European battlefields during 1939-42:

> The Germans may not have possessed deep knowledge of desert conditions, but they did possess a clear and well defined doctrine for armoured warfare which they had developed and refined during the Polish and French campaigns.
>
> When the 5th Light Division arrived in Libya it was able to execute those methods without change. The all arms combination of Panzer divisions had been tested and proved during the early years of the war. Each division was a fine balance of all arms, consisting of a reconnaissance unit, a Panzer regiment composed of two tank battalions, a rifle regiment of three battalions and an artillery regiment. The backbone of the Panzer regiments was provided by the Panzer III and IV, which were relatively well armed, armoured and reliable tanks which generally outmatched their British counterparts.
>
> There was also a generous allocation of antitank and anti-aircraft guns along with engineers and support services within each division.[73]

It was against the above-mentioned cutting edge features and capabilities of the Wehrmacht that the other forces engaged in the conflict in North Africa had to measure themselves against. The Germans were not only superior with some of their equipment but also with their tactics. Throughout the conflict both the Commonwealth and the Italians were constantly attempting to imitate German tactics and develop similar capabilities in terms of the mechanized equipment and weapons. The Italians in particular, had shown in prior campaigns that their infantry was effective when deployed in a static defensive fashion, but that despite its ability to unleash substantial artillery power its offensives had been less successful and had caused heavy casualties. Thus, despite the policy move toward mechanization of the period between 1938-40, the

---

70   Oscar E. Gilbert and Romain Cansiere, *Tanks: A Century of Tank Warfare* (London: Casemate, 2017), p.73.
71   *The West Point History of World War II, vol. I* (New York: Simon and Schuster, 2016), p.131.
72   Ibid.
73   Niall Barr, 'Rommel in the Western Desert' in Ian Beckett (ed.), *Rommel Reconsidered* (Mechanicsburg, Pennsylvania: Stackpole, 2013), p. 68.

Italian Army still had to demonstrate that it could adapt to a more mobile war, a war of movement. This required good inter-service collaboration, effective weapons and vehicles to support such an offensive and most importantly a strong focus by the officers on advanced reconnaissance and proper logistical planning of a prolonged offensive.

Italian Medium Tanks

Tank performance can be evaluated by narrowing in on three factors such as speed/mobility, firepower and armour thickness. Firepower is a function of the size of the tank and typically the bigger the tank the bigger the gun that it can carry. Two, the thickness of the armour protection will influence the weight of the tank and its overall mobility/speed. The bigger the tank, typically the greater its invulnerability to enemy fire. Third, the engine and the weight of the tank will determine its speed. Thus, tank design is based on the dichotomy between speed versus firepower and the degree of armour protection. The medium tanks produced by the Italians tended to favor since the inception a lighter construction over firepower for several reasons including a lack of suitable engines for larger tanks. In late 1939 and throughout 1940 the Army finally began to receive new tanks in the form of the M.11/39, an eleven-ton tank designed by Ansaldo and produced in a joint venture with Fiat. The tank was armed with a 37/40 (37mm *Vickers/Terni* L 40) gun and two machine guns (8mm *Breda modello* 38). The cannon was mounted on the hull and the machine guns in the turret. It was ideally designed to be operated in the mountainous or per-mountainous regions of Italy by a three-man crew given its relative light weight compared to other European medium tanks. The commander fired the machine gun, an operator drove the tank while the third member of the crew fired the gun. The hull was constructed of 30mm armoured plates that were riveted or bolted since Italian industry still could not weld on a mass scale, while the rest of the body averaged a thickness of 15mm. The armour protection was not adequate to stop the penetration of the standard British 2-pounder anti-tank gun. Military planners originally envisioned a radio set for each vehicle, but due to the delay in manufacturing the radios, the M.11/39 tanks that were fielded in North Africa did not have them.

By European standards of 1940 it was light for a medium tank with maximum armour thickness of 30mm in the turret. The tank's top speed was 34 kph (21.1 mph) on paved roads, while it achieved 15 kph (9.3 mph) on non-paved roads.[74] By mid-1940, 100 M.11/39 units had been built and delivered to the army with *Ariete* taking the lion share of these units. The desert conditions of North Africa, for instance, were not considered when the vehicle was designed and manufactured and its ineffectiveness in traveling long distances in the desert terrain was clearly demonstrated during General Graziani's advance on Sidi Barrani. Most of these tanks would eventually be lost in North Africa during Operation Compass, while twenty-four were lost during the campaign in Italian East Africa.

---

74 The tank's ineffectiveness was also caused by its mechanical reliability that was tested by the fact that military planners failed to developed a transporter for the M.11/39. Lacking a dedicated transporter; the tank crews had to drive from their bases to the frontline, which further limited the tank's effectiveness. This would be a recurring problem with other larger medium tanks such as the M.13 and M.14.

In late 1940 the production of the tank was discontinued since heavier and better armed tanks were required to fight the British armoured units and the choice was to build M.13 and later the M.14 tanks. But it is important to point out that "the M.11 tank bore most of the hallmarks of the subsequent Italian tank production; the hull was made of armoured plates at minimal angles, bolted or riveted (Italian industry lacked skills for welding, seldom used), with the bottom part of the hull made of a frontal nose plate and a frontal glacis plate connecting to the casemate, with two interconnected plates running on both sies of the hull from the sprocket wheel to engine compartment."[75] In fact, production was shifted toward the M.13 and M.14 tank designs even if they did not deviate too much from the model of the M.11. The first alternative to the M.11 was found in the M.13/40 tank which was a turret gun-mounted tank weighing more than the M.11 (14 tons) and equipped with the main armament represented by a more powerful 47mm gun and two 8mm Breda *modello* 38 machine guns.[76] The M.13 had a top speed on the road of 32 kph (19.9 mph) and off road of 15 kph (9.3 mph) with a slightly thicker armour around the main body of the tank with the turret plate being 30mm thick while most other plates were 25mm thick with the exception of the turret which was 42mm thick, while the roof was 15mm and the floor was 6mm.[77] The engine was a 12-litre, eight cylinder SPA 8 TM 40 diesel oil engine of 125hp.[78] It could be operated by a crew of four or three and it was hurriedly introduced into service in the fall of 1940 in both Greece and North Africa. Construction and assembly of the tank's body was like the M.11 achieved by bolting and riveting armour plates.

The M.13/40 was a somewhat reliable tank but as the campaign wore on it became largely outdated. "When this tank was designed, it was on par with contemporary designs in other nations and was adequate for the early period of World War II. Only after further tank developments and advances would this series of tanks become inadequate."[79] Some of its major technical and armament problem areas included: poor armour protection which was compensated by storing sandbags on the tank for extra protection, slow speed on non-paved roads, a modest gun, an engine that was not powerful enough and that was also frequently prone to mechanical breakdowns in the desert.[80]

Another major problem was the lack of radio equipment. Due to slow production of radio systems most Italian tanks lacked radios in 1940-41. It was only after the arrival of the DAK in early 1941 that new Italian medium tanks came with radio sets, while some tanks already deployed in North Africa were retrofitted with radios. By mid-1941 the new tanks M.13/40 came with a Marelli RF 1 CA radio that was located on the right side of the crew compartment. But poor two way communication between command centers and armoured and motorized battalions continued to plague the Italian units throughout the North Africa campaign. A report from mid-1942 from the Trieste Division states that: "We have taken the necessary steps to ensure the proper functioning of our telephone, telegraphy and radio communications. But the nearest command headquarters to the

---

75 Pier Paolo Battistelli and Filippo Cappellano, *Italian Medium Tanks* (Oxford: Osprey, 2012) p. 6.
76 Technical drawings and basic design work were completed in 1937 and the first prototype was delivered to in October 1939.
77 Pier Paolo Battistelli and Filippo Cappellano, *Italian Medium Tanks*, p. 10.
78 Ibid, p. 11.
79 Major Howard Christie, *Fallen Eagles: The Italian 10th Army in the Opening Campaign in the Western Desert*, p. 117.
80 Pier Paolo Battistelli and Filippo Cappellano, *Italian Medium Tanks*, p. 14.

area of operations will have to rely on dispatch runners on motorcycles or cars in emergency situations. Every unit must ensure the speedy communication of information especially under emergency circumstances. One must keep in mind that radio at short distances remains the slowest means of communication because of the need to cipher and decipher."[81] Initially the tank was equipped with a 125 hp engine that was underpowered to begin with also because the crews used, sandbags and spare track links to increase protection from the more powerful enemy guns. Although this solution, which was adopted locally in North Africa, made the tanks slightly more secure, it also created other problems. The increased weight of the tanks, for instance, further decreased its speed. Then in late spring of 1941 a new 145 hp engine was used to retrofit existing tanks in North Africa which made them slightly faster by achieving a top speed of 33 kph (20.5 mph) on road and 16 kph (9.9 mph) off-road, but still far slower than comparable British medium tanks which were equipped with a 340 hp engine and a top speed of 26 mph (41.8 kph).

In 1940 the L.6 light tank also was delivered to the Army with a 20mm cannon mounted on the turret. This tank was introduced to progressively replace the L.3 light tanks that were armed with machine guns, but both were totally obsolete by then. Thus, the L.6 was used by the troops primarily for reconnaissance and very rarely was deployed in tank versus tank combat actions.

In 1941 the Army also received the M.14/41 tank which was slightly different from the M.13/40 but by the time it entered the battlefield it too was "already outdated because of insufficient gunnery and inadequate armour."[82] Both could match up fairly well against British Mark IV Cruiser A13, and not as well but still somewhat satisfactorily against the Mark VI Crusader A15 and United States M 3 Honey tanks. The M.14/41 sported a 47mm gun which had a rate of fire of 20 rounds per minute, a range of 700 meters, and its projectile could pierce 43mm of armour at a distance of 500 meters[83]. Still the Crusader had some technical specifications that made it a better all-around tank than the Italian medium tank series. The Crusader was a 19-ton tank with a 2 QF Vickers 2-pdr (40 mm/1.57 in) gun and a machine-gun. The gun had a penetration of 44mm at a distance of 915 meters or less and it had 40mm of armour on the turret. Its major downside was the frequency of mechanical trouble which was a constant thorn to the side of British armoured units. Both the M.13 and M.14, however, were slower than the 26 and 19 mph (off-road) speeds of the Crusader and were no match in terms of firepower to the Grant and Sherman tanks or the British Valentine tanks that were introduced in 1942. The Italian medium tank was vulnerable to the standard British anti-tank as attested in the following combat report which presumably refers to a combat action between Italian medium tanks pitted against an anti-tank screen comprised of 2-pdr guns. "The British 2-pounder proved a most effective antitank gun for small infantry units. As an illustration, the British were holding a position overlooking a well with one infantry platoon and a section (two guns) of 2-pounders; they were attacked by one British infantry tank (which the Axis troops had salvaged) and four Italian tanks. The 2-pounders got the infantry tank at 400 yards and then in turn the four Italian tanks, the last within 50 yards of the position."[84] During the North African campaign

---

81 Dattilo Ciampini, 'La fanteria motorizzata tra modello ed esperienze: la Trieste in Africa settentrionale 1941-1942', *Quaderno di Storia Militare*, Anno 2009, pp. 163-64.
82 Pier Paolo Battistelli and Filippo Cappellano, *Italian Medium Tanks*, p. 14.
83 Ibid. p. 14.
84 'The British Capture of Bardia (December 1941-January 1942): A Successful Infantry-Tank Attack', Military Intelligence Service, War Department, *Information Bulletin*, No. 21, March 1943.

the Italians would eventually manage to deal effectively with the 2-pdr anti-tank gun by putting forth medium tank attacks that were supported on the flanks by self-propelled artillery units armed with a 75mm gun that could effectively neutralize the British gun. But the medium tanks could never deal effectively with a defensive screen comprised of 6-pdr guns. In fact, the confrontations between the medium tanks against the heavier anti-tank guns introduced by the British after the first year of the war such as the 6-pdr gun were especially dire. The British gun could effectively pick out Italian medium tanks even at safe distances of 500 meters (547 yards) or greater and even the German tank units would suffer high casualties when confronting the 6-pdr gun. Even more troublesome for the crews was the British 25-pdr gun, which could penetrate 54mm of armour at 1,000 yards or less and was also particularly effective against the M series tanks which had a range frontal armour thickness that was much less than 54mm. It was a gun that was appreciated by the Axis units and when several of these guns fell into Axis hands, the Italian mechanized and motorized artillery units would use them extensively. The M.14/41 tank offered improved mechanical reliability due to its more powerful engine (the original M.13's 125 hp engine was replaced with a 145 hp engine) while it weighed just 14 tons. It also could carry more ammunition than the M.13/40 with 87 rounds and it had slightly thicker armour in some sections of the main body. Its main downside was its 47mm gun which was obsolete against the heavier American and British tanks of 1942. Moreover, the first batches of M.14/41, which began to be produced in August of 1941, still had no radio. The British tanks had the advantage of radio, unlike most of the M.11, M. 13 and M.14 tanks, which had to move against pre-determined objectives and then wait for orders. While waiting for orders the commanders had to dismount from the tank to enter into communication with their superiors.[85] This slowed down operations considerably and exposed the crews to enemy artillery and air fire especially when the tanks were idle. The American intelligence services, for example, while acknowledging the technical changes made by the Italians with the 1941 medium tank, did not consider the M.14 tank to be too technically different from the M.13: "Recent reports show that there have been changes in the Italian tank M.13/40. The modified version is known as M.14/41. The armour has been reinforced by additional plates, the basic armour remaining the same. In consequence of these modifications the weight is now reported to be 1 ton heavier, i.e. 14 tons. The engine of the M.14/41 is said to be 145 h.p."[86]

To overcome the weaknesses of the M.14 tank especially when pitted against Grant or Sherman tanks, the Italian Army sought the development of a heavier medium tank. Thus, in 1942 Ansaldo/ Fiat introduced the M.15/42 tank which was slightly heavier than the M.14 and could carry up of 111 rounds for its improved 47/40 gun. Its new 12-litre Fiat SPA 15TB 190 hp petrol fueled engine allowed the tank to travel at a top speed of 38 kph (23.6 mph) on the road and 20 kph (12.4 mph) off road and a range of 200 kilometers. It was armed with a turret-mounted 47mm Ansaldo L/40 gun and two hull-mounted 8mm Breda *modello* 38 machine guns.[87] According to historian Nicola Pignato: "The longer barrel provided increased muzzle velocity, which translated into a flatter trajectory, increased range, and greater striking power."[88] The tank

---

85 Kenneth Macksey, *Beda Fomm: The Classic Victory* (New York: Ballantine Books, 1972), p. 145.
86 'Italian Tank Modifications', Military Intelligence Service, *Tactical and Technical Trends*, Number 6, 27 August, 1942.
87 Pier Paolo Battistelli and Filippo Cappellano, *Italian Medium Tanks*, p. 14.
88 Nicola Pignato, *Italian Armoured Vehicles World War Two* (Carrollton: Signal, 2004), p. 41.

was meant to replace the M.14/41 tank, but the first batches of the M.15/42 were delivered to the Army in early 1943 when the situation in North Africa had changed dramatically. Unfortunately, the tank although heavier than the M.14 was still no match to the medium American tanks such as the Grant and Sherman units and thus the Army cut the initial order of 280 to 220 units. Thus, the Army finally realizing that the medium tank series had brought Italian armoured units at a dead end in terms of tactics and firepower, instructed Ansaldo/Fiat in 1943 to focus production efforts on the *semovente*, self-propelled gun, the only Italian manufactured unit that could perform satisfactorily against the American medium tanks. It must be reiterated that Italian medium tank production was hampered by several factors, with the development of a viable engine being one of the main obstacles delaying the construction of a heavier medium tank. The original 105 hp engine that was used on the M.11/39 tank was unsuitable for a larger tank. The M.13/40 tank was assembled with a 125 hp engine and the M.14/41 with a 145 hp engine. Other attempts, for instance, the development of the P-40 infantry tank also were delayed in part by the lack of a suitable engine. Throughout the war the Italian technicians looked to Germany for help. One recommendation that was flouted was to use German Maybach engines for Italian tanks. Another was to convert aircraft engines for tank production. For various reasons both proposals were not implemented and the engine remained one of the biggest problems impacting upon Italian tank performance making them less mechanically reliable and slower than comparable German or British/American medium tanks that had more powerful engines.

Self-propelled Artillery

Regarding the development of the Italian self-propelled gun, an effective weapon against the Allies, there are two different versions about its origins. First, according to the official history of the war of the artillery branch[89], the weapon was the brainchild of one of its officers *Colonnello* Sergio Berlese, who had previously designed several artillery guns for the Army (such as the *Obice da 75/18 modello* 34, a 75mm howitzer) and that in 1940 was in charge of the *Servizio Tecnico Artigleria*, the Army technical evaluation agency. According to this interpretation Berlese encouraged *Comando Supremo* to authorize the construction of an armoured fighting vehicle in the mold of the German *Sturmgeschutz* III. One of the keys to German success, he noted, in the West against France had been the deployment in May 1940 of assault guns carrying a 75mm short barrel gun mounted on the chassis of the medium tanks. As a result Berlese was quick to propose to the army the construction of an Italian self-propelled model that would have similar characteristics. Second, according to Ansaldo, they were the first to propose its construction: "On 10 February 1941 we proposed along with the 90/53 truck mounted gun the first design prototype of the 75/18 howitzer mounted on the chassis of the M.13 tank (semovente da 75/18). We had begun to design this weapon in September of 1940 together with our business partner Fossati."[90] Thus according to Ansaldo, Berlese backed their idea and teamed up with Ansaldo technicians to implement the project. From the archive documentation available it is not possible to determine which version is to be believed and it is likely that the effort behind the self-propelled gun was the work of both parties.

---

89   Carlo Montu', *Storia della'artiglieria italiana* (Roma: Rivista artiglieria e genio, 1955).
90   Ceva and Curami, *La meccanizzazione dell'esercito*, p. 329.

On 18 March 1941 the Army would then approve a purchase order for an initial thirty assault guns and eighteen command vehicles (same design but two machine guns instead of the gun) to be delivered no later than April or May of the same year. A month later the first prototypes would pass the shooting range test which was held at Cornigliano and shortly thereafter they would be rushed into service. Whilst these vehicles were built on the chassis of an already existing tank model, the celerity with which they were designed and then pressed into service demonstrates that despite its many shortcomings the Italian military industry complex was not always ineffectual during the war. The *semovente* was indeed an excellent weapon that represented much more than a stop gap solution to be used prior to the introduction of the heavy tank. In Berlese's view a 75mm self-propelled gun would not only furnish the artillery and the armoured divisions with greater punch, but possibly also allow the Italian Army to adopt some of the advanced German combined arms tactics which had proved to be very successful during the French campaign. According to Nicola Pignato: "This vehicle was developed to provide the field forces with both an anti-tank and an armoured artillery vehicle and as an interim step before the development of the heavy P-series tanks."[91] The first model[92] produced in mid-1941 was the *semovente M 40 da 75/18* which was based on the chassis of the M.13/40 tank and equipped with a 6.5mm Breda machine gun along with the 75mm gun. It retained the hull and the engine of the M.40 tank with a redesigned casemate with large frontal armour comprised of two bolted plates that were 25mm thick. It weighted 13 tons and was equipped with a Marelli RF 1 CA radio.[93] There were only sixty of these *semoventi* built during the conflict. Production was quickly shifted to a more powerful *semovente* M 41 *da 75/18* because it also had a 75/18 howitzer capable of firing both high explosive and armour-piercing rounds along with a 8mm Breda *modello* 38 machine gun but it was based on the chassis of the M.14/41 tank. It weighted 13.5 tons and it had a top speed of 34 kph (21.1 mph). "The 75/18 gun had a reduced rate of fire, only ten rounds per minute, and a low muzzle velocity of only 425 meters per second, but this made it perfectly suitable for hollow charge rounds like the 5.2 kg EP, which enabled it to penetrate 70mm of armour at 500 meters."[94] It was more heavily armed than the M.14 tank but it had some of the same weaknesses such as not thick enough armoured plates and the same mechanical problems in the engine compartment. It was also subjected, just like the M.14, to overheating forcing the crews to frequently fight with the hatch open. This was very dangerous and exposed the crews to terrible injuries especially from splinters or machine gun volleys ricocheting into their compartment. The *Semovente da 75/18* was operated by a three men crew. The driver sat to the left of the 75mm gun, while the commander/gunner was on the right and the ammunition carrier and loader sat behind them. Each *Semovente da 75/18* carried 44 rounds of high explosive and armour-piercing shells.

The *Carro Comando* (command tank) vehicles for the *semoventi* units were also designed and built based on a turretless M.13/40 (later M.14/41) chassis. These originally retained the twin

---

91 Ibid., p. 41.
92 One L.3-35 was modified into a prototype self-propelled gun vehicle – the *Semovente da 47/32* in 1939. The top of the tank was removed and a 47mm Breda Cannone da 47/32 M35 gun was mounted on the front hull. Although several trials were conducted, military planners did not give the green light to the manufacturer for the Semovente da 47/32 to go under mass production.
93 Paolo Battistelli and Filippo Cappellano, *Italian Medium Tanks*, p. 19.
94 Ibid., p. 35.

8mm machine guns, which was later in 1942 replaced by a 13.2mm Breda *modello* 31 heavy machine gun.

In late 1941 a heavier *semovente* with a 90/53 gun was also manufactured and it was also based on the chassis of the M.14/41 tank. Although this self-propelled gun was heavier (weighing 15.7 tons and carrying heavier shells), it had a top speed of only 25 kph (15.5 mph) because of its heavier constitution. Despite its more powerful gun, it was not a completely successful model and few units were built. Its major downside was its greater weight which rendered it a slow moving vehicle. It was built with the Soviet T-34 tank in mind as the Italian *semovente* had to have similar firepower and heavier construction. The *Semovente da 90/53* mounted a 90mm *Ansaldo Cannone da 90/53* dual-purpose (anti-aircraft/anti-tank) gun. Its gun was similar, if not slightly superior, to the German 88mm Flak 36. For example, the Italian gun had an "impressive rate of 12 rounds per minute, a muzzle velocity of 758 meters per second and a range of 2,000 meters, which enabled its 12.1 kg armoured-piercing shell to penetrate 140mm of armour at 500 meters and 120mm at 1,000 meters."[95] It thus had tremendous firepower and could go head to head with any Allied medium tank in 1942. Its interior was made to accommodate two crewmen in front and two in the back but it was cramped and could only carry eight rounds. This required a modified L. 6-40 ammunition carrier with 24 rounds towing a trailer with additional rounds of ammunition. Of the first three models of self-propelled guns the Army ordered 60 *semoventi da 75* and 40 *carri comando* built on the chassis of the M.13 tank. 130 *semoventi* and 66 *carri comando* built on the chassis of the M.14 tank and 30 *semoventi da 90/53*.

Shortly thereafter 190 units were built of the *semovente* M.42 da 75/18, which was based on the chassis of the M.15/42 tank.[96] In quick succession a new *semovente* based on the chassis of the M.15/42 tank was also placed into production. The M 42 *da 75/34 semovente* was designed with the 75/34 gun that was originally intended for the P.40 heavy tank. This self-propelled gun had 50mm thick frontal armour, a weight of 15.3 tons and a maximum speed of 38.4 kph (23.9 mph). The inability by the Italian industry planners to finalize technical specifications from the P.40 tank led Ansaldo to focus production on the M 42 and then the M 43 *semovente* series. The latter was still based on the M.15/42 tank chassis and with a 105/25 gun, it weighted 15.3 tons and welded plates. The latter was nicknamed the *bassotto* (the short one) because of its extremely low silhouette. With a 190 hp petrol fueled engine, they had a top speed of 38 kph (23.6 mph) on the road and were also of a very thick construction with 70mm of armour in the casemate, 55 in the front nose and 45mm on the hull sides. They were the most powerful self-propelled artillery guns produced by the Italians during the war and with a very low silhouette, even lower than the M 42 da 75/18 self-propelled gun, which made for a terrific tank hunter. Unfortunately, these guns came too late into the war and they were only fielded by the Army just before the Italian surrender of 1943. The *Semovente* da 105/25 was generally well liked by

---

95 Paolo Battistelli and Filippo Cappellano, *Italian Medium Tanks*, pp. 35-36.
96 At approximately the same time, the Army ordered production of the Semovente da 47/32 which mounted a 47mm Ansaldo 47/32 gun on a turretless L. 6-40 chassis. It was ordered into production in early 1941 but did not enter service until late 1942. By that date, it was hopelessly ineffective against most enemy tanks it faced on both the Russian and North African fronts. Ansaldo also produced a Carro Comando L 40 (command company vehicle) version of the Semovente da 47/32. It had a similar design to the light semovente with the only exception that it had no gun. It had a fake 47mm gun concealing an 8mm Breda Modello 33 machine gun.

the crews because it was not only the most heavily armed assault gun in Italian service, but it was also well protected and reliable. The Germans liked the *Bassotto* as well and ordered several of them after the Italian surrender.

Initially the role of these assault guns was intended as one of artillery support to give firepower to the *bersaglieri* regiments of the armoured units. In this role, the weapon would be used in a more static position first as an anti-tank weapon and secondly as a support weapon as the motorized infantry advanced against an enemy anti-tank screen. But after the first battle experiences, the *semovente* was deemed as an above average weapon that could also flank the armoured battalions during offensive operations as well as go head to head against enemy tanks. A final role for the *semovente* was the deployment of one or more of the self-propelled gun batteries to strengthen the reconnaissance units. Since these units were primarily composed of light skinned vehicles, the *semovente* was there to provide the firepower in case the reconnaissance team encountered enemy units comprised of light to medium tanks. As the Allies introduced more powerful and thicker skinned medium tank vehicles with 75mm guns, the *semovente* became the only reliable Italian armoured vehicle that could be successfully deployed. The weapon would play a key role during the Axis counteroffensive of 1942 often going head to head against primarily against American medium tanks. General Giovanni Messe, who commanded the Axis forces in North Africa after Rommel's departure, stated in 1943 that the "the self-propelled 75/18 unit, not only has greater firepower than the M.14 tank and a reduced vulnerability but also has greater maneuverability and improved technical features."[97] Thus self-propelled guns retained their effectiveness even in the face of increased improvement from the Allies which were building heavier medium tanks and self-propelled guns of their own and despite its relatively slow speed.

In Search of New Medium Tanks

Given the delays related to the development of the P-Heavy tank and the feedback received from the front regarding the moderate to low mechanical reliability of the M.13/40 tank, the Italians, on the heels of Operation Compass asked for German assistance in obtaining improved medium tanks. The impulse came directly from *Generale* Alfredo Guzzoni that at the time held the number two position within Comando Supremo (*Sottocapo di Stato Maggiore Generale*) but was essentially the temporary head of *Comando Supremo* given Cavallero's involvement in Greece. In addition the frontline reports submitted by Generale Roatta in the spring of 1941 would also contribute to the Army looking for alternatives to the M series tanks. According to historian Lucio Ceva it was mainly Guzzoni who introduced a sensible change in industry/armed forces relationships opting for a more distant relationship between the duopoly of Fiat and Ansaldo[98] and the military with the establishment of more rigorous purchasing practices and the attempt to establish another

---

97   Nicola Pignato, *I mezzi blindo-corazzati italiani 1923-1943 (*Parma: Albertelli, 2007), p. 121.
98   The duo of Fiat and Ansaldo not only was against other domestic suppliers working for the military such as Lancia, Officine Reggiane etc. … but also opposed foreign companies. For instance, Ford was prevented from competing with Italian automobile company Fiat, which, along with its partner Ansaldo, retained the monopoly on the Italian production of tanks. See MacGregor Knox, *Hitler's Italian Allies*, pp.40-42.

industrial conglomerate led by Lancia and Reggiane to build German tanks in Italy[99]. Guzzoni's work would result not only in the evaluation of alternatives to the M series tanks produced exclusively by Ansaldo and Fiat who since the 1930s had a hold on the lionshare of the military commissions for tanks and armoured vehicles but also in the introduction of the 75 mm self-propelled guns, the purchase of more armoured cars and mobile artillery. The first attempt to secure better tanks was to gain German assistance. The Italian attaché in Berlin was tasked with securing French captured tanks, which the Germans did release to the Italians although not the quantity (800 were originally requested) that the latter were looking for. In addition, the French tanks came with few spare parts thus were inoperable for long periods of time and thus it was decided to deploy them in Italy to train armoured crews rather than ship them to the frontline troops in Africa. Given the fact that only 130 French tanks were secured, a second attempt was made with the Germans to obtain medium tanks and self-propelled guns from Skoda, the Czech industrial conglomerate that was now under German control. The latter provided the Italians with a Skoda T12 tank that was tested extensively in June 1941. The opening toward other manufacturers, especially foreign ones, was a belated attempt by *Comando Supremo* and military planners to open up the tank production market beyond Fiat and Ansaldo. Ugo Cavallero, who came from industry, and had now replaced Badoglio at *Comando Supremo*, is often credited with this move, but in reality the real propulsor of the effort was his number two Guzzoni who saw as one of his missions to expand the Italian armoured fleet by way of the domestic market, such as exploring the feasibility of awarding tank construction commissions to Lancia, OTO, and Alfa Romeo, and also by way of the international market. According to the study on Italian mechanization by Ceva and Curami, Skoda was the first non-Italian firm that was considered, mainly by a directive issued by General Guzzoni which outlined not only the speed of the tank at 47.2 kph (29.3 mph) but also that given its performance it offered the crews much better protection vis a vis the M series tanks.[100] Skoda was very eager to gain a commission from the Italian government to build armoured vehicles also because the Germans were not interested in purchasing the T-12 at the time. Cavallero initially was also appreciative of the tank's performance especially its speed and its armoured protection but ultimately the offer was turned down after much pressure from Fiat and Ansaldo. For the two historians, the Skoda T-12 was a more effective tank than the M.13/40 with increased firepower and speed. Its only downside was its fuel efficiency. Moreover, in the field it proved to be a worthy tank used by both the armies of Hungary and Romania until late into the war. In a chapter titled the 'The Victory of the Monopoly' they conclude by arguing that Skoda was ultimately turned down for spurious reasons by Cavallero who had been open initially to other producers but ultimately was apparently too close to Ansaldo and its president Agostino Rocca: "The issue appears to be very clear. Cavallero ultimately did not want the Skoda tanks, but his arguments against them are less clear. His arguments against the Czech tanks are not only debatable but full of inaccuracies."[101] Another attempt to develop a more effective medium tank took place in August 1941 when the Italians considered to begin construction under German license of the *Panzerkampfwagen* III tank and temporarily abandoned or put aside the plan to build a domestic (the P40) heavy tank. Italy had never built a heavy tank even after the Matilda II tank

---

99   Lucio Ceva, 'Rapporti fra industria ed esercito' in *Italia in Guerra*, vol. 2, (Rome: Ufficio Storico, 1995), p. 223.
100 Ibid., p. 225.
101 Ceva and Curami, *La meccanizzazione dell'esercito fino al '43*, p. 353.

performed so well against the Italian infantry during Wavell's offensive in 1940. Several designs were considered and analyzed but production had always stalled. When in the summer of 1941 the plan to begin producing the P-40 tanks again was put on the backburner, "the Germans agreed to authorize licensed production of their Panzer III tank on the condition that the Italians produced it without armaments and gunsights. These would have been supplied by the Germans together with half the raw materials needed for the tank production. These restrictions, along with the competition between Ansaldo and Fiat, and the general staff's reluctance to put Italian industry in German hands, soon brought the project to an end."[102] Thus, this first attempt to build the German tank fell through when the Axis allies could not agree on the deal and because of the opposition from the domestic manufacturer Ansaldo against it. One of the deal's main sticking points was that the Germans along with the license were also to furnish the raw materials to the Italian Fiat factories for the production of the tanks. By providing the raw materials the German industry could in essence control the production flow within Italian factories and ramp it up or down according to German and not necessarily to Italian production priorities. Also, the Italians had also hoped to sway Germany to furnish the hull and other components of captured Soviet tanks whose material would have been reused to produce the German tanks in Italian factories. It is not clear from the documentation whether Cavallero believed that the Germans would have readily agreed to furnish the parts requested. The lack of such parts and of the raw materials represented a potential threat to the meeting of quota production within Italian tank factories and would also make Italian industries captive to those in Germany. Ansaldo also opposed the plan because it would have relegated it to a secondary domestic manufacturer at the expense of a partnership between Fiat and German industry. Its president Rocca, for example, mobilized the Genoa branch of the party and its affiliated unions to lobby Rome against the production of German tanks which would have, in his view, detrimental effects on production levels and employment in the Ansaldo factories. Ceva and Curami, for instance, maintain that this pressure by the Genova based Ansaldo was one of the main factors that led to the rejection of the German offer.[103] For both political and economic considerations, along with strong domestic opposition from the duopoly the German offer was ultimately rejected. By this time General Guzzoni's position had been eliminated by the centralizer Cavallero that wanted to assume greater power of control over all branches of the armed forces and on purchasing decisions especially while the former was placed in retirement and shortly thereafter Roatta would be assigned to the Balkans. Many of Guzzoni's independent initiatives such as looking abroad for better tanks as a result were cancelled or fell to the wayside. "Only in February of 1942 did the Germans return to the issue, this time with a proposal for licensed production of the Panzer IV tank, but between March and April 1942 both sides agreed to quit the whole matter."[104]

It is unclear whether in 1942 the same conditions set in 1941 applied but the deal ultimately also fell through. Historian Emilio Faldella argues that in this case the Germans were more than willing to provide the license and the assistance for the production of such a tank and that Ansaldo had committed to manufacturing fifty tanks per month by the spring of 1942. "But such a tank required a 300 HP engine that Fiat at that time did not have. Lancia had such an engine and had a stock of over 300 engines. The problem appeared to have been resolved. But

---

102 Paolo Battistelli and Filippo Cappellano, *Italian Medium Tanks*, p. 14.
103 Ceva and Curami, *La meccanizzazione dell'esercito fino al '43*, p. 353.
104 Ibid.

ultimately the parties could not come to an agreement since Ansaldo had a preexisting agreement to source the engines exclusively from Fiat."[105] As Knox asserts Italian industry was much inferior when it came to technology innovation or mass production with respect to tanks and German equipment was superior to the Italian M tank series. As a result, Italian crews equipped with German tanks would likely have performed better in North Africa. But again, political and economic considerations regarding excessive Italian industry dependence on German production of key mechanical components continued to weigh upon the Italian chief of staff. In addition, Fiat and Ansaldo (the two most consistent military suppliers) "successfully if covertly resisted production in Italy of the Panzer III and IV, for which Germany and Hitler in person, intermittently offered designs, patents and even machine tools."[106] Later in the year (November) the Germans even allowed the construction in Italy of the Panther tank. This would have meant that other domestic manufacturers such as Reggiane, OTO, Lancia and Alfa Romeo could have aspired to win tank construction and assembly commissions since Fiat and Ansaldo were by then working under full capacity assembling primarily M series tanks. Ultimately, the duopoly did enough to dissuade the Italian military leadership against the Panther tank and sway them in favor of once again resurrecting the P-40 tank and while the two continued to produce obsolete M tanks even in 1943 and put forth plans for a technically more advanced P.40 tank, the production of German tanks never took off mainly due to a lack of political will. Strong pressure against the Panther tank was exerted by industry but it is not clear what other requirements came with the offer and whether they would have restricted the autonomy of the domestic manufacturing sector. Thus, whether we consider the Skoda tank or German armour two issues appear fairly clear. First, both Ansaldo and Fiat did exert undue influence over the purchasing decisions of the military by shielding their contracts from outside interference. They used the local party branch in Genova and Torino to advance their position on their behalf or the president of Ansaldo Rocca often did the bidding himself by lobbying key military and government figures. Second, the military and the political authorities failed to oversee and properly regulate the industry ultimately by being too close and too reliant on it. Since the feedback from the armoured crews on the M.13/40 had been negative since 1940, it appears that both the political authorities and *Comando Supremo* should have pushed back harder against the duopoly Ansaldo/Fiat or they should have opened the tank design and production industry to other manufacturers or to source product from Germany or Czechoslovakia. Historian Frederick Deakin has argued that: "Cavallero had attempted to standardize the production of Italian tanks based on German models, but he encountered strong opposition from Italian industrialists."[107] Similarly, Roatta wrote that "Comando Supremo while aware of the issues, ordered the continuation of the production of the M tanks."[108]

From the documentation reviewed it appears that the option to source tanks from Skoda would have been more beneficial to the armoured units. The tank that Skoda had put on the table was largely an improvement over the M.13 tank and the Czech option did not come with all the contractual and mandatory purchase requirements of the German tanks. Thus, the

---

105 Emilio Faldella, *L'Italia nella seconda Guerra mondiale* (Bologna: Cappelli, 1967), p. 588.
106 Macgregor Knox, *Hitler's Italian Allies*, p. 43.
107 Frederick Deakin, *The Brutal Friendship: Musssolini, Hitler and the Fall of Italian Fascism* (New York: Weidenfeld and Nicolson, 1962), p. 161.
108 Mario Roatta, *Otto milioni di baionette* (Rome: Mondadori, 1971), p. 80.

military could only have benefited from sourcing a more effective tank and at favorable conditions. Another option that came too late was the carro sahariano, which was developed into a prototype after evaluating the British Crusader tank series. Several of these captured vehicles were dispatched to Rome's research and development facility and were used to develop a prototype that was very similar looking to the British unit. It was designed for the North African terrain but it was eventually abandoned once Italy in late 1942 was evicted from Tripolitania.

P.40 Tank

The P.40 tank had a long and tortuous gestation despite the clear difficulties that Italian troops faced early on in the North African campaign when pitted against the British Matilda II infantry tank. The P.40 history in fact was characterized by numerous delays, design changes and the scarcity of primary material which ensued that the first prototype was only manufactured in 1943 when Italy's war effort was on the vane. By that time the P.40 was already obsolete in both technological design and firepower since by then Allied forces could deploy heavier, faster and more powerful medium sized tanks. Their technological advances made the P.40 tank in comparison a slower moving, softer skinned medium tank. The P.40 was first conceived in 1938 when General Pariani had argued for the development of an 8 tons' light (reconnaissance), a medium tank weighing anywhere between 8 and 15 tons (tank to tank confrontations) and a heavy tank (mobile artillery) with a weight greater than 15 tons.

The latter was to provide advanced artillery support by firing heavy shells into the enemy's positions. The Circolare n. 3446 titled "Impiego delle unita' carriste" (the deployment of tank units) stated that the P.40 shall weigh between 20 to 25 tons, reach a maximum speed of 32 kph (19.8 mph), shall have a crew of six and armed with three machine guns and one 47mm gun. But for two years no action was taken to advance the design of the tank or to assemble a prototype. In 1940 *Comando Supremo* began to consider again the P.40 but by this time its basic design had already changed reflecting the advances in tank technology in continental Europe. Its 47mm gun, for instance, was largely obsolete by late 1940 and shortly thereafter the technicians had changed its gun to a 75mm caliber gun that guaranteed greater firepower and had the potential to align Italian tank units to those of the Commonwealth or the German Wehrmacht. In 1941 design work was continued on the basis of 75mm gun and the work centered on evaluating several engines that could best serve the higher tonnage vehicle. In 1942 when the Allies introduced medium tanks with a 75mm gun and several self-propelled guns with even larger caliber guns, P-40 tank designers were forced to go back to the P.40 option in late 1942 and then again in 1943. Finding a suitable engine was still the main dilemma facing the design team. By then the newly redesigned heavy tank was to have a 75/34 gun, a weight increase to 25 tons, and 50mm frontal armour. "Weight increase meant the development of a suitable engine, which contributed to delays. Fiat-SPA had many problems in developing a diesel oil engine with more than 300 hp, and as a replacement the petrol fueled Fiat model 262 engine and the 300 hp German Maybach HL 120 were considered."[109] Eventually, in 1943, Fiat succeeded in providing the first prototypes with one 330 hp SPA eight-cylinder engine, which was later

---

109 Paolo Battistelli and Filippo Cappellano, *Italian Medium Tanks*, p. 18.

replaced with a V-12 SPA 420 hp petrol engine that could provide an average speed of 40kph (24.8 mph).

The last P-40 model took inspiration from the Soviet T-34 from which it shared several design features. At the same time that the final design of the P.40 tank was completed, Ansaldo also began the design for a *semovente* with a 149/40 gun, but both never underwent mass production. *Maresciallo d'Italia* Cavallero observed in one of his 1943 diary entries with regard to the heavy tank:

> I received General Horstig which offered the German Panther tank. I informed him that we already have the design of the P.40 and the M.15 tanks. I point out that we plan to phase out the production of the M.15 in favor of the P.40. I also told him that we were grateful for the German offer. I then told him that it would take up to three months to begin planning for the construction of the Panther in Italy and that we also must order the material ahead of time. It would be useful, I argued, if the Germans could ship us a few of these tanks so our technicians can study them up close. General Horstig concurs with my line of reasoning and states that he will inform the German High Command of our discussion. We also agree that two Italian technicians will travel to Germany to inspect a Panther tank, while two German technicians will come to Italy to examine the P.40 design.[110]

It is clear from Cavallero's entry that the Italian military leaders believed that the P.40 was comparable to the German Panther or that at least it was not inferior to it. It also appears that even late into the war the Italian High Command was still shielding Ansaldo and Fiat from domestic or foreign competition by placing a strong focus on the production of the P.40 tank rather than purchasing the license to the German heavy tanks. It was decided that a battalion of P.40 tanks (*I Battaglione Carri P.40*) was to be formed by August 1943 and headquartered in Vercelli. The production of the P.40 tank officially began in May 1943. By the time of the armistice of September 1943 the Italian Army had received only one prototype of the P.40, while five additional P.40 tanks were seized by the Germans in September of 1943. According to historian Nicola Pignato:

> Both Italy and Mussolini placed their armoured forces' future on this heavy tank. Unable to match Allied production, they placed their fortunes on a technically superior design. The P.40 could have affected the tide of the war for Italy had it been produced in numbers in 1941 or 1942, The reason it didn't was due to the research and design problems, plus the excessive time from conception to finished product. Lacking operational heavy tanks to meet the increasing number of newer and heavier British and American tanks, Italian armoured forces were doomed to defeat in North Africa. Even after the long research and design period, Italy had no heavy tanks to face the Allied invasion of her homeland in 1943. By the time the P.40s were in service, the Duce was no longer in power and Italy sued for peace with the Allies.[111]

---

110 Bruno Benvenuti, 'La chimera del Regio Esercito: Carro P.40', *Storia Militare*, n.6, 1994, pp. 26-33.
111 Nicola Pignato, *Italian Armoured Vehicles World War Two*, p. 14.

The production of the P.40 yielded twenty-eight tanks in 1943 and an additional sixty tanks in 1944. These machines were utilized by the military forces of the *Repubblica Sociale Italiana*. The effort behind the P.40 tank clearly showed a lack of a strategic vision for the armed forces as the whole process was characterized by delays and several radical redesigns. Once it was ready too few numbers were produced and also by then the P.40 was no longer the heavy tank that it was originally meant to be as the Allies had upped their game. As tank historian Nicola Pignato asserts it is difficult to gauge the effectiveness of the P.40 tank in combat since it was produced in very small numbers and it did not see any significant combat action while the Italian Royal Army was still at war: "Lacking detailed reports on the P.40 combat performance, it is difficult to establish how it performed. We might compare the P. 40 to its contemporary, the American M4 Sherman. Both tanks had identical armour, ground pressure, and speed. Their main guns had the same hitting power, but the Sherman possessed a larger ammunition capacity of 95 rounds versus the P.40's 65 rounds."[112]

Armoured Vehicles

Italy was also late to the game with the development of armoured cars and the Commonwealth was to exploit this weakness to the fullest from the beginning of the North African campaign by harassing Italian troops on the Egypt-Libya frontline with their more mobile and unpredictable reconnaissance units. This delay was the result of poor post war planning even though during the First World War armoured cars had been used extensively. The Italian Army had a long and distinguished history with regard to the use of armoured cars. The first units built by Lancia and Fiat were used during the First World War and were used extensively especially during 1917-18. During the Caporetto retreat many were used as stop gap solutions to halt the enemy advance and deployed to cover the retreat of the Italian forces by having armoured vehicles counterattack the enemy with their mobile machine gun units. Then during the Battle of Vittorio Veneto in October-November 1918 the same units were used within the Assault Army Corps to give chase and cut off the retreat of the Austro-Hungarian soldiers. Following the end of the war, three different types of armoured cars were used during the Libyan war in the immediate post war period.

During the interwar years and even though the Italian Army had used armoured cars widely during the First World War, its planners failed to innovate the armoured cars/vehicles fleet and instead focused on commissioning light tanks. This approach was ultimately abandoned when in the second part of the 1930s the Italian military developed a mechanized force committed to maneuver warfare, the so called *Armata del Po'*. In addition, Italian colonies in North Africa comprised by very vast territorial areas had to be patrolled extensively after the 1938 Munich agreements from the potential threat of nearby stationed British forces and hence armoured cars came back in favor.

Thus the Army commissioned Ansaldo in 1937 to advance an armoured car based on a four-wheel drive design and equipped with 8mm machine guns housed in the vehicles' turret.

112 Ibid.

Ansaldo committed to develop two models: a lighter one for the military police and one for the Army named *Autoblindo 40* (AB 40). The Army ordered 176 units which were to be delivered in March 1941 at the Armoured Car Training Center of the School of the Cavalry of Pinerolo. After commissioning the units, the Army planners changed their minds and urged Ansaldo to upgrade the main weapon from an 8mm machine gun to a 20mm gun which was capable of firing both thin armour piecing and high explosive ammunition. This new version was delivered during 1941 and renamed AB 41.

The AB 41 provided the Army with a reliable, fast and highly autonomous (it could travel for more than twice the distance of other Italian armoured vehicles) armoured car that could be used in a multitude of functions spanning from reconnaissance to escorting supply columns. The AB 40 and 41 vehicles were used together with motorcycle patrol units, *semoventi* units and light tanks to equip the reconnaissance units of the armoured divisions. They could carry out reconnaissance and surveillance roles as well as take part in small scale offensive operations or employed to protect armoured or infantry battalion flanks.

The vehicle came in three models the AB 40, which was armed with machine gun, the AB 41, which mounted a 20mm gun, while the AB 43 had a 47mm gun. A total of 700 units were built during the war. The AB 40 was a four-wheeled armed vehicle armed with three 8mm Breda *modello* 38 machine guns. Two of the machine guns were mounted in a fully revolving turret which had an armour thickness of 6mm to 18mm while the hull armour ranged between 6mm to 15mm plates. It was powered by an 88 hp SPA six-cylinder gasoline engine mounted in the rear. The AB 40's top speed was 76 kph (47.2 mph). It was also equipped with a RF 3M radio that was installed for communications, with its antenna mounted on the left side of the vehicle. It was well regarded by the troops especially the *Polizia Africa Italiana* units (Italian African Police) that were deployed with the reconnaissance battalion (RECAM) within the *Corpo d'Armata di Manovra* in North Africa at the time of Operation Crusader. The AB 40 was reputed by the troops to be a fast and mobile vehicle both on road and cross-country while its only downside was that it lacked firepower. Thus, the AB 41 was then introduced, whose design was modeled on the L 6-40 light tank with a 20mm *Breda modello* 35 gun and a co-axial 8mm *Breda modello* 38 machine gun.

The AB 40 and 41 both were introduced in 1941, a year after Italy had entered the war. Both were widely distributed to a range of units in North Africa. First and foremost, to the reconnaissance units of the *Corpo d'Armata di Manovra* first and then to the XX *Corpo d'Armata*. Reconnaissance units were typically comprised of a range of combat units but for the most part were equipped with AB 41 units, small detachments of *Semoventi da 47/32* or later in 1942 with *Semoventi da 75/32* built on M tank chassis. They were also widely used by *Bersaglieri* motorized infantry units, *Trieste's Bersaglieri* units, for example, also made extensive use of these vehicles. The AB 41 was considered by both Italian and enemy troops to be a very well designed vehicle that was suited for North African type-operations and: "They proved highly suitable for reconnaissance, security, and escort duties."[113] The vehicle was further up gunned with the AB 43 model which sported a wider turret with a 47/40 tank gun that was used to ward off enemy tank attacks as well as to pounce upon enemy surveillance units. The AB 43, however, was introduced into service just before the Armistice of September 1943 and hence was not properly deployed

---

113 Ibid., p. 17.

in North Africa. Similarly Italian light trucks for use in North Africa were developed late in the game and introduced in small numbers beginning in July 1942. Developed jointly by SPA and Viberti and using a AB 40 car chassis they came to be known as *Camionetta modello 42* and was armed with 8mm Breda machine guns. In addition some vehicles were fitted with a 20mm Solothurn rifle. Later on some vehicles were fitted with 20mm *Breda modello* 35 guns or 47mm guns. These vehicles were primarily used by the *Arditi* motorized units in Tunisia and in Sicily, but also by select other elite units.

When Italy entered the Second World War many of the tactical uses of the armoured car had been lost since in the 1930s the Army had failed to develop or update its armoured tactics. Thus, during the beginning of the North African campaign the Italian Army had very little capabilities in the field of surveillance and reconnaissance. This was pointed out by an early report that stressed how the Commonwealth was better prepared in the field of reconnaissance and Italian units lacked speedy armoured cars to locate and destroy enemy positions and field artillery batteries. This was due to outdated tactics and the lack of vehicles and dedicated reconnaissance units and the report underlined how the troops were using makeshift solutions such as using *Dovunque* trucks fitted with a machine gun to conduct reconnaissance. General Roatta, for instance, in his report compiled during his tour of the North African front urged the army to fully enhance the reconnaissance capabilities using a more fit for purpose and less bulky armoured car. Another area on which Roatta focused was training; specifically to fill the gap due to lack of proper training of officers using compasses and other tools to locate enemy positions. Ultimately armoured cars were introduced in 1941 and a major gap that existed between the Italians and the Commonwealth was narrowed.

ITALIAN RECONNAISSANCE UNITS IN NORTH AFRICA

1°, 2°, 3° and 4° *plotoni autonomi Nizza* (Nizza autonomous platoons). The platoons were active in 1942 and with sixteen armoured vehicles.

III *Gruppo Corazzato Nizza* (III Armoured Group *Nizza*). It was active between 1941-43 with forty-two armoured cars. It was originally named *132° Battaglione Autoblindo* for the *Ariete* Division.

III *Gruppo Corazzato Monferrato* (III Armoured Group *Monferrato*). It was active between 1941-43 with forty-two armoured cars. It was originally attached to the 132° *Battaglione Autoblindo* for the *Ariete* Division.

VIII *Battaglione Bersaglieri* (8th *Bersaglieri* Battallion). It was active between 1941-43. It was originally named 133° *Battaglione Autoblindo* and CXXXIII *Battaglione*. It was attached to the *Trieste* Division.

III *Gruppo Corazzato Novara* (III Armoured Group *Novara*). It was active between 1942-43 with only two armoured cars and was attached to the Italian I Army.

R.E.Co. Lodi (*Lodi* Reconnaissance Group). It was active between 1942-43 with thirty-six armoured cars and it was attached to the *Centauro* Division.

Source: https://www.modellismopiu.net/m+contenuti/fabio/Autoblinde_mod._40_41_e_43.pdf

The other factor that limited the potential of the armoured units during the first year of the war was the way these units were deployed, which was in a purely piecemeal fashion that saw them never in combat as uniform units.

Brief Overview of Italian Armoured Units 1940-43

The deployment of the Italian armoured units was gradual during the war. Initially, the bulk of the armoured units were held back in Italy to be used as a strategic reserve[114] and as a result both in North Africa during General Graziani's tenure as well as in other theaters the troops suffered extensively from this decision. As Battistelli and Crociani assert with regard to deployment of the armoured units: "The fate of these commands and formations, and the subsequent raising of other armoured and motorized units during the war, revealed a piecemeal, fragmented and badly managed employment of the Italian Army's mechanized assets."[115]

The splitting of units and their piecemeal deployment in Greece, North and East Africa was the result of the limited numbers of Italian motorized and mechanized assets compared to other nations at the beginning of the war.

With regard to overall situation of June 1940 historian John Gooch writes: "The army could mobilize seventy-five divisions. The two armoured divisions had only seventy medium M11 tanks between them, the rest being light tanks and no heavy vehicles or armoured cars....The army was almost 8,000 trucks short of the number it needed to mobilize and had only seven to eight months' fuel when it needed at least a year's worth."[116]

From this original sin followed a number of decisions that never saw the concentration of the armoured forces in one key area of operation. *Littorio* was deployed in France first and then in Yugoslavia while *Centauro* was involved in the Greek campaign and both suffered heavy losses throughout 1940-41. In North Africa, initially the Italian Army unexpectedly did not deploy its armoured formations but relied upon a quickly assembled ad hoc combat group called *Brigata Corazzata Speciale* under General Valentino Babini which initially fought satisfactorily in the second armoured confrontation of the campaign but later was destroyed at the battle of Beda Fomm by a combination of inexperience, lack of fuel and the effectiveness of British anti-tank guns. A few *Ariete* units were shipped to East Africa but were inconsequential given their limited numbers to alter the direction of the campaign. Then later the bulk of *Ariete* was hurriedly deployed in North Africa in early 1941 following the debacle of *Maresciallo d'Italia* Graziani's Army but initially it was only equipped with light tanks. The unit was first deployed during Rommel's counter thrust in Cyrenaica in March-April 1941 and would continue to fight in North Africa until its destruction at El Alamein. Following the stalemate in Greece in 1941 and the defeat at the hands of the Commonwealth troops in January 1941 in North Africa,

---

114 An interesting biography of Ciano, for example, argues that because of the parallel war concept the armoured units were initially held in reserve in Italy as a preventive measure against Germany. The Duce and Ciano did not trust Germany and opted for the Vallo Alpino and large troop and armoured reserves to be held in northern Italy in case of a German attack in 1940-41. Eugenio di Rienzo, *Galeazzo Ciano* (Salerno: Salerno Ed, 2018).
115 Filippo Cappellano and Pier Paolo Battistelli, *Italian Medium Tanks*, p. 6.
116 John Gooch, *Mussolini's War* (New York: Simon and Schuster, 2020), p. 89.

the Italian Army began a major reorganization of its armoured forces. In July 1941 *Centauro* Division was transferred back to Italy and was completely overhauled. Its 31º *Reggimento* was deeply reorganized losing its two light tanks battalions which were merged to form the LI medium tank battalion, which was attached to the preexisting XIII and IV battalions to form a medium tank regiment. The reorganization was slowed down by not having large numbers of M tanks and initially some of its units trained with captured Renault R35 tanks[117]. *Littorio* was the next unit to be reorganized. Its *133º Reggimento Carristi* was reformed in September 1941 with the X, XI, XII *Battaglioni Carri Medi* all equipped with M tanks. The unit also received the DLVI and DLVII *Gruppo Semoventi*.

Finally, after several changes to the strength of the standard Italian division and by fighting alongside Rommel and his forces in 1941, the Italians moved to form combined arms armoured corps first with the *Corpo d'Armata di Manovra* in 1941 and then with *XX Corpo d'Armata in 1942*. Both aimed to create elite, or highly specialized mechanized and motorized army corps units that could combine armour, mobile anti-tank artillery and special infantry units and advanced reconnaissance units that could be deployed independently both in offensive and defensive operations against enemy armoured divisions.[118]

On 23 May 1942 *Comando Supremo* issued a directive titled "Potenziamento delle forze in Africa Settentrionale" ('strengthening the units in North Africa') which called for a general but gradual transition to more powerful armoured units under the *XX Corpo d'Armata*. The unit was to be comprised of one full strength mechanized division, one understrength mechanized division, one motorized division and one reconnaissance unit. The *Ariete* mechanized division was to be strengthened considerably comprised of one medium tank regiment, one *Bersaglieri* regiment, and an artillery regiment. The latter was to be equipped with a first group of *semoventi* da 75 and 105/28 guns, and a second one of 90/53 and 20mm guns. The tank regiment was to receive greater numbers of M.14/41 and M.15/42 tanks to replace the M.13/40 tanks and as a stop gap solution until the deployment of the heavy tank. The *Trieste* motorized division was to be grounded on two partially motorized infantry regiments and one artillery regiment, plus one tank battalion and one reconnaissance unit. Its artillery was also strongly reinforced. This transformation comprised a considerable up gunning of the armoured divisions, but as we will see with *Ariete* and *Littorio* the domestic industry was never fully capable of supplying the desired number of guns and tanks and the partial reinforcement brought about by the creation of the *Corpo d'Armata* represented only a partial rearming and up-gunning of the Italian armoured divisions considering losses in battle and at sea.

---

117 The Renault R35 was a French light tank developed during the early thirties to replace the aging FT tank. It was used by the French Army in 1940. Many captured units fell in German and Italian hands. While the R35 was well protected with 40 mm-thick cast armour, it had little firepower (it had the same 37 mm gun as the FT), it lacked radio and it was also characterized by a slow speed engine.
118 Battistelli and Crociani in their book on Italian elite units of the Second World War consider the armoured corps deployed in North Africa as an elite unit of the Italian Army.

Artillery and Anti-Tank Weapons

The lack of adequate numbers of medium armour was compounded by the lack of heavy artillery and effective anti-tank weapons. When it entered the war, the Army had few modern artillery weapons as the clear majority of its field artillery was comprised by pieces that had been built prior to 1918. A reorganization of the artillery arm was conducted prior to June 1940 which entailed retrofitting some of the major artillery guns with more modern wheels so that they could be towed by trucks to the battlefield. In a further bid to improve the effectiveness of the artillery some guns were later also truck-mounted to ensure greater mobility and the capacity to intervene more quickly. The majority of the Army's field artillery was comprised of the *cannone da* 65/17, *cannone da* 75/27 *modello* 06 and *modello* 11, *Obice da 100/17 modello 14* howitzer, and 105/28 field guns. The 65mm gun was initially designed as a light mountain gun before the First World War. The 75mm gun was used to equip the standard infantry divisions and was based on a design from Krupps. At the start of the war many of them still had the original spoked-wheels but were progressively upgraded to wheels with steel rims and tires. The gun saw extensive service throughout the war. It weighed 1,076 kg and fired a 6.3 kg shell. The *cannone da 75/27 modello* 11 was of French design and had a ballistic performance that was similar to the *modello* 06. The 100/17 howitzer was manufactured by Skoda and the Italians acquired large numbers of this gun as war reparations from Austria-Hungary. The weapon weighed 1,417 kg and fired a 13.8 kg shell to 9,200 meters. The Allies, for instance, maintained that the 100/17 piece, which was used extensively in Libya and Egypt by both motorized and standard infantry divisions, was an accurate and effective howitzer.[119] Italian reports while stating that the howitzer was highly reliable also argued that its range was "inadequate compared to the artillery it faced."[120] The *cannone da* 105/28 was an Italian field gun derived from the French manufacturer Schneider *canon da 105mm de campagne*. The 105/28, for example, was considered by the British to be the most valuable battalion artillery piece in the Italian Army given its range of 11,425 meters and the rate of fire of one round per minute. The 105/28 weighed 2,170 kg in action and fired a 16.24kg shell.[121]

Given its modest artillery strength made up in great part of captured Austro-Hungarian guns from the First World War, the German Army came to help the Italians by furnishing 38 batteries of 149/28 Krupp guns which had a range of 14,545 yards (13,300 meters) which was unmatched by most Italian guns. In addition, several units of 88/56 Flak 36 were also supplied to the Army which utilized them in North Africa initially in the anti-aircraft role in the defense of Tripoli and later in the anti-tank role. In the early stages of the North African campaign the Italian infantry experienced many difficulties when facing the enemy armour as the troops were not trained in the anti-tank defense. The Italian infantry was surprised by the Matilda II tanks in December 1940, whose presence was unknown at the time to the SIM, the intelligence service. In addition, Italy in the early phase of the North African campaign lacked a mobile anti-tank gun that could pierce heavier British infantry tanks such as a Matilda II or

---

119 'Artillery in the Desert', Military Intelligence Service, War Department, *Special Series* No. 6, November 1942.
120 Massimiliano Afiero and Ralph Riccio, *The Italian Army in North Africa* (Warwick: Helion and Company, 2022), p. 264.
121 Ibid

later the Valentine. As historian Nicola Pignato asserts, about the North African theater the Army suffered tremendously in the first encounters with the British tanks because of a lack of viable anti-tank weapons and because of poor use that it made of its anti-aircraft batteries which could have been converted to the anti-tank defense:

> The only tank that could not be pierced by the standard 47mm and the 65 mm guns was the infantry unit armoured vehicle (Matilda II or Senior). But the heavier British infantry type tanks could be effectively neutralized by the 75/46 anti-aircraft modello 34 gun, which inexplicably was not utilized in 1940-41 in the anti-tank mode. Even though some of these units lacked armoured piercing shells capable of penetrating thick armour, they had projectiles that were nonetheless powerful and very fast (750 meters per second) and could pierce 70mm of armour at certain distances……According to British sources, Italian infantry troops were not aware in 1940 that the British could deploy heavy infantry tanks and were taken by complete surprise during the early part of the campaign. However, by December the Italian troops had become aware of the British heavier tanks but still failed to field the guns that could have stopped them. At Bardia on 12 December, the X Army, for example, still had as many as 28 pieces of 75/46 guns and 76 pieces of 105/28, that were comparable in performance to the most modern and lightweight 88/27 gun, but still failed to use them.[122]

The Italian Army and its planners had focused their major efforts in 1939-40 on the production of the 47mm gun assembled by Breda factories in Northern Italy. Although many units including the paratroopers of the *Folgore* swore by this gun, it was a reliable gun but with many limitations in the anti-tank defense. In the early stages of the campaign it could be deployed satisfactorily against the light British tanks like the A9, A10 and A13 Cruisers tanks but once the Commonwealth deployed heavy infantry tanks such as the Matilda II during Operation Compass the 47mm could no longer be utilized effectively.[123] The situation became even more precarious when the Commonwealth began to deploy American medium tanks (Grant and Sherman) as well as the British manufactured Valentine tanks in 1942. The gun could only be deployed successfully against these medium units if its servers aimed at the tracks of the tanks and from extremely close range. If successful, the 47mm gun would be able to at best immobilize the tank and then it was up to combat engineer units to torch it or blow it up before the Commonwealth forces could recover it. But fighting at close range was very difficult and risky leading to exceedingly high casualties amongst the artillery crews.[124]

Despite an antiquated artillery arm that was based on several batteries of First World War vintage Skoda captured guns, the Italian artillery did manage to introduce several successful motorized anti-tank weapons during the war. In fact, the *Regio Esercito* had a rich and fruitful expertise in building *autocannoni*, truck mounted guns that dated back to the First World War. The dearth of viable mobile anti-tank guns and of self-propelled guns at the beginning of the North Africa campaign pushed some forward-thinking officers to come up with improvised

---

122 Nicola Pignato, 'Prime esperienze italiane di guerra corazzata in Africa Settentrionale', *Quaderno 1999 Societa' Italiana di Storia Militare*, p. 124.
123 Ibid.
124 Ibid.

solutions that could be deployed with some degree of effectiveness until new weapons from Italy were ready to be deployed. The first improvised weapon was the result of the technical ingenuity by a few of the more forward thinking junior officers in North Africa which referring back to the *autocannoni* of the First World War attempted to overcome the lack of proper anti-tank weapons with a makeshift solution. Their quest to find suitable weapons began when they first retrofitted L.3 tanks with Solothurn 20mm anti-tank rifles instead of their original machine gun. This allowed the L.3 tanks to escort supply columns and thanks to their increased firepower they could be deployed to ward off raiding British armoured vehicles. Another innovation was the equipping of simple *Dovunque* trucks with Breda 20mm and 47mm guns that could also be used in the anti-tank mode. These truck mounted guns allowed the crews to fire upon the enemy from non-static positions thus gaining some degree of mobility and speed when targeting enemy troops or vehicles. Another relevant use of these truck mounted guns with the 20mm gun was to escort supply columns by warning off enemy planes when they dove down to machine gun Italian vehicles. These weapons were effective during 1940 and 1941 because British armoured vehicles were for the most part, soft-skinned and lightly armed. Things began to change when the enemy upgraded to heavier weapons. *Generale* Gastone Gambara of the *Corpo Armato di Manovra* announced in the summer of 1941 that "he had fitting out a squadron of 24 captured all-terrain camionette, on each of which a 65/17 gun was being mounted for use in the anti-tank role, as well as for other purposes as the case might warrant."[125] This resulted in *12° Autoraggruppamento* (a motorized group with its own workshop) forming a unit called *Batterie Volanti* (flying columns) which used several captured British armoured vehicles to conduct reconnaissance, enemy surveillance and anti-tank and anti-aircraft gun functions. Captured Ford FT15A and a few Chevrolet C15 vehicles, for instance, were retrofitted with Breda *cannone-mitragliera da 20/65 modello 35* guns, while several Morris CS8 vehicles were retrofitted with 65/17 guns. The 65mm armed vehicle was intended as self-propelled artillery weapon "suitable for fast movements for support and protection of our light tanks against British armoured cars."[126] The flying columns had less formal organizations and often were lightly staffed than the other *autocannoni* groups, but they filled vital functions. A flying battery typically consisted of four Morris CS8 trucks armed with 65mm guns. Finally, in the same fashion they assembled other makeshift *semoventi* with 100/17 Skoda howitzers[127] and 75/27 *modello* 11 guns mounted on Lancia 3RO trucks. These last two were purely makeshift solutions since the gun lacked a defensive shield and its rather tall silhouette made it an easy target for the enemy airplanes, artillery and tanks. Despite these limitations, the weapons, especially the 100/17 gun, were used effectively on numerous occasions to good effect against enemy tanks and armoured vehicles. It's not clear how many of these units were assembled at the headquarters of the 12° *Autoraggruppamento* in Berta throughout the campaign but we can confirm that there were at least twenty-four 65/17 and sixteen Breda 20mm guns mounted on Morris CS8 vehicles (plus an unspecified number mounted on Chevrolet C15) and twenty-eight 65/17 guns on Ford FT15A vehicles and seven 100/17 howitzers on Lancia 3RO.[128] Furthermore, it appears that most of this equipment was

---

125 Ralph Riccio and Nicola Pignato, *Italian Truck Mounted Artillery in Action* (Carrollton: Squadron, 2010), p. 31.
126 Ibid., p. 32.
127 Skoda made howitzers captured during the First World War from the Austro-Hungarians.
128 Filippo Cappellano and Nicola Pignato, *Andare Contro i Carri Armati*, p. 110.

lost due to attrition during Operation Crusader thus leading the *Corpo d'Armata di Manovra* and later the XX *Corpo d'Armata* to rebuild the *batterie volanti* fleet in early 1942. In March 1942 in anticipation of the Gazala battles the truck shop installed an additional twelve 75/27 and twelve 100/17 howitzers mounted on SPA TL 37 and Lancia 3RO vehicles respectively.[129] The *Batterie volanti* were initially merged into the RECAM in September 1941, the reconnaissance unit of the Italian armoured corps and later in the XX *Corpo d'Armata*. Initially there were seven batteries, all of which were under the RECAM but at times one or more battery could be put at the disposal of other divisions. Each battery of 65/17 guns typically was comprised by four truck mounted guns, two small ammunition carriers, and some included also two 20mm truck mounted anti-aircraft guns. In 1942 when the *Corpo d'Armata di Manovra* was disbanded and its units merged into the XX *Corpo d'Armata* the organization of the *batterie volanti* was further fine-tuned. By that time, it was comprised of a command/headquarters unit, three 65/17 truck mounted batteries, four truck mounted 20mm guns, and an undefined number of support vehicles including ammunition carriers. This change reflected primarily a response to the increased threat from the sky as the RAF not only increased the number of aircraft in the theater but also began to support in a major way ground operations.

Of all the above mentioned models, the truck mounted 100/17 guns were particularly successful. Deployed for the first time during Operation Crusader, on several occasions they demonstrated their combat worth both as anti-tank weapons as well as assault artillery weapons used in raiding type operations against enemy supply depots. The 20/65 Breda gun was used in the anti-aircraft mode and it was particularly effective against low level attacks as attested by the following American Command Headquarters in North Africa report: "As antiaircraft protection for the motorized column….there is evidence that the 20mm gun is used independently and is very effective. Large numbers are used on the march and it is generally known that in Libya pilots did not like to attack columns because the intensity of fire of the 20mm guns."[130]

On the heels of the introduction of these new mobile anti-tank and anti-aircraft weapons there were further developments when the North African truck workshop mounted seven 1914 vintage Schneider-Ansaldo 102/35 guns, that were originally used on battleships, on Fiat 634 N trucks. These guns belonged to the *MILIMART/X Legione* and were attached to the *Corpo d'Armata di Manovra* prior to the beginning of Operation Crusader. At first the *1° Batteria Mobile* was formed with three guns in September 1941 which was followed by the *6° Batteria Mobile* with four guns. The 102mm gun had a range of 10,900 meters (11,920 yards) and fired a 13.35 kg. (29.4 pound) shell.[131] The gun's firepower and its long range allowed the *Ariete* artillery to fire upon the enemy's Cruiser and Crusader tanks, which were equipped with a 2-pdr gun, often to good effect and from a safe distance. In turn, the British tanks at such distances could not effectively target the guns. During the Battle of Bir el Gobi, for instance, in November 1941 *Ariete* achieved some measure of success with these units by putting out of action several enemy tanks. This battle represented an important turning point for the Italians thanks to this first innovation in the field of powerful anti-tank artillery. The lack of great numbers of these guns, *Ariete* for instance had only seven of them at Bir el Gobi, forced the Italian Army to come up with a more viable truck mounted gun. One of the first solutions was

---

129 Ibid.
130 Ralph Riccio and Nicola Pignato, *Italian Truck Mounted Artillery in Action*, p. 46.
131 Ibid., p. 6.

found by Ansaldo with the dual purpose *Cannone da 90/53* gun which was also employed extensively in an anti-tank role especially in North Africa. On 20 January 1941 *Comando Supremo* had outlined the need for a mobile 90mm gun that could engage enemy armour at extended ranges.[132] In less than a month Ansaldo presented the first prototype of a *Terni modello* 39 dual purpose *cannone da* 90/53 gun mounted on Lancia 3 Ro and later on Breda 51 trucks. Then on 10 February firing trials were held that passed successfully. The Army initially ordered thirty *Autocannoni da 90/53*. These were shipped to North Africa to equip the *Ariete* Division (DI *Battaglione*) and shortly after the *Littorio* Division (DIII *Battaglione*). In May 1941 a further order was placed for seventy *Autocannoni da* 90/53, this time to be mounted on the chassis of the Breda 51. By late 1942 the *Centauro* Division also could field a battalion (DII *Battaglione*) equipped with these guns. In 1943 the DV *Battaglione* fought in Sicily against the Allies equipped exclusively with these guns. A standard 90/53 battery consisted of four *autocannoni*, one reconnaissance vehicle, six heavy trucks some of which carried the ammunition, three SPA 38R light trucks, three CL 39 light trucks, six motorcycles, two machine guns and two radio stations. The unit included four officers, seven NCOs, 105 artillery men and 31 drivers. Usually two *autocannoni* batteries were paired together to form a group. The gun's performance was similar to the German 88mm weapon with a "muzzle velocity of 840 m/s gave the 10 kg (22.2 pounds) HE shell a range of 17,465 meters (19,100 yards). The practical rate of fire was between 15 and 20 rounds per minute….An AP shell was reported to penetrate 112mm (4.41 inches) of plate at a 30 degree angle at 457 meters (500 yards) and 140mm (5.53 inches) at the vertical."[133] It was a true tank killer which was deployed extensively especially during the battles on the Gazala Line in mid-1942 where on several occasions the servers of the 90/53 gun batteries, mainly from the *Ariete* Division, repulsed several Commonwealth armoured attacks. Even at El Alamein and in Tunisia the gun retained its effectiveness against heavier Allied tanks. At El Alamein both *Littorio* and *Ariete* artillery groups were equipped with several of these batteries and they effectively countered the enemy's numerical superiority with the accuracy and reliability of this gun which time and time again functioned effectively as a tank killer. The only downsides to this weapon was that the Army never had too many of these units at its disposal, its tall silhouette made it highly visible to counterbattery fire and enemy planes and the vehicle would often get stuck on wet, desert terrain. First, only approximately 150 *Autocannoni da* 90/53 were produced during the war. This was an irrisory inventory of a very relevant weapon. Throughout the North African campaign, for example both the Germans and the British had much higher quantities of 88mm and 25-pdr guns respectively. The gun was very heavy and its assembly required many expensive mechanical components and industry could not keep the pace to replenish units that were lost or captured in combat. Second, in combat its major downside was its height and hence its high visibility on the battlefield. Because it was one of the Italians' most effective weapons, it was frequently the most sought after target of enemy aerial assaults or enemy counter battery artillery fire. The Commonwealth forces, for instance, had formed special task oriented air force units dedicated to identifying and taking out the 88mm and the 90/53 batteries. Thus, many units were destroyed either by enemy aircraft or by counter battery fire. Third, Italian reports in mid-1942, for example, also report of the excessive

---

132 Ralph Riccio and Nicola Pignato, *Italian Truck Mounted Artillery in Action*, p. 15.
133 Ibid.

weight of the weapon and how often the truck would get stuck on soft and wet terrain.[134] Overall, despite the shortcomings, an Italian document of 1943 reported that "the 90/53 gun was always effective in the anti-tank role and it always took the lead in counter battery fire against the 88mm and 114mm British guns. Numerous members of the *bersaglieri*, infantry and the armoured units have attested to the effectiveness of this weapon."[135] Another 1942 report stated that the Army should consolidate its anti-tank defense upon three weapons and ditch altogether the 47mm gun:

> The motorized infantry units lament the fact that they are without an effective and mobile anti-tank gun since the only piece at their disposal, the 47mm gun, must be hand towed which takes time to make it combat ready and it also takes considerable effort. It is necessary to focus our production effort upon the 47/58, the 75/34 for the *semovente* and the 90/53 on a lower silhouette platform that can be towed by the newly built Breda trucks.[136]

Another weapon that was used extensively in the anti-tank defense was the *Semovente* self-propelled gun in the various models that were discussed above. It proved an excellent weapon that could be deployed against both heavy and medium tanks. Its lower silhouette made it more difficult for the enemy to locate than the 90/53 gun. By 1942 it was deployed across the board to most units fighting in North Africa and even the non-motorized infantry divisions, even though in small numbers, received them. The *Brescia* Division, for example, was first strengthened by a motorized *Bersaglieri* company, then by a few M.14/41 tanks, and then by two *Semoventi* da 75/18 and the Menton German motorized unit. Similarly, other infantry divisions in North Africa received similar reinforcements to enhance the anti-tank defense.

After the first year of battlefield experiences with the 47mm anti-tank gun had not been encouraging, the Army began to address the issue not only by introducing new weapons but also by improving the effectiveness of the ammunition. In fact, another improvement was the introduction of new hollow charge round which the Italians labeled the *effetto pronto*, or the prompt effect projectile. This was used first in late 1941 to increase the effectiveness of the 75mm, 90mm and 100mm field guns and then it was later extended to the 47mm and 65mm caliber guns and to complement the initial HE high explosive shell. Then, these special projectiles were also used by the large caliber field guns such as the 105mm and 149mm guns. M.14/41 tanks also used prompt effect shells in 1942. Later in the year the *effetto pronto speciale* shell was also introduced that was even more effective. The first *effetto pronto* shells deployed by the 75mm guns during Operation Crusader were fairly effective while those for the 47mm gun were not completely successful and they only partially bolstered the anti-tank combat role. In fact the trials that were held against captured enemy tanks and the battle field experiences revealed that the shell for the 47mm gun was only marginally more effective than the prior ammunition used in damaging the hull of enemy tanks. But used by a 100mm Skoda howitzer the shell was able "to blow off the turret from the main body of Matilda II tank at a distance of 500 meters" and it was reputed

---

134 'Relazione sul Gruppo da 90/53', Maggiore P. Oliva cited in Filippo Cappellano and Nicola Pignato, *Andare Contro i Carri Armati*, p. 117.
135 Ibid.
136 'Notizie circa l'impiego dei carri e autoblinde in A.S.', colonnello Mario Bizzi cited in Filippo Cappellano and Nicola Pignato, *Andare Contro i Carri Armati*, p. 226.

"to be perfect in the anti-tank role and much superior to the standard shell."[137] Thus, these new shells proved only effective when used by select larger caliber guns, while the crews of the 47mm guns continued to struggle in the anti-tank defense.

Finally, in late 1942 the Italians shipped to Tunisia a number of *cannoni 75/46 modello* 34 anti-aircraft guns which were converted to the anti-tank defense by mounting them on TM40 tractors. They were deployed by five artillery battalions (XIV, XXXV, XL, XC and XCI). These guns could penetrate at a distance of 500 meters 90mm of armour and 55mm at a distance of 1,500 meters. A report by the Italian First Army in Tunisia in February 1943 stated that: "Given that this type of anti-tank gun is one of the most effective weapons at our disposal for the troops deployed on the Mareth line, we urge the shipment by fastest mean possible of 100,000 shells."[138] Unfortunately due to some high grade components used to manufacture the gun, industry was only able to produce limited numbers.

The Americans intelligence services also held high opinions of this weapon: "While this is primarily an antiaircraft gun, successful experiments in engaging ground targets have been carried out. The weapon is mechanically sound, and practically no maintenance has been required. The muzzle velocity is probably 2,500 feet per second, although it may be higher. The gun has a high rate of fire, and with a trained crew it is estimated that 20 rounds per minute can be fired. The silhouette is satisfactory and it is believed that it would be difficult to hit from a tank at 600 to 1,000 yards. The Italians camouflage the gun with light gray and dirty white colors, and from a range of 500 yards it is practically invisible, even on level ground."[139]

Italian artillery units, including the anti-tank gun units, were probably the most well-trained of the Army. Even the Allies frequently pointed out that they represented Italy's most effective branch. Their field intelligence reports detail how Italian anti-tank guns, in particular the smaller caliber units, were generally well positioned, excellently sited and dug in and they made extensive use of camouflage. Often, they were hard to spot as the muzzles just cleared the ground. Frequently they also took advantage of the terrain as the guns were usually located on a reverse slope or entrenched in a deep gun pit. In Tunisia self-propelled guns and 90mm guns were often concealed behind trees and high shrubs to pounce upon enemy armour. The artillery also used a unique tactic that was even highly regarded by the Germans which consisted in the centralized control, at the army corps and division level, of the artillery fire.

Training

Experienced tank crews were lacking when the conflict erupted and to address this issue the directive of 1940 ('*Dispositive sul reclutamento*') established that individuals with the following requisites were encouraged to be recruited into the armoured units:

- Individuals small in stature such as those between 1.50 and 1.54 meters tall.

---

137 Ufficio Storico: Foglio n. 04/434, 'Munizioni E.P. da 75 e 100 e col fucilone Solothurn', X Corpo d'armata, Colonnello Arrigo Grillo, 2 Aprile 1942.
138 Ufficio Storico: Comando 1a Armata nota 9 di servizio, 4 Febbraio 1943.
139 'Use of Captured Italian Weapons' from Military Intelligence Service, War Department, *Tactical and Technical Trends*, Number 7, 10 September, 1942.

- Individuals that had prior driving experience holding a valid license and that could also read and write.
- Individuals with experience driving agricultural equipment such as tractors.
- Lastly, individuals with technical high school degrees in mechanics, electrical technologies or heating systems.

Men recruited for armoured units came from all over the Army, whilst the officers came primarily from the military academy in Modena or the Cavalry school in Pinerolo. The latter in particular, had by the 1930s transitioned to such motorized specialties as reconnaissance, artillery observation, scouting and surveillance. Some were also trained by Ansaldo beginning in July 1940 when the new medium tanks M.13/40 were introduced.

In August 1940, two months after Italy entered the war, the mechanized army corps conducted summer maneuvers deploying two armoured divisions (*Ariete and Littorio*) and two motorized divisions (*Trento and Trieste*). The training took place again in mountainous terrain and the various exercises that were conducted demonstrated that the units could work together in a coordinated fashion, although the absence of heavy infantry tanks was keenly felt. Tank against tank combat encounters were not envisioned then due to the light weight of the Italian tanks and as Sadkovich asserts amongst the top ranks of the military: "There was a consensus among them that armoured divisions were best used against weakly-held positions, to widen gaps in the enemy's front, and to exploit positions that had already been breached by catapulting "waves" of mechanized and motorized units through the breaches." [140]

At the time a doctrine focused on tank versus tank combat engagements had not been developed even though in the French campaign the Germans had shown how important this aspect was to modern tank warfare. Similarly, a reconnaissance doctrine for the armoured units was still in its infancy.

For a *carrista* officer of the *Centauro* Division that would go on to fight in Greece, the training received by the M.13 crews was brief. According to the trainee, the training took place at Sestri Ponente at the Ansaldo plant. Here the trainees were instructed by an old colonel that:

> Fire and movement should drive our tactical thinking in the realm of tank deployment. Moreover, that you must lunge at the enemy and destroy his defensive positions by running them over and crushing them. This is the proper strategy for the deployment of the M tanks. The strength of the M tank resides in its ability to maneuver while firing all its weapons (the gun and the machine guns). While operating these tanks in combat you must be like mad demons. You should never stop moving keep the tanks running and drive at the enemy. The only stops you can make are the dynamic ones, the ones where you let the tanks behind you quickly pass you by while continuing to fire at the enemy. A tank that is not maneuvering is as good as dead. Always move forward and when the enemy's tank and antitank screen is met, the one that fires first is the one that wins. If you let the enemy fire first it's likely that your tank will be put out of action.[141]

---

140 James J, Sadkovich, "Some Considerations Regarding Italian Armoured Doctrine Prior to June 1940," p. 69.
141 Rolando Panetta, *Il ponte di Klisura* (Milan: Mursia, 1974), pp. 102-03.

In 1940 tank crews were generally given twenty-five days of training before being dispatched to the front. Some received even less. The XXI *Battaglione Carri*, for instance, was hastily trained for two weeks and was then thrown into battle with obsolete L. 3 light tanks. In July of 1940, for example, given the need to dispatch armoured troops to North Africa several M.13/40 tanks were assembled and hurriedly pressed into service. The first armoured battalion equipped with the M.13s was sent to North Africa lacking any training for desert-like conditions. Meanwhile the *VII Battaglione Carri Medi* was formed on 1 February 1941 and for the most part up to two thirds of its ranks lacked any armoured experience and did not possess any specific technical or mechanical skills. The *VII Battaglione Carri* trained for twenty-five days before being transferred to the front. Its drivers received only two hours of practical tank driving throughout the twenty-five days, while the gunners held shooting practice only six times. "Units were employed piecemeal without an overall structure to provide support, particularly lacking recovery vehicles, while coordination was almost impossible given the lack of radio sets."[142] General Babini's armoured unit (*Brigata Corazzata Speciale*) in North Africa was a classic example of a poorly assembled and trained armoured combat unit. Formed in 1940, it lacked a full command staff, its troops had hardly conducted any training or tactical exercises prior to being deployed in combat and its tanks were slightly inferior to the British Crusier tanks they faced at Beda Fomm. But as Battistelli and Cappellano argue that: "Despite these shortcomings, Italian tank crews were thrown into combat, and gained experience on the battlefield."[143]

Thus, it was not uncommon for the tank regiments to receive the same limited training administered to the infantry divisions in preparation for the war. The limited training combined with the mechanical failures of the M series tanks[144] would ensure a poor showing of the armoured units during the first year of the North African campaign. The training regimen improved as the war progressed. In March of 1941 a training school for tank personnel was created at Civitavecchia and it was administered by a training battalion that had experience fighting with armour in Greece and North Africa. Then in February 1942 the High Command in North Africa created a special training school for armoured personnel fighting in the desert.

The artillery units within the armoured divisions were a different story. Here the crews were generally better trained as the Army's most competent recruits were typically dispatched to the artillery branch, which necessitated technically able soldiers. Their biggest challenge was to get accustomed to the anti-tank defense with the 47mm, and 75mm guns that were administered to *Ariete* during the first year of the war. Things improved in 1941 when long range, more powerful artillery weapons were introduced.

Conclusion

In conclusion, it can be argued that armoured strategy and tactics in the Italian military during the pre-Second World war era was characterized by the following factors: lack of experience in using tanks in a major conflict, outdated war plans, the conservative views and orientations of

---

142 Pier Paolo Battistelli and Filippo Cappellano, *Italian Medium Tanks*, p. 34.
143 Ibid., p. 38
144 For the most accurate and detailed English language assessment of the M tanks see Ralph Riccio, *Italian Tanks and Fighting Vehicles of World War Two* (Aberdeen: Roadrunner, 2011).

Comando Supremo and limited industrial capabilities. First, unlike Great Britain, Germany or France during World War One the Italian Army did not deploy tanks and therefore in 1940 there was no prior real major experience of armoured warfare in a major war. Tanks had been used prior to the Second World War by the Italian Army such as during the Spanish Civil War but that conflict had been a proxy one for the major powers that limited themselves to lending support and equipment to the two fighting factions. The Second World War also started on the heels of the Spanish Civil War and the Army did not have enough time to fully flush out that experience and the lessons learned. Second, "Italian strategy and doctrine in the interwar period focused on the concept of war in the mountainous northern regions of the country."[145] Simulated war plans thus limited tank development primarily to light tanks that could cross small and narrow bridges and could travel on steep and unpaved mountain roads. When North Africa became the critical theater of operations for the Italian military in 1940, its armoured units where not trained to fight in the desert landscape. Nor did they have large numbers of medium tanks that were more suited in match ups against the British tank force.

Third, the chief of staff of the armed forces in 1940 Pietro Badoglio and many top generals held conservative views with regard to military strategy and armoured conflict. For many years' tanks were perceived by the military elite as support weapons for infantry not to be deployed in autonomous combat units. Between 1925-27 General Grazioli had attempted to shake up the *Comando Supremo* by introducing new ideas and by emphasizing the importance of armoured warfare, but his innovations had been largely rejected. The Spanish Civil War finally favored a much needed debate on the role of tanks in modern warfare and many lessons learned were incorporated. Unfortunately the Second World War ensued and the Army was largely unprepared for it having spent so much energy and resources in Spain. The latter was one of the reasons behind the much anticipated policy shift of 1938 and as a result the Italian Army's thinking about tanks began to change which led to the formation of the first autonomous armoured divisions. Moreover, even the German victories of 1940 in France, in which the armoured units had played a central role, failed to spur a more substantial policy change on the need to upgrade armoured warfare and the Italian *Comando Supremo* continued to maintain a conservative tactical outlook. Other lower levels 'innovators' had rightfully anticipated the outsize role of the tank in modern battles, but their influence was limited and not well represented within the upper echelons of the army. When Italy declared war, for instance, in North Africa there were no armoured divisions ready to strike and the armoured strength was basically comprised of light tanks. If only General Grazioli had stayed on as the number two within the *Comando Supremo* the Army's overall preparation and its procurement plans would have likely better prepared it for armoured warfare. Unfortunately, Badoglio's centralized control of the High Command together with his tendency to stifle dissent and isolate opponents did not serve the interests of the Army. Mussolini's deference to Badoglio in many military matters and especially personnel promotions and dismissals ensured the marginalization of capable military thinkers such as Grazioli and others.

Fourth, limited industrial capabilities and the lack of innovation within industry also limited the development of new tanks. For example, the army continued to purchase the light *carri veloci* throughout the 1930s and only in 1940 did the army began to receive in limited numbers the

---

145 Filippo Cappellano and Pier Paolo Battistelli, *Italian Light Tanks: 1919–45*, p. 1.

M.11/39 and then the M.13/40 medium sized tanks. Thus, the military arrived at the critical juncture of the Second World War largely unprepared and with a modest medium tank fleet. This delay was the result of several factors but since Italy was heavily involved in the Spanish Civil War where its troops faced heavy Soviet manufactured tanks, it can be argued that the military should have done more to push for the introduction of heavier medium tanks sooner.

Lastly the Army after the outbreak of the war had only one, largely untrained, armoured brigade that was ready to be deployed in Italy's main theater of operations (North Africa) while two armoured divisions in training were held back in the mainland to be deployed as a tactical reserve in defense of the homeland. *Ariete*, would be the first armoured division to be deployed in Africa but only in early 1941, sometime after Graziani's debacle. All of the above factors would lead to the lackluster performance of the armoured units deployed in France, Greece and especially North Africa during the first year of the conflict.

2

Minor Armoured Campaign

France

After Italy entered the war in June 1940 the first operation carried out by its military forces was the brief campaign against France in the Western Alps, the so-called Battle of the Alps between 10-26 June 1940. Here the army mobilized primarily several *alpini*, infantry and Blackshirts divisions and battalions which were charged with capturing the Little Maginot Line of the Alps, the French fortified bunkers and pillboxes that dotted the border between France and Italy. The goal was to overcome these French defenses and advance against Menton and ultimately capture Marseilles by attacking along three main roads; Little Saint Bernard Pass, Colle della Maddalena and Corniche. The plan entailed to capture as much territory as possible before the signing of a peace deal between France and Germany.

Even though the Germans had already overrun French territory by the time Italy entered the war, the objective assigned to the infantry forces was not an easy one since the campaign had been launched with little or no planning and the French positions were extremely well sited and difficult to reach: "Although most of the petit ouvrages of the Little Maginot Line in the Alps consisted of little more than a few infantry weapons positions, they were well sited. A few gros ouvrages included reinforced forward firing artillery casemates as turrets were impractical in the mountainous terrain."[1]

The fortified positions were not only situated in difficult to reach key positions such as on mountain passes or peaks but were also well equipped and armed. Each blockhouse of the alpine line, for instance, consisted mainly of two 149mm field guns, two antitank guns, several machine guns and automatic rifles. Although the field guns were not anti-tank weapons per se, from their privileged positions they could block any tank advance which could only take place on highly exposed main roads. Under the command of General Renè Orly, the French deployed the "Armeè des Alpes" which was comprised of highly skilled units in mountain warfare. The French units included 70 platoons of mountain scout-skier troops, the garrisons manning the forts and other smaller units for a total of 180,000 men.

---

1 Kaufmann, Kaufmann and Potocnik, Lang, *The Maginot Line* (Barnsley: Pen & Sword Military, 2017), p.154.

Given that the French controlled the high ground, this campaign would in fact result in an extremely tough engagement for the Italian Army, and for the armoured units in particular which had to advance along rough and narrow uphill roads to reach the mountain peaks. Most roads were unpaved and the high mountain environment meant advancing under very poor weather conditions. In fact, it was a fight that the Royal Army would engage not only against determined French opposition, but also against the mountains and their bitter climate. Even though the attack took place in June, the temperatures in the high peaks were still below zero and snow storms were a daily occurrence. The only way to proceed forward was for the mountain troops "to force the mountain passes between the coast and the Swiss border" and to do this under the watchful eye of the enemy.[2] The declaration of war had also come very precipitously and the High Command had not made any meaningful pre-war operational plans. To give just one example, when Italy entered the war, the High Command had yet to develop a plan to capture the vital island of Malta and no extensive reconnaissance of the French mountain positions had been made.

Badoglio's orders were to attack decisively across the Piccolo San Bernardino Pass while the attacks against Colle della Maddalena and Corniche were to be carried out only if favorable conditions emerged. These attacks were to be pressed forward 'decisively' in concurrence with the German armoured thrusts toward Grenoble and Chambery from Lyons. Thus the troops were divided into two major armies. The IV *Corpo d'Armata* under the command of *Generale* Alfredo Guzzoni would be deployed in the northern sector between Monte Dolent to Monte Granero, while the I *Corpo d'Armata* under the command of General Pietro Pintor, from Monte Granero to the sea. This final edition of the offensive plan had thus only two main actions, Operation M through the Little Saint Bernard and Operation R along the Riviera, the action in the Maddalena Pass being reduced to a diversionary advance. The immediate objective of Operation M was Albertville, while that of R was the town of Menton. Italy had a total of 22 divisions equivalent to 300,000 men, and 2,900 cannons of various caliber and the "Alpine Wall" garrisons.

On the first day of operation, 21 June, the Italian artillery launched a preparatory fire against the French positions near the border which was also supported by thirty-nine bombers which released their payload ahead of the infantry attack. During the preparatory phase an armoured train equipped with four 120/45 railway guns was also utilized to shell French defenses. The train shelled the enemy positions for several hours, but it was also targeted by the counter-battery fire of the French artillery which scored some direct hits. The infantry then moved forward in the area of the Little Saint Bernard Pass but could not proceed very far due to enemy artillery fire and the high snow. The next day the infantry and alpine units began to inch closer to the enemy positions, but again losses were sustained and the infantry had to attack by itself since the bad weather grounded the air force bombers. The third day of operations saw the spearhead of the attack undertaken by the armoured units mainly equipped with the L.3/35 light tanks.

The units involved were nine L.3/35 tank battalions, five of which belonged to the *Raggruppamento Celere* and the four remaining were from the *Littorio* Division, while the *Ariete* Division was kept in reserve.

2   Ibid.

The first deployment of the I *Battaglione*/33 *Reggimento Littorio* took place on the third day of the offensive when at 0500 on 23 June this unit advanced against two rounds of barbed wire defenses. The objective was to advance in cooperation with the *Trieste* Division along the Little Saint Bernard Pass toward the town of Seez.

In anticipation of the Italian attack, the French had placed numerous obstacles on the main road along with barbed wire entanglements and antitank mines. The engineers had thus been deployed ahead of the tanks to clear the way, but even after they had completed their tasks, the advance by the tanks was slowed by snow fall and persistent French artillery fire.

Then when the L.3 tanks arrived at Hill 1942, on top of the mountain pass leading to Seez, the first tank at the head of the column blew up when it struck an undetected land mine. At the same time the remaining tanks came under heavy fire from French guns. After a brief interruption, the advance resumed. But as the battalion kept moving forward the French artillery knocked out of action two more tanks because as they climbed higher, their pace slowed down considerably exposing them even more to enemy fire. Having reached the highest altitude, the tanks could not advance any further as they were immobilized along the main road and remained exposed to the concentrated fire coming from forts on Bourg-Saint Maurice.

The offensive thus stalled and the battalion was withdrawn during the evening while the damaged tanks could not be recovered. Since at the time the mechanized units did not possess tractors or heavy duty trucks to tow the damaged tanks and recover them to the rear, four tanks had to be abandoned.

The next day the IV *Battaglione/1 Reggimento Fanteria Carrista* was deployed as the spearhead to advance past the Moncenisio pass to reach the Arc valley in support of the *Trento* Division. The L.3 tanks were heavily targeted by blistering fire from the onset by 81mm mortars and mountain guns. The L tanks come under strong enemy fire just like what happened at the Little Saint Bernard Pass and could not proceed further as several units were lost.

By the fourth day of operations in the northern sector the troops had advanced for two miles into enemy territory. Meanwhile in the southern sector, in the area of the French Riviera, the advance had been more precipitous. The troops by the end of the campaign, after overcoming numerous defensive positions, had occupied Menton after heavy fighting penetrating five miles into French territory. The fighting had cost the Italians 642 dead, 2,631 wounded, and 616 missing, while 2,151 suffered from frostbite. [3]

The brief campaign highlighted some of the major shortcomings of the Italian army in 1940. A lack of adequate numbers of modern artillery pieces, especially motorized ones meant that the infantry advance was fraught with difficulties. The binary divisions also demonstrated that they were stretched too thin in the field of battle and that without an additional regiment these divisions had to be taken in the rear fairly quickly after they had suffered their first losses. Overall, the contribution of the armoured units to the campaign was marginal mainly because their pace during the advance was slow due to the rough terrain and it was always conducted under the heavy counter battery and anti-tank fire of the French mountain artillery. Advancing on lone roads against mountaintop and pass positions the tanks were always at the mercy of the enemy guns. The Italian official history of the campaign states that the deployment of the tanks was largely unsuccessful given the rough terrain and the inability of overcoming fortified defenses.

---

3   John Gooch, *Mussolini's War*, p. 103.

East Africa

The Duca d'Aosta, Viceroy of Ethiopia and Supreme Commander of all armed forces in *Africa Orientale Italiana* (Italian East Africa) territories had at his disposal in 1940 approximately 90,000 Italian troops and approximately 200,000 colonials. The two major Italian divisions were the *Divisione Granatieri di Savoia*, and the *Divisione Fanteria d'Africa*, while other units included several battalions of the MVSN and other Royal Army units. The remaining forces were comprised by local troops that were well regarded by the Italian command but were for the most part not motorized and carried most of their artillery with pack mules. In 1940 the army possessed in East Africa 8,600 machine guns, 670,000 rifles, four 149/13 howitzers, four 120/45 guns, twenty-six 120/24 guns, fifty-nine 105/28 guns, 216 77/28 guns, sixteen 75/46 guns, ninety-two 70/15 guns, 312 65/17 mountain guns, twenty-four 20mm anti-aircraft guns, fifty 81mm mortars and approximately an additional 100 guns of various calibers.[4] The few armoured vehicles in the theater consisted of a total of twenty-four M.11/39 medium tanks and thirty-nine light tanks and 126 armoured cars. In fact, one company from the I/32º *Reggimento Carristi* of *Divisione Ariete* fought in East Africa until the end of the campaign in March-May 1941 when it was virtually[5] destroyed during the British counteroffensive. It was split into two companies (321º and 322º *Compagnie*) which fought alongside another armoured unit equipped with L.35 tanks (a company from the *3º Reggimento*). Initially, they were deployed separately, one stationed in Eritrea and the other at Addis Ababa and for the most part throughout the campaign the light and medium armour was not consolidated into one combat unit. Thus, despite the fact that the force possessed a modicum of medium tanks, light tanks and some mobile artillery no one within the Duca d'Aosta command staff pushed for the constitution of a mobile reserve by assembling these assets into a new combat unit. Instead the assets were deployed in a piecemeal fashion which vastly reduced their combat power.[6] The Air Force had approximately 300 planes. According to the Italian Official History; "The combat units had adequate numbers of rifles and machine guns, but they possessed few mortars, and their anti-tank and anti-aircraft weapons were almost nonexistent. Moreover, they had few radios and their supply/logistics units relied primarily on pack mules. There were few trucks that were constantly rotated to the units most in need."[7] The artillery arm was for the most part not motorized, only few units of 105/28 guns were motorized, while the mass of 65/17 guns was transported by pack mules. These units enjoyed excellent mobility in the mountains but were not prepared for a rapid deployment in the non-mountainous sectors because they lacked motorized transport. Like the artillery, the infantry troops, for the most part, were not motorized and given the very low number of trucks it was not possible to create even a small mechanized and motorized special force.

In 1940 Britain, held approximately 27,500 soldiers in Sudan, 35,000 in Kenya and 7,500 in British Somaliland. The Italians had more troops but their position was nothing to rave about because it was so far away from its supply bases that the British Navy could easily cut it off from Europe or North Africa. As the British Official History states: "The unpreparedness

---

4   Alberto Rovighi, *Le operazioni in Africa orientale*, vol. 1, part 1 (Rome: Ufficio Storico, 1995), p. 39.
5   Filippo Cappellano and Nicola Pignato, *Gli autoveicoli da combattimento dell'esercito italiano* (Rome: Ufficio Storico, 2002), p. 95.
6   Ibid.
7   Alberto Rovighi, *Le operazioni in Africa orientale*, Vol. 1, part 1, p. 41.

of Italy to face a long war was nowhere more acutely felt than in Italian East Africa. The situation of Somalia, Eritrea, and Ethiopia was strategically weak because the sea communications could easily be cut, and even the air communications were liable to be interrupted, by an enemy based in the Middle East….. It was not as if Italian East Africa had the industries, the natural resources, or the accumulated reserves to offset a prolonged interruption of the normal routes of supply."[8]

Given the precarious supply situation the *Duca d'Aosta*'s plan was to effectuate a swift strike bringing to bear all available attacking forces with the invasion of British Somaliland and the capture of Berbera which was not only the capital city but also a key port facility. Others within his staff opposed the plan and maintained that the Italian forces should take a defensive position while building up a mechanized/motorized brigade. Their views however, represented a minority opinion and the offensive operation began in August of 1940 with three major columns of attack under the overall command of *Generale* Guglielmo Nasi, who was the commander of the Eastern Sector of *Africa Orientale Italiana*, and could rely upon three Italian and twenty-three colonial battalions, and three light field howitzer batteries. The mechanized component was comprised by the *Polizia Africa Italiana* on five Fiat 611 armoured cars, eleven M.11/39 tanks of 322° *Compagnia*, and fifteen L.35 tanks of the *Compagnia Carri Veloci Cavalieri di Neghelli*. As historian Nicola Pignato asserts in relation to the armour at the disposal of this force that "it is evident that such a modest armoured force could not exert a key role in the offensive."[9] The operation was also supported by the air force, fifty-seven aircraft in support, which flew several bombing missions against the British frontline positions ahead of the main infantry attack.

The main column, under *Generale* De Simone and comprised of eleven battalions, was to seize Hargeisa, establish a jumping off platform and finally seize Berbera. The eastern column, comprised primarily by three battalions under *Generale* Bertello was to play a support role protecting the flank of the main column. On the western flank *Generale* Bertoldi's column with eight battalions was to seize Zeila and then converge upon Berbera. The campaign can be broken down into three phases: 1. From 3 to 6 August when the troops made contact with the enemy's forward elements, 2. From 7 to 16 August with the battle of the Tug Argan Gap and finally 17 to 19 August with the capture of Berbera.

Order of Battle Italian Forces in East Africa

Command: *Generale* Guglielmo Nasi
Western Column-*Tenente Generale* Sisto Bertoldi
    LXX Colonial Brigade
    XVII Colonial Brigade
Eastern Column-*Generale* Arturo Bertello
    1 Colonial Battalion

---

[8] I.S.O. Playfair, *The Mediterranean and Middle East, Volume I: The Early Successes against Italy to May 1941*, p. 165.
[9] Filippo Cappellano and Nicola Pignato, *Insegne, uniformi, distintivi e tradizioni delle truppe corazzate* (Rome: T&T, 2005), p. 23.

    2 Dubat Battalions (irregular troops)
    1 artillery battery
Central Column- *Tenente Generale* Carlo De Simone
    XIII Colonial Brigade
    XIV Colonial Brigade
    XV Colonial Brigade
    Polizia Africa Italiana
    322° *Compagnia Carri Medi*
    Compagnia Carri Veloci Cavallieri di Neghelli
    149/13 heavy field artillery battery
    105/28 heavy field artillery battalion
Coastal Column- *Console Generale* Giovanni Passerone
    XI *Legione* CC.NN (two Blackshirt Battalions)
    LXVI Colonial Battalion
    Reparto Speciale
    Artillery company
Reserve-*Colonnello* Orlando Lorenzini
    II Colonial Brigade

The troops moved forward on 3 August and initially the enemy forces fell back and therefore there were only brief skirmishes against machine gun strongpoints that aimed to slow down the pace of the advance. The bulk of the fighting was carried out by *Generale* De Simone's column where the initial assault on Hargeisa was held up by the machine gun and the field gun fire of Camel Corps. Despite some losses, the attack was continued on 5 August and with the aid of the light and medium tanks the Camel Corps and a company of the Northern Rhodesia Regiment were forced to evacuate the position and fall back further. For several days, the advance was then put on hold because of the rough terrain, there was only one main road on which to advance and the heavy rains had made it almost impossible to proceed. The advance was resumed on 8 August when Italian columns pursued the enemy and prepared the main sally against the enemy's resistance positions. "It was during this phase that the presence of Italian medium tanks was first reported. Because there were no anti-tank guns the Captain of H.M.A.S. Hobart offered a 3-pdr saluting gun with 30 rounds of ammunition—an offer which was gladly accepted."[10]

The battle for the Tug Argan gap, so called from the name of the river that ran across the front, began in earnest as the Italians advanced on the valley floor while the enemy troops occupied the surrounding hills which gave them not only excellent observation points but also the ability to dig in small artillery in the form of several Bofors guns. In fact, British Lieut.-Colonel Arthur Chater had five infantry battalions, four Bofors guns and the 3-pdr Hotchkiss gun dispatched from HMAS Hobart. On 11 August the Italians began their operation with a preparatory barrage and then charged against the enemy positions on Punjab Ridge driving off a company of 3/15th Punjab Regiment. The next day the advance was resumed with the

---

10 I.S.O. Playfair, *The Mediterranean and Middle East, Volume I: The Early Successes against Italy to May 1941*, p. 175.

capture after fierce fighting of Mill Hill as well as the seizure of several howitzers. By now the Italians had captured the majority of the high ground positions and were on the verge of coming down from the opposite side of the pass. The next day there were other attacks which led to high casualties on both sides. Locked in an impasse the Italians turned to their artillery to pave a way forward. Since at the time the British forces did not have any heavy artillery and relied primarily on small caliber anti-tank guns, the Italian guns were able to batter the enemy lines with impunity forcing a further pull back by the enemy. According to the British Official History it was the preponderance of the Italian artillery which turned the tide at Tug Argan Gap: "It was now clear to General Godwin-Austen that not only was the enemy almost in a position to cut the road along which all supplies and water had to come, but that his marked preponderance in artillery, which outranged the light howitzers and so was able to fire without interference, meant that he could concentrate against each defended locality in turn."[11] On 15 August the Italians concentrated their main efforts in overcoming the defenses of two forts that were defended by machine guns and some field guns that had previously blocked all progress by the attackers. After the artillery had intervened with a preparatory fire aimed at subduing the enemy, the troops lunged forward invading the two forts and then clearing all the caverns surrounding the forts of any enemy presence. Then on the 17th the Italian troops continued to advance and finally broke through the enemy defenses forcing the Scottish 2nd Black Watch units to retreat. During this phase of the battle the tanks performed their standard combat role by advancing behind the infantry and taking on machine gun nests. By that time a heterogeneous combat group had been created centered on the LXX *Brigata* which included all available mobile elements such as light and medium tanks, armoured cars and truck borne infantry that was responsible in breaching the enemy defenses at Laferung Pass. No major losses of tanks were recorded during this period. On the 19th Berbera was evacuated by the British just in time before the arrival of Italian troops. The Italians there captured five howitzers, five mortars, 101 machine guns, 5,396 rifles, three tanks, and 108 trucks. They suffered 2,020 dead, while the British had 260 casualties, of which the majority were in the Northern Rhodesia Regiment and the Camel Corps, along with 100 men missing.

The operation had entailed a long range maneuver of over 270 kilometers conducted in approximately ten days (excluding the few days when the heavy fighting occurred) that tested the soldiers physical resistance since they had to march on foot with limited provisions and facing very challenging weather. The overall coordination between armour, infantry and air forces was good as the operation was preceded by aerial bombardments and the armoured vehicles force for the most part kept the same pace of the infantry during the advance but then broke loose in chasing the enemy forces during the last two days of the campaign. The logistics aspects of the operation were extremely challenging and the supply columns could only advance at night given the RAF's menacing presence during the daytime. Extensive wear and tear had been placed on the vehicles to the point that it was necessary to halt operations for a period of time and regroup.

After the conquest of British Somaliland, the Italians adopted a more conservative posture dictated primarily by their low supplies of ammunition by retreating to more easily defensible positions such as the mountain passes on the Kassala–Agordat and Metemma–Gondar roads.

---

11 Ibid., p. 176.

This was dictated primarily upon a calculus by the *Duca d'Aosta* that the strength of *Africa Orientale Italiana* was slowly dwindling due to equipment not being replaced and an overall lack of new troops and weapons. In fact, very few reinforcements came from Italy at this time and this contrasted sharply with a steady buildup of Commonwealth troops in the Sudan and Kenya which were being rapidly strengthened with also the addition of armoured units. The *Duca d'Aosta* thus was forced to rely almost exclusively upon his own troops. In Eritrea, General Frusci had three colonial divisions and three colonial brigades. At Gallabat and Metemma he could count upon three colonial brigades and in Gondar upon five Blackshirt battalions. In Gojjam (Ethiopia) General Nasi had four colonial brigades. At Addis Ababa, there were the *Savoia* and *Africa* divisions, some Blackshirt battalions and twelve colonial battalions.

In September strong British reinforcements arrived in the Sudan including B Squadron 6th Royal Tank Regiment equipped with cruiser and light tanks and the 5th Indian Division. The reinforcements gave rise to a plan due to start on 6 November that entailed the 3rd Royal Garhwal Rifles, with B Squadron/6th Royal Tank Regiment in support, capturing Gallabat Fort and then advancing against Metemma, a town in northwestern Ethiopia, on the border with Sudan. The attack was repulsed with heavy casualties mainly due to the fact that the Italian artillery was equipped to deal with the Cruiser tanks. The latter advanced toward the Italian fortifications but then were heavily targeted by the artillery forcing them to initially operate on the flanks and then to retire.

In early January 1941, the Italian intelligence services reported that another buildup of Commonwealth troops had occurred thus sounding the alarm of an imminent attack. In fact, the British had 75,000 forces at the start of the campaign but by the winter of 1940-41 their forces had been augmented considerably to 254,000. At the same time, the Italian forces were approximately 265,000. "On 11th January the Viceroy explained that the British mechanized troops would have such an advantage on the flat ground that he wished to withdraw most of his forces from the Sudan-Eritrea frontier to the eastward of Tessenei, Sabderat, and Keru; none of the ground west of Agordat and Barentu would hamper mechanized action sufficiently."[12] This resulted in the preemptive evacuation of Kassala and the consequent build out of strong defensive positions in the strategically sited mountain passes dominating vast valley floors.

Meanwhile, the British command after having pushed back the Italians in North Africa decided to take the initiative also in East Africa by launching an ambitious offensive. General William Platt decided to begin his advance on 19 January with the 4th Division (Major-General Beresford-Peirse) which was to progress to the area east of Kassala while the 5th Indian Infantry Brigade was to support its flank and B Squadron/4th Royal Tank Regiment (equipped with sixteen Matilda II tanks) was to provide the cutting edge once the mountain ranges and hill top positions had been overtaken. Gazelle Force, the advanced column of the Commonwealth deployment, reached Biscia on the 24 January and then continued toward Agordat. The brigades of the 4th Indian Division reached Agordat on the 27th, while 10th Indian Infantry Brigade was to head toward Barentu. The scene was set for the major showdown of the campaign with the battle of Agordat when on 31 January 1941, troops from the 4th Indian Division mounted a major attack on the mountain ranges and broke in the plains. As the Italian tanks were drawn

---

12   Ibid., p. 170.

into the open plain to repulse the infantry attack, they were met by several Matildas which thanks to their heavier construction were impervious to Italian tank fire.

The fortified Italian defenses were held primarily by the CLI *Battaglione* at Laqoutat and Chocen which came under attack on the left flank by a combination of infantry and medium tank armoured units. The initial enemy thrust was successful but further progress was halted by the accurate targeting of the 105mm gun crews which put down a repressive fire that forced the attackers halt the advance. The enemy artillery began to then pound again the Italian positions which had been already battered by the RAF in the early morning hours. At approximately 0830 a number of infantry tanks, that had never been seen before in East Africa, were observed by the Italian defenders from the distance. Once these tanks were spotted the Italian commander ordered his tank units to get ready for a potential counterattack while the frontline positions were buttressed by the arrival of some Blackshirt companies. At 1000 the first armoured clash of the day took place between a few Italian medium tanks that counterattacked led by *Capitano* Chisari. During the counter the Italians suffered the loss of a few tanks including the one led by the *Capitano* who was also killed in the action. By this time the left flank of the Italian defenses had been breached and a quickly assembled group comprised of Blackshirts, medium tanks and III *Battaglione* led by *Tenente Colonnello* Luziani was tasked to commit to another counterattack to halt the heavy tanks which were now advancing in full force. The final clash took place at 0100 when the Matilda tanks continued to push on and overran the Italian defenses on the resistance line. They then shot at and destroyed additional M.11/39 (nine) and several light tanks that had intervened in vain to try to halt the advance. The Italian Official History reports that initially the artillery crews equipped with 77/28 guns attempted in vain numerous times to stop the heavy infantry tanks from approaching the resistance line but their armour was so thick that the shells would simply bounce off and couldn't stop them. The heavy British infantry tanks could only have been stopped by proper large caliber anti-tank guns but the Italian colony did not have any at its disposal. In May 1940 at Arras/France the Germans had initially bolted when they had come up against the same infantry tanks and had to subsequently make recourse to the 88mm Flak 36 anti-aircraft guns to halt them. It is most likely that the Italian intelligence services did not know of the presence of these heavy tanks in East Africa as the battle report states that all of a sudden the enemy infantry came forward supported by sixteen heavy infantry tanks "the size of which hadn't been seen before that procured an extremely dangerous situation."[13] Once it was determined that the tanks could not be stopped by the artillery, the Italians deployed their tanks but they too were no match.[14] "Heroic was the sacrifice of our tank crews since the enemy tanks weighing three or four times more where putting them mercilessly out of action in a short time and without sustaining any losses of their own."[15] After the breakthrough from the hills of Cochen, Laquotat and Hill 726 there were other attempts made by the artillery crews to halt the advance of the tanks on the plain. The 77/28 gun crews managed to score some hits but none of the enemy tanks were damaged. Being impervious to the gun fire, the tanks managed to continue their advance to reach the Agordat-Keren road, where they were shortly thereafter joined by their infantry units. The enemy was now in complete control of the valley floor. At 1400 the enemy planes bombed the divisional headquarters with impunity

---

13   Alberto Rovighi, *Le operazioni in Africa orientale*, Vol. 1, part 1, p. 209.
14   Ibid.
15   Ibid. p. 210.

as they were the uncontested masters of the sky. The battle for Agordat was lost. By the end of the day the Italians had suffered the following losses: 1,500 Italians and 14,000 colonials killed or captured, nine medium tanks, fifteen light tanks, 231 machine guns and 96 guns of various caliber had been overrun.

The British official history furnishes a very similar account of the events that took place on 31 January. According to this document: "The same morning 5th Indian Infantry Brigade and the newly arrived 'I' tanks struck northward across the plain, carried the defenses, and destroyed a number of Italian tanks concealed for counter-attack. By 4.30 p.m. they had taken their objective and cut the Keren road, but most of the enemy's 4th Colonial Division escaped by a track farther north. It had lost about two battalions, twenty-eight field guns and a number of light and medium tanks. Gazelle took up the pursuit at dawn next day, greatly delayed by heavy mining and demolitions."[16]

Meanwhile, a second Commonwealth column attacked the Italian positions at Barentu, held by colonial troops from the 2nd Colonial Division and supported by 36 light tanks and armoured cars. After tough fighting the Commonwealth troops took the Barentu position forcing the Italians to retreat. Because of this serious breach of their defenses, the Italians were forced to retreat to Keren in central Erithrea, while the Commonwealth troops pushed forward towards Agordat, which was captured on 1 February. According to a British regimental history the Matildas proved decisive and "no more Italian armour appeared for the rest of the campaign."[17]

The following final siege of Keren, which lasted several weeks given the strong opposition put forth by the remaining Italian troops, ultimately determined the loss of Italian East Africa. The battle began on 5 February 1941 with the RAF making several flights to bomb and soften up the Italian positions which were mainly occupied by the *Granatieri di Savoia*, Blackshirts and colonial troops. The two-month long siege of Keren was fought by the Italians as a defensive rather than a battle of maneuver. During the prolonged engagement the few Italian tanks still standing were utilized on the defensive line as they were dug in and employed to repulse the infantry attacks. After the British troops stormed the Italian defenses all the tanks were either captured or put out of action. At Keren, the Commonwealth losses were of 536 killed and 3,229 wounded, while the Italians had 3,000 killed. "The battle was not the last of the campaign, but it was decisive, for although the Italians managed to withdraw a large amount of their artillery, and some of their infantry, they never fought with the same determination again."[18]

An analysis of the campaign in East Africa must begin with the fact that the Italians enjoyed the advantage of defending from hilltop positions which were ideally suited for an army that had fought that kind of defensive war before. On the flipside, there were too many weaknesses which the British would exploit to their own advantage which consisted mainly in the control of the airspace by the RAF which bombed with impunity the Italian positions and the presence of the heavy infantry tanks which were the game changers on the ground in the attrition-like battle of Agordat. On 16th March the *Duca d'Aosta* had written to Mussolini outlining his many difficulties, notably the lack of transport, the dearth of anti-tank weapons, and aircraft.

---

16   I.S.O. Playfair, *The Mediterranean and Middle East, Volume I: The Early Successes against Italy to May 1941*, p. 401.
17   Cited in Andrew Stewart, *The First Victory* (New Haven: Yale University Press, 2017), p. 159.
18   I.S.O. Playfair, *The Mediterranean and Middle East, Volume I: The Early Successes against Italy to May 1941*, p. 439.

In February 1941, for example, the Italians had 188 aircraft but only 67 were serviceable, while in March they had dropped to 150 and only 39 were serviceable. This allowed the British to conduct their ground operations with little or no interference from the enemy air force which not only could not intercept the RAF's bombing forays but also could not halt or degrade the ground forces.

The other major issue for the Italians that was apparent from the beginning of the campaign was the dearth of anti-tank weapons. Six months later the troops would face the heavy Matilda II tanks, with a limited number of anti-tank guns such as four 47/32, thirty-one 20/65 guns and thirty 37/40 guns"[19] and the field guns with which it had begun the campaign. The Matilda was invulnerable to the projectiles of the standard Italian anti-tank gun, the 47/32. Moreover, the standard Italian field guns in the caliber range of 75-100 with their standard projectiles were also not particularly effective against the 30 ton British tanks. Only the heavy field guns 105/28 could achieve sporadic success against these heavy infantry tanks. The standard Italian division, including the armoured divisions, at the start of the war were equipped primarily with the *cannone da 75/27 modello* 06. According to an artillery specialist this gun "is antiquated and is particularly not effective against armour that is moving. Given the absence of armoured piercing projectiles, this gun is even ineffective against medium tanks that are in a stationary position."[20]

The battle of Agordat, the key battle of the campaign, was decided after the heavy infantry tanks brushed aside the Italian medium and light tanks and then continued to rumble on toward the crossroad leading to Keren while the Italian artillery located in the nearby hills could do nothing to stop them. The failure to create a strategic reserve by assembling all mobile and mechanized forces into one unit was one of the major blunders committed by the Italians in the campaign. A second mistake was the failure to constitute a mobile artillery regiment that could in some way halt the enemy armour. Both mistakes were paid dearly with the loss of East Africa.

Greek Campaign

Another campaign that saw the deployment of the armoured units was the offensive against Greece in the fall of 1940. The Greek campaign was haphazardly planned and mainly launched to achieve strategic political objectives aimed at balancing German influence in the Balkans and in the Mediterranean, especially after the latter had initiated a strong military mission to Romania and had taken control of the oil fields. Another reason was to gain greater control of the Eastern Mediterranean, occupy the island of Corfu and gain possession of Greek coastal towns. This would have allowed the Italian Navy to better control the shipment of supplies to North Africa and to reduce the influence of the British naval base of Malta. Presumably there were other reasons why the Italian government decided to attack Greece and some of them are still today shrouded in secrecy. Its timing, however, late October 1940, was horrendous as the infantry troops found themselves fighting in grave conditions such as the mud, snow and icy rains of the Epirus mountain ranges. During the planning phase of the campaign the

---

19 Filippo Cappellano and Nicola Pignato, *Andare contro i carri armati*, p. 94.
20 Ufficio Storico: Comando Divisione Corazzata Ariete, Sezione Operazioni, informazioni e servizi, 'Dati d'esperienza circa impiego divisioni motorizzate e corazzate', 11 Agosto 1941.

Map 1 The Greek Campaign: Italian Plan of Attack, 28 October 1940.

High Command underestimated Greek strength and initially fielded an infantry force of only nine divisions that was roughly half the size of the mobilized troops by the Greek government by late November 1940. In fact, initially the Italians mobilized 90,000 men against 36,000 Greek soldiers stationed at the frontier with Albania. Then in less than a month the Greeks were able to call up and mobilize their reserves and by then they could deploy sixteen divisions at the Albanian/Greek front. Each Greek division had three infantry regiments against the standard Italian binary division which had only two. This prompted the Italian High Command to dispatch more troops to the front as a means of propping up the offensive and replacing losses. Lastly, logistics were also vastly underestimated as the ports in Albania did not have the capacity to handle the flow of troops and supplies coming from Italy that were required to support the offensive.

Italian Invasion

The launch of the campaign was decided on 15 October 1940 when *Generale* Sebastiano Visconti Prasca, who had been tasked by the government to plan the operation, stated that it would entail nine divisions plus the support of the air force to overcome Greece. Visconti Prasca claimed that the swift operation he had planned would meet with little resistance by the Greeks because large sections of the society and some politicians were sympathetic to the Italian regime. The major limiting factor was from the rains and the potential snow storms in the mountains, which could hamper troop movement. Given these considerations the operation, in his view, had to be launched as quickly as possible to avoid the winter season. Its strongest proponent was Galeazzo Ciano, the foreign minister, while it is believed that Badoglio and *Generale* Mario Roatta, his number two at *Comando Supremo*, were both initially lukewarm. Badoglio, in particular, stated in his diary (but after the war was over) that the Italian Army to be successful had to go beyond the occupation of the Epirus and that this would require twenty divisions. He thus was not apparently fully convinced that Visconti Prasca's plan would work but he did not object to the plan at the time and went along with everyone else stating that Greece had to be attacked. It was ultimately decided that the first objective would be to seize the Epirus region followed by an advance upon Athens. To this end the nine divisions were to launch a series of infantry attacks against the Greek army border positions from launching pads located in Italian occupied Albania and they were to be deployed as follows:

- XXV *Corpo d'Armata Ciamuria* led by Generale Carlo Rossi, comprised of one mechanized division (*Centauro*) and two infantry divisions (*Siena and Ferrara*), was tasked with leading the main offensive in the Epirus in the southern sector of the Albanian / Greek front to reach the Kalamas River and Ioannina and then further exploit the breakthrough toward the capital. The *Centauro* Division was to participate in the main attack in the Epirus and was mainly assigned the role of overcoming barbed wire and machine gun defenses to open a path for the infantry. Specifically, to provide the infantry with advanced covering fire to allow the latter to approach and close in with the Greek defenses. The role of the armoured forces was thus to support the infantry and once again the rough and hilly terrain of the southern Epirus region would dictate the pace of the operation. Most importantly, the autumn weather would pose a heavy challenge upon the progress of the armoured units. The plan of operations entailed that *Centauro*'s tank units to initially shadow the infantry of the *Ferrara* and *Siena* Divisions as they advanced toward the Greek lines in the direction of Kalibaki, Ioannina and Arta. Once the battle was in full swing the tank units were to act autonomously by bypassing the infantry to take on enemy defenses directly. The *Siena* Division had two main columns, while the *Ferrara* Division was to move in four columns.

The fact that the Greek army did not field armoured units nor did they demand them from the British in the campaign is a strong indication that the terrain was highly inhospitable to armoured warfare and maneuver. Even the British Army later in the campaign deployed troops to aid the Greeks in the defense against the Axis forces but given the impervious terrain the British Army also did not commit large numbers of armoured units to the campaign. At the start of the operations the 131º *Centauro* Armoured Division was comprised by the 31º *Reggimento Carristi* with its tank battalions equipped with L.3 tanks, the 5º *Reggimento Bersaglieri* (XXII, XIV, XXIV battalions) and the 131º Artillery Regiment also based on three groups (I-II-III) armed with twenty-four tractor mounted or trained 75/27 guns and eight 47mm guns. At the beginning of the hostilities in Greece *Centauro,* like many of the infantry divisions, was severely understrength with 5,000 men, 137 L.3 tanks and 33 flamethrower tanks. At the time the unit did not have medium tanks. Meanwhile both the *Siena* and *Ferrara* units were standard Italian infantry divisions each with just two infantry regiments and one artillery regiment and approximately 10,000-12,000 soldiers each. Each infantry regiment had approximately 3,450 soldiers, 108 light and 25 heavy machine guns, six 81mm mortars and four 65/17 guns. The standard infantry division had minimal motorized resources, no mobile reconnaissance units and very little in terms of support services such as combat engineers or specialized crew served weapons units.

> XXVI *Corpo d'Armata* led by *Generale* Gabriele Nasci was comprised of two infantry divisions (*Piemonte, Parma*). It was deployed on the extreme Italian left in the area of Korçë and it was to move along the border to invade north-west Macedonia.
>
> The *Alpini Divisione Julia* was to act on the left flank of the main attacking column to force the mountain passes in the central sector of the Pindus range and ultimately reach Drisko and Metsovo passes. This advance would have enabled the Italians to cut the Greek forces in two between those of the Epirus and those of Macedonia and then from Metsovo they would also gain control of the main Greek supply lines. The *alpini* would later be supported by the *Bari* and Venezia Divisions.
>
> The *Raggruppamento del Litoriale* (*Brigadiere* Carlo Rivolta) was deployed along the coast and comprised of two cavalry regiments (6th/*Aosta* Lancers, 7th *Milano*/Lancers), one of artillery and one of 3rd *Granatieri di Sardegna*, and was to be initially held back in reserve.

Order of Battle – XXV *Corpo d'Armata Ciamuria Generale* Carlo Rossi 28 October 1940

51º *Divisione Siena* (*Generale* Gualtiero Gabutini)
    31º *Reggimento Fanteria.*
    32º *Reggimento Fanteria.*
    51º *Reggimento Artiglieria.*
23º *Divisione Ferrara* (Generale Licurgo Zannini)
    47º *Reggimento Fanteria.*

    48º Reggimento Fanteria.
    14º Reggimento Artiglieria.
    Gruppo Solinas (5º Reggimento Bersaglieri/ Centauro).
131º *Divisione Centauro* (*Generale* Giovanni Magni)
    31º *Reggimento Carristi*
    131º *Reggimento Artigleria Corazzata.*

As Italian intentions to amass troops and build up the force on the border between September and October became known, the Greek government mobilized initially four divisions which were mainly deployed along the Albanian frontier and especially on each side of the Pindus mountain range. Twelve infantry divisions were initially kept as reserve troops. Five were kept in Eastern Macedonia and their role was to watch over the border with Bulgaria to negate any potential threat from a combined German / Bulgarian force. The remaining seven divisions were dispersed over the rest of the country. The standard Greek Army Corps had four infantry divisions and one heavy artillery regiment typically equipped with eight 85mm, eight 105mm and twelve 155mm guns. The equipment of the Greek soldiers was not too different from those of the Italians, although they lacked adequate numbers of anti-aircraft and anti-tank weapons and transport. Moreover, the Greeks did not have an armoured force (just a few older tanks) and possessed a very limited air force with approximately 160 planes. What the Greeks did possess was not only the capability of defending from the high ground but also, based on their excellent knowledge of the terrain, they had pre-registered their artillery guns to the point that all major roads, valley floors and mountain passes along the Albanian-Greek front were under their watchful eye.

    The Italian plan was handicapped from the beginning because it presumed that the campaign would be quick and that the Greeks would not sternly oppose the Italian offensive. It also did not envision that the fighting would last more than a few weeks and therefore did not initially foresee the consequent need to reinforce and reequip the troops at the front. The possibility of bad weather slowing down the operation was partly neglected also because the Italians after the initial stalemate lacked adequate transport. If the operation bogged down fresh forces were needed but the low handling capacity of the ports of Durazzo and Valona would further hamper operations. From a tactical perspective, according to military historian Mario Montanari, the plan did not consider the rather limited pre-war training administered to both armoured and infantry units aimed at achieving some degree of cooperation. He writes: "A close collaboration between tanks and infantry was not part of the tactical doctrine of the army in 1940. Not only had the units not trained to fight in such a fashion but also their cooperation would have been difficult to achieve since both lacked radios."[21]

    The fighting against Greece began on 28 October 1940 with *Centauro* representing with the two infantry divisions of the *Corpo d'Armata Ciamuria* the spearhead of the Italian offensive. Their initial goal was to advance toward Kalpaki, then Ioannina and finally Arta. On the first day of operations the armoured units moved slowly since the Greeks had earlier sabotaged bridges on the main road along the Drino River valley. "Unsurprisingly, the infantry columns

---

21 Mario Montanari, *L'esercito italiano nella campagna di Grecia* (Rome: Ufficio Storico, 1999), p. 112.

moved faster than the motorized ones."²² On 1 November, the infantry forces of the *Ferrara* attacked against the Greek positions but the accurate artillery fire, mainly from well concealed dug in guns in mountain caverns, blocked much of their progress. The infantry took heavy shelling which procured losses. On 2 November tanks and *Bersaglieri* of *Centauro* spearheaded the attack near the Kalamas River to establish a bridgehead but its advance on three main columns was blocked by enemy fire, deep anti-tank ditches, barbed wire defenses and muddy roads. The infantry put forth a frontal attack but it also lost several casualties to the blistering fire of the enemy artillery that given its well sited positions could not be neutralized. Having failed to cross the river, the next day *Centauro* was split into two battlegroups. The main group was to attempt again to cross the Kalamas River while I *Battaglione* was sent to attack the Kalpaki crossroads. The only success of the day was achieved by this latter group with the seizure of the Kalpaki crossroads by two tank companies equipped with twenty-six L.3 tanks which overcame stiff Greek opposition. This success came at the cost of eight tanks which could not be recovered. The attacks were made without bridging equipment, which had been furnished instead to the *Raggruppamento del Litoriale,* a major tactical error that prevented the bulk of the armour and of the *Siena* and *Ferrara* divisions to advance and achieve a potentially strategic breakthrough.²³ The Italian official history states that "despite the admirable effort put forth by all units, the progress of the advance was extremely slow. The attackers were persistently bogged down by the difficulty in moving through muddy roads and by the accurate enemy fire."²⁴ By the evening of 2 November the situation was unchanged and the Italians had not been able to advance past the Kalamas River and against the enemy's main resistance line. On the 3rd *Centauro* attacked again in the direction of Kalpaki but the lack of artillery support stifled this advance as well.

The operation was resumed at 1000 on 5 November when columns of *Centauro* supported again by the infantry of the *Ferrara* attacked in the direction of Kalpaki Palioka-Ioannina. The operation entailed a pincer movement with *Centauro* coming from the south and *Ferrara* infantrymen from the north. The XXV Army Corps had ordered *Centauro* to break through the enemy defenses by advancing on the main road on two main battle groups. The left column led by *Colonnello* Costa and comprised by two battalions of light tanks, XXII *Battaglione Bersaglieri*, a company of 47mm guns and a platoon from the *genio* had to conquer Hill 620, a fortified Greek position overlooking the main road. Meanwhile, the right wing column led by *Colonnello* Anzini was comprised of one tank battalion, XXIV *Battaglione Bersaglieri*, one platoon of 47mm guns, and a platoon of the *genio* had as ultimate objective the capture of the town of Negrasez. The attack was to begin promptly after an artillery barrage pounded the enemy positions which was to be followed by aerial bombings by the air force. The operation did begin in time but things began to go wrong from the inception because the *Regia Aereonautica* due to the severe weather had to cancel most of its aerial bombing operations. Thus, from the onset, the advance by the tanks was bogged down by the Greek artillery that had not been neutralized and that with pinpoint accuracy harassed the troops throughout their maneuver. The Greek 105mm guns, concealed in the mountains, and with longer ranges than many Italian artillery batteries, tore through entire units of infantry causing large losses. The left flank column of the *Centauro* slammed against three rounds of barbed

---

22 Pier Paolo Battistelli, *The Balkans 1940-41* (Oxford: Osprey, 2021), p. 32.
23 Ibid., p. 38.
24 Mario Montanari, *L'esercito italiano nella campagna di Grecia*, p. 161.

wire in an area that was water logged and had deep anti-tank ditches, while the right-wing column lost its way and wound up on the banks of the Kalamas River. *Centauro*'s war diary states that: "The combat action began at 1000. As soon as the tanks reached the crossroad to Kalpaki, the enemy reaction became very intense with strong machine gun and artillery fire. The L.3 tanks, protected only against light machine gun fire, could not advance any further. The movements to reach the ultimate destination carried out by both tanks and Bersaglieri were not effective. Along the main road several water canals made it very difficult for the tanks to advance and forced them to stay on the main road without the possibility of making flanking attacks."[25] The major success was made by elements of the *Siena* Division which were able to gain a bridgehead on the other side of the Kalamas River into the enemy's resistance line. While the Greeks launched limited counters in the area of Western Macedonia, the Italian attack on the Epirus sputtered due again to a lack of bridge casting equipment to allow the bulk of the troops to bypass the river and put further pressure on the Greek forces. This is where a closer collaboration between armour and infantry forces was required but was clearly lacking and especially keenly felt was the lack of adequate numbers of *genio* and combat engineer troops and their specialized equipment that could have put the armour in a position to continue the advance more expeditiously. Thus, in these early stages, the penetration into Greek territory along the Kalamas river could not be fully exploited by the armour in particular: "In Epirus the Italians succeeded in driving in the Greek covering forces and secured a bridgehead across the Kalamas river; had this success been exploited there might have been a chance for the Centauro (armoured) Division to make its weight felt."[26] During this early stage the main merit of the armoured unit was that despite the broken terrain of Western Greece which did not allow the tanks to fully maneuver, the Italian armour forced the Greek infantry to take a defensive position and prevented it from organizing strong counterattacks because of the risk of facing the tanks in the more open terrain. Meanwhile the *Julia Alpini* Division had also made progress and had reached an area situated twelve miles of the strategically relevant Metsovo Pass. But ultimately, it too had been held before its final objective by strong enemy fire.

Thus, despite the forces thrown at it the Greek army during the first week of operations had fought very hard and with considerable determination to contain the Italian advance. Their courageous stance had harried the advance of the armour and of the infantry. Accurate enemy fire, for example, caused losses during the five days of fighting as one armoured battalion lost to a combination of wear and tear and enemy artillery sixty percent of its tanks while a second lost thirty percent. At the time, the Italian armoured units still did not have dedicated mobile tank recovery teams and the few damaged tanks that were brought back to the rear had to be towed by other tanks. Thus, many units that could have been salvaged were abandoned on the battlefield. Thus, the losses were made worse by this inability to recover damaged tanks.

---

25   Ufficio Storico: Diario storico della Divisione Centauro, 'Relazione dei fatti d'armi dell'offensiva dell'Epiro', 20 Novembre 1940.
26   I.S.O. Playfair, *The Mediterranean and Middle East, Volume I: The Early Successes against Italy to May 1941*, p. 233.

Greek Counteroffensive

Having halted the Italian advance, on 14/15 November, the Greeks went on the counter-offensive with a three-pronged move that was supported by preliminary bombings by the RAF. The Greek I Corps acted on the coastal sector, the II Corps in the Pindus sector and the III Corps in western Macedonia. The main thrust was to be made by the latter with twenty infantry battalions and thirty-seven artillery batteries. Given the fact that the Greeks lacked tanks or mobile anti-tank weapons to face *Centauro*, the commander of the Greek Army decided to advance along the mountain ranges and not in the open on the valley floors in the advance toward Korçë. This slowed down the Greek advance considerably by forcing the infantry to advance on the icy and/or muddy terrain, but it avoided potential confrontations between infantry and armour. During the Greek counter *Centauro* entered a very difficult phase where the unit was deployed in a piecemeal fashion mainly for defensive tasks. By 21 November the Greek operation had achieved some measure of success pushing back the Italian troops in the Epirus considerably and *Centauro* was committed at first to cover the retreating *Ferrara* and *Modena* divisions. Then it was deployed piecemeal in support of other units. The bulk of its artillery group, for example, was dispatched to support *Bari* Division in the Desnizza valley, two of its armoured battalions supported the *Ferrara* Division as it slowly withdrew, while the *bersaglieri* were deployed with the *Modena* Division where one its officers Aldo Fiorini/5° *Reggimento Bersaglieri* would be awarded the gold medal of military valor for stubbornly defending some infantry positions against the Greek counter and allowing the bulk of his comrades to retreat in an orderly fashion. Those days saw some very sharp fighting that allowed the Greeks to capture Konitsa and Leskovik and retake the area near the Kalamas river. *Centauro* suffered huge casualties and lost several tanks and artillery pieces.

The attack against the Italian left flank had been the one that had progressed the furthest with the Greeks advancing to Korçë in Albania on 2 December. It was at this point that given the slow flow of supplies and reinforcements from Italy, the Greek command held several options after the eviction of the Italian forces from Greek territory. In fact, the Greek High Command faced two options: continue the offensive in the Korçë sector or shift focus on their left flank and drive towards the vital Albanian port of Valona in the south. Ultimately, the choice would fall on the latter option although initially the Greek High Command took some time to allow the troops to regroup.

On 4 December Badoglio was sacked. He had been preceded by the dismissal of Visconti Prasca. Badoglio's substitute was *Generale* Ugo Cavallero, who had been designated *Capo di Stato Maggiore generale* and later would also be responsible for taking over the Greek campaign after Visconti Prasca's (*Generale* Ubaldo Soddu) replacement resigned in January. Cavallero would confide to his son that: "We are at Caporetto once again. Just like then I am now called to fix Badoglio's mistakes."[27] Cavallero, who had very good organizational skills, would ultimately shore up the Italian defenses, stabilize the situation and adequately reinforce the troops. His most immediate problem, however, was to bring much needed supplies and weapons to the frontline troops. The supply situation for the troops at the front was poor because expecting a lightning campaign the Italian command had secured supplies for only a few weeks of fighting

---

27 Ugo Cavallero, *Diario 1940-1943* (Rome: Ciarrapico Editore, 1984), p. 51.

so that when the offensive stalemated the troops were left with ammunition, food and medical equipment shortages. The capacity to bring supplies from Albanian ports to the troops was also initially very poor. Albania's two main ports, Valona and Durazzo, created bottlenecks for supplies and reinforcements given their inability to handle large shipments. Airlifts initiated between Italy and Tirana could only transport troops and limited supplies but not heavy equipment. Lastly the support units on the ground in Albania lacking adequate number of trucks, horses, and mules experienced several difficulties in handling the volumes required by the troops.

Meanwhile at the front the situation slowly stabilized when the Greek 3rd Division advanced against the Italian XXV Corps at Tepelene and was pushed back by a combination of fire from both *Centauro* and *Modena* divisions.

Until the end of December, the *Centauro* division continued to fight a piecemeal fashion until it was withdrawn in early January and concentrated in Dukasi, where it began to reorganize. *Generale* Carlo Geloso of the XI Army Corps at the time stated that: " I do not have a tactical reserve because both Bari and Centauro divisions have been tested tremendously and are in need of a period of rest and reorganization. Meanwhile the Ferrara Division is now comprised of only a few infantry companies."[28] Thanks to Cavallero's efforts the ports of Valona and Durazzo were slowly but incrementally expanded so that some of the first reinforcements to pass through them were the new M.13/40 medium tanks of the IV *Battaglione Carri Medi* which although originally earmarked for North Africa was dispatched to Albania to reinforce the *Centauro* Division. In addition to the M.13 tanks fifteen light tanks also arrived by late January 1940.

The officers and soldiers of this medium tank battalion had expressed their surprise when they were communicated the news that they would be deployed in Greece: "When we heard the news our eyes darkened. If the Epirus is comprised by mountains and valleys what are we going to do there? The M13 tanks were designed and built to operate on the terrain were we can maneuver. To this end the North African desert was highly suited for the medium tanks. But there are no answers from the top brass to our objections."[29]

Klisura Pass

The medium tanks were first deployed during the counteroffensive in the battle of the Klisura Pass on 27 January 1941. The pass located near Këlcyrë Gorge and the Vjosë river was the gateway to the recapture of the town of Këlcyrë. By then the Greek command because of the bad weather and the stiffening enemy opposition had decided to bring to a halt its major counteroffensive. Its aim in early January had been to conduct a limited operation to improve its positions with the capture of the Klisura Pass, a position of strategic importance in the middle of the Italo-Greek frontline and barring the passage toward Valona, by II Corps. The latter attacked on 8 January, with two main columns and with the main thrust by the 15th Division, followed by the 11th Division which faced the *Julia* Division in defense of the pass. After heavy fighting the Greeks occupied the pass on 9/10 January forcing the Italians back in the Desnizes valley.

28　Mario Cervi, *La guerra di Grecia* (Milano: Mondadori, 2005)..
29　Rinaldo Panetta, *Il Ponte di Klisura*, p. 7.

This not only opened a dangerous gap but gave the Greeks a platform from which to launch future attacks.

Given the delicate situation, on 26/27 January the Italians counter-attacked, after two failed attempts in the middle of January, to recover it from the defenders of the II Corps reinforced with elements of the 5th Division. The main thrust was to be made by the *Legnano* Division north of Këlcyrë while the tanks of I and II Battalion/*Centauro* and the medium tanks of IV Battalion where to swing around from the south and travel on the main road to force the Klisura bridge on the Desnizes river (which streams into the Vojussa) behind which were stationed the Greek infantry troops. The infantry forces were to act on each mountainous flank of the main road. *Alpini* troops of *Monte Cervino*, 67º *Reggimento/Legnano* and the blackshirts of *Raggruppamento Galbiati* were to advance toward Mount Groppa while *alpini* of the *Val Natisone* together with the 68º *Reggimento Legnano* were to attack the Brezhanit. According to the plan the operation was to be conducted in two steps: "Capture of the advanced positions of Mount Groppa and Mount Brezhanit supported by a massive intervention by the artillery in support of the assault troops. This first phase of the plan was to be followed by a powerful assault by the medium tanks against Klisura conducted from the Vojussa valley floor."[30] The armour was only going to be deployed after the two flanks had been occupied by the infantry. If the former failed in the endeavor the tanks would have been easy prey from flanking artillery fire.

The two mountain positions were stormed between 26/27 January by the infantry. Mount Groppa fell after heavy fighting while the Brezhanit was taken by the Italians only temporarily after heavy fighting. On the morning of the 27 January the tank units were ordered to move forward. As the medium tanks began to advance on the valley floor they were targeted from the onset by enemy artillery fire which implied that the infantry had failed to secure all flank positions. "We can't hear the explosions because of the noise of the tank engine. But the valley floor is littered by huge flames from the explosions of the enemy shells. We are met by grenades, by mortar rounds, and by the 20mm machine gun rounds. Then I realize we are being targeted also from behind and from the castle. Damn it. The Greeks are still there, while the soldiers of the Legnano have failed to neutralize the enemy guns."[31] As most of the tanks attempted to reach the Greek lines, their path was obstructed by barbed wire, by boulders placed by the enemy on the main road and by an anti-tank ditch. Also they could not advance off the main road because the river was impassable with very swollen waters.

Two tanks managed to reach the bridge but observed that the middle section of the bridge had been destroyed by the Greeks. Based on their observation and due to the ongoing blistering enemy fire that was taking its toll on the tanks it was decided to retire and regroup the armoured units.

At 1200 Italian artillery batteries near Dragoti bridge began to bombard the Greek positions surrounding Klisura in preparation of a renewed attempt by the armour. But despite the preparatory fire the armour was unable once again to bypass the bridge or silence the enemy guns. This second attack by a reduced force could not overcome the determined enemy resistance. At the pass they were subjected to murderous fire which caused heavy casualties.

The following is a reminiscence of the battle of Klisura by one of the *carristi* officers:

---

30 Mario Montanari, *L'esercito italiano nella campagna di Grecia*, p. 485.
31 Rinaldo Panetta, *Il ponte di Klisura*, p. 85.

> The tank is moving along a very bumpy road because of a multitude of small craters caused by the enemy shells. As we approach the bridge a hailstorm of fire greets our arrival as the Greek medium gun units follow our every move. We respond by firing all our weapons while I try to follow with the periscope the movement of the tanks that preceded us. Shells are exploding all around us as we try to negotiate our way through the narrow path. We respond to the enemy fire by targeting the mountain area from where the shells are coming from but it's to no avail since it's impossible to locate exactly their positions. Then suddenly, the tank is hit by a medium size shell and we come to a dead stop. The inside of the tank quickly fills up with steam and I'm forced to open the turret to get some fresh air in.[32]

For the next hour, the tank continued to attract enemy fire but mysteriously its engine would start up again and the crew would return to safety.

Finally, on the third attempt the medium tanks managed to overcome enemy defenses comprised of an anti-tank ditch and several barbed wire defended machine gun and anti-tank gun positions and penetrate into Klisura. Has the Italian official history of the campaign states: "The medium tanks were able to breakthrough while the light tanks were not able to overcome the obstacles."[33] But the success was only temporary has the Italians were unable to ultimately occupy the position leaving a few tanks behind.

The following is the post battle report of the *Centauro* Division:

> On the night of 26 January 1941, the commander of the Legnano Division ordered the II Battalion of the 31st Carristi, equipped with L and M tanks, to press home an attack against Klisura. This thrust was to be launched in conjunction with other infantry attacks against Mount Groppa and Bregianit. After having agreed on a plan of attack on the morning of 27 January a platoon of M tanks began its approach march toward Klisura. From the beginning the operation was opposed by the enemy guns which located on hilltops near Klisura mercifully targeted the tanks. By 1000 the first tank had been immobilized by the enemy artillery but the commander of the Legnano insisted that Klisura must be captured at all costs. On the main road toward Klisura shells were raining in one after the other at a very quick pace and anyone exposed to such fire was almost guaranteed a quick death. A second platoon was then called into action and began to aggressively charge against the outskirts of Klisura. The enemy fire continued unabated forcing a second tank to desist and return to our line. But another three tanks continued to advance to bypass the Desnizes river to arrive at the enemy antitank screen. The commander of the company Tenente Ugo Passalacqua arrived on the field of battle just as another tank was being blown to bits. The burned out remains of several tanks signaled that it was impossible to proceed any further. Another tank was then targeted and its right flank was blown open. Two crew members were pulled from the vehicle but both are dead. The driver was heavily injured while the officer was also saved but with terrible injuries to his leg and arm.[34]

---

32 Ibid, pp. 102-03.
33 Ibid.
34 Ufficio Storico: Diario storico della Divisione Centauro, 'Relazione dei fatti d'armi di Klisura', 27 January 1941.

The Greek Army official history of the campaign reported the following: "On the morning of 27 January a unit of Italian tanks, this time involving larger medium tanks came forward toward Klisura but were targeted by our antitank guns. The tanks were forced to retreat while three were immobilized on the field of battle." [35]

It appears from both Greek and Italian documents that six tanks were damaged during the Italian counter, of which three were lost because they were immobilized near enemy lines and could not be recovered, while the remaining three were damaged but were towed back to the Italian rear. *Tenente* Ugo Passalacqua of the *Centauro* Division would later be awarded of the gold medal of military valor for leading the medium tanks into the attack and later bringing the remaining crews to safety despite having suffered grave injuries from enemy fire.

Throughout the last week of January *Centauro's* light and medium tanks were committed to a series of rapid raids and offensive thrusts against enemy frontline positions in the Vjosë River sector. The continuous shelling and machine gunning of the Greek frontline positions by the tanks deployed in multiple raids yielded numerous casualties amongst the enemy ranks. No tank losses were sustained.

At the beginning of February *Centauro* was brought again to the rear for a complete reorganization. Now, it received an additional batch of M.13/40 tanks from Italy. On 15 February a number of *Centauro's* light and medium tanks supported *alpini* troops from 7º *Reggimento* in an assault in Zagorais valley against a fortified enemy position. The Greeks suffered heavy losses but two tanks were damaged and several *alpini* lost their lives. On 17 February, its 2a *Compagnia/II Battaglione* was involved in a defensive action against a Greek attack on Mount Golico. The unit acquitted itself well in helping the infantry repulse the enemy attacks. However, two days later one tank was blown apart by a large enemy artillery shell and another tank, while attempting to bypass a damaged tank, ran off the road and plunged near a river. In late February the Greek army focused yet again its attention primarily on the southern sector of the front by attempting for several days to penetrate the Tepeleni basin and reach Valona. Here the positions were mainly defended by the *Divisioni Legnano, Ferrara* and *Sforzesca* and backed up by *Centauro's* artillery regiment and its tank units.

To the great disappointment of the Greeks their main offensive that had begun on 13 February with the aim of arriving to Valona was ultimately halted with severe losses by a combination of the weather, which became very bad after the attack was launched, and by the Italian defensive wall. It is estimated that the Greeks lost over 6,000 casualties and were the forced to suspend their operation.

On 18 February the 2a *Compagnia/*31º *Reggimento* was stationed in the Zagorias valley were it held up a large enemy force that was bent on taking from the Italian infantry the top of Mount Goliko. The next day an M tank was damaged beyond repair by an anti-tank Greek unit. For several days and until the end of the month *Centauro's* tank units supported the infantry in repelling several enemy attacks. Two L tanks were destroyed and one medium tanks was also heavily damaged during this phase.

After having repulsed several heavy Greek attacks (in which the latter bled profusely) aimed at advancing toward Valona, on 9 March the Italians of the VIII *Corpo d'armata* launched their 'Spring Offensive' in the area of Klisura, in the central sector of the front. Cavallero prepared

35 Ibid.

the major offensive after a buildup of forces had been achieved during a month-long operation where the Italian Navy had brought record number of supplies and men to Albania. 3,000 tons of supplies were brought in on a daily basis for a period of three weeks and the Army was reinforced reaching a total of 400,000 men. At 0700 on 9 March 1941 over 300 field guns, followed by the air force that dropped bombs on the Greek positions, opened the hostilities. VIII *Corpo d'armata* of *Generale* Gastone Gambara supported by XXV *Corpo d'armata* in the south and IV *Corpo d'armata* to the north-east then assaulted the enemy positions. In total the Italians deployed 50,000 soldiers from twelve divisions. The initial stages of the operation were quite promising as several Greek positions were overrun and on the 11th the vital hills 717 and 731 were captured, but soon the attack bogged down after a number of close quarters engagements were sustained that produced heavy casualties on both sides. Ultimately, Gambara's men were able to occupy several advanced positions but could not make a major breakthrough. Heavy casualties were sustained and at the front there was an impasse again. During this operation, *Centauro* was held back as a strategic reserve given that a breakthrough had not been achieved. By the 15th, the offensive ground to a halt and the armoured units did not see any action.

Monastir/Hill 731

On 19 March, *Centauro* and the IV *Battaglione Carri Medi* participated to another Italian attack around Monastir and hill 731 (near the central sector of the Albanian / Greek border), but once again it suffered losses when it lost two tanks. The plan was to advance to clear the Desnizza valley and thus thrust though the Greek lines. To accomplish this breakthrough the peaks on both sides of the valley had to be dealt with first. These were Hills 717 and 731, the latter called Monastir by the Italians because it was the site of an ancient monastery, these were the same two positions that had been occupied temporarily during the Spring Offensive. The attack took place after an intensive bombardment of the Greek positions by the Italian artillery. After the preparatory fire, *arditi* of the *Siena* Division supported by *Centauro's* light tanks attacked the highly-contested Hill 731, while other elements of the division attacked the other hill. By 0620 Hill 731 had been captured with a combination of artillery fire from the armour and an infantry assault involving hand grenades and bayonets: "The hilltop was seized by a frontal assault by Capitano Borbone-Parma and his men that launching countless hand grenades at the Greek positions while shouting the battle cry Savoia. Galli and Riccardi opened up a tremendous fire from the Breda machine guns and the 47mm tank guns on board their tanks. Meanwhile, *arditi* and trench busters inch closer toward the enemy positions and in a few minutes the position is seized. The machine guns begin to scan the trenches while the Greeks, after having attempted to resist the charge, are now throwing themselves downhill to avoid capture. Carrera is firing from his tank against the remaining enemy machine gun strongpoints. On the top he is by himself because the tank of sottotenente Campus experienced engine trouble and turned back, while Fettini's tank has partly overturned given the soft and wet terrain."[36]

While the Italians captured Hill 731, they suffered tremendous losses from Greek counterattacks and artillery shelling. The tanks and the *arditi* remained on Hill 731 for most of the day

---

36 Rinaldo Panetta, *Il ponte di Klisura*, pp. 180-181.

separated from the bulk of the infantry battalion of the *Divisione Bari* which were supposed to come to their aid and occupy the pinnacle of the mountain but were barred from advancing by the Greek blocking fire. Despite remaining isolated, the tanks continued to pour fire against the approaching Greek infantry, while the *arditi* company had already lost over seventy percent of its force but managed to hold the pinnacle. Ultimately, the attack stalled as the *Bari* Division troops were caught in no man's land and prevented from coming to the aid of the attackers due to heavy fire and the Italian troops on the pinnacle were forced to retreat. During the latter stages of the operation only two of the five remaining tanks were still in working conditions. As they retreated one hit a mine and two members of the crew died instantly while one tank was destroyed, while another was the only one able to make it back. One more tank had been lost during the first attack, while two other tanks, although damaged, were later recovered. If properly supported the operation could have allowed the troops to advance much further and capture Klisura. But the failure to consolidate the position forced the assaulting troops to ultimately retreat. As Sadkovich asserts the overstretched Italians did not have enough troops or equipment to achieve a breakthrough. "Consequently all the Italians could achieve was parity; by March 1941 there were 72 Italian battalions in twelve divisions facing sixty three Greek battalions in seven divisions. Given the nature of the terrain, this was simply not enough to assure an Italian victory."[37] A long war of attrition awaited both sides without the intervention of a mightier power. Total Italian losses during the campaign were: 13,755 killed, 115,000 wounded, and 25,067 missing in action. Greek losses were: 13,325 killed, 62,663 wounded, and 3,755 missing.[38]

At the end of March the situation in the Balkans precipitated as a result of German involvement in the region. While the Germans were planning for Operation Barbarossa they came to the conclusion that they should secure their position in the Balkans first by defeating the British forces in Greece deployed at the northern border, and force Yugoslavia into a forced alliance or a German takeover. This was all intended to prevent Britain from bombing the Romanian Ploiești oilfields, that Germany used as one of its main energy supplies. Yugoslavia's Prince Paul agreed to an alliance with Germany on 25 March 1941. This decision, however, was not very popular with the military that executed a coup d'état on 27 March and forced Prince Paul to abdicate prompting a German intervention.

Yugoslavia

The next objective of *Centauro* Division was to take part in the invasion of Yugoslavia together with *Littorio* armoured Division and two army corps. *Littorio* was equipped with ninety-three L tanks, twenty-four flamethrower L tanks, and fifteen M.13/40s. Meanwhile *Centauro* had eighty-nine light tanks and twenty-five M.13/40 tanks.

The former was to attack from bases in Italian occupied Albania, while *Littorio* was to attack from the northern frontier of Istria. On 6 April 1941 the German air force executed a devastating carpet bombing operation against Belgrade. This was followed by the invasion of Yugoslavia

---

37   James J. Sadkovich, 'Military Incompetence through Italian Eyes', *War in History*, vol. 1 no. 1, 1994, p. 41.
38   Mario Montanari, *L'esercito italiano nella campagna di Grecia*, p. 241.

from its northern borders by two German mechanized and motorized army corps. The Italian operation was coordinated with the German intervention. As a result, the II Army with nine infantry divisions, four motorized and one armoured (*Littorio*) division began its advance from its bases in Venezia Giulia, Istria, and Zara, while the IX Army first fought off enemy incursions into Albania and then proceeded to attack from bases in Albania with three infantry divisions and one armoured (*Centauro*). The plan envisaged that the two armoured units would meet somewhere in the middle in the pincer movement of western Yugoslavia.

Southern Front

The forces from the south confronted fierce enemy resistance which initially took the form of a counterattack. German intelligence had informed the Italian High Command that the Yugoslavian Army, even before the German advance, was gearing up for a preventive strike against the Italian units deployed in the Drin River area. To parry the blow General Cavallero ordered the *Centauro* Division to bring most of its armour near the banks of the river. In fact, *Centauro* was transferred to Scutari on 4 April with the I, II, and *IV Battaglioni Carri Leggeri* and the IV *Battaglione Carri Medi*, while the III *Battaglione Carri Leggeri* was held at the front with the Greeks. In addition at Scutari the armoured component was also supported by 1° *Reggimento Bersaglieri* (that took temporarily the place of the bulk of the 5° *Reggimento* that was held at the front with the Greeks), the XXII *Battaglione Bersaglieri Motociclisti*, 131° *Compagnia Genio*, and 131° *Reggimento Artiglieria Corazzata*. The troops were deployed on a defensive line spanning from Scutari to the mountain ranges near Kossovo to halt any potential threat posed by the Yugoslav army, while the artillery regiment was positioned further back. The terrain was very favorable for the armoured units because even though it was surrounded by hills the valley floor was wide with an ample road network and the rivers were wadable with their very shallow waters. On the night of 7/8 April the Yugoslav army made a frontal and a flanking attack against the Italian troops on Scutari. The attack was made by Yugoslav troops that had crossed the lake and emerged from a number of boats to suddenly assault their enemies. The latter were initially caught off guard but then after a time they reorganized and repelled the Yugoslavians with heavy losses. *Bersaglieri* and the tank units contributed to push back the enemy infiltrations. On 10 April both light and medium tanks conducted a number of reconnaissance patrols and several enemy platoons were captured. One of the officers taken prisoner was found with the imminent plan of attack by infantry supported by aircrafts against Scutari. The next day the armoured battalions were dispatched on the main defensive line to support the infantry units in preparation of the attack. "Very heavy fighting. Tanks are vulnerable to antitank guns but they are deadly against infantry and our Breda 38 and Fiat 14/35 of the L tanks have inflicted heavy casualties against the enemy troops concealed in the forested areas nearby."[39] For several hours the Yugoslav troops continued to launch attacks in this fashion against the Italians which heavily engaged both the light and medium tanks in multiple counter-attacks. *Carrista* officer Rinaldo Panetta reports one of these typical clashes with the enemy infantry on 11 April near Scutari: "A platoon of M tanks led by Camera together with a number of L tanks from I Battaglione

---

39 Rinaldo Panetta, *Il ponte di Klisura*, p. 212.

surprised a number of enemy infantrymen north-east of Kopliku and attacked them decisively. Ten men were killed and twenty were made prisoner. The latter, mostly Bosnians, had given up because they were terrorized by Breda 38 guns and declared that they have lost the commander, the vice commander and several of their comrades in the last few days."[40]

On 12 April three tanks were disabled by the Yugoslav infantry near Ura Zaies. Boulders had been placed on the road so that the tanks could not get by and when the crews exited the tanks to remove the boulders they were gunned down by the enemy. At 1200 reinforcements were dispatched, including one medium tank unit, which were able to salvage some equipment and rescue two *carristi*. The next day the Yugoslavian infantry with one of its main elite units in the forefront, *Zetska* Division, attacked all sectors of the Italian defensive line severely testing the artillery and infantry units. Attacks were made on Mount Khrriles, in the Prrhoni That and on Phrrhoni Banush. Centauro's artillery units were active all day in bombarding the enemy attack waves, while *Bersaglieri* units manned the forward positions. Meanwhile, the armoured units were tasked with committing several counterattacks throughout the day to push the enemy back. In one incident, several medium and light tanks ambushed from concealed positions behind bushes the enemy infantry that was coming forward in large numbers. In a separate operation a L flamethrower tank unit (1 *Compagnia*/3° *Reggimento*) penetrated into the enemy lines by targeting an hanger where the troops were stationed. The hanger was torched and some of the enemy troops captured. On 14 April, the *Zetska* Division repeatedly attacked in waves but was thrown back without achieving any relevant result in large part due to the fact that it did not have armoured support. During this defensive action, the medium tanks, backed by the divisional artillery, completed several sorties against the enemy infantry forcing them to scatter and retreat.

> Tonight the divisional artillery hammered the enemy positions on Mount Khurriles, Kondra Luges and Jvanai. We never stopped. In our numerous attacks where we were moving forward 200 meters at the time we just kept going. The enemy must truly hate us carristi since the Scutari plain is full of enemy soldiers that want to target our tanks. They come at us launching hand grenades hoping to disable the tanks. Chiamenti was lucky to have dodged one by going inside his tank in the nick of time. The enemy threat that poses the most dangerous to us, however, is from the anti-tank units. It's a cat against mouse game. The anti-tank units do not want to reveal their position but when they can they shoot armoured piercing shells that if well aimed can debilitate our tanks. But the blistering fire of our Breda 38 machine guns really terrorizes the enemy to the point that the gunners typically are not very accurate. As of today, they have only inflicted slight damages to our medium tanks, while a few light ones have been blown up. They are a continuous and present danger.[41]

The Italian official history states that: "The Centauro's strong reaction, especially by its armoured battalions, inflicted large casualties and forced the enemy to retreat."[42]

---

40   Ibid., p. 213.
41   Ibid, p. 241.
42   Ufficio Storico, Diario Storico Divisione corazzata Centauro, Aprile 1941.

On 15 April, Yugoslav parliamentarians reached the Italian lines in an apparent attempt to come to terms for the surrender. At the same time the Yugoslav army moved anti-tank artillery units forward on the Prrhoni Phat. In a bid to dispatch troops into Yugoslavian territory, *Centauro*'s general Gavino Pizzolato, convinced that the Yugoslavs were on the verge of surrendering, mobilized his units (three tank battalions) to cross the border and penetrate deeply into enemy territory but without artillery support or without the *Bersaglieri* supporting the armour. Once the armour advanced it soon became apparent that the Yugoslav army had laid a trap and the calls for a Yugoslav surrender were a pretext since their artillery continued to fire artillery shells into the Italian ranks causing losses to the tank battalions. Despite the blistering enemy fire, the Italian forces, mainly the *Centauro* supported by the *Marche* infantry Division, continued to advance expeditiously against the enemy defenses in a two pronged assault. The IV on the right, the I on the left and the II *Battaglione Carri* on reserve. "While advancing at dawn under a heavy artillery barrage the second wave equipped with L tanks bypassed a main bridge and then overcame the Yugoslav defenses from behind which were obliterated."[43] The *Zetska* Division was thus overcome from the two pronged assault. The armoured units then continued to advance against the Yugoslavian anti-tank screen and on the 16th they reached Jvanai. The two pronged armoured operation succeeded, but the gamble of dispatching the tanks without artillery support was paid dearly. Because of accurate enemy fire eleven L.3 and three medium tanks were knocked out of action, while five were damaged. The losses were three officers dead and five wounded, seventeen carristi dead and seven wounded.[44]

On the 16th in the afternoon the advance continued although by this time *Centauro* was advancing at reduced ranks: three tank battalions with seventy percent of their initial strength. On the 20th this force arrived at Ragusa (Dubronick) where the remains of the *Zetska* Division had retreated to. Its soldiers here surrendered.

Northern Front

Meanwhile in the north the advance had been more decisive given the scant opposition encountered. "On 11 April, the Italian II Army attacked from the vicinity of Trieste down the coast of Yugoslavia. It had become clear that no enemy resistance worth mentioning was to be expected and that the Italian High Command's estimate of thirteen Yugoslav divisions opposing their II Army was incorrect. Their attack encountered almost no resistance and found 30,000 Yugoslav soldiers concentrated near Delnice waiting to surrender."[45] It then continued its deep maneuver into the heartland of Yugoslavia by advancing a further 1,000 kilometers. On the 20th this force linked up with *Centauro*. By then Yugoslavia had sued for peace with the Axis. According to American historian John Sweet the Yugoslavian campaign was the type of operation that the Italian armoured units had trained for before the war. The troops had trained to deploy in armoured maneuvers in both hilly and flat terrain in the Apennines and the Po Valley and

---

43 Filippo Cappellano and Nicola Pignato, *Gli autoveicoli da combattimento*, p. 98.
44 Ibid.
45 Michael Barefield, 'Overwhelming Force, Indecisive Victory: The German Invasion of Yugoslavia, 1941', Fort Leavenworth, Kansas: School of Advanced Military Studies, United States Army Command and General Staff College, May 1993.

unlike the Greek campaign, they had conducted drills mainly on paved roads. Thus, unlike the French and Greek campaigns, the Yugoslavian campaign, although brief and characterized by the haphazard politically driven pincer movement, was conducted according to pre-war drills and hence the armoured units accounted themselves well. It is important to note how two factors distinguished this campaign from all the others such as the fighting that took place on favorable terrain and the armoured units fought mainly against enemy infantry defenses and not against tank units as the original tactical dispositions envisioned. The light Italian tanks could perform satisfactorily against infantry defenses and against troops that had no armoured support as the personal accounts tell the story of how the enemy infantry and artillerymen were vulnerable to the machine gun fire emanating from the tanks. After Yugoslavia was dealt with the focus was again on the Greeks. The latter continued to deploy the majority of their troops on the Albanian frontier even though the Germans were building out their forces on the opposite frontier. By tying down a large number of Greek troops the Italians facilitated a German victory when its armoured units barreled through the three weak Greek divisions deployed on the Metaxas line and then dealt with the Commonwealth forces. When the Germans broke through the Italians began to drive toward Athens and Greece sued for peace.

Conclusion

Once again, as in other theaters of operation, the Greek campaign witnessed a limited participation of the armoured units which were deployed sporadically in battle and when they were deployed they suffered from mechanical problems and by their light constitution. Tank officer Rinaldo Panetta, for example, asserted that medium tanks broke down quite often in Greece and Albania because the treads could not negotiate the mountainous terrain and that armoured warfare and tactics were not suited for such a theater of operations. According to a British account of the campaign even the Commonwealth armour units experienced several technical difficulties and that the few tanks that were used by the British in Greece also frequently broke down.[46] The campaign revealed once again how difficult it was to operate the armoured units in a mountainous environment where the narrow and unpaved roads, highly visible to the enemy from mountaintops, slowed down the advance of the tanks and made them an easy target for the Greek artillery. The tanks had a terrible time in maneuvering in such a challenging environment made even worse by the timing of the campaign. Swollen rivers and muddy roads on mountainous terrain made it very hard for the tanks to advance while they also could not rely on the support of the air force since the planes were mostly kept in the hangars due to the bad weather. On the Battle of Klisura, for example, the *Centauro*'s official history states that the armoured action ordered by the head of *Divisione Legnano* was suicidal: "To proceed forward on the main road to enter the curtain of fire and iron that has become our path means to commit oneself to certain death."[47] The armoured units, in particular, but also the whole army could not adopt the lightning war tactics for which they had counted upon to force a quick conclusion to the campaign. Thus, high losses were incurred especially for the L.3 tanks and even the relatively

---

46   Robert Crisp, *The Gods Were Neutral* (London: Pelican, 1960), pp. 110-111.
47   Rinaldo Panetta, *Il ponte di Klisura*, p. 280.

sturdier M.13 tanks did not perform any better. Strategically the campaign was a huge drain on resources at the expense of the North African front which was Italy's main theater of operations and the effort against Britain and the Commonwealth. The IV *Battaglione Carri Medi*, which was originally earmarked for Graziani's army, was rerouted to Albania. Similarly, many trucks and artillery pieces were dispatched there as well. In the fall of 1940, for instance, 10,000 vehicles were dispatched to the Greek front while North Africa received only 2,500. An estimated 30 light tanks were lost during the campaign and up to 16 medium tanks were also left behind. In addition "two armoured divisions in the spring of 1941 remained in the Balkans, *Centauro* in Albania and *Littorio* in Dalmatia even though they were ill suited to operations there."[48] In contrast, initially only one Italian armoured division was dispatched to North Africa in early 1941 after the British offensive against the Sidi Barrani line had succeeded. For several months, Greece, not North Africa became Italy's core theater of operation and while it ultimately forced Britain to shift resources away from North Africa it starved the Italian Army in North Africa of useful mechanized and motorized resources at a critical juncture of the campaign. On 30 October 1940 *Generale* Roatta, who at the time was responsible within *Comando Supremo* to organize the deployment of forces in North Africa and Greece, had wrote that: "Yes we have suspended the shipment of a second medium tank battalion to North Africa as well as a vessel carrying several trucks that are both destined to Albania. The 5th Army Corps will have to be reorganized and reinforced and this will put a heavy strain on the resources available in Italy."[49]

As historian Alessandro Massignani has observed: "The campaign cost Italy reinforcements to North Africa, especially in equipment, which went instead to Greece. Thus, the British successes in North Africa in large part resulted from the Italian invasion of Greece."[50]

Similarly, Pier Paolo Battistelli has argued that at the time the Germans believed that "Italy lost a huge amount of prestige in the war against Greece....it was this fatal blunder that led to the British Operation Compass offensive in North Africa."[51]

Soviet Union

Although Italy made a major commitment by siding with the Germans during Operation Barbarossa in 1941 it failed to send to Russia a self-sustaining tank force. Initially, on the heels of the start of Operation Barbarossa, Mussolini dispatched the *Corpo di spedizione italiano Russia* to support the German army. This unit was comprised of 60,000 soldiers, several artillery batteries of different sizes and a fleet of bomber and fighter planes. In 1941, however, the only Italian unit dispatched to Russia equipped with tanks was the *3. Celere Divisione Principe Amedeo d'Aosta*. The division was a *celere* unit therefore it was not an armoured division per se but a mixed combat unit with some infantry regiments, some motorized elements and a light tank battalion. The unit's L.3 light tanks were totally inadequate for the Eastern Front and were

---

48   James J. Sadkovich, 'The Italo-Greek War in Context: Italian Priorities and Axis Diplomacy', *Journal of Contemporary History*, vol. 28, n.3, July 1993, p. 444.
49   Cited in: Lucio Ceva and Andrea Curami, *La meccanizzazione dell'esercito italiano*, p. 308.
50   Spencer C. Tucker, *World War II: The Definite Encyclopedia and Document* (New York: ABC CILO, 2016), p. 331.
51   Pier Paolo Battistelli, *The Balkans 1940-41*, p. 91.

no match for the much more powerful Russian T-34 tanks. The armour belonged to the III *Gruppo Corazzato San Giorgio*, which at the start of the campaign had sixty-one x L.3 tanks. The unit participated to the initial Axis advance in the southern sector of the Russian front (Ukraine) alongside German units during the summer and fall of 1941. Since the Axis advance was extremely rapid, several tanks were lost due to mechanical breakdowns. The machines that did survive the initial advance carried out several activities including reconnaissance of enemy positions, raids against enemy strong points and the mop up of scattered Russian soldiers. Most light tanks were idled during the winter due to lack of proper lubricants and fuel. In March 1942, it was decided that these tanks were obsolete and they were substituted with a battalion equipped with nineteen *semoventi da 47/32* called *XIII Gruppo Cavalleggeri di Alessandria* and by *LXVII Battaglione Bersaglieri Corazzato* equipped with sixty L. 6/40 tanks. The second unit was involved in its first combat action near Gorbatowo where a company of thirteen tanks was cut to pieces in less than a half an hour by Soviet anti-tank rifles. Both units would experience heavy fighting during Operation Little Saturn in December 1942 which aimed to overcome Italian defenses and penetrate deeply into the Axis rear. The aim of the Soviet army was to overtake the weaker Italian and satellite armies deployed on the Don River to surround the German Sixth Army deployed at Stalingrad. Several L.6 tanks were lost during the beginning of the offensive used in a dug in anti-tank role as they attempted to halt the Soviet advance. The tanks were mostly positioned on the frontline positions held by the *3. Celere* and the *Ravenna* Division and were knocked out of action by Soviet tanks. The *semoventi* suffered the same fate and were deployed during the Soviet attempts to breakthrough in the sector held by the *Ravenna* Division during 16 and 17 December. Their 42/32 gun was no match for the T-34 tanks and all units were lost during heavy fighting. In March 1943, the official war diary of the ARMIR stated that "after a month of heavy fighting, the Soviets finally broke through our lines in large part due to the deployment of heavy tanks."[52]

As Italian historian Lucio Ceva has pointed out, the decision to dispatch an Italian force in the Soviet Union in support of Operation Barbarossa had a detrimental effect upon Italy's main theatre of operation (North Africa), where it had concentrated most its infantry and armoured forces. The campaign against the Soviet Union represented a huge dispersal of forces especially with regard to the artillery arm. Italy's largest and newest field and anti-tank guns were dispatched to the Soviet Union at the expense of the North African campaign. In the Soviet Union, the Italian artillery units faced the powerful Russian T-34 tanks but such units would have been equally useful in North Africa both in an anti-tank and field artillery role.[53] The only benefit that arose from the campaign against the Soviet Union was that it forced Italian military planners to come up with more durable anti-tank weapons in orderly to properly confront the T-34 tanks which had caused several problems even to the better equipped German Army. The result of this campaign was that the Italian domestic industry hastened the production of the *semovente* da 75/18 (M 13/40) and the M 14/42 still with a 75/18 gun but built on the chassis of the M 14/41 tank. These two units were to replace obsolete *semoventi* with the 47mm gun. Then later the Italian industry also designed in late 1941, on the chassis of the M14/41 tank a self-propelled gun armed with a 90/53 anti-aircraft gun modeled on the German 88mm Flak

---

52 Filippo Cappellano and Nicola Pignato, *Gli autoveicoli italiani da combattimento*, p. 97.
53 Lucio Ceva, *La condotta Italiana della Guerra* (Milan: Feltrinelli, 1975).

36. Thirty of these units were produced in late 1941 and early 1942 and were intended to be deployed against the Soviet Union on the Eastern Front. Because of the defeat of the Italian forces in the winter of 1942-43 the heavy *semoventi* were transferred instead to Sicily to face the Allied invasion of the summer of 1943.

The campaign against the Soviet Union was not a successful campaign for the minuscule force of Italian armour. The equipment dispatched to Russia was totally inadequate since the tanks were few, they were light units and they had little firepower compared to the Russian armour and guns. In addition, they were not suited for the Russian winter and its deep-freezing temperatures and thus were idled for long periods of time.

Conclusion

With regard to armour in these campaigns there are two factors that must be considered. Although, these campaigns were very important for the Italian Army and the Italian position especially in the Balkans and southern Europe they did not involve large amounts of armoured units because either the terrain was unsuitable for tanks or because the campaign took place largely without tanks (Soviet Union) because the majority of them were concentrated in North Africa. Second, the Italian East African, to some extent, and Yugoslavia are the two exceptions. In both campaigns the Royal Army would have performed better if only its armoured and motorized units had been better prepared for the campaigns. In East Africa, for example, the few motorized and mechanized resources at its disposal could have performed more effectively if only the Army had concentrated vehicles, mobile artillery and tanks into an armoured brigade. Similarly, in Yugoslavia the armoured units could have fought more effectively if they had been deployed together with motorized artillery and special infantry units in true combined arms fashion.

3

North Africa

The North African campaign against the forces of the British Commonwealth represented Italy's biggest commitment during the war and where most its armoured units would be incrementally concentrated between 1940-1943. The Italian colony of Libya was surrounded by hostile forces since it bordered Algeria and Tunisia (French North Africa) to the west and British-controlled Egypt to the east. The North African colony was run by Italo Balbo, who in 1937 had developed the first set of offensive plans which envisioned dispatching motorized and mechanized columns along the coast to Alexandria and inland to the Nile. Initially, *Comando Supremo* did not back this plan nor began simulated attacks in support of it and limited the Army's overall preparations to building defensive fortifications in Tripoli, Tobruk and Bardia. In 1938 General Pariani developed his own war plans to attack British forces and reach the Suez Canal, with the capture of the latter being viewed as a decisive move in any future war. Then in 1939 the situation changed dramatically after the crisis of 1938 in Munich when Italy's focus was redirected again toward Europe and to a potential conflict with France. Thus, plans against the British in North Africa were shelved. By 1940 things had changed again. Now Italy wanted to launch a parallel war where Italian troops would fight exclusively for Italian interests in North Africa and primarily by battling Commonwealth forces in defense of the Suez Canal and Egypt. The capture of key natural resources was the aim of the campaign which would have made Italy more autonomous from the energy profile and much less dependent on Germany. In 1940 the Italian authorities anticipated that Germany would not have a substantial role in Africa and that Italy would conduct an autonomous campaign. Thus, they considered North Africa as their sphere of influence and no joint planning had been conducted with the Germans to wage a campaign against Britain. The major limitation of this plan was that at the time Italy had only three fledgling armoured divisions, which initially where considered as a strategic reserve based along the Po' River and to be deployed either against France or Yugoslavia. Since there were only three divisions at the time and they were to be deployed in Europe, the whole North African strategy lacked the necessary means to achieve such a major objective. Thus, "In June 1940 the Italians had no strategic plan for the war in North Africa, other than waiting to defend themselves against anticipated French and British attacks."[1] When France collapsed on 20 June, however, Balbo began to pressure the military and political authorities into shipping equipment to North Africa to initiate a preventive offensive against French Tunisia or against the British in Egypt. He wrote: "Dear Badoglio you are perfectly aware of our situation in Libya and I do not need to belabor to describe it to you. Our light tanks are vulnerable to the 12.7 caliber machine guns of the British armoured cars and it would be opportune if we could receive at least fifty German Panzer tanks and armoured vehicles to launch this offensive to reach the main British defenses in Egypt..... With 100 tanks we could carry out an important offensive operation that could give us the initiative."[2] He even proposed as an alternative, if the major offensive was not authorized, to seize the Sollum plateau along the Egyptian border which would have allowed the Italians to control from above the movements of British troops, thus denying them the ability to lead raids into Italian positions. But even this limited plan was not authorized by *Comando Supremo*, which initially ceded the initiative to the enemy. Badoglio was less convinced about the chances of success of a major offensive and argued that "If things become very serious for Britain in Egypt we could then launch a major offensive."[3] His strategic plan was based on a major German success in the Battle of Britain that would then open up an opportunity for the Italian forces to strike in Egypt. As historian Mario Montanari correctly asserts it was a purely defensive strategy that depended upon a wait and see approach regarding the Battle of Britain.[4] As far as Badoglio was concerned, Balbo was "to shut the door"[5] and prevent any major incursions of British mobile forces into Libya. This hesitant approach changed almost overnight however, when the Duce thought that the time was right to strike in North Africa after the French collapse. Subsequently, Mussolini authorized the main offensive against Britain in North Africa and instructed a recalcitrant Badoglio to send reinforcements to North Africa such as medium tanks, anti-tank guns and other new equipment. At that point Badoglio decided to dispatch seventy-two medium tanks (M.11/39) to North Africa in support of Balbo's offensive, which were to arrive during the first week of July. Unfortunately, the offensive, which was to commence on 15 July 1940, was put on hold after Balbo died by friendly fire on 28 June in Tobruk. An early attack against the Commonwealth forces envisioned by Balbo was sound from a strategic point of view. This is because although the Italian forces in North Africa were still understrength, the same can be said about the British forces. The 7th Armoured Division, for instance, at that time had only sixty-five of the 220 divisional Cruiser tanks at its immediate disposal plus some additional light and heavy tanks. If there was ever a time to attack Egypt it was probably July 1940 although the Italians lacked several key equipment and weapons and most importantly towing equipment for the tanks. It would later become apparent that the M.11/39 tanks were generally not suited to travel for large distances in off road conditions in the desert without experiencing technical problems of all kinds. Even if the Italians enjoyed some slight numerical advantages in June-July 1940, it is unlikely that its tank force could have functioned well in a long-distance offensive against Egypt without the necessary tank towing or transportation

---

1 Andrew Sangster and Pier Paolo Battistelli, *Myths, Amnesia and Reality in Military Conflicts, 1935-1945*, p. 66.
2 Mario Montanari, *Le Operazioni in Africa Settentrionale*, vol 1, Part, 1, Sidi Barrani, p. 68.
3 Andrew Sangster, Pier Paolo Battistelli, *Myths, Amnesia and Reality in Military Conflicts, 1935-1945*, p. 67.
4 Ibid, p. 71.
5 Ibid.

equipment or due to the lack of self-propelled artillery and heavy tanks. These would have been some of the major obstacles to the success of the offensive, but on the flipside the enemy was very weak. [6] Traveling large distances in the desert while being able to supply the army moving forward would have been another major problem as General Wavell's and Rommel's offensives in 1940-41 and 1942 respectively would later reveal.

Balbo's place was taken by Rodolfo Graziani who became Commander-in-Chief of Italian North Africa and Governor General of Libya. In the view of several historians such as Giorgio Rochat and Arrigo Petacco, Balbo's death was a fatal blow as he was a very energetic and bold leader cut in a very different mold than Graziani. Although not a military tactician, Balbo had not lacked initiative and was considered a good planner: "He might have made a difference in the upcoming fighting, as he was an inspirational and aggressive leader, and long an advocate of invading Egypt."[7]

Graziani went to work on the offensive but his planners, has they began to organize the North African forces, realized that the Army lacked key resources and advised Graziani to bide for time. The Army in North Africa, for instance, in late July had 3,500 trucks at its disposal, but it was estimated that the offensive required over 5,000 trucks, while the armoured force, being based mostly on light tanks, was not adequate for a major offensive against British forces. Graziani pointed out to Badoglio that he lacked many of the necessary resources, notably anti-tank, anti-aircraft, and long range field artillery, medium tanks and vehicles of all kinds. As Battistelli correctly point out at this point "Ideally, Mussolini or his chief of staff should have decided to send part of the strategic reserve, the Po' Army to Libya. This was not done. Instead, only piecemeal reinforcements, weapons, equipment and vehicles were sent."[8] Lacking adequate mechanized and motorized resources Graziani held on until September and then, only after several solicitations from Mussolini, finally launched his offensive.

Desert Warfare

The war was fought primarily in the Western Desert, the area of the Sahara which is located to the west of the Nile River, and Libya's eastern region (Cyrenaica), an area that is approximately 240 miles wide and that stretches from Gazala on the Libyan coast to Mersa Matruh in Egypt. Most of it is comprised of barren desert terrain with only one main road that at the time was called Via Balbia that cut across from the Egyptian border to Tripolitania. The vast area was delimited to the north by the Mediterranean Sea and to the south by the Great Sand Sea and the two oases of Giarabub and Siwa. Given the barren landscape, navigation, even for

---

6   A 1941 report by Divisione *Ariete* outlined that one Italian tank battalion arrived at its destination during the race to El Mechili after a long-distance operation with 14 operational out of 40 tanks with which it started the operation, while a German tank battalion concluded the operation with 8 working tanks out of 60. But unlike the Italians which only recovered six tanks and dispatched the others to the repair shops for long term retrofits, the Germans later recovered the majority of their tanks thanks to their recovery crews and the greater availability of spare parts. The report also added: "we lack the means to transport the armour nor do we have tractors to tow them." Ufficio Storico, Relazione Andreani "Impegno Operativo M.13/40" 21 April 1941.
7   Jack Greene and Alessandro Massignani, *Rommel's North African Campaign*, p. 132.
8   Ibid., p. 87.

experienced units, was always a challenge and often the troops relied upon the position of the stars, the moon and the sun and on compasses to travel across the Western Desert. The weather also presented a challenge with very hot, humid daytime temperatures and very cold temperatures at night. Because of its specific characteristics, warfare on such a vast terrain would give a central fighting role to the armoured units. Prior to Operation Compass, the British strike against Graziani's army in the winter of 1940-41, the potential for tank warfare and maneuver in the desert terrain had not been fully envisioned. The Italians maintained that warfare in such terrain could only be carried out in consequential leaps where each move forward would halt at some relevant location to allow the army to re-supply and then after a period of rest and recuperation would move to the next objective. But after Operation Compass, which jettisoned the Italian leap frog approach, the tank would take center stage in a series of British attacks followed by Axis counters and with the initiative passing to both armies at different times. In this flat and barren landscape, the absolute visibility both from above and from the ground of motorized or mechanized columns, necessitated land based forces to rely on speed, and maneuver at every level to avoid detection. In such an environment, free of natural obstacles and shelters, the tanks, self-propelled guns and armoured vehicles comprised the basic offensive combat means of both Axis and Commonwealth armies. In contrast, non-motorized troops were obviously disadvantaged compared to the motorized ones, which by exploiting their greater mobility could put forth bold flanking and encirclement maneuvers against both static and non-static defenses. In the desert landscape, where the troops had to be fed and supplied from far away bases, the mass of infantry soldiers represented a major drain on resources. The mechanized assets on the other hand, were typically comprised of fewer soldiers and had the means to travel long distances.

With regard to his desert experiences Rommel, for example, observed:

> One of the first lessons I had drawn from my experience of motorized warfare was that speed of maneuver in operations and quick reaction in command are decisive. Troops must be able to carry out operations at top speed and in complete co-ordination. To be satisfied with norms is fatal. One must constantly demand and strive for maximum performance, for the side which makes the greater effort is the faster and faster wins the battle.[9]

Factors such as the mechanical reliability of tank engines, tank speed and their capacity to travel long distances quickly came to the fore. The future course of the continuous seesaw like campaign in North Africa indicated that the decisive role in the desert warfare was to be played by the tanks and mobile artillery. With no natural barriers of any sort the tank's possibilities to maneuver were unrestricted and the factors leading to victory were the mobility, maximum range and the caliber of the guns together with the overall number of tanks that each side possessed. For the tanks to succeed, however, an all arms or combined arms approach worked best. While taking on entrenched defenses, tanks greatly benefited from the support provided by special infantry units, by mobile artillery and by fighter planes and bombers. These ideas would take some time to take hold in North Africa and the German forces would be the first to

---

9   Basil Liddell Hart, The *Rommel Papers* (New York: Harcourt, Brace and Co., 1972), p. 225.

implement them in detail, although both Graziani's and Wavell's offensives had already experimented with some degree of combined arms mechanized warfare prior to the arrival of the Germans.

On the defensive level the desert campaign enabled certain heavy weapons of the infantry units to also have a key impact, in many instances even more important than the tanks. Even Rommel's fast moving Panzer columns, for instance, could not overtake the formidable defensive screen set up by the Commonwealth armies during the first two battles of El Alamein. As Paddy Griffith asserts: "In a field artillery against tank duel, the latter often did not prevail especially if faced by a British 25-pounder, a German 88mm Flak 36 gun or an Italian 90mm gun. AT fire suffered by British tanks did not come from other tanks at all, as perhaps British tacticians liked to assume, but from towed (ground mounted) AT guns."[10]

After the first few major tank maneuvers, the campaign became a battle ground between the major armies and their artillery arm soon played a central role in the fighting. One of the factors, for instance, that enabled the *Das Afrika Korps* (DAK) to prevail in many duels with the Commonwealth tank formations was its offensive use of the artillery based on the practice to have towed guns being brought forward with the armour and provide an advanced anti-tank screen. Another key factor for the artillery arm was the effectiveness of certain anti-tank guns especially the German 88mm Flak models 36 and 37 originally designed for anti-aircraft use, especially when facing the larger and more heavy medium tanks that were introduced in 1941. An army with effective guns could repel an enemy tank attack much better than one that had light anti-tank weapons and the Italians given their intelligence lapses and the use of obsolete guns would pay a heavy price in 1940-41 for not having the proper equipment. They would eventually introduce heavier anti-tank guns beginning in mid-1941 and their artillery would go to play an important role in major encounters with the Commonwealth armour. Motorization of the artillery arm was another key factor allowing for a mobile defense against the enemy and the capability to shift resources where they were most needed. A high degree of motorization also enabled the infantry to sustain long winded battles and provide soldiers with the ability to be brought to an offensive operation in fresh conditions by avoiding long approach marches.

In offensive operations against entrenched infantry defenses, movement and maneuvering by the tank columns was the only way the latter could survive when facing a formidable anti-tank screen. Defensive positions comprised by well-prepared infantry with dug in guns and machine guns were not easily detectable by the tank crews. Thus, they could pick out tanks at random and from a distance and destroy them piecemeal.

Armour also was more successful when involved in combined arms operations where the tanks were supported by forward positioned artillery and by specialized infantry units that could decommission mines and degrade the enemy's defenses. In addition, specialized infantry could also deal with the enemy's anti-tank units that often-used camouflage and well sited defenses to attack and destroy tanks in close combat. In such multi-faceted attacks the armour had greater chances of success but true combined arms operations were a novelty during the first phase of the campaign and it took considerable time before both sides could produce such capabilities. Many of the units involved in combined arms operations such as special reconnaissance units, tank hunting platoons or the engineer combat units simply did not exist at the beginning

---

10 Paddy Griffith, *World War Two Desert Tactics* (Oxford: Osprey, 2008), p. 27.

of the war and they were established progressively. Rommel had understood the need for a combined arms approach earlier than other commanders. During the Battle for Bir Hacheim, for example, Rommel relied on a variety of forces to take the fortress. An immediate attack by armour alone was out of the questions since "tanks cannot be sent into minefields that are protected against clearance by strongpoints."[11] By mid-1942 the so-called "All tanks" approach had been abandoned even by the British tank commanders who had been initially influenced by JFC Fuller's theories on armoured warfare. During the night of 24/25 October 1942, for example, in the midst of the El Alamein III battle, the British assault of infantry and engineers over the Miteiriya Ridge did not progress. Despite having agreed to Montgomery's battle plan, Lieutenant-General Herbert William Lumsden refused to launch his X Corps armoured units against the Axis anti-tank screen and uncleared minefields. Lumsden ordered his tanks to pull back and then to send them into battle once the motorized infantry and engineers had dealt with the screen. Despite having the correct approach to combined arms warfare Lumsden was sacked by Montgomery and replaced by General Horrocks. Out of this diatribe night fighting became more prominent especially for combined arms operations against strong defensive positions which allowed the special infantry units to advance in the dark to face the enemy tank screen with mobile artillery, mortars and detonation charges.

Another factor that contributed to strengthening the defensive position was the control or the possession of the field of battle. In the Libyan desert after a battle was concluded the side that occupied the field of battle, often the army that was on the defensive, could reap significant material benefits such as the recovery of damaged but not destroyed tanks that could be towed back to the rear to be salvaged by the armoured repair shops.

In the latter stages of the campaign, Allied air supremacy would also play a vital role in the fighting and particularly upon harassing the Axis tank units from above. According to Rommel, air power played a decisive role in the final battle of El Alamein by forcing Axis tanks to maneuver much less freely than before. The barren desert landscape also presented huge logistical challenges as the troops had to be fed, the tanks and the armoured columns needed to be refueled and the ammunition and weapons had to be transported to the frontline. First, everything that the troops needed to conduct operations (fuel, water, ammunition, repair parts, weapons, uniforms, and medical equipment) had to be moved into the theater over sea and air lines of communication from Italy to North Africa and then forwarded by trucks to the fighting units at the front. Since material had to be flown or shipped in there were always losses that were sustained due to enemy attacks by sea or by air. The Italians shipped equipment mostly through naval convoys in the Mediterranean, while the British used the Atlantic Ocean sea lanes going through the Cape of Good Hope and up the Red Sea to reach the Egyptian ports. While the Italian sea route was more direct, it was also heavily targeted by the British Navy and the RAF. Naples and Taranto were the two naval bases from which convoys were dispatched to North Africa. Malta, given its position in the Mediterranean, assumed for the British a central role in the interdiction of Axis supply convoys. It was slowly transformed in an island fortress with a submarine flotilla, naval destroyers and RAF bomber units. Beginning in August 1941 the British Navy began to mount major attacks to the point that Italian monthly losses ramped up considerably (28 percent of all cargo lost in August versus 50 percent in September). In October

---

11 Basil Liddell Hart, *The Rommel Papers*, p. 218.

62 percent of the total supplies that were shipped from Italy were lost at sea due to enemy attacks.[12] In November, as Operation Crusader unfolded, the Italians suffered tremendous losses with the total destruction of the Duisburg convoy. The overall supply situation was made worse by Ultra intercepts which furnished the British with key intelligence to interfere with Axis convoy operations. In turn, unloading supplies required adequate port facilities to handle large volumes as well as viable roads or rail system to transport it from the ports to the fighting troops on the frontline. The North African area lacked both as railways were sparse and there was only one main coastal road, the Via Balbia that was in full view of enemy aerial attacks. This exposed the supply columns to further losses forcing them often to travel only at night and at a very slow pace given that it was forbidden to use headlights to avoid detection. The side that advanced the furthest and was thus further away from its supply depots was at a considerable disadvantage since it could not be readily supplied of fuel, food, water and ammunition. Thus, the strategic aspect of the campaign comprised these key logistics considerations which dictated the size, reach and the volume of offensive operations.

> **ITALIAN TANK MARKINGS FOR AERIAL RECOGNITION**
>
> Stato Maggiore Regio Esercito
> Ufficio Addestramento
>
> N. 4900 di prot P.M. n. 9, 12 Agosto 1940
>
> To the High Command Armed Forces in North Africa, High Command in East Africa, High Command Aegean Islands and High Command Army Corps.
>
> Subject: Markings to recognize our tanks by airplanes
>
> To allow Italian planes to recognize our tanks while on offensive action it is ordered that a white circle shall be painted on the turret of M.11, M.13, and L.6 tanks and on the turret of the motor section of the L.3 tanks. All units are hereby ordered to paint such markings on all their armoured vehicles by 31 August 1940. For those units deployed in North Africa and East Africa the timing of the implementation of this order will be determined by local command.
> Note that there were five different tank markings that were considered prior to making a final decision upon the white circle symbol. These included, amongst other, a white cross and a white fascio.

---

12 Mario Montanari, *Le operazioni in Africa Settentrionale*, vol. II, Part II, p. 642.

Italian Forces

Just a few weeks after the declaration of war had been lodged, Italian forces in North Africa included the following units, weapons and equipment:

> V and X Army with fourteen infantry divisions and one tank brigade. The V Army occupied the area of Tripolitania while the X Army was in Cyrenaica closer to the Egyptian border and thus would carry out most of the initial fighting.
> 390 anti-tank pieces (47mm and 65mm) with 880,000 shells;
> 34 truck mounted anti-tank guns;
> 250 tanks comprising seven battalions of L.3 light tanks.
> 780 heavy trucks;
> 555 light trucks;
> 224 Dovunque trucks;
> 120 tankers;
> 40 ambulances.
> 200 × 20mm guns;
> 62 × 47mm guns;
> 72 × 65/17 guns;
> 440 artillery divisional pieces (192 × 75/27, forty-four 77/28, twelve 88mm and ninety-six 100/17;
> Plus 182 miscellaneous pieces (48 × 105/28, 52 × 149/35 and other varied caliber guns).

The key factors of note here is that in June 1940 not only was the Italian Army in North Africa comprised in large numbers by infantry soldiers with almost no means for transport and little in the way of effective anti-tank guns against the enemy tanks but also its armoured assets were primarily light tanks armed with a machine gun rather than a cannon. Such an armoured force lacking medium tanks was ill suited for a wide sweeping offensive across the Egyptian frontier. According to Italian tank doctrine the light tanks were supposed to conduct reconnaissance of the enemy lines and make the first contact with the enemy. The medium tanks were to be employed for long-range maneuver operations and support in engaging enemy forces, while the heavy tanks were to reinforce the medium tank action. The lack of adequate numbers of medium and heavy tanks, which were necessary to exploit and breakthrough the enemy defenses, would have made an advance into Egypt highly prohibitive.

The infantry based units of the Italian Army in North Africa was short of motor transport, which meant that the soldiers were often stranded in the desert in their foxholes or fortified positions and could not be deployed for large scale offensives spanning large swath of desert territory. As historian Paddy Griffith aptly summarizes: "They were short of motor transport, which meant that their infantry was almost completely immobile and often short of supplies. They were also badly deficient in amour: alongside 14 infantry divisions there was only one Italian armoured brigade in Libya in January 1941, and its vehicles were of poor quality."[13] Other factors that would influence on the combat performance of the Italian units in 1940

---

13 Paddy Griffith, *World War Two Desert Tactics*, p. 13.

was inadequate anti-tank weaponry and an almost complete lack of reconnaissance units. With regard to anti-tank weapons the situation was similar to the one in East Africa where the 105/28 guns had been somewhat effective against the British medium tanks, while the standard 47/32 and 75/27 gun crews having no stocks of armoured piercing shells had been less effective when facing medium enemy tanks. Apparently, the significance of the German campaign against the French army which had more effective anti-tank weapons but had still succumbed to the German Panzers had not sinked in with *Comando Supremo*. It is unlikely that by 1940 the Italian Army could have deployed more powerful anti-tank weapons but with more haste it could have supplied the frontline artillery crews with armoured piercing projectiles that would have improved the effectiveness of the available guns. The army had no armoured vehicles for reconnaissance during the early stages of the campaign. These would be introduced only in 1941. As a result, the reconnaissance function was primarily carried out by small units equipped with trucks, motorcycles and light tanks that were generally slower moving than their British counterparts. In contrast, the Commonwealth forces under General Wavell in Egypt had approximately some 36,000 soldiers. The 7th Armoured Division, the main tank force in Egypt, was constituted upon two understrength tank brigades that each had two regiments, instead of three, and these were only partly equipped. In late July, the unit had approximately 120 medium Cruiser tanks[14], 50 light tanks and was awaiting the arrival of the Matilda II heavy tanks. The Commonwealth force was augmented by the 4th Indian Division and a New Zealand Division which were both understrength initially. There were also fourteen battalions of British infantry and two artillery regiments. Most importantly the frontline troops were motorized with Rolls-Royce, Morris, Ford vehicles and Bren carriers equipped with either a machine gun or a Boys anti-tank rifle.

To alleviate the lack of medium tanks in Graziani's army on 7 July 1940 the arrival of the *Comando del 4° Reggimento Fanteria Carrista,* with two battalions of M.11/39 tanks (these had been promised initially to Balbo) immediately strengthened X Army's armoured component.

The seventy-two medium tanks reinforced units equipped with L.3 tankettes[15] already in Libya. The *Comando Supremo* and Graziani debated on how best to structure an armoured brigade in preparation for the Italian offensive in North Africa. At first, Graziani requested additional armoured reinforcements such as *Ariete or Centauro* but was rebuffed as these units were to be held by Badoglio in Italy to be utilized as a reserve against Greece or Yugoslavia. Graziani then returned to Balbo's idea of constructing an armoured brigade in North Africa by assembling Italian and/or German medium tanks.

Graziani, to get the most out of his armoured units, ordered them to be organized as a *colonna celere*, which was a combat group roughly equivalent to the strength of an armoured brigade. But a few days later, Graziani unexpectedly suspended the implementation of such an order. The units were then placed under the orders on 29 August 1940 of *Generale* Valentino Babini

---

14 The Cruiser Mark IV A13 Tank was the main medium tank of the British armoured units from the start of the campaign in North Africa until the fall of 1941. It was a 14.8 ton tank armed with a QF Vickers 2-pdr gun (40 mm/1.57 in) with 87 rounds 0.303 (7.7 mm) Vickers machine-gun with 3,750 rounds. It could reach a top speed of 30 mph. In North Africa the Cruiser tank force was also comprised of Cruiser A9 and A10 tanks.
15 The lightly armoured L. 3 was vulnerable to the 14mm British Boys anti-tank rifle mounted on armoured cars.

and his *Comando Carri Armati della Libia (*Libyan armoured command*)*. The latter was at that point only an administrative unit without experienced tank commanders and officers thus other precious time was lost in the selection and training of new personnel and the assembly of these officers within the new unit. But most importantly the units were split up into four ad hoc main combat groups during the first offensive, thus diluting their combat power.

> *1° Raggruppamento* (*Colonnello* Aresca) comprised of one battalion of M.11/39 (24 vehicles) and three battalions of L.3 tanks were to fight alongside the XXIII Army Corps;
> *2° Raggruppamento* (*Colonnello* Trivioli) comprised of the same strength as Aresca's unit but fighting alongside the Libyan divisions;
> *I Battaglione* comprised mainly of one company of light tanks which was to operate with General Maletti's group.
> *LX Battaglione* carri L.3 which was to operate with the XXI Army Corps.

At the same time, the Italians also formed a second smaller armoured group within the Libyan Corps that was independent from Babini's brigade. This was the so-called *Gruppo Maletti* commanded by *Generale* Pietro Maletti which was composed of six battalions of Libyan infantry and of two armoured battalions. One armour battalion had thirty-five L.3/33 light tanks (I *Battaglione*), while the other (II *Battaglione*) had twenty-four M.11/39 medium tanks. This latter unit was to operate very close to the frontier, while the unit under Babini was to act as the main armoured combat arm and it was to be headquartered in Tripolitania. At this point the Italian armoured strength in Libya was comprised by 72 medium tanks and a few hundred light tanks. The army had no heavy tanks or self-propelled guns and lacked a true reconnaissance arm.

As Greene and Massignani assert in reference to the various plans to build an autonomous armoured brigade in Libya that Graziani lacked initiative and could not organize and train his mechanized and motorized assets to fight under a single command during the Italian advance and subsequently during the major Commonwealth counter-offensive.

Referring to General Wilhelm Ritter von Thoma's August 1940 visit on behalf of the German High Command to North Africa they write that "After von Thoma's visit, Graziani gave some thought to concentrating vehicles and tanks into a division. But the most he ever implemented was a motorized force which, in part, was created due to the successful skirmishing of the British armoured cars."[16]

The German General inspected the Italian frontline troops and completed an extensive tour of their frontline positions and finally in a detailed report advised the German High Command not to get involved in the campaign since in his view the Italians were bereft of all major equipment required to conduct a proper mechanized campaign. Despite opposing the involvement of German forces, von Thoma argued that if the German High Command eventually decided to send troops to North Africa a minimum of four or five mostly armoured divisions were required to properly conduct the campaign. Less than four divisions would result in leaving the initiative to the British, while the tight supply situation could not, in von Thoma's view, satisfy the supply demands of six or more divisions.

---

16 Jack Greene and Alessandro Massignani, *Rommel's North Africa Campaign*, p. 30.

General von Thoma had observed that the Italians had obsolete equipment and too many non-motorized infantry units that were literally stranded in their frontline positions. The first battle encounters, where the motorized Commonwealth units, had the upper hand against the Italians appeared to vindicate his view.[17]

First Shots

After Italy entered the war in June 1940, the British forces defending the Egyptian frontline achieved some local successes by raiding and harassing the Italian frontier outposts in large part thanks to their greater mobility and their extensive use of Bren carriers and light and medium tanks. The other factor that led to this outcome was Badoglio's initial directive, which incorrectly relying upon Italian intelligence service (SIM) estimates of the presence of a major Commonwealth force in Egypt, ordered Balbo to maintain a defensive posture and forbidding any preventive strikes. In contrast, the enemy would soon take advantage of this predicament. On 14 June, a bold action by British motorized units seized Ridotta Capuzzo (Fort Capuzzo) and Ridotta Maddalena, two Italian infantry outposts close to the border. In another episode, which took place three miles from the frontline on the night between 15-16 June, an Italian tactical group was dispatched to reconnaissance the frontier and was ambushed by several enemy tanks and armoured vehicles near the locality of Gabr Saleh. Upon spotting the enemy, the Italian *Raggruppamento* led by *Colonnello* D'Avanzo and comprised by the XI *Battaglione Libico* with 378 soldiers, two companies of L light tanks (eighteen tanks) of IX *Battaglione Carri*, one battery of 77/28 guns with two motorcycles, and fifty-five trucks halted its movements and assumed a defensive position. This took the form of a square formation with the field artillery deployed on each side while the infantry units stood in-between the artillery while the light tanks patrolled around the deployment. Regarding this very defensive and static position taken by *Colonnell*o D'Avanzo the Italian Official History states that it inhibited a combined arms response to the threat posed by the enemy: "The decision to form a square in the open, knowing the ability, mobility, co-ordination and aggressiveness of the British armoured units was a great mistake by the Italian commander, especially considering how these aspects of how the British operated were regularly emphasized by the Italian commands during this period."[18]

As a result of this feeble disposition, the Commonwealth force led by armoured units pounced on the Italian column which was initially defended by the light tanks. Without the aid of the artillery or motorized infantry the Italian tanks countered alone while the bulk of the column remained back. While attacking the enemy with considerable dash, the light tanks were all destroyed or disabled by the Commonwealth unit which possessed tanks, mobile anti-tank guns and armoured vehicles. After having dealt with the tanks the combined arms enemy force

---

17 The Germans had already considered whether to help the Italians with equipment in June/July 1940 mainly through their Military attaché in Rome Major-General Enno von Rintelen. He considered the North African theater to be of vital importance to the Axis war effort and was widely supportive of the Italian objective to drive the British out of Egypt. In his view it was necessary to protect the sea routes with a massive naval effort and air superiority over northern Egypt. The problem of supply would be exacerbated by a major advance by troops well beyond the available ports.
18 Mario Montanari, *Le Operazioni in Africa Settentrionale*, vol. 1, part 1, pp. 65-66.

began to advance against the Italian infantry which fought back with the field artillery but was ultimately overwhelmed. Unfortunately for the Italians, the column had no anti-tank guns or even truck mounted anti-tank Solothurn 20mm rifles which would have been effective against the armoured vehicles. Some infantrymen managed to escape, but most of the members of the tactical group were either captured or killed including the commander of the unit *Colonnello* D'Avanzo.[19] Regarding this first tank versus tank engagement the commander of one of the light tanks reconnaissance unit wrote that:

> The Vickers tanks were more or less the same category of the CV.35 but when the first A9 medium Cruiser tanks arrived things started to become difficult for us. The battalion formed a circle, with the CV.35s facing outwards. The enemy started to circle around firing against us. The battalion fought hard until the end, refusing to surrender, until the last CV.35 was destroyed and Colonnello D'Avanzo was killed. Colonnello D'Avanzo improvised, under enemy fire, a defense of infantry and artillery, counterattacking with the few remaining light tanks under his command. I commanded a small reconnaissance party in the area and I took some pictures of the light tanks destroyed, still positioned in a circle and with some of the bodies of the crew members still in the tanks.[20]

It appears that the *Raggruppamento* had been hastily put together with little or no training. Most critically it had no mobile anti-tank weapons and its defensive disposition forced the tanks to fight a solitary battle, unsupported by the artillery and the infantry. As Major Christie asserts: "The main failures of these initial combined arms columns or raggruppamento were in training, equipment, and their doctrinal use. The lack of training as a cohesive force was critical. These formations were ad hoc formations with no standard battle drills. They were organized based on the current conditions and lacked the necessary training in combined arms warfare as called upon in Italian doctrine."[21]

On 16 June, a transport column with twenty-two empty trucks was captured by Commonwealth armoured units near Bardia. In addition, the British had knocked out of action between 11 and 25 June seven more Italian light tanks and sustained no losses of their own. Early successes by the Commonwealth forces spurred the creation by the charismatic Lieutenant Colonel J.C. 'Jock' Campbell of the so-called 'Jock Columns' in August 1940. These units, which consisted of a battery of 25-pdr. gun company, a troop of armoured cars, a troop of anti-tank guns (2-pdr.), a section of light anti-aircraft guns (40mm Bofors), and some other motorized units, gave rise to an early development of the all arms concept which proved to be one of the major innovations in the desert campaign. These highly motorized and mobile units would play a key role in antagonizing enemy troops often laying ambushes to enemy soft skinned supply columns and in interfering with the enemy artillery operations. In addition, the Commonwealth forces also deployed mechanized formations which made several forays against Italian positions causing casualties and destroying some of their equipment.

---

19   Nicola Pignato, 'La Colonna D'Avanzo', *Storia Militare*, N. 55, April 1998.
20   Ibid.
21   Major Howard Christie, *Fallen Eagles: The Italian 10th Army in the Opening Campaign in the Western Desert*, p. 17.

The early actions by Commonwealth mobile columns brought attention to some of the weaknesses of the Italian Army in North Africa as related to mechanization and motorization. In a highly mobile environment Italian defenses were based on static strongpoints without an armoured reserve to oppose and check major enemy breakthroughs. Moreover, the Italians lacked adequate reconnaissance teams and vehicles to preempt enemy raids and conduct proper counter reconnaissance. The AB series armoured car produced by Ansaldo would make its appearance only in 1941 and for the first year of the war the Italians used simple trucks and light tanks to carry out the reconnaissance and surveillance functions. Most importantly, dedicated reconnaissance units like the Jock Columns fit for that purpose had not yet been constituted when Italy entered the conflict. The tanks still relied on flags to signal when they should advance or halt and were generally more prone to breakdowns than enemy tanks or armoured cars. Another problem that plagued the Italian armour in North Africa was the lack of dedicated recovery and repair units that could tow damaged tanks out of the battle field.

To make matters worse collaboration between the air force and the armoured units was not very effective and rivalries between the services did not improve cooperation. With regard to these first Italian light tank units engagements, Major Christie states that lack of training and of true collaboration between infantry and mechanized forces were two elements responsible for the early defeats:

> The main failures of these initial combined arms columns or raggruppamenti were in training, equipment, and their doctrinal use. The lack of training as a cohesive force was critical. These formations were ad hoc formations with no standard battle drills. They were organized based on the current conditions and lacked the necessary training in combined arms warfare as called upon in Italian doctrine. The new doctrine called for medium tanks working in cooperation with motorized infantry and artillery that had trained together to perform their specific mission. No prior training or cooperation existed with these units. Complete command and control relationships were not developed and poor communications nets supported them.[22]

On 21 June Balbo began to reverse the initial directive that had maintained his frontline troops on a defensive posture by ordering them to increase the rate of frontline patrols. Incidentally, on that same day while on a frontline reconnaissance Balbo's SM79 plane spotted a British Rolls Royce armoured vehicle which was shortly thereafter captured. In late June, the Italian armoured and reconnaissance units were ordered to intensify their patrolling activities even further along the frontier to check Commonwealth raids into the Italian positions. He also ordered that the captured enemy vehicles be shown around to the frontline troops to demonstrate that they were not impervious to machine gun fire or from the fire of 20mm anti-tank rifles. This initiative was to dispel the mistaken belief by many infantry troops, who had never fought against such armoured vehicles, that indeed they could be damaged and even destroyed by their crew served weapons. On 2 July near Fort Capuzzo a clash took place between Commonwealth armoured cars and *1a Divisione Libica* units which resulted in losses on both sides. On the 3rd Commonwealth tanks attacked near the fort but they were repulsed. On the same day,

---

22 Ibid. p. 21.

motorized elements of the *Marmarica Divisione* raided enemy positions in Sollum repulsing a counter by mobile artillery and armoured vehicles. On the 6th *2a Divisione Libica* successfully repulsed an armoured attack near Bardia capturing one tank, one armoured vehicle and damaging two more. On the 16th and the 20th the enemy attacked again with tanks near Fort Capuzzo overcoming several Italian positions and inflicting casualties.

On 5 August near Sidi Azeiz-Capuzzo the first deployment of Italian medium tanks took place when they met a British Cruiser tank formation that led to a brisk but deadly engagement for both sides. The Italian post combat report asserts that: "The fighting was very lively and the enemy lost four tanks two of which were towed back to our lines,"[23] while the Italians suffered three damaged (by infantry fire) but repairable medium tanks. The Italian vehicles were from the I and II *Raggruppamento* and it was the first time the British tanks faced the Italian M.11/39 medium tanks. The Italian combat unit this time had greater firepower being also comprised by mobile artillery and motorized *Bersaglieri*. Its post-battle report written by *Colonnello* Aresca stated that with the medium tanks it was possible to win engagements against the enemy especially, like in this instance, when the vehicles were utilized in a combined arms role. By cooperating closely with the other units of the combat group, the artillery, infantry and anti-tank units (the latter were not present in the earlier engagement of 15 June along with the medium tanks), the medium tanks were able to surprise and overwhelm the enemy force. Despite the success, the author of the post-battle report, *Colonnello* Aresca, commander of the unit engaged, listed some of the technical deficiencies of the M.11/39 tanks. He first described how the poor hull design and the limited traverse of the gun diminished the M.11/39 tank maneuverability and also had limited range when shooting against enemy tanks. Another point that was made was how the lack of tractors to tow the tanks to and from the battlefield negatively affected the M.11/39's mechanical reliability. From a tactical perspective, the lack of radio communications between tanks for the synchronization of combat unit operations was considered a significant shortfall. Given the lack of radios (only the commander had a radio) tank maneuvers could only be organized with signal flags.[24]

The British or Commonwealth official histories do not mention this engagement, while only one British author mentions it in detail. In 'Beda Fomm' historian Kenneth Macsey furnishes the following account of the battle:

> The Italians were getting stronger and stronger toward the end of July, and felt able to start the ball rolling themselves, sending up to two infantry divisions supported by a few tanks – Medium M11/39s. This force presented the British tanks for the first time with something they could not easily overcome, particularly since the Italian artillery was handled with both aggression and skill. Keeping the British at long range they posed a tactical problem which was clearly stated in the history of the 7th Hussars, who had two tank squadrons engaged: 'if the tanks halt so as to engage the guns accurately, they in turn become targets for the guns. If they do not halt, they are still quite good targets and at the same time nothing but a fluke shot from the moving tank would hit an enemy gun.' So the 7th Hussars were persuaded to pull back while the tanks of the 6th Royal tank Regiment, 7th

---

23 Mario Montanari, *Le Operazioni in Africa Settentrionale, vol. 1, part 1*, p. 119.
24 Lucio Ceva and Andrea Curami, *La meccanizzazione dell'esercito dalle origini fino al 1943*, volume II, pp. 211-215.

Armoured Division, sent forward to support them, were ordered to refrain from rushing the three Italian batteries which were putting up a truly formidable display, Nevertheless, as dusk began to fall, it was decided to attempt a night attack … And 'rush at speed against the enemy batteries using Vickers machine guns continuously during such an advance,' to quote orders from the 7th Hussars. At once there came a dazzling blaze of fire from the Italian guns, tracer flying all over the place and, out of the gloom, three Italian M11s advancing, one of which rammed a British Tank. Again, the British backed off after one of their cruisers had deflected a 37mm shot at point blank range, and still the Italian gunners stuck it out, through now being fired at by British 25 pounder artillery from long range.[25]

Although the engagement was not a major one, it was nevertheless relevant because it contributed to the ongoing development of a mechanized doctrine. According to Ceva and Curami the Italian tank commander involved in the combat action emphasized in his post battle report that: (1) There was a need for air reconnaissance and surveillance which was to guide forces on the ground, (2) the need for an English-speaking officer or NCO to gather information on enemy movements from POWs to help guide the commanders' decisions whether to continue or disengage from the combat action, and lastly, (3) the need at all times for anti-tank guns to accompany the mechanized forces.[26] These appear to be sound guidelines and most of them had already been experimented and put into practice during the Spanish Civil War. It appears that these useful lessons learned had not been administered at the time to the Italian units fighting in North Africa.[27]

Operazione E

After the postponement or the strong hesitation in launching Operation Sealion the German High Command floated the idea of dispatching to North Africa one of its panzer brigades. Hitler, urged by his High Command, had presumably by then shifted his attention from the Battle of Britain to other areas of operation. After the Italian military attaché' in Berlin Alfisio Marras requested additional German support for the North African theater, General Alfred Jodl on 31 August 1940 offered one or two panzer divisions. At this point *Comando Supremo* was considering the idea of forming an armoured striking force for North Africa made of German and Italian units. Despite the offer of support, no immediate decision was made by the Italian chief of staff likely because he desired German tanks but was hesitant, as was Mussolini, about the deployment of German troops in Italy's military sphere.

Thus, Operazione E, whose ultimate objective was to seize the Suez Canal, began on 9 September 1940 with Italian forces alone. The operation opened with aerial bombings put forth by *Regia Aeronautica* followed by a rolling barrage that trailed the advance by both armoured and infantry troops. The Italian force was led by The XXIII Army Corps of *Generale* Annibale Bergonzoli, that advanced along the coastal road with his non-motorized and motorized

---

25 Kenneth Macksey, *Beda Fomm: The Classic Victory* (New York: Ballantine Books, 1972), p. 19.
26 Lucio Ceva and Andrea Curami, *La meccanizzazione dell'esercito dale origini fino al 1943*, volume II, pp. 211-215.
27 Ibid.

formations. The infantry troops advanced in a very uneven way since some infantry units were motorized while the majority was not. This led the non-motorized troops to leapfrog advancing twelve miles per day on foot while carrying all crew served weapons. The British forces rather than oppose the advance fell back to rear positions and thus there were few clashes between opposing troops. Graziani's X Army suffered the loss of 500 soldiers but managed to reach Sidi Barrani, less than 100 miles into Egyptian territory, on 16 September. Here the troops were ordered to halt the advance and to build fortified camps. Graziani also envisioned building a pipeline to transport water from the rear and sought to further augment his forces to resume the offensive at a later date.

The following is the experience of *Colonnello* Aresca's main column during the advance which was plagued by the extreme heat inside the tanks during the day and by the difficulty in coordinating an advance by light and medium tanks that traveled at different speeds:

> Raggruppamento Aresca – Both medium and light tanks advanced as one single column. The two-day advance caused several difficulties for the crews. The extremely warm weather during the day greatly complicated the maneuver as inside the tanks temperatures reached 70° degrees Celsius, causing several drivers to faint. The average speed maintained by the motorized column was too fast for several vehicles causing several breakdowns. The pace of the advance was dictated by the fastest moving vehicles which forced the slowest tanks to keep an exceedingly high pace to allow the column to advance as one. It is therefore appropriate that in the future the motorized column should base its pace on the top speed of the slowest vehicles to avoid breakdowns and a disjointed advance. There was an overall lack of coordination between M and L tanks which was especially keenly lacking during the final advance on Sidi Barrani. This was due to the nature of the rough terrain and to excessive engine and other types of failures of the L tanks whereby only 17 out of 52 retained their efficiency during the operation. Considering the enemy's use of the armoured units as one large cohesive group, it is an imperative that future breakthrough offensive actions can only succeed if our tanks units act in unison. They should be placed under one coordinated command and if they are to complete wide-ranging maneuvers the efficiency of the light tanks must be greatly improved.[28]

Refusing German support, the Italian offensive did not achieve significant military results. Not only did the Italian units fail to capture large numbers of retreating British soldiers but also were not able to degrade or capture the enemy's rearguard. On the flipside, the offensive extended Italian supply lines from their main bases in Libya. On this new frontline position troops were ordered to build fortified camps and to prepare for the next phase of the offensive which aimed to capture Mersa Matruh. The only strategic advantage gained by Graziani's offensive was the capture of the air base near Sidi Barrani which allowed the Italian air forces to provide fighter escorts to its bombing missions deep into Egypt.

According to Commander-in-Chief Middle East Archibald Wavell's records the Commonwealth lost only fifty men and a very small number of vehicles during the enemy

---

28   Ufficio Storico, Carte Graziani, b. 59. Comando 10a Armata – Uff. Operazioni, 'Operazioni per la presa di Sidi Barrarni' – Relazione n. 01/8769 prot., Bardia, 20.10.1940 XVIII, p. 28.

offensive. According to Graziani's records the enemy's losses were higher. A total of thirteen British armoured vehicles were destroyed or lost during the withdrawal, while seventy-eight tanks were destroyed, idled, and abandoned during the same time.[29]

According to Graziani the main cause behind the slow Italian advance was the design shortcomings of the Italian tanks which revealed to be much less effective in maneuvering over the sandy terrain than the enemy's armoured force. He goes on to argue that the medium tanks could have been deployed more cohesively while the light tanks revealed themselves to be prompt to recurrent breakdowns in the desert. The advance was in fact characterized by several incidents where the armour got stuck in the sand or experienced engine malfunction.[30] Regarding the M.11/39 tanks historian Nicola Pignato asserts that at the termination of the advance to Sidi Barrani they came under heavy criticism:

> The M.11-39 was not considered successful for several reasons. African conditions were not considered when the vehicle was designed and tested and its reliability suffered. Additionally, the M.11/39 lacked a dedicated transporter; the tanks often had to drive from the African ports to the front, which further eroded their reliability. The hull-mounted main armament, limited armour protection, and the absence of radio equipment compromised its tactical value.[31]

At the end of the offensive Italian medium tank strength had fallen to sixty-eight (out of the original seventy-two) tanks, mostly as a result of mechanical failures.[32] Losses of light tanks are unclear.

As the front stabilized at Sidi Barrani, infantry units were organized into isolated *capisaldi* (strongpoints) along the frontline that separated the Axis from the Commonwealth/British forces. The isolated strongpoints were comprised of artillery and infantry forces that were kept informed of any enemy activity only by the actions of the reconnaissance patrols that traveled throughout the line and fed the infantry commanders of any important insight on enemy movements. It is important to note that Graziani had no motorized reserve unit that could be deployed to prop up a strongpoint attacked by an overwhelming enemy force, nor did he have a reserve armoured brigade to send into a gap.

One of the first significant encounters between British and Italian armoured units prior to the British counteroffensive took place on 18 November 1940 after an Italian reconnaissance team had alerted *Generale* Maletti's staff of an infiltration of British tanks at Alam Abu Hileuat (a position on the Sidi Barrani line). Because of this sighting, Graziani ordered the *II Battaglione* (M.11/39 tanks) to reach the area immediately. The latter, comprised by twenty-seven officers, 420 soldiers, twenty-seven medium tanks, six 47mm guns, four 65mm guns and four × 20mm guns mounted on vehicles arrived in the area at 1240 and it soon drew considerable enemy fire by both artillery and tank units. A second unit from the 2nd Libyan Division with no tanks but comprised by seventeen officers, 252 soldiers, four 47/32mm guns, four 65mm guns, four 75mm guns and four 20mm anti-aircraft guns was dispatched shortly thereafter to lend support

---

29   Ibid.
30   Ibid.
31   Nicola Pignato, *Italian Armoured Vehicles World War Two*, p. 23.
32   Paolo Battistelli and Filippo Cappellano, *Italian Medium Tanks*, p. 24.

and after arriving in the threatened sector was virtually surrounded by enemy troops and fired upon by both tanks and artillery. The situation was finally resolved with the arrival of a third motorized column and by the intervention of the *Regia Aeronautica* which used bombers and fighters to disperse the enemy troops. Losses amongst the Italians were considerable: 3 dead and 4 wounded officers, 3 dead, 25 wounded and 12 missing amongst Italian soldiers, 6 dead, 24 wounded and 4 missing among the Libyans. Moreover, five armoured vehicles were lost along with two 75/27 guns. In turn, the Italians claimed to have shot at eight enemy vehicles and to have damaged two of them.

This first skirmish on the Sidi Barrani line was most revealing and outlined how the defensive line could be breached by overwhelming one of the outposts with a superior mechanized and motorized force before Italian motorized columns could come to its aid.

It is worthwhile quoting at length the observations of a German war correspondent Dr. Franz Reichner, who had patrolled the Italian frontline at Sidi Barrani a few days prior to the British offensive. Marshall Graziani had told the German correspondent that he had enough troops and equipment to parry the British blow and that in a few days his troops were to go on the attack themselves.

> The frontline was not comprised of a continuous line of defense but instead of several individual fortified islands connected to each other by small patrol units ... Each infantry division or unit of a certain size was isolated in the desert and constituted a caposaldo (strongpoint). I am not going to mention the difficult conditions of the Italian troops of Sidi Barrani which had to endure all kinds of privations in the dust and filth of these fortified islands. Each caposaldo was maintained by patrol units and even supplies had to be delivered through no man's land and their columns were subjected to continuous enemy raids. It was obvious that every caposaldo would be endangered by an attack put forth by superior enemy forces. On the other hand, I was not sure that an effective and uninterrupted defensive deployment from the sea on one end and to the desert on the other was possible given Graziani's exiguous forces. It was impossible with the forces available to safeguard a line that was 100 kilometers long and to effectively prevent any attempt to infiltrate it. Surprisingly, I found a complete lack of armoured forces. The 1st Libyan Division was completely devoid of both armoured cars and tanks, while the 2nd Libyan Division was equipped with a few anti-tank gun units. I saw a few colonne celeri (fast moving columns) which consisted of simple large trucks on which 20mm machine guns or 4.7cm and 6.5cm anti-tank guns were mounted. The latter could be quickly dismounted and positioned on the ground to face an enemy attack....These trucks lacked any armour protection and were also very slow especially compared to British armoured units. In turn they appeared to be superior to the British in terms of firepower.[33]

After the capture of Sidi Barrani the dilemma of how best to organize the armoured force in North Africa resurfaced once again. On 4 October 1940 Mussolini met Hitler at the Brenner Pass and the latter, according to Galeazzo Ciano's diary, offered a German panzer division in

---

33 Nicola Piganto, "Prime esperienze italiane di guerra corazzata in Africa Settentrionale", Quaderno 1999 *Societa' Italiana di Storia Militare*, p. 124.

support of the Italian effort in North Africa and in exchange for the efforts made by Italy's *Corpo Aereo Italiano* that at the time was providing support to the *Luftwaffe* in its confrontation with the RAF in the Battle of Britain. But Mussolini declined the offer. This was followed in late October by another odd decision which was likely influenced by Mussolini's desire to fight the parallel war in North Africa without support from the Germans. Responding to Mussolini's guidelines, Badoglio in mid-October stated that "a German Panzer division was not necessary"[34] for an offensive with limited goals such as the seizure of Mersa Matruh. He argued that for such an offensive Italian troops and tanks were adequate for the task at hand which was to be another limited leap forward rather than a major push into Egypt. Thus, Graziani proceeded once again in strengthening the armoured brigade in North Africa exclusively with the "armoured units already in Cyrenaica." [35]

At the end of October he wrote to *Comando Supremo* stating: "I have studied the possibility of constituting an armoured brigade with the material that is already here in Cyrenaica. In fact, with this material together with the additional equipment that is being shipped to us from the mainland, I will be able to constitute an armoured unit of a certain consistency. To enhance its effectiveness, however, this unit should be equipped with two additional combat elements: a motorized regiment on three battalions and a unit equipped with armoured vehicles."[36] Both according to Graziani were to be equipped with vehicles that were to be supplied ideally by the Germans since the Italian AB armoured vehicles were still under production and large numbers of trucks could only have been made available if stripped from the *Armata del Po'*. On one hand, the trucks that Graziani requested were being rerouted to Greece at the expense of North Africa. On the other, the Germans had seized a large number of Panhard 178 from the French Army but were not willing to put this equipment under the disposal of the Italians. The only offer on the table by the German High Command was to dispatch an armoured division as a way to gain a foothold in North Africa as well as to maintain control of their armoured equipment.. With no additional equipment coming from Germany because of the Italian refusal to also accept the presence of German soldiers in North African soil, Graziani was forced to make the best of the situation in light of the equipment that was already in North Africa. As historian Pignato asserts "the short lived special armoured brigade will originate from this fatal decision, a unit that would be destroyed in just a few weeks of fighting."[37] Inexperience of combat methods associated with armoured warfare together with the lack of proper anti-tank weapons and heavy tanks would indeed prove fatal during Operation Compass. But at the origin of this debacle was, as Pignato points out, the decision not to seek German armoured support at a time when such support could have been vital.

During November 1940, historian Giovanni Cecini argues that Graziani in vain wrote several letters to General Roatta demanding more equipment, but his demands were largely rebuffed as the Greek campaign had taken centerstage. In his replies Roatta stated that the tanks and trucks under production were to be rerouted to Greece to prop up the Italian position there. Roatta advised Graziani to be patient.[38] In anticipation of the next offensive sally, Graziani not only continued to

---

34 Ibid
35 Ibid.
36 Ibid
37 Ibid.
38 Giovanni Cecini, 'Sciabole e veleni. Intrighi del Regio Esercito nel carteggio segreto Roatta-Graziani (luglio-agosto 1940)', *Bollettino dell'Ufficio Storico 2018*, USSME, Roma 2019, pp. 43-98.

demand that more medium tanks and armoured vehicles be shipped to North Africa but he also continued the process of assembling under one brigade all available motorized and mechanized forces in Libya often by stripping other units of their transport resources. The plan entailed training both the crews of the L.3 and the medium tanks to operate in a more cohesive fashion, improve the firepower of the L.3 tanks by mounting 20mm and 47m guns to replace the machine guns, repair the M.11/39 tanks that had broken down during the advance toward Sidi Barrani, create a centralized mobile organization to recover tanks stranded in the field of battle and assemble the few M.13/40 tanks that had just been shipped to North Africa under the new brigade. This was a tall order especially because it was a run against time. The special unit was officially constituted on 6 November 1940. It was a month later named *Brigata Corazzata Speciale "Babini"*, (Babini's special armoured brigade) taking the name from its commander *Generale* Valentino Babini (who had already commanded the *Comando Carri Armati della Libia* and had then succeeded *Generale* Miele in December) and it assembled under its command all the equipment previously attached to the *Comando Carri Armati della Libia*.

The unit was based on two *raggruppamenti*, each comprised of one medium and three light tank battalions. These were the original two units of the *Comando Carri Armati della Libia* that had spearheaded the advance to Sidi Barrani. It also was reinforced with the initial thirty-seven medium M.13/40 tanks that belonged to the *32° Reggimento Fanteria Carristi* of the *Ariete* Division which had been shipped to North Africa in late October and early November 1940, while the light tanks were those that had been assigned to Libya since the start of the war. Several M.11/39 tanks were also incorporated into the brigade mostly from the earlier tank formation, although many of them were under repair in workshops in Tripolitania. Then in late November the V *Battaglione Carri Medi*, bringing from Italy an additional undefined number of medium tanks M.13/40, also arrived to be merged into Babini's unit. Its standard medium tank battalion was to be comprised of one medium tank in the battalion headquarters and two tank companies with approximately sixteen tanks each. In addition, the unit also had an infantry regiment (*10° Reggimento Bersaglieri*) of three *Bersaglieri* battalions, a motorcycle battalion, an artillery regiment (with units and equipment coming from several artillery regiments such as I *Gruppo* da 75/27 from *12° Reggimento artiglieria*), two anti-tank gun companies, an engineer company and various supply units.

Its main armoured units included:

1° Raggruppamento carri (*Colonnello* Pietro Aresca)
I Battaglione Carri Medi with medium tanks.
XXI Battaglione carri L.3/35.
LXII Battaglione carri L.3/35.
LXIII Battaglione carri L.3/35.

2° Raggruppamento carri (*Colonnello* Antonio Trivioli)
II Battaglione Carri Medi with medium tanks.
IX Battaglione carri L.3/35.
XX Battaglione carri L.3/35.
LXI Battaglione carri L.3/35.[39]

---

39 VI *Battaglione Carri Medi* arrived in early February 1941 to bolster Babini's unit with twenty-four M.13/40 tanks. The unit was destroyed at Beda Fomm.

But despite Graziani's order Babini's unit initially remained "more an administrative unit than a combat unit."[40] Many of its ranks were inexperienced and some of the equipment was obsolete. Most importantly, Babini's unit lacked key elements of an advanced armoured brigade such as a command company comprised of experienced senior officers, a reconnaissance company with modern mechanized and motorized equipment and a fully motorized infantry regiment and some mobile anti-tank guns that could be effective against large to medium sized infantry enemy tanks such as the Matilda II.

Both the training and the repair work of Babini's special unit was begun only after considerable delay. A memorandum written on 2 December by General Miele, who had been nominated on 8 November as commander of the newly constituted mechanized brigade before Babini's arrival, communicated to Graziani that "training will commence on 5 December for the armoured units."[41] Thus, two months had passed since the conquest of Sidi Barrani and the training for the newly formed armoured unit had not even commenced.

Another letter dated 4 December written by Graziani to *Generale* Roatta lamented the poor state of several M.11/39 tanks that were reputed to be "too fragile and prone to malfunction," and urged the latter to dispatch a groups of qualified Ansaldo mechanics to repair them.[42] It is unclear from the documentation whether these mechanics arrived at all in North Africa.[43] The British counteroffensive would start before these M.11/39 tanks were put back into service and up to 30-35 of them could only be fielded in Bardia in a dug in, non-mobile artillery mode. In addition, in December Graziani had received fresh intelligence on enemy tank strength which advised to hold off the offensive until Italian tank strength was improved. SIM warned of a major enemy buildup. This strengthening of the British position in Egypt was obviously taking place but the intelligence reports were not accurate by vastly overestimating enemy strength. In addition to the delays in training the troops, Graziani had another problem which was related to the low degree of motorization of his infantry. Between September and December 1940 Graziani received a total of 329 light vehicles, 1,589 trucks, 502 motorcycles, 73 tractors and 57 medium tanks.[44] If we add to this tally of approximately 2,500 vehicles that were deemed operational and already in North Africa in the beginning of September 1940 three important considerations emerge. First there were not enough numbers of standard transports such as Dovunque trucks which had a carrying capacity of twenty soldiers to motorize an infantry regiment. As a result, the majority of Graziani's infantry was not motorized and the majority of units would be forced to travel again on foot during the next offensive. Similarly to the advance to Sidi Barrani this second offensive would be conducted in very challenging circumstances such as the very hot and dry weather. This also meant that from a defensive standpoint Graziani's troops could not parry the blow as best as they could because if faced by a British attack against the line with limited motor transport they could not shift large amounts of troops from one strongpoint to another. Second, the Greek campaign siphoned a tank battalion (IV *Battaglione Carri Medi*)

---

40   Jack Greene and Alessandro Massignani, *Rommel's North African Campaign*, p. 85.
41   Ufficio Storico, Generale Miele, Promemoria per il Comandante Superiore, 2 December 1940, A.C.S., Carte Graziani, b. 60.
42   Nicola Pignato,'Prime esperienze di guerra corazzata in Africa settentrionale', p. 120.
43   Ibid., p. 121.
44   James J. Sadkovich, 'The Italo-Greek War in Context: Italian Priorities and Axis Diplomacy', *Journal of Contemporary History*, vol. 28, n.3, July 1, 1993, p. 457.

of approximately fifty medium tanks that was originally earmarked for North Africa along with a vast number of vehicles and special infantry units. Graziani was thus forced to plan his next leap forward with the troops that he had as of November 1940 as the Greek theater took center stage as far as the Italian government was concerned. This decision had implications on the number of lorrie-borne infantry that Graziani could deploy as well as on the number of medium tanks. Third, the delay in developing the P tank on the part of Fiat and Ansaldo would be detrimental to Graziani's army during Operation Compass when facing the British infantry tanks. Graziani would be forced to face the enemy counter with light and medium tanks thus putting him at a considerable disadvantage. In mid-December, relying on SIM over blown estimates of enemy strength, he again requested trucks, tractors, an armoured brigade and at least one motorized division. He also demanded more artillery units to unleash "an imposing mass of fire."[45] But his call went to no avail as the Greek/Albanian front absorbed the majority of Italian reinforcements. Instead of the organizational and training delays experienced by the Italians, the Commonwealth had not played for time and decided to strike by surprise and early against their opponents.

Operation Compass

When Operation Compass commenced, the opposing forces were somewhat evenly matched with regard to their medium armoured strength, while the British units could also field heavy infantry tanks. The British had sixty armoured vehicles, 145 Vickers Mark VI light tanks, equipped with .5inch or .303inch machine guns, eighty medium Cruiser tanks and fifty-five infantry tanks (Matilda II) from the 7th Battalion Royal Tank Regiment. The latter were the only tanks that were impervious to the standard Italian anti-tank weapons such as the 20mm Solothurn rifle and the 47mm gun. Thus, they would achieve against the poorly equipped Italian infantry anti-gun units "an enormous shock, being virtually impregnable."[46]

Even though the British 7th Armoured Division was not at full strength in late 1940 it was better organized and equipped than Babini's tank brigade. Its armoured force was comprised of three types of vehicles:

1. Light tanks that were lightly armoured and equipped with machine-guns. These were used primarily for reconnaissance or to be deployed against the infantry.
2. Medium tanks (Cruiser) armed with a gun and machine-guns that were suited for tank versus tank combat.
3. Heavy tanks that were heavily armoured hence were slower but armed with a gun and machine-guns. These were intended to be used in support of the infantry and specifically to take on machine gun and artillery strongpoints and barrel through infantry defenses.

While the Cruiser tank force matched up well with Babini's medium tank force, the British armoured units had better reconnaissance support and could count upon the detachment of the

---

45 John Gooch, *Mussolini's War*, p. 159.
46 Jon Latimer, *Operation Compass 1940* (Oxford: Osprey, 2000), p. 23.

Matilda II heavy tanks that the Italians lacked. Most importantly, the 7th Armoured Division had trained extensively. Wavell stated a few days before the launch of the offensive that "we are more highly trained … we know the ground and better accustomed to desert conditions."[47] Wavell's length of service in North Africa epitomized how better prepared the Commonwealth troops were to the Italians. Wavell had been nominated to his command post of General Officer Commanding-in-Chief of Middle East Command in July 1939, while Graziani was thrusted into North Africa after Balbo's death and expected to lead an offensive shortly thereafter. For the Commonwealth troops training was conducted in repeated rehearsed assaults against a full-scale model of the standard Italian camp on the Sidi Barrani line. In addition, a plan for the placement of forward fuel and ammunition supply dumps was put in place to facilitate the movement forward of motorized infantry and tanks.

The X Army by December 1940 could count upon approximately thirty-seven M.11/39 tanks[48], fifty-seven M.13/40 tanks and seventy L.3 tanks that had been retro-fitted with the 20mm Solothurn rifle. Thus, even though the Matilda tanks were impervious to anti-tank fire and were more than a match to the M. 13/40 tanks in terms of durability and firepower, the Italian armoured brigade was slightly larger than the British Crusier force and if the M.11/39 was not considered to be a good match, the M.13/40 tank could fairly match up to the turret mounted gun of the Cruiser tank. In addition, by early December additional medium tanks were in transit from Italy to North Africa to augment the strength of Babini's brigade.

Babini's unit major problems were an almost complete lack of training, lack of radios inside the tanks and the poor serviceability of many older tanks that lacked spare parts or had not been retrofitted in time with more powerful guns. Many of these problems could have been addressed after the capture of Sidi Barrani if only the leadership of the Army in North Africa had shown more initiative, urgency and drive. His other major weaknesses was the lack of heavy tanks and of proper reconnaissance vehicles.

The British forces had a clear advantage in artillery. Field artillery was equipped with the excellent, long range 25-pdr gun, the 4.5in. (114mm) and 6in. (150mm) medium artillery pieces, along with approximately 200 2-pdr anti-tank guns. In contrast, the Italians, who had a total of 2,301 guns, had nothing comparable to the 25-pdr and their medium guns were for the part obsolescent and residuals from the First World War.

This above data has to be placed in relation to the two army corps deployed in North Africa with the X Army Corps being split into two groups with one closer to the frontier in Cyrenaica and comprised of 45,000 troops and approximately twenty-two medium tanks, and up to thirty working light tanks. This force had to self-sustain itself in case of an enemy operation because it was unlikely that the bulk of the X Army could come to its aid in a speedy manner given that it was deployed in Tripolitania or on the western section of Cyrenaica. As Kenneth Macksey asserts the Italians although more numerous were less mobile and overall possessed tanks that were of an inferior quality: "Yet to begin with, there was little in the way of tank-versus-tank action, chiefly because the Italian Tenth Army in Cyrenaica was equipped with 200 of the L.3 carriers, (which had been so outclassed in Spain) reinforced by 60 extremely poor 11-ton 37mm

---

47 Neal Dando, *From Tobruk to Tunis* (Solihull: Helion and Co., 2016), p. 53.
48 The M.11/39 tank force was comprised of 22 tanks with the Maletti combat group, 32 in Bardia that were not operational and an unknown limited number (15 or less) of operational tanks that were with Babini's combat group.

self-propelled M.11/39 guns, neither of which were a match for the Cruiser tanks of British Western Desert Force under Lieut.-Gen. Richard O'Connor."[49]

The Commonwealth forces that counter-attacked with Operation Compass had multiple aims. First, the 4th Indian Division and 7th Royal Tank .Regiment units would pass through the Nibeiwa—Rabia gap on the main defensive line and then concentrate their forces on attacking the Nibeiwa camp, where the Italians held several tanks. If the attack was successful the second phase entailed a thrust towards Sidi Barrani, while the 7th Armoured Division along with the 6th Australian Infantry Division would be ordered to exploit the gap and advance against the Italian rear. As Greene and Massignani assert "General O'Connor organized an assault on the Italians, built around the Matilda II tank, which would bring about a brilliant victory."[50] In fact, the heavy infantry tank would not be deployed primarily in the few tank versus tank battles of the campaign but primarily in overcoming Italian defensive strongpoints in a way similar to the battle of Arras in France when German infantry forces were forced to retreat under the pressure of the heavy infantry tanks.[51] While the Matilda II tanks were to accompany the infantry and attack the Italian fortified positions, highly mobile teams comprised of tanks, mobile artillery, reconnaissance units and motorized infantry were set to outflank the Italian positions and envelop them with their great mobility.

Presumably, the Italian intelligence services were not aware or failed to warn the North African High Command of the presence in North Africa of the Matilda II tank, while the Germans, who had faced them in France at Arras failed to warn their ally in time. Thus, a major intelligence blunder that could have possibly been avoided greatly aided the Commonwealth offensive.

Prior to the assault of 7 December the RAF began to bomb Italian frontline positions, airfields and supply depots, while the infantry and armoured units began to move forward. A few days later the infantry tanks of 7th Royal Tank Regiment raided Nibeiwa Camp, where a unit of twenty-four M.11/39[52] tanks had set up camp during the night. The attack was swift and took the Italians by complete surprise as the British armour overran and shot up the camp while most of the Italians were still sleeping or were making their way into their vehicles. "The crews were surprised before they could mount up and in no time, the Matildas were into the camp."[53]

All the medium tanks were destroyed or captured and the soldiers able to survive the onslaught were captured. The commander of the unit, *Generale* Maletti, was also killed during the raid as he was shot while firing a machine gun. According to the British official history:

---

49   Kenneth Macksey, *Tank Versus Tank*, p. 80.
50   Jack Greene and Alessandro Massignani, *Rommel's North African Campaign*, p. 30.
51   Niall Barr has observed, the 'Germans had also panicked when first confronted with the Matilda during the Arras counterattack in France.' Niall Barr, *The Pendulum of War* (London: Random House, 2010), p.45.
52   This battle appears to be the only one where the medium Italian tanks faced the Matilda II tanks. The latter were especially useful to the British in breaking through the infantry defenses. As Kenneth Macksey asserts:" The very few tank-versus-tank engagements inevitably ended with British victory since the Matilda's 40mm gun could penetrate the M.11/39's 29mm armour at any range while the M.11/39's 37mm gun made no impression on the 80mm armour." Kenneth Macksey, *Beda Fomm*, p. 32.
53   Ibid, p. 33.

At 7.15 a.m. 72 guns opened with concentrations on selected targets and at that moment two squadrons of 7th R.T.R. supported by 31st Field Battery R.A. bore down upon the north-west corner of the perimeter. On the flanks of the 'I' tanks were the Bren carrier platoons of 2nd Battalion The Queen's Own Cameron Highlanders and 1/6th Rajputana Rifles, firing as they advanced. Outside the camp were about twenty medium and a few light Italian tanks, unready for action; these were quickly overrun. Not until the 'I' tanks entered the camp were they opposed or obstructed at all; but immediately afterwards the Italians opened artillery and machine-gun fire, and a few gallant but useless attempts were made to check the 'I' tanks with grenades. At 7.45 a.m. the Cameron Highlanders, who had moved up in lorries to little more than half a mile away, were ordered to advance, followed by the Rajputana Rifles. Tanks and infantry now quartered the camp methodically, helped by a section of 31st Field Battery R.A. firing at point blank range at a few stubborn and isolated centres. By 10.40 a.m. all was over. General Maletti had been killed, and some 2,000 prisoners taken. Large quantities of supplies and water were found intact. British casualties were eight officers and forty-eight men.[54]

That same day (9 December) a number of British Cruiser tanks also lunged against the Alam el Tummar strongpoint which was defended by infantry and IX *Battaglione*'s light tanks. The latter fought bravely but in vain as one by one its armoured vehicles were shot up leading to the British capture of the position on the 10th.

The larger base at Sidi Barrani was attacked on 10 December by an infantry Brigade supported by Matildas. Once again, the strongpoints were overrun by the heavy infantry tanks followed by the infantry which dealt with the smaller infantry outposts. The Italian anti-tank guns could only damage but not stop the heavy infantry tanks and since the guns had no protective shield the gunners of the 47mm units suffered huge losses. Other Italian positions were similarly methodically overrun during the month of December with the heavy infantry tanks playing the predominant role to the point that the entire defensive line ultimately collapsed leading the Commonwealth forces to take other important fortifications such as Bardia (5 January) and Tobruk (22 January). The capture of Tobruk, for example, again highlighted the importance of the British heavy infantry tanks. As John Gooch asserts: "At 540 am on 21 January the attack began. Helped by a wind which raised clouds of dust and blinded the defenders, Australian troops accompanied by heavy Matilda tanks quickly broke through the weak defensive ring. Poorly coordinated, blinded by the sand and with only 110 anti-tank guns, not all of which had perforating munitions, the Italian artillery was unable to protect the strongpoints."[55] Thus what had started as a raid against frontline Italian positions had by then become a major offensive with the Commonwealth forces penetrating deeply into Cyrenaica. Despite the numerical superiority of its infantry, the Italian Blackshirts and standard Royal Army units could do little to stop a smaller but highly mobile armoured and motorized formation hitting their strongpoints from the flanks. The Italian units could not counter the British tanks and mobile artillery units because they could not buttress individual defenses lacking the means to move units into

---

54   I.S.O. Playfair, *Mediterranean and Middle East, Volume 1: The Early Successes Against Italy, to May 1941*, p. 268.
55   John Gooch, *Mussolini's War*, p.172.

troubled spots and also because their lighter tanks could not go head to head with the British heavy infantry tanks.

The second encounter battle between British and Italian armoured units during Wavell's offensive took place at El Mechili on 24 January 1941. By that time the 6th Australian Division troops had advanced deeply into Cyrenaica but had been halted at Derna. Babini's unit was positioned near Derna, at El Mechili, when Italian intelligence had found out by radio intercept that the 4th Armoured Brigade had advanced deeply into Italian held territory with the aim of striking Babini's *Brigata Corazzata Speciale*. On 17 January 1941, this armoured brigade had the following strength: 138 officers, 2,200 soldiers, eight 75mm guns, eight 100mm guns, eight 47mm guns and sixteen 20mm anti-aircraft guns. Fifty-Seven M.13/40 tanks, twenty-five L.3 tanks, six armoured cars, over 200 trucks and 180 motorcycles. Based on the intelligence information gathered Babini's unit was to set up an ambush aimed to surprise and overwhelm the enemy. Initially the British put forth probing attacks by light tanks that were easily repulsed by the Italian units with their guns which knocked out six enemy tanks. Then it was the Italians turn to counter the British and as the M tanks closed in against their opponents they destroyed two Cruiser tanks and damaged four. Initially on the losing end of the confrontation, the British were forced to dispatch more Cruiser tanks into battle. These charged against the Italian tanks firing their guns and knocked out of action seven M.13/40 tanks, three of which were later recovered. By 1300 the battle ended abruptly as both sides disengaged.

The accounts of the two sides diverge when dealing with the losses at El Mechili. The Italian sources claim ten British tanks destroyed against seven Italian vehicles, while British sources indicate the loss of one Cruiser and six light tanks lost in the face of eight destroyed Italian medium tanks.[56] On the same evening, there was an additional clash between Italian tanks and 11th Hussars, at Bir Semander, where the latter lost eight armoured vehicles. But even regarding this battle encounter, the sources diverge. The Italian sources claim the battle happened at approximately 1800, while the 11th Hussars own diary does not report any losses. At any rate, the *Brigata* had repulsed a major British armoured attack, but it failed in very favorable circumstances to pursue the retreating British tanks due to the lack of resources and reserves. The main factor holding it back, however, was a failure to properly reconnaissance the enemy's true tank strength and as a result Babini's force was held back by Graziani's staff because the British forces were incorrectly reputed by his intelligence service to consist of 150 or more tanks. The British unit having suffered some losses and also experiencing breakdowns during the advance was much less consistent than what was estimated by the Italians which could have pounced upon it but instead deliberately allowed the unit to get away with no further losses.

Despite Babini's rearguard action at El Mechili, the rapid British advance during Operation Compass continued forcing the Italian X Army to initially retreat and later to evacuate Cyrenaica altogether. The first tactical error committed by the Italian command during this phase of the counteroffensive was to order the armoured brigade to evacuate El Mechili, which was a strong, funnel like position from which it was possible to attempt to check the enemy advance. The second mistake was to split up the armoured brigade into two main components, one to assist the

---

56 'The same day a large force of the enemy, including about fifty medium tanks, was encountered by 4th Armoured Brigade to the north of Mechili. A tank v. tank fight ensued, in which the enemy lost eight medium tanks destroyed and one captured; the British losses were one cruiser and six light tanks.' I.S.O. Playfair, *Mediterranean and Middle East, Volume 1: The Early Successes Against Italy, to May 1941*, p. 353.

rearguard of the retreating Italian column and the other at the head of the column. As the Italian column was retreating it was bogged down by the foot soldiers with their slow pace, prompting the British commander to devise a plan to cut them off along the Via Balbia. Accordingly, the 7th Armoured Division was to drive at the Italians from the desert, while the 6th Australian Division was to advance along the main coastal road. On 5 February 1941, the British ambushed the Italians by encircling them and reaching the location of Beda Fomm ahead of the main Italian contingent. Here the fighting became very intense as the Italians attempted to break out of the encirclement, while the British took up position on a ridge with their machine guns and artillery. On the first day of battle the British forces managed to capture several Italian soldiers from the *Bersaglieri* units who had tried in vain to attack the ridge position and breakthrough but without the help of the armoured units. On the 6th the Italians attempted to organize another break out of the encirclement by utilizing their armoured unit. Unfortunately, the *Brigata Corazzata Speciale* had been split into two groups; a first group of thirty M.13/40 tanks had been held back to protect the rear of the Italian column at Benghazi, while the second group at Beda Fomm could count upon twenty-five medium tanks. By this time the brigade had received additional reinforcements from Italy such as VI *Battaglione Carri Medi* and the XXI *Battaglione Carri*, that was already in Libya but was equipped with a few medium tanks. The brigade's sparse force of medium tanks was sent into combat in a piecemeal fashion such as five or ten machines at the time to break through the British machine gun, mortar and anti-tank screen. But such a penny-pinching use of tanks only facilitated the work of the British artillery cordon, which led by the 25-pdr guns inflicted large casualties upon the Italian armour. Despite mounting losses, the Italian tanks persisted in attacking in a disjointed, piecemeal fashion for most of the day. By attacking in this way, the 25-pdr guns had all the time in the world to pick them out and put them out of action. As the tanks came in proximity of the British lines, they were one by one shot at by the British heavy guns and tanks which had a further range.

On the 7th there were only about fifteen Italian medium tanks that were still operational. Some were heavily targeted and damaged once again when they met the British guns and the tanks, while others ran out of fuel and had to be abandoned. These units were later recovered and used by the Commonwealth. In the final desperate cavalry like charge to escape the encirclement only four medium tanks successfully broke through the enemy defenses along with several motorized units of *Bersaglieri* and reached the safety of the rear. The bulk of the infantry however did not escape the Commonwealth trap. The following passage is the British account of the fighting:

> At daybreak on February 7th the enemy made a final determined attempt to escape, when thirty tanks heading a column of lorries advanced straight down the road. The tanks broke through the forward companies of the Rifle Brigade, and so tense was the moment that the officer commanding C Battery R.H.A. asked for, and received, permission to engage targets in the areas occupied by the infantry. The anti-tank guns, which now numbered eleven, gradually knocked out the advancing tanks, the last one being stopped a stone's throw from the Officers' Mess.[57]

---

57   I.S.O. Playfair, *Mediterranean and Middle East, Volume 1: The Early Successes Against Italy, to May 1941*, p. 353.

As Nicola Pignato asserts, "the British defeated nearly all Italian tank units, which were scattered among the infantry instead of concentrated into a dedicated armoured force."[58] If more medium tanks had been dispatched in time to North Africa and if the tanks had been properly concentrated along with the guns, instead of their piecemeal deployment, the result might have been different. However, nothing should be taken away for the bold British armoured drive whereby British tanks had covered over 1,000 miles in a prolonged armoured maneuver to outflank the Italian infantry.

The result of Operation Compass was the destruction of Italian medium tank strength in North Africa along with the loss of many units from the non-motorized infantry divisions. The Italians had also lost some of their most important positions in Cyrenaica such as Fort Capuzzo, Tobruk and Benghazi. The main culprits for this debacle were both Pietro Badoglio and Graziani, who lacked experience in commanding and deploying tank forces, and had obviously not been able to launch a successful maneuver offensive by armoured forces in a timely manner. The delays in training the armoured units, in shaping them into a viable cohesive combat unit and in equipping the light tanks with more powerful weapons were some of their major responsibilities. Another initiative which was not taken in time by the Army in North Africa was the consolidation of all available towing equipment, armour and motorized assets of all kind into the *Brigata Corazzata Speciale* in preparation for the offensive. Graziani was not responsible for receiving troops that were not fully trained for armoured warfare from Italy nor can he be held responsible for the failure of *Comando Supremo* to dispatch early on to North Africa a trained and equipped mechanized, armoured formation, but shares some of the blame in the slow speed with which the *Brigata Corazzata Speciale* came together as a fighting unit. In contrast, it is largely still unexplainable (and not Graziani's fault) why senior top officers back in Italy such as Badoglio did not deploy from the onset of the campaign the more experienced armoured divisions that could have better accounted themselves than Babini's hastily assembled brigade. Babini was an experienced armoured commander, but he lacked equally experienced officers, ncos and armoured personnel and most of all heavier tanks and mobile anti-tank guns. British tank tactics had been more flexible and adaptable to the terrain. Most tank crews opened fire when they were sure of their targets. While advancing at full speed against the enemy tanks, they would get within shooting range and then halt temporarily and fire. This would allow them to score more direct hits from a stationary position. In contrast, as it appears from the soldiers' recollections, some of the Italian tank crews were firing from moving tanks which made their shooting less accurate. Artillery commanders also were responsible for failing to deploy some of their anti-aircraft guns in an anti-tank mode which could have stopped the Matildas even though they were not equipped with armoured piercing shells, while the intelligence services also failed having little or no knowledge of the presence of the heavy infantry tanks and thus allowing them to become game changers during the offensive. Graziani and Badoglio's failures were compounded by the serious deficiency in training and tactical doctrine that characterized Italian tank formations in 1939-40, especially the units dispatched to North Africa. According to a British intelligence report the Italians had failed to properly incorporate a modern motorized or mechanized tactical disposition so that the armour could cooperate well with the infantry. Infantry tactics in particular had shown little mobility: "The principal characteristic of Italian

---

58 Nicola Pignato, *Italian Armoured Vehicles*, p. 21.

tactics in both theaters Libya and East Africa, has been rigidity. They have remained attached to one principle, the concentration of the greatest possible mass for every task that faces them. In the attack, they deploy this mass in line and rely solely on weight on numbers to clear the way."[59] The British official history also makes the same point: "It was, of course, true in general that in the desert the army with the superior mobile troops possessed the means of turning the enemy's flank, and whereas the British had an organized armoured formation the Italians had not; they habitually used their tanks in penny packets." [60]

Mobile warfare had clearly been an impediment to the Italian troops, but so was the defensive, more static aspect of the campaign. During the First World War the Italian infantry had performed well in this role, but in North Africa it suffered tremendously especially against the British heavy infantry tanks. In the desert, non-motorized infantry was capable only of a static defense and was also poorly equipped.

Rommel Arrives

Operation Compass had been a heavy loss for the Italian mechanized force in North Africa which had been wiped out almost completely. In addition, Wavell's forces advanced 500 miles into Italian held territory and captured 100,000 Italian soldiers, 180 tanks and 845 guns while suffering only 2,000 casualties. The destruction of the Italian X Army forced *Comando Supremo* to transfer almost immediately to North Africa the bulk of the *Ariete* mechanized division along with the *Trento* motorized infantry division. This was done in concurrence with stabilizing the front lines in Tripolitania, by building a defense belt around Tripoli and constructing new defensive positions. *Comando Supremo* this time also sought German assistance by requesting more than 800 captured French tanks (both Renault R-35 medium tanks and heavier Somua S-35 tanks). In the view of *Comando Supremo* these French tanks were to form the backbone of a newly formed armoured division. After extensive negotiations, the Germans supplied only 109 Renault R-35 tanks and thirty-five Somua S-35 tanks. Although the initial thought had been to form a tank brigade with these French tanks to be dispatched to North Africa, the final decision was to retain these tanks in Italy and form a local defense brigade. The French tanks were mechanically sound and their firepower was greater than many Italian tanks, but spare parts and ammunition were in short supply. Hence the decision not to send them to Africa in a terrain of combat where the armour was expected to travel for long distances. The Italians also requested more direct German support. Indeed, the defeat had also led the German Army to transfer an initial force to North Africa to prop up the Italian ally. Hitler's operational order, issued on 11 January 1941 as Directive No. 22, reflected a defensive mindset: "The situation in the Mediterranean makes it necessary to provide German assistance, on strategic, political, and psychological grounds. Tripolitania must be held."[61] The *Deutsches Afrikakorps* (DAK), under *Generalleutnant* Erwin Rommel, equipped with tanks and armoured vehicles was meant to

---

59   Allan R. Millett, Williamson Murray (eds.,) *Military Effectiveness: Volume 3, The Second World War*, p. 162.
60   I.S.O. Playfair, *Mediterranean and Middle East, Volume 1: The Early Successes Against Italy, to May 1941*, p. 364.
61   Ibid.

provide some of the fire and the movement that the static Italian infantry lacked. Their mission was a purely defensive one to help safeguard Tripolitania and then conduct limited counterattacks to take back Cyrenaica. The German troops were experienced in armoured warfare, made extensive use of the numerous mobile anti-tank guns at their disposal in forward positions to debilitate enemy armour (a tactic that early 1941 was not well known to the British or to the Italians, had excellent communication systems allowing commanders to truly guide their troops in the heat of war and lastly had first rate reconnaissance units even aerial reconnaissance.

When Rommel reached Tripoli, he was not well known but he was already a senior officer of the German Army who had distinguished himself during the campaign against France and had experience in commanding armoured units. Rommel and his troops were initially subordinate to Italian commander-in-chief General Italo Gariboldi, who had replaced Graziani after the Operation Compass debacle. When, the newly appointed commander of the German units landed in Tripoli one of the first things he observed was the poor state of the Italian equipment which in his view was particularly deficient in heavy artillery and armour: "Perhaps the best example of the inferior quality of the Italian armament apart from the grave technical defects of their tanks," he wrote, "with their short-range guns and underpowered engines, was to be found in the artillery, with its low mobility and short range."[62]

Rommel's first impressions were also that the Italian Army was better disposed toward a defensive war rather than a war of movement that was more appropriate in the North African theater:

> The Italian soldier is disciplined, sober, an excellent worker and an example to the Germans in preparing dug-in positions. If attacked, he reacts well. He lacks, however, a spirit of attack, and above all, proper training. Many operations failed solely because of a lack of coordination between artillery and heavy arms fire and the advance of the infantry. The lack of adequate means of supply and service and the insufficient number of motor vehicles and tanks is such that during some movements Italian sections arrived at their posts incomplete. Lack of means of transport and service in Italian units is such that especially in the bigger units, they cannot be maintained as a reserve and one cannot count on their quick intervention.[63]

His big challenge was now to mold this force into a more mobile army capable of keeping up with the faster moving and better coordinated German units. Meanwhile, as previously mentioned, *Comando Supremo*, had already decided by then to field to North Africa the mechanized and motorized assets that had not been made available to Graziani. In addition, additional artillery units were also to be dispatched to North Africa to enhance the army's anti-tank fight and this last decision would also have an important influence upon the campaign. These initiatives along with the overstretched and tenuous British hold on Cyrenaica, whose troops were now positioned on far away strongholds from their supply bases in Egypt, would place Rommel in a much better condition than Graziani and enable him to attack the British at a very favorable time.

---

62 Basil Liddell Hart, *The Rommel Papers*, p. 101.
63 Ibid.

The first formation to arrive was the 7,200 soldiers strong *Ariete* Division which landed in Tripoli on 24 January 1941 even though it initially lacked medium tanks. Its main armoured combat element initially was its *32° Reggimento Carristi* that had ninety-three L.3/35 tankettes and 24 × L.3/Lf (flamethrower units). It also disembarked, according to Italian High Command documents, with fourteen 47/32 guns, twenty-four 75/27 guns, sixteen 20mm guns, 716 trucks, and 542 motorcycles.[64] Meanwhile German estimates of *Ariete*'s strength at the time diverged widely from the numbers furnished by the Italian High Command. According to a German intelligence report *Ariete* had disembarked with only 3,500 soldiers, 900 trucks, 63 anti-tank rifles, 254 machine guns, twenty-six 37mm guns, six 81mm mortars, eight 47/32 guns, eight 20mm guns, thirty-six artillery pieces, and 134 tanks.[65]

Within a short time, on 7 March, *Ariete* began to conduct its first operation of the campaign when it was asked to monitor frontline positions in the Agedabia area. A few days later, 11 March, other elements of *Ariete* arrived in Tripoli when *VII Battaglione Carri Medi* (7th Medium Tanks Battalion) offloaded forty-six medium M.13/40 tanks, 21 officers, 51 NCOs, 296 soldiers, six cars, six *Dovunque* trucks, six large transporters, forty-six tank transporters, and ten motorcycles. *Ariete* was commanded by *Generale di Divisione* Ettore Baldassarre who came from the artillery branch. In the 1920s Baldassarre had written the artillery's arm main technical instructions manuals "*Istruzioni di Artiglieria*" which served to train artillery officers in the 1920-30 period. Subsequently, he was given command of an artillery army corps and in 1940 he was nominated as the commander of the *Ariete* Division. Meanwhile the Germans had also moved troops into North Africa by dispatching the 5th *Leicht* Panzer Division with 9,300 soldiers, 55 light (Panzerkampfwagen I and II) and 130 medium (Panzerkampfwagen III or IV) tanks. In addition, twenty-seven armoured cars, and fifteen motorcycles for the reconnaissance battalion. Two Panzerjaeger battalions equipped with sixty-seven 37mm and 50mm anti-tank guns. Two machine gun battalions. One field artillery battalion and one anti-aircraft battalion, plus support services that were fully motorized.

Whilst the Germans dispatched a 'blocking force' meant to halt further British offensive sallies and help Italy maintain a position in North Africa, the Italian *Comando Supremo* had committed to the North African campaign its most effective armoured unit. In fact, while the *Brigata Corazzata Speciale Babini* was a hurriedly put together mechanized brigade, *Ariete* was a more balanced and better trained mechanized division that possessed tanks, mobile anti-tank guns and *Bersaglieri* units. In addition, Italy also committed the *Trento* (later the *Trieste* as well) motorized Division as well as other reinforcements and implemented the reorganization of the infantry divisions (*Brescia, Bologna, Savona,* and *Pavia*), that already had fought under Graziani.

Rommel's Counteroffensive

With the British command forced to halt the advance in North Africa and dispatch some of its troops to Greece to parry the Axis offensive in the Balkans, Rommel decided that an opportunity had opened to strike right away. At the time of Rommel's first counter offensive to reach

---

64 Nicola Pignato, *Gli autoveicoli da combattimento dell'esercito italiano*, vol. 2, p. 22.
65 Oberkommando des Heeres, en St D H, abt, Fremde Here West Nr. 960/39, das Italienische Krigsheer, Januar 1940, Militararchiv RHD 18/169.

the Egyptian frontier he had at his disposal appropriately 25,000 soldiers, 231 medium tanks, seventeen light tanks, twenty-seven armoured vehicles, seventy-two field guns and 220 antitank guns. Since initially the 5th Leicht possessed a limited number of field guns and *Ariete* had few medium tanks, Rommel decided not to deploy them as individual combat units but to form tactical groups by pooling diverse capabilities from different units to fill the weapon gaps. This explains why originally *Ariete* was split into several units that took the name of their commander such as the *Raggruppamento or Colonna Montemurro* and these were paired up with German units. With regard to the mixed combat groups the Australian Official History of the war states that: "The impetuous Rommel's purposeful organization of the German and Italian forces had been marked by an extreme degree of improvisation. New groupings and new commands were set up almost every day. Each of the major formations—the German 5th Light Division and the Italian Ariete and Brescia Divisions—was split into several independently operating groups."[66]

At the time and, despite dispatching some units to the Balkans, the Commonwealth still could count upon the 4th Division and the 7th Armoured division, one French infantry brigade, one British infantry division and several Australian infantry battalions. Despite this Commonwealth deployment Rommel had more effective tanks such as the *Panzerkampfwagen* III and IV which were considered superior to the British Cruiser tanks. Also, Rommel detained another considerable advantage which was comprised by the fact that the German armoured forces had displayed superior armoured tactics during the campaign against France. It was this armoured experience and technical know-how that Rommel would rely upon against the Commonwealth force.

The Axis counteroffensive began on 24 March 1941 when the 5th Leicht Division struck Commonwealth troops at El Agheila to then quickly advance on the Via Balbia capturing 800 enemy soldiers as they were retreating east. Rommel had divided his troops into several mixed (German and Italian) major columns. The 3rd Reconnaissance Battalion and the *Brescia* Infantry Division were to drive to the objective from the via Balbia. The right flank consisted of the motorized elements of the 5th Leicht, the Fabris motorized column from *Ariete* as well as the *Santamaria* Reconnaissance Group, while the center columns were led by the Ugo Montemurro's unit from *Ariete*, the 5th Panzer Regiment, and the 2nd Machine Gun Battalion. His basic plan "called for a triple converging movement on the huge enemy supply dump at Mechili."[67]

Rommel's advance was conducted at an extremely fast pace which prompted General Gariboldi, fearful of a repeat of a Commonwealth counter and of another Beda Fomm, on 2nd April to send Rommel a message: "From information I have received I deduce that your advance continues. This is contrary to my orders. I ask you to wait for me before continuing the advance."[68] The message forced Rommel to halt, but only for a short time. After he had halted the advance for a couple of hours, an aerial surveillance unit informed him that the enemy withdrawal was continuing at a fat pace thus forcing him into action again to exploit the favorable situation. On 3 April *Ariete* had its baptism of fire. At approximately 1230 Rommel went out to the forces of the *Ariete* Division that were stationed on the track from Agedabia to

---

66 Barton Maughan, *Australia in the War of 1939-1945 Vol. III: Tobruk and El Alamein* (Canberra: Australian War Memorial, 1987), p. 122.
67 Samuel Mitcham, *Triumphant Fox: Erwin Rommel and the Rise of the Afrika Corps* (New York: Stein and Day, 1984), p. 74.
68 Mario Montanari, *Le operazioni in Africa settentrionale*, Vol II, Part I, p. 81.

the Trigh el Abd and ordered one of its tactical groups to conduct an advanced reconnaissance to Ben Gania and then reach the main road leading to Msus. In the evening Rommel had dispatched the 3rd Reconnaissance Unit to advance along the coast road and upon learning that Benghazi had been evacuated he ordered the unit to press on toward the city. This it did, but it entered the town during the night preceded by *Colonna Fabris*, consisting of III *Battaglione Motociclisti/ 8° Battaglione Bersaglieri*, 142° *Compagnia Cannoni* da 47mm, 2nd Artillery battery of the 132° *Reggimento* with 75/32 guns, and a section of 20mm guns, which arrived first. This was a major propaganda coup since the unit along with platoons from the *Sabratha* Division arrived in Benghazi ahead of the German DAK units. As the Commonwealth tank forces were retreating many individual vehicles were lost due to lack of fuel and breakdown. Some were overpowered by the German motorized and mechanized units and captured. Given the disorganized state of the enemy forces, Rommel decided upon the capture of the whole of Cyrenaica in one fell swoop by advancing across the desert towards the British rear which stood at El Mechili. As a result, *Colonna* Fabris was ordered to continue to press on to El Mechili, as the advanced guard of the *Ariete* Division which was to follow as soon as possible by the same route. Another force, placed under the command of Lieut-Colonel von Schwerin, and backed by a stronger force comprising the headquarters of the 5th Leicht Division with a machine-gun battalion, an anti-tank company and a squadron of tanks was also ordered to converge on El Mechili. On the 5th, Rommel ordered some tanks of the 5th Armoured Regiment and forty tanks from *Ariete* to break away from the main column headed toward El Mechili and instead head for Msus, the vital enemy supply depot. This tactical group was placed under the command of Colonel Olbrich. The next day Msus was captured. As the British Official History asserts by 6 April: "The 3rd Armoured Brigade was no longer of any use as a fighting formation."[69] The British rear was also in considerable disarray as an Axis motorized unit captured the British Commander in Chief Cyrenaica, General Philip Neame and General Richard O'Connor, who had so valiantly led Commonwealth troops during Operation Compass. As the Commonwealth forces continued to pull back, it was decided that a large detachment would be left at El Mechili to act as a rearguard and check the Axis counteroffensive. The El Mechili position was held by General Gambier-Parry's 2nd Armoured Division headquarters, the 3rd Indian Motor Brigade, M Battery of the Royal Horse Artillery and a detachment of the 3rd Australian anti-tank Regiment. The purpose of this unit was to halt the advance of the Axis forces into Egypt, thus allowing the bulk of the Commonwealth units to retreat in an orderly fashion. Since the Commonwealth force lacked armour (the 22nd Armoured Division had still not reached El Mechili on the 7th of April) and was deficient in antitank weapons, Rommel ordered an attack by the Axis columns that were in hot pursuit of the retreating enemy forces near the Egyptian frontier. The attack began on 8 April and it culminated with an important success for the Axis forces. The operation was meticulously prepared by the Axis troops in the days preceding the attack as reconnaissance units were utilized to identify the location of enemy guns and clear several isolated enemy outposts.

On 6 April, the column led by *Colonnello* Fabris had already engaged advanced enemy elements near El Mechili. It was quickly followed by the column of *Colonnello* Montemurro's

---

69   I.S.O, Playfair, *The Mediterranean and the Middle East Volume 2: The Germans Come to the Help of their Ally (1941)* (London: Her Majesty's Stationary Office, 1966), pp. 23-24.

which was comprised by a Command Company, XII *Battaglione Bersaglieri*, the 72° *Compagnia Cannoni* da 47/32, 1st Artillery battery of 132° *Reggimento Artiglieria*, and a section of 20mm machine guns. This column had raced for over 350 miles in the desert to reach the Egyptian frontier. The following day (7 April), at 1500 Montemurro's unit finally reached El Mechili and surrounded the enemy positions.

The two *Ariete* units were also supported by Major Santamaria's column, an ad hoc mobile combat group that also took the name of its commander, and by two armoured units of the 5th Panzer Regiment. One of the German units, the Schwerin Group, was located north of the Commonwealth position, the *Fabris* column was positioned to the east, along with the *Santamaria* Reconnaissance Group, the German 5th Panzer Regiment Headquarter unit was to the west, while to the south the *Montemurro* column had also taken up position. At dawn on 8 April at 0400 behind a thunderous concentration laid down by Italian artillery, the motorized groups and the infantry moved forward. The enemy, sensing that it had been encircled, attempted to break out by dispatching platoons to probe several enemy positions in a bid to identify their weak points.

The first probe was broken up by the machine gun and artillery fire of the *III Battaglione Bersaglieri*, while the second probe was successfully fought off by the Schwerin group. The following break out attempt, aimed at breaching the south-east meeting point between the two *Bersaglieri* columns, was initially successful in overcoming several machine gun strongpoints. This deft maneuver allowed the Commonwealth infantry platoons to sally the rear positions of *Fabris* unit, but the prompt intervention of several batteries of 75/27 guns readily foiled the attempt promptly beating back the enemy's armoured vehicles.[70] *Montemurro*'s group was then given the order to advance and close in on the enemy. The troops advanced under the curtain of fire provided by the artillery units pinning down the enemy in its positions. Then the *Bersaglieri* emerged from their trucks and deployed around the enemy perimeter firing all their weapons such as the machine guns, mortars and light artillery. Under heavy fire and unable to escape to the north or west, the Commonwealth unit was forced to surrender.

> During the day, General Gambier-Parry was twice summoned to surrender and twice refused. He and Brigadier Vaughan agreed that the force must fight its way out. They decided to attempt this at dawn, when the going could be seen and some surprise might perhaps be hoped for. The advanced guard, Captain Barlow's squadron of the 18th Cavalry, successfully broke out and turned back to deal with some Italian guns which were firing on the main body of vehicles. Although in the confusion some units managed to get away, by now the enemy were thoroughly roused and General Gambier-Parry, Brigadier Vaughan, and most of the Indian Motor Brigade and Divisional Headquarters were taken prisoner.[71]

As Buckingham asserts: "The victory must have been especially sweet for the men of the Ariete Division, partly as recompense for past humiliations at British hands, and partly because it was an all-Italian triumph; Generalmajor Streich, Oberstleutnan Dr. Olbrich and Panzer Regiment

---

70   In this combat action *Maggiore* Giuseppe Romano, Commander I *Gruppo da* 75/27 would be posthumously awarded a gold medal of military valor.
71   I.S.O., Playfair, *The Mediterranean and the Middle East Volume 2: The Germans Come to the Help of their Ally (1941)*, p. 30.

5 arrived too late to take part in the action and Gambier-Parry actually surrendered to Colonna Montemurro."[72]

The Commonwealth suffered the loss of 1,200 soldiers that were captured and approximately 200 casualties. For his unit's key contribution, *Colonnello* Montemurro was decorated by Rommel with an Iron Cross Second Class. However, despite Montemurro's column main role in the fight, the DAK War Diary makes no mention of the Italian contribution: "At 08.00 hours 5th Panzer Regiment/5. Leicht Div. led by Major Bolbrinker (8 tanks) took Mechili. One English general, 60 officers, and about 1,700 men were captured, an immeasurable volume of booty consisting of vehicles, weapons, ammunition, and rations fell in our hands."[73]

In the words of British historian Niall Barr in its first campaign the DAK "had bundled the Western Desert Force out of Cyrenaica in a matter of days….." The British loss of Cyrenaica was due primarily to Rommel's audacity in mounting an attack with inadequate forces. Rommel "had torn up the orthodox military rule book and achieved an astonishing success precisely because of his boldness."[74] A boldness that had been supported by the Axis motorized and mechanized units which raced to the frontier for hundreds of miles in the desert to pursue the enemy. The operation was a top speed maneuver covering a huge area in less than two weeks. Rommel had seized the initiative after conducting reconnaissance, including aerial recon, of the enemy positions where he found an enemy in considerable disarray. Once Rommel decided to counter-attack he brilliantly led his troops in pursuit of the Commonwealth forces. His boldness and his tactics of maneuver warfare showed the more defensive minded Italian senior officers what a combined Axis mechanized and motorized force could achieve even by placing a huge strain on its supply lines and stretching to the limits its thin motorized resources. It's important to note that Rommel's victory had also been aided by Prime Minister Churchill's diversionary support of Greece which had weakened the Commonwealth force in North Africa. One area particularly impacted by Churchill's decision was the air campaign over the Mediterranean and North Africa: "The Royal Air Force had sent the best squadrons in the Middle East to support the operations in Greece, leaving the bombers and fighters of the Regia Aeronautica a free hand to harass the retreating British mercilessly."[75]

After the Axis forces had completed their first major operation, Rommel immediately requested that *Comando Supremo* send in reinforcements to enhance *Ariete*'s capabilities and align it to the standard German Panzer division. It's lack of aerial and land based reconnaissance capabilities, the need for bolstering its antitank and anti-aircraft defenses and the lack of communication and engineering functions were keenly felt. He urged the reinforcement of the antitank function with the addition of two batteries of 150mm guns, of the sapper and engineer units by bringing them up to the strength of a battalion while also requesting several reconnaissance airplanes. He also suggested that the North African command attach additional vehicles, artillery and support units to *Ariete* to enhance its firepower and mobility. General Gariboldi

---

72 William F. Buckingham, *Tobruk: The Great Siege* (London: Random House, 2010), p. 107.
73 DAK War Diary <https://rommelsriposte.com/2016/04/10/d-a-k-war-diary-entry-8-april-1941/> (accessed 12 May 2019).
74 Niall Barr, 'Rommel in the Western Desert' in Ian Beckett (ed.), *Rommel Reconsidered* (Mechanicsburg, Pennsylvania: Stackpole, 2013), p. 68.
75 Daniel Allen Butler, Field Marshal: *The Life and Death of Erwin Rommel* (New York: Casemate, 2015), p. 210.

was generally receptive to Rommel's suggestions and demand for more weapons but all he could do at the time was to substitute the light tanks with the medium tanks.[76] Unfortunately, Rommel's demands could not be satisfied in a timely manner given the scarcity of resources in the Italian Army. In fact, it would take another six months to fully rearm the *Ariete* Division as well as enhance its fighting capabilities. This inability by *Comando Supremo* to satisfy Rommel's demands created a second friction point between the former and the Italian High Command in North Africa. By mid-April General Gariboldi had already warned Rommel of not advancing too fast against the enemy since the Italian command could not guarantee supplies nor the requested reinforcements. The German High Command at the time was planning the invasion of the Soviet Union and had more important priorities and considered the North African campaign as secondary. Thus, Rommel was unlikely to receive major reinforcements from Germany. General Halder, Chief of the General Staff, OKH, was particularly opposed to further offensives in North Africa. Halder noted in his diary on 23rd April: '. . . Rommel has not sent in a single clear report, and I have a feeling that things are in a mess . . . All day long he rushes about between his widely scattered units and stages reconnaissance raids in which he fritters away his strength . . The piecemeal thrusts of weak armoured forces have been costly . . . His motor vehicles are in poor condition and many of the tank engines need replacing . . . Air transport cannot meet his senseless demands, primarily because of lack of fuel . . . It is essential to have the situation cleared up without delay."[77]

But as we will see, Rommel will disobey Gariboldi's order as well as take a different approach from the German High Command's cautious position on North Africa by appealing directly to Hitler and bypassing both the German and Italian High Commands.

At the time, several issues divided the Italian command in North Africa and Rommel and their differences of opinion demonstrated the divergent priorities within the Axis alliance. First, General Gariboldi lamented the fact that many non-motorized Italian infantry troops were deployed in isolated, inhospitable sections of the frontline and demanded that these troops be better supplied and that mobile armoured units be placed at their disposal. His fear was a repeat of Graziani's offensive when the Commonwealth countered and cut off and captured stranded Italian infantry troops with no motorized or mechanized support deployed in the frontline.

Rommel on the other hand, had other preoccupations mainly related to his desire to go on offensive again and was not primarily concerned about the Italian infantry. He requested that *Comando Supremo* furnish a new armoured division such as *Centauro* or *Littorio* and that *Ariete* was to be equipped with at least 200 medium tanks. Moreover, he requested that Italian infantry units be fully motorized and that 88mm or 90mm truck mounted guns be introduced into service as soon as possible.

Rommel's requests for a general strengthening and greater mechanization of the Italian units were timely and opportune demands, but the status of the troops and their equipment had already been compromised after the initial battles. *Ariete*, for instance, was down to 5,700 soldiers, three infantry units and two armoured ones and its losses of machines due to breakdowns and destruction in the field of battle had been pronounced. All standard infantry units were also all under strength. The task to rearm and bring these units up to full strength was a

---

76 MacGregor Knox, *Hitler's Italian Allies*, p. 126.
77 I.S.O., Playfair, *The Mediterranean and the Middle East Volume 2: The Germans Come to the Help of their Ally (1941)*, p. 41.

tall one primarily because the North African desert caused a high wastage of equipment. As we will see, Rommel's requests would only be partially fulfilled. The lack of an adequate number of trucks was the number one problem afflicting the infantry divisions but due to the slow moving Italian industry and to commitments in other areas it was a problem that would persist throughout the campaign.

Notwithstanding the difficulties surrounding the low degree of motorization and mechanization of the Italian troops in North Africa, the defeat at Beda Fomm must be seen as a turning point of the Italian campaign in North Africa as several factors were changed almost overnight. First, the training of new recruits to the theater would improve as a result of the setting up of training centers for desert warfare. Second, beginning in early 1941 several combat-effective units were brought in from Europe. Third, the five infantry divisions under Graziani that remained in North Africa were slowly reinforced and partially up-gunned especially with regard to artillery. Moreover, Italian troops benefited from Rommel's experienced leadership which just in a few weeks had initiated a highly successful military offensive which boosted morale. Most important of all, was the arrival of the DAK *Ariete*, and then later of *Trieste* motorized division, and much later of the *Littorio* armoured division "making the first serious commitment of Italian mechanized forces to this theater. These were veteran formations, including units originally blooded in combat during the Spanish Civil War under the command of General Bastico, who later came to Libya himself."[78]

Tobruk

After the recapture of Cyrenaica Rommel believed, based on information received from his intelligence services, that the retreating Commonwealth forces could no longer withstand any further attacks and that the Axis forces ought to pursue them all the way to Alexandria and the Suez Canal. But Rommel and especially his intelligence services had not accounted for the strength of the Tobruk garrison which stood in the way of the Axis advance and its fortress was defended by tough Australian infantry units. Tobruk was a vital supply depot and with its port infrastructure located between Tripoli and Egypt it had the potential to greatly shorten the travel time for some of Rommel's supply needs. Its recapture was vital if the Axis troops planned to advance into Egypt since fuel provisions coming from the ports of Benghazi and Tripoli were not adequate to fully supply the German and Italian forces. In addition, supply columns from these ports had to travel longer distances to reach the front extending the time that it took to deliver provisions and fuel to the troops. In the worst case scenario some of the supply could be lost due to the interference from the RAF. The longer the route, the greater the chance of the potential for disruptions caused by RAF bombings.

By April 1941, the garrison at Tobruk, commanded by General Leslie Morshead, consisted of the 9th Australian Division comprised of three infantry brigades (20th, 24th, and 26th) and by the 18th Brigade of the 7th Australian Division and several thousand British and Indian troops. In total the garrison had approximately 30,000 soldiers, forty-eight 25-pdr guns, twelve 18-pdr, twelve 4.5-inch howitzers and 113 antitank guns, half of which were captured Italian

---

78 Paddy Griffith, *Desert Tactics*, p. 11.

guns. Its armoured brigade consisted of four Matildas II, twenty-six Cruiser and fifteen light tanks. Tobruk was thus heavily defended and fortified and definitively a tough fortress position to overcome for Axis troops attacking prepared defenses. Initially held by the Italians under Balbo, Tobruk had been fortified in 1940. The forts had been built with the best concrete material possible in consideration of a defense from modern siege and heavy artillery weapons. In addition, the numerous works which surrounded Tobruk, like the defensive belt that had been dug in and camouflaged in such a way that it could only be recognized by way of aerial reconnaissance, made its defenses almost invisible. These consisted of a system of underground trenches which connected several antitank or machine gun positions. The Commonwealth forces had further built upon the Italian fortifications. Their first line of defense was comprised of small outposts and bunkers set in a zig zag fashion, with one in the forefront and two at the back. Behind the first line of defense, called the Red Line, there was an antitank mine field to prevent deep armoured penetrations. Two miles behind the Red Line was the Blue Line, or the resistance zone, defended by the three reserve battalions. "General Morshead's concept of defense was based on four principles: no ground should be given up; garrisons should dominate no-man's-land by extensive nightly deep patrolling; no effort should be spared in improving the defensive positions and obstacles; and the defense should be organized in depth, with a large mobile reserve."[79]

In this endeavor Morshead could rely upon experienced and well drilled units of infantry soldiers that could hold their ground by adopting a dynamic defense based on frequent counterattacks to reestablish positions. In the First World War the Australians had excelled in this type of defense and now they were facing again German troops but in a very different context. In turn, the Axis forces that ringed the fortress were positioned in rocky outposts and exposed to the hot sun. The troops were instructed to keep still for most of the day so not to offer a target to the excellent Australian sharp shooters. Most troops faced privations of all kinds especially the lack of adequate water and food. The deployment of Italian troops was as follows: *Savona* Division was at El Aghelia, *Bologna* Division at Barce, *Pavia* at Derna while the *Ariete, Brescia and Trento* divisions surrounded Tobruk. They had a total of 135,000 soldiers with 7,000 machine guns, 780 mortars, 1,848 artillery pieces and approximately 5,000 trucks.

The first Axis probe of the Tobruk defenses was made by the 5th Leicht and *Ariete* on 11 and 12 April but being a minor operation it did not achieve any success. The Australian official history reproduces Captain Balfe's account of the action:

> About 70 tanks came right up to the anti-tank ditch and opened fire on our forward posts. They advanced in three waves of about twenty and one of ten. Some of them were big German Mark IV's, mounting a 75mm gun. Others were Italian M 13's and there were a lot of Italian light tanks too. The ditch here wasn't any real obstacle to them, the minefield had only been hastily re-armed and we hadn't one anti-tank gun forward. We fired on them with anti-tank rifles, Brens and rifles and they didn't attempt to come through but blazed away at us and then sheered of east towards the 2/13th's front.[80]

---

79 Ward A. Miller, *The 9th Australian Division versus the Africa Corps: an infantry division against tanks-Tobruk, Libya, 1941* (Fort Leavenworth, Kansas: U.S. Army Command and General Staff College, 1985), p. 12.
80 Barton Maughan, *Australia in the War of 1939-1945 Vol. III: Tobruk and El Alamein*, p. 133.

The Commonwealth commander then dispatched the 1st Royal Tank Regiment, with its Cruiser tanks, to help support the artillery in heading off the Axis tank attack near the El Adem road-block. At first on this position one Italian medium tank was knocked out. Then in quick succession a few others were hit by anti-tank fire and a light tank was disabled by small-arms fire demonstrating once again how obsolete the L series tanks really were. After attracting considerable enemy fire, once arrived at El Adem road the Axis tanks stumbled upon a mine-field and were forced to turn away from the Tobruk defensive perimeter. As they retreated, a clash took place between the British tanks and the last wave of ten Axis tanks. During this rear-guard combat action three light and one medium Italian tanks were knocked out by the British tanks and a German medium tank was destroyed by gunfire. In turn, two British cruisers were knocked out of action. The assault failed miserably and it clearly demonstrated that superior forces were needed to overcome an imposing enemy defensive system.

The next attack, a prepared operation backed up by prior aerial reconnaissance and bombings on 13 April, allowed the German troops to enter the defensive perimeter. But even this more prepared attack ultimately bogged down due to heavy enemy artillery fire. The 8th Machine Gun Battalion initially succeeded in breaking through the belt of fortifications just west of the road El Adem – Tobruk, but it could not overtake the successive defensive belts. The operation then progressed with the launch of a tank attack by the 5th Panzer Regiment but has soon as the operation got into full swing the tanks had to turn back as they were targeted by very heavy and unabating concentrated anti-tank and artillery fire. The infantry troops of the 8th Battalion where then surrounded and cut off in the break-in area. A large part of these troops was captured or killed.

The first major attack against Tobruk demonstrated that the Axis forces were dealing with a well-fortified position and that even the well-trained German armoured units and infantry could not easily prevail in frontal attacks against prepared defenses.

The following attempt to breech Tobruk was then undertaken by *Trento* and *Ariete* Divisions.

It began on 15 April when a battalion of the *Trento* Division was engaged to penetrate the defensive perimeter. At dawn attacks were undertaken by small successive groups of infantry and sappers which were broken up by machine gun fire. According to the Australian official history:

> Throughout the morning group after group of infantry, each group seeming larger than the last, approached the perimeter; each as it came into view through the dancing mirage, was in turn halted by the guns of the 51st Field Regiment. All appeared to be Italian. By midday the front was quiet.[81]

At 1700 the same battalion of 62nd Regiment of the *Trento* Division sallied again against the perimeter and initially overran one enemy outpost, but then it came under fire again by Bren machine guns and artillery pieces and the attack once again bogged down.

On the 16th the attack was resumed but this time the infantry battalion was supported by *Ariete*'s tanks. Once again, the infantry found no openings from which to carry out the attack against the perimeter and the troops came under heavy fire. *Ariete* was then thrown into the

---

81 Ibid., p. 162.

fight with the remaining seven M.13/40 medium tanks of *VII Battaglione Carri Medi* and twelve L.3 tanks of *I/32° Reggimento Carristi* that had not broken down due to mechanical problems during the recapture of Cyrenaica.[82] At first the tank attack progressed well, as they overran some Australian positions and seized their main hilltop position, Ras el Medauar (Hill 209). But once reached this exposed position, however, they came under the concentrated fire of the enemy's anti-tank weapons and were forced to retreat. The Australians then closed in on the infantry troops that had been left stranded in the isolated forward positions. Despite explicit orders from Rommel to intervene, *Ariete*'s men refused to continue the fight since their deployment could not help the infantry breakthrough, which were now surrounded, and the operation quickly stalemated. As the official Italian history states: "The armoured unit was not able or unwilling to intervene in the battle out of fear that it would fire upon the Italian soldiers that had been boxed in by the enemy fire and because of the inadequacy of its light tanks."[83]

The Australian Official History states that: "As the Italians moved in towards the perimeter, four of the tanks came forward. A 'few spiteful rounds,' which appeared to the Australians to come from the enemy tanks, were then fired into the Italian infantry.

The Australian carriers were also engaged. But retaliatory gunfire from the British artillery quickly put an end to the enemy's shooting; his fire had, however, caused several casualties among the Italians and wounded two Australians of the 2/48th Battalion, one mortally."[84]

Over 200 Italian soldiers were captured and over 100 were either wounded or dead.

The DAK War Diary blamed *Ariete* for failing to advance toward the designated point of attack by stating that: "The attack failed because of the hesitant advance of the armoured battalion of Div. Ariete."[85] But it was the paucity of the attacking forces and especially their few means of combat (lack of tanks, armoured vehicles and heavy guns) involved that determined the outcome. The DAK Command failed to recognize that even better equipped Germans had experienced the same difficulties in penetrating the fortress a few days earlier.

On 17 April Rommel met with *Generale* Ettore Baldassarre of *Ariete* and after having expressed his disappointment for the failed attempt of 16 April demanded a more forceful offensive probe by the Italians. The latter committed to a new offensive and promised Rommel that he would field all available forces. The new plan entailed a frontal attack against enemy troops to take Ras el Medauar (Hill 209), the highest point occupied by the Commonwealth (2/48th Battalion's sector) in the Tobruk perimeter which stood more than 600 feet above sea-level and was a commanding position. Immediately behind the position was a large minefield which represented the outer perimeter of the Tobruk defenses. The armoured troops involved in the Axis operation were to be supported by a German machine gun company and two German infantry companies. At the time *Ariete* only had four M.13/40 and seven L.3 tanks in working order

---

82 Rommel states: "The Ariete, although they had not yet seen any action, now only had ten tanks left out of the 100 odd with which they had started the offensive. The remainder had fallen out, due to engine failure or some other mechanical trouble. It made one's hair stand on end to see the sort of equipment with which the Duce had sent his troops into battle." Basil Liddell Hart, *The Rommel Papers*, p. 127.
83 Mario Montanari, *Le operazioni in Africa settentrionale* (Rome: Ufficio Storico, 1985), vol.II, Part I, p. 139.
84 Barton Maughan, *Australia in the War of 1939-1945 Vol. III: Tobruk and El Alamein*, p. 165.
85 DAK War Diary <https://rommelsriposte.com/2016/05/03/desaster-at-sea-d-a-k-war-diary-entry-16-april-1941/> (accessed 12 February 2019).

and therefore given the paucity of forces available the assault was again likely to be doomed to fail from the start. In fact, the attack began in the worst possible way and ended in an even greater disaster. The machine gun company did not arrive, while the German infantry companies arrived late to the meeting point. The tanks began their approach march from Acroma at noon and opened a path into the enemy's defenses with their firepower and with contribution from combat engineers. Bust soon the coordination between infantry and tanks became [86] disjointed to the point that it prejudiced the whole operation: "The attacking force had instructions to advance from one dip in the ground to the next, waiting each time until supporting fire had been secured. But the company commanders ignored their instructions and made a blind dash straight at the enemy. The *Ariete*'s armour was led by Lieut. Wahl, an interpreter on the 5th Light Division's staff. Contrary to their orders to remain behind the infantry, they pushed on far ahead and soon vanished out of sight."[87] By this point both the German infantry and the tanks were met by heavy enemy fire mainly artillery and anti-tank guns and as the tanks retreated, raising thick clouds of dust and sand, they were targeted by German 88mm guns, the servers of which had mistaken them for British Cruisers. Thus, two tanks were damaged by friendly fire. It turned out that the attack of 18 April against non-identified positions failed miserably. *Ariete* lost several men and tanks. The thrust had failed primarily because the troops were attacking frontally against strong prepared positions and because the attack had not been supported by field artillery and by prior Luftwaffe or *Aeronautica* bombing probes. According to *Maggiore* Andrea Andreani[88] of VIII *Battaglione Carri Medi* the combat action had been prejudiced by the slow speed of the Italian tanks: "During the combat action against quota 209 west of Tobruk, the only tank that survived was the one that was more efficient than the others and that could operate on third gear, while the others operating on second and first gear were easy preys to the enemy fire." He also goes on to say that the tanks were shot at multiple times by 37mm enemy guns which given the slow pace of the Italian tanks had plenty of time to aim accurately at their targets.[89] In his view, the engine that moved the M.13/40 tank was the critical component that needed improvement. An improved, more powerful engine was necessary to build a heavier, better protected vehicle and the lack thereof of such an engine was one of the reasons why Italian tank production could not go beyond vehicles weighing more than 15 tons. The production of the P.40 heavy tank for instance, was held back by several factors one of which was the lack of a viable engine. This appeared to be a problem facing Italian tank design in general and involving several ranges and one that could not be readily addressed in a timely manner. Intensive research and design was necessary to change the engine compartment.

Following the debacle Rommel reported that "It was now finally clear that there was no hope of doing anything against the enemy defenses with the forces we had, largely because of the poor state of training and useless equipment of the Italian troops."[90] It is important to note

---

86 Basil Liddell Hart, *The Rommel Papers*, p. 127.
87 Ibid.
88 *Maggiore* Alberto Andreani was one of the most experienced tank commanders of *Ariete* Division. He had graduated from the Military Academy in Modena and in 1937 was promoted to *Capitano* and served in the 3° *Reggimento fanteria carrista* and then with *Comando del Corpo d'Armata* in Genoa. He was promoted to Major in 1940 and he fought with the armour units during the French campaign. In 1941 and 1942 he was the commander of *Ariete*'s VII *Battaglione Carri Medi*.
89 Ufficio Storico, Relazione Andreani 'Impegno Operativo M.13/40', 21 Aprile 1941.
90 Basil Liddell Hart, *The Rommel Papers*, p. 128.

that Rommel's post-battle analysis was not completely correct since both the German and the Italian offensive probes had failed against consolidated enemy defenses and both troops had suffered heavy losses. In addition, the Italian troops in contrast to the attack put forth earlier in the month by 5th Leicht, had been sent into the attack without aerial support and against enemy objectives and positions that were not known to the officers through prior reconnaissance. Basically, in an attack hastily prepared that since its early stages had little or no chance of success. The German attack had been a prepared attack involving both the *Luftwaffe* and superior armoured forces. But the latter had also failed miserably against the stout enemy defense. Rommel's propensity to attack as soon as possible and by surprise this time had not beared any fruits and had costed high casualties.

After the succession of failed attacks, the seizure of Tobruk was thus placed on hold by Rommel as he waited for reinforcements from Italy. General Leslie Morshead instead effectively employed this time of Axis operational stasis by implementing a series of raids against Axis forces situated outside the Tobruk perimeter. These were attempts to relieve the pressure on the defenders of Tobruk by making a further Axis attack against the perimeter even more prohibitive. On the night of 19 April Commonwealth troops made their first attempt to push back and inflict losses upon the Axis troops besieging the fortress. The blow fell upon *Colonna* Fabris (*Ariete's III Battaglione Bersaglieri*) south of Ras el Medauar. The latter fought back two separate attacks together with the infantrymen of the *Trento* Division and the few tanks still in operational order of the VII *Battaglione Carri Medi* which were instrumental in inflicting heavy casualties upon the enemy. The most forceful raid was undertaken on 22 April when three separate Axis positions were attacked simultaneously. To the south, the Commonwealth operation was repulsed by *V Bersaglieri* and by the tanks of the *VII Battaglione Carri Medi*. Here a mixed force comprised by an infantry company of the 2/17th Battalion, a squadron of cruiser tanks, two troops of light tanks and a company of the 2/1st Pioneers, supported by a battery of the 1st Royal Horse Artillery attempted a surprise attack at dawn. The objective was to attack and destroy a battery of enemy field guns. The force set forth before dawn but when daylight came its troops were targeted by heavy fire from three sides. It thus began to withdraw but was then counterattacked by medium tanks. During the withdrawal a British light tank was knocked out by a well-concealed anti-tank gun and the unit suffered only few casualties.

Another raid was attempted in the same direction the following day but the prompt response of the defenders sealed the initial breech by laying down heavy gun fire. In the north in a separate sortie, the Australians were also beaten back but after very heavy fighting. The 2nd Company/23rd Battalion was divided into two forces that were to converge upon a wadi that was located west of the defensive perimeter. The Italians here held strong positions from which intense machine-gun fire was brought to bear on the advancing Australians. Machine gun fire was followed by mortar and gun shells which inflicted casualties upon the assailants. Despite the fire the Australians advanced in the open with bayonets and grenade and irrupted into the Italian position where they made some prisoners. From there the Australians attempted to advance further but were met by intense fire to the point that they were forced to turn back. Meanwhile the second Australian force advanced on the left flank against an anti-tank/anti-aircraft battery, behind which were two batteries of field guns. The Italian defenders held their fire until the enemy was within 500 yards. Then all weapons, field guns, anti-aircraft guns, machine-guns and mortars, targeted the Australians with concentrated fire. Some Australians managed to reach an advanced Italian position and capture its occupants. They then continued to advance but once again were subjected to heavy artillery fire. They were supported by four carriers which aimed to destroy the enemy strongholds. By this point the Australian force had been halved while the carriers charged bravely with the infantry. They came under heavy fire. And two were knocked out. The infantry losses included 24 casualties, and 22 dead.

Meantime, the main position Hill 201 was attacked by a much more forceful Commonwealth unit which comprised the 2/48th Australian Battalion supported by five carriers, four 2-pounder guns, four Matildas II and several medium tanks. These forces overtook the positions of *III Battaglione Bersaglieri* and assaulted the artillery batteries of the I/132° Artillery Regiment of *Ariete*. This fierce counter taking by complete surprise the Italians knocked two guns out of action and yielded the capture of 200 prisoners. *Colonnello* Fabris, the Italian officer in charge of *III Battaglione*, was one of those killed during the fighting. With regard to this raid the Australian Official History states that: "For a short time the Italians stood to their positions and engaged the Australians with infantry weapons at short range but could not halt them, and the sight of the assaulting infantry coming forward with fixed bayonets soon proved too much for the Italians. Generally, they surrendered though isolated pockets continued to resist."[91]

After this initial success, however, the Australians were then beaten back by a mixed unit of infantry troops, four M.13/40 tanks and three *Panzerjager*. During the retreat the Commonwealth troops lost nine tanks and two armoured vehicles. The 2/48th Battalion, had three killed and seven wounded, and several soldiers missing and it also suffered the loss of an anti-tank gun and a portee. Italian weapon losses were also very high: The booty included four 20-mm antitank guns, machine-guns, motor transports and motorcycles. The bold attempt had ultimately been foiled, but at a high cost to the enemy. In Rommel's view the defeat of *Colonna Fabris* was the result of the inability to call up immediately tank support to beat back the Australians: "The six Italian tanks which had been put there to protect the position, and which should have been perfectly capable of engaging and driving off the enemy tanks, had been sent back by Fabris." [92]

Battle of the Salient- Ras el Medauar (Hill 209)

After the first series of attacks against the Tobruk garrison petered out, *Comando Supremo* and the German High Command agreed that Tobruk had to be captured before resuming the advance against the Egyptian frontier. Rommel wanted to press the attack against Tobruk but conscious of the limited forces in his ranks, demanded reinforcements especially more *Luftwaffe* support to not only carry ammunition, fuel and water for his tired troops, but also to bomb the fortress. He was still intending to take Tobruk by a quick assault. "My plan now," he wrote in his memoirs, "was to take the hill, Ras el Medauar, using elements of the Ariete and Trento and several German companies attacking under strong artillery support."[93]

On 27 April, Major-General Friedrich Paulus a Deputy Chief of the German General Staff, arrived in North Africa to meet Rommel. Through Paulus, the German High Command wanted to verify the options open to the German and Italian units in North Africa and to

---

91 Barton Maughan, *Australia in the War of 1939-1945 Vol. III: Tobruk and El Alamein*, p. 176.
92 Basil Liddell Hart, *The Rommel Papers*, p. 130.
93 John Pimlott, *Rommel in His Own Words* (Oxford: Amber Books, 2018), p. 63.

ensure that Rommel would pursue the defensive minded campaign to prop up the Italians as was originally envisaged by Hitler in early 1941. After having examined the situation, however, both Paulus and Gariboldi were unable or unwilling to stop Rommel and allowed a new attack to go ahead against Tobruk. Although both Generals gave the green light on Tobruk they were opposed to having Suez as an ultimate objective. General Paulus remarked that if Tobruk fell he would order the DAK to secure Cyrenaica by halting Rommel's forces at Sollum on the frontier with Egypt.

Since 25 April Rommel had worked out a new plan of attack. After receiving the green light from Paulus, he then gathered his direct reports to lay out the tactical instructions to breech the Tobruk defenses. The plan entailed the deployment of two battle groups: one to the left led by the newly arrived troops of the 15th Panzer Division and one to the right led by the 5th Leicht and *Ariete*. The main thrust was to be made in the direction of Ras el Medauar by the two converging columns, while diversionary thrusts were to be executed against other sections of the Commonwealth defenses. All around Tobruk the terrain was flat but in the south-west, at Ras el Medauar, there was a small hill which was surmounted by a blockhouse which was the highest defensive position on the defensive perimeter. The objective was the capture of the Ras el Medauar hilltop fort to create a lodgment in the enemy defenses and control much of the Commonwealth line to then widen the breech. The front-line divisions were the Kirchheim Group of the 5th Leicht Division on the right flank and the 15th Panzer Division on the left. The *Ariete* Division was to follow in the wake of the Kirchheim Group, while *Brescia* Division was to follow in the wake of the 15th Panzer Division. *Ariete*'s column was comprised by the *V Bersaglieri* Battalion and by two platoons of light tanks, two medium tanks, five German tanks and supported by the preparatory fire of the *132° Reggimento Artiglieria*.

On the evening of 29-30 April this column along with their German allies went into the gap created by the preparatory fire and by Stukas dive bombing against the enemy positions to first tackle the minefield and the outer defenses. Thanks to special teams of combat engineers Axis troops from *Brescia* Division open a path in the minefields protected by barbed wire that stood in defense of Redoubt 3. They then surprised the enemy by assailing its positions which were conquered utilizing flame throwers and hand grenades. Shortly thereafter a similar penetration was made by the *Bersaglieri* on Redoubt 7. Soon after they then attempted to widen the gap by penetrating to the nearby positions and Redoubt 6 and 8 also fell when the Commonwealth soldiers, who had been encircled, raised white flags and surrendered. A *Bersagliere* of *Ariete*'s *V Battaglione* recalls: "The vigorous thrust of *Maggiore* Gaggetti's Bersaglieri supported by a few light tanks, anti-tank companies, and by teams of flamethrowers broke through the enemy defenses. The first objective was redoubt n. 4 which despite the very alert enemy fire was overrun forcing the enemy to raise the white flag. But the Bersaglieri were not intent in stopping there. With a great leap forward three more small forts were occupied and then at dawn Tenenti Bertolini and Padovani occupied redoubt n. 7, the most solid section of the advanced enemy defensive works. Major Gaggetti's men were then tasked with occupying it."[94] As soon as these positions were captured the Axis tanks came forward to widen even more the breech but both the infantry and the tanks came under heavy fire and could not advance any further. By dawn the tanks unable to proceed and in clear view of the enemy guns were forced back to the Axis lines,

---

94 Giulio Bedeschi, *Fronte d'Africa: c'ero anch'io* (Milan: Mursia, 1979), p. 168.

as Rommel sensing that any further progress was doubtful, called a halt to the operation. Thus, on 30 April the troops that had been designated to take hold of the captured bridgehead, mainly the *Bersaglieri* and other Italian infantry troops, found themselves isolated into the inner perimeter of Tobruk. During the night, they were subjected to strong enemy fire especially machine gun rounds which poured in unabated helped by special night lights for improved targeting. The next day, given that a decisive breakthrough was unlikely, further attacks were called off but the Axis forces had managed to take redoubt 3, 4, 6, 7 and 8 from the Commonwealth troops and had advanced a little closer to Tobruk.

The Australian Official History reports the results of the Axis attack in the following terms: "In about 24 hours of operations Rommel's forces had seized and obtained a firm hold on an arc of the perimeter of Tobruk spanning three miles and a half, including its highest point; they had captured or killed about one-half of one of the garrison's battalions; of the garrison's small tank force they had destroyed four tanks; they had sliced off a part of the front but had failed to carve right through the defense."[95]

On 3-4 May the Commonwealth troops (2/9th Battalion of the 9th Australian Brigade) mounted a major counterattack to retake possession of the redoubt positions. The battalion was to attack in two phases. The first phase included the capture of the four posts: Redoubts 8, 7, 6 and 5, while the target of the second phase were the remaining Redoubts: 4, 3, 2 and 1. According to the Australian Official History: "The area to be attacked was found to be garrisoned mainly by Italians."[96] The positions were in fact held by *V Battaglione/Ariete* under *Maggiore* Gaggetti.

The first phase of the assault got soon underway after a blistering preparatory artillery fire as the Australians rushed an enemy position in front of Redoubt 7 with hand grenades and then charged in with bayonets. As they rushed the defenses the Australians killed several infantrymen and drove out the rest of the garrison. They then concentrated their attention on Redoubt 7. At that point, however, *Ariete* counter-attacked with strong defensive fire and with three L.3 tanks that were quickly put out of action by the Australian guns. During the close combat, the latter temporarily reoccupied redoubt 7 but were quickly pushed back by a counter-thrust by the *V Battaglione Bersaglieri* and supported by one M tank and several armoured cars. The Australian Official History states that: "The post was assaulted, most of the garrison were slain and two prisoners were taken. Four 47mm guns and a heavy Breda machine-gun were found in the post. Almost immediately, however, the Australians were counter-attacked by a medium tank and three armoured cars, probably attracted by the burning blankets. The Australians fell back."[97]

Maggiore Gaggetti described the fighting in the following terms:

> After more than three hours of a barrage of iron and fire there were bloody gaps opening in the ranks of my Bersaglieri. I was gravely wounded in turn; conscious of the delicacy of the situation, with all the section commanders wounded or fallen, I remained among the survivors who were engaged in furious hand to hand fighting. The epic struggle of V Battaglione was bitter, arduous, and to the death. It took place in a continuous stream of brilliant acts of valor. Redoubt R7, in which I found myself, was surrounded and the enemy repeatedly attacking it because it was the mainstay of the position. They finally succeeded in

---

95 Barton Maughan, *Australia in the War of 1939-1945 Vol. III: Tobruk and El Alamein*, p. 222.
96 Ibid., p. 233.
97 Barton Maughan, *Australia in the War of 1939-1945 Vol. III: Tobruk and El Alamein*, p. 234.

penetrating it, but only for a moment, then the handful of survivors succeeded in repelling them once and for all.[98]

After being pushed back the Australian troops, which had lost between wounded and dead half of the battalion, regrouped to implement the second phase of the counterthrust, but the operation was then called off by General Morshead. As the Australian Official History asserts: "In view of the enemy's defensive strength and dispositions it appears that any further large-scale infantry operations will require the support of many more guns and tanks"[99] Thus, the frontline became quiet again and the Battle of the Salient came to an abrupt conclusion.

The next day Rommel visited *Ariete*'s headquarters eager to learn what had happened during the night. To his surprise, he received the welcome news that the frontline positions had been held by General Baldassarre's men who in turn asserted: "The communication links with the frontline positions have been reestablished. You can communicate directly with the commanders in each redoubt if you so wish."[100] The positive outcome prompted Rommel on 6 May to issue the following communique: "My personal thank you and recognition goes to the proud members of Ariete Division that with an excellent defensive combat operation beginning on 3 May have stifled every enemy attempt and kept possession of their strongholds."[101]

Even though the siege of Tobruk was maintained and the Axis forces were still deployed like a ring of steel around the port town, the offensive had taken its toll. *Ariete*, for instance, had lost 87 soldiers, 73 wounded and 115 missing between April and early May, in addition to 200 captured by the enemy. The III and V *Battaglioni* were the units that had been hardest hit and were each reduced to the strength of one infantry company. The VII *Battaglione Carri Medi* had only five M.13/40 tanks that were still effective, while the 32° *Reggimento Carristi* had less than thirty light tanks in working order. Several artillery pieces had also been lost during the siege. The 32° *Compagnia Controcarri* anti-tank company had only one gun out of the ten with which it had started the campaign, while the *132° Reggimento Artiglieria Corazzata* had only five 75mm guns. The Germans had lost a total of 658 soldiers, while the Italian Divisions (*Trento, Ariete and Brescia*) had collectively lost 740 soldiers. The *Colonna Santamaria* had also sustained heavy losses and would shortly thereafter be relegated to train armoured personnel. Its commander had been gravely injured and it had only five small platoons remaining with two machine guns and two Solothurn anti-tank rifles, three 47mm guns and two 75/27 guns.

Tobruk proved to be an impregnable position that the combined strength of Italian and German units could not overtake. Rommel was forced to call off additional offensives and requested further reinforcements from Europe. According to the authoritative source of the United States Combat Studies Institute: "The prime causes for the German failure at Tobruk were piece meal of forces, a poor assessment of the garrison's defensive strength, and overconfidence. These factors affected the ability of the assault forces to retain the initiative and to hold, reinforce, and expand their penetration."[102] The Axis had only approximately 25,000 troops to

---

98 Ian Walker, *Iron Hulls, Iron Hearts*, p. 75.
99 Barton Maughan, *Australia in the War of 1939-1945 Vol. III: Tobruk and El Alamein*, p. 234.
100 Mario Montanari, *Le operazioni in Africa Settentrionale*, Vol, II, Part I, p. 167.
101 Basil Liddell Hart, *The Rommel Papers*, p. 167.
102 Ward A. Miller, *The 9th Australian Division versus the Africa Corps: an infantry division against tanks-Tobruk, Libya, 1941*, p. 12.

siege Tobruk, a force that was inferior to that of the defenders. In addition, they lacked heavy siege artillery. Against prepared defensive positions the Axis forces could only have succeeded by blasting Tobruk with heavy artillery and bombers and then by dispatching a major concentrated tank attack supported by specialized infantry and by engineer/sapper detachments with detonation charges. Instead, Rommel's overconfidence resulted in the execution of several surprise piecemeal attacks carried out by small sized units that were unable to make a dent in the Commonwealth defenses. Rommel ultimately blamed the Italians for the failure to take Tobruk and especially the light tanks of *Ariete* which were prone to breakdowns. A more balanced analysis of the siege would indicate that the Axis did not have enough troops and tanks to effectively capture the Commonwealth garrison. The lack of heavy artillery by both German and Italian units meant that the Axis could not degrade Tobruk's defenses enough to enable the infantry and the armour to overtake its defenders.

Operation Brevity

In late spring and summer of 1941 the fighting moved to the border between Egypt and Libya as the Axis forces maintained the siege of Tobruk but were not able to make any further progress. A quick offensive operation conducted by the newly formed German Herff Combat Group (led by Colonel von Herff), had resulted in the capture of Fort Capuzzo and Halfaya Pass on 26 April. The first position was a fortified outpost that had originally been built by the Italians to guard against a British attack into Libya, while the pass was a strategic high altitude position that overlooked the main road between Egypt and Libya in the so-called Sollum position. Fort Capuzzo had been previously captured by the Commonwealth during the Operation Compass counteroffensive, and the pass had been fortified by British troops at the end of their major operation. The Germans by seizing them with a surprise attack had scored a major coup with very few losses. Based on ULTRA intercepts that revealed that more German troops were being transferred to North Africa, the British commander Wavell opted for a preemptive strike to recapture the two positions and to relieve the pressure upon the Tobruk garrison. He was also made aware through the ULTRA intercept that the Axis troops maintaining the siege front against Tobruk were weak after weeks of fighting and that therefore Rommel eagerly awaited reinforcements. To counter the arrival of more German troops to North Africa the British navy dispatched a major convoy of reinforcements. "By 28th April 1941, 300 new tanks and over 50 Hurricanes were on their way to the Nile Delta, so General Wavell decided that he would counter attack against the enemy positions at Sollum and Fort Capuzzo, with the aim of pushing Rommel back from the frontier and relieving Tobruk."[103]

Both frontline positions were defended by an ad hoc Axis combat group composed of some of the troops of Herff's unit armed with a battery of 88mm Flak 36 guns and the 8° *Reggimento Bersaglieri/Ariete* of *Colonnello* Montemurro plus a small unit of *Arditi*. Although the positions (Sollum, Halfaya Pass, Fort Capuzzo) had not been hardened, the Axis soldiers, numbering

---

103 Desert Rats: Engagements 1941 <http://www.desertrats.org.uk/battles1941.htm#Brevity> (accessed on 1 June 2019).

6,000, were dug into their well camouflaged posts and had interspersed German and Italian anti-tank guns to better parry the enemy blow.

Halfaya Pass was defended as follows: two *Bersaglieri* platoons held the base of the pass along with two platoons equipped with 47mm guns. On the pass at Point 191 there were two companies of the 15th German motorized Battalion and an Italian battery with 105mm guns. North of the pass the *6ª Compagnia Bersaglieri* occupied numerous isolated rifle and machine gun positions. Sollum was also occupied by the bulk of *Colonnello* Montemurro's *Bersaglieri*, which also manned the fort's defenses. The *Comando XII Battaglione Bersaglieri* and elements of the *6ª Compagnia Bersaglieri* occupied the highest point in Sollum, while Montemurro's headquarter along with several regimental companies, including two platoons of 47mm anti-tank guns occupied Fort Capuzzo. Herff Combat Group headquarters was based at Bardia.

The operation began on 15 May when three Commonwealth columns advanced against the Axis positions. As the troops quickly moved forward the artillery, mainly 25-pdr guns, shelled the pass and Fort Capuzzo. Finally, several Blenheim flew over the *Bersaglieri* positions and bombed them repeatedly. The major thrust was put forth by the center column comprised of twenty-four Matildas II of the 4th Royal Tank Regiment and the 22nd Guards Group which aimed to capture the pinnacle of the Halfaya Pass, secure Fort Capuzzo and ultimately advance northwards. 2nd Scots Guards and a tanks squadron of 4th Royal Tank Regiment overran the position above the Halfaya Pass but suffered heavy losses in the process. At 6000 the 105mm battery communicated to their headquarters that: "Enemy tanks have attacked the positions of a German company that has pulled back. Our most effective and only functioning gun fired seven or eight shots before jamming. Position under enemy attack."[104] At that point both the *Bersaglieri* units north of Point 191 as well as those positioned at the bottom of the pass had been encircled and were each fighting their individual battle. The *6ª Compagnia* was first subjected to artillery fire then saw the Matilda II tanks advancing. At a distance of 400 meters the 47mm guns opened fire but to the dismay of the crews the heavy tanks continued to rumble on as the shots just bounced off the armour. "When the Bersaglieri realized, at 400 yards, that their 47mm AT guns were worthless against the Matilda's hull, they shifted the targets to the Matilda's tracks and undercarriages when they came up crossing the low stone walls and rocks of the position. Seven Matildas were knocked out in this fashion."[105]

Likewise, historian Brian Perrett states that the Italian artillery was still learning how to deal with the heavy infantry tank Matilda II in the spring of 1941 and that on Halfaya Pass the artillery men demonstrated composure. They fired and did not panic. They then waited until the tanks had approached the anti-tank ditch and had then exposed their thin underbelly to go into action and knocked seven tanks out of action.[106] This was the first time that the Italians had found a way to deal effectively with the heavy infantry tank that had been the game changer in Operation Compass.[107]

---

104 Mario Montanari, *Le Operazioni in Africa Settentrionale*, Vol.II, Part I, p. 195.
105 Greene and Massignani, *Rommel's North African Campaign*, p. 70. The British official history also points out that: '2nd Scots Guards and a squadron of 4th Royal Tank Regiment soon overran the position above the Halfaya Pass, although seven tanks were knocked out or damaged.' I.S.O., Playfair, *The Mediterranean and the Middle East Volume 2: The Germans Come to the Help of their Ally (1941)*, p. 160.
106 Brian Perrett, *The Matilda* (London: Allen, 1973), p. 637.
107 According to the History of the 7th Armoured Division: "The attack started on 15th May and the assault on Halfaya Pass, the achieved complete surprise, only being held up by some Italian gunners,

By 0930, however, *6ª Compagnia* had been completely decimated by the concentrated fire of enemy guns and tanks. The remaining heavy tanks along with the Scottish infantry charged the pass and finally breached its defenses. The infantry tanks then overran the remaining Italian defenses while only some of the defenders managed to escape to the rocky terrain north of the pass and there continued to fight. This forced the Commonwealth infantry to engage in hand to hand combat for most of the day to finally subdue the remaining *Bersaglieri* at 1745. Heavy losses were incurred in the process while the Commonwealth captured 150 mostly wounded *Bersaglieri*.

With regard to the fighting on the pass the DAK situation report issued in the evening in a first instance stated that on Halfaya Pass a company of German infantry was still holding out despite being surrounded. The next day the report changed by stating that "the defenders of Halfaya pass were Italian and most likely they were captured last night."[108]

Meanwhile the 9th Durham Light Infantry and A Tank squadron also equipped with infantry tanks headed for Capuzzo and captured the fort after a sharp fight. The operation began at 0730 as both the Commonwealth infantry and the armour surrounded the position. While besieging the fort nine more Matildas II were knocked out as Axis guns of all sizes (37mm, 47mm, and 75mm) opened fire at a distance of 300-400 meters.[109] As a result, only two Matildas managed to enter the fort to clear out the enemy position once the resistance of the last defenders had been overcome. Meanwhile, on the desert flank the 7th Armoured Brigade Group had advanced towards Sidi Azeiz.

As a countermeasure to the enemy infiltrations Rommel responded by ordering the 2nd Battalion of the 5th Panzer Regiment to check the advance. In a fierce counter near fort Capuzzo the former charged against the enemy infantry inflicting heavy casualties upon the Durham Light Infantry and forcing its soldiers to scatter. Meanwhile on the Sollum front the Italian positions were also attacked by infantry accompanied by Matildas. The Commonwealth forces seized most positions but were not capable of subduing one last remaining strongpoint held by the *7ª Compagnia Bersaglieri* which held out until it received the support by several German tanks.

Conversely, the Australian official history summarizes the outcome after the first day of battle:

> Meanwhile the centre force had sent a detachment (Nire Column, with which was Lieutenant Scanlon's troop) with two infantry tanks to Sollum, which was taken with 123 prisoners, while a battalion of the Durham Light Infantry with nine or ten tanks set off for Capuzzo. Capuzzo was captured but most of the tanks were temporarily disabled. Even with reinforcements brought up from Halfaya only six tanks in fighting state could be spared to guard the infantry at Capuzzo.[110]

---

who knocked out seven tanks before being overrun." *Desert Rats: Engagements 1941* <http://www.desertrats.org.uk/battles1941.htm#Brevity> (accessed 26 January 2019).

108 DAK tele 421, 16 May 1941.
109 "Bir Wair and Musaid were quickly taken, and 1st Durham Light Infantry and another squadron of tanks made for Capuzzo. Contact between tanks and infantry was lost, but after a sharp fight the position was captured. Nine tanks had now become casualties and no exploitation to the north was possible." I.S.O., Playfair, *The Mediterranean and the Middle East Volume 2: The Germans Come to the Help of their Ally (1941)*, p. 159.
110 Barton Maughan, *Australia in the War of 1939-1945 Vol. III: Tobruk and El Alamein*, p. 241.

On the 16th the fighting continued. The Axis infantry and artillery managed to hold the line until Rommel unleashed his own tank units (I/8th Panzer) which were followed by the motorized elements of *Colonnello* Montemurro which readily countered the Commonwealth troops and pushed them back both from Capuzzo and Sollum. Ultimately, the Commonwealth only retained the position on the pass with the Coldstream Guards and nine Matildas. Ultimately, "Brevity" failed in achieving its goal of relieving Tobruk and destroying large amounts of Axis guns and armour.

The Germans had lost three tanks, twelve dead and sixty-one soldiers wounded, while 185 soldiers missing. The Commonwealth lost eighteen tanks (five Matilda tanks had been lost, and thirteen others damaged) and 160 men. Italian losses were of 395 soldiers mostly from the *Ariete*'s *Bersaglieri* battalions while no Italian tank units were deployed in the operation.

Despite the heavy losses for the Axis troops, the Commonwealth attack had been stopped on its tracks by the defensive fire of the artillery and the anti-tank guns. As the British Official History asserts: "Operation 'Brevity' was therefore a failure; the only British gain was the Halfaya Pass."[111] Even though the Axis units defensive effort succeeded, it is necessary to point out that the positive outcome was aided by two factors: the deployment of a relatively weak attacking force by the Commonwealth and by the fact that the Axis troops were defending from advantageous uphill positions. Despite these advantages the operation shed a different light on the defensive capabilities of the Italians which in 1940 under Operation Compass had performed very poorly. As Greene and Massignani correctly point out: "The Italian official war historian Mario Montanari gives several reasons why the Italians defeated the enemy in this action, in contrast to the battle of Sidi el Barrani in 1940. He states that the Italians fighting here were better trained, had superior officers, showed a higher level of esprit de corps, and had some victories (such as El Mechili) under their belt. Furthermore, they had the German example to follow, and they had confidence in German tanks and in Rommel."[112]

With regard to *Ariete*'s *Bersaglieri* units fighting under his command, von Herff wrote to Rommel stating:

> I would like to specifically recognize the great example set by each unit of Colonel Montemurro's regiment. Since the beginning of the operation, when they fell under my command, I have formed a very positive opinion of them. Similarly, the Frongia unit also fought admirably. The company assigned to defend hill 191 fought alongside their German comrades and ceased fighting only when it was encircled by enemy tanks. The company defending Sollum was active from 0530 to 1800 and it also fought to the end and surrendered only after all its officers had fallen and their ammunitions exhausted. A few of its soldiers even managed to resist until darkness descended and then forced the enemy encirclement to reach our lines. At Capuzzo the soldiers under the direct command of Montemurro repulsed two tank attacks supported by infantry. They then engaged the enemy with hand grenades until they were joined by Axis tanks. The regiment has sustained heavy losses, but has soon as Colonel Montemurro reorganized it, the unit, or the fragment

---

111 I.S.O., Playfair, *The Mediterranean and the Middle East Volume 2: The Germans Come to the Help of their Ally (1941)*, p. 162.
112 Jack Greene and Alessandro Massignani, *Rommel's North Africa Campaign*, p. 70.

that remained, was ready to be deployed again….I therefore propose that the Colonel be awarded the Iron Cross First Class."[113]

Operation Battleaxe

Operation Battleaxe was launched by General Wavell to recapture positions in Cyrenaica as well as to relieve the pressure upon the Tobruk garrison. Wavell had been pressured by Prime Minister Churchill to launch another offensive to weaken the Axis siege of Tobruk and to push back Rommel's forces. Wavell had considerable misgivings about a renewed offensive arguing on 28 May that "Our infantry tanks are really too slow for a battle in the desert, and have been suffering considerable casualties from the fire of the powerful enemy anti-tank guns."[114] But eventually at the beginning of June he relented and let the offensive go ahead. Meanwhile, the arrival of the Tiger naval convoy in mid-May to Alexandria with its impressive cargo of 82 Cruiser, 135 Matilda II and 21 light tanks, made it possible to replace the losses sustained by the 7th Armoured Division as well as launch the new offensive.

The plan was to attack the frontline positions of Sollum, Fort Capuzzo and the Halfaya Pass and once the enemy defenses had been overcome the 7th Armoured Division would lead the break through to Tobruk. The main aspect of the plan consisted in a second attempt to overtake the strategic Halfaya Pass (it had been recaptured by another surprise raid by Colonel Herff's unit on 26 May) which was occupied by Axis artillery units, including *Maggiore* Leopoldo Pardi's *2° Reggimento motorizzato artiglieria Celere*, (2nd Celere motorized artillery regiment). The latter had been dispatched to reinforce the understrength *Ariete* Division and it was comprised of:

- One group with three batteries of 100/17 howitzers,
- Two groups with two batteries each of 75/27 guns.

The pass was a position of critical importance since supply columns to Tobruk had to cross it therefore its capture was imperative for the Commonwealth troops which by seizing it would have cut the enemy's supply line and help relieve the siege of Tobruk.

Positioned on the pass along with a German artillery unit commanded by Major Bach and armed with four 88mm guns, the Italian artillery unit had deployed its truck mounted guns. It was thus one of the few Italian units that were fully motorized and that could keep pace with the more fast moving German mobile artillery forces. The guns had been camouflaged on the hilly terrain on the pass and dug in concealed positions with the barrel just a few inches from the ground while others had been placed higher up entrenched in stone sangers with their muzzles barely visible. Italian units also held the other main strongpoints situated on the Axis frontier line, those of Sollum, Musaid, Fort Capuzzo and Bir Hafid. The defensive deployment was based on its most important pillar, which was Halfaya pass, but the Axis defensive disposition was also based on the armoured units providing support where need be along the line. The big difference with Brevity was that the German 88mm guns along with Pardi's unit had been moved forward alongside the Pak 50mm and the 47mm guns to deal with the enemy armour directly.

---

113 Mario Montanari, *Le operazioni in Africa settentrionale*, Vol. II, Part I, p. 197.
114 Basil Liddell Hart, *The Rommel Papers*, p. 141.

On the morning of 15 June, the British attacked with a three-pronged surge: the 11th Indian Brigade against Halfaya, the 4th Armoured Brigade against Fort Capuzzo, while the 7th Armoured Brigade was operating wide to the left. Both armoured units were part of the rebuilt 7th Armoured Division that was based on both Cruiser and Matilda II tanks.[115] On Halfaya pass the 2nd Battalion of the Camerons supported by 4th Royal Tanks were advancing slowly on the edge of the escapement. The artillerymen were ordered to initially held their fire until the enemy tanks were within range of their guns and then opened a blistering barrage. Here eleven out of twelve Matildas were destroyed by the upper defenses, while four out of six were destroyed by the lower defenses through a combination of artillery fire and mines.[116] The German and Italian guns, positioned on a strategically sited ridge overlooking the roads, thus destroyed fifteen Matilda tanks and damaged several others as they debouched. At 1000 the commander of the 4th Royal Tanks Major Miles radioed that "my tanks have been blown to bits."[117] By this time, the motorized infantry of the *Trento* Division (62nd Regiment) had also come to the aid of the defenders with some heavy truck mounted guns of its own: one 105/28 truck mounted naval gun and several truck mounted 47mm guns. The large caliber gun, in particular, had played an important role in targeting the heavy infantry tanks and further buttressing the defense of the pass. As the operation bogged down, the Commonwealth artillery opened a tremendous fire concentrated upon the pass and aimed to suppress the Axis guns. "Even though submerged by enemy fire, the battery of 100/17 guns, commanded directly by Maggiore Pardi continued unabated to spit out fire."[118] The reaction of the Axis artillery was so fierce that only two Matildas were left standing which together with the Camerons sought shelter in a wadi close to the pass. Although these troops were not too far from the main Axis positions, the Axis artillery continued to pound away pinning down the Commonwealth soldiers. As a hail of fire overwhelmed the Commonwealth soldiers, several losses were sustained and the attackers were forced for two days to suffer from the enemy fire while taking mounting casualties. The timely barrage against the infantry concentrations by the Axis artillery had been even more important to the outcome of the first day of battle than the concentrated fire against the tanks. As Rommel, had instructed during the battle: "Victory depends on your holding the Halfaya Pass and the coastal plain"[119] and by inflicting heavy losses on the enemy infantry the Axis guns were instrumental in retaining the possession of the pass. In the afternoon, the Commonwealth attacked again with the 7th Armoured Brigade but again its forces were repulsed by a timely intervention of the artillery which knocked out seventeen more tanks. During the latter stages of the battle the Italians had almost run out of artillery shells when they made recourse to an old supply dump in one of the wadis which contained vintage artillery shells.

Meantime, Fort Capuzzo was besieged by the 7th Royal Tanks which bypassed Point 206, which was occupied by *Bersaglieri* with anti-tank guns, and arrived at the fort at 1200. After a

---

115 The 7th Armoured Brigade had two regiments of Cruiser tanks, the 4th Armoured Brigade with two regiments of 'I' tanks, and the Support Group.
116 "The attacks by the 11th Indian Infantry Brigade Group on the Halfaya Pass position failed, mainly because of the powerful anti-tank defense; above the Pass the German guns accounted for eleven out of twelve tanks engaged, while the minefields below trapped four out of six." I.S.O., Playfair, *The Mediterranean and the Middle East Volume 2: The Germans Come to the Help of their Ally (1941)*, p. 171.
117 *History of the 4th and 7th Royal Tank Regiments* <http://www.4and7royaltankregiment.com/1941-1942/> (accessed 1 June 2019).
118 Mario Montanari, *Le operazioni in Africa settentrionale*, vol, II, Part I, p. 242.
119 Ibid., p. 73.

brief fight, they overcame the enemy resistance and made their way into the fort. The following counterattack by a battalion of the 5th Panzer Regiment was unable to recapture it. Having captured the fort the Commonwealth forces then focused their attention on Point 206, which was occupied by a small contingent that was still holding out. The first attack was put forth by the A Tank squadron (4th Royal Tanks) which had only four Matildas left in operational order. The tanks mounted their attack against the position but were unable to overtake it and three tanks were put out of action. To subdue it, the commander of the 4th Royal Tanks had to deploy B Tank Squadron, which had been held in reserve. The latter tank squadron also attacked the enemy but it was also rebuffed. According to the units own war diary the attack had taken a heavy toll on the British armour: "By the end of the 15th out of the 100 Matildas that had started the battle only 37 were operational, but by morning hard work by the fitters had increased this number by another 11."[120]

The Commonwealth plan for the next day was for the 4th Indian Division to attack again the Halfaya Pass, while setting up a defensive screen in the Fort Capuzzo area. Meanwhile, the bulk of the 7th Armoured Division was to continue to advance on the desert flank. As a result, further attacks against the pass were made on the morning by the 11th Indian Brigade but both attempts were repelled.

Through counterattacks by German armour, the mechanized Commonwealth columns were also checked and pushed back with losses, especially the one led by the 7th Armoured Brigade. Rommel states that: "The 5th Light Division, which was attacking toward Sidi Suleiman from the area west of Sidi Azeiz, was soon heavily engaged with the 7th Armoured Division six miles west of Sidi Omar. The violent tank battle which ensued was soon decided in our favor and the division succeeded in fighting its way through to the area of north-east of Sidi Omar and continuing its advance on Sidi Suleiman. This was the turning point of the battle."[121]

According to historian Roland Lewin throughout the engagement the Commonwealth commanders thought that "the panzers were responsible (an impression of superior fire power which was by now indelibly stamped on the minds of the British tank crews), the damage was done by the 88mm guns, though the excellent 50mm PAK may have contributed."[122] Similarly, historian Niall Barr also argues that the Axis guns first and foremost won the battle: "This time, when the lumbering Matilda infantry tanks, which had proven invulnerable to every Italian anti-tank and artillery gun, rumbled forwards to assault the German defenses at Halfaya Pass, they were knocked out at long range by the well dug in German 88mm guns."[123]

The Axis artillery, strongly anchored to its positions, had played an important contribution in halting the Commonwealth attack and the Italian guns had played their part by knocking out several Matildas and two Cruisers. The artillery had held out enough for the tanks to come to their aid and deal the final blow to the enemy. This role was recognized by Rommel himself which decorated *Maggiore* Pardi with a German Iron Cross First Class because of his leadership skills demonstrated on Halfaya Pass. In the Rommel Papers, he states: "The crucial position in this battle was the Halfaya Pass, which Captain Bach and his men held through the heaviest

---

120 *Desert Rats: Battleaxe* < http://www.desertrats.org.uk/battles1941.htm#Battleaxe> (13 February 2019).
121 Basil Liddell Hart, *The Rommel Papers*, p. 144.
122 Ronald Lewin, *The Life and Death of the Afrika Korps* (Barnsley: Pen and Sword, 2003), p. 65.
123 Niall Barr, "Rommel in the Western Desert," in Ian Beckett (ed.), *Rommel Reconsidered*, p. 72.

fighting. Major Pardi's artillery battalion also rendered distinguished service in this action, thus showing that Italian troops could give a good account of themselves when they were well officered. Had the British been able to take the Halfaya Pas as they had planned, the situation would have been very different."[124]

The Western Desert Force lost 122 officers and men killed, 588 wounded, and 259 missing. They also suffered four guns lost, 27 Cruisers and 64 Matilda tanks were lost from enemy action or breakdown, many of which were recoverable. The Germans suffered 93 officers and men killed, 350 wounded, and 235 missing and 12 tanks destroyed. The Italians suffered 112 dead, 218 wounded and 189 missing.

As the West Point history of the war asserts, Operation Battleaxe failed and the Commonwealth lost 91 tanks mainly due to the Axis skillful deployment of the antitank guns. It would not be the last time during the desert campaign when the antitank guns would have the upper hand against the tank brigades. Brevity and Battleaxe were good defensive battles for the Italians especially with regard to the anti-tank defense which had so much troubled Graziani's army in 1940. One of the reasons Italian morale collapsed during Operation Compass was because the standard infantry soldiers had little or no experience in fighting Commonwealth armoured units. At the time, Matilda II tanks, which were too hard skinned for the Italian 47mm guns, overran Italian fortified defenses on several occasions by circumventing their defenses and cutting off large pockets of soldiers that were later captured by the Commonwealth motorized columns. Several factors account for the improved performance of the Italian troops fighting against enemy armoured units in mid-1941. The most important factor was that the Italian soldier, both in the infantry and in the armoured units, had received better training. Beginning in 1941 training was administered in the North African instruction centers in Libya to increase the fighting performance of all troops. The first center was created at Barce for infantry and combat engineers while another center was created near Benghazi for the artillery units. Finally, a tank crew training center was constituted near Derna that included a repair shop, a school for drivers, and a recovery squad to salvage tanks. According to historian Richard Carrier[125] both infantry and armoured units received better training and improved equipment. He furnishes the example of the anti-tank defense where soldiers were trained on how to use the 47mm anti-tank gun more effectively from an uphill position and by deploying it at very close range against vulnerable parts of an enemy tank. This was coupled with the creation of dedicated tank hunter teams amongst the infantry and the *Bersaglieri* using improvised explosive devices such as incendiary bombs, anti-tank rifles, and heavier anti-tank weapons to fight off enemy tanks. "Given the delay in developing an anti-tank gun that could replace the now outdated 47mm, the Italian infantry developed (in contrast to German and British forces, which relied more and more on new anti-tank guns) a whole series of close range, individual anti-tank hand grenades and devices, mostly developed with ingenuity in the field."[126] In addition to the 47mm guns, the heavier caliber 100/17 and the 105/28 guns had been skillfully deployed and inflicted heavy losses. The latter, in particular, deployed as a kind of

---

124 Basil Liddell Hart, *The Rommel Papers*, p. 147. Also cited in John Pimlott, *Rommel in His Own Words*, p. 76.
125 Richard Carrier, 'Some Reflections on the Fighting Power of the Italian Army in North Africa, 1940–1943', *War in History*, 2015, vol. 22, n.4, pp. 503–528.
126 Pier Paolo Battistelli and Piero Crociani, *Italian Soldier in North Africa: 1940-43* (Oxford: Osprey, 2013), p. 18.

self-propelled gun had changed position several times during the combat action to better target the enemy tanks. Another factor that improved the soldier's performance was the arrival with *Ariete* and of the DAK of armoured reinforcements to prop up the anti-tank defense by deploying its units in counter-attacks against enemy tanks. An additional factor that increased combat effectiveness was provided by the support and example provided by the Germans, especially in their use of maneuver tactics and the forward use of anti-aircraft guns deployed in the anti-tank defense. Lastly, the energetic Rommel also contributed to boosting troop morale through his battle field example and presence.

THE ITALIAN ARMY AND CAPTURED ENEMY TANKS AND ARMOURED VEHICLES

During the war the Italian Army captured 5,833 enemy vehicles of all sizes and types. Of these many of the tanks and armoured vehicles that were easily repairable were used by the troops in the frontline, while many more units that were damaged or were not easily repairable were transferred to the rear either to be studied and evaluated by technical staff or used for target practice by Italian tank and anti-tank gun crews.

The largest mass deployment of captured British vehicles occurred when the Italians seized thirty Morris Commercial and Ford F.5 vehicles which were fitted with 65/17 guns and 20mm guns and operated by the *12° Autoraggruppamento* in its *batterie volanti* (flying artillery columns) units. After the first seizure more enemy vehicles were acquired over time. The largest seizures were obtained in early 1942 with the recapture of Cyrenaica and then in mid-1942 after the recapture of Tobruk.

The Italians also used several captured Mark IV and A 15 Crusader II tanks. The latter was evaluated extensively. Several units were shipped to Italy where the Army requested Ansaldo/Fiat to develop a 15 tons' medium tank, with thicker armour, a petrol fueled engine, and a top speed of 55/Kph. This led to the design of the *Carro M Celere Sahariano* (Saharan fast track medium tank) which was a "carbon copy of the British A 15 Crusader II tank."[127] A prototype was built in mid-1942 equipped with a 47/40 gun and a Breda model 38 machine gun. Trials where then conducted in early 1943 but the plan for mass production was ultimately abandoned when Italian troops were evicted from North Africa and there was no longer a need for such a tank. One Bren Carrier and two Universal Carriers were transported back to Italy and were used to develop Italian prototypes. Both were studied for many months but the prototypes developed were never produced in mass due to lack of funding and materials. The Italians also extensively evaluated the Matilda II infantry tank but also never got around to developing a mass produced heavy, infantry tank.

The Italians also seized 109 Renault R35 tanks, and 33 Somua S35 tanks from the French Army because of the agreements between the two countries in 1940. Initially the French armour was destined to equip a newly formed armoured division, but then the lack of spare parts and ammunition induced the Italians to use them for training and then for the defense of Sicily in 1943 and most were destroyed by the Allies.

---

127 Pier Paolo Battistelli and Filippo Cappellano, *Italian Medium Tanks*, p. 14.

Summer 1941: Training and Re-equipment

During spring-summer of 1941 *Ariete* was reorganized with the arrival of additional troops and equipment (mostly medium tanks and heavier artillery) from Italy. This reorganization would culminate with the reorganization of the 132° *Reggimento Carristi* comprised of the VII, VIII and IX *Battaglioni Carri Medi* on 1 September 1941. The VII had already been in North Africa since the winter of 1941 and had participated to Rommel's first offensive which led to the recapture of Cyrenaica, while the other two battalions came from Italy during the summer. The newly formed regiment, comprised in its entirety by medium tanks, was intended to become the breakthrough and maneuver mechanized unit of the division. The commander of the regiment was *Tenente Colonnello* Enrico Maretti.[128] While some, especially VII *Battaglione Carri Medi* crews were experienced, others had not gone through any combat action operating the medium tanks especially in the desert terrain and this prompted a renewed focus on training. Even the arriving tank crews of the medium tanks from Italy necessitated training since the drivers had only operated their vehicles four times and the gunners had fired only three rounds apiece in the brief training sessions held in Italy. Thus during this time *Ariete* focused extensively on training and on the incorporation of the new soldiers and equipment that came from Italy into its ranks. *Tenente* Enrico Serra of *Ariete* recalls from that period that:

> We are profiting by the pause in activities to intensify the training of our units. We chose land that is variegated and irregular, and we prepare dummies made of shells of abandoned vehicles. I explain the lessons repeatedly. Our tanks must approach the enemy at a sustained speed. they must pause for a moment to allow the tank commander to fire his gun, and then leave as quickly as possible …I explain repeatedly that it is useless to fire while the tank is in motion, as the rolling motion makes it impossible to aim.[129]

Another *Ariete* officer argued that to properly operate in an armoured battle the division's various combat units had to train and fight as one. "Anti-tank and anti-aircraft units must accompany the armoured units. Each unit is mutually supportive and must complement the divisions capabilities."[130] Tactics also evolved at this point. As Greene and Massignani assert the Italian units learned German tactics which were assimilated primarily by conducting joint operations with the panzer units:

> Italian doctrine envisioned the use of M tanks to punch holes in the enemy line with L tanks acting as scouts, while the P tanks, which were essentially non-existent, were to act as mobile artillery- the semovente substituted in many ways for this lack. The artillery doctrine, fuoco da manovra (maneuvered fire), called for the employment of anti-tank guns and field artillery forward close to the front and using massed fire, compensating in part

---

128 *Tenente Colonnello* Maretti was an experienced commander of tank units that had fought in the Spanish Civil War with the Littorio Division which was the main Italian Division that deployed tanks during the campaign. In North Africa Maretti would enjoy a close working relationship with Rommel who decorated Maretti with an Iron Cross second class.
129 Ian Walker, *Iron Hulls, Iron Hearts*, p. 71.
130 Giulio Bedeschi, *Fronte d'Africa: c'ero anch'io*, p. 340.

for the lack of range and older guns. This would be combined with celere (a light, partially mechanized division not sent to Africa) and infantry division support. The concept was close to German Blitzkrieg and lacked only tactical airpower.[131]

When the Fiat 3000 B were first introduced in the 1920s the High Command had issued an instruction document stating that "during an offensive operation the tank (to be assigned to every platoon) is destined to neutralize the antitank screen, machine gun posts and enemy tanks."[132] The document, barely mentioning the tank, did not assign to it an autonomous combat role but one that was in close support of the infantry.

In 1938 the Army updated its tactical plans and envisioned the use of tanks in three circumstances: in cooperation with infantry, together with a celere unit or within a tank brigade. In the first circumstance, a few tanks were to support an infantry battalion to overcome defensive obstacles in the latter stages of an advance. This was a traditional combat role, much akin to First World War strategies adopted in the Western Front, assigned to the armoured units.

In the second circumstance *celeri* units would make a frontal attack while tanks were to attack the enemy flanks. This second approach was popular during the 1930s after the *celeri* units had been formed but it still perceived the tanks as being deployed in a piecemeal fashion mainly in a support combat role. It still had limitations but it represented nonetheless an improvement over the First World War armoured tactics.

In the third circumstance tanks were to be deployed in deeper maneuvers aimed at reaching the enemy rear and destroying its infrastructure such as fuel depots and ammunition dumps. This last approach was the most innovative of the three even though in 1938 Italy still could not field medium tanks that would have been central to the success of such an ambitious maneuver.

The 1941 directives updated the 1938 document and other older technical manuals reflecting the new circumstances of war in North Africa. They stressed that armoured divisions were not only expected to confront enemy defenses but also to engage enemy tanks and other armoured units in protracted battle. "Tanks can fire both in a static as well as while moving. Given limited ammunition and the necessity to use resources wisely, it is advised that firing while maneuvering is to be preferred than firing from a static position. The best defense for the tanks is their mobility not their armour therefore they should never be used in a passive defensive role."[133] Since Italian tanks had less firepower than many Commonwealth tanks they could only succeed by getting as close as possible to enemy armour or by maneuvering at their flanks or the rear. They were also softer skinned than medium Commonwealth tanks and thus they had a greater chance of survival if they moved quickly and expeditiously in the battlefield thus offering less of a target than when deployed in a static position.

The 1941 directives assigned to the armoured units the task of breaking through the enemy defenses in combined arms operations by following the lead of the German panzer units:

"The function of the armoured division is the rupture of the enemy's frontline. The rupture must be effectuated by the armoured unit or by the armoured unit in combination with other combat elements of the army. The operation's objective is to penetrate deeply into the enemy's

---

131 Jack Greene and Alessandro Massignani, *Rommel's North African Campaign*, p. 236.
132 Filippo Cappellano and Nicola Pignato, *Andare contro i carri armati*, p. 171.
133 Ufficio Storico, Stato Maggiore Regio Esercito, Ufficio Addestramento, 'L'Impiego delle unita' corazzate', circolare n. 18000, Aprile 1941.

rear by deploying greater fire power to overwhelm the enemy's defenses. In addition, when faced by an enemy armoured unit the objective is to first attack it with air and artillery power and then to attack it resolutely with the armour deploying all of its resources to surprise and overwhelm the enemy."[134]

For it is important "in the open desert to take the enemy under effective fire earlier and hit him earlier than he, himself, is able to do." To be "further from the enemy than he from you is a cardinal principle in the desert."[135] The instructions here appear to refer to the British Matilda II tank, which was feared because it had such heavy armour that it was almost impenetrable by the 47mm guns. There was also renewed interest in the reconnaissance function with the publishing of a tactical document for the deployment of special units titled *"Impiego del raggruppamento esplorante corazzato RECO"* (deployment of reconnaissance unit RECO). This function was to be carried out by units equipped with light and medium tanks, motorcycles, armoured vehicles and support services acting as a tactical group on behalf of an armoured division or army corp. The essence of their mission was to act with 'extreme mobility and rapidity which were necessary not only to capture intelligence swiftly but also to quickly disengage if and when they encountered an enemy unit." Such units were required to have heavy guns such as *semoventi* or medium tanks and artillery in their ranks since it was expected that successful reconnaissance deep into the enemy lines would frequently involve clashing and disengaging from similarly organized enemy units.[136]

Reconnaissance was now recognized as a key capability in desert warfare. To take the enemy under effective fire as soon as possible and hit him suddenly thus impeding his reaction was a key feature of the North Africa battlefield that could only be carried out by relying upon good reconnaissance. To hit first and to do so with longer range guns so that the friendly armour was further from the enemy than he from you was a key tactical principle of warfare in the desert.

While the tactical instructions were being updated, General Ugo Cavallero dispatched to North Africa General Mario Roatta who was charged with inspecting Italian frontline troops and to issue a report with recommendations to improve combat effectiveness. He was not only to assess the morale and preparedness of the infantry, but also to focus upon the armoured units and how they could be better organized, trained and equipped. Roatta issued two reports, a preliminary one on 15 March 1941 and a more detailed report on 28 July, which promoted reforms to enhance combat performance.[137] The first issue that he raised was training which is in his view had to be intensified and should reflect actual combat situations. Then he focused upon the anti-tank defense and how artillery and anti-tank guns were to cooperate more fully with infantry in halting enemy tanks. He reminded how in Spain the anti-tank defense had been perfected by the Italian troops by bringing anti-tank guns forward and employing them at short range against the massive Soviet hulks. Another issue was reconnaissance how it could be improved by relying upon dedicated mobile units and on greater reliance upon the air force. Finally, how the offensive operations had to rely more on advanced surveillance and greater cooperation between armour, artillery and infantry. With regard to armour one of the first

---

134 Ibid.
135 Ibid.
136 Ufficio Storico, Stato Maggiore Regio Esercito, Ufficio Addestramento, 'Impiego del raggruppamento esplorante corazzato RECO', Maggio 1941.
137 Ufficio Storico, "Lacune rilevate," 17 Marzo 1941, and 'Addestramento e operazioni', 28 Luglio 1941.

things Roatta noticed was that many tanks were not properly maintained and serviced, while the Germans had dedicated recovery teams and could return to combat a much higher rate of tanks in a much shorter time. In one sector of the front, for instance, Roatta noticed that there were twelve tanks in the repair shop, nineteen tanks that had been left scattered along the Trigh Capuzzo road waiting to be repaired and only eleven that were deployed at the front and could be considered combat ready. Roatta learned from the crews of the typical mechanical and technical failures of the M.13/40 tanks which included several issues. The performance of the Italian M.13/40 tank, mainly during the siege of Tobruk in April 1941, was reviewed extensively by *Maggiore Comandante VII Battaglione Carri Medi/Ariete* Alberto Andreani. His report is very worthy because it is brutally honest in accounting for the mechanical and design failures of the tank. The major issues were that the engine was underpowered (125 horsepower versus the 320 horsepower of a German panzer tank) and had to overhauled after 500 km given the lack of suitable air filters. Moreover, every fifty miles the tank needed an oil change thus impeding fast paced operations. Water did not circulate well in the engine, filters had to be cleaned out every two hours because of the sand, and the electrical panels were not effective and often shut down unexpectedly.[138] The damning report on the technical defects of the M.13 tank by *Maggiore* Andreani concluded by observing:

> Ultimately, this tank is equipped with an engine that certainly would work well in Italy or in an urban type of environment. The engine of the M.13 tank was designed originally for an 8-ton tank and is unsuited for a 14-ton tank. In the North African territory, with the ghibli, the sand, and a number of other adverse environmental conditions it is utterly unsuitable despite the care and the precautions taken by the crews. The tank crews must operate under enemy fire and they cannot and should not be worrying about the reliability of their vehicle. They should not worry whether the tank engine will start, whether the gear shift will operate properly or whether the tank will lose too much water or leak too much oil. In short, after the maintenance crews get the tank going the crews are often forced to operate at below full speed and they cannot perform the offensive tasks they had been assigned. This tank cannot carry out the tactical objectives which the Army expects because of its underpowered engine. It needs an efficient and powerful engine worthy of our proud automobile heritage. With regard to a recent operation, a German Major told me: 'You guys performed a miracle with your primitive vehicles. I was able to accomplish the mission with only eight out of the sixty-four vehicles with which I started the operation, while you guys were able to complete the mission with fourteen tanks out of forty … Ultimately, the Battalion must be reorganized completely while all the vehicles still operational must be overhauled with new engines coming from Italy, other vehicles must be recovered and we need to obtain the spare parts. We must replace the fallen soldiers and officers with new trainees from Italy. For all this work, I estimate it will take a while probably no less than

---

138 Ufficio Storico, Relazione Andreani 'Impegno Operativo M.13/40', 21 Aprile 1941. It is interesting to note that not everyone in the armoured forces was critical of the medium tanks. The medium tanks utilized by IV *Battaglione Carri Medi* were reputed by the commander of the 31° *Reggimento* De Lorenzis, to have performed effectively during the Greek campaign and of being of "appreciable quality." This assessment is likely the product of the fact that the writer had not operated them in the desert terrain but in Greece.

40-50 days and this will also depend upon how long it takes to receive the new engines and the spare parts."[139]

General Gambara, who would shortly thereafter be put in command of Italian armoured units in North Africa, toured the front and on 25 May 1941 and he also wrote a very critical report on the technical and performance shortcomings of the M.13/40 tank. The report was based on feedback he had received from the crews of the armoured units. In it he wrote: "The troops, believe it or not, still prefer the L.3 tank! At least, they say, the light tank is fast and therefore offers less of a target. Ariete still has about twenty of these light tanks and the crews prefer driving them over the M.13/40. The latter they say has a good hull, firepower and decent armoured thickness, but its engine does not work well. It's too weak and on non-paved terrain its maximum speed is only 8 kph. Given its low mobility it is often the target of even the puniest anti-tank gun which can in most cases penetrate its armour. The engine needs to be overhauled from diesel to petrol. With this change the power of the engine would hover approximately between 130-150 hp."[140]

After receiving the valuable feedback provided by the crews regarding the technical issues experienced while operating the M.13/40 tanks in the desert terrain in the spring of 1941, Roatta decided to conduct tests between four *Panzerkampfwagen* III and four M.13/40. The first test involved a race at top speed between the tanks. Whilst the Panzers had no problem reaching their destination, the M.13s experienced several difficulties. Two tanks were stuck at the start line because of engine failure, one tank took off but only travelled a few meters before it broke down and one tank completed the race but at a considerable slower speed than the German units. The second test was based on the firepower of the respective tanks. Each German tank fired six shells consecutively against a captured Matilda tank, while the M.13s could fire only a few shots before the gun jammed. It is reported that Roatta was shocked by the results of the tests and that he wowed to equip the Italian Army with a more effective tank. His efforts, however, were not successful since the M.13/40 (or the slightly improved M.14) remained the mainstay tank of the Italian Army for the duration of the war.

The Germans, like Roatta, also viewed the M.13/40 tank as a very ineffective weapon: "The M series was called Rollende Saerge, or rolling coffin, by the Germans, due to lack of armour and poor quality of the bolted plate. Dr. Monzel, a German interpreter in the Italian *Ariete* said that: 'the chance of surviving an attack in such a tank, lay beyond the realms of courage which can morally be demanded."[141] Another German tank specialist argued that the M tanks were "obsolete, slow, had limited armour and were an obstacle to effective armoured attack."[142] Even Rommel admitted that no German crew would ever want to ride in an M.13/40 tank which were considered too slow and light skinned offering little protection when pitted against Commonwealth units.

With regard to Italian armour, Roatta noted in his report not only the mechanical failures but also the lack of adequate reconnaissance capabilities by Italian tank battalions especially in

---

139 Ibid. Other specialists argued that the Italians should procure German engines for their tanks, but the Germans never agreed to supply them most likely because they were needed in German factories.
140 Lucio Ceva, *Le forze armate* (Rome: Ufficio storico, 1988), p. 573.
141 Ibid, p. 236.
142 Hermann Büschleb, *Operation Crusader: Tank Warfare in the Desert, Tobruk 1941* (Philadelphia: Casemate, 2019), p. 20.

North Africa and the weakness of communication, especially two way radios for the armoured unit's commands. In his tour of the front the crews of the armoured units and of the infantry had noted that armoured vehicles were as essential as tanks in North Africa and that there was a desperate need for them. Another officer noted that: "our troops .... lacking both speedy armoured cars with which to locate the enemy and air reconnaissance ...end up steering toward the enemy more or less randomly, using above all what evidence there is of the direction of the incoming enemy artillery fire, which however emanates from extremely mobile British batteries spread over a wide front." [143]

It was also recognized that the lack of adequate light armoured vehicles and jeeps had delayed the creation of proper specialized reconnaissance units to support the tank formations. The feedback received by the troops on the ground, the reports by technical specialists on the performance of the medium tanks and the joint training exercises conducted with the Germans were all factors that led to a reorganization of the troops in North Africa. This introduced a change of personnel at the top as well as a reorganization of the Army.

General Baldassarre of *Ariete* also made a number of recommendations following the experience of Operation Battleaxe. First, he argued that the light tanks were obsolete and their crews should be transferred immediately to the medium tank regiment as new M tanks were being shipped from Italy to North Africa. Second, the M tanks needed improvement in the form of a more powerful engine. Specifically, he argued for the development of a petrol engine to replace the existing diesel engine. Third, he expressed the need for a new 18 tons tank to slowly replace the 13 and 14 tons tanks. Four, he argued that the personnel and the weapons of the Santamaria and other ad hoc mobile combat groups be disbanded and integrated into *Ariete*. *Comando Supremo* replied positively to these demands but cautioned on disbanding the light tank regiment since the transition for the crews to medium tanks was not seamless and required at least two months of training. Moreover, General Cavallero was of the opinion that both the introduction of the 18 tons tanks and a more powerful engine would take time and that Ariete had to make do with the vehicles that were presently in North Africa.[144]

As part of the vast reorganization of the Italian units there was a shakeup in the command structure when on 12 July 1941 General Ettore Bastico was nominated *Comandante Superiore delle Forze Armate in Africa Settentrionale* (superior commander of the armed forces in North Africa). Bastico, born in Bologna in 1876, replaced Gariboldi which did not have good relations with Rommel and was also reputed by the Italian chief of staff not to be suited in maneuver and tank warfare. Bastico was reputed to be a better fit for the North African campaign because he had prior experience with armoured warfare. In 1937 Bastico had been the commander-in-chief of the Italian volunteer corps in Spain and led the Nationalist troops during some of the most important stages of the campaign where the Italians also deployed tanks. While in Spain he thoroughly reorganized the Italian forces eliminating several positions and streamlining the decision-making process within certain units. Bastico won some key victories in Spain before being torpedoed by Franco, who had demanded the handover of Italian captured Republican soldiers to the Nationalists. Bastico had refused to counter the rules of war and had therefore been forced to resign. In 1939 he was appointed commander of the new mechanized and

---

143 Giuseppe Mancinelli, *Dal fronte dell'Africa settentrionale* (Milan: Rizzoli, 1970), p. 65.
144 Mario Montanari, *Le operazioni in Africa settentrionale*, Vol, II, Part II, pp. 319-320.

motorized army corps the so-called *Armata del Po'* (Sixth Army). Then he was responsible for commanding troops in the Dodecanese islands in the Aegean, preparing them against a potential Greek-British attack. Largely based on Roatta's recommendations on 15 August 1941 it was announced that a new *Corpo D'Armata di Manovra* (maneuver army corps) was to be constituted by the *Ariete* and the newly arrived *101° Divisione Motorizzata Trieste*. This was a further shakeup, a profound change of the Italian organization in North Africa. The newly formed unit was to be led by *Generale* Gastone Gambara who had a prior working relationship with Ettore Bastico during the Spanish Civil War where he also gained experience commanding armoured and motorized units. Gambara had graduated from the Italian military academy in Modena and was promoted to Major of an *Arditi* battalion during the First World War. In 1935 he took part to the campaign in Ethiopia then in 1937 to the Spanish campaign when he was nominated *Capo di Stato Maggiore* of the Italian troops in Spain. Because of his participation to the Spanish campaign, Gambara was promoted to General of an army brigade. He then participated to the brief campaign against France and in 1941 he was appointed *Capo di Stato Maggiore del Comando Superiore Forze Armate Africa Settentrionale*, as second in command to General Bastico. *Ariete* was to be commanded by the newly appointed *Generale di Divisione* Mario Balotta, while the *Trieste* Division by *Generale di Divisione* Alessandro Piazzoni. Balotta came from the artillery branch. Prior to the Second World war, Balotta had been the commander of *7° Reggimento d'Artiglieria da Campagna Pisa* (7th Field Artillery Regiment Pisa) and then had been assigned to constitute another artillery regiment, the *Reggimento di Artiglieria Leonessa* based in Brescia. After that, Balotta was named *Comandante della Scuola Centrale di Artiglieria* (commander of the Army's main artillery academy) and in this capacity, he wrote several articles on artillery tactics on numerous military journals such as the *Rivista di Artiglieria*. In 1939 he took part to the invasion of Albania followed by his transfer into the armoured units.

As a result of Roatta's recommendations *132ª Divisione Corazzata Ariete* was deeply overhauled. The *32° Reggimento* was left with its three obsolete light tank battalions (I, II, and III), while the *132° Reggimento Carristi* was completed with initially two (later three in October 1941) medium tank battalions (VII, VIII and IX). Each tank battalion was to have ideally fifty medium tanks plus four tanks in the battalion's HQ. In mid-July, there were 113 L.3 tankettes and ninety-one M.13/40 (later by September there were ninety-seven L.3 and 141 M.13/40 tanks).[145] The *8° Reggimento Bersaglieri* retained its three motorized infantry battalions (III, V and XII) and also its anti-tank unit: 132ª *Compagnia Controcarri* 47/32 guns. Its artillery arm *132° Reggimento Artiglieria Corazzata* which was also considerably reinforced and could field sixteen 105mm guns, thirty-two 75mm guns, eight 47mm guns, and eight 20mm anti-aircraft guns.[146]

The *101ª Divisione Motorizzata Trieste* was organized as follows:

> *65° Reggimento Fanteria Motorizzata* (motorized infantry grounded on 3 battalions).
> *66° Reggimento Fanteria Motorizzata* (3 battalions).
> *9° Reggimento Bersaglieri* (XXXII Motorcycle Battalion, XXVIII and XXX Motorized Battalions).

---

145 Pier Paolo Battistelli and Filippo Cappellano, *Italian Army Elite Units*, p. 10.
146 One battalion of 75/27 guns came from *Pavia* Division, while one battalion of 105/28 guns came from 24a *Raggruppamento Artiglieria*.

21° *Reggimento Artiglieria Motorizzata* (I and II Gruppi with 75/27 guns, III Gruppo with 100/17 gun.)
LII Battaglione Misto.[147]

Moreover, the newly formed army corps also included for the first time a standalone reconnaissance group that allowed the Army Corps to match some of the capabilities of the German and British armoured units. The *Raggruppamento Esplorante del CAM* (RECAM) was comprised by the *Reggimento Fanteria Giovani Fascisti* (Young Fascist) volunteer unit, *Battaglione PAI Romolo Gessi*, which acted as a police force, the *LII Battaglione Carri Medi* with medium tanks and the *III/32° Battaglione Carri* armed primarily with light tanks and armoured cars and two battalions of mobile artillery with 65/17 and 100/17 guns. This unit was by the fall of 1941 able to conduct several tasks such reconnaissance, escort of supply columns, raiding and surveillance that could not be carried out before due to lack of men and equipment.[148]

Rommel welcomed the strengthening of the Italian units in North Africa and authorized a number of joint training sessions with DAK, although he disagreed with the fact that the CAM was placed under Bastico's control. Soon both would engage a turf war for the day to day control of the Italian armoured units in North Africa which was fueled in part by Cavallero. Both Bastico and Gambara were well placed. Bastico was a personal friend of Mussolini, while Gambara was closely linked with Mussolini's son in law Ciano. Both were experienced having worked together during the Spanish campaign, but both had poor relations with Cavallero. Especially Bastico had a strong dislike for Cavallero since the time that the latter held positions of prestige in the Italian military-industrial sector. After Bastico was nominated as supreme commander in Libya, Cavallero began a campaign to streamline the decision-making process by proposing that there should be one armoured commander on the frontline and one in the rear in charge of the overall organization. According to Cavallero, Rommel was to be nominated the commander of all frontline troops, while Bastico was to remain in overall command in the rear. Rommel's bid to take control of the CAM was further fueled when he was appointed in August by Hitler as commander of the newly created *Panzergruppe Afrika*[149] (*Gruppo Corazzato Africa*), with Fritz Bayerlein as his chief of staff. The DAK, comprising the 15th Panzer Division

---

147 Pier Paolo Battistelli and Filippo Cappellano, *Italian Army Elite Units*, p. 10.
148 Other reconnaissance units followed. The *18th Reco Bersaglieri*, formed on 1 February 1942, was attached to *Centauro* Division, which began to operate in North Africa in late 1942. The 15th *Reco Cavalleggeri di Lodi* was formed on 15 February 1942 and was also later attached to *Centauro*. The *8th Reco Lancieri di Montebello* was formed in July 1942.
   These reconnaissance units were equipped with the following:
      Command/Headquarters with one platoon.
      I Gruppo, with an armoured vehicles unit typically armoured cars, motorcycles, and L.3/40 tank squads.
      II Gruppo, with a motorcycle squad, a squad of L.3/40 tanks, a squad of anti-aircraft 20mm guns and a squad of *semoventi da 47/32* with two batteries.
   In addition, two batteries of *semoventi da 75/18* were also added later.
   Other smaller cavalry units were also equipped with light tanks and self-propelled guns and were for the most part dispatched to North Africa to support the armoured divisions.
149 The *Panzergruppe Afrika* was formed officially on 1 September 1941. This combat unit included the German armoured and infantry units in North Africa, as well as the Italian infantry divisions deployed at the front (*Pavia*, *Bologna*, *Brescia* and *Savona* Divisions). The Italian CAM would come

and the 5th Leicht Division, now reinforced with the 21st Panzer Division, was put under the command of *Generalleutnant* Crüwell. In addition to DAK, Rommel's Panzer Group had the 90th Leicht Division and four Italian infantry divisions (*Pavia*, *Bologna* and *Brescia* at Tobruk, while the *Savona* was at Bardia). *Ariete* and *Trieste* and the entire army corps remained under the command of *Generale* Gambara, but were to operate in close cooperation with the German commander. Rommel also obtained a strengthening of his DAK when Major-General Alfred Gause was nominated chief of staff to Rommel and with him arrived from Germany several experienced officers to strengthen the planning, logistics and the overall organization of the DAK. Rommel was also promised by the German High Command that his army would be brought up to the strength of four German armoured divisions. But as the war continued and the conflict with the Soviet Union expanded the requirements of the other Axis theatres of operation never made the considerable strengthening of the DAK possible and Rommel would later write that: "If these reinforcements had in fact come to Africa in the autumn of 1941, with their supplies guaranteed …We would have been strong enough to destroy the British in Egypt in the spring of 1942 and could have advanced in Iraq and cut off the Russians from Basra."[150]

The Mussolini's ill-advised invasion of Greece (28 October 1940) and the German invasion of the USSR, Operation Barbarossa, (22 June 1941), were two Second World War milestones that had relevant repercussions on the Axis war effort in North Africa. Hitler's "decision to attack the USSR adversely affected the Axis war effort as a whole."[151] Because of this monumental decision, the German war machine became focused primarily upon the Eastern front forcing the concentration of German materials and men to defeat the Soviet Union. The Germans, much like in the First World War, found themselves fighting a multifront war again. The entry of the United States into the conflict further exacerbated the difficulties of a two front war for the Axis forces which were by the fall in 1941 even more overstretched. The Italians were adversely affected. First, the focus of the German war effort became the conflict with the Soviet Union which limited what the Germans could spare in terms of material and men for the Mediterranean theater. Second, Mussolini's decision to dispatch an Italian contingent to the Eastern front on the heels of the start of Operation Barbarossa also reduced available reinforcements of trucks, guns and men that could be shipped to North Africa. By mid-1941 Mussolini's decision to invade Greece was also adversely affecting the Axis campaign in North Africa. By then both Greece and Yugoslavia had been subdued but large numbers of Italian forces were needed to maintain the occupation of the two countries, a huge burden until 1943. Earlier in October of 1940 up to twenty-four M.13/40, that were originally destined for North Africa, were dispatched to Greece and were placed into service in early 1941. Progressively more medium tanks were absorbed by the Balkan theater. Likewise, other heavy weapons such as artillery guns, trucks etc…. were dispatched to Greece at the expense of North Africa. Historian James Sadkovich has pointedly argued regarding the Greek campaign that: "The Italo-Greek conflict was of particular importance because it diverted Italian land, air and sea forces at a time when they were desperately needed in North Africa to parry the British attack there.[152]

---

into the *Panzergruppe Afrika* during Operation Crusader. It was redesignated *Panzerarmee Afrika* on 30 January 1942 while Operation Theseus was in progress.
150 Basil Liddell Hart, *The Rommel Papers*, p. 148.
151 James J. Sadkovich, 'Rebuttal to Bagnasco Q&A', *Global War Studies*, vol. 7, issue 1, 2010, p.17.
152 James J. Sadkovich, 'The Italo-Greek War in Context: Italian Priorities and Axis Diplomacy', *Journal of Contemporary History*, vol. 28, n.3, July 1, 1993, p. 440.

In 1941-42 the Italians began to also transfer record numbers of trucks and artillery batteries to Russia. Some of the large caliber guns, for example, were originally earmarked for North Africa but were later re-routed to the Eastern Front. In contrast to the Axis allies dispatching troops in multiple directions and operating in multiple theaters, the British during the summer of 1941 began to prepare Operation Crusader and to support it they began to amass tanks, guns and men in North Africa. As the United States became more engaged in the European/Mediterranean theater its military began to ship record numbers of weapons to Egypt to support the Commonwealth effort further outmatching the number of weapons that the Axis could deploy.

Order of Battle Corpo Armato di Manovra- November 1941

Corpo Armato di Manovra
Comandante Generale di Corpo d'Armata, Generale Gastone Gambara
Generale Addetto, Generale di Brigata Alberto Mannerini
Capo di Stato Maggiore, Tenente Colonnello Carlo Scaglia

132° Divisione Corazzata Ariete, Comandante Generale di Divisione, Generale Mario Balotta
Vice Comandante di Divisione, Generale Ismaele Di Nisio
Capo di Stato Maggiore, Maggiore Giuseppe Rizzo

8° Reggimento Bersaglieri
III Battaglione Bersaglieri
V Battaglione Bersaglieri
XII Battaglione Bersaglieri
Battaglione armi accompagnamento
132° Compagnia Battaglione controcarri (47/32)
132° Compagnia Mista Genio

132° Reggimento Carristi
VII Battaglione Carri Medi M.13/40
VIII Battaglione Carri Medi M.13/40
IX Battaglione Carri Medi M.13/40

32° Reggimento Carristi
I Battaglione Carri
II Battaglione Carri

132° **Reggimento Artiglieria**
I Gruppo Artiglieria (75/27)
II Gruppo Artiglieria (75/27)
1 Gruppo/3° Celere Artiglieri (75/27)
1 gruppo/24° Raggruppamento Artiglieria d'armata (105/28)
MILMART (102mm guns)

101° ***Divisione Motorizzata Trieste***, *Comandante Generale di Divisione, Generale* Alessandro Piazzoni
Vice Comandante di Divisione, Generale Arnaldo Azzi
Capo di Stato Maggiore, Tenente Colonnello M. Guido

65° **Reggimento Fanteria**
I *Battaglione*
II *Battaglione*
Battaglione Anticarro

66° **Reggimento Fanteria**
I *Battaglione*
II *Battaglione*
Battaglione Anticarro

9° **Reggimento Bersaglieri**
XXVIII Battaglione Bersaglieri
XXX Battaglione Bersaglieri
XXXII Battaglione Bersaglieri

21° **Reggimento Artiglieria**
II Gruppo Artiglieria Motorizzata da 75/27
I Gruppo Artiglieria Motorizzata da 100/17

DVII *Battaglione armi d'accompagnamento*
Compagnia Artiglieria Controcarro da 47/32
Batteria Artiglieria Contraerea da 20 mm

***Raggruppamento Esplorante del CAM (RECAM)**, Comandante-Colonnello* Mario De Meo
Vice Comandante Colonnello Giuseppe Follini
Comando e plotone comando (command platoon)
Compagnia Mitragliatrici Autocarrata (Truck bourne machine gun company)
Reggimento Giovani Fascisti (I and II *Battaglione*)
Battaglione PAI Romolo Gessi
LII Battaglione Carri Medi
III/32° Battaglione Carri leggeri
Una Compagnia Autoblindo. (Armoured vehicles and L.6 tanks Company)
Due Compagnie Motomitragliatori. (Two Machine Gun Companies)
Raggruppamento Batterie Volanti:
I Gruppo da 65/17 guns su tre batterie. (I Group with 65/17 guns on three batteries)
II Gruppo da 65/17 guns ed una batteria da 20/35. (II Group with 65/17 guns on three batteries plus one battery of 20/35 guns)
11ª Batteria Autonoma da 65/17. (11th Autonomous Battery with 65/17)
13ª Batteria Autonoma da 100/17. (13th Autonomous Battery with 100/17)
14ª Batteria da 20/35 guns (14th Battery of 20/35 guns)

> Support Units:
> Three Batteries *cannoni da* 102/35 guns for *Ariete* (Milimart)
> Mobile Combat Engineer Battalion
> 67° *Gruppo*
>
> (Sources: Picozzi 1949, Montanari 1985)

Operation Crusader

By mid-November 1941 *Ariete* had 6,200 men, 63 L.3 tankettes, and 141 M.13/40 tanks. *Trieste* in turn had 11,000 soldiers and no armour while the RECAM had 43 L.3 light tanks, 19 M.13/41 medium tanks and 23 armoured cars.[153] This recently formed (*Corpo d'Armata di Manovra*) mechanized and motorized army corps together with the DAK under Lieutenant General Crüwell, comprising the 15th Panzer Division, and 21st Panzer Division (total of 260 tanks) would be deployed in its entirety during the British offensive Operation Crusader. Meanwhile according to historian Mario Montanari's estimates the Axis in mid-November possessed a slightly smaller tank force. His estimate was based on only working tanks that could be deployed right away: 35 Panzerkampfwagen IV, 139 Panzerkampfwagen III, 70 Panzerkampfwagen II, five enemy tanks, 143 Italian medium tanks and 162 Italian light tanks.[154]

Following the costly failure of Operation Battleaxe, General Wavell was sacked as Commander-in-Chief Middle East Command and replaced by General Claude Auchinleck. Wavell's highly successful Western Desert Force was reorganized and renamed the Eighth Army. The latter was comprised by two main battle groups: the 13th and 30th Corps. The former included the New Zealand and the 4th Indian Divisions with a brigade of infantry tanks. The latter included the 7th Armoured Division with two armoured brigades (the 7th and 22nd), the 4th Armoured Brigade Group, the 22nd Guards Motor Brigade, and 1st South African Division, while the 2nd South African Division was kept in reserve. It is estimated that the Commonwealth in early November 1941 possessed a force of approximately 770 tanks (including Crusader tanks, Matildas, Valentines, and newly arrived American M3 Stuart[155] light tanks). In contrast the Axis armoured units were heavily outnumbered almost two to one and could muster only approximately 420 medium tanks (of which 160 were Italian medium tanks). The commander of the Commonwealth mechanized and motorized forces was General Alan Cunningham whose immediate task was to lead General Auchinleck's desert counteroffensive. According to General Cunningham's pre-battle estimates the Commonwealth in the planned offensive would face approximately 250 German Panzer tanks while discounting completely *Ariete*'s M.13/40 medium tanks which were reputed to be "not very formidable."[156] At the time, the Italian medium tanks, given their performance during Operation Compass, were evidently

---

153 Pier Paolo Battistelli and Filippo Cappellano, *Italian Army Elite Units*, p. 11.
154 Mario Montanari, *Le operazioni in Africa settentrionale*, Vol. II, Part II, p. 451.
155 Approximately 170 M3 Stuart light tanks were used during Operation Crusader with mixed results. The 15 tons' tank had a 37mm gun.
156 Mario Montanari, *Le operazioni in Africa settentrionale*, Vol. II, Part II, p. 429.

not seen as a threat by the British general or his command staff. According to British intelligence sources, the only advantage held by the Axis was in the realm of anti-tank guns since *Ariete* had some heavy truck mounted naval guns armed with armoured piercing shells and the Germans had the lethal 88mm Flak 36 guns. In contrast, the Commonwealth could field a high number of 2-pdr guns and the more effective 25-pdr guns, but in limited numbers. According to their estimates Commonwealth troops had a clear advantage with armour, armoured vehicles and with aircraft.

The Operation Crusader objectives were twofold: to degrade the fighting capability of Axis armoured forces in Cyrenaica and to lift the siege of Tobruk. To achieve these objectives, the British commander would deploy all the forces under his disposal. The 13th Corps would pin down with artillery and infantry the Axis forces defending the frontier positions and was to later converge on Tobruk, while the 30th Corps would sweep around the flanks of these frontier defenses through the southern desert with the goal of engaging and destroying the German Panzers and later to turn north west to support a breakout at Tobruk. On the first day of operation, the British armoured brigades, 4th Armoured Brigade Group, 7th Armoured Brigade, and 22nd Armoured Brigade, all part of British 7th Armoured Division under Major General William Gott, would fan out in three separate directions and then converge to Gabr Saleh, a central point about 30 miles west of Sidi Omar. After destroying the German tank forces that were assembled nearby, they were to march north to Tobruk. Once the enemy tank forces had been defeated, the garrison from Tobruk would commence breakout operations. First, it would capture the El Duda escarpment. Then it would assist the 30th Corps to take the Sidi Rezegh escarpment. With the occupation of these two main southern ridges Commonwealth forces would seize control of the main enemy line of communication, thus completing the breakout operations. The initial part of the plan involved the Commonwealth armour driving toward the German Panzer units and entice them toward an armoured pitched battle in the desert where Commonwealth tank superiority was likely to prevail over a battle hardened but less powerful enemy. *Ariete* and *Trieste* positioned by Rommel in front of the German Panzer units stood in the Commonwealth armour's way since they were tasked in an advanced position to protect the German Panzer units assembled in the rear as well as the Axis units that were positioned around the Tobruk defensive belt.

As Walker asserts: "This plan would take the British armour right past the *Ariete* Division, but the British were unduly concerned about this, although they were aware of its presence."[157]

In mid-November, the Axis forces were deployed as follows: the Sollum front was held by non-motorized mixed Italo-German troops (mainly *Savona* Division), while the fortress of Tobruk was besieged by Italian infantry divisions (*Brescia, Pavia, Trento* and *Bologna*) and backed up by the German 90th Leicht Division to prevent a breakout on the part of the enemy. The mechanized and motorized forces had been split up, with the *Trieste* Division near Bir Hacheim, the German mechanized troops were nearby at Gambut, the RECAM at Berta while *Ariete* was near Bir el Gobi. Rommel had instructed *Ariete* to act as a strategic reserve and keep watch of enemy movements in the area west of Tobruk and then, to cover the flank of the German armoured units. Bir el Gobi was also instrumental to Axis deployment because there was a supply dump nearby of ammunition and fuel.

---

157 Ian Walker, *Iron Hulls, Iron Hearts*, p. 80.

At the time General Bastico had expressed opposition to Rommel's plan for another major offensive against Tobruk arguing that the British had enough troops to strike the Axis troops from the flanks as they lay siege to the port city. The Italians, unlike Rommel, were also particularly concerned of the potential for a large scale British offensive due to the buildup of tanks and artillery pieces through the Tiger and other convoys. Meanwhile, the German intelligence service in early November dismissed Italian concerns about an imminent Commonwealth offensive. While Rommel and the DAK command staff were busy devising a new plan to siege Tobruk and did not believe that the Commonwealth forces were about to launch a massive counter thrust, the frontline Italian troops and their intelligence services had observed a steady buildup of troops and equipment by the Commonwealth on the frontier. Thus, General Mario Balotta of *Ariete* had disposed his troops defensively to face the potential enemy onslaught by organizing an anti-tank screen and sixteen machine gun strongpoints that were well sited and highly camouflaged. An artillery officer recalls that: "We could understand the importance of the Bir el Gobi position as it was the meeting point of three major tracks leading to Tobruk and as a huge supply dump. Our senior officers instructed us early on in November to dig in and construct deep, communicating trenches and machine gun strongpoints. They were very observant and attentive to our work which lasted several days."[158] As a result of this work *Ariete*'s artillery and anti-tank units had been emplaced as close as possible to the ground and some guns had been dug in so that no ground observer could see them. Many foxholes were covered with camouflage nets and in many artillery positions the ground was covered by sand color blankets so that they could minimize the dust raised by the firing of the guns. *Ariete*'s position was centered on three main strongpoints called lozenges due to their shapes, each consisting of trenches, weapons pits, and connecting communication ditches. Each was occupied by a battalion of *Ariete's Bersaglieri* Regiment (from a southern direction the III was on the left, the V in the middle and the XII on the right flank) and backed by the divisional artillery. The 75 mm guns were behind the lozenges while the heavy naval guns of MILIMART were positioned further north of these main positions. Unlike Rommel, the Italians were thus waiting for an enemy attack to be unleashed at any moment and most units had taken the necessary precautions.

While Rommel on 13 November had outlined a plan of attack against Tobruk to his subordinates and discounted intelligence reports that the Commonwealth was ready to attack, *Generale* Gambara the following days insisted that "Ariete should deploy as quickly as possible along the crossroad/Bir el Gobi."[159] This disposition was based on intelligence received from Italian surveillance aircraft which on 15 November had spotted over 3,000 armoured vehicles parked in three main assembly areas between Mersa Matruh and fort Maddalena. Furthermore, CAM's intelligence services released on the eve of Crusader, the following report on 18 November:

> On the Sollum Front at 0800 several enemy vehicles were spotted south of Sidi Omar and some foot soldiers units had been observed building trenches and gun pits. In the afternoon, Savona artillery fired 1,000 shells against enemy motorized and mechanized

---

158 Giulio Bedeschi, *Fronte d'Africa*, p. 130.
159 Livio Picozzi, 'Memorie del Corpo Armato di Manovra', *Rivista Militare*, n.7, 1949, p. 28.

concentrations. Intercepted enemy communication leaves us to surmise that an enemy attack is imminent south of Sidi Omar and in the direction of Bir el Gobi.[160]

In fact, on 18 November the 22nd British Armoured Brigade with the 11th Hussars in the vanguard and scouting out the terrain were riding forward toward Bir el Gobi where the next day they would clash against the Italians. On the same day 13th Corps had already surrounded the *Savona* Division positions and begun to shell them with its heavy artillery pieces.

As the 22nd British Armoured Brigade inched forward towards the Italian positions some of its elements belonging to 11th Hussars were spotted by RECAM armoured cars. This led to the first clash between the opposing forces which occurred at 1400 when elements of 3ª *Compagnia/* VII *Battaglione Carri Medi* commanded by *sottotenente* Benito Fabbri sighted a group of armoured vehicles belonging to B Squadron/11th Hussars as they were scouting the area between Got el Belchonfus and Bier el Dleua, approximately ten kilometers south-east of Bir el Gobi. The Italian tanks suddenly assumed their combat formation and opened up a lively fire from the maximum range of their 47mm guns. This forced the enemy armoured vehicles to quickly pull back. At 1500 a second tank platoon from 3ª *Compagnia* led by *tenente* Umberto Sobrero sighted for a second time another group of enemy vehicles and opened fire. As the enemy retreated once again, the medium tanks gave chase but were unable to catch up with the faster enemy vehicles. Later in the afternoon the British unit pushed forward a number of 25-pdr guns in an attempt to neutralize the Italian medium tanks, but as darkness descended only a few gun rounds were exchanged, and shortly thereafter both sides retreated. Once the Italian patrol unit made it back to base it immediately reported their findings to their superiors.[161] With this information on the evening of the 18th *Generale* Gambara once again furnished Rommel the details of the skirmish and in vain attempted to persuade him to postpone his planned attack against Tobruk and to focus attention on a likely Commonwealth largescale operation. Rommel discounted what *Generale* Gambara told him, telling him not to worry about any Commonwealth troop movements against Bir el Gobi since German intelligence had heavily discounted the potential for an enemy armoured attack. Gambara, who had been following closely the enemy's movements since early November, chose instead to heed what his own intelligence agency was telling him and instructed the *Ariete* division "that a British attack was imminent and that the Division should react energetically to any enemy attempt against its right flank, while Trieste was to keep an eye on the Mechili position and the meeting point between Trieste and Ariete."[162]

As a precautionary measure the 132° *Reggimento Carristi* was moved near Bir el Gobi behind the artillery positions. This measure ensured that for the first time *Ariete,* after all the training drills conducted in the summer, was going to be deployed in its entirety rather than in the earlier piecemeal fashion when it sieged Tobruk. Most of its men were cognizant that a major enemy attack was most likely about to commence and were waiting in anticipation to see how the division, at almost full ranks and fighting for the first time in its entirety, would fare. "As

---

160 Mario Montanari, *Le operazioni in Africa settentrionale, Vol. II,* Part, II, p. 439.
161 Ufficio Storico, Diario Storico 132° Reggimento fanteria carrista, Comando VII Battaglione Carri Medi, 'Relazione sull'avvistamento, inseguimento e tiro contro camionette autoblindo', 18 Novembre 1941.
162 Livio Picozzi, 'Memorie del Corpo Armato di Manovra', *Rivista Militare*, n.7, 1949, p. 28.

tenente Roberto Rosselli of the VIII *Battaglione Carri Medi* remembered, his driver made a simple remark when advancing against enemy tanks the next day: 'the time has come, we've been waiting for this for a long time.'[163]

Bir el Gobi I

The next morning a unit of sixteen M.13/40 tanks was tasked to reconnaissance the terrain in front of Bir el Gobi and spotted what appeared to be the advance guard of the British armoured unit which was menacingly approaching their defenses. The latter was comprised by three tank regiments of 22nd Armoured Brigade (158 Crusader tanks in total with 2nd Royal Gloucestershire Hussars on the Italian right flank and the 3rd and 4th County of London Yeomanry on the Italian left flank)[164], one battery of 25-pdr guns, and only one infantry company of the 4th County of London Yeomanry. Thus, this combat unit it was heavy with armour but it lacked adequate numbers of foot soldiers and guns.[165] Nonetheless according to the post-battle report of the British unit, the Commonwealth force was full of confidence and when it spotted the Italian positions it attacked them head on with little or no prior reconnaissance. In fact, on the morning of the 19th, General William Gott, the commander of the 7th Armoured Division instructed Brigadier General J. Scott Cockburn, commander of the 22nd Armoured Brigade[166], to initiate a vigorous attack on the *Ariete* positions. The division commander aimed to remove *Ariete* from its position and then install in its post the 1st South African Division, thus securing his left wing. The aim was to cut the Axis communication lines which relied heavily on holding the Bir el Gobi position, and to force the German armour from its positions to support their Italian allies thus pulling away from Tobruk this most important Axis resource. According to the War Diary of the 4th County of Yeomanry the objective of the operation was to eliminate an enemy supply dump occupied by a few tanks and guns.[167] Thus the units were aware of the presence of Axis forces at Bir el Gobi but their reconnaissance of the position obviously had underestimated the strength of the positions held by the enemy.

The first skirmish of the day took place once *Ariete*'s reconnaissance unit, even though outnumbered, decided to lunge against the first wave of Commonwealth tanks (H Squadron/2nd Royal Gloucestershire Hussars) that were sighted.

The *132° Reggimento Carristi* post-battle report states:

> At 0700, 19 November … 3rd Company under *Tenente* Lieutenant Pracca left the Lozenge accompanied by Capitano Arturo Zanolla and reinforced with a 75/27 gun section.… At 0800 enemy artillery opened fire on the Italian tanks from a fair distance. A duel

---

163 Pier Paolo Battistelli, and Piero Crociani, *Italian Soldier in North Africa* (Oxford: Osprey, 2013), p. 46.
164 The brigade had begun with 163 tanks but during the approach march of 80 miles some tanks had experienced mechanical breakdowns.
165 The British unit was not balanced being tank heavy, but it had only eight artillery guns and one small infantry unit. Thus, it lacked the combined arms force to properly deal with a defended position equipped with an anti-tank screen and backed up by tanks and mobile artillery.
166 John Connell, *Auchinleck* (London: Cassell, 1957), p. 342.
167 War Diary of the 4th County of Yeomanry, Operations in Libya 18 November 1941-30 November 1941, wo 169/1399, National Archives, Kew.

180 Steel Centurions

followed with attacks and counterattacks. At 1100 a group of forty Cruiser Mark VI tanks approached from a position four kilometers to the north-east at high speed. Our tanks turned around to face them, and though outnumbered, attacked head on. A ten-minute-long fight followed, during which the enemy lost eight tanks before retiring. Three of our tanks were hit and their crews killed. Seven were hit by anti-tank fire but returned to our positions. Three of these bore their dead commanders: Capitano Zanolla, *Tenente* Umberto Sodero and *Sotto Tenente* Fabbri Benito. A fourth commanded by *Tenente* Pracca,[168] barely reached our lines as had been hit in the engine.[169]

Thus on the morning the Italian tanks clashed with the enemy's vanguard and halted, at least temporarily, their advance. After having engaged forty enemy tanks in a brief (10-minute) but fierce duel, which left eight British vehicles destroyed for three Italian machines put out of commission and seven more damaged, the outnumbered Italian tanks began to pull back to Bir el Gobi.

At the same time the eight 25-pdr guns began the preparatory fire against the frontline enemy positions of A*riete*. As the Italian tanks retreated, the British armoured units pursued them at great speed in a cavalry like charge or as historian Basil Liddell Hart puts it "in a too gallant assault."[170] Like a team of fast racing cars, the 2nd Royal Gloucestershire Hussars with H Squadron in the middle, F Squadron on the right and G Squadron on the left pitted itself against the positions held by the III and V/8° *Bersaglieri* on the left while the 4th County of London Yeomanry targeted the flank positions of XII/8° *Bersaglieri*.[171] The last two *Bersaglieri* units where the ones that at the moment of the attack were well entrenched into their positions and could therefore respond almost at once to the enemy's thrust. While the III *Battaglione* had just set up its defensive strongpoints but many of its the guns were still on the trucks. These were 47mm guns that were usually dismantled when in transport from one position to another. "This created problems most notably the unsuitability of the gun for because it had to be towed by a motor vehicle. The Italian 47/32 gun had to be carried on lorries, with all the consequences imaginable when it came to loading and placing it in position."[172]

Predictably, on the Italian left flank and in the middle as the British tanks advanced they were met by the fire of all of *Ariete*'s 47mm and 75/27 guns which shot at point blank range, less than 250 yards away. As the Italian official history reports: "The Italian defense was well organized and could effectively react from defilade positions from which they could hit the 22nd tanks at an angle."[173]

Ariete artillery Tenente Coglitore recalls that:

> The fire by our reliable 47/32 guns was accurate and efficient, although we kept noticing, with some degree of disappointment and bitterness, that some tracer-piercing shells,

---

168 NO FOOTNOTE TEXT
169 Ufficio Storico, "Relazione Enrico Maretti sul comportamento del 132° Ariete in A.S.," Cartella 1160, prot.1809, Novembre 1942.
170 Basil Liddell Hart, *History of the Second World War* (New York: GP Putnam's and Sons, 1970), p.186.
171 War Diary of the 2nd Royal Gloucestershire Hussars, wo 169/1397, National Archives, Kew.
172 Andrew Sangster and Pier Paolo Battistelli, *Myths, Amnesia and Reality in Military Conflicts, 1935-1945*.
173 Jack Greene and Alessandro Massignani, *Rommel's North African Campaign*, p. 103.

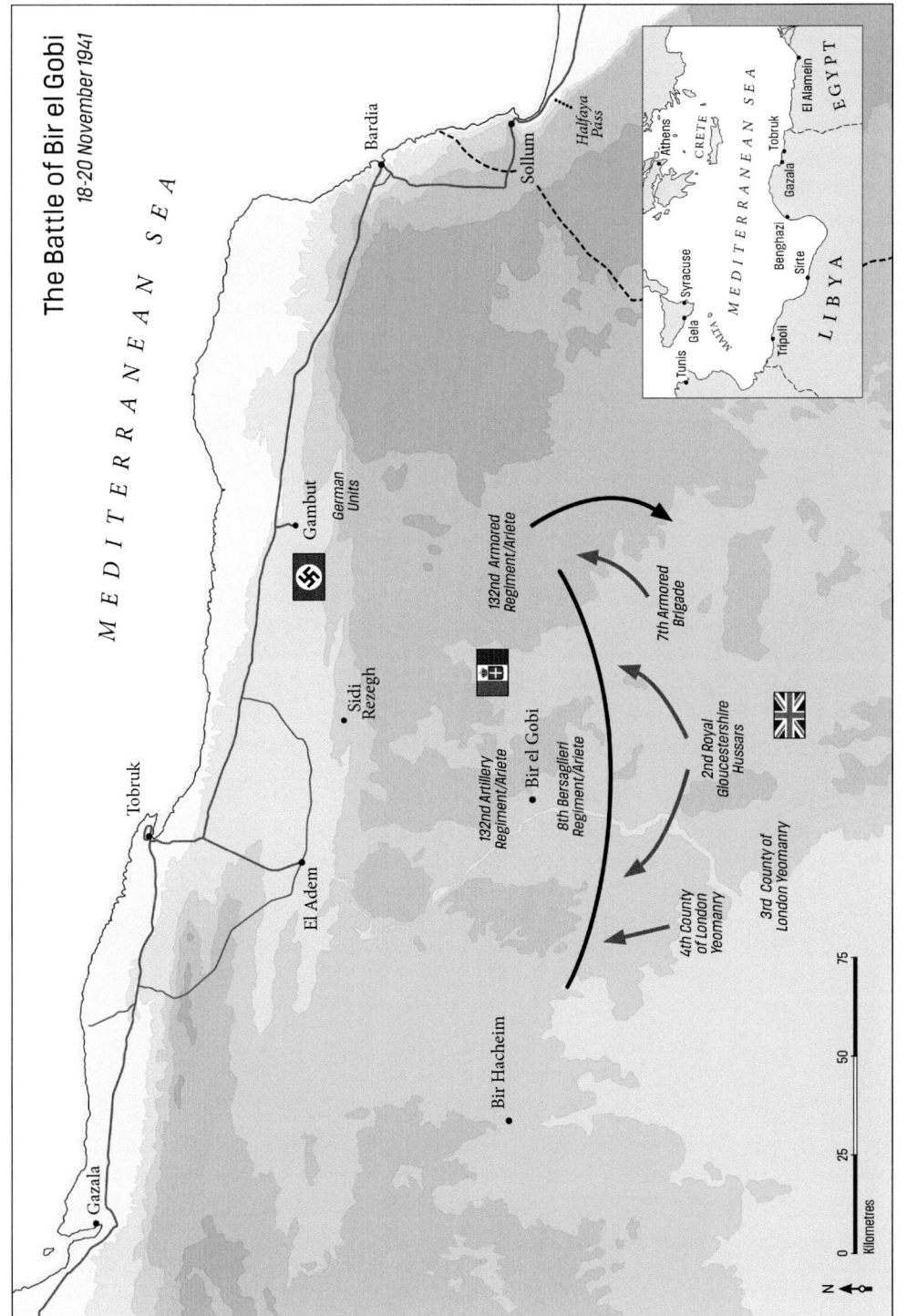

Map 2 The Battle of Bir el Gobi, 18–20 November 1941.

although reaching their target, only ricocheted off the steel armour. The field artillery was also in action and from my observation post, I could see the 75/27 guns shooting at the enemy. Artillery Capitano Morgante's battery was particularly effective with the speed and accuracy of its guns.[174]

The artillery strongpoints on the Italian right flank were able to halt and redirect the enemy attack toward the center mainly thanks to the 75/27 guns. As the British vehicles moved from the flank toward the center they lost tanks from flanking fire. *Capitano* Piscitelli Taeggi's recollections of the battle remark that the 20mm, 47mm and 75mm gun units were: "dug into camouflaged gun pits with the weapons barely visible to the adversary. Some enemy tanks wound up wandering around our positions and were subjected to deadly fire. One of them drove in the direction of our car park and began to overturn some tractors only to be immediately struck by a grenade. Another one was struck at close range when it wondered close to a gun pit."[175]

While the British account states that: "Despite unheeded warnings from the 11th Hussar screen, 4 CLY came up on the left in what one officer described as "the nearest thing to a cavalry charge seen during the war". 'C' Squadron 4 CLY had lost eight out of eleven Crusaders."[176]

Although pushed back in the center by a combination of divisional and anti-tank artillery fire, the British tanks of 2nd Royal Gloucestershire Hussars exploited the lighter defenses of the *III Bersaglieri* on the left flank which was still deploying and had failed to unload many of its heavy weapons from the trucks. With the tanks in their midst, taken by surprise, many soldiers surrendered. "Regiment was ordered to advance towards Bir el Gubi. Here some 100 MET were encountered by our leading Squadron. There was no opposition and a considerable number of Italians gave themselves up."[177] By 1330 the position of *III Bersaglieri* had almost been completely overrun as the Commonwealth tanks were driving amongst the Italian troops but could not round them up since they had no infantry support to collect them. At 1500 the bulk of the British armoured brigade, mainly from 2nd Royal Gloucestershire Hussars and 3rd County of London Yeomanry in support, regrouped and resumed the advance into the Italian positions. But as the British tanks moved further ahead they stumbled on what appeared to them from the distance to be an enemy truck park. Instead it was a well disguised anti-tank position manned by the MILIMART led by *Capitano* Priore equipped with seven truck mounted 102/35[178] guns firing armoured piercing shells that immediately opened fire at almost point blank range.[179] Within minutes, six Crusaders were smoldering in front of the Italian anti-tank position. The war diary of the British unit continues: "Regiment advanced three miles North of Bir el Gubi

---

174 Davide Zambon, "Bir El Gobi," *Ligne du Front Magazine* <http://www.qattara.it/Zambon_files/17_Art_Bir%20el%20Gobi.pdf> (accessed on 23 April 2019).
175 Oderisio Piscitelli Taeggi, *Diario di un combattente nell'Africa settentrionale* (Bari: G. Laterza & figli, 1946). p. 38.
176 *Desert Rats: Bir el Gubi* <http://desertrats.org.uk/battles1941.htm#Crusader> (accessed on 12 June 2019).
177 TNA WO 169/1397, 2nd Royal Gloucestershire Hussars War Diary.
178 These were the naval guns converted by necessity into an anti-tank role which could fire special shells that could pierce even the heaviest of the enemy's tanks.
179 The naval guns mounted on trucks were deadly but also very visible due to their size and height. Luckily for the Italians the British tank attack had not been supported by RAF. The 102/35 truck mounted guns were vulnerable when attacked by enemy planes.

and two Squadrons became engaged with a very large force of enemy tanks estimated between 140 and 160, plus numerous concealed anti-tank positions. H Squadron was held up by strong anti-tank and artillery positions on the left and did not join until late in the afternoon. Wireless communication with 22nd Armoured Brigade broke down at 1530hrs and was continued until 1630hrs. For at least two hours heavy fighting ensued."[180]

While the heavy naval guns were continuing to pour fire into the enemy tanks, *Ariete*'s tanks gathered and organized the counterattack. At first the VII and VIII *Battaglioni Carri Medi* engaged the enemy tanks for almost one hour in tank duels of great but inconclusive intensity with the armour of the 3rd County of London Yeomanry and 2nd Royal Gloucestershire Hussars. While pinned down by both tank and artillery fire the most advanced tanks of 2nd Royal Gloucestershire Hussars were then struck from behind and from the flank by *IX Battaglione Carri Medi* of the *132° Reggimento Carristi,* which had initially been held in reserve. As the latter completed this arduous and unexpected maneuver, the British tanks, shot at from different sides, were forced to fight in a disorganized fashion and without the aid of their heavy artillery. *Ariete*'s *Maggiore* Giuseppe Rizzo recalls that the final phase of the battle turned when the armoured battalion made a wide sweep that surprised the bulk of the 22nd Armoured Brigade tank units:

> The IX Battaglione was ordered to make a long-range maneuver to strike upon the enemy from the flank and rear ... During an extremely violent artillery duel between the enemy tanks and ours, the Battaglione having completed its wide sweep lunged at the enemy tanks. The latter were taken by surprise. In that instance, most of the enemy tanks being fired from behind retreated in a disorganized fashion while approximately thirty enemy tanks were surrounded, fired upon from multiple sides and ultimately boxed in and destroyed. The bulk of the enemy units were retreating fast and furiously in a southern direction while our artillery continued to target them with withering fire. The hell of Bir el Gobi had come to an end.[181]

Meantime, *Tenente* Roberto Rosselli of VIII *Battaglione Carri Medi* similarly recalls that: "That day fortune was on our side. As we advanced the wind blew a lot of sand and dust in the air which greatly shielded our movement. When the wind died down our tanks were positioned on the flank of the enemy tanks. Since the distance between us and the British tanks was not great the latter were within range of our 47mm guns. Thus, we had a field day when we suddenly opened fire and the shells penetrated the less protected flanks of the enemy tanks."[182] During this phase of the fighting a small number of medium tanks from the IX *Battaglione* moved toward the positions of the III *Bersaglieri* in an attempt to support that unit under duress. But by separating themselves from the bulk of the Italian armour they were shot to pieces by G and H Squadrons/ 2nd Royal Glouchestershire Hussars. Most of its medium tanks were lost.

As the British tanks began to disengage and retreat they were also fired upon by the Italian artillery and several other tanks were lost during this last stage of the fight. The war diary of the British 2nd Royal Gloucestershire Hussars armoured unit states that: "While withdrawing

---

180 TNA WO 169/1397, 2nd Royal Gloucestershire Hussars War Diary.
181 Giuseppe Rizzo, *Buche e croci nel deserto* (Verona: Aurora, 1969), p. 200.
182 Giulio Bedeschi, *Fronte d'Africa*, p. 85.

through Gubi anti-tank fire was encountered from Italian personnel who had previously surrendered but had re-manned anti-tank guns mounted on lorries and engaged our withdrawing tanks from the rear."[183]

The 3rd County of London Yeomanry war diary, which was originally held in reserve and then was dispatched in support of the 2nd Royal Gloucestershire Hussars when the latter came under heavy fire, tells a similar story:

> During this action, C Squadron, had been ordered to move up on the right of A Squadron, and B Squadron, consisting of five tanks under Major Godson, Capt. Vaughan, Lt JC Holcroft, Sgt Gregory and Sgt Medlar, to remain in a hull-down position 1500 yards behind A Squadron, to observe the left flank of the Regiment and to watch for 2nd RGH. From 1500 wireless touch was lost with B Squadron. This Squadron advanced from hull-down position to reconnoiter and was engaged by heavy anti-tank gunfire from the fort at Bir el Gubi. Almost at once Major Godson's tank was hit and the track blown off. The tank continued to fire for a while and was then hit on the turret and silenced, Major Godson and his operator both being wounded. Immediately after this Mr Holcroft's tank, which had gone further forward was hit on the turret at close range and all the occupants (Mr Holcroft, Tpr Mammen and Cpl Dixon) killed, except the driver, who brought the tank out of action. Sgt Hansford and Cpl Reddish treated Major Godson's wounds under fire and evacuated him from his tank. He was brought out of battle by a tank of 2nd RGH. In the meantime, Capt. Vaughan's and Sgt Medlar's tanks were hit by anti-tank gunfire. At 1650 the Regiment received orders to encircle Gubi and accordingly rallied at 181 423369. B Squadron was still silent and did not come to the rallying point. The Regiment advanced to 42037 and deployed facing West. Visibility was becoming bad and at 1750 orders were received to close leaguer in the area.[184]

Ariete's Tenente Enrico Serra describes in detail the tank versus tank engagement with the vehicles of 2nd Royal Gloucestershire Hussars outlining how brittle the Italian medium tanks were with their thin armour that often exposed the tank crews to terrible injuries:

> My command tank is within minutes in the thick of the action. To better observe where the enemy is shooting from, most officers leave the hatch open from the turret and, from time to time, observe in an exposed position instead of using the periscope which offers only limited visibility. Although indispensable, this system of observing enemy movements, is too often fatal. At one point, a sudden jolt rattles us and we fear that our tank has been hit by an armour piercing shell. But it's nothing serious and we continue to move forward. But a second later, a heartbreaking blow shakes us badly. I feel a warm liquid sliding down on my neck: I stroke my hand against the neck and when I withdraw it my hand is soaked with blood. I turn around and I now realize what happened. The armour piercing shell has made a huge hole in the turret, while several splinters have hit the crew. Pilot Lucchesi and I, bowed down in the lower part of the cockpit, are mostly unscathed, while the gun server

---

183 TNA WO 169/1397, 2nd Royal Gloucestershire Hussars War Diary.
184 TNA WO 169/1399: 3rd County of Yeomanry War Diary.

is badly wounded and the driver has an injury to his leg. Despite the wound, driver Casale seized the moment by continuing to advance. I will never forget the screams of the gun server who continued to lose blood profusely. His look of anguish, despair, and supplication will forever stay with me. We cannot stop, however. At one point, I even thought that the only way to save his life would be to throw him out of the tank, hoping that one of the four good motorcyclists who follow us can retrieve him. The work of these reckless bikers is of vital importance to our crews. A biker for instance, managed to locate two damaged tanks, with dead and wounded on board, and brought them back to the base. The battle is still unfolding. Indeed, the British are trying to regain their spirits and regroup to restart the assault. In order; not to give the enemy the time to reorganize our divisional artillery is called upon to barrage the tanks. But the call is to no avail since all communication with the rear has broken down. One after the other, the three British regiments finally withdraw as the day dies down. At the same time, Colonnello Maretti places IX Battaglione on high alert; in the event of a new attack, it will be necessary to bring it into play. Its tanks are the last available reserves. In the event of a rout, the entire German-Italian system would be threatened with encirclement from the south. As dusk falls, continues Enrico Serra, we learn that a new enemy attack is unleashed. We can see the cloud of dust of a moving column. Maretti decides to send all the tanks available to attack. [...] The fight is brief. It is a column of British trucks loaded with supplies, escorted by some tanks and armoured cars and heading to Tobruk. Most likely the British truck column was dispatched by senior commanders who believed that el Gobi had been overrun. The next day, other trucks and armoured cars are captured as they end up driving by our positions for the same reason.[185]

The post operation diary entry of *132° Reggimento Carristi* states:

After the initial retreat the enemy began to plan a new attack against our positions with a large tank formation estimated at 100 tanks. Our positions were attacked head on and the enemy pitted himself against our *132° Reggimento Carristi* which represented our only unit that could maneuver against the enemy tanks. The armoured unit was struck by the enemy and the clash of armour gave way to a confused melee. The enemy suffered larger casualties and after one hour of heavy fighting it was forced to retreat to its lines. At night, the smoldering enemy tanks (over 40 of them) could be seen on the battlefield surrounded by large clouds of smoke. We also captured several prisoners, including one captain and two majors. In addition, several armoured vehicles were abandoned by the enemy during the battle and were later recovered by us. [186]

Viscount Cranley, a commander of the tank squadrons of the 4th County of London Yeomanry, provides the following account of the battle outlining how the attack was made for unknown reasons but that likely stemmed from an underestimation of the enemy strength:

---

185 Davide Zambon, 'Bir El Gobi', *Ligne du Front magazine* <http://www.qattara.it/Zambon_files/17_Art_Bir%20el%20Gobi.pdf> (accessed on 23 April 2019).
186 Ufficio Storico, 'Relazione Enrico Maretti sul comportamento del 132° Ariete in A.S.', Cartella 1160, prot.1809, November 1942.

At about 1500 in the afternoon the Regiment's (4 CLY) and 2nd Royal Gloucester Hussars were ordered to attack a formation of vehicles that had been sighted. I afterwards heard that B Squadron 11th Hussars, Major Bill Wainman's squadron, desert veterans of great experience, had warned our Brigade Staff Officers, who were new to the game, that they were attacking Bir el Gubi, which was a defended strong point. But our staff thought that they knew better and disregarded the warning, being confident that they had come across a mobile force still five miles to the east of Gubi. The attack was launched, the 2nd Royal Gloucester Hussars on the right and the 4th County of London Yeomanry on the left, and at last the Regiment had its first taste of real warfare, moving forward strictly according to the drill book and full of confidence. I can see them now, A Squadron leading, B Squadron echeloned back on the left and C Squadron on the right. On approaching what turned out to be Gubi, exactly as the 11th Hussars had said, we found it to be a heavily fortified strong point, screened by dummies which were covered in turn by dug in anti-tank guns; A Squadron having been fired on halted in tactical positions to give battle, and C Squadron was ordered to attack the enemy's flank where, through the haze, a stationary column of enemy Mechanized Transport, known in the desert as Met (subsequently discovered to be dummies) could be seen in the distance. Meanwhile, B Squadron was to make a wide sweep and attempt to get in to the enemy's rear … As we sailed in the enemy guns opened and very shortly afterwards my tank struck a trap, consisting of a large patch of sand which had been dug over and heavily soaked with oil so that we bogged down. However, thanks to Jackson's brilliant driving we somehow managed to get out. At the same time, I got message that N.1 troop, which had come in from the flank, had had all their tracks shot off, except Sergeant Jones' tank, but were still fighting hard. No. 4 troop, consisting of two tanks owing to earlier breakdowns, was still moving and was also heavily committed. No. 1 troop had gone off the air and was not seen or heard again. We subsequently learned that all their tanks had been taken prisoner.[187]

After the Italians had completed their counterattack the British units began to retreat further. The first unit to pull back was the 2nd Royal Glouchestrshire Hussars which suffered the highest losses. It began to pull back at 1630 under the fire of the MILIMART guns. Shortly thereafter 4th County of London Yeomanry also began to retreat after its commander had in vain requested the support of the 25 pdr guns to support another attempt to overrun Bir el Gobi. This unit was followed by the 3rd County of London Yeomanry which at 1730 received the order to also pull back. It is clear from the account that whatever the respective losses, the Italians were still in possession of Bir el Gobi on the night of 19 November and that the 22nd Armoured Brigade had not only lost several tanks but it was, as one leading historian wrote, 'considerably disorganized afterwards."[188] The highest losses were sustained by the 2nd Royal Glouchestrshire Hussars with the death of eleven of its personnel, nineteen wounded including its commander Lieutenant Colonel N.A. Birley and twenty soldiers captured by the enemy. 4th County of London Yeomanry lost four and twenty-two captured or missing, while the 3rd

187 Michael Carver, *Tobruk* (London: B. T. Batsford LTD, 1964), pp. 52-53.
188 Ibid., p. 53.

County of London Yeomanry had six dead and an unknown number of captured and/or missing personnel.[189]

This was the first major encounter of the newly reconstituted *Ariete* Division and it ended in an important success with the Commonwealth offensive clearly blunted. The Italians claimed the loss of thirty-four M.13/40 tanks, and claimed the destruction of fifty enemy tanks of which fifteen were estimated to have been destroyed by the 102/35 *autocannoni* who had been "a nasty surprise for the British."[190] *Ariete* had clearly stood its ground but suffering the following losses: forty tanks (six of which were repairable), eight 47mm guns, four 75mm guns, 15 dead, 80 wounded and 82 missing.[191] In addition, they claimed to have captured 100 enemy soldiers, including two majors and one captain from the armoured units, and the destruction of several armoured vehicles."[192]

"The enemy that was coming from the direction of El Cuasc," according to the CAM war diary, "after having made contact with Ariete's defensive screen launched a serious of armoured attacks against said division aimed at overtaking its flanks. The enemy attack was blunted by the defensive screen deployed in the middle of the Italian line while it was counter-attacked on the flank and forced to abandon the field of battle with severe losses."[193] According to the war diary of the CAM the battle was won because of two factors: The detection of the enemy movements early on which lead to the occupation of the Bir el Gobi position thus anticipating the enemy thrust. Second, a new combat tactic that was adopted by the artillery that by abandoning its traditional concentrated indirect fire role had assumed a more pronounced anti-tank role. It was realized that the British tanks were the most dangerous elements within the enemy deployment and that the defensive effort should be concentrated against them. This new tactical predisposition had been filtered down in the chain of command even to single batteries. This lead to the forward positioning of the field guns together with the anti-tank guns to concentrate their combined power against the enemy tanks.[194]

Meanwhile, the British 22nd Armoured Brigade post battle report admitted the loss of twenty-five Crusader tanks and the destruction of forty-five Italian tanks. The 2nd Royal Gloucestershire Hussars alone, for instance, reported the loss of thirty of its own tanks, while the 4th County of London Yeomanry war diary reports the loss of eight tanks, thus these individual by unit figures appear to contradict the Brigade's collective figures.[195] This data would imply, even considering losses to mechanical failures, what was later asserted by some British historians such as Basil Liddell Hart, General Verney and Correlli Barnett that the losses were higher than those furnished in the official numbers. These accounts vary widely

---

189 Brian Pitt, *The Crucible of War* (London: Cassell, 2001), p. 51.
190 Ralph Riccio and Nicola Pignato, *Italian Truck Mounted Artillery in Action* (Carrollton: Squadron, 2010), p. 32.
191 According to Basil Liddell Hart, "In a series of gallant charges, it [XXII Armoured Brigade] drove back the Italian tanks but suffered heavily from the enemy's dug-in guns, losing more than forty of its 160 Crusaders." *The Tanks: The History of the Royal Tank Regiment and its Predecessors, Heavy Branch, Machine-Gun Corps, Tank Corps, and Royal Tank Corps, 1914-1945*, Vol. II (New York: Praeger, 1959), p. 106.
192 Livio Picozzi, "Memorie del Corpo Armato di Manovra," *Rivista Militare*, n.7, 1949, p. 28.
193 Ibid.
194 Ibid.
195 War Diary of the 2nd Royal Gloucestershire Hussars, wo 169/1397, National Archives, Kew.

from those written in the immediate post-war period. One of these for instance, asserted that the Commonwealth had won the battle. Playfair, for example, in the British Official History stressed that the 22nd Armoured had been deployed at Bir el Gobi as a training exercise to improve its tactics and to gain a valuable experience prior to encountering German troops. Moreover that it destroyed 34 Italian tanks while it suffered the loss of only 25 tanks. A second account stated that the Italians were led by German officers, while a third stated that German tanks stationed at Bier el Gobi fought against the 22nd Armoured Brigade. As Greene and Massignani correctly state: "German troops were not present and Rommel was unaware of the action for hours."[196]

A more recent account, that of W. G. F. Jackson, does not argue that Germans were present but stated that if the British units had more infantry it is likely they would have won the battle: "Had there been any infantry with the British tanks the Italian position might have collapsed."[197] Jackson's account appears not to have fully flushed out what happened after the British tanks advanced past the III *Battaglione* positions when they ran into the defensive shield provided by the artillery. In contrast, historian Paddy Griffith has taken a different view regarding the battle of Bir el Gobi: "This battle," he writes, "should have delivered a body-blow to the popular stereotype of the Italian soldier, formed by the earlier photographs of acres of cheerfully complacent prisoners of war strolling into captivity; but it was not really recognized as such at the time, and it has remained largely under-reported in the British literature right up to the present day." Then he also summarizes the battle in the following terms:

> The wake-up call for the British came at Bir el Gubi on 19 November 1941 when Brig. Scott-Cockburn's 22nd Armoured Brigade blundered into their midst without reconnaissance and with just eight field guns in support. The Italians fought back tenaciously, and their 132nd Tank Regiment launched a telling counter-attack. Within the space of less than four hours the British brigade had been reduced to about half of its tank strength, and according to one report had only ten 'runners' left by dusk.[198]

In conclusion, it can be argued that during the battle the Italians adopted some of the tactics learned from their German ally by using mixed combat groups comprised of tank battalions, mobile artillery batteries and anti-tank and anti-aircraft guns used for bolstering the anti-tank screen in advanced positions. Both light and heavy naval guns, the latter a stopgap solution to the lack of proper mobile self-propelled artillery, had been brought forward and had been well camouflaged to conceal their existence to the enemy tank crews. As Battistelli and Cappellano assert: "Lacking infantry support the British A 15 Cruiser tanks were soon outflanked by the Italians, who, with their artillery firing in close cooperation, destroyed 25 enemy tanks and damaged another 25."[199] In turn, the Commonwealth units lacking special infantry and sapper units and with few truck mounted heavy artillery guns in support of the armour could not adequately destroy the enemy anti-tank screen and thus its armour had a difficult time once it advanced against it. DAK's war diary states that ultimately the encounter battle at Bir El

---

196 Jack Greene and Alessandro Massignani, *Rommel's North Africa Campaign*, p. 105.
197 William Jackson, *The North African Campaign* (London: Batsford, 1975), p. 129.
198 Paddy Griffith, *World War Two Desert Tactics*, p. 18.
199 Pier Paolo Battistelli and Filippo Cappellano, *Italian Medium Tanks*, p. 39.

Gobi had brought the initial phase of the Commonwealth counteroffensive at a stalemate: "The Italian garrison at Bir el Gobi succeeded in repulsing strong enemy attacks and thus preventing an enemy advance into the area west of Tobruk."[200] Moreover, the battle derailed the initial plan of drawing the German armour in a pitched battle against superior Commonwealth tank forces. Given the dynamics of the tank versus tank battle, Commonwealth losses at Bir el Gobi could have been even higher. But the "limited capacity"[201] of the Italian tanks allowed many enemy tanks to get away. Unfortunately, for the Italians their M.13/40 tanks were slower than the Crusaders and they could not trap the clear majority of the enemy tanks in the Bir el Gobi positions. It was thanks to the Crusader tank greater maneuverability and speed which allowed some of the armour of the 22nd Armoured Brigade to escape the encirclement. This same dynamic was to repeat itself in other circumstances as the M.13/40 tanks were not only decisively slower but were prone to mechanical failures while operating in the desert like their British counterparts. It became a well-known fact during the North African campaign, for instance, that whenever the Italians or the Commonwealth units began to disengage from an armoured pitched battle it was always the latter that lost fewer tanks during the latter stages of a pullout. When the Italians tanks were first to disengage they typically suffered higher casualties due to slower speeds. When the Commonwealth tanks disengaged first the clear majority of those armoured units could typically get away. In any case, as historian Arnold Blumberg asserts:

> The Battle at Bir el Gubi affected the entire Crusader campaign. Ariete remained in position for a few days guarding the Axis flank and diverting British armour and infantry to watch it. This prevented the full weight of 7th Armoured Division from concentrating its strength against the German panzers barring the gate to Tobruk at Sidi Rezegh. Helping to keep the enemy armour dispersed, Ariete also allowed conditions to exist for German tank victories over isolated British armoured units—against 4th Armoured on November 20th, 7th Armoured Brigade and 7th Support Group on November 22, and the destruction of the 5th South African Infantry Brigade south of Belhammed on the 23rd and 24th, in which Ariete took part.[202]

On the same day that the clash at Bir el Gobi occurred, the British 7th Armoured Brigade captured the Sidi Rezegh airfield, while the 7th Support Group was more hesitant to move forward given that the 22nd Armoured Brigade had been halted. Meanwhile the 4th Armoured Brigade at Gabr Saleh had halted a German armoured counter. According to General Cunningham the Commonwealth troops had achieved a tactical surprise against the Axis forces but it was too early to tell whether the latter were retreating to the Bardia-Sollum positions.[203] DAK General Ludwig Crüwell also examined the situation at the end of the day and ordered his armoured troops to conduct counter-attacks in the next few days to push back the Commonwealth forces,

---

200 US Marine Corps, *German Experiences in Desert Warfare of World War II* (Washington DC: Dept. of the Navy, 1990), p. 8.
201 Ibid.
202 Arnold Blumberg, 'Battle at Bir el Gubi' <https://warfarehistorynetwork.com/daily/wwii/battle-at-bir-el-gubi> (accessed December 26, 2018).
203 John Connell, *Auchinleck*, p. 342.

while the Italian infantry besieging Tobruk was ordered to fight off potential enemy breakout attempts.

The next day the offensive resumed. While the 4th Armoured Brigade clashed with German tanks at Gabr Taieb el Essem, on 20 November, other Commonwealth forces renewed their attack against the Bir el Gobi defenses. This time the 1st South African Brigade was tasked with putting forth the main thrust. But as the unit's infantry and vehicles moved forward they were first battered by Axis fighter planes and later by the timely fire of *Ariete*'s artillery units. The *132° Reggimento Artiglieria Corazzata* then finally repulsed the attack by concentrating fire against the forward elements and the vehicles of the South Africans. A few forward vehicles were split open in this hail of fire. Thus, by midafternoon the South Africans were ordered to not press forward with further attacks as *Ariete*'s positions appeared to be solid and entrenched.

On the 21st the two units continued to lob artillery fire against each other but no major attacks were attempted. Then *Ariete* dispatched two small tank units of M.13s to reconnoiter the terrain and to attempt to anticipate future enemy movements. In one instance a team of twelve M.13s encountered several armoured vehicles and anti-tank units of the South Africans travelling toward Sidi Rezegh. The encounter resulted in a protracted exchange of fire that led to the destruction of two Commonwealth guns and two M.13 tanks. Largely outnumbered by the South African force, the Italians then retired to their line. In another incident at 1530 a unit of M.13/40 tanks advanced toward the positions held by the 5th South African Brigade, which had been deployed to block any enemy advance toward Sidi Rezegh. As the Italians inched closer to the enemy positions they opened fire and a lively exchange of fire ensued. Then as the same unit was retreating they ambushed an enemy supply line from the 22nd Armoured Brigade and captured several trucks and their precious supply. Meanwhile, on the same day a strong Commonwealth tank unit put forth a surprise attack against the German Panzer units south of Sidi Rezegh. *Maggiore* Pardi and his unit, who had been ordered by Rommel to help siege Tobruk, shielded the German units by driving in the direction of the enemy and positioning their guns in their path. The Commonwealth tanks, targeted by the guns, were forced to slow down their advance and this bought time and allowed the Panzers to reorganize. Four enemy tanks were destroyed, while five damaged vehicles were later recovered after the battle and salvaged by Commonwealth engineers.

Meanwhile, on 21 November the Commonwealth forces made the first major attempt to breakout from Tobruk by taking control of the El Duda escapement. Here the defenses surrounding Tobruk were comprised of five German and Italian posts called by the British 'Butch', 'Jill', 'Jack', 'Tiger' and 'Tugun.' All of them were protected by minefields, wire and anti-tank ditches and proved difficult to take or bypass. Preceded by a fierce artillery barrage the forces of the 70th Infantry Division of General Scobie (2nd/King's Own, 2nd Black Watch, 2nd/Queen's and 4th Royal Tank Regiment with thirty-two Cruisers and sixty Matilda II tanks) began to advance against the Axis positions. Initially, the infantrymen of *Pavia*, and *Bologna* Divisions were stunned by hundreds of artillery shells falling on their trenches and causing large casualties. And soon after a company of the *Pavia* was overrun and captured in the predawn darkness. But as the artillery barrage gradually tapered off the troops of the *Bologna* Division held their ground and secured the 'Tugun' strong point by halting the enemy attack. As the New Zealand, Official History states: "The more elaborate attack on Tugun went in at 3 p.m. and gained perhaps half the position, together with 256 Italians and many light field guns; but the Italians in the western half could not be dislodged and the base of the break-out area remained on this account uncomfortably narrow."²⁰⁴ The resistance by the infantry had stymied the first breakout attempt forcing the New Zealand troops back into their original positions. Thus, *Comando Supremo* issued the following communiqué on 22 November: "Repeated enemy attempts to break out from Tobruk failed, owing to the work of Italian divisions which besiege the fortress."²⁰⁵ On the 22nd there were also several clashes between German and Commonwealth armour in the vicinity of Sidi Rezegh as the Axis forces attempted to clear the base.

Sidi Rezegh: Tank Battle on Memorial Day

On the night of 22 November Rommel, who had now become convinced that the Commonwealth offensive was real and in full swing, issued orders to both German and Italian armoured units to conduct an offensive operation the next day aimed at the enemy forces assembled at Sidi Rezegh. Two days earlier Rommel had learned of the unfolding Commonwealth offensive from listening to a broadcast from the BBC, which went into great details in listing all the units and weapons involved in the operation. Now focused on beating back the enemy, Rommel temporarily put on hold the plan to attack Tobruk.

His detailed plan to dislodge the enemy forces from the airfield was as follows:

> (..) 2. The Panzergruppe will resolve the battle on November 23 in the south-east of Tobruk by a concentrated attack of DAK and part of Corps Gambara. The Corps Gambara will attack with the divisione corazzata « Ariete » at 0800, from el-Gobi towards Gambut.
>
> 3. The DAK will attack at 0700, weighting the effort on the left, in the direction of El Gobi, attack the enemy and destroy him …
>
> 4. 3rd Reconnaissance Group reinforced to open the way to Bardia away and will carry out an armed reconnaissance of Bardia, advancing towards Capuzzo. The 33rd Reconnaissance Group … will carry out an armed reconnaissance in the direction of Sidi Bin Oman-Ghirba.²⁰⁶

As a precautionary move his instructions also warned the German panzer commanders that *Ariete* had several captured enemy vehicles that should not arouse any suspicions once the Axis mechanized forces met at the rendezvous point in the morning of 23 November. The CAM adhered to Rommel's plan by communicating to its units that: "Ariete shall deploy a large, armoured force along the road from Bir el Gobi to Gambut at 0800 the next morning to provide support to the German Panzer units for a concentric attack against the enemy forces deployed at Bir Bu Cremisa."²⁰⁷ *Ariete*'s other units were ordered to remain at Bir el Gobi to secure its

---

204 W.E. Murphy, *The Relief of Tobruk* (Wellington: Historical Publications Branch, 1961), p. 94.
205 USSME, *I bollettini del Comando supremo* (Rome: Ufficio Storico, 1984), p. 121.
206 Mario Montanari, *Le operazioni in Africa settentrionale*, vol. II, Part, II, p. 623.
207 Livio Picozzi, "Memorie del Corpo Armato di Manovra," *Rivista Militare*, n.7, 1949, p. 22.

possession while some elements of the RECAM were directed to reach Bir el Gobi by 0700 on 23 November to provide support to the infantry.

These orders were communicated directly to the divisional commanders bypassing *Generale* Bastico and his staff. The latter on the evening of 22 December accused Rommel of bypassing his command and giving operational directives directly to the Italian units divisional commanders. The disagreement would later be one of the causes, along with the necessity to streamline the decision-making process in a top down direction, to lead Rommel to demand one chain of command for the Axis mechanized forces.

Sidi Rezegh was an airfield of strategic interest to both contenders. The Commonwealth armour had captured it at the start of Operation Crusader thus depriving the Axis of a critical supply and operational base near Tobruk. On the night of the 22nd, *Ariete* was still in Bir el Gobi, while *Trieste* occupied the area of Bir el Hacheim – Bir Harmat and there it was tasked to prevent the enemy from penetrating into the area west of Tobruk. The Axis attack was meant to catch off guard the enemy forces with an envelopment maneuver by the armour. To prevent and block an Axis counter-attack, the British commander had deployed the 5th South African Brigade in a box (a fortified stronghold) within the Sidi Rezegh airfield. At the time, the British commander aimed to regroup his forces to then attempt another attack against the Axis forces surrounding Tobruk.

Given the difficulties of communication, Rommel's final plan did not arrive in time. Thus, partly due to a timing issue, the operation took the form of a disjointed attack by Italian and German units that throughout the day of the 23rd had trouble communicating and coordinating operations with each other. The objective was the recapture of the airfield and the *Ariete* units that took part to the operation consisted of the Headquarters of 132° *Reggimento Carristi* (Tank Regiment) with VIII and IX medium tank battalions; (each with 2 companies), V/8th *Bersaglieri* reinforced by I *Gruppo*/132° *Reggimento Artiglieria Corazzata*, one *Gruppo batterie volanti* with 65/17 guns, a battery of truck mounted 100/17 howitzers detached from the RECAM, and one with 102/35 guns (while the remainder of the unit was stationed at Bir el Gobi to watch the other South African units). According to Rommel's plan *Ariete* units were to attack the box from the left flank, while the 15th Panzer were to attack from the center and 21st Panzer from the right. In Rommel's plan the main thrust was to be put forth by the 15th Panzer Division, together with the *Ariete* Division, which were to lead the main attack, enveloping the South African positions and then throwing the Commonwealth armour against the front of the 21st Panzer Division.

Despite the detailed plans, the attack against the positions held by the 5th South African Brigade resulted in a confused melee giving way to a huge clash of armour made worse by the Italians lack of modern communication equipment such as vehicle radios and by their slower vehicles. As the German account of the battle asserts by midday the Axis units had finally linked up despite Italian delays and were advancing toward the objective: "The Ariete assault spearheads had meanwhile arrived with 120 tanks and General Crüwell now launched the combined German and Italian armoured forces northwards into the enemy's rear, with the object of bottling him up completely and forcing him back against the 21st Panzer Division's front at Sidi Rezegh."[208] But as the Italian tanks, advanced with some delay because they could not keep the pace of the faster German tanks against the South African positions they also came under heavy

---

208 Ibid.

enemy artillery fire, while moments later they were counter-attacked on the flanks by elements of the 22nd Armoured Brigade, including several tanks from the 3rd County of London Yeomanry. Thus, while the German Panzers attacked head on at 1500 the South African line, *Ariete* washeld up and engaged by thirty British tanks.[209] The tank against tank encounter materialized when the British force, despite being vastly outnumbered, courageously charged against the Italian medium tanks. To counter the threat, shortly thereafter, the Italian medium tanks opened fire as the British armour crossed their path dangerously exposing their sides to *Ariete*'s tanks and anti-tank guns. Within thirty minutes a few British tanks were shot to pieces and several vehicles were left smoldering in the desert as the survivors of the unit retired from the battlefield. Up to three British tanks were destroyed to no loss for the Italians and the lion share of the enemy tanks had been hit by the deadly 100/17 truck mounted howitzers. While the Italians were busy facing some of the echelons of the 22nd Brigade, some of the latter's elements also attacked the most advanced units of the German Panzers from the exposed left flank which according to the original plan had to be covered by *Ariete*. "This intervention took place just as the panzers broke over the front lines of the South Africans. It was a difficult time for the German formation, not only because there was a danger of a gap between the tanks of the 8th Panzer and the companies of 115th Rifles, but the rear of the infantry was also very vulnerable."[210] Meanwhile a German intelligence officer reported that the battle hung in the balance precisely because of the failure of *Ariet*e to keep the same pace as the German Panzer units:

> A terrifying fire front of more than a hundred guns focused on the two attacking tank regiments and the two rifle regiments which followed closely on the vehicles. A mass of pieces' anti-tank unusual in this theater of operations, and cleverly hidden during enemy vehicles placed out of action in the morning, inflicted heavy losses to the two regiments. Particularly annoying was the fire from the left side, the sector assigned to the divisone corazzata « Ariete », not even immediately in the fight.[211]

Given the harassing action of the British armour and the slower pace of the Italian column, *Ariete* managed to attack the South Africans only a half hour after the German units had lunged forward.

The following is a detailed description of the operation carried out by the tank units of *Ariete* that culminates with the final clash against the enemy defenses:

> On higher orders, under the command of Brigadier General di Nisio[212], Deputy Commander of the *Ariete* Division, an armour-mechanized column was formed, consisting of two companies of the VIII Tank Battalion and two of the IX Tank Battalion, one group of 75/27 guns, one light detachment of portee trucks with 65 guns, two battalions

---

209 Agar-Hamilton, J.A.I. & Turner, L.F.C, *The Sidi Rezeg Battles: 1941* (Cape Town: Oxford University Press, 1957), p. 231.
210 Mario Montanari, *Le operazioni in Africa settentrionale*, Vol II, Part II, p. 627.
211 Ibid.
212 Brigadier General Ismaele di Nisio had a distinguished military career. Prior to the war, as Ten. Colonnello, he was one of the few Italian officers to specialize in armoured warfare. He authored two training pamphlets; one on armoured combat and the other on motorized reconnaissance patrols.

of Bersaglieri, and two sections of 20mm guns. Its task was to move into the area of Bir bu Cremisa, to work with the German forces coming from Gambut. At 0830, leaving behind in the zone of Bir el Gobi the remainder of the tanks and vehicles, the column, pointing east, moved to reach the target destination.

At about 0950, after only a few kilometers, enemy vehicles coming from the north-east were recognized. The column continued its march with the tanks in the vanguard, and most of the vehicles closing. The tanks pushed forward decisively, and soon were in contact with the enemy elements, leading to lively engagements which the adversary however managed to extract himself from thanks to the higher speed of his vehicles. – About 1000 the column had to stop because of signs of violent artillery fire from flying enemy batteries from the center of resistance. The halt in operations was protracted until 1300 and the tanks, in reaction to the situation, formed a defensive front with the two companies of the VIII facing north, and the two of the IX facing out. At about 1340, coming from the north-west, a great dust cloud announces the arrival of a column with a certain strength of numerous vehicles. At 1400 the Italian and German forces made contact, fusing into a block of steel that now points, in straight union, at the enemy forces advised to be in the area. After a brief halt, the German forces moved pointing in the direction of Bir bu Cremisa, and the Italian forces remained on their left, with the same objective. At 1425 the Germans closed with the enemy from the north, while our armoured vehicles found themselves embroiled with similar English vehicles. At 1600 the fight showed itself to be violent and decisive. The tanks moved on the attack in waves, in combat formation, and sustained the collision with resoluteness, stopping various British vehicles in the area. The light artillery of the C.A.M. was then launched on the left flank and in-between the M.13 with the order to support with anti-tank fire of our armoured vehicles. The German forces meanwhile continued their operation to annihilate, with their flank protected by our forces. Intense fire from the field artillery continued amid the clash of tanks while dense high columns of smoke engulf the horizon. Close-knit formations of planes survey the area incessantly in search for opportunities to strafe but are frustrated by the immediate intervention of the anti-air artillery.

At 1700 the struggle did not abate but rather increased in fury and intensity like that which happened during the encounter at Bir el Gobi. Regardless, all the tanks proceeded orderly with their advance extinguishing the last resistance of the adversary. At 1730 the English wavered and rescued the last surviving vehicles, by moving to flee. During this time the daylight diminished, and the dark gathering on the horizon rendered the flames of the fires even more lively. An endless line of similar fires on many places showed the line of retreat of the enemy. German and Italian forces, cooperating closely, now found themselves among the remains of the defeated enemy, as they were during their decisive action of destruction. Also during this action, like the previous one, the tank men have been above any praise. They demonstrated their superb aggressive intent and their sense of unity with their weapon up to making the supreme sacrifice. Against the numerous but unquantifiable losses of the English and an immense number of prisoners stand one dead and four wounded, and two tanks lost and three lightly damaged.[213]

---

213 Ufficio Storico, 'Relazione sul comportamento del 132° Reggimento Carri nei cicli operativi del 18/11/1941 al 03/07/1942 da me comandato', n. 5498, Enrico Maretti, 4 luglio 1942.

Lieutenant Schmidt of the 15th Panzer Division recorded the following recollection of the battle:

> The armoured troop carriers, cars of various kind, caterpillars, hauling mobile guns, heavy trucks with infantry, motorized anti-aircraft guns, thus we roared towards the enemy's barricade ... tank after tank split open in the hail of shell ... tank against tank, tank against gun, or anti-tank nest, sometimes in frontal, sometimes in flanking attack, using every trick of the mobile warfare and tank tactics, the South Africans were overcome.[214]

At the height of the fighting, the broad area of Sidi Rezegh airfield had been transformed by the tank clashes and gun duels in a pool of dust, steam and smoke. Visibility was almost non-existent and neither side could distinguish friend or foe. Whilst British armoured forces managed to breakout of the pocket, a large part of the South African troops were not able to escape, however, and were captured or killed/wounded during the night. Thus, the 5th South African suffered heavy casualties while *Ariete* captured a battery of 25 pdr guns and some enemy vehicles, while destroying a few enemy tanks. Overall its performance was mixed as it arrived on the battlefield with some delay, while it did in the latter stages of the melee manage to overrun several enemy positions. However, its role in battle had been secondary to that of the German armoured units, which endowed with greater speed and mobility, attacked the enemy first and achieved greater success. Relying on the timely intelligence provided by the reconnaissance units and by speedily moving forces to the decisive position using radios, the German armoured units could concentrate their forces at the point of decision to be able to successfully overwhelm the enemy positions.

When the battle was over the commander of the 30th Corps General Norrie was forced to withdraw his forces to Gabr Saleh after an estimated 100 of his tanks had been destroyed or damaged. The battle turned out to be a relevant success for the Axis forces which collectively knocked out a high number of enemy tanks and had at least temporarily reestablished numerical parity with the enemy tank strength.

Meanwhile at Tobruk another breakout attempt was made by 70th British Division and 32nd Tank Brigade. This time Rommel himself had personally directed the defensive battle and had rushed from Gambut four 88mm anti-tank guns to halt the Matildas from advancing against his infantry. Despite a protracted and bloody fight by mid-afternoon the El Duda escapement was still held by Axis troops.

On the night of the 23 November Rommel, who had lobbied to have operational control of all armoured units in North Africa arguing that "it is necessary to immediately substitute the dual command of the operations by a unitary command of all units that are located in Marmarica and Cyrenaica. I ask that I be charged with this command,"[215] had won his political battle against Bastico and Gambara. As a result, Mussolini finally agreed to put the CAM under him. In the Duce's view and influenced by Cavallero, this was a difficult but necessary decision to make to streamline the decision-making process in the field. The Commonwealth troops, for instance,

---

214 Agar-Hamilton, J. A. I., and Turner, L. C. F., *The Sidi Rezeg Battles, 1941*, p. 243.
215 Mario Montanari, *Le operazioni in Africa settentrionale*, Vol II, Part II, p. 634.

were all under the commander of Eighth Army and it was logical for all Italian and German units to also be under one operational commander as well.[216]

Dash to the Wire

On the morning of 24 November General Crüwell informed Rommel of the outcome of the "Day of the Dead/Memorial Sunday" battle stating that in his opinion the enemy had been destroyed at Sidi Rezegh and only a few elements had been able to get away. Unfortunately, this was not the correct reading of the situation as a few days later, after the losses sustained during the first phase of Operation Crusader, the Commonwealth would resupply its depleted armoured units with the arrival to the front of two hundred tanks thus rebuilding the strength of 22nd Armoured Brigade almost overnight. Rommel, however, in complete disagreement with General Bastico who urged caution, seized upon his subordinate's intelligence report and by taking advantage of the disorganization amongst the retreating enemy forces, ordered his mechanized units to drive toward the Egyptian border to surprise and box in the retreating Commonwealth units. The unexpected order for a "Dash to the Wire" involved all mechanized units of the Axis but once again *Ariete* was unable to keep up with the faster moving German tanks. Despite the combat exhaustion of the men and the heavy casualties suffered in the fighting of the last few days, at about noon on 24 November the German mechanized forces began to march across the desert in the direction of Sidi Omar "which they reached in the evening after a complete disregard of the British threat to their flanks."[217] *Ariete* had received the order a few hours later and it too began to move towards the same destination. It appears that the reasons for the delay in receiving Rommel's order were twofold. One was that the unit, unlike German or British armoured units, lacked a command tank with a radio whose range exceeded 100 kilometers. Second, it relied upon the CAM for direction but the latter had its own problems to deal with. Gambara's dual role, for example, as both CAM commander and as second in command to Bastico often overburdened CAM's HQ. Second, Rommel's tendency to give orders directly to the divisional heads without also informing the CAM often did not allow the latter to conduct its command function in an orderly and harmonious way. In the afternoon of 24 November both CAM units (*Ariete* and *Trieste*) were separated from each other and were not able to communicate with HQ, which received Rommel's order three hours after it was issued. While traveling to the frontier *Ariete* on 25 November reached the vicinity of Taieb el Esem which was occupied by the 1st South African Brigade. Upon sighting the enemy force, *Ariete*'s motorized artillery began to barrage the South African positions, which came under heavy fire, and then prepared for an attack. Following the bombardment, *Ariete*'s commander dispatched a small tank unit which was sent out on patrol to reconnoiter the enemy positions, but it too came under heavy fire and was forced to retreat. Because of the assessment of the reconnaissance unit, which reported back that the enemy was dug in with heavy artillery, the planned tank attack against the Commonwealth position was canceled. In a precautionary move to watch *Ariete,* the 4th Armoured Brigade was dispatched during the morning to support the

---

216 Ibid.
217 Basil Liddell Hart, *The Rommel Papers*, p. 163.

1st South African Brigade at Taieb el Esem. The arrival of the British armour further deterred the Italians from attacking. The next day the standstill persisted as both sides continued to fire artillery shells against each other, but no one moved. *Ariete* was thus again involved in a heavy firefight against the South Africans, fifteen miles south of Bir el Gobi for most of the day. As far as *Trieste* was concerned it was moving toward the frontier but at an exceedingly slow pace. The unit was equipped with mainly Lancia 3RO and SPA38R trucks, which were the standard trucks of the Italian infantry, these had fairly prominent silhouettes which made them a highly visible and attractive target for the RAF forces. This often caused the unit to halt its march forward to defend against enemy attacks extending the time it took to link up to other units. Once it was deployed for operations and especially when pitted against enemy armoured units, *Trieste* had a difficult time in its approach march toward the enemy. The infantry, being only partly motorized, could not keep the pace of the faster German or Italian armoured units as some of its units advanced on foot. Moreover, many of its anti-tank guns were not motorized and had to be unloaded from the trucks and be placed in position by the crew hand-towing them into position.

At the same time the standoff involving *Ariete* was occurring, several German units had followed Rommel's order advancing toward the frontier. But even though they made it to their destination the troops were exhausted and poorly equipped. Thus, ultimately, Rommel's "Dash to the Wire" resulted in a dangerous operation that did not yield significant results as the Axis troops were too disjointed while driving at the Egyptian frontier to constitute a serious threat to British armour. Instead of concentrating his armour to destroy Commonwealth tank strength near Tobruk, Rommel's gamble to overtake the enemy's rear failed.[218] Historian Basil Liddell Hart argues that Rommel's counterstroke was a brilliant tactical maneuver that failed because some German units and all Italian units did not execute the order in a timely manner. In contrast, recent research has rather highlighted that Rommel's move was extremely risky and brash given the precarious situation at Tobruk where Axis troops ringing the city were just barely hanging on after successive Commonwealth attacks and also because Rommel's staff car and entourage had risked capture during the latter stages of the dash to Egypt.[219] Thus, *Ariete*'s operation (which was unintended because of the standoff) against the South Africans must be seen in a different light. Rather than the failure to heed Rommel's order, *Ariete* by standing against the South African forces "arguably played a more important role in the battle than DAK by effectively preventing the South Africans from moving north to support the New Zealanders and by distracting the 4th Armoured for a time."[220]

The CAM war diary states that it was oblivious to what was happening near the frontier because all communications with Rommel had broken down on the 25th and that "CAM's unity of command had been temporarily interrupted by Rommel's counterstroke that directed Ariete to head toward Sollum. All attempts to communicate via radio with Ariete had been unsuccessful."[221] The Commonwealth forces especially the infantry units deployed in numerous

---

218 "Instead of concentrating upon collecting or destroying the helpless mass of disabled enemy tanks, he left the field clear for the British to repair their damaged tanks and reconstitute their armoured force at Sidi Rezegh." Kenneth Macksey, *Tank Versus Tank*, p. 94.
219 Ian F. W. Beckett (ed.), *Rommel Reconsidered* (Mechanicsburg: Stackpole, 2014).
220 Ian Walker, *Iron Hulls, Iron Hearts*, p. 96.
221 Livio Picozzi, "Memorie del Corpo Armato di Manovra," *Rivista Militare*, n.7, 1949, p. 22.

strongholds put up a very determined opposition to Rommel's advance, indicating that Rommel's estimate that the enemy was in full retreat was erroneous. The enemy had quickly recovered from the shock occasioned by the Sidi Rezegh tank battle, and General Auchinleck, the Commander in Chief of the Middle East, by personally intervening and blocking the decision of General Alan Cunningham, the Commander of the Eighth Army, to evacuate the frontline positions and fall back to Egypt, had saved the situation preventing Rommel from obtaining a decisive victory. Shortly thereafter, General Auchinleck sacked General Cunningham in open disagreement with the latter's order to retreat his troops to Mersa Matruh and promoted General Neil Ritchie to command the Eighth Army.

Meanwhile as events were rapidly unfolding at the frontier, on 25 November heavy fighting erupted at Tobruk again as the enemy countered against the besieging Axis force with a simultaneous pincer movement frontally from the southeast and in the rear from Tobruk. By utilizing all available Italian infantry forces the Axis managed to repulse the Commonwealth thrust and finally the enemy breach was halted by a counter thrust. Since further attacks by the Commonwealth were to be expected, the Axis made a change in tactic necessary.

This critical situation at Tobruk in essence forced Rommel's hand which called off the fighting on the Sollum front near the Egypt border and transferred all available elements at or near Tobruk to face further breakout attempts. The first unit to engage the enemy troops was the RECAM which was dispatched by Gambara from Bir el Gobi to Sidi Rezegh to try to stop the advance of the New Zealand infantry units into Tobruk. After an hour of heavy fighting in which the unit deployed its mobile guns to ward off enemy attacks, it pulled back to the line held by the *Pavia* Division. Then the 9° *Reggimento Bersaglieri/Trieste*, under the command of Major General Karl Böttcher of the 21st Panzer Division who led a combined Italian-German combat group (Kampfgruppe Böttcher), was also dispatched to Sidi Rezegh, about twenty kilometers east of el Adem, to block the passage to the enemy, who was advancing toward Tobruk. The New Zealanders continued to attack south of Tobruk on 26 November with the 23rd and 28th Infantry Battalions making frontal attacks against several Axis positions. 9° *Bersaglieri* was particularly tested on this day, when because of a sudden armoured sortie from the garrison of Tobruk, the unit had to sustain attacks on both its front and rear. Despite this dual envelopment, the unit retained a hold on its positions with a counter-attack supported by tanks:

> The commander of the 9° *Reggimento Bersaglieri* ordered two groups of 105mm guns to target the attacking enemy troops and to support the counter of XXXII battalion, which was immediately launched. The roar of the engines joined the roar of the artillery. The mass of the attackers hesitated at first then continued heading toward the plains. The enemy, subjected to the effective shooting of the 105mm guns and surprised by our sudden counter, did not withstand the thrust of XXXII Battaglione and four German tanks. After a brief fight, the enemy retreated.[222]

On the evening of the same day the XXVIII *Battaglione Bersaglieri* sustained another strong enemy attack against its positions which was rebuffed with losses. In this operation it was

---

222 Enrico Scala, *Storia delle fanterie italiane, vol. VII* (Rome: SME Ispettorato dell'Arma di Fanteria, 1954), p. 535.

supported by RECAM motorized units which had been dispatched by the CAM from Bir el Gobi to Bel Hamed with the objective "of attacking the enemy head on"[223] with the *autocannoni* da 65mm. CAM war diary goes on to state that "RECAM attacked from the rear the enemy troops which sustained losses in equipment and men."[224] At dawn on the following day, Major General Böttcher, ordered *Bersaglieri* infantry units, who had effectively carried out the task of arresting and counter-attacking enemy forces until the arrival of the German armoured divisions, to maintain their positions. However, on the 27th the New Zealanders were finally able to link up with the other Commonwealth forces, mainly with the 32nd Tank Brigade at El Duda, but only after again encountering very stiff opposition from *Bersaglieri* manned positions. The 6th New Zealand Brigade, for example, fought a fierce battle with a battalion of the 9° *Bersaglieri Regiment*, who had emplaced their machine guns near the mosque at Sidi Rezegh and kept on firing at the enemy despite being on the receiving end of a heavy barrage. The attack was undertaken by the 24th and 26th Battalions which enveloped the enemy position after a long preparatory barrage. With regard to the action of the 26th Battalion the New Zealand official history states that:

> Both battalions struck opposition almost at once, flares rose in front of them, tracer bullets cut the intervening ground into jagged patterns of light and dark, the air was filled with a deadly rustling, whistling and shrieking, and then anti-tank guns and mortars joined in and the streaking gun-flashes and shattering explosions told their ominous tale of an enemy ready and waiting. A and B Companies of the 26th came to grips with the enemy in the first wadi, getting showered with grenades as they mounted the far slopes, and charged all signs of movement. The crest gained, they rallied to the calls of their officers and NCOs and especially to Major Milliken's roars of encouragement, and then ran into more bullets and grenades as they descended into the next hollow—'all bayonet, small arms, very tough fighting', it seemed to Tolerton, the adjutant.….From the plumed hats of those lying dead they were identified as Bersaglieri and closer examination showed them to be 9th Regiment (Trieste). Many of those who went through this night and saw these dead foes in the morning had occasion to sharply revise their opinion of Italians as fighting men.[225]

The 24th Battalion had a similar experience while advancing through the enemy positions:

> The advance of 24th Battalion across the flat was, if anything, a grimmer ordeal for some platoons than that of the 26th along the escarpment. The men came under fire almost at once and on the right, as Tomlinson says, had 'hand-to-hand fighting practically all the way to our objective.' The enemy fought their guns to the last. 'Few prisoners were taken that night as all Coys were so below strength by this time that we simply had not got the men to look after them', he adds…. The Bersaglieri regiment fought with much greater determination than is usually found among Italian troops and the numbers of their dead and the position in which they lay showed that they had kept their guns in action to the

---

223 Livio Picozzi, 'Memorie del Corpo Armato di Manovra', *Rivista Militare*, n.7, 1949, p. 21.
224 Ibid.
225 W.E. Murphy, *The Relief of Tobruk* (Wellington: Historical Publications Branch, 1961), p. 289.

last. Indeed, it was reported from several of our men that the first to break under our onslaught were the German troops and the Bersaglieri had been the last to yield. [226]

The *Bersaglieri* Regiment after three days of hard resistance had sustained the following losses: 61 dead, 127 wounded and 80 missing and three of its soldiers would receive gold medals of military valor (*Bersagliere* Settimo Di Battista, *Tenente* Giuseppe Regazzo, and *Caporal Maggiore* Aurelio Zamboni).[227] Despite the heavy losses *Divisione Trieste*'s units had held up the enemy advance for several days forcing the New Zealanders into a bitter fight for every inch of terrain and thus slowing them down. Further attacks against the Axis garrisons surrounding Tobruk were feared and the German general in charge dispatched the following message to Rommel: "Kampfgruppe Böttcher with heavy loss back on both sides. Allow 8th Panzer Regiment to come immediately. Recovery of the situation possible only thereby."[228]

Second Battle of Sidi Rezegh

Rommel and his staff evaluated the evolving situation at the siege front and decided on a plan to encircle the New Zealand forces near Tobruk. As a result *Ariete* was tasked with advancing on a high ground position Point 175 while the 15th and 21st Panzer were to make the major attack against the Commonwealth troops. On 28th November, the mechanized DAK and Italian elements raced to return to Tobruk and help relieve the besieged infantry at Sidi Rezegh, El Duda and El Adem. *Ariete* began its long march back harassed from the onset by several encounters with enemy jock columns and mobile artillery units which inflicted casualties. The Support Group of 7th Armoured Division equipped with several batteries of 25-pdr guns was the main battle group to hold up *Ariete* Division by engaging about forty medium tanks which came under heavy gun fire. Then the bulk of the 4th and 22nd Armoured Brigades were deployed to interfere with the Axis retreat from the frontier. Their field artillery and mobile gun units continued for most of the day to exchange fire against the Axis forces, but no clear winner emerged.

Despite harassment by enemy jock columns, on the 28th the German tanks arrived near Tobruk in the evening and in the process overran the 5th New Zealand Brigade headquarters capturing 696 soldiers and killing 93. The remaining bulk of New Zealand forces, which had broken through and were positioned on the corridor to Tobruk were attacked by Axis tanks on the 29th and the 15th Panzer captured, albeit only temporarily, the El Duda escapement. It was at this point, while *Ariete* was covering the rear of the Axis tank columns, that it achieved

---

226 Ibid., p. 293.
227 Aurelio's Zamboni motivation for the gold medal reads: "As a machine gunner facing an enemy attack and under heavy enemy artillery fire, and though seriously wounded, Zamboni did not abandon the weapon and refused any medical care. He continued undaunted to shoot his gun. Wounded a second time by a grenade that injured his leg and struck him in several parts of the body, with admirable stoicism he had his almost severed arm amputated on the spot and shortly thereafter continued to fight. When his comrades counterattacked, he stayed on the field of battle refusing additional medical care and shortly thereafter died of his wounds.
228 Hermann Büschleb, *Operation Crusader: Tank Warfare in the Desert, Tobruk 1941* (Philadelphia, Pennsylvania: Casemate, 2019), p. 61.

an important success against the New Zealanders by capturing Point 175 near Bir el Gobi with no losses. This coup was facilitated by the fact that by then *Ariete* had many captured enemy vehicles at its disposal which likely caused some confusion amongst the enemy ranks. In fact, the enemy infantry positioned on Point 175 initially thought that *Ariete* was a friendly unit mainly because it was using many captured enemy vehicles in its ranks. When the New Zealanders realized that they were indeed enemy troops, the latter were already in their midst. At that point, the Commonwealth artillery opened fire at close range. Two Italian tanks were quickly put out of action by truck mounted guns but it was too late for the anti-tank screen to halt *Ariete*. By then, many infantry soldiers had already emerged from their trenches to greet the mobile unit and were defenseless against *Ariete*'s machine guns. Indeed, *Ariete*'s tank crews opened machine gun fire at close range, and later the *Bersaglieri* dismounted from the trucks and were soon disarming and rounding up enemy troops. Some infantry soldiers attempted to flee down the escarpment to safety; but many were quickly captured by armoured cars equipped with machine guns.

> The *Ariete* approached a local highpoint which had exchanged hands several times, Point 175, and in the gathering gloom, mistaken identity on the part of the New Zealanders (due in part to Ariete having substantial amounts of captured Commonwealth equipment), allowed the Ariete, virtually in a coup, to capture the position from the 21st New Zealand battalion. The Ariete inflicted heavy losses, captured 200 men as well as liberating about 200 prisoners of the 21st Panzer. It then proceeded to hold off an attack by the weak 4th and 22nd Armoured Brigades which never closed to decisive ranges.[229]

The New Zealand official history tells a similar story:

> Major Fitzpatrick was looking over the position when a runner brought a message from Second-Lieutenant Cairns to the effect that a column was approaching from the east. The CO returned to Battalion Headquarters while the Adjutant got through to Brigade with the information. Brigade said it was probably the South Africans who had been expected all day. The column approaching at a steady six miles an hour was keenly watched. Brigade had mentioned that the South Africans would be easily identified by their Marmon-Harrington armoured cars, and there were cars with high turrets leading the column. The turrets were open and men wearing berets were sitting on top waving friendly greetings. The guns were given a range and bearing and a carrier patrol was ordered out to make a positive identification. D Company, quite sure that the South Africans had got up at last, left their trenches and ran forward to welcome them with their steel helmets held high on their rifles, the recognized method of identification. Suddenly the turret lids were slammed down and the astounded troops were being fired upon. The forward observation officer yelled for fire, but his set must have failed for no fire came. Fitzpatrick put a frantic message through on the telephone to the guns but could get no connection. As a last resort he rang Brigade to get the guns firing. Still no fire came, and the tanks behind the armoured cars were among the troops with their guns trained on the helpless men. Those who were

---

229 Jack Greene and Alessandro Massignani, *Rommel's North African Campaign*, p. 122.

furthest from the enemy ran an 80-yard gauntlet to the edge of the escarpment and scrambled down into the wadis.[230]

Recalling the loss of the 21st Battalion, Lieutenant-Colonel Howard Kippenberger, who later rose to command the 2nd New Zealand Division, wrote that, "About 05.30 p.m. a damned Italian Motorized Division (Ariete) turned up. They passed with five tanks leading, twenty following, and a huge column of transport and guns, and rolled straight over our infantry on Point 175."[231]

After this combat action and on the afternoon of the 29th, *Ariete* proceeded to parry an armoured attack by the 4th and 22nd Armoured Brigades which failed to close in on the Italian units. Regarding this combat action the war diary of the *Ariete*'s armoured regiment reports: "In subsequent stages, where it engaged with its remaining armoured units a number of enemy units, the regiment arrived without stopping in the area of Sidi Rezegh on the evening of 29 November. Here it engaged the second major armoured battle encounter of the month long campaign against the enemy armoured masses. The importance of this combat action is documented by bulletin n. 550 issued by the headquarters of the Comando Forze Armate which furnished the number of casualties inflicted upon the enemy of twenty-five enemy tanks destroyed along with forty armoured vehicles some of which were captured."[232] *Ariete*'s losses are not reported but were likely to be considerable.

On the morning of 30 November *Ariete* Division was deployed around Points 175 and 176 that had just been conquered the prior day. Since the early morning hours, it was subjected to a heavy enemy bombardment. Soon the toll began to mount with three tanks immobilized, two dead officers, two dead tank drivers and three injured. Thus, to prevent further losses elements from the *132° Reggimento Carristi* were dispatched to reconnaissance the immediate area to locate and destroy the enemy guns. According to the regimental war diary:

> While on patrol M tanks encountered approximately 120 tanks of the British 4th Brigade. Although Ariete was heavily outnumbered it rushed the British tanks to engage them. It attempted to overtake them on the right flank but for almost an hour the two sides exchanged fire. Ultimately after prolonged fire the battle encounter was inconclusive and no clear winner emerged.[233]

At 1100 the British tanks counterattacked against the VIII and *IX Battaglioni Carri Medi* and the battle lasted until dawn with very confused fighting on both sides. The British account furnishes the following losses sustained by the Italian armour: "Here nineteen enemy tanks were destroyed and set on fire, with most of the damage was done by a squadron from 5th RTR who got around the enemy's flank, with their twenty-six Stuarts fell on an Italian tank group

---

230 J. F. Cody, *21st Battalion* (Wellington: Historical Publications Branch, 1953), p. 138.
231 Howard Kappenberg, *Infantry Brigadier* (Oxford: Oxford University Press, 1949), p. 101.
232 Ufficio Storico, 'Relazione sul comportamento del 132° Reggimento Carri nei cicli operativi del 18/11/1941 al 03/07/1942 da me comandato', n. 5498, Enrico Maretti, 4 luglio 1942.
233 Ufficio Storico, 'Relazione Enrico Maretti sul comportamento del 132° Ariete in Africa. Settentrionale', Cartella 1160, prot.1809, Novembre 1942.

knocking out thirteen M-13s and five light tanks, without loss to themselves. The brigade also suffered no other casualties on the day either."[234]

By nightfall *Ariete* had lost several M tanks, while the British tank losses are unknown, but by then the Italians had retained control of Points 175 (Bir Sciuerat) and 176 (Baten Bel Cor).

During the night between 30 November and 1 December *Ariete*'s units in cooperation with German panzers were involved in maneuvers against the 1st South African Brigade positions near Point 175. A company of M.13/40 tanks made a flanking attack but came under intensive fire from enemy guns losing four tanks. Then on 1 December it was the South Africans turn to attack the Italian positions on Point 175 but the former were repulsed by the combined fire of the *Ariete*'s artillery and tanks in a hull-down position. Rommel had also communicated orders to Trieste Division to support Ariete and the German divisions but the former took most of the morning in getting organized prompting Rommel once again to lash out at the division commander for this delay. Meanwhile on the same day the RECAM effectuated a raid against an enemy supply dump that was targeted specifically by two 100/17 truck mounted guns which caused damage before being chased away by enemy tanks.

By then the German Panzer divisions had surrounded the New Zealand forces and wiped out several of their outposts. The latter had retreated from Tobruk along the Trigh Capuzzo ridge. With this German maneuver and the consequent New Zealand infantry retreat, the garrison of Tobruk was again encircled by the Axis forces. Rommel's assessment of the situation was that the Crusader battle appeared to be finally turning in the Axis favor especially after the enemy had been chased into Egypt and its Tobruk garrison was once again under siege. But the Axis losses were substantial. For example, particularly troubling were the losses sustained by the Axis artillery: forty-one howitzers, thirty-four guns, sixty mortars, and most importantly eighteen 88mm Flak 36 guns. In addition it lost 142 German tanks of which twenty-five were *Panzerkampfwagen* IV, the most lethal weapon of the German divisions.[235] Italian losses in the CAM were also severe. On 3 December 1941, the Italian Official History reports the strength of *Ariete* as follows: Ninety-Two M.13, of which only fifty were fully efficient, fifty L.3 tanks of which only a third were efficient, thirty-six artillery pieces and twenty-five 47mm guns.[236] *Trieste*'s losses were also significant.

Bir el Gobi II

On 3 December strong words were exchanged between Gambara and Rommel. The former had gone to the German headquarters in the morning to meet with Rommel and receive further directions on where to deploy his mobile force, but Rommel was nowhere to be found. Many German and Italian generals, and Gambara was one of them, found Rommel's style of command difficult to work with because the latter was always in the field on the move. This absence prompted Gambara to state to Rommel's chief of staff that: "It was not admissible for a commander to virtually disappear for a day causing confusion and disorienting the division

---

234 Desert Rats <http://desertrats.org.uk/battles1941.htm#AxisWithdrawal> (accessed on 2 May 2019).
235 Mario Montanari, *Le operazioni in Africa settentrionale*, Vol. II, Part II, p. 625.
236 Ibid.

commanders. Another inadmissible fact is that every issue that needs to be addressed immediately cannot be dealt with until Rommel's return." [237]

On the night of 3 December Gambara finally met Rommel at his headquarters where a heated face to face took place. According to the former, Rommel asserted that he was no longer concerned about keeping forces at Bir el Gobi because his intelligence service had told him that they had spotted over 800 enemy vehicles retreating east behind Trigh Abd. When Gambara argued that evacuating Bir el Gobi was not a good idea because it would give the enemy the opportunity to attack the Axis flank, Rommel further stated that the enemy had been beaten and was evidently disengaging his forces away from Bir el Gobi and Gabr Saleh. "Rommel then urged me to free up the Giovani Fascisti forces that were hunkered down at Bir el Gobi."[238] Gambara goes on to state that despite Rommel's assessment of the situation he ordered his troops to maintain the occupation of the Bir el Gobi position even after the *Panzergruppe* had decided that the position was no longer of interest given the enemy's apparent defensive movements. His orders were to "engage the enemy, resist at all costs and only if overwhelmed retreat toward the Axis main positions."[239]

In fact, after the failed November attempts to capture Bir el Gobi, the Commonwealth forces were bent on attacking the same position in early December. General Norrie aimed at tearing a hole in the Axis defenses by hitting its flank position in anticipation of a subsequent move toward el-Adem. For the purpose, he had assembled a new force at Bir el Gobi with the objective of thrusting through the area west of Tobruk and to dislodge the Axis troops deployed in the siege front. The plan was for 11th Indian Brigade supported by sixteen heavy infantry tanks to capture the Bir el Gobi position, with 4th Armoured Brigade deployed north-east of Bir el Gobi and ready to hold off the enemy armour. After the capture of the position, 22nd Guards Brigade was to carry the attack on northwards. At 1200 on 3 December, Commonwealth artillery began shelling the Italian positions with great force causing some losses. At the time, Bir el Gobi was occupied by a 1,454 strong infantry unit comprised of volunteer university students of the *Reggimento Fanteria Giovani Fascisti* (Young Fascist Infantry Regiment based on I and II *Battaglione*) which faced a large, enemy force without the aid of the Axis armour. The *Giovani Fascisti* were equipped with eight 47mm guns, twenty-four *Breda modello* 30 machine guns, twelve heavy *Breda* machine guns, eighteen anti-tank rifles, eight 81mm mortars and two large cases of Pazzaglia bombs.[240] In addition, the Italian positions were further buttressed by two MILIMART 102/35 guns, an anti-tank platoon equipped with four 47mm guns and a battery of 20mm guns. This battle also saw the participation of the few forces remaining of the RECAM/*32° Reggimento Carristi* of the *Ariete* which had been left behind to solidify the defensive position of the Young Fascist Regiment as well as provide mobile security to the fuel and ammunition dump. Given the huge losses sustained this unit at the time of the battle equaled the strength of one company with twelve L.3 tanks and one M.13/40 tank.[241] Another small detachment from RECAM commanded by *Colonnello* Di Meo (two M.13/40s, a few light tanks and several 'flying batteries' including one truck mounted 100/17 howitzer)

---

237 Ibid., p. 629.
238 Ibid.
239 Ibid.
240 Alpheo Pagin, *I ragazzi di Mussolini* (Milan: Mursia, 1999), p. 120.
241 Mario Montanari, Le operazioni in Africa settentrionale, vol. II, part II, p. 631.

was to perform patrol duties in the area of Bir el Gobi and was also assigned to safeguard the supply dump. During one of its operations on the afternoon of 3 December this small unit came under attack at Hagfet Gueitenat from an enemy reconnaissance unit from, presumably 4th Armoured Brigade, which was positioned to the north-east of Bir el Gobi. According to De Meo's post battle report as the unit was traveling north it was approached by up to five enemy tanks and several armoured vehicles which opened fire and then closed in. As the enemy tanks were inching closer, the M.13/40 tanks and the truck mounted guns responded and the 100/17 unit saved the day by damaging two enemy tanks and forcing the rest of the enemy unit to flee. On 7 December *Colonnello* De Meo would write a report to CAM in which he expressed high praises for the performance of the truck mounted 100/17 howitzer: "I am still located at Point 176 North-west of Bir el Gobi and I believe my unit has carried out its assigned task. The battle is still unfolding and my worn-out vehicles will likely not make a difference anyway. The valiant battle of the 100/17 piece against the flank of an enemy armoured brigade cannot be repeated because the gun has been destroyed."[242]

At dawn on 4 December, after the artillery of the 7th Regiment had resumed its preparatory fire the Commonwealth forces launched two attacks against Bir el Gobi. During the barrage several Italian positions had been damaged. The first victim of the enemy fire was a volunteer from Istria Adelmo Pribaz who was decapitated by a splinter from a grenade. Other soldiers also fell under the powerful enemy shelling. Amongst the numerous wounded there was the commander of the unit Maggiore Fulvio Balisti who was taken to the rear by an ambulance. The first assault was conducted by the Queen's Own 2nd Cameron Highlanders (11th Indian Infantry Brigade) supported by three Valentine tanks and sevral Bren carriers which attacked Point 176 defended by the first battalion of Blackshirts, while the 1st Battalion/ 6th Rajputana Rifles and the 2nd Battalion/5th Mahratta Light Infantry with the support of thirteen Valentine tanks attacked Points 188 and 184 defended by the second Blackshirt battalion. At 0800 the infantry trailing the tanks and armoured vehicles moved forward towards Points 184 and 188. Alpheo Pagin an eyewitness recalls that: "I could not believe what I was seeing. They were all in front of us and they were maneuvering against our strongpoint in a noisy and dusty column comprised of tanks, armoured cars, Bren carriers, guns, truck borne infantry units and armoured vehicles."[243] Initially the operation proceeded well to the point that the attacking infantry reached the antitank ditches without suffering losses. But once they continued to inch closer toward points 188 and 184 they were subjected to fierce rifle and crew served weapons fire. Because of non-abating fire, the Commonwealth troops were forced back and had to call in their artillery to further soften up the enemy positions. Meanwhile the Camerons had advanced toward point 176 in the belief that the position had been evacuated during the heavy artillery bombardment. At 1000 meters the infantry had dismounted from their trucks and was slowly and carefully following the lead of the heavy tanks and the Bren carriers. Suddenly, however, when they were at a distance of 400 meters of Point 176, the defendants came to life forcing

---

242 Ufficio Storico, *Seconda offensiva brittanica in Africa settentrionale e ripiegamento italo-tedesco* (Rome: Ufficio Storico, 1949), p. 180-181. The truck mounted 100/17 was an improvised but effective anti-tank weapon, but it was vulnerable to enemy aerial fire because of its prominent silhouette. On 23 November RECAM had deployed its 100/17 battery effectively but then it lost several of these guns to RAF fire. One gun had also been put out of action by mistake by friendly fire from a Stukas.
243 Alpheo Pagin, *I ragazzi di Mussolini*, p. 120.

the Camerons to the ground. The troops defending dug in and highly camouflaged positions concentrated the fire of the crew served weapons against the enemy tanks, some of which were immobilized by the 47mm guns and later torched with Pazzaglia bombs and flamethrowers:

> Suddenly when the enemy was at 400 meters from our positions, Sottotentente ordered to 'open fire!' His voice could barely be heard when the first shots of our cannons were fired. Meanwhile, at that same moment the enemy's tanks and armoured cars also opened their fire giving way to countless rounds moving on a straight trajectory and culminating in huge sparks and flames. It first appeared to us that those huge iron hulls facing us where about to breach our positions by focusing upon a single point. But no, targeted by the first well-aimed shots of our 47/32 guns and under the hail of fire of our mortars, the enemy tank formation, which was very compact at first, fanned out while the infantry soldiers went to the ground.[244]

Later at 1400, a third attack was launched against the Italian lines supported by a heavy artillery barrage. Volunteer Antonino Calvaruso recalls that: "Numerous rounds were reining in destroying our defenses. Sand and smoke dispersed in the sultry air to the point that it was difficult to see anything."[245] After the barrage died down, the infantry came forward in large numbers but even though the volunteer unit suffered casualties it could maintain the main positions losing only advanced Point 188. During the afternoon, L.3 tanks were thrown into the cauldron and effectively scattered infantry and small engineer units forcing enemy soldiers to retreat. But after this initial success, they were targeted by a counter put forth by ten Valentine tanks which readily shot to pieces the so-called sardine tins. The Italian tanks were defending the CAM's supply dump and truck park which was shot up by the British tanks after they had overrun them.

Whilst the Commonwealth troops had not succeeded in breaking down the Axis resistance, the situation for the Bir el Gobi garrison was becoming tenuous. By the evening the garrison had not only sustained heavy losses but had also been cut off from being able to communicate with the CAM and even the two *Giovani Fascisti* battalions being surrounded were unable to communicate with each other. In addition food and water provisions were running exceedingly low to the point that the commander did not believe that the troops could hold on indefinitively. Stocks of anti-tank ammunitions were also very low.

The next day (5 December) the attacks against Bir el Gobi resumed. The first operation began as an early dawn raid undertaken by a company of Camerons and one of the Mahratta Light Infantry with a surprise bayonet attack without the aid of the artillery against Point 176. But even at the early hour the defenders were alert and opened fire immediately repelling the attack.

The second more massive operation began in the afternoon when 1/6th Rajputana Rifles backed by a company from the Camerons and four Valentine and one Crusader tank surged against the defenses of II *Battaglione*. The latter immediately opened a blistering fire and stopped the first surge in its tracks. The only openings found by the enemy were those made by the tanks that entered with brute force into the defensive perimeter. The defenders, even with

---

244 Ibid., p. 128.
245 Ibid.

tanks behind, concentrated their efforts upon the advancing infantry whose progress was met with machine gun and rifle fire. Immediately the infantry attack was repulsed and the tanks, left stranded in open ground, were forced to retreat out of the infantry stronghold. During the pullback one Valentine tank was hit at close range and its crew was captured.[246]

At 1600 the two strongpoints of Bir el Gobi were targeted again by a heavy artillery bombardment which was followed by several bombing raids by the RAF. After the devasting fire the infantry menaced again the Italian positions. This time five enemy tanks barreled their way through the infantry positions and began to use their machine guns at close range to decimate the infantrymen in their foxholes. The reaction by the defenders was again very fierce comprised by the fire at close range of the 47mm and 20mm guns. Some defenders even came out of their foxholes by launching Pazzaglia bombs against the armour. One of these infantrymen Ippolito Niccolini was able to damage two tanks before being struck down by the enemy fire. He would later be awarded a gold medal of military valour. To better understand the dynamics of the battle it is worth quoting at length the official history of the 11th Indian Armoured Brigade:

> At 1245 hours, the artillery laid a smoke screen on the southern approaches to el Gobi; behind it two companies of the 1/6 Rajputana Rifles moved to the attack. Four I tanks accompanied the assault, but owning to wireless failures fought independently and were not on call by the infantry. After initial progress the Rajputana Rifles were held up. A company of Camerons joined the fray on the left flank. At 1430 hours Lieutenant Colonel Butler (Rajputana Rifles) reported that he had reached the outskirts of a comprehensive defense position organized in depth. His tanks and carriers (Bren) had penetrated the outpost line but were unable to deal with the enemy in their deep and narrow slit trenches. Several tanks had been knocked out by Molotov cocktails. A similar report came from the Camerons, who added that enemy machine gun squads had occupied one of the disabled I tanks and were enfilading them. At 1600 hours, the Rajputana Rifles commander again reported the situation as stalemate. A few minutes Lieutenant Colonel Butler was killed by a mortar.[247]

A letter written by an officer of the *Ariete* states that "the enemy subjected our position to a very intense bombardment. After the preparatory fire wave after wave of enemy tanks and infantry were repeatedly thrown at us. But all attempts to take our positions were nullified. It's almost a miracle that I am still alive."[248]

The operation resulted in over 400 infantry casualties and several knocked out tanks that were suffered by the British/Commonwealth forces. CAM war diary claimed the destruction of six medium tanks, six light tanks and fifty vehicles and argued that it suffered thirty dead, sixty wounded and the loss of several anti-tank guns and light vehicles. "The enemy's attempt to outflank the Axis deployment by overcoming the Bir el Gobi position had been frustrated by the CAM's early decision to not vacate the position and then by the Giovani Fascisti regiment and

---

246 Alpheo Pagin, *I ragazzi di Mussolini*, pp. 165-166.
247 Jack Greene and Alessandro Massignani, *Rommel's Desert Campaign*, p. 124.
248 Andrea Rebora, *Carri Ariete combattono. Le vicende della divisione corazzata Ariete nelle lettere del tenente Pietro Ostellino. Africa settentrionale 1941-1943* (Milan: Propsettiva, 2016), p. 140.

the support units that blunted the numerous attacks."[249] *Giovani Fascisti* losses were up to a third of its initial strength. British historian Michael Carver wrote that the action of the *Giovani Fascisti* contributed in halting Operation Crusader, the first major British counter-attack against the Axis forces commanded by Rommel: "Although Norrie had an overwhelming superiority in every arm in the area of Bir el Gubi, the failure to concentrate them and coordinate the action of all arms in detail had allowed one Italian battalion group to frustrate the action of the whole corps and inflict heavy casualties on one brigade."[250] Historian John Gooch has argued that the action of the *Giovani Fascisti* and of the disparate forces of *Ariete*'s light armour is a valid example that illustrates why "Italy's military component was so different in the first and second stages in the campaign in North Africa."[251]

According to Gooch the change in performance of the Italian units stemmed mainly from increased battle field experience, coordinated and centralized artillery action that stifled more effectively enemy armoured attacks and a greater assimilation of German tactics by Italian armoured and motorized units.[252] By that time, following the German lead, the Italians had understood the full ramifications of using primarily the anti-tank guns and not tanks to knock out enemy armour. In the specific case of Bir el Gobi I the leading part was played by the MILIMART naval guns which used armoured piercing shells to debilitate enemy tanks with some degree of success. The 47mm had also been effective because the *Giovani Fascisti* at Bir el Gobi II had used them in a different fashion than Graziani's X Army. At Bir el Gobi the anti-tank guns had been deployed in forward positions, sometimes at less than 400 meters of the enemy, and they had been used to shoot at the tracks of the enemy tanks rather than at their impervious armour. Once the tank was immobilized it was dealt by dedicated teams of tank hunters that emerged from their concealed foxholes with Pazzaglia bombs and Molotov Cocktails to permanently put it out of action.[253]

On 4 December Rommel reacted to the British move toward Bir el Gobi by ordering the German Panzer units to concentrate their forces at Bir el Gobi by way of El Adem. His intent was that: "The attack on Gobi was to be made in conjunction with the Italian Motorized Corps coming up from north-east, but the Italians neither assembled nor in a fit state to attack, the Afrika Korps had to strike the blow alone ..."[254]

On the afternoon of 5 December the German armoured forces conducted forceful counter-attacks to retake Point 188, which they did recapture after a fiery clash between German and British tanks. After this combat action, the German tanks headed towards the other Bir el Gobi positions to come to the aid of the infantry. Once this task had been completed Rommel decided to immediately attack the Commonwealth force near Bir el Gobi in what he expected to be the final battle engagement of Operation Crusader. "The Afrika Korps' attack has inflicted no decisive damage on the enemy at Gobi, largely because of the absence of the Italian Motorized

---

249 Livio Picozzi, "Memorie del Corpo Armato di Manovra," *Rivista Militare*, n.7, 1949, p. 28.
250 Michael Carver, *Tobruk*, p. 124.
251 John Gooch (ed.) *Decisive Campaigns of the Second World War* (London: Frank Cass, 2004), p. 101.
252 Ibid.
253 *Caporal Maggiore* Ippolito Nicolini would be post-humorously awarded a gold medal of military valor for his actions on 5 December knocking out two tanks with an anti-tank gun and forcing a third tank, that had come too close to the gun position, to retreat by throwing against it several hand grenades.
254 Basil Liddell Hart, *The Rommel Papers*, p. 170.

Corps.….Nevertheless there still appears to be a chance of gaining a decision, by launching all the remaining German and Italian panzer and motorized divisions in a concentrated attack against the British at Gobi."[255] He aimed to strike at the enemy force with all the available Axis mobile elements. The *Ariete* and *Trieste* Divisions were also dispatched for this concentric attack, which was to take place on 6 December at 0800, but the former was halted by 7th Support Group artillery shelling near Gast el Arid, while the latter lost its way in the desert. Thus, on 6 December DAK again had to continue the attack on the Commonwealth armour at Bir el Gobi without the assistance of the Italian armoured corps. The Italians on their way to El Aden reported that they had again been shelled by enemy fire from both sides once its units reached Sidi Rezegh on the morning of 6 April. At 0800 a thirty strong *Ariete* medium tank force clashed with the British 4th Armoured Brigade, but the flanking fire of *Ariete*'s artillery did enough to disperse the enemy force. In the morning Trieste division was still not in sight and had clearly missed the link up with *Ariete* at the rendezvous point.[256] Since the German Panzer Divisions were quick to execute Rommel's order while the slower moving Italian units, which were also hampered by their antiquated communication systems, failed to show up on time they prompted Rommel to ask rhetorically: "Where are the Italians?" And General Crüwell specifically to ask, "where is Gambara?" This would be a recurring problem for the Axis alliance since Italian tanks and communication systems were technically inferior, while Rommel continued to demand from them quicker responses and movements. In addition, the Italian units had to cover twice the number of miles than the DAK forces to reach Bir el Gobi while also doing it with low stocks of fuel and a higher number of wastage of tanks and vehicles with several of them breaking down. In response to the German request for support Gambara issued a pointed directive to the three commanders under him (Piazzoni, Balotta and de Meo) that in essence stated that the division commanders were to be held responsible and even fired if some of their units failed to arrive in time or bypass the meeting point for future operations.[257]

The DAK attack was nonetheless continued but it led to an inconclusive encounter that resulted in heavy casualties on both sides. With the Axis armoured units stationed at point 188, the Commonwealth forces began to withdraw sensing that it was impossible to break the Axis position of Bir el Gobi.

Because of the delays caused by the Italians on 6-7 December 1941 the DAK war diary states that "the offensive undertaken against the enemy near Gobi failed mainly because of a lack of cooperation from the Italian mechanized army corps."[258]

On 7 December, Rommel stated that "Ariete and Trieste have suffered few losses up to now. But during the maneuvers they are very slow and need days to reach their destination."[259] Because of this delay in reaching the German Panzer units in a timely fashion, the Axis did not have the strength, as Rommel argued, to deal the much-needed decisive blow of Operation Crusader. Taking into consideration the strong enemy superiority and the heavily fatigued and

---

255 Basil Liddell Hart, *The Rommel Papers*, p. 171.
256 In the Rommel Papers the German general argues that: "The Afrika Korps launched their attack on the 6th December, once again alone. The Italians reported that their troops were exhausted and no longer fit for action", p. 171.
257 Jack Greene and Alessandro Massignani, *Rommel's North African Campaign*, p. 125.
258 Mario Montanari, *Le operazioni in Africa settentrionale*, Vol, III, Part II, p. 665.
259 Ibid.

depleted ranks of his troops, Rommel decided to abandon the siege of Tobruk which was no longer feasible and fall back to the Ain el Gazala position. The factor that clinched Rommel's decision to back away from Tobruk was a report from *Comando Supremo* that stated that the much needed armoured reinforcements could only be dispatched in January 1942. This led Rommel to "break off the action outside Tobruk on account of the Italian formations and also the badly exhausted German troops."[260] The Gazala positions were established defensive works but its southern flank, in Rommel's view, was exposed and subject to a potential flanking attack. Thus, it was not clear at that point whether Rommel aimed make his defensive line there or only to occupy the position temporarily to cover a further retreat west.

The delays on the part of the Italian armoured units would later prompt Rommel to call for the dismissal of General Gambara from the *Corpo d'Armata di Manovra*. The latter was relieved mainly because he had countermanded one of Rommel's orders which demanded that *Pavia* Division was to withdraw from Tobruk. Again there were strong words exchanged between the Italians and Rommel on 8 December, when *Generale* Bastico challenged the German officer by arguing against the retreat at Ain el Gazala especially on the heels of Rommel's proclaiming victory at Sidi Rezegh on 23 November. Both Rommel and Bastico lost their temper and the conversation quickly degenerated in a shouting match. Shortly thereafter, Gambara handed over his position to *Generale* Alessandro Piazzoni of *Trieste* Division and became chief of staff to Bastico. Operation Crusader had been blunted by the Axis, but the latter was unable to go on a major counter-attack again for lack of reinforcements and troop fatigue. In contrast to Rommel's assessment of the situation the Italian troops had suffered heavily and even if they had arrived on time on 5-6 December to Bir el Gobi[261] it is doubtful that the DAK together with the Italian armoured corps could have destroyed the Commonwealth armour in a decisive battle. The Italians, for instance, had lost a total of 6,813 soldiers and particularly severe had been the losses of the *Corpo d'Armata di Manovra*. *Ariete* in mid-December had only 1,500 soldiers and less than forty M.13 tanks in working order, while *Trieste* had 2,200 soldiers (losses on 5 December are less clear). The units were depleted by three weeks of constant fighting many of the German and Italian vehicles necessitated overhauls and fuel supply was persistently low. According to Basil Liddell Hart on 7 December the British 4th Armoured Brigade could count upon 136 tanks "almost three times the remaining strength of the Afrika Korps."[262] Adding up the forty odd Italian medium tanks still in working order to the DAK's forty-five tanks there was a combined force that was still inferior to the British armoured brigade. In addition, the British had additional tanks in other brigades deployed not too far from the border so therefore it is doubtful whether the combined Axis tank force was in a condition to deal a fatal blow to the enemy.

Rommel's first battle maneuver on 23 November that concentrated all available armoured forces against the Commonwealth at Sidi Rezegh, had paid huge dividends. But his second decision, the race to the Egyptian frontier had not only dispersed Axis armour in a multitude of disparate forces but also given the Commonwealth garrison at Tobruk the opportunity to break

---

260 Basil Liddell Hart, *The Rommel Papers*, p. 172.
261 According to the Italian Official History it was almost impossible for Ariete and Trieste to comply with Rommel's order to gather at Bir el Gobi in such a timely fashion due to the distance between their initial position on 5 December and the interference of enemy Jock columns.
262 Basil Liddell Hart, *History of The Second World War*, p. 196.

out of its encirclement. Most importantly it had not engaged the Axis armour with the British tank units that were still in the area of Sidi Rezegh. Rommel's counter order on 5 December, aiming to prop up the siege of Tobruk, and deal a decisive blow to the Commonwealth armour came too late when most Axis forces were depleted by the constant fighting. Thus, Rommel decided to take up defensive positions falling back to the Gazala line and there wait for reinforcements. The Commonwealth, on the other hand, had suffered terrible losses in both men and machines but had nonetheless successfully pushed back Rommel's forces thus putting an end to the siege of Tobruk.

The Axis withdrawal commenced on the night of 7-8 December with the Italian infantry moving on a northern column, a middle column comprised of the Italian armoured units and the DAK on the southern column. On 9 December at Sghifet en Naama, north of Trigh Capuzzo, the *Corpo d'Armata di Manovra* was involved in a very fierce pitched battle against enemy tanks of 4th Armoured Brigade and several infantry units that attempted to cut them off from the bulk of the Axis forces. The attack was put forth by up to forty armoured vehicles against the positions of the 66th Regiment of the *Trieste* and also involved a battalion of *Giovani Fascisti*. The British armour attacked four times and on the last attempt they made considerable headway into the Axis defenses to the extent that Commonwealth tanks irrupted into the strongholds of *Trieste*:

> The enemy has far more preponderant forces, especially in the realm of self-propelled batteries and tanks and it could suddenly fall upon the rear of the retreating Axis troops and on the artillery batteries that are vacating the area around Tobruk. The English armoured troops are the fiercest amongst the Commonwealth troops deployed. And they prove it by stubbornly attacking, with their heads down, four times a day even though they are sustaining heavy casualties.[263]

To stem the enemy attack an *Ariete* tank battalion, supported by the mobile anti-tank guns of *Batterie Volanti*, was called in to try to push back this infiltration. The tanks rushed to the scene and began to engage the enemy armour in a spirited artillery duel where the dust and the smoke obfuscated the tanks from the fire. By the time the *Ariete*'s armour came to the scene several infantry strongpoints had already been overrun and Trieste was in desperate need for reinforcements. The intervention of the armour resulted in a reduction of the enemy pressure upon *Trieste*'s line and the knocking out of action six enemy tanks with no loss to *Ariete*.[264] By the end of the day the British brigade had lost the chance to cut off Rommel's forces: "It was checked by an enemy rearguard eight miles short of Knightsbridge and showed more concern to protect itself than to trap the enemy."[265]

As Rommel's army was able to slip away, it wound up taking position on the Gazala line. These defenses, that the Axis forces now occupied, were a complex fortification system that had been built prior to the war. The forts started at Ain el-Gazala (a coast oasis) and continued on a straight line for a dozen miles to Alem Hamza. The Italian infantry divisions were positioned

---

263 Ufficio Storico: Divisione Trieste, 'Fatto d'arme di Sghifet en Naama', V.E. Borsi, cartella 906 allegato 5.
264 Ibid.
265 Basil Liddell Hart, *History of the Second World War*, p. 196.

as follows: X Corps was positioned on the coast and XXI Corps inland. The CAM (*Ariete* and *Trieste*, both very much understrength) was at Alem Hamza and DAK lay behind the southern flank, ready to counter-attack. Meanwhile the *Savona* Division still held very advanced positions near the border at Sollum and Halfaya. Initially the Commonwealth forces dispatched several reconnaissance units whose task was to ascertain if Rommel aimed to make a stand at Gazala or merely use the position as cover for a further retreat.

The first test against the Gazala line, which saw the Italian infantry units in the northern sector, the Italian armoured units in the middle and the DAK to the south, came on 13 December. The major thrust was put forth by the 5th Indian Brigade which attacked the meeting point between *Trieste* and *Ariete* Divisions around Hill 204 on the Ain el Gazala line. The Commonwealth unit snatched Hill 204 from the Axis after heavy fighting and some of its reconnaissance units reached Sidi Breghisc, fifteen miles behind the Axis defensive line. The bold move preoccupied Rommel which had feared all along a flanking move by a mass of armoured enemy forces against the Axis line. *Ariete* then countered on the next day. A unit of twelve M.13/40 tanks attacked Hill 204 at approximately 1100 but came up against nine Matildas II and a troop from the 31st Field Regiment. Thus, in the engagement three Italian tanks were damaged by enemy fire in a courageous but reckless assault against heavier enemy tanks. Then in the afternoon fifteen Italian tanks overran a troop of six 25-pdr guns capturing them but they too were unable to occupy Hill 204.[266]

The New Zealand official history notes:

> After the setback to 7 Indian Brigade at Sidi Breghisc on the 13th, when a field battery was overrun and an Indian battalion narrowly escaped the same fate, 5 Indian Brigade met more trouble next day near Point 204, a few miles to the east, this time from the remnants of Ariete. The nine I tanks and three cruisers of 1 Royal Tanks and a troop of 31 Field Regiment, RA, helped to repulse an attack at midday by ten or twelve tanks (wrongly reported to be German) and claimed to have put three of them out of action. Then fifteen Italian tanks renewed the attack and overran the troop of six 25-pounders.[267]

Even though the Axis troops had fended off the enemy attacks, Rommel maintained that resistance on the Gazala line was not sustainable in the long run, given that the positions could have been easily outflanked by the enemy and they were still located at quite a distance from the Axis main supply bases. While General Crüwell gave a positive assessment of the situation on the Gazala line and described the enemy situation as dire, Rommel was much more pessimistic. The Italians shared Crüwell's position and maintained that resistance at Gazala was favored over a retreat.

On the 15th the following Commonwealth units renewed the attacks against the Italian positions on the Gazala line: 4th and 5th Indian Brigades, 7th Armoured Division, the Polish Brigade and the 5th New Zealand Brigade. The main attack was put forth by the 5th Indian Brigade. Initially its Buffs Battalion charged the Italian positions with bayonets and machine guns and achieved some success by snatching several forward posts and overrunning machine

---

266 W.E. Murphy, *The Official History of New Zealand in the Second World War*, p. 499.
267 Ibid, p. 500.

gun points. As the Buffs continued to advance however, they were countered by *Ariete* with thirty-five M.13/40 tanks and some fifteen Panzers forcing the attackers to scatter and retreat. One of the reasons the Commonwealth infantry ranks were reduced was because the 4th Armoured Brigade failed to support them when they came up against the Axis tanks. The British brigade experiencing a number of vehicles breakdowns and losing its way never arrived at the rendezvous point. On the northern sector of the Gazala line the Polish Brigade and the 5th New Zealand Brigade put in a more forceful attack which broke through the Italian infantry defenses creating a huge bulge. These troops advanced for over four miles and captured several Italian infantry strongpoints. Overall, however, the Commonwealth attacks were checked as the *Trento* Division was rushed in to plug the hole by using its mobile artillery against the infantry. Thus, during the day's operations approximately 1,000 Commonwealth soldiers either died or were captured, along with forty guns, many trucks and other equipment such as machine guns and rifles.

Ariete's war diary states that the unit was then ordered to counter-attack again Hill 204 and link up with the isolated outposts of the *Trieste* Division:

> Only thanks to the maneuverability of the armour it was ultimately possible to retake Hill 204. For two days, the position had been heavily targeted by the artillery and subjected to numerous attacks. This was followed up by a fast-paced tank attack which overcame several enemy positions. A general, 500 prisoners and forty enemy tanks were captured. The field of battle, on the night of 15 December, was littered with burning vehicles. There was an eerie silence as the enemy retreated. The *Ariete* had won the battle for Hill 204 on Ain el Gazala and the unit was praised for its effort by the commander of the 15th Panzer Division.[268]

On the night of 15 December despite the success of Hill 204 "Rommel was depressed by dwindling supplies, the battle-weariness of his troops, the ever-present danger of being cut off by strong British mobile forces, and the inevitable loss of the 13,000-odd troops in the frontier area. On the other hand, Crüwell was ready, after overrunning the Buffs, to turn and strike the British amour, and the new commander of the Italian Mobile Corps, General Piazzoni, was in high spirits."[269] After carefully pondering the situation, Rommel ultimately issued orders for the Gazala line to be abandoned. According to Axis estimates 800 trucks were needed to supply the troops in Cyrenaica. Moreover, by that stage DAK had only thirty tanks left in working order. Based on these estimates Rommel gathered that *Comando Supremo* could not guarantee such volume of supplies before the end of December and thereby decided to shorten his supply lines and thus justified his general retreat a hundred kilometers to the west to the line of Ain el Gazala, where his tried and tested troops stood between 12 and 15 December 1941. Since the burden of both supplies and fuel was so high, Rommel had wisely decided to retreat and regroup closer to the Axis supply bases hence the retreat from Cyrenaica. Thus, the siege of Tobruk had to be definitively abandoned. The decision was not taken well by the Italians which wanted to make a defensive stance closer to the frontier and because they feared that the retreat

---

268 Ufficio Storico, 'Relazione sul comportamento del 132° Reggimento Carri nei cicli opertaivi del 18/11/1941 al 03/07/1942 da me comandato', n. 5498, Enrico Maretti, 4 luglio 1942.
269 W.E. Murphy, *The Official History of New Zealand in the Second World War*, p. 501.

by the Panzers would lead the less mobile Italian formations to be sacrificed to save the German troops, but Rommel was adamant in pulling back much further closer to the Axis ports.

On the 16th the enemy attacks resumed especially against the positions held by the 7º and 9º *Reggimenti Bersaglieri* but the latter could contain the numerous attempts to overtake their positions with machine gun fire.

The 9º *Reggimento* was particularly tested sustaining heavy casualties between 12 and 16 December 1941, while it held the rearguard. These amounted to 126 dead, 164 wounded and 67 missing. But the enemy losses had been equally high as the *Bersaglieri* fought back with considerable energy to prevent an enemy breakthrough. In his report, *Colonnello* Bordoni estimated the losses inflicted on the enemy in a few hundred men wounded or killed, seven tanks and various vehicles destroyed, one tank and three armoured vehicles immobilized.[270]

An emergency meeting took place on the 16th between Cavallero, Kesselring, Bastico and Gambara to discuss Rommel's intentions. At the meeting, it was made evident in addition to the stretched supply situation that no significant reinforcements would be coming from Italy before the new year. Although Kesselring and Cavallero both wanted unjustifiably to hold on at Gazala, Rommel ultimately correctly determined that to retreat even further back to Agheila and as soon as possible was the right choice to make given the depleted supplies. At that point Bastico posed the problem of the more static Italian infantry troops and whether they would be sacrificed to cover the retreat of the German mechanized units. But Rommel, adamant that remaining on the Gazala line was not sustainable due to dwindling supplies and given the large distance between Italian supply bases and Gazala, forced the decision upon everyone else stating that the retreat was already underway. The final retreat in fact commenced on 17 December, after Rommel formed a combat group comprised of the *Bersaglieri* and buttressed by four 88mm guns that was tasked to cover the Axis retreat. The Axis even made recourse to a special Italian unit made up of Italian *Carabinieri* paratroops which made a stand on the Jebel Akhbar Mountains as all other units were orderly falling back. The paratroopers engaged the enemy from 18 to 20 December facing two battalions of the 4th Indian Division supported by tanks and armoured cars. The former "held back the 3/1 Punjabis throughout December 20th, but at dusk a bayonet charge overran the last stubborn defenders."[271] While the bulk of the Axis forces escaped the Commonwealth counter, the Italian *Savona* Division which occupied the advanced frontier defenses was totally cut off from Rommel's army and was ultimately forced to surrender in mid-January after being surrounded by the enemy and running out of food and water.

Operation Crusader was a Commonwealth victory but Rommel won the tactical engagement. "He made better use of his tanks because he kept them concentrated by using antitank guns with his infantry. The British, while keeping some of their armour concentrated, insisted on stationing some tanks with infantry formations to counter panzers."[272] Even though the Germans won the most important battle of the Crusader Operation on 23 November 1941 the dynamics of the fighting demonstrated the long term untenable Axis position in North Africa. Since the German High Command did not give the theater the same resources given to the

---

270 Ufficio Storico, "Relazione sui fatti d'arme dei giorni 12, 13, 14, 15 e 16 dicembre 1941 redatta dal colonnello Umberto Bordoni," 5 gennaio 1942.
271 I.S.O. Playfair, *Mediterranean and Middle East, Volume 3: British Fortunes Reach Their Lowest Ebb* (London: Her Majesty's Stationary Office, 1962), p, 71.
272 Ibid.

German army deployed against the Soviet Union while the Commonwealth could count upon massive support from the Americans, the Panzer Armee could not likely afford to engage the Commonwealth in a long-term battle of attrition. Thus, the Day of the Dead battle had resulted in an Axis victory although at too high a cost in the loss of tanks and other equipment that could not be readily replaced. The British tank units, for instance, had suffered more than double the losses of vehicles of the Axis forces but could replace these losses more quickly throughout the month-long battle. Losses of men were also revealing. The Italians lost 1,320 dead, 3,100 wounded and 13,000 missing. In addition, in January of 1942 another 8,000 soldiers would fall in the hands of the Commonwealth as the surrounded frontier fortifications finally surrendered. The German lost 1,000 killed, 3,500 wounded and 10,100 missing. Commonwealth losses were 2,900 dead, 7,300 wounded and 7,500 missing. Both had suffered heavy losses in men but the Axis losses were significantly higher on a percentage basis with regard to armoured vehicles that were not easily replaceable. Thus, Crusader had set the stage for the El Alamein battles and the final defeat of the Axis in North Africa through a drawn-out war of attrition. According to Basil Liddell Hart Operation Crusader had shown Rommel's brilliance as an armoured commander since he had dealt a heavy blow to a more numerous enemy force through the concentration at the right point and time of his armoured force, while the British tank commanders had failed by deploying their tanks in more of a piecemeal fashion. At the time, the Italians saw thing differently. Knowing that their infantry was mostly non-motorized and without significant tank and mobile anti-tank support, they had feared all along a repeat of Graziani's offensive when a quick advance into Egypt had been followed by a powerful enemy counter by greater motorized and mechanized forces leading to the capture of large numbers of Italian infantry units. Although Rommel had achieved two major successes during his rapid advances, the first one being the battle of El Aghelia and the second the destruction of a Commonwealth force on 23 November, he had ultimately suffered a reversal. A reversal that was not as dire as the one suffered by Graziani, but one that nonetheless had led to the capture of the *Savona* Division. According to the Italian Official History Mussolini, Cavallero and other Italian generals admired Rommel's style of leading his troops from the front but were fearful that another major leap forward would ultimately result in another Axis reversal.

With regard to the behavior of the Italian troops as Battistelli and Crociani assert about Operation Crusader "The battles that followed produced mixed results for the CAM; the corps demonstrated both a good level of combat experience and the inadequacies of Italian equipment and command systems."[273] On the one hand, the stand at Bir el Gobi I demonstrated that the *Ariete* had become a more effective combined arms unit than the armoured units under General Babini during Operation Compass. While the M.13/40 tanks were, apart from some slight improvements, the same equipment used in the winter of 1940-41, they were deployed more effectively by *Ariete*. Due to enhanced training and greater experience operating the medium tanks, *Ariete* maneuvered as a unit with the mobile artillery in close support rather than dispatching tanks in the attack in a piecemeal fashion. The Italian medium tanks also revealed themselves to be slightly less effective than the British Crusader tanks but that they could still hold their own in tank to tank battles. As such Operation Crusader clearly demonstrated that even though the Crusader tanks were slightly superior to the Italian medium tanks, the latter

---

273 Pier Paolo Batttistelli and Piero Crociani, *Italian Medium Tanks*, pp. 12-13.

were still somewhat competitive. The British Army's A 15 Crusader I (Cruiser Mark VI) tank was operated by four-man crew, weighed 19 tons, it had an armour plating of 49mm on the turret and most importantly it was fast moving (27 mph on main roads) compared to Italian tanks. In contrast, the M.13 tank was protected by only 30mm of armoured plating on the turret and was powered by a less reliable, underpowered engine capable of an average speed of 19.9 mph. Both the British and the Italian tank had similar armament. The M. 13/40 was equipped with a 47mm gun, while the Crusader with a puny 2-pdr (40mm) main gun.

To compensate for the weak medium tanks during the Crusader battles *Ariete*'s *Bersaglieri* and artillery units provided strong support during the attacks especially because the Italians now had more mobile artillery that could be deployed near or in support of the tanks. The artillery units in fact played a key role both at Bir el Gobi I and II making an important contribution to the erosion of British tank strength during Operation Crusader. The flying columns equipped with 100/17 howitzers, for example, had carried out a relevant anti-tank role and the same could be said for the truck mounted naval guns and their special projectiles. On the downside, the Crusader battles revealed already known Italian deficiencies. The underpowered M.13/40 tanks traveling at a much slower speed than German tanks and subject to greater numbers of breakdowns often could not keep up with their Axis companion units. In fact, on one occasion (23 November) they arrived late at the point of decision and when the battle was already unfolding. The situation was made worse by the lack of vehicles radios and by the cumbersome Italian communication system. Two of the factors that also delayed *Ariete* and *Trieste* from reaching Bir el Gobi on 5 December. According to the Italian Official History the Crusader battles demonstrated that the main problems influencing the performance of the elite unit, the *Corpo d'Armata di Manovra* was not the lack of combativeness or the shortcomings of the medium tanks but the lack of overall command and control of the unit by its commanders. "The large scale, elite unit at the disposal of *Comando Superiore Africa*, did not offer in that first period of operational activity the type of superior performance that was originally expected."[274] The work cites the lack of effective communication systems and the absence of a true experienced armoured staff in support of the CAM as the two factors impeding its leadership during Operation Crusader: "Lacked energetic initiative. This coupled with the poor status of communications and problems in the Italian command structure led to the slow arrival and execution of orders."[275] The work is also critical of Gambara's role during Operation Crusader. The CAM unit was particularly found wanting when it came to mobility and effective communication and that an armoured commander "must remain in standing communication with his staff. Reliance on his staff is an important requirement if he wants to integrate his decisions effectively into operational leadership. Every staff must remain mobile. Staff and troops must not lose contact."[276]

Some of the same critiques against the CAM were made in the war diary of the *Panzergruppe Afrika* which in summarizing Operation Crusader stated that the Axis plans to concentrate the troops against the Commonwealth forces failed due to the slowness in the decision-making process of a coalition alliance and the lack of fuel supplies. Both problems were attributable to the Italians and their inability to fully provide for the troops during operation Crusader:

---

274 Mario Montanari, *Le operazioni in Africa settentrionale*, Vol III, Part II, p. 761.
275 Ibid.
276 Hermann Büschleb, *Operation Crusader: Tank Warfare in the Desert, Tobruk 1941*, p. 78.

> The operational leadership of the Panzerarmee was guided by the effort to bring its numerically inferior forces to bear at the decisive point and the correct point of main effort and in the most effective possible defense posture. This effort was somewhat limited by both the nature of coalition war and the sometimes difficult supply situation.[277]

This criticism reflects the various operational delays of the CAM in execution of the orders during Operation Crusader, although its impressive stand at Bir El Gobi I was not even mentioned. The battle diminished Commonwealth combat strength and as a result fewer tanks reached Sidi Rezegh. As a result Rommel's forces pounced upon this reduced Commonwealth force on 23 November. Operation Crusader might have turned out differently had the bulk of the Commonwealth tank force hit Rommel's DAK when he least expected it during the early stages of the battle when he was still planning his winter offensive.

The Italian units had performed well in head to head confrontations against enemy tanks both in the realm of tank against tank engagements such as at Bir el Gobi I or in the anti-tank versus tank type of battle such as the *Ariete*'s and *Giovani Fascisti* stance had Bir el Gobi II in December. What the unit lacked was an overall more effective command system during battle that was amplified by the lack of modern communication systems. This prevented the commanders of both *Ariete* and *Trieste* and of the CAM overall from significantly influencing the battle as it unfolded. Another problem that was identified was the way Rommel continued to deploy these units. In some engagements, they were deployed in ad hoc mixed (German and Italian) combat groups rather than the deployment of the *CAM* as a whole. These mixed combat groups often demonstrated the inherent weaknesses of the Italian units versus their Axis allies also because in many instances Rommel's orders or expectations exceed what was achievable with underpowered and under gunned M tanks and 47mm anti-tank guns.

The greatest Italian complaint against Rommel, however, was not the way troops had been deployed in battle. The latter in fact always followed his orders and had great respect for a commander that led from the front. Their major gripe, as *Generale* Gambara pointed out, was that when things went well Rommel often stated that it was because of the more positive role played by the DAK or the German Panzer units, while when things did not go well Rommel always blamed it on the Italians. Lastly, Rommel was always worried about intelligence leaks and always communicated his orders to the Italian commanders at the last minute frequently without their input. This type of behavior was a continuous source of strain between the two armies. His falling back to Tripolitania after Operation Crusader was a prime example, so argued the Italians, of Rommel's excessive pessimism that resulted in giving up the territories occupied during his fast-paced campaign in the spring of 1941.

Final Considerations

Although the Italian armoured corps had trained extensively prior to the operation it nevertheless demonstrated that its troops were more effective while holding a defensive position rather than when being called to conduct maneuver warfare. On one hand, at Bir el Gobi, Sidi

---

277 Ibid.

Rezegh and Bir el Gobi again in December their defensive effort not only prevented the British armour from attacking the flanks of Rommel's panzers but also engaged the enemy in a battle of attrition which reduced its combat power. On the other, when the CAM was tasked with conducting wide sweeping tank maneuvers its effectiveness was hampered by the mechanical reliability of the Italian tanks, by the slower pace of their vehicles and by the absence of effective communication systems. Moreover, Italian infantry being for the most part not motorized, also fought with reduced speed and effectiveness. In the month long Crusader battles it can be argued that the Italian troops accounted themselves well but their reduced number of tanks and mobile artillery would not have been able to halt the British offensive without the aid of the German Panzers. Rommel's decision to strike on 23 November effectively countered and halted the enemy operation, but then his "Dash to the Wire' diluted Axis combat strength and ultimately the Commonwealth prevailed in the extended attrition battle by being able to quickly replace the losses while steadily reducing the Axis armour and artillery units.

General Francesco Saverio Grazioli. The commander of the arditi army corps in the First World War. In the 1920s and 30s Grazioli became the main advocate of the progressives within the Italian Army who advocated for the formation of mechanized divisions.

General Ettore Bastico awards a medal of bravery to a *Giovane Fascista*. Born in Bologna, Bastico had the tough assignment during the North African campaign of tempering Rommel's desire to always go on the offensive as well respisibilities for supplying the frontline troops with weapons, fuel, water and food.

Victory parade at the end of the Spanish Civil War. The Italian trucks are towing 37/45 and 47/32 guns.

Top: Fiat 2000 tank. This is the first tank designed in Italy immediately after the end of the First World War.

Middle: Renault FT-17 tank in the service of the Italian Army.

Bottom: Blackshirts at a parade. These were volunteer units separate from the Royal Army. In 1943 these units would form an armored division equipped with German tanks and motorized artillery.

Top: Blackshirts at a parade.

Middle: Fiat 3000 tank testing anti-tank defenses. The first Fiat 3000s were designated as the *carro d'assalto Fiat 3000*, Mod. 21 and their armament, consisted of two 6.5 mm machine guns. Later some tanks adopted a 37 mm gun as main armament.

Bottom: Fiat 3000 tank testing anti-tank defenses.

Top: Italian soldier and anti-tank defenses somewhere in Sicily.

Middle: *Breda* 20/65 anti-aircraft gun mounted on SPA-38 truck. The Breda 20/65 was developed during the 1930s to be deployed as a dual-function weapon. It could be used both in an anti-aircraft role and against ground targets. It was similarly effective against lightly armoured vehicles such as trucks, armoured cars and light tanks. The *Breda's* ammunition could penetrate armour up to 30mm thick.

Bottom: *Cannone* da 75/32 being pulled by a light tractor TL-37.

Top: *Bersaglieri* strongpoint in North Africa. These were the elite infantry units of the Army in North Africa. Most units were motorized.

Middle: Italian M 13/40 tank testing anti-tank defenses.

Bottom: M13/40 tank in Greece in 1941.

Top: *Carristi* during the Greek campaign.

Middle: 47/32 gun manned by *Bersaglieri*. It was effective against armored vehicles and British Cruiser and Crusader tanks but it became obsolete, lacking firepower, when facing Lee, Grant and Sherman tanks in 1942. It had a particularly difficult time against Matilda II tanks during Operation Compass.

Bottom: Anti-aircraft position in North Africa.

Top: *Autocannone* da 90/53 abandoned in the desert. It proved an excellent anti-tank weapon thanks to the powerful 90 mm gun during the North African campaign. During the Allied landing on the shores of Sicily some *Autocannoni* da 90/53 on *Breda* 52 were used in the indirect fire role against Allied vessels.

Bottom: Howitzer 100/17 mounted on a *Lancia* 3-Ro. The weapon played a key role during Operation Crusader. It was originally designed by Skoda and several batteries were given to the Italians at the end of the First World War.

Top: Medium tank fighting in Greece.

Middle: *Carristi* during the Greek campaign.

Bottom: *Bersaglieri* on the march in North Africa.

Top: *Bersaglieri* handling enemy soldiers. During the Second World War the *Bersaglieri* regiments were organized in armoured, motorized and fast divisions. They fought on all fronts, showing their capabilities and dedication. The Field Marshal Rommel, the Italian-German Army Commander in Northern Africa, is believed to have said: " the German soldier has astonished the world, the Italian Bersagliere soldier has astonished the German one…"

Middle: Italian tank perforated by enemy shell.

Bottom: Captured *autocannone* da 102/35 captured by the British.

Top: M13/40 on the move.

Middle: *Semovente* da 75/18 a successful weapon introduced by the Italians in early 1942. It belonged to a family of Italians self-propelled guns based on the chassis of the Italian medium M13/40, M14/41, and later M15/42 tanks armed with a 75 mm Ansaldo cannon in the casemate. It is the most widely produced self-propelled gun in the Kingdom of Italy during the Second World War, capable of fighting against almost all opposing armored vehicles. It was used in various roles by the Regio Esercito for infantry support and as a tank destroyer.

Bottom: *Semoventi* da 105/25 at Ansaldo factory in Genoa ready to be shipped out to the Army. More than 600 *semoventi* vehicles representing different models were produced in total by the Italian industry during the war. It was also appreciated by the Wehrmacht, which captured several of them and put them back into service in its armored divisions in 1943.

Top: Prototype of *semovente* da 90/53 on a Breda 501. This was an early prototype built by Ansaldo with colaboration from Breda factories.

Middle: M3 Lee tank captured by the Italians.

Bottom: *Semovente* with extra protection. The use of more protection made the vehicle more impervious to enemy fire but it made it also slower. The vehicles main advantange point was its low silohuette but it was hampered by its underpowered engine.

Top: Giovani Fascisti at Bir el Gobi. These were volunteer units primarily comprised of university students. The photo depicts them in their slit trenches as an armored vehicle burns in front of their position.

Middle: Italian armored unit on the move.

Bottom: *Giovani Fascisti* with anti-tank gun.

Top: Captured A15 Crusader.

Bottom: Tank hunting training.

Top: *Semovente* da 75/34 on the chassis of a M42.

Middle: Captured self-propelled gun.

Bottom: Tank shooting practice.

Top: *Ariete* parade in Tripoli.

Middle: *Semoventi* training somewhere in Tunisia.

Bottom: British tank immobilized by the *medaglia d'Oro* Ippolito Nicolini at Bir el Gobi.

Top: Italian artillerymen with a German 88/56 gun battery in Egypt.

Middle: *Bersaglieri* strongpoint in North Africa.

Bottom: Anti-tank hunters training.

Top: Captured 25-pdr gun used by the Italians.

Middle: *Arditi* mortorized unit in Tunisia. These soldiers fough well at the Battle of Primosole in Sicily in July 1943. They used their armored vehicles to counter-attack the British near the important bridge.

Bottom: *Arditi* mortorized unit in Tunisia.

Top: Officers of the *Arditi* motorized units.

Bottom: Officers of the *Arditi* motorized units.

Top: Officers of the *Arditi* motorized units.

Middle: Italian artillerymen with a German 88/56 gun battery in Egypt.

Bottom: Italian anti-aircaft position in North Africa.

Top: Captured Pak-40 gun in Sicily.

Middle: *Giovani Fascisti* position at Bir el Gobi.

Bottom: Skoda da 47 captured by the Americans in Sicily.

Top: Captured 6-pdr British gun.

Middle: *Semovente* da 47/32 in Tunisia. The *Semovente* L40 da 47/32 was developed by Ansaldo and built by FIAT between 1942 and 1944. It was designed to support assault infantry units of the *Regio Esercito* in the form of direct fire support from the *Cannone da* 47/32 *modello* 1935 medium support gun.

Bottom: Italian *cannone* da 75/34 *modello* 97/38 in the defense of Sicily.

Top: *Batterie Volanti* unit. In order to provide anti-tank support against the technically superior British armored forces, the availability of captured British vehicles from spring of 1941 on led to mount on them 20mm and 65mm guns.

Middle: *Autoblinbo* AB41. The AB41 was the standard reconnaissance armored car of the Royal Italian Army which used it with excellent results in the African Campaign, the Russian Front and the Balkans from mid-1941 to September 8th, 1943.

Bottom: Blackshirt M division.

Top: Italian officer during the defense of Sicily.

Bottom: Italian *cannone* da 75/34 *modello* 97/38 in the defense of Sicily.

Top: Italian artillery piece in Greece.

Middle: Anti-aircaft crew in Greece.

Bottom: Renault R 35 knocked out in Sicily. These captured vehicles equipped a battalion of Italian armored personnel.

Top: *Cannone* da 75/34 *modello* 97 in the defense of Sicily.

Middle: *Cannone* da 105/25 in position in Sicily.

Bottom: British officer inspectes Italian anti-aircraft position.

Autocannone da 75/27 modello 11. Along with the modello 6 this was the standard gun of the artillery regiments of the mechanized divisions during the war.

(Credit for all images: Ufficio Storico, Rome)

4

Further Advance

In January 1942 Rommel's intelligence services reported an incremental building up of Commonwealth forces and supplies that likely was the precursor to a large-scale attack against the Axis forces in Tripolitania. In fact, at the time Auchinleck was in the midst of planning Operation Acrobat, which entailed the capture of Tripoli. The bulk of the Commonwealth forces where in the rear and away from the frontline which was thinly held and by troops that were not experienced. Evidently, the Commonwealth commander believed at the time that Rommel's forces were not strong enough to mount an offensive. Despite Italian objections, Rommel decided that the best remedy against further Commonwealth attacks was to go on the offensive with a preemptive strike in the form of a spoiling attack to capture and box in enemy troops and equipment in Cyrenaica. His final objective was always Tobruk, whose capture had eluded him in spring of 1941, but his initial plans were more limited. At the time, the DAK and the Italian armoured units were assembled at El Aghelia after their retreat in December. On 20 January, the *Corpo d'Armata di Manovra* had eighty-nine M.13 tanks, while DAK had 111 *Panzerkampfwagen* III and IV, twenty-three armoured vehicles and an additional twenty-eight *Panzerkampfwagen* IV that were in transit from Italy and were due to arrive at the front shortly. Despite this reduced armoured strength, Rommel aimed to launch a pincer movement whereby the German amour would travel south, while the Italians would drive north. Ultimately, they were to converge at Agedabia between the Via Balbia and the El Faregh wadi to destroy the Commonwealth troops there deployed. Since this was a preemptive strike the element of surprise was the key to an early success which in Rommel's view was designed to box in large quantities of enemy troops and machines. To maintain secrecy Rommel did not communicate his plans nor obtained prior authorization from *Comando Supremo*, the German High Command or Bastico. The only one that was warned of Rommel's plans was Kesserling who was told on the day the operation began. The only other general that was fully aware because he had participated to the planning of the operation providing the fuel necessary for the vehicles to operate was *Generale* Gambara. He was now back in favor with Rommel but was shortly thereafter dismissed by *Comando Supremo* for having failed to warm them of Rommel's plans with Operation Theseus.

The operation began on 20 January 1942 as the Axis tank units moved forward at the head of the infantry. For historian Correlli Barnett[1] Rommel began one of his most impressive tactical operations of the campaign that demonstrated all of his brilliance and impulsiveness. He ordered his troops to advance into two separate columns one on the Via Balbia (CAM now under *Generale di corpo d'armata* Francesco Zingales) and one in the interiors (German units) across the desert to surprise and overwhelm enemy pockets of resistance. While the German troops were initially traveling at top speed, the Italian columns proceeded more slowly mainly due to their equipment. The CAM moved from Mersa Brega along the Via Balbia, while the bulk of the German units advanced on the rougher Wadi Faregh. The Commonwealth forward positions were evacuated just in the nick of time by the 200 Guards Brigade leading the CAM war diary to report that "the advance was conducted at a fast pace but the enemy had already pulled back. The tracks of the Commonwealth vehicles were clearly noticeable in the terrain pointing to the fact that the enemy has escaped southeast and northeast directions."[2] In fact, the bulk of the Commonwealth troops fell back to the east after their advanced reconnaissance units had spotted the Axis troops on the move. By the 22nd the Axis troops had reached Agedabia facing little if no opposition.

Realizing that the Commonwealth troops were retreating in disarray Rommel opted to continue the operation. As Major General von Mellenthin, DAK Intelligence Officer, asserts Rommel turned his forces north in the direction of Benghazi: "The Italian armoured corps was to hold the Agedabia area, the Afrika Korps was to try and establish a cordon along the line Agedabia-Antelat-Saunnau, and Group Marcks was to move south east of Saunnau, and endeavor to close a ring on the eastern flank."[3] The move was meant to encircle the 200 Guards and the 2nd Armoured Brigade. But as the troops moved forward once again the enemy units were able to escape from the trap set by Rommel by anticipating their moments even though they had to abandon, ammunition supplies, trucks and other equipment behind. On the 25th the pursuit resumed after, as the CAM War Diary reports, *Ariete* had been forced to stop and regroup as up to fifteen percent of its tanks had experienced mechanical failures of some sort. On the 25th *Ariete* reached Antelat while *Trieste* remained between Agedabia and Antelat. Meanwhile, DAK encountered in a sharp fight the 2nd Armoured Brigade and inflicted heavy casualties on its enemy.

This defeat gave way to the next leap forward which was the drive to Benghazi. The 90th Leicht, CAM and the Marcks Group headed respectively north and north-west, while a number of German mechanized units moved toward El Mechili. On 28 January CAM was deployed into two columns: *Ariete* on the left and *Trieste* on the right. By midday they reached Sceleidima where they opened artillery fire against the Commonwealth garrison of the 4th Indian Division holding its position. At the same time 21th Panzer Division units reached Regima and also made contact with the enemy forces. The first position to fall was Sceleidima which was captured by the *Bersaglieri* units of the *Trieste* Division, while *Ariete* was launched on the pursuit of several enemy units that were fleeing toward Soluch. The latter was captured shortly thereafter. Supported by the divisional artillery, *Ariete*'s tanks together with motorized elements from *Trieste* made a flanking move against the enemy garrison. The action against

---

1   Correlli Barnett, *The Battle of El Alamein* (London: Macmillan, 1964).
2   Mario Montanari, *Le Operazioni in Africa Settentrionale*, Vol. III, Part I, p. 53.
3   Ibid.

Sceleidima offers some interesting insights on the improved tactical deployment of the Italian motorized and mechanized troops and how they were fighting much more cohesively as all arms teams than in 1940.

Rommel had ordered the Italian armoured corps to pin down the enemy to prevent him from escaping to the east. *Trieste* came into contact with the troops from the 7th Brigade/ 4th Indian Division and reinforced by a mechanized/motorized tactical group of the 5th Brigade after marching on foot because of the strong enemy fire and the rough terrain.

The battle began around noon, when reconnaissance elements of the 9° *Bersaglieri* signaled the presence of enemy forces at fort Sceleidima and on the surrounding hills. The plan entailed the deployment of three attacking columns, a frontal attack by the XL *Bersaglieri* Battalion, an envelopment from east to west by the XXVIII *Bersaglieri* Battalion and finally the infantry of I/66° *Reggimento* encircling the enemy from the right flank, supported by divisional artillery. Meanwhile *Ariete*'s tanks were to concentrate for an envelopment from the west flank. At 1300 the frontal attack began as the troops rushed the enemy defenses, while by 1400 *Ariete*'s tanks had outflanked the enemy positions. Meanwhile the column belonging to 66° *Reggimento* was moving forward on trucks but experienced some difficulties when it encountered a minefield. But by 1430 the enemy position had been encircled completely and while some managed to escape, the majority of the enemy soldiers fell into the trap.

It was at this point that General Tucker of 4th Indian Division ordered the evacuation of Benghazi. Thus, as a result of this order the 7th Indian Brigade managed to flee and avoid Rommel's pincer movement, while the 2nd Armoured Brigade could not escape in time and was deeply battered. Despite the lack of surprise, the Axis forces continued to advance and on 29 January captured Benghazi where 1,000 more enemy soldiers were taken into custody. According to the War Diary of *132° Reggimento Carristi* its capture was achieved with relatively few losses: "On 29 January after having overcome rearguard enemy forces left in place to slow our advance and with some losses on our side we finally entered Benghazi."[4] In quick succession on 3 February Derna was captured. Then on 6 February, the Italians arrived at El Mechili where they clashed against enemy reconnaissance units. On 8th February the enemy attacked El Mechili with a combination of artillery and tank fire but the assailers were dealt with by the Axis artillery. According to the British Official History the Commonwealth from 21 January to 6 February had suffered 1,309 casualties, lost 42 tanks knocked out and another 30 due to damage or breakdowns and lost forty field guns.[5] Italian and German records indicate higher enemy losses such as 150 enemy tanks, 192 artillery pieces, and 3,300 prisoners.[6]

The CAM, for example, who had started the campaign with 750 vehicles, by 10 February its vehicle tally had risen twofold to 1,300 because of the high number of captured vehicles. Its commander, *Generale* Zingales, lamented the fact that his units during this operation did not have adequate vehicles for the reconnaissance function: "The reconnaissance function had to be carried out primarily with light tanks, semoventi and regular trucks that were clearly

---

4   Ufficio Storico, 'Relazione sul comportamento del 132° Reggimento Carri nei cicli operativi del 18/11/1941 al 03/07/1942 da me comandato', n. 5498, Enrico Maretti, 4 luglio 1942.
5   ISO Playfair, *The Mediterranean and Middle East: British Fortunes reach their Lowest Ebb* (London, HMSO, 1960), pp. 139-153.
6   Mario Montanari, *Le operazioni in Africa settentrionale*, vol III, Part I, p. 70.

inferior to the much faster enemy armoured vehicles. The enemy using very fast moving vehicles (40 to 50 kilometers per hour versus our vehicles that did not exceed 15 kilometers per hour) was able to direct its artillery fire much more effectively."[7] As a result of this deficiency the numerous vehicles captured during this operation would be put into service as a stop gap solution until the arrival in large numbers of the AB series vehicles. They would be used extensively up until July of 1942. During this operation, which forced the Commonwealth back to the Ain El Gazala line, the Axis forces deployed for the first time in North Africa the self-propelled gun units which performed relatively well. The Italians deployed the *DLI and DLII Gruppi Semoventi* with 75/18 guns installed on M.13/40 and M.13/41 tank chassis within *Ariete*, while the Germans used a 76.2mm Soviet gun mounted on a *Panzerkampfwagen* IV tank. During Operation Theseus, the self-propelled guns were used in flanking support of the German panzer units and the batteries were all concentrated with the column travelling on the Via Balbia. Especially for the Italians, the *semoventi* could achieve what the medium tanks no longer could against up gunned British tanks. Equipped with a 75mm gun the self-propelled guns had greater range and firepower than the Crusaders and could go toe to toe against the tanks that the British would later field in the spring of 1942. These heavy Italian guns were in fact intended to fight alongside the tanks by assuming an aggressive tactical disposition rather than a more traditional defensive posture. They were to play two main combat roles. Tactically the self-propelled guns were to be used as mobile artillery but they could also be used in offensive operations providing fire while covering the flanks of the medium tanks. The weapon, given its firepower, was thus seen as a great improvement over the 47mm gun mounted on the standard M tank and its performance during this brief operation fully proved that the Italians now had a more effective weapon for the desert campaign. The commander of the *Ariete* Division reported that the "semoventi represent an important step forward despite their shortcomings, like the low muzzle velocity of their guns, insufficient range especially in comparison with the British guns and excessively slow speed when moving in rough terrain."[8]

Both the DLI and the DLII *Gruppi Semoventi* had been constituted on 16 April 1941 and had originally been assigned to the *Littorio* Division. Each had two batteries of eight *semoventi*, and four *semoventi* within the command company. In addition, they had two *semoventi* and one command company *semovente* as a reserve. Upon their arrival in North Africa they were assigned to the post-Crusader depleted *Ariete* Division.

With the reconquest of Cyrenaica Rommel had completed a brilliant maneuver pushing once again the Commonwealth forces back to Tobruk, and the Ain El Gazala line. He had inflicted heavy losses even though the Axis troops had not been able to deal the major blow. Rommel was now poised for further advances and sought again to siege Tobruk. Rommel's views differed significantly from those of the Italian commanders that were more concerned about another major leap forward which Bastico opposed due to low stockpiles of supplies. Moreover, Bastico again was worried about the Italian low mobility of the infantry troops that had followed the armoured advance and now were strung out along the frontier in several isolated outposts. The fear was that these largely immobile troops would become again the first victims of a

---

7   Ufficio Storico, CAM, 'Relazione sulle operazioni del corpo d'armata di manovra' Generale Zingales, 29 Marzo 1942.
8   Paolo Battisatelli and Filippo Cappellano, *Italian Medium Tanks*, p. 36.

Commonwealth mechanized counter-attack. To avoid a repeat of a debacle along the lines of Graziani's stalemated offensive, Bastico had asked Cavallero to fly to North Africa to dissuade Rommel from committing the Axis troops to a major advance. *Generale* Cavallero met Rommel on the 22nd of January but ultimately agreed with Rommel's assessment and was supportive of the operation that was to lead to the recapture of Cyrenaica.

5

Gazala and Tobruk

Further Training

During the period between February 1942 and the beginning of the Gazala Line clashes in May the North African front was quiet. This gave the Italian Army the opportunity to further refine its tactics through more training as well as a reorganization of its forces. A document dated 20 April 1942 from *Trieste* Division, for example, outlined how training was now tailored to the north African environment and also for defeating armoured formations. Training was focused on improving physical fitness and troop morale, drills centered on dismounting from trucks and unloading the crew served weapons in position, moving with vehicles at night and improving the anti-tank defense with target practice. Troops were trained at travelling on foot with full pack for over ten kilometers as well as doing the same on trucks. Particular attention was also placed on using the anti-tank weapons deployed at a distance of approximately 400 meters from captured enemy tanks used for target practice and less than 1000 meters for artillery weapons. The report went on to state: "The necessary measures have been taken to ensure that units commanders have improved phone, and radio communication systems and when that is not available they have available dispatch runners equipped with motorcycles or armoured cars to relay urgent messages. In any case, it is essential that all units are in a position to communicate effectively."[1]

The reorganization was primarily a response to Rommel who had urged it in the past especially after the siege of Tobruk in 1941. But it was also a response to the Commonwealth which had made several efforts to improve the firepower of its armoured units and the fighting quality of its infantry with a focus on specialization. First, the Commonwealth had seen an increase in the number of tanks due to ramped up production in Britain as well as its greater capacity to salvage tanks from the battle field by towing them back to the rear.

Second, the United States began furnishing the Commonwealth armies with record numbers of Stuart tanks in the winter of 1941-42 and later in mid-1942 with Grant and Sherman tanks that would prove to be a real challenge even to the mighty German *Panzerkampfwagen* IV tanks. Another factor that was contributed to the Commonwealth build up and later to the increased combativeness of its troops was the fact that more elite units, such as for example the

---

1 Ufficio Storico: Divisione Trieste, Documento 47, Cartella 921, N. 01/6231/op., 20 aprile 1942.

28th Maori Battalion of the New Zealand Army were getting accustomed to desert warfare and to fighting in conditions that they had not experienced before.

The introduction of the newly made Stuart tanks in the spring of 1942 and improvements in tank technology by British industry spelled trouble mainly for the Italian medium tank units, that risked becoming obsolete. But the challenge was also posed to the Germans. A report published by *Colonnello* Mario Bizzi, one of Italy's foremost weapons and munitions experts, described in detail the equipment pitfalls experienced by the armoured crews during the Operation Crusader tank battles. The problems pointed out in the report would become even more pronounced in mid-1942 as the 47mm guns of the Italian medium tanks lacked range and firepower while the engine compartment only saw slight improvements.

> The British tanks opened fire at a distance of 1,500 meters from our positions and closed in to 1,000 to halt the tanks to better aim their guns. Given the lack of effectiveness of the 47/32 gun, Italian crews held their fire until closing to less than 1,000 meters from the British positions. At this range their fire was more effective and it allowed the crews to spare ammunition. At this point the two tank formations closed down at a slower speed, with the British tanks exploiting their superior speed and maneuverability to attack the Italian tanks on the flanks, at distances down to 200 meters, while other tanks approached frontally, closing in at some 300-400 meters. The final stage was the climax of the combat action, where one of the two sides, both suffering from tank losses, crew casualties and ammunition shortages, would break off the engagement first and withdraw, avoiding the frontal clash. It was at this stage that the Italian tanks were especially vulnerable as the faster and more mobile British tanks were able to outrun any pursuit or, if victorious, catch and overwhelm what was left of the Italian armour.[2]

To overcome the shortcomings in equipment the report recommended that Italian armoured units be reorganized and strengthened with improved anti-tank and mobile artillery weapons. It also outlined that since the main anti-tank weapon of the Italian infantry (47mm gun) was effective only at 300 meters or less,[3] that the infantry units too were to be bolstered with mobile weapons with greater range and firepower and that could be brought forward to fight alongside the armoured units.

A vast reorganization was begun with a view to increase the elite status and the tactical specialization of the units deployed in North Africa. The focus was on equipping these units with greater amounts of mechanized and motorized assets as well as new weapons while maintaining or reducing the manpower of each division. This was to ensure a greater mobility and firepower of the Italian units fighting in the desert landscape where speed and powerful guns rather than the number of infantry soldiers could yield better results. The buildup, however, could only take place gradually due to limited industrial capacity, logistical difficulties and continued losses at the front. "Bastico's staff calculated that turning the Army in North Africa from a static into a dynamic one would require 6,650 motor vehicles. Bringing it to its full complement would require an additional 55,000 men. Shipping 1,200 trucks a month (and allowing 300 for wastage)

---

2   Ufficio Storico: Maggiore Bizzi foglio 1710/op. del 29 Marzo 1942.
3   Ibid.

and 10,000 men a month, it would take seven months to get the army in North Africa up to full strength."[4] In the spring *Ariete* and the other Italian armoured divisions were reorganized and their total number of weapons and machines were significantly improved. This was part of a much wider plan which had been contemplated by *Comando Supremo*, of an Africa Army Corps which would never be put in place given the scarcity of equipment and the ultimate reversal of fortune at El Alamein. According to the Italian Official History, *Comando Supremo* had an ambitious plan that aimed to strengthen the Italian forces in North Africa by constituting two armies.

A V Army comprised by four mechanized divisions such as *Ariete, Centauro, Littorio* and *Freccia* was to be constituted first followed by a VI Army comprised by six motorized divisions such as *Trento, Trieste, Piave, Pasubio, Torino* and *Pistoia* and by several infantry divisions (*Pavia, Brescia, Bologna, Savona, Puglie, Marche, Firenze, Forli', Ravenna, and Messina*). By mid-1942 some of these units were already present in North Africa while others were under formation in Italy, thereby the plan in order to be put into practice required time and greater production output by industry. This undertaking would have required 2,350 medium tanks, 190 *semoventi*, 1,600 light tanks, and 1,200 armoured cars to be produced within a period of six to twelve months. The ambitious plan also entailed a further strengthening of the mechanized divisions with the inclusion of a larger share of 75mm guns. For example, each armoured battalion was to receive a company of 75mm self-propelled guns and each armoured platoon was to have at least one *semovente da* 75/18. Spurred on by Bastico's *Comando Forze Armate Africa Settentrionale* (the Italian High Command in North Africa) the introduction of greater number of self-propelled guns was seen as a way to strengthen the armoured battalions not only during offensive operations where the *semoventi* were to provide flanking and covering fire but also in the anti-tank action where the same units could utilize the E.P. (*effetto pronto*) shells to good effect against British and American medium tanks. Each mechanized battalion was to receive one *semoventi da* 75 company comprised by three platoons with three self-propelled guns each. The armoured divisional artillery was to receive two *semoventi* da 90/53 and one group (with three units) of *semoventi da* 100/17 that at the time were still under design. Then after more debates and after Mussolini had intervened, *Comando Supremo* decided for a ratio of forty percent medium tanks and sixty percent *semoventi* da 75/18 for each *battaglione carri*.[5] The heavy losses sustained in mid-1942 and the slow production quotas for new weapons and mechanized assets would eventually torpedo this plan. "Not only did the estimated production by the end of the year suggest that this program could not be completed, but actual production fell much shorter than expected and the plan had to be abandoned. Production in June yielded only 95 medium tanks and semoventi, but of these fifteen were used to supply non-armoured units, thus leaving only twelve semoventi, eight company command vehicles and sixty tanks for the armoured units."[6] The long term ambitious plan was thus never realized, while a more limited reinforcement of the armoured units was made just in time before the start of the Gazala line battles in May 1942.

---

4   John Gooch, *Mussolini's War*, p. 305.
5   Ufficio Storico, Stato Maggiore Regio Esercito, Circolare Ufficio Ordinamento n. 54908/3, 18 Decembre 1942. Later in the year Mussolini ordered that each armoured battalion was to have one company equipped with M. 14/41 tanks and the other two companies with *semoventi* (self-propelled guns). This contradicted the Army's proposal for two tank companies and one assault company in each tank battalion.
6   Pier Paolo Battistelli and Filippo Cappellano, *Italian Medium Tanks*, p. 30.

The CAM was renamed *XX Corpo d'Armata* (20th Army Corps) on 10 March 1942 and its RECAM reconnaissance unit was disbanded and its ranks re-organized on smaller reconnaissance units which were made detachments of the two divisions (*Ariete and Trieste*). On 15 March, *Generale* Zingales would resign and his position was taken by *Generale* Baldassarre, who became *Generale del XX Corpo d'Armata*.

Thus, by March 1942 the *Ariete* Division had 8,000 soldiers, 1,000 vehicles, 210 light and medium tanks (137 M.13/40 tanks), forty-seven armoured cars, twenty self-propelled guns (*Semoventi* da 75/18), eight *Cannoni da* 90/53, forty-two 47mm anti-tank guns, thirty-two 75mm artillery pieces and ten 105/28 guns. It was still based on a three-pillar structure comprised of: *132º Reggimento Carristi* (*Tenente Colonnello* Enrico Maretti with VIII IX, and X *Battaglioni Carri Medi*), *8º Reggimento Bersaglieri* (V and XII *Battaglioni Motorizzati* and III and IV *Battaglioni Controcarri*), and *132º Reggimento Artiglieria Corazzata* (I and II *Gruppo* with 75/27 guns, III *Gruppo* with 105/28 guns, I *Gruppo* 90/53 guns, V *Gruppo Semoventi da* 75/18, VI *Gruppo Semoventi da* 75/18, CXXXII *Battaglione Misto Genio*).

The *32º Reggimento Carristi* was dissolved while the *Raggruppamento Esplorante Corazzato* (recon unit) was established with III *Gruppo Lancieri di Novara*, based on two companies with L.6 light tanks and the III *Gruppo Autoblindo Nizza Cavalleria* based on two squadrons equipped with forty armoured vehicles AB.41 armed with a 20mm gun and two 8mm machine guns. The latter with the newly arrived armoured cars would prove their worth during the campaign.

As far as the armoured regiment was concerned with the disbandment in early 1942 of its VII tank battalion, the limited options available were to either merge one of *Littorio*'s tank units or to form a new battalion mainly from the reinforcements coming from Italy. Given Rommel's insistence on going on the offensive as soon as possible and on rebuilding quickly the *Ariete* Division, the Italian command opted for the first option even though the second option was initially preferred. Initially it was an imperative not to dismantle *Littorio*, whose units were arriving in different stages to North Africa, but Rommel was very insistent on his immediate need for fresh troops. Therefore, it was decided to transfer X *Battaglione Carri* equipped with M.14/41 tanks from *Littorio* to *Ariet*e, while XI *Battaglione Carri* M. 13/40 was transferred to *Trieste*.

The *Bersaglieri* of *Ariete* were also deeply reorganized in the spring of 1942. The two motorized battalions were retained while the motorcycle battalion was dropped and a new heavy weapons battalion was formed. The latter was formed by three antitank 47mm gun companies and named III *Battaglione Armi d'Accompagnamento*. The V and XII *Battaglioni* were based on three companies each with four platoons, one machine gun platoon with six guns, three anti-tank platoons with three 20mm guns, and one platoon with 47mm guns. The *8º Reggimento* was completed by a headquarters company, one 81mm mortars company with nine pieces and various signal and service platoons.

The *Trieste* overall composition was shrunk considerably with less manpower but more weapons and vehicles. The inspiration behind the change were the *Panzerjager* units or the British commando units which were comprised of better trained troops equipped with armoured vehicles, tanks and mobile self-propelled guns and anti-tank guns. It had 6,700 soldiers, fifty-two M.13/40 tanks, thirty-six 47mm anti-tank guns, and forty-eight artillery pieces. It was still based on the 65º and 66º *Reggimenti Fanteria Motorizzata* and the *21º Reggimento Artiglieria* (I and II *Gruppi* with 100/17 guns and III *Gruppo* with 75/27 guns) as the two main pillars. But it also received the VIII *Battaglione Bersaglieri Corazzato* equipped with fifty-six armoured cars and thirty-eight motorcycles, and the XI *Battaglione Carri Medi* (originally from *Littorio*) with fifty-two M.13./40 tanks, seventy-seven vehicles, and thirty-eight motorcycles. It also received a higher number of trucks for the motorized infantry regiments with 235 vehicles and sixty-tow motorcycles.[7] The overall purpose was to make it more like a specialized infantry unit with less but better equipped and trained soldiers that were supposed to be integrated into fully motorized companies. For this purpose, it was renamed *Divisione Trieste Motorizzata A.S. 42* (Northern African 1942 type *Trieste* Motorized Division).

The main problem during the reorganization was to overcome the low level of mechanization and motorization of the *Trieste* Division which limited its operational offensive capability as well as its ability to pursue the enemy or to simply conduct reconnaissance. A *Trieste*'s war diary entry reports that: "On the eve of the 1941 offensive, the Armed Forces Command in North Africa had alerted Comando Supremo of the difficult task faced by its reconnaissance units which lacking suitable vehicles could not check the enemy's raids and explorations in the area of the Jebel mountains and in the oasis area."[8] At the time there were no proper vehicles to conduct proper reconnaissance and there were also a limited number and range of vehicles available to transport its infantry battalions that relied on two main models: the SPA38R and the Lancia 3RO, which were standard trucks.[9]

STANDARD MOTORIZED INFANTRY REGIMENT "tipo AS" 1942

Infantry
compagnia comando (command company);
due battaglioni fucilieri (two infantry/sharpshooter battalions)
    compagnia comando; (command company)
    tre compagnie fucilieri; (three sharpshooter companies)
    un plotone mortai da 81; (81mm mortar platoon)
    battaglione armi accompagnamento e controcarro (anti-tank and crew served weapons battalion):
    compagnia comando (command company);
    compagnia mortai da 81(81mm mortar company);
    compagnia cannoni da 47/32 (47mm guns company);
    compagnia da 20 mm.c.a. (20mm anti-aircraft company)

---

7 Ufficio Storico, *Divisione Trieste*: cartella 921, N. 3004/op. E.D.C.Q., 26 maggio 1942, allegato 5.
8 Dattilo Ciampini, "La fanteria motorizzata tra modello ed esperienze," *Quaderno della societa' Italiana di storia militare*, 1999, p. 165.
9 These were very basic vehicles that lacked machine guns, or any other weapon for that matter, and were soft skinned. On main paved roads, they traveled at an average speed of 52 km/h, while on more rough roads their top speed could vary from 18 km/h to 6-8 km/h.
The former weighed 3200 kg (over 7,000 lbs), and with a load capacity of 2500 kg of supplies and/or ammunition and it could carry twenty-five men. The engine was inefficient with its high fuel consumption keeping it at a range of 290 km.
The latter weighed 5610 kg and had a load capacity of 6390 kg of supplies or ammunition or it could carry forty-two soldiers. However, given that it had a prominent silhouette it offered a pretty good target to enemy guns or planes. Rubertini, "La Divisione di Fanterìa Catanzaro nel secondo conflitto mondiale," *Studi storico-militari-1990*, USSME, 1993, p. 258.

> Bersaglieri
> compagnia comando (command company);
> compagnia motociclisti (motorcycle company);
> due battaglioni bersaglieri autoportati (two truck borne bersaglieri battalions):
> compagnia comando (command company);
>> due compagnie bersaglieri (two bersaglieri companies);
>> compagnia cannoni da 47/32 (47mm guns company);
> Battaglione armi accompagnamento e controcarri su (anti-tank and crew served weapons battalion):
>> compagnia comando (command company);
>> due compagnie mortai da 81 (two 81mm mortar companies);
>> compagnia da 20 mm c.a (20mm anti-aircraft company).

The first problem, the lack of mechanized assets, was addressed by incorporating into the division the *XI Battaglione Carri* equipped with M.13/40 tanks that originally belonged to *Littorio*. With this medium tank unit, *Trieste* could in the future not only conduct combined arms operations, but also better repel enemy tank attacks by using a combination of tanks and heavy artillery fire. The second problem, the lack of trucks to bring into battle its infantry units in a timely manner, was only partially addressed. The few trucks available forced the infantry to suffer above average losses during Crusader since they were typically dropped far away from the battle zone and had to advance for many miles on foot and under the constant threat of the Commonwealth artillery. This was partially addressed by introducing a few more Dovunque trucks per infantry battalion. This was stop gap solution as the Eastern front was absorbing the majority of new vehicle production. Finally, *Trieste*, through its *Bersaglieri* unit, was also able to constitute its own reconnaissance unit with AB.41 armoured vehicles. This had represented one of its main problem areas in the past.

Advanced reconnaissance of the enemy positions with fast moving armoured vehicles was since the inception of the campaign one of the strengths of the British Army. The Italians were slow to develop similar capabilities such as the Long-Range Desert Group or the Jock Columns. First, they created RECAM, the first unit which was solely to be deployed for reconnaissance purposes. The unit represented an important innovation in desert warfare but its capabilities in 1941 were limited as it relied for the reconnaissance function to teams comprised of slower moving vehicles such as ordinary trucks, truck mounted gun units and light tanks.

"Reconnaissance was carried out by tanks, semoventi and truck mounted gun units which were not ideally suited for the function and were much slower moving than comparable enemy reconnaissance units. The enemy units could move at a top speed of 40-50 kilometers per hour while our units did not exceed 12-15 kilometers per hour on the desert terrain."[10] The first limited batch of AB.40 armoured vehicles arrived in North Africa in August 1941 and were used primarily by the local police force, the PAI. Then, beginning in 1942 Italian units began to receive AB.41 armoured vehicles which were not only just as fast as the vehicles used by the enemy but also had considerable fuel efficiency enabling them to travel longer distances. These

---

10   Filippo Cappellano and Nicola Pignato, *Andare contro i carri armati*, p. 121.

units were also effectively deployed to harass enemy reconnaissance vehicles. "One of the lessons learned from the recent operations in Libya is that it has become essential to equip our troops with autoblindo (armoured cars) at the direct command of the commander of celeri units."[11]

According to historians Cappellano and Pignato the introduction of AB.41 vehicles was vital in strengthening the reconnaissance function: "Autoblindo AB.41 enabled the army to thwart the enemy's surveillance, reconnaissance and raiding functions and to repress the enemy's mobile artillery batteries which relied on forward observers, experienced British officers, riding on armoured vehicles."[12]

Perhaps the major problem affecting the Italian troops between 1940-41 had been their reliance on the 47mm anti-tank gun and other makeshift solution when confronting enemy armour. The issue would come to the fore even more in mid-1942 when the Commonwealth fielded more durable tanks such as the American Stuart, and later Grant and Sherman tanks. This problem was partly alleviated, because of the low numbers, by the arrival to North Africa of self-propelled artillery and long range guns.

With the reorganization both *Ariete* and *Littorio* (later in 1942) could quickly integrate truck mounted 90mm guns and 75mm self-propelled guns in their tactics where the former alleviated the lack of firepower of the M.13 and M.14 tanks and of the 47mm anti-tank guns. During the first battle of Bir el Gobi, given the lack of mobile guns with comparable performances to the German 88mm Flak 36 anti-aircraft gun, *Ariete* improvised by mounting field artillery or naval guns on trucks. These were 102/35 field guns mounted on Fiat 634 trucks that performed well given that their field of fire exceeded that of the lighter British Crusader tanks equipped with 2-pdr guns. Such weapons proved their worth during the battle enabling *Ariete*'s artillery to knock several enemy tanks out of action.

The successful deployment of the 102/35 guns first led the Italian Army to develop the Lancia 3ro truck which mounted a *Cannone da* 90/53 anti-aircraft gun. This resulted in an extremely powerful weapon with performances that rivaled or even exceeded that of the German 88mm gun and could knock out of action even the heavier American tanks. According to an Italian technical report the only drawbacks of such a weapon was its excessive weight and its low mobility which made it a target for both the Commonwealth artillery and aerial forces.[13]

While some of these guns were truck mounted, others had to be towed and here the excessive weight caused some inconveniences especially in muddy terrain after heavy rains. The wheels of the trailer would plunge into the mud and the vehicle would get stuck as reported below:

> The highly effective 88 German gun and the 90/53, even though we still have not found an ideal truck to tow them, were used extensively during the offensive of end of August 1942. Having to travel through sandy terrain the Ariete division had to rely at times upon improvised solutions especially when it brought forward its 88mm, 90mm and 105mm guns.[14]

---

11   Ibid, p. 121.
12   Ibid, p. 164.
13   Ufficio Storico, Comando XX Corpo d'armata- Stato Maggiore "materiale da 90/53," foglio n.2475, 2 giugno 1942.
14   Ufficio Storico, Generale Franceso Arena, "Considerazioni sulla campagna in Africa settentrionale," foglio 41, Maggio 1942.

The 90/53 gun had been built by Ansaldo from an earlier model that was used on ships. The majority of these guns were used for defensive purposes in static positions near harbors, airports, coastal defenses, etc. ... but in North Africa some were truck mounted others were towed and they were used extensively by the armoured corp.

The 90/53 gun was the Italian most successful anti-tank weapon and was highly rated by both Axis and Allied troops. An Italian report of June 1942, for example, stated:

> An attack put forth by the enemy's armoured units against the Ariete Division (on the eve of the conquest of Bir Hacheim) was undertaken by a large unit with heavy American tanks that according to the enemy's propaganda were invulnerable moving fortresses. The attack against Ariete was extremely violent since it involved up to forty tanks that attempted to overcome our division's defenses from the flank. But a timely deployment of our antitank screen was not only able to stop the attack on its tracks but it also managed to immobilize over twenty tanks and forced the others to flee. The operation confirmed without any doubt, the importance of the 90/53 artillery gun especially as an antitank weapon.[15]

Even the Americans thought highly of the Italian gun and their intelligence services were compelled to write the following article for the United States Army Magazine Tactical Trends which was used to warn American units of the potential of this new weapon:

> Shortly before the beginning of the last British offensive in Egypt, the Italians put into service a 90mm multipurpose gun ... It is now known that the length of bore is 53 calibers rather than 50, and that the practical rate of fire is 15 to 20 rounds per minute.
>
> The gun has a steel monobloc barrel with a detachable breech ring, allowing the barrel to be changed. The weight in action is given as 11,220 pounds.
>
> Normally, the gun is tractor-drawn on a four-wheeled Lancia Ro trailer, although a self-propelled model, utilizing a standard Italian tank chassis, has also been reported. In the case of the latter model, the tracks of the tank are apparently locked before the gun opens fire. Since the characteristics of this gun are like those of the German 88mm weapon, a correspondingly similar tactical employment may also be expected.[16]

Thus, with the *Cannone da* 90/53 gun the Italians by mid-1942 finally possessed a true tank killer, a weapon that represented a formidable threat to Allied tanks.

Another key anti-tank weapon was the 75mm self-propelled gun, another effective tank killer, even with regard to medium tanks. Deployed for the first time during the recapture of Cyrenaica: "The semoventi da 75 were deployed during the offensive and throughout the advance they kept pace with the first wave of tanks. Since their footprint and height is smaller than that of the tanks while their gun has a greater punch, these self-propelled guns damaged several enemy vehicles and made a great impression upon the enemy. According to captured enemy soldiers the Italians had deployed newly motorized artillery."[17]

---

15 Cited in Nicola Pignato, *Italian Armoured Vehicles*, p. 34.
16 'Italian 90mm Multipurpose Gun', *Tactical and Technical Trends*, No. 12, 19 November, 1942.
17 Ufficio Storico, 'Notizie circa l'impiego di carri ed autoblinde in Africa Settentrional', Mario Bizzi, maggio 1942.

Another Italian report also praised the performance of the new weapons: "The *semoventi da 75/18* have proved to be an excellent weapon with greater firepower, they are more impervious to enemy fire and are built upon an improved technological platform."[18]

By mid-1942 these weapons were found to be highly suitable for the North African campaign, unfortunately the large numbers envisioned by *Comando Supremo* were never produced by a domestic industry that had limited capacity. But according to historians Cappellano and Pignato the industry and the military which oversaw its plans, also contributed to the problem by continuing the dispersion of production efforts in 1942 on obsolete models such as the M series tanks.[19] Rather than concentrating all production on the self-propelled guns they continued to also manufacture medium tanks as well as continue experimenting with other light tank models. As a result, because of a less effective and resourceful domestic industry and the constraints of fewer quantities of raw materials due to the war economy the forces in North Africa never had enough quantities of *semoventi* to turn the tide of the campaign.

The reorganization also brought about a change in tactics with the formation of new tactical units which were tasked oriented like their German counterparts and represented a novelty in the highly rigid hierarchical structure of the Italian Army. These groups were to be formed by *Bersaglieri*, mobile artillery, engineer and armoured units and offered several advantages such as the swiftness with which they could be deployed in combat.

The *Ariete* was one of the first units to experiment with tactical units in 1941. Initially by forming ad hoc teams that were later disbanded when the objectives of their mission had been achieved. Then in February 1942 *Ariete* formally constituted its first official tactical unit comprised by an M tank company, a *semovente* battery of 75/18 guns and three captured Bren carriers. This unit would provide several services during the Axis counteroffensive which culminated with the Battle of Gazala such as advanced reconnaissance, the disruption of enemy activities such as those of forward positioned artillery observers, and the surveillance over minefields and resistance lines.

Later in 1942 *Ariete*'s General Balotta wrote that the experimentation with the tactical combat groups, inspired by the German model, had been very positive and urged the creation of more formal tactical groups within all Italian divisions fighting in North Africa:

> In the deployment of the armoured units the raggruppamento misto has shown to be a foundational tactical element constituted generally by: a tank battalion, a Bersaglieri battalion, an artillery group, a company of 47mm, and a 20mm battery. These raggruppamenti, constituted ad hoc and spontaneously have demonstrated to be only partly reliable and have often fought without a commander. Moreover, such units have had no prior military training. I am totally in support of creating such units in a more formal way and to replace the regiments with more mobility centered tactical units. This will result in the creation of two or three tactical groups per division that can act independently during reconnaissance and raiding missions. They could be useful both as small offensive parties as well as when united under an armoured mass capable of breaking through enemy defenses.[20]

18 Filippo Cappellano and Nicola Pignato, *Andare contro i carri armati*, p. 121.
19 Ibid.
20 Ufficio Storico, Divisione Corazzata Ariete, 'Dell'esperienza circa impiego divisioni motorizzate o corazzate', Sezione operazioni, Generale Balotta foglio n. 1828, 11 Agosto 1941.

Because of these recommendations and experimentation on the field in North Africa, the Italian Army would later introduce a major change by authorizing the constitution of such units at the division level.[21]

This move represented an important shift in tactical and strategic thinking given that in the past the Italian Army had been highly hierarchical and centralized. For instance, the new disposition more closely aligned it to the German army which frequently used these task and objectives oriented tactical groups to conduct operations. Generally, mid-level officers in the German Army enjoyed greater freedom of action and were less reliant on their superiors during combat operations. The introduction of looser formal command structures within the Italian Army brought benefits to combat operations. It better enabled these units to fight as a single combat group whether led by an Italian or a German senior officer and together with other units in the DAK.

The concept was even further expanded in July 1942 by the creation of a tactical mobile reserve unit that could be deployed for specific defensive or counterattacking operations. This resulted in the constitution under the command of General Becuzzi of a unit equipped with two M tank battalions, an infantry battalion, a *semovente* battery of 75/27 guns, an artillery unit made up of captured of 6 and 25-pdr guns and a special communications specialist group. This unit was used to intervene to prop up feeble defensive sectors or to protect the headquarters of the *XX Comando d'armata* or of *Ariete* Division during an enemy attack.

All these innovations were made against a backdrop of new recruits coming to North Africa with a much deeper preparation in armoured warfare than their predecessors in 1940. *Ariete* was one of the first units to benefit from improved training as attested by the following testimony: "One morning III Battaglione received brand new tanks and the commander of the drivers, Capitano Clemente, remarked that the real training could now begin. Thus, began an exhausting number of sessions which dragged on into the night, in many cases past 2300 where we learned everything about the mechanics of the tank, its components, the use of devices such as a compass, and a bit of astronomy which was very handy once we arrived in North Africa. In many cases, we would drive the tanks past highway 11 to San Bonifacio. The training was held near San Michele where we would maneuver the tanks past various caves either filled with water or small rocks. In June 1942, the course terminated and the selection process was extremely rigorous as only twenty-eight drivers or 30% of the class was selected."[22]

As Greene and Massignani assert: "This general upgunning and reduction of manpower was an attempt to respond to the desert war with its heavy demand on supplies, hence the desire to reduce manpower but increase firepower because of the heavy use of armoured fighting vehicles."[23] Thus the 1942 reorganization had brought more heavy weapons and fewer but better trained soldiers to thrive in the challenging conditions of the desert were fuel, supplies and provisions were at a premium. It was a move intended to satisfy Rommel's desire for more mobile and powerful Italian units.

---

21 Ufficio Storico: Stato Maggiore Regio Esercito, Ufficio Addestramento, circolare n. 12800, 'Gruppi Tattici', 8 luglio 1942.
22 'Ricordi di Antonio Tomba' in Andrea Tallillo, *Carro M: carri medi M11/39, M13/40, M14/41, M15/42: semoventi e altri derivati* (Trento: Gruppo modellistico trentino di studio e ricerca storica, 2010), p. 147.
23 Jack Greene and Alessandro Massignani, *Rommel's North African Campaign*, p. 37.

The improved training and the greater availability of *semoventi* artillery batteries and long range anti-aircraft and anti-tank guns would enable, as described in the next section, the Italian Army to obtain some measure of success during the combined Italian German offensive of May/June 1942, the high point of the Italian Army in North Africa. Regarding the improved, organizational status and good morale of *Ariete*'s tank units in mid-1942 the commander of the *132° Reggimento Carristi* would assert that: "To counter the enemy buildup in North Africa and together with the German units with which we saw eye to eye, we would deploy a strong force that had reached its maximum effectiveness after four months of intense and continuous training. The force was fueled by units that were close to full rank and could rely on new equipment which had been brought in by way of the Mediterranean from the fatherland under the vigilance of our Navy. We had to anticipate the enemy buildup by striking first."[24]

The equipment and manpower buildup of Italian forces which took place in the spring of 1942 although an important feat in itself was not complete by the time Rommel decided to go on the offensive again. *Ariete* and *Trieste*, for example, "were almost complete, but the infantry divisions lacked trucks."[25] Some improvements were made by the infantry divisional artillery regiments with the introduction of 88mm and 90mm anti-tank guns but there weren't enough of these guns. Also the tank problem was equally serious. *Ariete*, for instance, had paired the losses by receiving a batch of new medium tanks, but a second armoured division that was supposed to be dispatched to North Africa did not have enough tanks to be operational. Industry was also having difficulties producing enough self-propelled guns to fully arm all North African units.

Operation Venezia

An agreement between Germany and Italy was brokered by Cavallero and Kesserling in the spring of 1942 which took the name of Operation Venezia. This plan called for a three-step process. First, the capture of Tobruk by the *Panzerarmee*. Then plans had been made for the implementation of Operation Hercules (Operazione C3 for the Italians), the airborne and seaborne invasion of the British occupied island of Malta. The Axis planners maintained that once Malta was taken, supplies would be easier to dispatch from Italy to North Africa. Cavallero would in fact state that: "The assault on Malta will cost us many casualties but I consider it absolutely essential for the future development of the war. If we take Malta, Libya will be safe."[26] Then with an easing of the supply situation, Rommel would be authorized to invade Egypt. Operation Venezia entailed a massive Axis counter-attack deploying the clear majority of the armour available in North Africa and whose ultimate objective was to retake Tobruk. The Axis plan of attack consisted in a flanking maneuver by the tanks around the Bir Hacheim box at the southern extremity of the Gazala line to then end up at Acroma where the major armoured confrontation was expected to take place. Finally, after having destroyed the Commonwealth tanks the Axis troops were to surround and overcome the fortress of Tobruk. *Ariete* was tasked with overtaking the Bir Hacheim box, while the 21st Panzer Division and

---

24 Ufficio Storico, 'Relazione sul comportamento del 132° Reggimento Carri nei cicli operativi del 18/11/1941 al 03/07/1942 da me comandato', n. 5498, Enrico Maretti, 4 luglio 1942.
25 John Gooch, *Mussolini's War*, p. 306.
26 Ufficio Storico, *I diari del Comando Supremo*, p. 311.

15th Panzer Division would advance through the desert south of Bir Hacheim and engage and destroy the Commonwealth armour and cut off the infantry divisions positioned on the defensive line. To the south of the tanks, units of specialized infantry and motorized groups were to advance toward Tobruk and tie down the Commonwealth troops with diversionary moves.

Expecting a strong Axis offensive, the Eighth Army had built a defensive network of mutually supportive boxes or strongpoints that spanned from Gazala, near the coast, to Tobruk and to Bir Hacheim in the south. Each box was defended by an infantry brigade situated behind minefields and barbed wire works. Each brigade had its own artillery and machine guns and motorized patrol units. It is estimated that the Commonwealth had 110,000 men, 843 tanks and 604 aircraft in May 1942 deployed on or near the Gazala line.[27] They roughly outnumbered the Axis tank strength by two to one as the Germans had seven armoured regiments and the Italians two and a half to the Commonwealth fourteen armoured regiments. The Commonwealth had also received new weapons just in time for the enemy offensive such as the new American Grant tanks with a 75mm gun and thicker armour. By May 1942 each tank regiment of the 7th Armoured Division, for instance, was equipped with twenty-four Grants and twenty Honeys that could readily be deployed. In addition, more 6-pdr anti-tank guns were being brought into service although at a slower pace than originally envisioned. According to the pre-battle estimates the Axis had forty-eight 88mm Flak 36 guns (including the ones operated by the Italian artillery that would be shipped to the front a few days after the launch of the operation), twelve *Cannoni da* 90/53mm, eighteen *semoventi da* 75, 320 German tanks, of which nineteen were *Panzerkampfwagen* III Ausf.J with the long barrel 50mm gun and four *Panzerkampfwagen* IV with the long barrel 75mm gun, and 228 Italian M.13 or M.14 tanks. *Ariete* and *Trieste* had most of the M.13 tanks while *Littorio* which would be deployed later in the campaign had the bulk of the M.14/41 tanks, which further added to the 228 tally. In contrast the British armoured formations had approximately 900 tanks, this is counting the replacements that came into action during the fighting. The most important Commonwealth asset, however, were the 200 Grant[28] tanks with a 75mm gun and which "had a stronger punch than any of Rommel's."[29] By mid-1942 Rommel had totally discounted the Italian medium tanks especially in the tank versus tank battle engagements arguing that: "The 240 Italian tanks were no sort of match for the British and the troops had long talked of them as self-propelled coffins."[30] Rommel most likely counted first of all on the German medium tanks and then on the strength of the Axis artillery and the self-propelled artillery which in his view still held a tactical edge over the enemy.

As the Axis was on the verge of mounting its operation the 1st South African Division was deployed at Gazala, while the 2nd South African Division garrisoned Tobruk. The Bir Hacheim box, the main objective of the Italian units, was defended by the 1st Free French Brigade of General Marie-Pierre Koenig. Its defensive forces consisted of approximately 4,000 French soldiers subdivided into six battalions of infantry, one artillery battalion and an anti-tank company. The heavy weapons included: twenty-four 75mm guns, eighty-four antitank

---

27 Michael Carver, *Tobruk* (London: Pan Books, 1964), p. 167.
28 The M3 General Lee/Grant tank preceded the M4 General Sherman. It was mechanically similar to the M4 and it was armed with a medium-velocity 75mm gun. One of the main differences amongst the two tanks was that the M3 Grant had the gun mounted in the hull instead of the turret, because this could be put into production more quickly at the time that the British needed tanks very urgently.
29 Basil Liddell Hart, *The Rommel Papers*, p. 196.
30 Ibid. p. 197.

guns, forty-four mortars, seventy-two Hotchkiss machine guns, eighteen Bofors anti-aircraft guns and eight heavy machine guns.

By mid-May the defensive perimeter surrounding the fort was comprised of approximately 1,200 positions including: foxholes, gun emplacements, underground bunkers, machine gun pits and other highly camouflaged supply dumps. Finally, the British 1st and 7th Armoured Divisions were deployed to the rear of the Gazala line to be used as mobile counter-attacking forces.

As Walker asserts "The Axis forces now faced an entirely new challenge at Gazala, a fixed enemy defensive line protected by barbed wire and extensive minefields like those of World War One." [31] This line represented a challenge to the Axis tank units that in the past had outflanked or outmaneuvered enemy tanks or positions to win battles. In mid-1942 this tactic, the hallmark of Rommel's Blitzkrieg offensives, appeared to offer limited possibilities of success while pitted against a fortified, continuous line of defense. Also, maneuvering around the enemy defenses on both northern and southern flanks was not an option since in the north the Commonwealth defenses bordered into the sea, while in the south into the Qattara Depression which was impossible to negotiate because of the soft sands.

PanzerArmee Afrika Order of Battle 26 May 1942

Commander, E. Rommel
X Army Corps (General N. Gioda)
Brescia Infantry Division (General G. Lombardi)
Pavia Infantry Division (General A. Torriano)

XX Army Corps (General E. Baldassarre)
Trieste Motorized Division (General A. Azzi)
Ariete Armoured Division (General G. De Stefanis)
support units

XXI Army Corps (General E. Navarini)
Trento Infantry Division (General C. Gotti)
Sabratha Infantry Division (General M. Soldarelli)
15th Schutzen Brigade (Colonel Menny)
support units

Deutsches Afrikakorps (General W. Nehring)[32]
15th Panzerdivision (General G von Vaerst)
21th Panzerdivision (General G. von Bismark)
support units

90th Leicht Division (General U. Kleemann)

---

31 Ian Walker, *Iron Hulls, Iron Hearts*, p. 110.
32 Ludwig Crüwell arrived from leave a day after the launch of the operation and was captured a few days later.

Artillery Command Unit 104
Italian Artillery Command (General Nicolini)
Hecker Group
Support units.
Source: Montanari 1985

XX CORPO D'ARMATA
Comandante di Corpo d'Armata Generale Baldassarre
Ariete Armoured Division
Comando di Divisione, *Generale di Divisione* De Stefanis.
RECo Ariete (LII *Battaglione Carri Medi*, III *Gruppo Corazzato Nizza*, III *Gruppo Carri* L.6 *Lancieri di Novara*, Batterie volanti)
132° Reggimento Carristi (VIII, IX, X *Battaglioni Carri Medi*).
8° Reggimento Bersaglieri (III *Battaglione anticarro, V Battaglione autoportato, XII Battaglione autoportato*).
132° Reggimento Artiglieria Corazzata (I – II *Gruppo da 75/27, III Gruppo da 105/28, IV Gruppo da 90/53, V (ex-DLI) Gruppo Semoventi da 75/18, VI (ex-DLII) Gruppo Semoventi da 75/18 and V/1a Artiglieria Contraerei e Controcarri da 88/55* (added a few days after the start of operations).
CXXXII Battaglione misto genio *(132.a Compagnia artieri, 232.a Compagnia collegamenti).*
4° Battaglione controcarro Granatieri di Sardegna.
132° Sezione Sanità.
132° Sezione Sussistenza.
82° Autogruppo misto.
13° e 14° Squadriglia pilotaggio per zone desertiche.
Trieste Motorized Division
Comando di Divisione, Generale di Divisione Azzi
VIII Battaglione Bersaglieri Corazzato
XI Battaglione Carri Medi
65° Reggimento Fanteria Motorizzata *(I and II Battaglioni)*
66° Reggimento Fanteria Motorizzata *(I and II Battaglioni)*
9° Reggimento Bersaglieri *(XXVIII, XXX, XXXII Battaglioni)*
21° Reggimento Artiglieria *(I – II Gruppo 100/17, III Gruppo 75/27)*
XXXII Battaglione Misto Genio

Bir Hacheim

Operation Venezia began on 26 May when at 1400 all motorized and mechanized units of the *Panzerarmee* roared toward the frontline in the direction of Bir Hacheim. According to General Baldassarre the *XX Corpo d'Armata* left its base with 228 tanks, seventy-eight armoured vehicles and eighteen *semoventi*.[33] All units were close to full strength while the only unit that was at full strength was the X *Battaglione Carri Medi* that had recently arrived from Italy. Its strength was as follows: 24 officers, 465 NCOs and soldiers, 51 M.14/41, 17 Lancia 3 RO, 12 Viberti trailers, 8 SPA Dovunque trucks, 2 large model 1100 trucks, 1 Breda tractor and 1 spare parts truck. The unit travelled north of Trigh Capuzzo and initially found little enemy opposition, mainly some jocks columns which did not create much trouble. The war diary of *Ariete* reports that the Italian units, but especially *Trieste*, despite finding weak opposition had difficulties in keeping up with the faster moving German units:"*Ariete* is barely keeping up with the DAK and has to follow the Germans on the right flank, while Trieste is further afield because it is marching forward at a slower pace."[34] Due to delays *Trieste* would arrive at the rendezvous point only on the morning of the 27th, prompting Rommel to again bitterly complain against his Italian allies.

Rommel knew full well that the enemy held a numerical advantage in both men and equipment but he was confident that his superior tactics would enable his troops to succeed:

> On certain assumption … that the British would not dare to use any major part of their armoured formations to attack the Italians in the Gazala line (while strong German Panzer forces stood able to threaten their rear) …. thus, I foresaw that the British mechanized brigades would continue to run their heads against our well organized defensive front and use up their strength in the process. [35]

Rommel maintained that success could be had with a decisive and speedy offensive operation. "Despite warnings from Italian intelligence (SIM) that British armour was positioned behind the Ain el Gazala line to intervene quickly, and despite Bastico's misgivings, Rommel estimated that he would need only two days to wipe out the RAF, three to eliminate British armour and five to capture Tobruk."[36] While Rommel was confident going into the Gazala line battles, the Italian command was more hesitant. Rommel based his optimism on his troops superior tactics. As his troops attacked, Rommel was expecting strong counterstrokes against them, but he also expected that the British tanks units would continue to be deployed in a piecemeal fashion like they had been deployed during Operation Crusader and thus could be more expeditiously dealt with by his anti-tank and artillery units. The Axis artillery would in fact play a key and skillful role in the battle, a much more pronounced role than in Operation Crusader. General Ritchie

---

33 Some vehicles were kept in the rear especially those of *Littorio* that was still training in May 1942 and only some of its units would be deployed in battle. In May *Ariete*'s strength was of 193 tanks (123 M.13/40 and 70 M.14/41), while *Littorio* had 157 tanks (39 M.13/40, 117 M.14.41 and one M.15/42). *Trieste* had fifty-two M. 14/41 and 17 M.13/40 tanks some of which were held in the rear.
34 Basil Liddell Hart, *The Rommel Papers*, p. 203.
35 Basil Liddell Hart, *The Rommel Papers*, p. 211.
36 James J. Sadkovich, 'Of Myths and Men: Rommel and the Italians in North Africa', *The International Review*, vol. 13, n. 2, 1991.

in the Gazala line battles would disregard his superiors' instructions to concentrate the British armour force. Instead, Ritchie, even though his tank force outnumbered Rommel's force, would waste his advantage by not using his tanks en mass and thereby losing the initiative.

The Siege of Bir Hacheim thus began on 27 May when the 15th and 21st Panzer Divisions and, the bulk of the DAK swung around it, while *Ariete* began to attack the southern flank of the French defenses. While driving toward Bir Hacheim, *Ariete's* reconnaissance units spotted a fortified enemy box in the distance, which was initially mistakenly taken to be the French position. The position was Point 171, a high-altitude position located four miles south-east of Bir Hacheim. It was held by approximately 1,200 troops of the 3rd Indian Motor Brigade, which were equipped primarily with thirty 2-pdr guns. Although, these Commonwealth troops were organized into a well-positioned and fortified box, they lacked heavy guns and were vulnerable to armoured attack. The former nonetheless opened a tremendous barrage immediately after spotting *Ariete's* reconnaissance team. Soon after the Commonwealth unit suffered return fire as it was shelled by an equally fierce counter battery fire by the Italian 88mm and 90mm guns. Following a brief but fierce exchange of fire, *Ariete's* command gave orders to its armoured units to charge against the box. The IX and VIII *Battaglioni Carri Medi* were in the forefront, while X was at the back. Stunned by superior and longer range artillery fire, the box was surprised at 0630 and then overrun by the M tanks. Initially the enemy infantry surrendered but seeing that the tank crews were unable to round them up, many retook their weapons. But just in the nick of time *Ariete's* motorized infantry units arrived to capture the enemy infantry. Commonwealth losses were estimated at 200 dead, and 1,000 taken prisoner. A key contribution was made by the *semoventi* units paving the way for the M tanks to advance by firing at close range and from flanking positions against the enemy antitank screen. Their role was recognized with the award of a gold medal for military valor to *Tenente* Aldo Scalise who commanded one of Ariete's *semoventi* units, and who fell during the operation. His tank driver Tritto recalls the last stages of the attack against the enemy position:

> After a very hard fight and after we had penetrated the enemy's first line of defense, our vehicle was hit by an anti-tank shell that penetrated the cabin and injured our tenente (the twenty-two-year-old Aldo Maria Scalise) and poor Cicognani. Upon seeing Cicognani in such grave conditions, tenente took control of the weapon and began firing at the enemy.... We were a few meters away from numerous enemy positions and several Indian soldiers that were surrendering in droves. But we were not paying any attention to them as we were focused instead on those enemy strongpoints that were still fighting. Tenente kept firing the machine gun as I drove rough shod over the enemy positions. Suddenly, a second armoured piercing shot penetrated the armour and wounded tenente's arm which blew away in a matter of seconds. He did not realize that I had been wounded as well and even though he was more severely wounded than I he raised his other arm and ordered to drive on. The tank was travelling at top speed, without anyone from the crew commanding it. Suddenly it smashed against an enemy position and came to a dead stop. I tried to help our tenente escape from the tank but he had already passed away.[37]

---

37 'Ricordi del conduttore artigliere Tritto', *Italia Giovane*, Novara, Maggio 1943.

The *Ariete* division's post battle report observed:

> After a prolonged exchange of fire, the 132º Reggimento assaulted the enemy positions with the VIII Battaglione deployed on the right while IX Battaglione deployed on the left. Both units were supported respectively by a self-propelled gun company such as the 552º and 551º Gruppo Semoventi. X Battaglione was also involved as it breeched the central enemy positions.
>
> At 0710, after overcoming with a swift charge the very strong enemy reaction, Ariete tanks penetrated deeply into their positions.
>
> The garrison, composed of colored and Congolese troops, surrendered for the most part, including about a thousand men and one general and three colonels. Ariete's losses included 23 tanks, 30 dead, 6 missing, and 40 wounded.[38]

The following is the post battle report of the *132º Reggimento Carristi* detailing the experiences of the unit during the counteroffensive:

> At Rugbet el Atasc (Bir Hacheim) the first major clash against the enemy took place during the operating cycle of summer 1942. Here the enemy had built numerous strong points that were to be used to halt our advance while giving his troops a launching pad for a counterthrust. Our units were to break through the enemy defenses with extreme force and together with other troops of the Axis carry out a wide-ranging encirclement maneuver to surround and isolate the British strongpoint. Once these positions had fallen we would have cleared out the main road toward Egypt to continue our advance. The 132º Carristi attacked with decisiveness the enemy position at Rughet el Ataso with its three battalions. Once it approached the main positions, the enemy situated in dug in positions in the desert, fired at us at close range with its anti-tank weapons. But as we continued to advance the enemy positions were overrun and the tracks of the tanks barreled over many enemy weapons and positions. The enemy was forced to surrender and we managed to capture 1,000 soldiers, while several dead soldiers were left on the battlefield along with burning vehicles and destroyed equipment of all kind. The losses in our ranks were also considerable with only 124 tanks remaining in working condition.[39]

The report also mentions that most of the tank losses came from the VIII *Battaglione Carri Medi*, while the IX suffered fewer losses. It lists the following losses: twenty-three tanks and one *semovente*, thirty dead, seven missing, forty-two wounded. According to the Commonwealth's unit war diary it was originally estimated that the attack had been put forth by 200 German tanks. It was only later realized that the tanks were Italian and that only a few German tanks had participated in a marginal way to the operation. The Commonwealth version of events states that there were two tank charges put forth by the Axis forces with up to 200 tanks, while the Italian account states that there was only one with no more than 120 tanks and the eighteen

---

38 Ufficio Storico, "Relazione Enrico Maretti sul comportamento del 132° Ariete in A.S.," Cartella 1160, prot.1809, Novembre 1942.
39 Ibid.

semoventi involved. Rommel's account states that the "Panzer units of the Afrika Korps"[40] put forth the attack against the Indian brigade, although the battle diary of the 21st Panzer Division which was deployed south of the Italians makes no mention of an encounter with the Indian infantry. Historian Ronald Lewin asserts that the Afrika Korps was responsible for seizing Rughet el Ataso: "Late on the 27th, therefore, the situation looked serious. After eliminating 3 Indian Brigade and savaging 7 Motorized Brigade DAK had fought intensive actions with large or small groups of British armour …"[41]

At any rate the success was clearly achieved by *Ariete* mainly by the fact that the enemy did not have heavier anti-tank weapons other than the 2-pdr guns to stop the medium tanks and the self-propelled guns. The encounter demonstrated that *Ariete* and the Italian tank units in general could still be deployed offensively in an effective manner against enemy defenses comprised of 2-pdr guns. Future encounters, however, would reveal that their tanks were too soft skinned to attack an anti-tank screen equipped primarily with 6-pounder guns.

After over-running the 3rd Indian Motor Brigade, *Ariete*'s armoured regiment moved to the north-east of Bir Hacheim and the *IX Battaglione* (*Tenente Colonnello* Prestisimone)[42] with sixty medium tanks under his command, unexpectedly changed direction or got lost and headed towards the fort. Once in proximity of Bir Hackeim *Tenente Colonnello* Prestisimone, it is not clear whether he received the order from *Ariete*'s tank regiment HQ or on his own initiative, ordered his battalion to make a direct attack against the fortress without conducting any prior in depth reconnaissance. To the surprise of the troops of the *IX Battaglione* the area surrounding the fort was littered with anti-tank mines which took a heavy toll on the tanks as they traveled toward the main enemy positions. Thus, by 0830 *Ariete* had already lost thirty-one tanks and an additional *semovente* self-propelled gun and had already sustained heavy casualties. Ten M tanks managed to emerge from the minefield but were then targeted by the heavy French 75mm guns and quickly put out of action. There were 124 casualties amongst the *IX Battaglione* before its tattered remains retreated back to the Axis positions. Regarding this attack historian Francesco Viglione wrote that: "Prestisimone, following his sanguine and impulsive nature, reverted 25 years back to his young Lieutenancy and the bayonet charges of World War I. He sought proof of his courage from those times in this attack. He forgot that he now had the responsibility of 60 tanks."[43]

French General Koenig would later state that his artillery did most of the damage to Prestisimone's men: "The enemy tanks charged our positions. Our armour piercing shells are exploding and raising huge dust clouds. Occasionally an enemy tank is hit followed by loud explosions."[44] With regard to this operation, the Italian Official History states that; "While the unit attacked very courageously, the operation and its final objective were not rationally thought over. It appears for reasons unknown that a rash decision was taken."[45]

---

40 Basil Liddell Hart, *The Rommel Papers*, p. 206.
41 Ronald Levin, *The Life and Death of the Afrika Korps*, p. 128.
42 After this battle the IX Battaglione was disbanded and Prestisimone became the commander of the VIII Battaglione, which took the place of the no longer existing unit.
43 Jack Greene and Alessandro Massignani, *Rommel's North African Campaign*, p. 157.
44 Mario Montanari, *Le operazioni in Africa settentrionale*, vol III, Part I, p. 211.
45 Ibid., p. 212.

At 1200 Ariete resumed its advance, while Trieste was still unable to move forward because its troops were dispersed and much disorganized. In the afternoon *Ariete*'s units, including the IX *Battaglione Carri Medi*, linked up and regrouped at Rugbet el Atasc, while the XX *Corpo d'Armata* HQ was finally able to communicate with the *Trieste* Division. Communication was especially difficult for the Italian units especially when in movement, thus when *Trieste* was finally reached its whereabouts where still North of Bir Hacheim and the minefields had yet to be surpassed. On the same day that *Ariete* made the first attempt to seize the French garrison the Germans had made considerable headway, although they had lost tanks and artillery. On the morning of 27th May they overran the 7th Armoured Division HQ and then inflicted heavy losses on the 8th Hussars and 3rd Royal Tank Regiment. The 15th Panzer Division then clashed against the 4th Armoured Brigade that for the first time was deploying a very high number of M3 Grant tanks. The Germans had a few Panzer tanks with a 50mm gun and even fewer with a 75mm gun and throughout the three-hour engagement suffered several casualties due to the preponderance of the Commonwealth tanks. Although the Germans survived the encounter in large part due to the effectiveness of their artillery, the new American tanks, thanks to their superior speed and 75mm gun, proved to be a heavy challenge to the panzers. Similarly, the 21st Panzer Division was involved in hard fighting against the British 22nd Armoured Brigade. But once again the British armour was committed piecemeal, leading the German 21st having the upper hand.

The alarm caused by the appearance on the battlefield of the medium M3 Grant tanks, forced the Italians to rush to the front two batteries of 88mm Flak 36 guns that had previously been deployed in defense of Tripoli's harbor in an anti-aircraft role and which were attached to *Ariete* Division (V *Gruppo* da 88/55, received as a reinforcement from *Divisione fanteria Brescia*). These weapons had been supplied by Germany to Italy in 1940 as it entered the war bereft of modern anti-aircraft guns to protect the large, populated cities from French and, later, British air attacks in the industrialized north.[46] The Italians now wanted to press them into service in the anti-tank role.

By the end of the first day of operation the situation for the Axis forces was uncertain. On one hand they had inflicted losses on the enemy and pushed him back. One the other, the Germans had lost a third of their tank strength, while *Ariete* had lost more than forty tanks. A pessimistic Rommel wrote that: "The advent of the new American tank had torn great holes in our ranks."[47] *Trieste* suffered no losses since it lost its direction and was not engaged.

---

46 In September 1940, two battalions of 88mm Flak 36 were formed in Florence and the personnel was trained by German artillery officers. The personnel then received further instructions at a special artillery school near Rome for two months, but due to the lack of ammunition only had two days of firing exercises. The training was entirely based on the anti-aircraft role as at the time it was not envisioned to use the guns in anti-tank role. After France surrendered the threat of bombing attacks somewhat diminished as Britain was fighting alone against the mighty Luftwaffe. It was then decided to dispatch the two battalions fielding a total of six batteries to North Africa and were originally intended for a strictly anti-aircraft role in the defense of Tripoli. The XVIII battalion was sent in October of 1940, while the XXIX arrived in December 1940. The former later was renamed V Gruppo and assigned to the Brescia infantry division, and then transferred to the Divisione Ariete.
47 Basil Liddell Hart, *The Rommel Papers*, p. 207.

The Cauldron

On May 28th *Ariete* was ordered by Rommel to move north to link up with the German DAK units and the 90th Leicht at Rigel Ridge in the Cauldron on the Gazala line. The Cauldron was the area comprising Sidi Muftah, Knightsbrige, Bir el Harmat and Got el Ualeb where the enemy fortifications stood in the way of an advance toward Tobruk. Thus, the division was stationed between Bir el Harmat and Aslagh Ridge when the first enemy counter-attack materialized. Rommel's strategy at the time was to defend against Commonwealth armoured counterthrusts, while reducing one by one the infantry boxes on the Gazala line. This is how *Ariete*'s tank regiment interpreted Rommel's order to stand in the Cauldron: "The enemy had built several strongly armed strongpoints whose purpose was to beat off our attacks and then to use them as jumping off platforms for counter-attacks. We had to break through this defensive network and then carry out a pincer movement together with the German units to capture the enemy positions. Once we had cleared the area we were to advance toward the Libyan-Egyptian frontier."[48] At approximately 1000 *Ariete* was attacked by several Valentine tanks from the 1st British Army Tank Brigade, which were met with a deluge of fire and iron by the artillery. In the afternoon, the British were back at it again. The 2nd Armoured Brigade, this time with a mixed force of Grant and Crusader tanks, attacked *Ariete*'s right flank but the 90/53 guns promptly repelled this attempt by shooting to pieces the leading tanks. Finally, the M tanks countered the enemy armoured force forcing it to retreat. In one of the counterattack actions "8th Compagnia, commanded by Ten. Carlo Rombola', suffered heavy casualties because it was subjected to heavy artillery fire amidst high winds up in a minefield. Its 2° Plotone, led by Ten. Francesco Viglione, was the first to emerge from the minefield and while continuing to the attack it managed to capture two armoured vehicles towing artillery guns."[49]

On the 29th the Axis supply situation had become very strained because the ammunition, water food and fuel, due to the offensive had to be moved from the rear over great distances in Commonwealth-dominated territory. Some of the columns, therefore, lost their way, others were shot up, and captured by the enemy. Thus, only an extremely small portion of the supplies had reached the frontline troops positioned deep in enemy territory on the Gazala line.

By this time *Ariete* was deployed at Aslagh Ridge sandwiched between the DAK at Rigel Ridge and the 90th Leicht at Bir el Harmat. The Axis forces thus formed a defensive line in the so-called Cauldron between Tobruk to the north and Bir Hacheim to the south to face any potential Commonwealth counter-attack.

Since enemy counters were highly anticipated especially when the German Panzer units attacked and left their flanks and rear thinly defended, *Ariete*'s commander had his troops deployed along several lines of defense in a semicircle. The *Bersaglieri* units were positioned on the ridge. Behind it laid the anti-tank screen comprised of 88mm, 90/53 guns interspersed with some older 76mm Skoda guns. The tanks of *132° Reggimento Carristi* were held in reserve behind the antitank screen, while the heavy field guns of *132° Reggimento Artiglieria Corazzata* were positioned behind the tanks.

---

48 Ufficio Storico, 'Relazione Enrico Maretti sul comportamento del 132° Ariete in A.S.', Cartella 1160, prot.1809, novembre 1942.
49 Ufficio Storico, Diario del X Battaglione Carri Medi, 'Operazioni del 1942', Il Comandante, Agosto 1942.

On 29/30 May the Commonwealth armoured brigades attacked in wave after wave the Axis lines again in a bid to relieve the pressure on the boxes held by their infantry. On 29 May, the British 2nd Armoured Brigade comprised of a mixed unit of Crusader and Grant tanks was the first to strike *Ariete*'s position in the morning. The aim of the former was to prevent the Italians from linking up with the DAK, but having observed that *Ariete* was well entrenched in its position it refrained from putting forth a major attack and limited itself to few piecemeal sallies.

Tenente Alberto Coglitore of the 8ª *Compagnia cannoni controcarro/XII Battaglione* recalls:

> The regiment is deploying in a new defensive position facing east. At 0800, as the troops are in the process of assuming the position, I spot far away what appeared to be a number of enemy vehicles heading toward us. As they inched closer they were clearly identified as enemy vehicles and the regiment opened up a blistering and timely gun fire that forces the enemy back to its starting line. Throughout the brief but very intense confrontation our position is plastered with enemy fire. But as the enemy tanks get perilously close to our position they are beaten back with force.[50]

Instead of a major tank attack for approximately an hour there was a brisk exchange of artillery fire which was inconclusive. After the British unit was countered from two sides (by 15th and 21st Panzer from the north and *Ariete's* tanks from the opposite direction) it was forced to retire. The X *Battaglione Carri Medi* was heavily engaged on the 29th and took part to the Axis armoured counter:

> On 29 May 1942 the Battalion linked up with the 8th Bersaglieri Regiment on the ridge of Hagiag Es Sidra, about 5 km north of Bir El Tamar and from there, at the explicit request of the Commander Rommel, was engaged in support of several German artillery units that were on the verge of being overrun by the British forces. Following this action the British forces, which were initially located 500 meters from the positions of the German artillery, fell back by about 2 Km. The enemy then reorganized its forces and launched a new attack that was repelled also thanks to the action of the self-propelled guns. Other attacks were made during the day but were repelled.[51]

In the evening of 29 May, the Commonwealth had concentrated their armoured forces in front of the German-Italian units deployed on a line in the Gazala front. Nonetheless, the latter's main worry remained the supply situation which had become very critical to the point that due to lack of fuel and ammunition the scheduled Axis attacks could not be initiated. The situation had deteriorated because while the Axis forces had created a bulge in between Bir Hacheim and the Commonwealth positions north of the Gazala line held by the 150th British Infantry Brigade, their supply columns could not easily reach them without risking capture by mobile Jock columns. To reach Bir el Harmat, where the Axis artillery and armour was concentrated they had to move south past Bir Hackeim then swing north on a tortuous journey. General Bayerlein reported the predicament of the Axis units in the following terms: "We were in a

---

50 Giulio Bedeschi, *Fronte d'Africa*, p. 132.
51 Ibid.

really desperate situation, our backs against a minefield, no food, no water, no petrol, very little ammunition, no way through the mines for our convoys; Bir Hacheim still holding out and preventing our supplies from the south. We were being attacked all the time from the air."[52]

At 0730 on 30 May the Commonwealth tanks in order to exert further pressure on a depleted opponent suddenly attacked again (this time with 22nd and 2nd Armoured Brigades) without the aid of a preparatory bombardment. Their aim was to reach the rear of the DAK including its command center. The attack stumbled upon the positions of the *V/1 Artiglieria Celere* equipped with the mighty tank killers 88mm and 90/53 guns.

As *Tenente* Calabresi of the *14ª Batteria* recalls: "tanks came suddenly attacking out of the cover of the Trigh's downward steps, firing all guns. We responded immediately with artillery fire. Three enemy tanks were hit almost instantly, while up to five tanks managed to get perilously close to our positions."[53]

Approximately ten M.13/40 tanks from *Ariete* intervened in the fighting in a bid to halt the enemy advance together with the artillery, but two were put out of action almost immediately. An officer of the 13 ª *Batteria V/1 Artiglieria Celere* equipped with the mighty German 88mm Flak 36 guns recalls:

> Under increasing enemy pressure the M.13 tanks began to move slowly and then a little while later responded to the massive enemy fire. Two of them were hit almost immediately and by the time they had positioned themselves on our line the artillery batteries had already opened fire. With some degree of ability and luck one of our first artillery shells hit a Matilda tank at a distance of 800 meters knocking it out of action. A few minutes later two Crusaders were also hit …Then more tanks were knocked out as the pace of the enemy attack slowed down considerably. Several Stuart tanks at 400 meters from our flank also pulled back. After half an hour of continuous enemy artillery fire an eerie silence descended on the battlefield. A few minutes of quiet were followed by the buzzing noise of the vehicles which could be heard in the distance and it was the prelude to a new enemy attack. In this phase of the battle an artillery observer of 1. pezzo (artillery piece) was shot to death by machine gun fire and an artillery server from the 3. pezzo was killed when struck by a shell. Then all of a sudden the huge amount of dust raised by the tanks subsided as they slowed down while facing our position and then opened fire. We spotted several tanks at a distance of 500 meters. Thus, our guns went into action again….We observed several tanks exploding while others made a dead stop and the crews bailed out of the vehicles. Meanwhile a Crusader kept on going at full speed until finally it was stopped by 1. pezzo at a distance of 200 meters from our position. In this second phase of the fight 1. pezzo put out of action three enemy tanks and hit two more. 2. pezzo knocked two out of action and damaged two more, while 3. pezzo hit three tanks completely obliterating one of them. 4. pezzo, although deployed in a less advantageous position, damaged two tanks. Two artillery men from 1. pezzo were seriously wounded while one had an arm blown off. 2. pezzo had two lightly wounded including myself, while 3. Pezzo and 4. pezzo crews suffered two

---

52   Basil Liddell Hart, *The Rommel Papers*, p. 210.
53   Jack Greene and Alessandro Massignani, *Rommel's North Africa Campaign*, p. 117.

dead. The enemy attack had been beaten back and twenty enemy tanks retreated to their starting line.[54]

The assault lasted over two hours. Finally, the last offensive probe was foiled by a combination of artillery fire and the intervention of two Stukas which dive bombed the enemy armour. Despite attacking by surprise the tanks suffered some losses, the 2nd Armoured Brigade, for example, after the battle was reputed to have only thirty tanks in working order. Another attack was conducted by the same units in the afternoon but it was also met with heavy artillery fire as reported in the war diary of 4th County of London Yeomanry, which had come out in support of 2nd Armoured Brigade:

> 1500 – 2nd Royal Gloucestershire Hussars reported in difficulties about Point 155. Extracted Grants and moved Regiment to that area. Decided with Lt. Col. Birley (2 RGH) to advance south and try and delay the enemy advance. Did so but visibility rapidly became less and we lost 2 tanks by running into enemy guns at close range unawares, when they could see our dust. Withdrew to B.230 to await better visibility. Very heavily shelled, so moved North.[55]

As the above report states elements of the 22nd Armoured Brigade provided support to 2nd Armoured Brigade in the afternoon attack by renewing the tank assault against the *Ariete* anti-tank screen. The tanks were met by point blank fire from 90/53 and 88/56 guns concealed in gun pits or positioned amongst derelict tanks that had been knocked out of action in the last days of fighting.

Although effective, the Italian armoured artillery also suffered huge casualties, mainly due to the close combat conditions which characterized this encounter. One battalion, for instance, lost forty-nine men and five precious 88mm guns. Several guns were involved in extreme close combat fighting as several Crusaders managed to infiltrate the Italian positions. At one point one Italian gun faced a British tank at almost point blank range at less than 200 yards. Despite the latter's adroit maneuvers and its ability to travel at top speed, the gun crew ultimately knocked it out of action just in the nick of time. Some other gun crews were not as fortunate. Some men were shot at close range by the machine guns from the tanks, while others had already been killed or wounded by the tank guns at a further range. The defensive action, which had taken place while the Panzer units were overrunning the defenses of the 150th Brigade, was praised by Rommel which awarded *Tenente* Calabresi with an Iron Cross second class. In his diary, he wrote that: "Nothing happened during the morning, except a few attacks on the Ariete, which the Italians beat off and a number of even weaker thrusts on the rest of the front. Fifty-Seven British tanks were shot up that day."[56] Rommel's tally is probably on the high end. It is more likely that total British tank casualties did no exceed twenty to twenty-five destroyed tanks on that day by the combined Axis artillery and tank forces, while several more were likely damaged but ultimately were recovered.

---

54   Giulio Bedeschi, *Fronte d'Africa*, pp. 152-53.
55   TNA WO 169/1399: 4th County of Yeomanry War Diary, Operations in Libya 20 May-20 June 1942 – 3 July 1941.
56   Basil Liddell Hart, *The Rommel Papers*, p. 212.

Ariete's anti-tank artillery officer *Tenente* Coglitore recalls that the unit was once again called upon on 31 May to beat back another enemy tank attack. "At 0445 an enemy armoured column coming from Trigh Capuzzo got very close to our artillery positions. This was followed by a heavy and thunderous fire from our guns which put out of action three armoured vehicles. Two additional armoured vehicles were captured along with an officer and eleven enemy soldiers."[57]

Despite losses sustained between 26-31 May, the Axis units were slowly gaining the upper hand in the Cauldron battle: several enemy tank formations had suffered casualties, while in the meantime elements of the XX Italian Army Corps had succeeded in getting through the Commonwealth blockade forming a bridgehead on the eastern side of them. *Trieste* Division had lost its way on the first day of operations and had stumbled upon an enemy minefield that stood between Bir Hackeim and el Chebir that was patrolled and defended by units of the 150th Brigade. On the 28th it began to attack the enemy front, which was centered on Point 182, but the heavy artillery fire of the British units stopped the advance on its tracks. A follow up reconnaissance of the enemy positions revealed that they were defended by several "dug in tanks placed in static positions that revealed only the barrel of the gun."[58] A second attempt to seize the enemy position was carried out on the early evening of the 28th but it was not successful. On the night between 28/29 June *Trieste* continued to pressure the enemy and this forced him to retire past Point 182. A rearguard of armoured vehicles was left behind but this action was countered by the VIII *Battaglione Bersaglieri* which pushed forward and cleared the area of Point 182. This action allowed the Axis sappers to begin to decommission some of the mines. By clearing a lane of several miles in the minefields to transport supplies the action enabled the Axis supply columns to advance toward the frontline. The lifeline proved to be of critical importance for the continuation of the operation even though the Commonwealth guns could still target Axis supply trucks with their well sighted artillery.

On the 30th Rommel had ordered an attack against Got el Ualeb where the 150th British Infantry Brigade had set up a major defensive position on the Gazala line aimed at halting the Panzers from reaching the north and the coast. It was critical for the Axis to take this box because it continually harassed the Axis supply line in the only passage that the combat engineers had cleared within the minefields. The attack, undertaken by the 90th Leicht Division and the *Trieste* Division, proved to be a very arduous operation as the British put up a very stubborn and dogged resistance. For *Trieste*, the operation began on 30 May at 0600 when it began its approach march toward the enemy positions with II/65° *Reggimento* acting on the right while the I/66° and II/66° on the left. After having advanced 800 meters the infantry units were halted by a British counter made by infantry and supported by tanks. *Trieste* made recourse to several truck-mounted 100/17 howitzers which were brought in advanced positions as "specific anti-tank support"[59] to check the counter. As a result of these guns one tank was shot up, two were damaged and others were dispersed.[60] The determined British opposition had also checked the German units that had suffered

---

57   Giulio Bedeschi, *Fronte d'Africa*, p. 132.
58   Ufficio Storico, cartella 921, ore 15, 28 maggio 1942, allegato 5, doc. 120.
59   Ufficio Storico: Cartella 921, 30 Maggio 1942.
60   Ibid.

casualties due to the swift enemy counterstroke. But the next day the attacks were resumed and Rommel states: "The attack was launched on the morning of 31st May, German-Italian units fought their way forward yard by yard against the toughest British resistance imaginable. The defense was conducted with considerable skill and as usual, the British fought to the last round. They also brought a new 57mm anti-tank gun (the 6 pounder) into use in this action. Nevertheless, by the time evening came we had penetrated a substantial distance into the British positions."[61]

The next day the Commonwealth defense crumbled after a series of devastating Stukas attacks and an artillery preparatory fire that lasted only twenty minutes but was very intensive. With the 90th Leicht to the right and *Pavia* to the left, the infantry units of the *Trieste* lurched forward and after a half hour they took possession of several enemy strongpoints which were seized after "hand to hand combat."[62] The fighting as reported by the war diary of the *Trieste* Division was very intense as the British soldiers fought tooth and nail forcing the *Bersaglieri* and the infantry to sustain many casualties as they cleared trenches and machine gun outposts. The anti-tank gun units then followed the initial advance and positioned their weapons in the captured outposts just in time as the enemy launched his expected counter. The enemy reacted by dispatching a mixed combat unit comprised by tanks, armoured vehicles and infantry to try to push back the Axis advance. Consequently, "thanks to some well-placed 100/17 gun units they were able to immobilize five tanks and 2 armoured vehicles by using these weapons forward and in close collaboration with the infantry."[63] The final phase of the operation saw the infantry push forward once again, while the *Trieste*'s tank battalion stormed the last remaining enemy strongholds forcing the surrender of its occupants. At the same time the units of 90th Leicht had also overrun the enemy positions on their front and reached their objective. Finally, the enemy surrendered. The Axis captured a total of 3,000 prisoners and had destroyed forty enemy tanks. XX *Corpo d'Armata* war diary reports that: "The attack ended in the afternoon with the complete destruction of the enemy which opposed a fierce resistance utilizing even hand grenades and pistols. The losses are heavy on both sides. Trieste has sustained sizeable losses including the commander of the 66th Infantry Colonnello Chiapuzzo."[64]

As of 31 May, the XX *Corpo d'Armata* losses included:

> *Ariete*: 42 dead, 119 wounded, 89 missing, 52 tanks destroyed, 43 tanks damaged but repairable, 6 *semoventi* destroyed and 5 repairable.
> *Trieste*: 55 dead, 170 wounded, 56 missing, 23 tanks destroyed, 14 tanks damaged but repairable.[65] The Germans also sustained heavy casualties. The battle had also a tremendous toll on the upper echelons of the army as Colonel Westphal and General Gause of the DAK General Staff were both wounded, while the commander of *Trieste*'s 66° *Reggimento* was killed.

---

61   Basil Liddell Hart, *The Rommel Papers*, p. 212.
62   Ufficio Storico: Cartella 921, 1 giugno 1942.
63   Dattilo Ciampini, 'La fanteria motorizzata tra modello ed esperienze: la Trieste in Africa settentrionale 1941-1942', *Quaderno di storia militare*, Anno 2009, p. 170.
64   Mario Montanari, *Le operazioni in Africa settentrionale*, Vol. III, Part I, p. 235.
65   Ibid. p. 236.

Final Advance on Bir Hackeim

During the night of 1-2 June, the 90th Leicht Division and the *Trieste* Division finally approached the French fort of Bir el Hacheim, the last box on the Gazala line still held by the enemy. *Trieste* advanced against the fort from the northeast, while the 90th Leicht Division attacked from the southeast. While the infantry was approaching the fort, the Axis artillery opened fire against the French providing the first round in a battle of unusual severity, which was to last for ten days.

As the infantry assault against the French position was taking place, it became apparent to Rommel that the Commonwealth would soon make a counterattack, either against Axis armoured units in the north or against the siege group in the south to help take the pressure off the French. He therefore ordered the Axis unit deployed in the Cauldron to be on high alert and take up defensive positions, warning them of major armoured attacks. The Axis forces were deployed as follows: 21st Panzer was at Hadiag es Sidra, 15th Panzer was at Got el Ualeb, while *Ariete* was stationed at Bir et Tamar and Aslagh Ridge.

The first attack came on 2 June when two squadrons of British tanks attacked *Ariete*'s position on the Gazala line. As the DAK war diary asserts: "The Ariete Division alone was attacked by them on 2 June, but it defended itself stubbornly."[66]

Operation Aberdeen

The second much more powerful and largescale attack came three days later. Operation Aberdeen, launched on 5 June 1942, was another attempt by the Commonwealth forces to counter the Axis advance by punching holes through their defensive line in the Cauldron. Since all previous Commonwealth attempts either with infantry or armour to penetrate the Axis positions on the Gazala line had failed, Operation Aberdeen was to see a major force deployment. The plan entailed a surprise attack by the 9th and 10th Indian Brigades against *Ariete*, which was to pave the way for a breakthrough in the Cauldron by the 22nd Armoured Brigade to deal with the bulk of the Axis armour. A diversionary action against the 21st Panzer by units of 13th Corps was also planned. According to the Commonwealth intelligence reports the position occupied by *Ariete* was presumed to be occupied by German anti-tank units most likely because of the Italian manned 88mm guns that were placed at its disposal. The plan entailed first the deployment of specialized infantry troops that were to degrade the anti-tank defense of the Axis so that in the second stage of the operation the tanks could roll through the enemy's defenses and then hook the flank and reach deeply into the rear. The 2nd Highland Light Infantry came through and began to form a bridgehead on the Axis side by dismantling mines and attacking strong point positions held by the *Ariete* Division's infantry. As the sappers and engineers were busily trying to open a path for the tanks, the British 107th Royal Artillery opened fire but due to bad reconnaissance it targeted positions that had been already abandoned by *Ariete*, who had fallen back as a preemptive measure to better parry the enemy attack. The Scots then dislodged the *Bersaglieri* from Aslagh Ridge after much hard close quarters fighting. Once the breech had

---

66 Ibid.

been made, the 2nd West Yorkshire was thrusted into the gap to penetrate the Italian defenses and reach the rear, but as soon as its infantry advanced it was met by heavy gun fire. The West Yorkshire unit, accompanied by a company of Matilda II tanks, initially overran the outposts of the *V Battaglione/8º Bersaglieri*, which was forced to surrender some of its positions and fall back. The Commonwealth troops then attempted to seize the resistance line manned by the *Bersaglieri*, but they were prevented from doing so by heavy machine gun and anti-tank gun fire. Then soon after the attackers were checked, they were faced by a combined Italian and German armoured counterattack which had been ordered directly by Rommel. This action was undertaken by the 21st Panzer on Bir el Aslagh and X *Battaglione Carri Medi* against Dahar el Aslagh to the south. With limited tank support, the British infantry was forced to pull back. The X *Battaglione Carri Medi* war diary reports that "On the morning of the 5th, the battalion was faced with a massive, combined infantry and tank attack. Despite the large deployment, the fighting ended with a clear success on our part but we suffered heavy casualties such as three tanks destroyed, and four dead: *Tenente* Radivoj Tavchar, *Sergente* Maggiore De Luca and *carristi* Ghinzelli and Corrado."[67] Further north up to 156 tanks (Crusader, Grants and Stuarts) of the 22nd Armoured Brigade came forward in between the meeting point between the *Ariete*'s and DAK anti-tank screen. The 22nd Armoured Brigade was deployed as follows: 3rd County of London Yeomanry was on the right flank, 2nd Royal Gloucestershire Hussars in the middle and 4th County of London Yeomanry on the left flank. Unfortunately, as von Mellenthin asserts, the armour had been ordered to attack too soon since its vehicles became entangled with the infantry that was still occupying the field of battle, and as a result the pace of the operation slowed down considerably.[68] As the British tanks were slowly moving toward the enemy positions, the combined force of the German and Italian anti-tank guns opened fire. The artillery response took them by complete surprise since they had attacked on the premise that Aberdeen's preparatory fire had seriously eroded Axis artillery strength. The lead vehicle was the first to be met by the blistering fire of the anti-tank screen comprised primarily by German 88mm, which were positioned to the north, and Italian 90mm guns, positioned south-west. Having immobilized the lead vehicle, the Axis artillery then reversed its focus upon the tanks at the back of the enemy columns to box them in. Several tanks were destroyed in this fashion and at almost point blank range and numerous Bren carriers where machine gunned by the infantry as reported in the Italian Official History: "The 22nd Armoured Brigade tanks fell under the concentrated anti-tank and field guns of the DAK and the *XX Corpo d'armata* positioned to the north and west. In the end, the brigade, faced by the counter of part of *Ariete* and the 8th *Panzerregime*nt lost many tanks and retreated back to Bir et-Tamar."[69]

By 1700 Rommel had ordered a further counterattack by 15th, 21st Panzer and by *Ariete*. Each unit was assigned a specific direction from which to encircle the 22nd Brigade. "The counter, preceded by a brief bombardment by Stukas, was carried out according to plan. Assaulted from multiple sides, the 22nd Brigade fell back in a disorderly fashion to Trigh Hacheim."[70] According to the tank crews of the *Ariete* Division the fighting was particularly intense during this counter-

---

67   Ufficio Storico, Diario del X Battaglione Carri Medi, 'Operazioni del 1942', Il Comandante, Agosto 1942.
68   Major-General F. W. von Mellenthin, *Panzer Battles* (New York: History Press, 2009), p, 123.
69   Mario Montanari, *Le operazioni in Africa settentrionale*, Vol. III, Part I, p. 246.
70   Ibid, p. 247.

attack because they encountered, new, heavier tanks: "The enemy fielded new American Pilot type tanks which were heavier and with a more powerful gun than our M tanks. As a result, the aggressiveness and the will to fight of our crews was severely tested during the fighting. But, after heavy fighting, the enemy fell back thanks to a combination of artillery fire, anti-tank guns, machine gun fire and successive waves of counter-attacking tanks."[71]

With regard to Operation Aberdeen historian Michael Craver observed that:

> 10th Indian Brigade crossed their start line at 0250 on 5 June and everything went smoothly. All battalions reached their objectives, the four gunner regiments moved into position and the leading battalion of the 9th Indian Brigade with a squadron of 4th Royal Tanks came up also to Aslagh Ridge, but this success had been gained so easily because the enemy's positions, or the distance to them, had been miscalculated. The attack had not reached them: the considerable volume of artillery support had fallen on empty desert and had served only to warn Ariete and the rest of the DAK of what was afoot. When therefore Carr's 156 tanks crossed the Aslagh Ridge in daylight, they were in full view of the enemy, and two miles further on ran suddenly into the concentrated fire of the Panzergruppe Army Artillery and all the anti-tank guns that the Afrika Korps could bring to bear. The brigade suffered heavily and veered off to the north-east.[72]

Flung in the midst of the fighting the armour of the 2nd Royal Gloucestershire Hussars was met by enemy barrages of great intensity:

> Our attack reached B.178 (Ariete's position ndr) where heavy anti-tank gunfire from guns dug in on the ridge prevented any further advance.........6 June. Broke leaguer at 0515 to find line of German tanks (25) with strong force of guns and anti-tank guns facing us on ridge T.185 to our South. Regiment formed up with 3 CLY on right, Gds Bde to our rear. No move was made by the enemy or our tanks but they were shelled by the Gds artillery. The enemy put down some HE amongst us causing us to lose 2 Grants and 1 Honey.[73]

An *Ariete* anti-tank unit officer recorded the following recollection of operation Aberdeen: "5 and 6 June were two memorable days that will be remembered vividly. From dawn to dusk massive artillery preparations were followed by enemy attacks, which were in turn followed by our numerous attempts to counter-attack. Numerous attempts were made by the enemy to overcome our positions with the brute force of the armoured units. In an apocalyptic scenario, the German and Italian units ultimately had the upper hand upon the enemy. The clear majority of our losses were sustained by the V *Battaglione* which while moving toward the enemy suddenly came under heavy enemy artillery fire that caused several dead and wounded amongst the infantry."[74]

71　Ufficio Storico, "Relazione Enrico Maretti sul comportamento del 132° Ariete in A.S.," Cartella 1160, prot.1809, novembre 1943.
72　Michael Carver, *Tobruk*, p. 197.
73　2nd Royal Gloucestershire Hussars War Diary <http://www.warlinks.com/armour/4_cly/4cly_42.php> (accessed 21 May, 2018).
74　Giulio Bedeschi, *Fronte d'Africa*, p. 135.

It is estimated that the 22nd Armoured Brigade lost sixty tanks during Operation Aberdeen. While 32nd Tank Brigade also lost a number of tanks. As Michael Carver asserts: "It was a blow from which 8th Army was not in fact to recover" and an important contributing factor to the defeat of the Commonwealth at Gazala.[75] The defensive stand by the artillery and antitank units of DAK and *Ariete*, holding the flank and protecting the lines of communication with the rear, was thus a turning point of the Gazala Battle as the batteries took a deadly toll on the enemy. Thus, the Commonwealth overwhelming tank strength prior to the start of the Axis operation had been eliminated. Rommel's war diary also remarked the positive role played by the Axis artillery during Operation Aberdeen: "In the face of heavy British pressure, their forces in this sector were several times stronger than ours, the Ariete fell right back to the Army artillery lines, where the British attack came to a halt under concentrated artillery fire."[76]

The next day *Ariete* and 21st Panzer mopped up the Cauldron of any enemy troops that had not been able to escape bringing the total tally of captured soldiers to 3,100 along with 96 artillery guns and 37 anti-tank guns seized from the enemy. On 7 June *Ariete*'s losses were 95 dead, 247 wounded, 102 tanks (of which 30 were repairable) and a seven *semoventi*.[77]

Rommel on the 7th ordered *Ariete* to take forward positions within the Cauldron and therefore *V Battaglione/ 8º Bersaglieri* was deployed between Trigh Capuzzo and Trigh Hacheim, while the *XII Battaglione/8º Bersaglieri* took positions at Bir el Harmat. The *132º Reggimento Carristi* stood in between the two units. *Ariete* would face in the upcoming days several more assaults by the 7th Armoured Division, as its advanced position was to become a thorn in the enemy's side. On the 8th several tank units from the 7th Armoured Division lunged forward against the *V Battaglione* positions forcing it to pull back to the west of Trigh Hacheim.

Bir Harmat

Then on 10 June 1942 *Ariete*'s *132º Reggimento Artiglieria Corazzata* faced a renewed attempt this time by the 4th Armoured Brigade, which was later reputed by *Ariete*'s commander De Stefanis to be one of the most powerful enemy attacks made against the Cauldron positions. The report mentions that the operation began with a large-scale artillery preparation by more than 100 heavy guns against *Ariete*'s positions and was followed up with an armoured thrust by up to forty enemy vehicles (thirty M3 Grant and ten M3 Stuart of 1st and 6th Royal Tank Regiment).

But as the tanks came forward, they were met almost immediately by heavy counter fire provided by antitank and self-propelled weapons which together with the barrage put forth by the field artillery positioned further back promptly faced down the enemy attack. Within minutes the Commonwealth tanks were in disarray. Several tanks were shot to pieces by the artillery guns and especially by 90mm gun projectiles as stated in 1st Royal Tank Regiment official history: "On June the 10th while acting as left flank guard to the remainder of the Brigade, the Regiment ran into a line of anti-tank guns at Bir Harmat and in a few minutes more than a dozen Grants were blazing furiously, besides 2 or 3 Honeys that had also been

---

75 Michael Carver, *Tobruk*, p. 205.
76 Basil Liddell Hart, *The Rommel Papers*, p. 216.
77 Mario Montanari, *Le Operazioni in Africa Settentrionale*, Vol. III, Part I, p. 249.

knocked out."⁷⁸ The 6th Royal Tank Regiment, who was also involved in the day's fighting on the right flank of the tank attack also sustained losses due to artillery fire. Its war diary reports the following:

> Regiment reached area west of unnamed BIR 382409 and came under fire from enemy tanks and anti-tank guns. C Squadron on left, B Squadron on right, A Squadron watching flanks.
> 09100 C Squadron pushed forward to engage enemy tanks.
> 0915 One enemy tank set on fire.
> 0940 Heavy fire from 88mm battery to left flank, two Grants knocked out.
> 0950 1 Grant and 1 Honey knocked out and another enemy tank set on fire. Very heavy and accurate fire from 88s, caused Regiment to withdraw slightly. Battery RHA gave support and engaged the enemy guns.
> 1030 Tank attack reported coming in on 1st Royal Tank Regiment on left. C Squadron moved round quickly to give support.
> 1100 Patrol of A Squadron sent out to look at 2 burning Grants and try and locate crews, driven off by anti-tank fire.
> 1400 Some crews of the tanks knocked out in the morning walked in and reported that Italian infantry had been sent to destroy the damaged tanks and presumably had captured Capt. RS Kemp, 2Lt Williams and 2Lt Wilkinson (wounded) and some of the crews. Remainder of the day was spent in this area, some slight shelling. After dark Regiment withdrew and leaguered some 3 miles back.
> Losses 3 Grants, 2 Stuarts.⁷⁹

The Italian post battle report asserts that twenty-eight tanks were destroyed and were reported to be smoldering in front of their positions. In turn *Ariete* had suffered 7 dead, 23 injured and 24 tanks had been hit by enemy fire and only some of them could be salvaged. *Ariete*'s action was mentioned in *Comando Supremo*'s war bulletin no. 742 of 12 June 1942: "... An attack put forth by British armoured forces north of Bir Hacheim was broken up by the *Ariete* Division. Its artillery guns put down a highly effective barrage by firing their weapons at point blank range of the enemy tanks. The artillery halted the attack on its tracks."⁸⁰ Rommel reported that: "In the morning, the Ariete suffered an attack by some 40 tanks at its strongpoint southwest of the supply route crossroads. The attack was fought off by the *Ariete* and the 15th Light Division with the destruction without loss of 25 enemy tanks."⁸¹

On the night of 10 June General de Stefanis reported that *Ariete*'s soldiers "had fought very well," while with the German divisions located on both flanks the degree of collaboration and coordination during the enemy attack "had been continuous and immediate throughout the

---

78 *1st Royal Tank Regiment History* <http://www.1rtr.net/1955%20Handbook%20RTR.html> (accessed 21 November 2018).
79 *6th Royal Tank Regiment History* <http://www.warlinks.com/armour/6th_royal_tank/6rtr_42.php> (accessed 21 November 2018).
80 Mario Montanari, *Le operazioni in Africa settentrionale*, Vol. III, Part I, p. 250.
81 John Philmott, *Rommel in his own Words*, p. 107.

combat action."[82] He also had very positive words for the newly arrived X *Battaglione Carri Medi* by stating: "In the victorious battles at Trig Capuzzo – Trig Bir Hacheim – Enver Bey, X Battaglione Carri M.14/41 has several times saved the day in situations that seemed to be already compromised. The unit was one our strongest elements and could be relied upon extensively."[83] According to historian Nicola Pignato the recently introduced *semoventi* also played a key role during this operation supporting the artillery arm in repelling the attack. The *Cannone da 90/53* along with the *Semovente da 75* represented the Italian response to the 75mm gun of the Grant tanks.[84]

Bir el Hacheim Final Conquer

Meanwhile the siege of Bir el Hacheim continued throughout the first ten days of June. Once the Axis troops had recovered from the first failed attempt on 3 June they managed to reach the minefields and there began a prolonged struggle to open gaps to get closer to the fort. British jock columns attempted several times during the day to interfere with the work of the German and Italian combat engineers, but the prompt action of the *VIII Battaglione Bersaglieri*, which patrolled the minefield areas throughout the day to counter the British mobile forces, heavily interfered with these forays. Despite the extensive work of the combat engineers the numerous attempts made by the troops to enter the fort were repelled by heavy fire. Of the siege of Bir el Hacheim Rommel wrote that: "The French fought in a skillfully planned system of field positions and small defense works-slit trenches, small pill boxes, machine guns and anti-tanks gun nests-all surrounded by dense minefields."[85]

Following the failed attempts by the 90th Leicht supported by tanks, on the 7th Rommel issued an order for a more massive attack which involved both 90th Leicht and *Trieste*. The latter was to see action on two columns: on the right the 65° *Reggimento* and the *XI Battaglione Carri Medi*, and on the left flank the 66° *Reggimento* with some armoured support were to conquer the northern ridge of Bir el Hacheim, which was located three kilometers north of the main fort. Meanwhile the 90th Leicht was also tasked with continuing its advance upon the main enemy position. This time Rommel also deployed a special artillery unit with 88mm guns whose role was to target the enemy defenses and breach them in several sectors. The unit was to be backed up by combat engineers and infantry units from the *Trieste* who were assigned to widen the gaps created by the artillery. At 0600 on 8 June the attack began in earnest but from the start it was carried out in such a disharmonious fashion, mainly due to the strong enemy reaction, that it did not have chances to succeed. The right flank column even though supported by several *semoventi* had trouble advancing through the gaps given the extensive enemy fire and its II/65° could not keep up with the I/65° which infiltrated the second minefield belt. Despite a large deployment of forces and numerous attacks by the German Stukas, the attack stalled and by the end of the day the troops had only been able to advance a depth of just one kilometer. On 9 June, the attacks were resumed but once again the troops were unable to proceed beyond the minefields

---

82   Mario Montanari, *Le operazioni in Africa settentrionale*, Vol. III, Part I, p. 250
83   Ibid.
84   Nicola Pignato, *Italian Armoured Vehicles of World War Two, p. 31.*
85   Basil Liddell Hart, *The Rommel Papers*, p. 213.

and were targeted by the enemy artillery for a great part of the day sustaining considerable losses. On the 10th the Axis troops further surrounded the fortress closing several escape routes to the French garrison. Thus, during the night between 10 and 11 June the French forces (2,700 soldiers) managed to flee from the fortress and reach the Commonwealth lines. This signaled that the siege was over and the Axis finally captured Bir Hacheim.

Once the fort had been seized, Rommel focused again upon the Cauldron. His battlefront along the Gazala line was now secure as all of the major enemy infantry boxes had been overcome. After the enemy had bled profusely and lost its armoured numerical supremacy, Rommel aimed to inflict the *coup de grace*. To this end, on 11 June, Rommel thrusted the 15th Panzer Division and 90th Leicht toward El Adem. These troops overran signal and command posts of the 7th Armoured Division and 5th Indian Division. The following day he ordered all the mechanized units to concentrate for the battle in the Cauldron. While the 29th Indian Infantry Brigade managed to hold off the enemy on the El Adem line, the 2nd and 4th Armoured Brigades were struck and were pushed back by the 15th Panzer and 21st Panzer Division. The Italian units experienced stronger enemy opposition. As *Trieste's* tanks were en route to the designated area they were harried by several Crusaders from 3rd County of London Yeomanry and Grants from the 4th Hussars. Together these British armoured units engaged *Divisione Trieste's* twenty-five medium tanks. As the Italian tanks outnumbered the British formation and also enjoyed the support of several anti-tank guns their combined firepower forced the enemy armour back. According to the unit's war diary Captain Buxton, of 3rd County of London Yeomanry, and his crew were captured and remained prisoner until they managed to escape the following day:

> At first light, enemy tanks were seen in the area 381409, but orders were given by 22nd Armoured Brigade that we were not to leave the ridge. About midday Capt. SL Buxton was ordered to carry out a reconnaissance due South from the ridge and to investigate a report of an enemy column in the area 171 388405. He reported 'no movement seen' and Brigadier WG Carr, DSO, ordered him to remain where he was and await the arrival of a Squadron of the 4th Hussars (Grants), which had been given a special task. Capt. Buxton met this party which was subsequently caught by many Italian tanks and destroyed. Capt. Buxton and his crew were taken prisoner but escaped the following day.[86]

On the same day *Ariete* too was also ordered to move forward. But before committing itself to Rommel's offensive it was called upon to eliminate an advanced enemy position that in the previous days had withstood several Axis attacks. *Tenente Alberto Coglitore XII Battaglione/8° Reggimento* recalled:

> Before resuming the advance toward east, the division was ordered to deal with an enemy strongpoint situated at the crossroads between Trigh Capuzzo and Trigh Hackeim. Our deployment saw the Bersaglieri in the forefront flanked by the tanks and the self-propelled guns. The operation began at dawn on 12 June ... Smokescreens were deployed by the enemy in front of our positions in preparation of the attack. Since this was the first time

---

86 War Diary of the 3rd County of Yeomanry, Libya Operations, wo 169/1399, National Archives, Kew.

that the XII Battaglione was faced with this new tactic it was placed on high alert in order to push back the enemy. At first there was this distant noise of motor vehicles that as time passed it got louder and louder. It was clear that enemy tanks were fast approaching but we could not see them because of the massive screen. We were all anxious about what unfolding in front of us because of the smokescreen which blocked our view. On the right flank of the 8th Compagnia Bersaglieri there were several medium tanks and semoventi deployed. As soon as the enemy tanks emerged from the artificial fog, the armour opened fire followed by our anti-tank guns. All of our 47mm guns, followed by machine guns, mortars and rifles were concentrated against the enemy tanks and the infantry advancing behind them. A wall of fire prevented the enemy from advancing any further and the latter was then forced to retreat … After the smoke further subsided we observed in the distance several smoking enemy tanks that had been immobilized. Several dense, acre columns of black smoke rose to the sky. [87]

On 13 June Commonwealth troops and armoured units were assembled in the rear position of Knightsbridge and Rommel aimed at dislodging them by deploying 15th and 21st Panzer, *Ariete* and *Trieste* as a concentrated tank force. Rommel's plan aimed at neutralizing the Commonwealth forces from the flanking positions (Maabus er-Rigel, el-Adem and Hagiag er-Raml) first, before thrusting forward to the main enemy position of Knightsbridge. Maabus er-Rigel was occupied by 2nd Scots Guards and it was to be attacked by the 21st Panzer Division. The el-Adem position was to be dealt with by the 15th Panzer Division, *Ariete* and *Trieste* Divisions, while Hagiag er-Raml box was to be assaulted by the 90th Leicht. Initially all three attacking columns were bogged down by Commonwealth anti-tank fire which caused several tank losses. However, these units persisted and the first breakthrough for the Axis forces came after the 21st Panzer Division swept away enemy resistance at Maabus er-Rigel. "The slaughter of British tanks went on. One after the other of the 120 or so which they probably now had left remained lying on the battlefield."[88] The Axis artillery was also brought forward in support of the tanks, including *Ariete's XII Bersaglieri* which recorded the following: "On the 13th we were again involved in heavy fighting in the same area. The deadly fire of our artillery once again wreaked havoc amongst the enemy tank crews. The latter, decimated in several successive combat actions, abandoned the Knightsbridge position, the vital position until then held by the British."[89] This opened the way for a major enveloping attack against Knightsbridge which however never materialized because the Commonwealth troops, aware that the flanking positions had fallen, evacuated it. Thus, after a series of armoured forays against Commonwealth positions and prolonged tank against tank combat engagements, the Axis finally forced the enemy from the position which was evacuated on 14 June. On the evening of 13 June the Axis command reported the capture of 3,100 prisoners, 115 tanks destroyed or damaged, 96 artillery pieces and 37 anti-tank guns.

The tank battles of 13 June had further seriously eroded the tank strength of the Commonwealth, which was now pulling back. Most importantly, with control of the Cauldron, Rommel had seized the key coastal road that led to Tobruk.

87 Giulio Bedeschi, *Fronte d'Africa*, p. 135.
88 Basil Liddell Hart, *The Rommel Papers*, p. 221.
89 Giulio Bedeschi, *Fronte d'Africa*, p. 135.

The post battle report of the *Ariete* Division mentions that the fighting for the medium tanks in the Cauldron became more complex and difficult because of the heavier M3 Grant and some Pilot tanks deployed by the Commonwealth, which even troubled the more robust German units and even the crews of the 75mm armed tanks.

The great disparity between the new heavy and medium American/British armour and the Italian medium series tanks was a factor in the battle which was countered by adopting more unpredictable tank maneuvers. Because of the longer range and greater durability of the enemy tanks, the Italian tank units had to ultimately change their tactics when engaging them. The only way for the anti-tank artillery or the medium tanks to properly fight against these bigger units was for the artillery guns to be concentrated in advanced positions to be within range of the enemy positions. The medium tanks too were forced to increase their maneuverability while fighting against the Grants by always moving quickly and hence becoming less of a target for them. While advancing the medium tanks had to zig zag across the desert to prevent offering the enemy a good clean shot. To put these larger tanks out of action, Italian tanks were forced to close in against them and focus their fire upon the tracks or the underbelly of the tanks which were their most thin skinned parts. Although, the strategy was at times successful, it exposed the medium tanks to a higher loss ratios than before because they were forced to get as close to the enemy tanks as possible to have any effect upon them. This also exposed Italian tanks to the counter battery fire of the enemy artillery which was often successful in immobilizing both the M.13 and the M.14 tanks. The *semoventi* on the other hand performed much better than the tanks largely due to their greater firepower (75mm versus a 47mm gun) and range. The *semoventi da 75/18* were designed with the German StuG III self-propelled gun in mind and they had a similar combat role. Deployed extensively during the Axis counter-offensive, the new weapon proved to be more effective than the Italian tanks with its 75mm gun that could pierce 70mm of armour at 500 meters or less and thus could penetrate M3 Grant tanks.[90]

An Italian post battle report stated that the *semoventi* "represented an important step forward despite their shortcomings, like the low muzzle velocity of their guns, insufficient range especially in comparison with the British guns, and excessively low speed when moving in rough terrain."[91]

Despite its limitations (namely its cramped interior and the insufficiently powerful engine in the M.40 and M41 variants), the *Semovente da 75/18* proved successful both in a direct support role and in anti-tank role; its main advantages, other than its sheer firepower, was in its lower silhouette that made it more difficult to hit.

Finally, the fear of the new more powerful American M3 Grant tanks had forced the Italian High command to transfer several gun units, previously used as anti-aircraft and naval defense in Tripoli, to the *Ariete* Division. The German 88mm Flak 36 guns were rushed to the front and were used effectively in the May and June period to bolster the artillery arm in its combat actions against Commonwealth tanks. The *Ariete*'s artillery, comprised of its field guns, the Italian and German anti-tank guns and the *semoventi* units, were to play an important role in campaign of mid-1942.

---

90 Pier Paolo Battistelli and Filippo Cappellano, *Italian Medium Tanks*, p. 19.
91 Ibid., p. 36.

Tobruk

The final attack on Tobruk began on 18 June 1942 as the Axis noose around the port city began to progressively tighten more and more. The Tobruk garrison, commanded by Major-General H. Klopper, at the time was comprised mainly of the 2nd South African Division, 201st Guards Division, 32nd British Armoured Brigade and the 11th Indian Infantry Brigade. Klopper had at his disposal approximately 35,000 men and a total of 2,000 military vehicles, including fifty light and medium tanks. The garrison also had plenty of supplies that were designed to last for over three months. The operation began after the *Trieste* Division had taken possession of the road that from the city led to the port, a move that isolated the enemy garrison. This together with the reduction of Commonwealth combat power after the Gazala Line battles presented Rommel with the unique opportunity to finally seize Tobruk. Because of the successful operation conducted by Axis combat engineers, Rommel issued orders for an attack against the Commonwealth positions in which all the armoured units of the Axis were to play a part. The infantry based XXI Italian Corps, which was given several tanks as support, was assigned to make a feint attack in the southwest of Tobruk, while DAK and *XX Corpo d'Armata* were to make the decisive attack on the fortress. The point of penetration in the southeast was to be bombed by all the German-Italian air forces available. When the infantry and combat engineers had overcome the fortified lines, and decommissioned the lanes in the minefield, DAK was to thrust past the crossroad to the harbor and capture the Via Balbia to the west. In conjunction with the DAK, *XX Corpo d'Armata* was to drive through to Ras el Medauar in the rear of the South African positions with the task of breaking through the enemy defenses at Redoubts 49 and 57. The two fortified positions targeted by the Italians were held by 2nd Cameroon Highlanders with 800 soldiers, six 6-pdr anti-tank guns and four batteries of field artillery. Thus, according to Rommel's plan "The group making the main attack consisted of the Afrika Korps and the XX Italian Corps."[92] Although still a formidable position, Tobruk's overall defenses were not as powerful as in mid-1941 when the Axis troops had been easily rebuffed by the Australians. In 1942 some of the fiercest Australian battalions had been deployed elsewhere while some of the defensive positions had been covered up by the strong desert winds while some had decayed over time. In addition, some of the anti-tank mines had been deployed elsewhere and some were no longer effective. Moreover, the RAF's Desert Air Force had been forced back to airbases that were further away from Tobruk and thus was unable to interfere with the Axis bombing raids on the fortress. Lastly, the Commonwealth garrison no longer had the number of heavy guns that were deployed in its defense in 1941 and at its disposal there were primarily about forty 2-pdr and fifteen 6-pdr guns.

As the Italians began to mount their attack against Tobruk, Rommel also deployed the newly arrived *Littorio* Division to the south of Tobruk to guard against a Commonwealth attempt to relieve the garrison. After the Yugoslavian campaign *Littorio* was transferred back to Italy where it trained for a long period in Parma and Reggio Emilia. The unit was re-equipped and most of its combat elements spent most of their time in improving the reconnaissance function which was particularly lacking during prior campaigns and especially during the French campaign. The reorganization of the unit lasted until November 1941. During this time (on 17 June 1941)

---

92 Basil Liddell Hart, *The Rommel Papers*, p. 229.

the *Littorio* received the 133° *Reggimento Carristi*, which was slated to take the place of the 33rd Armoured Regiment. The former was based on the X, XI, and XII *Battaglioni Carri Medi* all equipped with M.13/40 tanks and later in 1942 equipped with M.14/41 tanks.

The unit was then transferred piecemeal to North Africa beginning in January 1942. Initially *Littorio* was used to reinforce existing under strength divisions. In late spring, the X *Battaglione Carri Medi* was transferred to *Ariete*, while the XI was transferred to *Trieste* Division. The XII *Battaglione Carri Medi* was the last to reach the shores of Africa (March 1942) and was the only one at the time equipped with M.14/41 tanks. This unit arrived in Africa in a piecemeal fashion and on 13 December 1941 two Italian ships that were transporting some of its detachments were torpedoed in the gulf of Taranto and suffered the loss of thirty-six dead and several pieces of equipment were also lost. In March *LI Battaglione Carri Medi* joined *Littorio* along with the reconnaissance unit *Reggimento Lancieri di Novara* equipped with L.6 tanks.

Therefore, in mid-1942, *Littorio*'s was not at full strength. It had trained extensively upon arriving to North Africa, as some of its battalions had been reassigned. Commanded by General Bitossi, *Littorio* was to reinforce the armoured corps and finally in early June the unit was incorporated in the *XX Corpo d'Armata*. On 2 June, it was ordered to be deployed near Tobruk but at the time, according to the Italian official history, it had the strength not of an armoured division but of a tactical reconnaissance unit. It could count upon the 12° *Reggimento Bersaglieri*, XII *Battaglione Carri Medi* with thirty M.14/41 tanks, LI *Battaglione Carri Medi* with thirty-six M.13/41 tanks and a battery of 75/27 guns. Given the fact that in the past Rommel had used Italian units at will and had often asked of them more than they could deliver with their limited forces and few equipment, the Italian High Command was quick to point out to the German general that *Littorio* should not be deployed as a standard armoured unit as its collective strength only equalled that of a tank battalion. Additionally, because it only had sixty-six tanks and no engineer or sapper unit and no true reconnaissance capabilities, it could not be compared to a German armoured division. But Rommel, sensing that the enemy was off-guard and in disarray, demanded more troops to continue the offensive and *Littorio* as a result was thrown into the fight with its limited strength.

On 17 June, the DAK war diary reports of an initial maneuver towards Tobruk by the Axis mechanized forces to initiate the siege of the port city:

> To win and secure the necessary protection of the German rear, prior to the proposed attack against Tobruk, forces from the DAK and the Panzerdivision Ariete advanced in an easterly direction towards Gambut. This would eliminate any chances of the enemy air force being able to operate from airfields around Gambut. The German forces pushed the 7th Tank Division back along their whole front and then reached the area south of Gambut. The operations continued into the evening hours.[93]

While the tanks approached the port city, the Axis field artillery which ringed the fortress opened up a tremendous fire that forced the defenders to keep their heads down. This was followed by coordinated dive bombing attacks by the Luftwaffe and *Regia Aeronautica* that according to first-hand accounts were so fierce that they greatly destabilized the enemy defenses.

---

93 DAK War Diary <http://samilitaryhistory.org/vol076jm.html> (accessed 2 March 2018).

Several embrasures caved in, while fires began in several buildings. The initial shock caused much confusion in the ranks of the defenders which allowed the sappers and the special infantry units to go in and begin to decommission the minefield. In the sector were the German 15th Panzer Division was operating the *13ª Batteria* with its 88mm guns was called in by two German Generals to help soften up several fortified posts that stood in the way of the German pioneers. Within twenty minutes the three forts were knocked out of action and the pioneers were able to move further inside the defensive perimeter. As the Italian Official History states in the sector held by *Ariete*'s units such tight coordination witnessed in the German sector between the pioneer units and the divisional HQ of 15th Panzer could never have been achieved since the latter possessed much better communication systems that enabled its elements to work closely together. In the *Ariete/Trieste* sector things moved decisively more slowly. In the Italian sector the attack began with a slow start. This forced *Ariete*'s *8° Reggimento Bersaglieri* units to begin moving forward when it was already late in the morning. The troops were observed as they advanced and they were targeted by strong enemy fire. In one hour, they managed to decommission a section of the minefield in front of the Camerons' positions and then penetrated the forward defenses and finally arriving to the antitank ditch. The *Bersaglieri* units were then dispatched at the head of the attacking columns to deal with the antitank screen. But since the enemy was concentrated in mutually supportive strong points the battle became extremely costly as pockets of enemy resistance had to be overcome one by one after costly close quarter combat. The fighting was particularly bitter in the sector held by *Trieste* Division. Here "one infantry battalion was to operate at the forefront supported by a company of medium tanks and one of 81mm mortars. In turn, this first advanced guard was followed by another infantry battalion which was to remain in the second echelon with its trucks at the ready in order to exploit any initial breach. The infantry, even though supported by the artillery, could not move forward until the combat engineers had cleared a lane. Even the tanks could not move forward against an area where the minefields were backed up by several anti-tank guns. Despite strong enemy fire the operation got underway, but Trieste was unable to advance very far as the minefields and the blocking fire of the enemy artillery impeded any progress. At around 1030 the combat engineers had run out of explosives and Trieste's operation had come at a standstill."[94]

By this time after a massive air bombardment the German 15th and 21st Panzer divisions had already bypassed the antitank screen and the ditch and were heading toward fort Pilastrino and the port. At the fort the German advance however was halted by pinpoint British artillery fire which managed to destroy several tanks and forced the infantry to go to ground.

At 1200 *Ariete* also reported that the enemy was putting up considerable opposition but that a new attack would be attempted following another preparatory bombardment. After a second artillery barrage, *Ariete* renewed the attempt to overcome the determined opposition of the Camerons. But even this assault was broken up by considerable enemy fire. The infantry was pinned down by the enemy's machine guns and mortars, while the tanks also could not break the enemy's determined resistance. By mid-afternoon however the German advance had resumed after having breached the enemy defenses at fort Pilastrino and *Ariete* finally penetrated the fortress behind them thereby bypassing the Camerons' positions.

---

94 Dattilo Ciampini, 'La fanteria motorizzata tra modello ed esperienze: la Trieste in Africa settentrionale 1941-1942', *Quaderno di storia militare*, Anno 2009, p. 170.

Thus, on 21 June *Ariete* was inside the Commonwealth defensive perimeter but had still not overcome the Camerons, which although surrounded did not surrender. The latter were not aware that many of their comrades had already surrendered and were still fighting with great vigor. Their willingness to resist was in full display when at 0800 three M.14/41 tanks advanced toward the Scots' positions only to be knocked out by blistering antitank fire. Shortly thereafter, another three tanks were dispatched forward but when they came within a couple of hundreds of yards of the Camerons they too came under heavy fire and turned back. The attack was therefore called off until the next day.

The next day, 22nd June, a *Bersagliere* from *Ariete* Division recalled the massive deployment of Axis weapons that supported the siege and surrounded the port city: "I had never seen anything like this. The Axis forces had concentrated in front of Tobruk a most impressive number of guns of all types and sizes which were hammering the enemy positions repeatedly … In front of us I could clearly see the enemy position where the Tommies had lined up waiting for us to attack. I could clearly see their khaki colored helmets and the soldiers deployed in the trenches. We waited with trepidation the signal to move forward, while in other sectors the battle was being waged very fiercely as we could hear the sounds of heavy explosions. Then just after 1200, as we were to start the infantry attack, we received the counter order whereby the enemy had surrendered after a bold move by the Axis tanks."[95]

On the 22nd the Camerons finally realized that they were surrounded and surrendered. The war diary of the *132° Reggimento Carristi* observed:

> In two days of very hard fighting the enemy fortified position of Tobruk was finally overtaken by the combined effort of the Axis forces. Thanks to the timely collaboration of the air forces, the tanks, charged with dismantling the enemy's main two strong points, acted decisively by aggressively charging forward. Many tanks and crews were sacrificed during this battle but Ariete ultimately achieved its final goal. Many enemy positions have been literally smashed by our tanks opening fire at close range.[96]

The same maneuver is reported in the DAK war diary:

> The attack of the XX AK came to a standstill in front of the first bunker line, after crossing the minefield. To prevent further heavy losses, the Panzerarmee Ariete was withdrawn through the penetration sector of the DAK, and immediately deployed north of the bunker line to attack from the west.[97]

When the war weary, exhausted Axis infantry troops entered the fortress they were surprised when they found the enemy warehouses stocked full of foods of all kinds:

> There were stacks of tinned beer: huts, bursting with pure white flour, cigarettes, tobacco and jam; gallons of whiskey; priceless tinned food of all kinds; and tons of khaki clothing-that

---

95   Giulio Bedeschi, *Fronte d'Africa*, p. 121.
96   Ufficio Storico, 'Relazione sul comportamento del 132° Reggimento Carri nei cicli operativi del 18/11/1941 al 03/07/1942 da me comandato', n. 5498, Enrico Maretti, 4 luglio 1942.
97   DAK War Diary <http://samilitaryhistory.org/vol076jm.html> (accessed on 18 January 2018).

magnificent khaki, which looked so heavy and was so light and cool to wear. The first comers (armoured detachments of Ariete, 15 Panzer Division and Trieste), swiftly hit on a vast store of shoes -gorgeous shoes, just like those that had occasionally been seen on prisoners, soft elegant suede shoes with thick rubber soles.[98]

Meanwhile *Littorio*, put in charge of blocking any enemy attempt to relieve the Tobruk garrison, also saw action during the operation. Its units exchanged heavy fire with the 7th Motor Brigade. Both sides, however, limited themselves to shell each other without attempting to overrun their respective positions with the armour. The M.14/41 tanks lined up as if they were ready to charge the enemy but it was a faint operation meant to throw off the British force. The latter reported that "it had been held off by considerable forces" [99] and thereby unable to relieve Tobruk.

Final Considerations

The Cauldron Battle seriously reduced Commonwealth combat power allowing Rommel to achieve his victory on the Gazala Line on 13-14 June and then his triumph with the capture of Tobruk. Historian Ronald Lewin asserted that the capture of Tobruk demonstrated how the Axis forces were by mid-1942 fighting together much more harmoniously than in the spring of 1941: "One should emphasize the group achievement, for through DAK had provided the armoured spearhead which tore the Tobruk defenses apart, the Italians – Ariete, Trieste, Brescia, Pavia had played an important supporting role."[100] Within the Italian units the artillery had played the most important role when it ringed the fortress and softened it up in preparation of the armoured /infantry attack. *Ariete* and *Trieste* also made important supporting contributions to the capture of Tobruk although the former failed to fully penetrate the enemy positions and trailed behind the DAK. Together with the destruction of numerous enemy tanks at Gazala, the capture of Tobruk was one of Rommel's most brilliant operations of the desert war. Its capture allowed the Axis to seize 32,000 prisoners, several artillery batteries and anti-tank guns, machine guns and a few Bren carriers. It's important to recognize that although the war booty was considerable, the Axis forces captured very few stocks of petrol (less than 2,000 tons). This meant that once again the *Panzerarmee* was totally reliant upon the Italian logistics network for its fuel, ammunition and food/water supply. Although, they had captured the port of Tobruk, this dependence was accentuated by the fact that the forward troops were now further than ever from their supply bases in Tripolitania, while the port of Tobruk only had the capacity to receive and process a fourth of the army's total needs.

Throughout the Gazala line campaign the Italian *XX Corpo d'armata* demonstrated its positive evolution vis a vis the earlier experience of the CAM, both in terms of tactics and the ability to use all its units in a more organized and harmonious fashion. Once again its main threat was represented by its artillery arm which in several days of fighting accounted itself well and played a role in debilitating the enemy's tank strength. Its armoured units were less effective although

---

98   Paolo Caccia-Dominioni, *El Alamein* (London: Allen and Urwin, 1962), p. 28.
99   Michael Carver, *Tobruk*, p. 129.
100 Ronald Lewin, *The Life and Death of the Afrika Korps*, pp. 136-137.

they were able to overcome several enemy infantry boxes mainly defended by 2-pdr guns and took part to several armoured counters in support of the German panzer units.

Contributions to the Axis victory at Tobruk and especially the role played by *Ariete* during operation Aberdeen is hardly mentioned by historians of the likes of Michael Carver, William Jackson or Ronald Lewin.[101] Only more recently historians such as John Gooch have highlighted this role when he argues: "Joining up, the two Italian divisions and the Germans fought off poorly coordinated British attempts to encircle them in their turn, the Ariete's artillery giving particularly a good account of itself."[102]

Although not decisive without the contribution of the German armour, *Ariete* and DAK artillery carried out an essential task. In turn, the important role of the Axis artillery enabled Rommel to achieve his victory at the Gazala line in the great clash of armour at the battle of Knightsbridge.[103]

While facing the heavy Matilda II tanks with 2-pdr guns in 1940 Italian infantry and artillery units had collapsed. Why did they not collapse in 1942 when the armoured army corps faced Grants with their 75mm guns? Especially when these tanks so much more powerful compared to even the more advanced Italian M.14/41 tanks? The Italian Official History ventures to state that improved battle field experience played a part together with the introduction of new weapons such as self-propelled artillery, and the batteries of 88mm and 90mm guns. Lastly the increased alertness due to new vehicles and combat groups by the armoured corps reconnaissance units also contributed to the final outcome.[104]

Perhaps mid-1942 was one of the most opportune times during the campaign to decide its final outcome because there was still a balance of power between Axis and Commonwealth troops. But Rommel was denied additional Panzer units and even if he had been properly reinforced it's not clear whether the Axis logistic and supply organization could have had the wherewithal to support a prolonged campaign supporting four or more divisions involved deep into Egypt.

As Liddell Hart correctly argued Hitler's focus during most of the German war effort between 1941 and 1945 was the conflict against the Soviet Union and not North Africa where Rommel's troops could have possibly achieved something more significant if he had only been equipped with more armour. The same point is made by historian Lucio Ceva who has argued that the Italian military dispersed its combat strength by participating to the invasion against the Soviet Union. He argues that even though North Africa was Italy's main theater of war, when the political authorities decided to send to Russia an entire army corps they automatically weakened an army that already was at a severe technical and equipment disadvantage against the Commonwealth. Ceva, for instance, argues that while armoured strength was concentrated in North Africa, Italy's most well equipped artillery units were dispatched to Russia. Thus,

---

101 For example Sir William Jackson, *The North African Campaign* (London: Batsford, 1975), p. 215: Rommel ordered the Ariete on the Aslagh feature to dig in..Lumsden did attack again with 2nd and 22nd Armoured Brigade Groups on 30 May but could find no way of penetrating the German anti-tank defenses without further heavy loss of tanks."
102 John Gooch, *Mussolini's War*, p. 308.
103 Both the British Official History and Michael Carver accounts, for example, ignored the role played by the Italian artillery during Operation Venezia.
104 Mario Montanari, *Le operazioni in Africa settentrionale*, vol. III, part I, pp. 331-334.

participation to Operation Barbarossa came at a steep price since it diluted rather than concentrated Italian combat strength. The field gun batteries of 210/22, 149/40, the German Krupp 149/28 and the 75/46 anti-aircraft guns that were deployed in Russia by the Italian troops, for example, could have been useful in North Africa and the same could be said for some of the motorized units of *ARMIR* which were also deployed during Operation Barbarossa. In addition, the Italian troops in Russia absorbed 16,700 trucks, 4,470 motorcycles, and 1,130 tractors to tow artillery pieces which could have been of critical importance in mid-1942, the high point of Axis involvement in the North African campaign. Ansaldo, for instance, fast tracked the production of thirty heavy *semoventi* da 90 in 1942 which were specifically built to operate against the Soviet T-34 tanks but would have been extremely useful in North Africa. Every gun, hand grenade or rifle that was destined to the ARMIR was taken away from the army in North Africa. This is probably the biggest mistake made by Cavallero and the Italian High Command which did not oppose Mussolini's desire to prop the Italian position in the Soviet Union. "Cavallero," Ceva argues, "sacrificed guns, trucks, ammunition and anti-tank weapons in Russia. The Soviet troops not only trapped in a sea of mud 100,000 Italian soldiers, but also halted the German/Italian advance by impeding it from reaching the Suez Canal. It had destroyed six Italian divisions that lacked trucks and were abandoned during the retreat from the El Alamein line. The Italian army in Russia served the interests of the British more than the troops that came from India, Syria and Iraq in support of the Eighth Army."[105]

---

105 Lucio Ceva, 'ARMIR', *Rivista Italiana di Storia Militare*, N. 7, 1991.

6

El Alamein

What Next?

After the capture of Tobruk the Axis leaders in North Africa not having a unified command structure disagreed on what to do next. The issue whether to continue the attack or not divided Bastico and Rommel, whereby the latter wanted to continue the pursuit of the Commonwealth forces while the former urged caution and privileged the takeover of Malta prior and a steady buildup of the force in North Africa to further advances into Egypt. In Bastico's view, which represented the wishes of *Comando Supremo*, Malta had to be neutralized first or else it would pose a major threat and trap Rommel's army beyond its supply lines deep in Egypt. Kesserling was the first to meet Rommel when he flew into Tobruk on 21 June with the aim to convince Rommel that the conquest of Malta now took priority. He spoke about the need to rest the Axis troops after weeks of constant fighting and of transferring some of the *Luftwaffe* units for a focus against Malta. In Kesserling's view, Malta had to be conquered to secure the Axis supply lines and to enable the *Panzerarmee* to advance further in an ordinary way. Cavallero was not present at this meeting but on the 20th he had written a letter to Hitler with Mussolini's blessings in which he stated: "The action on Malta is more necessary than ever."[1] He also demanded that the German command put aside 70,000 of petrol for the Malta operation. On the 22nd Ciano's diary reports that: "The Duce is in good spirits and intends to go to Egypt."[2] On the same day Rommel, who by then had been promoted by Hitler to *Generalfeldmarschall*, met Bastico near Bardia and argued that with the fall of Tobruk British morale had collapsed and now was the time to pursue Commonwealth troops all the way to Alexandria. Bastico did not share Rommel's optimism stating that "we need to stop on the Sollum Halfaya line."[3] Rommel's enthusiasm was apparently shared by Hitler who wrote to Mussolini stating that the Axis troops had a unique opportunity to cause the collapse of the British position in Egypt. Then on the 25th of June Bastico, Cavallero and Kesserling met Rommel in Derna in an attempt to convince him to halt his advance. Concerning this meeting Carlo Cavallero, the son of Ugo Cavallero, stated that the following transpired:

---

1 Mario Montanari, *The Three Battles of El Alamein* (Rome: Ufficio Storico, 1991), p. 15.
2 Ibid.
3 Ibid., p. 22.

Kesserling and my father attempted to convince Rommel that because of the long distance separating from their objectives, an advance under such conditions would not allow the Axis to fully take advantage of its success. In fact, Rommel would face a refreshed enemy close to its bases, with a reduced and ragged Axis army that would be dangerously low in supplies. Kesserling pointed to the difficulty of effectively supporting the Axis ground forces with the new planes he had, hundreds of kilometers from their bases. The enemy would have the advantage of being very close to his own bases. He concluded by stating that: 'I am very skeptical of a deep advance. If I am given the order, I shall obey, but the end result in this case is very much in doubt.'[4]

Knowing that Hitler and Mussolini, who had by then come around to Rommel's position, both favored a continuation of the offensive, the three military leaders came to an agreement that the *Panzerarmee* would advance to El Alamein and there halt and assess the situation. Then in an effort to torpedo the invasion of Malta on 26 June, the German High Command informed the Italians that it could not provide the fuel for Operation Hercules. This likely reflected Hitler's ambivalent posture toward Operation Hercules and his general skepticism toward airborne operations. Prior operations such as the one against Crete, had caused heavy casualties, while the campaign against the Soviet Union was absorbing great amounts of resources and the fuel could not be spared. Hitler was also influenced by Rommel's argument that the captured supplies, including the fuel supplies (the amounts of which were not clear at the time to both the German High Command and *Comando Supremo)*, could sustain the *Panzerarmee's* invasion of Egypt. At that point even within the German High Command there were strong disagreements over which course to take. The German Navy and especially its head Admiral Raeder were proponents of a Mediterranean strategy aimed at taking Malta and the Suez area in order to break the deadlock. The *Luftwaffe* too was being challenged from its multi-front commitments arguing that it did not have the strength to neutralize both Malta, whilst also providing air cover to the *Panzerarmee* in Egypt. But it appears that Hitler favored the pursuit of the Commonwealth troops although he was not willing to commit major additional resources in North Africa. After communicating that the Germans could not undertake Operation Hercules, Hitler agreed with Rommel's assessment of the situation in Egypt, that the Commonwealth was on the run while the Axis was in the ascendancy, and that the theater was ripe for exploitation. Embracing this enthusiastic view of the campaign while also downplaying the advice of his generals, Mussolini ultimately authorized Rommel to continue his offensive. Thus, against the strong opinions of Kesserling and Cavallero, who opposed further advances into Egypt given the inability of the Axis inland transportation system to fully resupply the *Panzerarmee*, Rommel had successfully appealed to Hitler and Mussolini directly but did so over the head of his superiors thus in violation of the unity of command principle[5] and had ultimately received the green light to continue his offensive operation. Rommel ultimately won the argument by bypassing Bastico, Cavallero and Kesserling and gaining permission to advance by Mussolini and Hitler: "I requested the Duce, immediately after the capture of Tobruk, to lift the restrictions on the Panzer Army's

---

4   Santi Corvaja, *Hitler & Mussolini: The Secret Meetings* (New York: Enigma, 2002), p. 206.
5   Naumann, Klaus, 'Afterword' in Charles Messenger (ed.), *Rommel: Leadership Lessons from the Desert Fox* (New York: Palgrave Macmillan, 2008).

freedom of operation and allow us to advance into Egypt."[6] In Rommel's view it was essential to do everything possible to invade Egypt and bring about a Commonwealth defeat before any additional major shipments of arms and men could arrive from Britain or the United States.

Mersa Matruh

Based on intelligence reports that indicated a general weakening of the Commonwealth forces after the fall of Tobruk, Rommel decided to press his advantage and attempt to capture Egypt and deal a fatal blow to Britain in North Africa. Despite being on the defensive after the loss of Tobruk, it was estimated that Britain could resupply the troops at a much faster rate than the Axis given the proximity of its supply bases to the North African frontline and the strong support from America. It was partly for this reason alone that Rommel did not want to give the enemy the time to reorganize and replenish frontline troops and opted for a quick sally against the El Alamein line.

Auchinleck had been preparing defenses at Mersa Matruh, a fortress in the desert in front of the El Alamein line, since the fall of Tobruk. The 10th Indian Infantry Division was deployed in the fortress, while the 50th (Northumbrian) Infantry Division was positioned east of the fortress. Auchinleck instructed both commanders to offer the strongest possible resistance and to recur to flanking infantry and armoured attacks to push back any enemy infiltration. He had also reorganized the armoured units and had begun the process of emulating some of the German combat methods of pooling armoured and anti-tank resources.

The New Zealand Official History aptly observes that:

> Auchinleck held that the Germans used their tanks as the decisive weapon in close co-operation with the other arms, while the Italian tanks were used either against unarmoured troops or to cover Afrika Korps' flanks or rear. The British Grant tank was the equivalent of the German types and the Crusader, Stuart, and Valentine were the counterparts of the Italian tanks. In his reorganization Auchinleck concentrated the Grants in 1st Armoured Division, whose main tactical functions thereafter would be to neutralize the German amour and to take part in decisive attacks with infantry and with the Valentines, which were not as mobile as the Crusader, Stuart, and Italian tanks. In defense and attack, the division was to be supported by the greatest possible concentration of artillery.[7]

His reorganization effort would not stop Rommel at Mersa Matruh but would ultimately later check him at El Alamein.

As the Axis, mechanized forces advanced toward the fortress they were heavily harassed by the RAF which inflicted considerable casualties and destroyed much of the Germans supply columns. *Generale* Baldassarre, the commander of the *XX Corpo d'Armata*, was one of those killed during the advance along with several members of his staff when they were struck by an aerial bomb. Thus, command of the Italian mechanized unit passed to General Giuseppe

---

6   Basil Liddell Hart, *The Rommel Papers*, p. 235.
7   W.E. Murphy, *The Official History of New Zealand in the Second World War*, p. 572.

de Stefanis[8], who at the time was the commander of the *Ariete* Division. In turn, *Generale* Francesco Arena became the commander of *Ariete*.

Even *Littorio* was heavily targeted by the RAF which by the summer of 1942, given the proximity between the Commonwealth airfields and the El Alamein line, began to play a much more central and vital role in the campaign.

Littorio's war diary reports two incidents where heavy losses were sustained due to RAF bombing attacks and enemy counters:

> On 20 June Litttorio sustained an attack by an Indian brigade which drove from the south but was repelled from the onset. The major challenge faced on that day was the heavy enemy bombardment that Littorio's artillery had great difficulties thwarting due to lack of ammunition and guns.
>
> The night of 25 June was particularly difficult for the troops of the Littorio Division which suffered heavy casualties due to the enemy's aerial bombardment which was unopposed given the lack of anti-aircraft weapons. Numerous vehicles were burning during the night and this factor improved the enemy's visibility and hence his ability to target our equipment.[9]

On the approach march Rommel wrote that" the Italians were having their difficulties. On the 25th of June, the Ariete and Trieste had a grand total of 14 tanks, 30 guns and 2,000 infantry between them! The Littorio was immobilized for hours on end by lack of petrol and simply could not keep up."[10]

Notwithstanding heavy interference by the RAF, on 26 June the Commonwealth position at Mersa Matruh was in the process of being completely encircled by the Axis forces. A major contribution to the encirclement was made by the 90th Leicht Division which had been able to isolate the enemy garrison by occupying the coast road that connected the fortress to the sea. Despite opposition from Jock columns it destroyed one of them capturing 400 enemy soldiers and then penetrating deeply into the enemy deployment. The Italian *XX Corpo d'Armata* and the DAK arrived with some considerable delay but both managed to reach the desired position by late evening. In the morning, both had been held up by a combination of enemy air attacks and lack of fuel. Then later in the day the Italian unit together with the DAK while en route to Mersa Matruh were attacked suddenly near Kanayis by sixty tanks from the British 4th Armoured Brigade. While the attack was, sudden and undertaken primarily by a unit equipped with powerful American medium tanks, the Axis artillery promptly opened fire. Even though the British unit continued to launch several flanking attacks against the Axis formation, the latter's anti-tank screen destroyed several enemy tanks and ultimately forced the remaining tanks to disperse.

---

8   He was recruited in 1903 and graduated from the Torino artillery academy in 1905. As a Major he participated to the First World War while commanding several artillery units. In 1932 he was appointed as commander of the 8th Regiment of Artillery *Pasubio* based in Verona. He was further promoted in 1935 to commander of the VII *Corpo d'Armata* Artillery. He was promoted as *Generale di Divisione* in 1941 while fighting in Greece with the *Pinerolo* Division. He was then transferred to Libya where he assumed command of the Trento Division and then later of the *Ariete* Division.
9   Ufficio Storico, 'Relazione sul fatto d'arme della Divisione Littorio dal giugno a novembre 1942', Generale Gervasio Bitossi, Novembre 1942.
10 Basil Liddell Hart, *The Rommel Papers*, p. 241.

Despite suffering casualties from enemy artillery fire, the Axis forces pressed their attack forward at dawn on 27 June. The 21st Panzer and the 90th Leicht attacked the northern flank with *Littorio* in support, while 15th Panzer and the *XX Corpo d'armata* attacked the southern flank. The first attempt was blunted by the Commonwealth forces which opened destructive fire especially with the 25-pdr guns. A second attack proved more successful and allowed several armoured units to gain a foothold inside the fortress. On the 28th Axis troops attacked again in a bid to widen the breach but they were not successful. They were then counter-attacked by the enemy which attempted several times to escape encirclement. *Littorio*'s war diary reports of a wild melee that ensued that is also recorded in the Rommel's Papers:

> The enemy attacked several times in Mersa Matruh. Littorio oversaw defending the rear of the Axis deployment and of protecting Rommel's staff vehicles and men. The British made several attempts to reach Rommel's command but the Bersaglieri of the XII Battalion nullified all of them. We could capture several armoured vehicles and over fifty prisoners, while we destroyed several enemy tanks and two armoured vehicles.[11]

During the night between 28/29 June *Littorio* was positioned near Wadi Nagamish as the Axis troops had created a *cordon sanitarie* around the enemy positions. Its role was to prevent the British Commonwealth forces from escaping from Mersa Matruh.

According to British Tommy Les Davies:

> The next day we reformed and got ready, it was Sunday. Shells were coming over by the dozen and Jerry was closing in on us, so as soon as it was dark we made our mad dash to freedom and at a dear cost. Hell, was let loose, he knew we were coming out. We broke the way through. Trucks were burning, men were killed and wounded and screaming for hell, out our trucks.[12]

Thus, the Indian 10th Division attempt to break out of the Mersa Matruh positions was foiled primarily by *Littorio*'s and German units as they promptly opened fire when the Commonwealth units attempted to escape. The next day the Axis attack resumed and finally the capture of Mersa Matruh at 0930 by 90th Leicht and 7th *Bersaglieri* Regiment was achieved when they entered the stronghold, taking 2,000 Commonwealth prisoners.[13] The German war diary stated that: "The fortress of Mersa Matruh strengthened by installations organized in depth in the outlying area and by numerous minefields was taken by storm in the morning hours of 29.6 by 90 Lt. Div. in the face of stubborn enemy resistance."[14] In reality, the 10th and 11th Battalions of the 7th *Bersaglieri* Regiment had broken into the port of Mersa Matruh before the Germans guns and tanks and opened the way for the 90th Leicht to overcome the enemy resistance.

---

11 Ufficio Storico, 'Relazione sul fatto d'arme della Divisione Littorio dal giugno a novembre 1942', Generale Gervasio Bitossi, Novembre 1942.
12 *People's War:* <https://www.bbc.co.uk/history/ww2peopleswar/stories/46/a2181746.shtml> (accessed 21 May, 1018).
13 Mario Montanari, *Le operazioni in Africa settentrionale*, vol. III, part II, p. 345.
14 US Marine Corps, *German Experiences in Desert Warfare of World War II* (Washington DC: Dept. of the Navy, 1990), p. A-8-6.

Following the capture of the fortress Rommel observed that: "My troops had at all times given their best. But it had repeatedly been the superiority of certain German weapons over the British equivalents that had been our salvation. Now there were already signs, in the new British tanks and anti-tank guns, of a coming qualitative superiority of British material….For that reason alone, therefore, it was essential to do everything to bring about a British collapse."[15]

First Battle of El Alamein

At a meeting in Derna on 25 June both Cavallero and Kesserling had attempted in vain to convince Rommel that given the long distance that separated the Axis supply bases to the positions of the *Panzerarmee* a major advance into Egypt was extremely risky. Rommel did not openly contradict the two generals and stated that "he would consider each of his movements nothing more than a series of jumps forward: he was not willing to become engaged in a deep operation."[16]

In reality after the capture of Mersa Matruh Rommel was already thinking about his next offensive move which would pit his forces against the Commonwealth defenses at El Alamein. He would from now on continue to advance despite a depleted force and the loss of the valuable intelligence produced by the so-called 'Good Source,' the compromised by Axis intelligence (SIM) reports of Colonel Bonner Fellers, the American military attaché in Cairo. This source, which up to that point, had been vital for Rommel, dried up in early July 1942 when the British discovered it and has a result Rommel's future moves were based on much reduced intelligence with regard to enemy movements and planning.

On 29 June Rommel deployed *Littorio* on the left flank of the 580th Reconnaissance Group and on the right of 21st Panzer. The unit, while advancing against the enemy, sustained an assault by Commonwealth tanks from 4th Armoured Brigade which were retreating to the El Alamein road but suffered no losses. The next day it was not so fortunate. On 30 June, a British tank column presumably equipped with 75mm tanks while traveling east toward El Alamein bypassed *Littorio* which was travelling in the opposite direction in two separate columns. One was the armoured one, while the second was of truck mounted *Bersaglieri*. The British tanks did not hesitate and pounced upon the tanks and vehicles of *Littorio*. The encounter gave *Littorio* a very bloody nose as its armoured units were outgunned by the enemy's more powerful guns and tanks. Thus, it lost thirteen tanks (nine medium and four light tanks), 100 men and two of its commanders: *Tenente Colonnello* Salvatore Zappala', commander of LI *Battaglione Carri* and 133° *Reggimento Carristi* commander *Colonnello* Pietro Zuco. The unit's war diary reports that "the enemy's superiority with his 75mm tank and artillery guns determined an overwhelming defeat for Littorio."[17] Its commander furnished the following situation report to the North Africa High Command: "Situation day 30. Loss of a hundred men and twenty tanks. Division engaged for many days, all provisions have been used up. We are also lacking combat service

---

15 Basil Liddell Hart, *The Rommel Papers*, p. 245.
16 Santi Corvaja, *Hitler & Mussolini: The Secret Meetings* (New York, Enigma, 2010), p. 206.
17 Ufficio Storico, 'Rapporto sui fatti d'arme della Divisione Littorio dal giugno all'ottobre 1942', Generale Battista Arista, Novembre 1942.

support, without any supplies and we urgently need medical support, fuel and water."[18] Despite the losses the next day the unit arrived at Deir el Shein where it was reinforced with the addition of the IV *Battaglione Carri*.

Even though the Commonwealth had suffered additional losses, the three day stand in the fortress allowed the troops defending the El Alamein line/bottleneck to further improve their defenses. The Commonwealth commander had organized his troops as follows: the 1st South African Division was deployed on the northern end of the El Alamein line, the 6th New Zealand Brigade was deployed at Bab el Qattara while the 4th and 5th New Zealand Brigades were deployed south. The 1st Armoured Division, which counted 150 tanks in working order, was deployed as a mobile reserve. The line was fortified throughout and it was delimited in the north by the sea and in the south by the desert depression, thus it was a cleverly selected position that would force Rommel's armoured units to attack by way of a head-on assault into a bottleneck. Up to that point of the campaign Rommel had succeeded because he had been able to outflank the Commonwealth troops with his fast moving and unpredictable mobile columns. Now he and his troops faced a totally different situation having to attack against a very powerful anti-tank screen made up of 25-pdr and 6-pdr that could penetrate even the heaviest of the Axis tanks. The Commonwealth forces had built an intricate system of defense centered on the El Alamein railway station which consisted of a fortified position backed up by fall back positions. North of El Alamein railway station the defensive line was built along the edge of the coast road that ran all the way to the sea. To the south of the railway station the defensive line was developed along the sandy desert and it was centered on the two main ridges: Miteiriya and Ruweisat. South of Ruweisat the line finally ended by the Qattara Depression.

In contrast to the Commonwealth, at the end of June the Axis forces were seriously reduced and the troops were tired due to a general lack of rotations and for being deployed very far from their supply bases. The Italians had seventy medium tanks in working order mostly by repairing existing vehicles, 200 artillery pieces and 8,000 infantry soldiers, while the DAK could count upon fifty-five tanks, 330 artillery pieces, and 2,000 infantry soldiers. Their opponents, although severely beaten at Gazala were slowly reorganizing and rebuilding their strength. The fall of Tobruk, for instance, had hastened American support to the Commonwealth with the shipment of record numbers of Sherman and Grant tanks. It is estimated that up to 200 American new tanks were shipped to the Commonwealth during the month of July.

Rommel's intelligence reading of the situation was that the Commonwealth forces were on the run and were retreating with considerable disarray. He believed that one final push would see them off and he therefore urged his fatigued but battle hardened troops to commit to one final offensive advance. The DAK was to tackle head on the El Alamein line in the center, while the Italian forces were to attack in the south against the positions held by the 2nd New Zealand Division. But on 2 July the Axis attack was blunted by very precise and effective artillery fire. In the south three M tanks and some armoured vehicles managed to penetrate inside the enemy lines but were quickly beaten back and were then chased away by up to twenty Grants from the 4th Armoured Brigade. The next day the attacks continued and the Italian units were tasked with capturing the strategic position of Alam Nayil. *Ariete*'s tanks were the first to see action by engaging the 4th Armoured Brigade in a spirited artillery duel. To support the attack *Ariete*'s

18 Ibid.

artillery was moved forward on the right flank of the tanks providing supporting fire. The plan was for the *Trieste* Division to also advance and protect *Ariete*'s artillery exposed flanks but its motorized columns were pinned down by several RAF aerial bombings and could not proceed. Having reached the designated position General Arena communicated to *XX Corpo d'armata* headquarters that: "We have reached the position and had to assume a defensive posture because we can observe enemy units on the west, south and east of us. The German 15th and 21st Divisions are north-east of us at a distance of eight kilometers, while we have yet to see *Trieste*. Given our thinning infantry ranks and the necessity to face a three-pronged attack, our situation remains very precarious. I therefore urge that Trieste be moved up as quickly as possible."[19] But as soon as this message had gone out, the losses began to mount because of the heavy enemy shelling. Then the tanks of the 4th Armoured Brigade rolled in against *Ariete*, but they were checked by the units' own tanks. At 0800 Arena further communicated that "we are alone under continued enemy fire coming from multiple directions."[20] At 0830 the XII *Bersaglieri* faced the New Zealand infantry thrusting forward with two columns (19th and 20th Battalions) supported by a heavy rolling barrage. As *Ariete*'s artillery unit began to dismount and set up its guns, it was plastered by well positioned Commonwealth guns which inflicted further casualties. *Ariete*'s unit had basically arrived at a deep depression which was surrounded by the enemy fire. "All of sudden," states *Tenente* Ennio Calabresi *13ª Batteria V Gruppo da 88/56*, "there were a few minutes of silence that shortly thereafter were broken by the buzzing sound of machine guns mixed in with the explosions caused by mortar shells. It was clear that the enemy infantry was coming forward in numbers but everything seemed clear in front of our gun positions. Then one of my servers shouted out: 'Signor Tenente the 75mm gun crews are fleeing.' In fact, I could see a few Bren carriers driving around our 75mm guns while several soldiers were escorted into captivity…..The enemy infantry then reached within 100 meters of our gun positions. Given our desperate situation I gave orders to my crew members to flee as fast as possible."[21] *Tenente* Calabresi would shortly thereafter be captured along with several 88/56 guns, some of the cream of the crop of *Ariete*'s artillery. Apparently only the IV *Gruppo da 90/53*, thanks to the alert action of its commander *Maggiore* Arnaldo Polon, was able to escape along with other small anti-tank gun units. Since the artillery unit had advanced too far and too deep into the enemy's deployment, the New Zealanders had launched a successful bayonet attack put forth by an infantry battalion. In less than two hours they overran the batteries and captured both soldiers and guns:

> The Division Ariete, having just arrived in the positions assigned to it at dawn on the 3rd July and without any support from the Division Trieste, which had been unable to occupy its respective positions owing to delays caused by aerial bombardments, had been compelled to face a concentric attack from the east, the south and from the west, launched by the 2nd New Zealand Division and supported by the 4th Armoured Brigade (1st Armoured English Division).

---

19 Mario Montanari, *Le operazioni in Africa settentrionale*, vol. III, part. II, p. 446.
20 Ibid.
21 Giulio Bedeschi, *Fronte d'Africa*, p. 166.

> After strenuous resistance, with ammunition exhausted and practically all the guns lost and the left wing completely open, the remnants of Ariete withdrew to the assembly area of the Division Pavia.
>
> The Division Trieste, because the delay, was unable to mount a counter-attack and received orders to assemble to the east of Alam Dhimaya [Alam el Dihmaniya] in the rear of the German Panzer Divisions.[22]

The New Zealand official history, however, states that the resistance of the Italians was less pronounced:

> A Company, closely followed by D Company, moved to a low ridge about 900 yards to the east and south-east of the main point of resistance. The enemy had by now opened heavy fire with machine guns and mortars which the platoon of No. 2 Machine Gun Company endeavored to subdue, one section firing over the heads of the companies moving to the flank and the other giving supporting fire from the south. The battalion's three-inch mortars and four two-pounder guns were also brought forward. These engaged the enemy gun lines and, with the help of the small-arms fire, prevented the Italians from manning their artillery. Three tanks were also engaged by the two-pounders as they withdrew through the gun lines. As this supporting fire developed, A and D Companies advanced over the ridge and down the slope under a certain amount of enemy fire. On the appearance of B Company from the south resistance collapsed. Part of the enemy escaped, but about 350 prisoners were counted and sent to the rear. Their captors described them as 'a dirty, greasy unkempt mob, without fighting spirit.' Captured equipment included twelve 105-millimetre guns, eleven 88-millimetre and Russian 76·2-millimetre, sixteen 75-millimetre and five 25-pounders, a total of forty-four heavy artillery pieces, as well as some 20-millimetre dual purpose (anti-aircraft and anti-tank) guns, mortars, and other small arms. One M13 Italian tank and another which could not be identified were found damaged and abandoned.[23]

Because of this action *Ariete* lost much of its artillery equipment (37 pieces of several size including several 88mm and 90mm guns) although the *Bersaglieri* units, the tanks and some truck mounted artillery escaped the encirclement and avoided capture. Much of the blame for this debacle should be placed on combat fatigue as well as bad reconnaissance. As Greene and Massignagni properly assert: "This was a sign of the strain which affected this good unit, and the fault remained on the shoulders of her commander, General Francesco Arena, who pushed too far ahead without proper reconnaissance and support."[24]

According to the 15th Panzer Division war diary: "Ariete has lost all of its artillery and now has five tanks and two artillery guns available for the attack. The rest of Ariete is either

---

22 J.L. Scoullar, *Battle for Egypt: The Summer of 1942* (Wellington: Historical Publications Branch, 1967), p. 171.
23 Ibid.
24 Jack Greene and Alessandro Massigani, *Rommel's Desert Campaign*, p. 196.

weaponless or unfit for action."[25] This is probably an exaggeration but it is clear that by early July 1942 the unit was a spent force and for several weeks it could not be deployed by Rommel.

A detailed description of the poor conditions of the Italian troops by the New Zealand official historian reveals two things. First, that the continuous advance by the Axis forces had strained the morale and the combat effectiveness of the troops. Second, the decrease in combat effectiveness of the Italians was the result of many factors but one of them was clearly the lack of rotation of frontline troops. As Battistelli and Crociani assert in 1941 the lack of rotation out of service of troops was not a factor since reserve troops were available. In 1942 reserve troops, due to Italian commitments in both North Africa and in Russia/Ukraine, became a rare commodity and frontline troops remained in combat for much longer often even without a few days or weeks of leave. [26]

Along with this defeat of *Ariete*, the Axis had also been pressed back by the strong enemy resistance in the north of the El Alamein deployment where the 15th Panzer Division and *Littorio* suffered severe losses. On 3 July 1942, its *XII Battaglione Carri* attacked the enemy line on Ruweisat Ridge encountering a formidable anti-tank screen that did not yield an inch of terrain. *Tenente* Armando Luciano recalls that:

> We're lined up facing east, with the sun blinding us and making our tank armour shine. In the distance in front of us, I can make out the silhouettes of the enemy tanks backed up against a large mound. This is it, the moment of our first combat has come. Maggiore Dell'Uva gives the final orders, the battalion advances to get in range, then the exchange of fire starts and the platoons start moving. At the same time, we are bombarded by enemy artillery fire, which gets more and more frequent and well-aimed.[27]

The ensuing tank battle with the British tank brigades was a shock to many *carristi* of the *Littorio* Division which for the first time came face to face with several American Grant medium tanks. These *carristi* witnessed for the first time how impotent their units were against the enemy armour:

> In the distance in front of me I can make out an enemy tank flying a pennant from its radio antenna; it must be a command tank. Halt! I cry to Ramazzotti, 'Aim 600 fire! Following the trail of the tracer, I see the shell hit the enemy armour, but I wait in vain for the usual black smoke of burning fuel to pour from the tank, or to see the crew throw themselves out of the vehicle. Our armour piercing shells must have misfired – it is probably an American Grant tank, a beast with too thick a skin. I try again with another armoured piercing shell, but almost simultaneously I feel a blow on our right flank and hear the screams of the radio operator who seems to be going mad and whom Vizentini, the gunner, is trying to calm down. The tank has taken a hit, fortunately not a direct hit, but its right side, on the track,

---

25   Glyn Harper, *The Battle for North Africa: El Alamein and the Turning Point for World War II* (Bloomington: Indiana University Press, 2017), p. 45.
26   Pier Paolo Battistelli and Piero Crociani, *Italian Soldier in North Africa*, p. 14.
27   Armando Luciano, *Guerra dei corazzati in Africa settentrionale: Battaglie e ricordi* (Modena: Mucchi, 1982), p. 151.

which is now hanging uselessly with the exchange of fire is getting more intense and other tanks are being destroyed.[28]

Littorio's war diarist observed:

> Littorio's attacks against a formidable defensive line between the Quattara Depression and the sea (El Alamein) were all repulsed with heavy casualties by the enemy's very strong and determined defense. The Bersaglieri, the artillerymen and the carristi of Littorio attacked the enemy without artillery support, but a very powerful and energetic anti-tank screen stymied all their efforts.[29]

In three days of heavy fighting the unit lost most its tanks and only seven remained in working order on 7 July.

During the Axis offensive, the whole Commonwealth resistance line position did not yield terrain and its guns wreaked havoc upon the already thinned out ranks of the Italian and German armoured units. The Commonwealth had in effect stopped Rommel's advance on its tracks with a skillful performance from the artillery crews. Rommel blamed the Italians for the debacle:

> This reverse took us completely by surprise, for in the weeks of the fighting around Knightsbridge, the Ariete covered, it is true, by German guns and tanks – had fought well against every onslaught of the British, although their casualties had not been light. By now the Italians were no longer equal to the very great demands being made of them. The resulting threat to our southern flank meant that the Afrika Korps' intended knock out attack now had to be carried out by the 21st Panzer Division alone, and the weight of the attack was consequently too small.[30]

The Axis forces prior to the three-day operation were already a spent force too weak to make a major attack against prepared positions backed by heavy artillery. Rommel had gambled with a dilapidated force and had lost. He had badly underestimated enemy strength, especially with regard to the number of enemy artillery units and its troop morale which was bolstered by the C-in-C Middle East General Sir Claude Auchinleck) who made all of the correct decisions and urged his troops to remain on the defensive.

On 8 July Rommel gave the following tally of the Axis strength: DAK (15th and 21st Panzer Divisions) had fifty tanks, 600 infantrymen with twenty anti-tank guns and two artillery regiments with seven artillery batteries each. The 90th Leicht Division had a strength of 1,500 soldiers, thirty anti-tank guns and two field artillery batteries. There were also an additional three reconnaissance battalions with fifteen armoured cars, and twenty armoured troop carriers. The German artillery had eleven heavy and four light batteries, and forty anti-tank guns. The Italians of *XX Corpo d'armata* had fifty-four tanks and eight motorized battalions with approximately 1,600 men. Also, it had forty anti-tank guns and six light batteries. *Littorio* had seven

---

28 Ibid.
29 Ufficio Storico, "Rapporto sui fatti d'arme della Divisione Littorio dal giugno all'ottobre 1942," Generale Battista Arista, Novembre 1942.
30 Basil Liddell Hart, *The Rommel Papers*, p. 249.

medium tanks and 2,000 soldiers. The infantry Divisions of General Navarini *XXI Corpo d'Armata* had a total of 2,200 soldiers, eleven heavy and thirty light artillery batteries.[31] After Rommel's offensive operation had stalled he withdrew DAK and his mobile forces from front-line positions and inserted the Italian infantry divisions on the El Alamein line. This allowed for a reorganization of his armoured striking force in anticipation for a resumption of the offensive.

The New Zealanders were the first to counter the Italians after the major battle of 1-3 July in the southern sector after British intelligence services informed them that *Littorio* was getting ready to withdraw westwards. As a result, Auchinleck ordered on 6 July the 4th New Zealand Brigade to thrust towards the enemy's rear in a bid to surround it. The latter advanced without being spotted and at dawn positioned its guns on a ridge overlooking the enemy's position and began shooting up the *Littorio*'s leaguer before breakfast. The sudden artillery attack caused numerous casualties but later as *Littorio*'s artillery responded with counter-battery fire the New Zealanders also suffered losses and eventually retreated.

During the night on 8 July a German reconnaissance group broke into the positions of the New Zealanders at Qaret el Abd. This was followed by another Axis attempt to break the main enemy position at Bab el Qattara as Rommel wanted at all costs to resume the initiative and deal the fatal blow to the enemy. On the morning of the 9th 21st Panzer, *Littorio,* who had taken up positions previously held by *Ariete,* and 90th Leicht advanced against the southern flank of the Commonwealth positions. Although the operation was successful, the New Zealand infantry managed to prematurely abandon their positions and fall back to the resistance line thus avoiding the capture of its infantry. According to Ian Walker:

> This attack was led by a squadron of 3 Group Novara Lancers equipped with L.6/40 light tanks under Capitano Dardi. The fragile light tanks formed up in the open and moved forward at top speed. Dardi was having difficulty directing the attack through the narrow observation slits in the turret. He therefore decided to open the hatch and command from a better vantage point, clear of the smoke and dust caused by vehicle movement and enemy artillery fire. He guided his squadron to its objectives but was killed by shrapnel fragments from artillery fire. Unfortunately, the whole Littorio attack fell on an empty stretch of desert and encountered only artillery fire…. The position was then garrisoned by Littorio.[32]

After the brief but deadly encounter, *Littorio* took up position at Bab el Qattara, while the XX *Corpo d'Armata* took position on Ruweisat Ridge. Thus, another offensive thrust had failed to breakthrough and the Axis forces braced for enemy counters against its positions.

Tel el Eisa – Hill 33

Indeed, what followed this hasty operation was a series of counterattacks put forth by the Commonwealth forces which aimed primarily to degrade the fighting capabilities of the Italian infantry divisions deployed against the El Alamein line. This deliberate strategy, which was

---

31 Mario Montanari, *Le operazioni in Africa settentrionale*, vol III, part I, p. 402.
32 Ian Walker, *Iron Hulls, Iron Hearts*, p. 144.

meant to offset any gains obtained by the *Panzerarmee*, forced Rommel on the defensive for many weeks and to desist from putting forth further armoured attacks. The strategy was to launch attacks following massive artillery barrages concentrated upon selected Italian positions on the El Alamein defensive perimeter. The hurricane, First World War like, destructive barrages were meant to shock and overwhelm the defenders who then had to promptly face the infantry attack. In one instance, for example, an entire battalion from the *Sabratha* Division was overrun after a massive barrage causing panic for the Axis command of a potential enemy breakthrough. This for the Axis was a harbinger of worse things to come. The first enemy blow came on the afternoon of 9 July when elements of the 2nd New Zealand Division attacked the positions held by *Divisione Brescia*. The latter were saved in the nick of time by the intervention of 21st Panzer and Maggiore Pardi's mobile artillery unit, Heavy losses were sustained by the Axis unit, including the loss of Pardi, but the enemy was repelled. On 10 July, the Australians of 2/24th and 2/48th Battalions launched an attack against enemy positions on Tel el Eisa/ Hill 33 in the northern end of the El Alamein line. The very heavy barrage that preceded the infantry advance shocked the Axis defenders of the poorly trained *Sabratha* Division and some German infantry troops, and one battalion of the former, for instance, lost approximately fifty percent of its ranks due to the bombardment. The swift Australian operation yielded the capture of 924 German and Italian prisoners and 27 guns after they had penetrated all the way into the second line of defense held by 3rd *Celere*. In turn the Australian official history states that the 2/24th Battalion suffered relatively few losses such as six killed and twenty-two wounded and took more than 800 unwounded prisoners and much equipment, while the 2/48th also suffered light casualties. In the Rommel Papers, Rommel wrote that the infantry troops of the *Sabratha* were "throwing away arms and ammunition as they ran. It was primarily the Panzer Army's staff, led at the time by Lieut.-Col. von Mellenthin, whom we had to thank for bringing the British attack to a halt."[33] Following the barrage as Jack Greene and Alessandro Massignani assert "Navarini, commander of XXI Corps, immediately sent a battalion of the 7th Bersaglieri and a battalion of the 46th Artillery to block the road, while Rommel sent an ersatz battalion of the 90th Light."[34] This move plugged the hole caused by the destruction of the *Sabratha* battalion.

After the front was stabilized the decision was taken to recapture Hill 33 and the ridge parallel with the sea, which by that point had already been firmly occupied by Australian troops with machine guns and artillery. The task was entrusted to Major Verri's XI *Battaglione Carri Medi/Trieste* Division and specifically to its *3ª Compagnia* led by *Capitano* Vittorio Bulgarelli which was committed to make a surprise attack against Hill 33 across two miles of barren desert landscape. The plan was to charge at the enemy position and then scale the small hill to kill or capture its defenders. This straightforward plan, however, gave the Commonwealth guns an important advantage as they could target the advancing enemy tanks which were in full view of their positions. Under continuous fire from a multitude of well sited 25-pdr and 6-pdr guns the Italian medium tanks nonetheless advanced with considerable dash. In a cavalry like charge where the tanks continually zig zagged to avoid the enemy fire, the combat unit advanced for over two miles at top speed. As the operation quickly reached its crescendo, the desert night was lit by the clash of armour and guns as the Italian tanks stormed forward while

---

33   Basil Liddell Hart, *The Rommel Papers*, p. 253.
34   Jack Greene and Alessandro Massignani, *Rommel's North Africa Campaign*, p. 197.

the Commonwealth artillery fired many shells in rapid succession to stop them. As the shells began hitting the tanks or the ground, huge explosions lit up the battlefield. During the operation, the unit despite its bold maneuvering lost seventeen out of nineteen tanks which were put out of action by the enemy guns. The last two M.13/41 tanks then continued to advance again until they reached the enemy positions which were put under heavy fire. According to the 2/48th Battalion diary: "At approximately 2000 hours' enemy tanks–number unknown– and infantry attacked D Coy's front. They overran position and enemy infantry forced D Company to withdraw and occupied their positions."[35] A night attack by the Australians later recaptured the contested hill by surprising and capturing a 250-strong unit of *Trieste*.

Ruweisat Ridge

On 14 July, a squadron comprised of tanks from 90th Leicht and *Littorio* attacked from Bab el Qattara in the direction of Alam Nayil, on the southern flank of the Commonwealth defensive line. However, the tanks were blocked by a much larger force of the British 22nd Armoured Brigade which soon after began to mount a counterthrust of its own pushing them back to Bab el Qattara. In the meantime, Auchinleck, noting that Rommel was transferring armour to the north, set in train preparations for an attack from the south and center in the Ruweisat Ridge area. On night between 14/15 July, the 2nd New Zealand Division and 5th Indian Brigade launched a major attack against the Italian *Pavia* and *Brescia* Divisions at Ruweisat Ridge, in the center of the Axis defensive line. The attack broke through in two different sectors causing hundreds of casualties and the capture of over 1,500 soldiers, but because of the Axis spoiling tank attack the British 22nd Armoured Brigade was tied down and unable to support the New Zealanders who had reached Deir el Shein. But a major break could not be achieved by the infantry without the support of the British tanks. The attack was also met with fierce mortar and artillery fire until the infantry troops were relieved by the tank units. Elements from 15th Panzer and *Littorio* mounted a major counter which tore through the enemy defenses leading to the capture of 1,000 enemy soldiers. The Commonwealth troops were then forced to vacate the position and this allowed the Axis troops to recapture positions at Ruweisat Ridge.

On the night between 16/17 July, another successful counter-attack was conducted by the 24th Brigade/9th Australian Division at Miteiriya Ridge against positions held by the *Trento* and *Trieste* Divisions which again caused heavy casualties and the capture of 700 soldiers. These developments prompted a meeting at Derna between Bastico, Kesserling and Cavallero. The latter now offered a very pessimistic assessment: The Axis troops had been stalemated by the aggressive reaction of the Australian and New Zealand infantry troops and their counter-attacks had bared fruits inflicting grave casualties. The DAK armoured units were reduced to a bare minimum and the Italian *Ariete* and *Littorio* were unable to field more than thirty operational tanks. Kesserling and Bastico once again urged caution and stressed the need for consolidation of the Axis positions on the El Alamein line rather than incremental jumps forward.

---

35   48th Battalion War Diary <https://s3-ap-southeast-2.amazonaws.com/awm-media/collection/RCDIG1070086/document/5519415.PDF> (accessed 8 July 2018).

On 18 July, the 24th New Zealand battalion after a preparatory fire surged ahead against the 8° *Reggimento Bersaglieri* positions at Deir um Khawabir in the southern flank of the Axis deployment. The attack conducted under the cover of darkness at 2030 managed to capture several of the enemy's advanced positions. However, the nearby positions still manned by the Italian infantry responded to the sudden attack by opening fire. The New Zealand battalion responded by deploying several Bren carriers which began to move in the direction of Italian artillery and anti-tank gun positions. Initially the motorized unit managed to knock out of action an Italian 47mm gun and an 88mm gun. The Italian response, however, was first comprised by concentrated anti-tank fire which put out of action a Bren carrier and was later followed by a counter by several M.14/41 tanks which managed to destroy two Bren carriers and forced the others to retreat. Despite the loss of the Bren carriers and two soldiers killed, two wounded and six missing the 24th Battalion managed to capture forty-two *bersaglieri*.

On the 21st the Commonwealth sprang another surprise counter against the Axis on Ruweisat Ridge. The major attack was put forth by the 5th Indian Division, 2nd New Zealand and 1st Armoured Division with numerous tanks. As Rommel observes: "South of the strongpoint they overran our positions, after the German-Italian infantry holding them had fought to the end, and by 2100 were already dangerously far behind our front."[36] But as the tanks came forward in support of the infantry attack they were shot to pieces by the Axis artillery which destroyed several machines. On the 22nd after several units of *Trieste* Division had fought off several enemy attacks, the 21st Panzer Division mounted a major counter which yielded the destruction of several enemy tanks and the capture of 500 enemy soldiers. As a testament to their fierce resistance, posthumous decorations were awarded to *Colonnello* Gerardo Vairone de Piacenza, Commanding Officer 65th *Trieste* Infantry Regiment, and *Colonnello* Umberto Zanetti, Commanding Officer 66th *Trieste* Infantry Regiment. Meanwhile, the 18th New Zealand Battalion, which was covering the flank of the main attack, came under very heavy fire from *Ariete* Division at Ruweisat Ridge. Despite the heavy fire one company of attackers managed to infiltrate itself past the minefields and into the advance Axis line covered by *Ariete*'s *bersaglieri* units. As the New Zealanders charged in with bayonets, the *bersaglieri* manning mortars and machine guns opened fire at close range killing and wounding many. "The real surprise, however, awaited them just beyond the brow of the ridge: a line of Italian M.14s in hull down position. The New Zealanders had neither the numbers nor the firepower to face enemy armour…. The bersaglieri immediately laid down heavy machine gun fire and small arms fire on the exposed enemy, who then charged with the bayonet."[37] In a matter of less than thirty minutes an entire New Zealand company was completely wiped out. A little later *Ariete*'s tanks than came to the fore to capture the fleeing enemy soldiers. Several groups of soldiers were rounded up and brought to the rear.

---

36 Basil Liddell Hart, *The Rommel Papers*, p. 258.
37 Ian Walker, *Iron Hulls, Iron Hearts*, p. 147.

Sanyet el Miteiriya

Auchinleck's last effort came in the northern sector with an attack on the night of 26-27 July aimed at breaking through the Italian lines the Sanyet el Miteiriya. The plan entailed that a joint Australian and British force comprised of one infantry battalion/9th Australian Division and two battalions/50th British Division were to capture the ridge held by Italian troops.

The Australian 2/28th Battalion began to advance at midnight while a heavy artillery fire rained down on the positions of the *Trento* Division. Progressing through an area swept by enemy fire the Australians lost Bren carriers and suffered losses before coming to blows with the enemy infantry and taking 117 prisoners.

> Eight hundred yards from the start-line the battalion came under fire from field guns, mortars and machine-guns. Among the casualties were the commander of the right forward company (Captain Carlton), and the commander (Captain Stonehous) and one other officer of the right rear company. The vehicles bearing the supporting arms were fired on by anti-tank guns as soon as they began to advance and, when about Kilo 10, were halted by a minefield. Soon five vehicles, including three carriers, had been knocked out and some began burning.[38]

But once the Australians began to occupy the newly captured positions they were counter-attacked by the newly formed *Trieste* Division Reconnaissance group which together with the artillery guns of *Trento* Division repulsed the attack. The former was equipped for the most part with captured British armoured vehicles as most its original vehicles were under repair at the time. An eyewitness of the campaign Paolo Caccia Dominioni describes the unit in the following terms: "The names of certain units were on everyone's lips up and down the line following particularly brilliant actions, among them the Reconnaissance Group of the Trieste. It had been set up some time previously: it was hardly a homogeneous unit on the German pattern but did reflect admirably the Italian genius of improvisation. They had no more than nine vehicles–Morrises, Fords, Dingos and Jeeps, all captured from the enemy–armed with small caliber guns and machine-guns of all descriptions, British, Italian and German, together with two British 88 guns and their carriages, and two small supply lorries."[39]

The diary of Lieutenant S. A. Walker states that the attack was sudden and the swiftness of the attack caught the Australian 2/28th Battalion by surprise: "The Battalion was completely surrounded by armoured cars which worked forward under cover of fire from enemy tanks further back, while 20mm, MMG, and mortar fire kept the heads of our own troops well down. In this manner, the enemy was able to cut off and dispose of sections and platoons one by one."[40]

Similarly, the Australian official history reported that: "Then suddenly, at Godfrey's head-quarters, the 2/28th Battalion's wireless came on the air and began at 09.40 a.m. to pass a message. It was brief—only four words—but graphic. "We are in trouble."[41] The commander

---

38 Barton Maughan, *Australia in the War of 1939-1945 Vol. III: Tobruk and El Alamein*, p. 591.
39 Paolo Caccia Dominioni, *El Alamein* (Milan: Longanesi, 1962), p 137.
40 28 Battalion War Diary < https://s3-ap-southeast-2.amazonaws.com/awm-media/collection/RCDIG1070086/document/5519415.PDF> (accessed 8 July, 2018)
41 Ibid.

of the 2/28th Battalion then attempted to get artillery support, but by that time it was too late as *Trieste*'s Reconnaissance Group was already into the Australian position and began machine gunning the trenches. Thus, the battalion was soon overrun. Unsupported by its heavy guns and with a British tank Brigade that was dispatched to relieve the Australians but could not reach their position on time[42], the rapid counter yielded the capture of approximately 700 Commonwealth soldiers according to Italian sources. The Australian Official History meanwhile states that two officers and sixty-three other ranks of the 2/28th were killed or wounded, while twenty officers and 469 men were missing. This was last major operation of July as the frontline stabilized.

The situation was now at an impasse has both contenders were severely worn out and both lacked guns and tanks. On the Axis side four Italian divisions had been particularly tested by these assaults and had lost a high number of men and weapons. As a result Rommel announced further offensive action was impossible.[43] The Commonwealth troops, particularly the New Zealanders, felt that their attacks had not been properly supported by armour and accused Auchinleck of forcing them to be deployed in a piecemeal fashion. The Commonwealth had suffered higher casualties than Rommel's army (13,000 versus 12,000), but its overall strength was more considerable than the Axis forces therefore it was prevailing in the war of attrition. Churchill, who was not satisfied with how Auchinleck had conducted the campaign thus far abruptly removed him from command on 8 August.

Contrary to Churchill's interpretation of the campaign, Auchinleck had checked Rommel who admitted: "It was now certain that we could continue to hold our front, and that, after the crises we had been through, was at least something. Although the British losses in this Alamein fighting had been higher than ours, yet the price to Auchinleck had not been excessive, for the one thing that had mattered to him was to halt our advance, and that, unfortunately, he had done."[44]

After the heavy fighting of July both sides needed time to recover and reorganize. On the Commonwealth side the infantry continued to strengthen the defensive positions by laying thousands of mines in front of the El Alamein strongpoints, while record number of tanks shipments (300 Sherman tanks and 100 self-propelled guns) arrived from America during August. In addition, 368 tanks and 820 artillery pieces were shipped from Britain. Moreover, the clear majority of the frontline troops were now in possession of the 6-pdr anti-tank gun, which had proven to effective against Axis armour in July, and most of the troops were motorized. On the Axis side, there was a deep reorganization where the newly created *Deutsch-Italienisch Panzerarmee* or the *Armata Corazzata Italo-tedesca* was placed under Rommel's command who now reported directly to *Comando Supremo* and Marshal Cavallero. General Bastico's position was downgraded to that of *Comando Superiore Africa Settentrionale* (North African High

---

42 The Australian Official History states that "The 50th R.T.R. began its attack to relieve the pressure on the 2/28th at 9.55 a.m. but met with disaster. The leading tanks reached Point 30 and a ridge near the Ruin but saw no Australian troops and were forced back by fire from a ring of anti-tank guns; 22 tanks were knocked out of which 10 were recovered later. The men of the 2/28th witnessed the debacle." <https://s3-ap-southeast-2.amazonaws.com/awm-media/collection/RCDIG1070086/document/5519415.PDF> (accessed 8 July, 2018).
43 John Gooch, *Mussolini's War*, p. 313.
44 Basil Liddell Hart, *The Rommel Papers*, p. 260.

Command) and was assigned mainly defensive and administrative duties in the rear. Now the bulk of the Italian infantry divisions were under Rommel along with the armoured and motorized formations. Also on the Italian-German front there were some additional changes. Newly arrived troops such as the *Folgore* paratroopers' division, the 164th German infantry division, the 22nd German paratroopers Brigade under the orders of General Hermann-Bernhard Ramcke and more tanks originally assigned to *Littorio* were deployed on the frontline. The heavy losses sustained in July had made it necessary to dispatch these new troops with haste and fury to North Africa.

Rommel at the time was faced by a conundrum. On one hand the Commonwealth was building up its material and numerical strength day by day by improving its defensive positions and by bringing in record numbers of supply such as tanks and artillery. On the other hand, the Axis forces deployed far away from the supply bases desperately needed to either attempt one last offensive to break through the stalemate and invade Egypt or make an orderly retreat across the desert to more sustainable defensive positions in Libya. Since both Hitler and Mussolini had cancelled the plan for the invasion of Malta and believed that one last push could see off the Commonwealth in Egypt, they authorized Rommel, despite opposition from Kesselring and Bastico, to try to go on the offensive again.

> **Relative Tank Strength Commonwealth v Axis Per New Zealand Official History of the War**
>
> Comparisons of the qualities of British and Axis tanks are extremely difficult to make as there are so many factors involved. In most points of amour and armament, the Grant was a reasonable match for the German Mark III Special, Mark IV and IV Special, and the Crusader and Valentine for the lower Marks, while the Stuart could stand comparison with the Italian tanks. On this basis, a table of comparison of numbers and quality on 30 August 1942 would read:
>
> | | | |
> |---|---|---|
> | 164 Grants | versus | 109 Mk III Sp, IV and IV Sp |
> | 360 Valentines and Crusaders | versus | 124 Mk II, III |
> | <u>169 Stuarts</u> | versus | <u>281 Italian</u> |
> | 693 | | 514[45] |

Alama Halfa –El Alamein II

On 28 August, fully aware based on intelligence estimates which pointed to a steady enemy buildup, that time played in favor of the Commonwealth, Rommel instructed his senior officers that the new offensive was to start on 30 August. Although the Axis units had been replenished Rommel lacked large stockpiles of petrol given the disruption to Italian supply lines brought about by the continued intervention from the forces on Malta and the forward position occupied by the *Panzerarmee*. It is estimated that the Axis army necessitated between 600 to 2,000 tons of

---

45   Ronald Walker, *Alam Halfa and Alamein*, p. 79.

petrol per day depending upon whether on any particular day it was on a defensive or offensive posture. The army as a whole in North Africa necessitated 75,000 tons of overall supplies per month, which was considered the minimum necessary to guarantee day to day operations as well as guarantee two months of operational autonomy. In May 1942 88,200 tons had arrived, in June supplies dipped to 24,200 while in July 45,000 tons arrived. In August, the Italians lost four petrol cargo ships as the British Navy through the ULTRA intercept had adopted a new strategy which was focused on disrupting above all the fuel supply. The Royal Navy deliberately targeted cargo ships carrying petrol, while many other large cargo shipments of weapons and food made to port safely. Based on the losses sustained at sea supply was tight and the longer the army stayed at El Alamein the situation could not be improved. Thus, the maneuver Rommel had in mind was a swift leap forward that would initiate in the south and then convert to the north over the relief of Alam el Halfa to hit the enemy on his flank and rear. The main thrust was to be made by the German Panzer units, while the XX *Corpo d'Armata*, with the armoured divisions *Ariete* and *Littorio* and the motorized division *Trieste*, would advance on the left flank. The aim was of overcoming the minefield area, bypassing the entire Commonwealth line and ending up on the coast at the height of El Hamman, behind the Eighth Army.

The 15th Panzer and the 21st Panzer had 210 tanks, of which 47 were *Panzerkampfwagen* III type J and 15 *Panzerkampfwagen IV* type J. The XX Army Corps had 155 medium tanks, 25 L6/41 tanks, 25 armoured cars, and twenty-five 75mm self-propelled guns. *Littorio* was up to almost full strength with its recent losses in vehicles replenished by newly arrived equipment from Italy. It had the following organization/order of battle:

> *Compagnia Comando di divisione.*
> *III Gruppo Corazzato Lanceri di Novara with L.6 tanks*
> *133° Reggimento Carristi: IV, XII, and LI Battaglioni Carri Medi M.* In addition, to the *Comando di reggimento and Compagnia da 20mm.*
> *12° Reggimento Bersaglieri: XXIII Battaglione Bersaglieri, XXI Battaglione Bersaglieri Controcarro, XXXIV Battaglione Bersaglieri.*
> *133° Reggimento Artiglieria Corazzata: I and II Gruppo da 75/27, DLIV Gruppo semoventi da 75/18, DLVI Gruppo semoventi da 75/18.* And reinforced by *Comando 3° Reggimento Artiglieria Celere with CCCXXI Gruppo da 100/17 and XXIX Gruppo da 88/56.*
> *Compagnia Genio*
> *133° Sezione Sussistenza,*
> *133° Sezione Sanità*
> *85° Sezione Carabinieri.*
> (Source: Montanari 1985)

Conversely, *Ariete* was still largely understrength given the losses sustained during July. It is not clear how many tanks *Ariete* had at the time. At the start of the offensive General De Stefanis set out the guidelines to his mechanized force that mirrored Rommel's operational plan: "The success of the night operation depends upon overcoming the initial enemy resistance and then upon making good use of the supplies and petrol available during the subsequent advance."[46] The

---

46 Mario Montanari, *The Three Battles of El Alamein*, p. 242.

XX Army Corps advanced with *Ariete* on the left and *Littorio* on the right and in the forefront and *Trieste* in a second echelon formation and split up on two battle groups. The armoured divisions were deployed on three tactical groups, each had a tank battalion, a self-propelled artillery group, a truck towed artillery group and one of *Bersaglieri* transported on trucks, while the motorized division was subdivided into two combat groups each based on an infantry regiment.

Before midnight, the advanced reconnaissance units of 15th Panzer met the British defenses and the minefields. Instead of the weak forces expected, the German tank units stumbled upon deep minefields and strong enemy resistance. From the onset, the 1st battalion of the 115th Armoured Grenadier Regiment (15th Panzer), for instance, found itself under a powerful artillery barrage in the early stages of the advance and even before having to face a British infantry counterattack. Similarly, other units encountered strong opposition to the point that once they did advance it was too late and the possibility of a breakthrough elusive given the amount of fuel spent during the early stages of the operation.

The Italian units' experience of the battle was even more troublesome as stated by the New Zealand official history:

> In the early part of the night of 30 August, RAF bombers on routine harassing had noted and bombed concentrations of vehicles on the El Kharita plain, where the Italian 20th Corps was assembling. By the time these particular bombers had returned to their bases and reported their activities, Air Headquarters had heard from the army that the Axis attack was on its way and all available night bombers were got ready to take to the air. So great was the confusion, aggravated by the ground and air attack, that even Rommel himself was unaware of how his striking force was faring............ [47]

The bombing caused several explosions that were concentrated against the positions held by the Italian tanks and vehicles, some of which were lost even before they had a chance to move forward. Not only did they commence moving toward their objectives with some delay but subsequently then stumbled upon a deep minefield which further held them up. The deadly combination of heavy artillery fire and the minefield took a heavy toll on the troops. While the vanguards of the two German divisions by 0500 were clear of the main minefields, each gap was creating its own bottleneck causing huge traffic jams all the way back to the start line. *Ariete* and *Trieste* would emerge from the minefields only several hours had passed and only after having spent a great deal of petrol. Many of their vehicles had broken down or had been trapped in soft sand, and others had been damaged by shellfire or bombing. Thus, they were not able to join the other armoured units in the assault of the enemy positions. In fact, *Littorio* was the only Italian unit that managed to emerge from the minefields and reach the jumping off position for the attack albeit with a noticeable delay. At 0900 the 31st Reconnaissance Group and 15th Panzer Division had emerged from the minefield and were west of Samaket Gaballa and were already engaging British motorized and mechanized columns, 21st Panzer Division was still further west and had just passed the minefields, while *Littorio* was still threading its way through the last field on 21st Division's left. It eventually emerged from the minefield and joining forces with the 90th Leicht, it travelled north at twelve miles from the sea. But it was at this point that

---

47 Ronald Walker, *Alam Halfa and Alamein*, p. 95.

Rommel ordered the troops to return to base as the whole operation could not succeed given the lack of petrol and the stubborn enemy resistance. It had taken too much time and petrol to emerge from the minefields. The operation had been compromised.

On 2 September Rommel had to inform *Comando Supremo* of the failure of the offensive. The defeat at Alam Halfa was a huge reversal of fortune for the Axis in general and for the DAK specifically which had been successfully on the offensive for most of 1942. Rommel's flanking maneuvers did not reap any success as the combination of Commonwealth artillery guns, deep minefields and the harassing fire and bombing from the RAF took a deep toll on the German Panzer units. The Ultra intercepts also aided the Commonwealth defense since it is believed that the British commander knew ahead of time about Rommel's offensive intentions and the date and time of the attack. The latter held that someone in the Italian officer ranks had betrayed the operation by giving the Commonwealth forces warning of his plans. But several years later it was discovered that British intelligence by intercepting enemy communications with Ultra had been able on several occasions to anticipate Axis movements.

Because of the stalemate at Alam Halfa Rommel was forced on the defensive. His troops did not have the tanks required nor the fuel supply to attack again soon. Thus, Rommel ordered the troops to begin digging trenches, strongpoints and artillery emplacements to face a likely Commonwealth attack. His gamble, to continue the offensive at all costs, however, failed to achieve the breakthrough while his failure to see the neutralization of Malta as a key stepping stone to final victory, condemned the Axis forces to the static battle at El Alamein. Always oblivious to the supply constraints and the needs of his army, Rommel took the easy way out and blamed the Italian Navy for not readily supporting his army during the final offensive. Prior to the start of the final offensive he had gained authorization from Hitler and Mussolini by going above the heads of his superiors Kesserling and Cavallero and by embellishing the amount of war booty and fuel captured at Tobruk. Hitler and Mussolini gave the go ahead to his offensive without having a complete picture of the supply situation of the *Panzerarmee* that was by then very far from its supply bases and the major ports and had only captured 2,000 gallons of petrol at Tobruk. Rommel's miscalculation in mid-1942 cost the Axis dearly but so did the fatal decisions made by the two leaders Mussolini and Hitler who refused to listen to the cautious advice of their senior generals that had greater experience than Rommel in assessing the supply needs and the related difficulties in transporting them to North Africa. Their other great miscalculation was of not reinforcing Rommel's army with two additional armoured divisions and motorized artillery units in early 1942 and having failed to do so to privilege the campaign on the Eastern front. As the campaign with the Soviet Union absorbed an incredible amount of equipment and resources, the *Panzerarmee* suffered the consequences of this very uneven situation. Whereas the Soviet Army had by 1942 stopped the Axis advance on its tracks, Rommel's army, properly reinforced, could have possibly achieved more in early or mid-1942.

Mussolini and the Italian High Command initially in mid-1942 backed Rommel and ultimately even though with some reservations approved of his offensive plans with Operation Venezia. After the *Panzerarmee* was stalemated at Alam Halfa the dictator became more critical of Rommel's conduct of the campaign. Eventually after the final El Alamein, Mussolini stated rather opportunistically that Rommel was a good general worthy of commanding a few battalions but had shown to have lacked the strategic vision needed to command an Army Corps. A more balanced view would argue that Rommel was a general with great strengths and thanks to his audacity he often achieved important successes with relatively few resources. His major failure, which likely derived from his not being a cadet of the general staff school of the army, was probably in not taking into adequate consideration or fully understanding the Axis supply situation in North Africa. Moreover, his offensive at all costs mentality did not help either because it often led to advances for the sake of advancing without a strategic overall vision.[48] In driving his forces to exploit every battlefield success and spurring them on to continue the advance toward Egypt he ignored the advice of his superiors and increased the vulnerability of the troops under his command that were each time further away from their supply bases, while the enemy had superior numbers and was much closer to its bases. As military historian Citino asserts in reference to the North African campaign: "There was an iron logic at work, and neither side could escape its grip. Long advances did not simply take you away from the railhead, they took you entire time zones from it. Supply became not just a problem, but the problem. Rommel was more dangerous at El Aghelia, relatively close to Tripoli, than he was on the Egyptian wire, six-hundred miles east. Likewise, the British were never more dangerous than when they were fighting with Egypt at their back, and never more helpless than when they had just overrun Cyrenaica."[49]

It is believed that by September 1942 Rommel was of the opinion that the campaign in North Africa had come to a stalemate and the Commonwealth was in the ascendancy. Rommel, many argued, had now become highly pessimistic about the Axis ability to prevail in North Africa.[50] The supply situation was always one of the main concerns of both Rommel and the Italians. On 27 September a meeting was held by *Comando Supremo* to review the supply, weapons and manpower requirements of the Italian units deployed. With respect to North Africa it was determined that given the need for reinforcements for the armoured divisions it was impossible given the lack of experienced personnel to form a new armoured divisions. In fact, a plan had been in place to transform the *Giovani Fascisti* in a fully-fledged armoured division. But as a result of this review the plan had to be put on hold because of a lack of the necessary number of tanks in favor of bringing up to full rank the existing armoured units. It was noted that they lacked personnel in key areas such as drivers, experienced artillerymen and munitions experts. It was also decided that the production of the M.15 tank series was to be reduced considerably in favor of more *semoventi*. The L.6 tank production was also to be discontinued while the number of AB armoured vehicles produced was to be increased considerably. Thus, the focus of industrial production was on:

- Increasing the production of the 75mm self-propelled guns, while limiting production of the M.15 tanks.
- Accelerate production of the P-40 heavy tank.
- Increase production of armoured vehicles.

---

48 Robert Citino, 'Drive to Nowhere: The Myth of the Afrika Korps', *Military History Quarterly*, Summer 2012.
49 Ibid.
50 Giuseppe Mancinelli, *Dal fronte dell'Africa settentrionale 1942-1943* (Milan: Rizzoli, 1970).
    Niall Barr, 'Rommel in the Desert' in Ian Beckett (ed.), *Rommel Reconsidered* (Mechanicsburg, Pennsylvania: Stackpole, 2013).

"My criteria" argued Cavallero, "is to bring up to full rank the existing armoured divisions while putting temporarily on hold the constitution of a new armoured division (Giovani Fascisti) due to a general lack of reinforcements. At present time the composition of the armoured divisions is inadequate especially the available weaponry is insufficient for the current phase of the campaign."[51] Cavallero's overall directions for the continuation of the war were sound and the increased production of self-propelled guns would have served well the interests of the units deployed in North Africa as well as those deployed in the Soviet Union. The main problem was the slow pace of production due to a host of factors which did not help especially when both the Soviet Union and the Commonwealth launched massive offensives in late 1942 leaving the Italian units at the front with few reinforcements and replacement vehicles. The great irony in the campaign was that both *Comando Supremo* and Kesselring were aware of the need to halt the Axis advance and regroup but were not powerful enough in stopping the impetuous Rommel. Thus the dysfunctional command structure ultimately played in the hands of their adversary.

Comparison of Main medium tanks				
Tank Nationality and model	Crew	Petrol	Radio	Gun
Italian tank M.13/40 and M.14/41	4	Petrol	None	47mm
German pzKw IV	5	Petrol	Transceiver	75mm
British Mk VI Crusader 4	4	Petrol	Transceiver	57mm
American M3 Grant	6	Avgas	Transceiver	75mm
Source: Paddy Griffiths, *Desert Warfare*.				

EL Alamein III

Preparations

In early October General Georg Stumme, who was in temporary command of the Axis troops in North Africa as Rommel was away on sick leave, held a conference with all the divisional commanders warning them that a major enemy offensive was likely to take place. Stumme did not know when it would take place but his intelligence services had informed him of a great enemy build up. In the Axis forces, there were by then four German and ten Italian divisions in the advanced positions in Egypt and some at the rear in Libya. In the *Panzerarmee* there were the original DAK units (15th and 21st Armoured Divisions) and the 90th Leicht Division, 164th Leicht Division and the *Ramcke* Parachute Brigade. In the three Italian corps—X, XX, and XXI—were the *Ariete* and *Littorio* armoured Divisions, *Trieste* Division (motorized), *Folgore* Division (parachute troops), and the *Pavia*, *Bologna*, *Brescia* and *Trento* Divisions (infantry mostly non-motorized). The Young Fascists Division garrisoned the Siwa

---

51 Mario Montanari, *Le operazioni in Africa settentrionale*, vol. III, part I, p. 631.

oasis while the *Pistoia* Division was just across the Libyan frontier at Bardia. The Axis forces were about 100,000 strong, of which a little less than half were Germans; there were some 47,000 other Italian troops in the rear in North Africa. They had approximately 500 tanks, of which more than half were Italian. On the eve of El Alamein the Axis armour was divided into two battle groups: the 15th Panzer and *Littorio* were deployed in the northern sector of the defensive line while *Ariete* and the 21st Panzer were deployed in the south together with the 33rd Reconnaissance Group. The 90th Leicht was kept in reserve along the northern coast to prevent a potential enemy amphibious operation together with *Trieste* Division. Each mechanized unit was located close behind the main resistance and minefield line and its mobile artillery stood side to side with the forward positioned anti-tank units and even some of the tanks were deployed in a non-mobile fashion in dug in gun emplacement positions to face the enemy attack. The infantry divisions such as the *Brescia, Bologna, Pavia and Trento* were deployed on the main resistance line behind the minefields and special troops such as the *Ramcke* Parachute Brigade and the *Folgore* Division occupied key positions such as Ruweisat Bridge and the Munassib depression.

On 23 October, the Axis defensive line at El Alamein from north to south was organized as follows: In the north, near the coast, the resistance line was backed up by the LI *Battaglione carri medi* which was deployed behind Point 22, whereas the main line of defense in front of the minefields was comprised by the X *Battaglione/7° Reggimento Bersaglieri* which was at Mersa el Hamra, while the XI *Battaglione/7° Reggimento Bersaglieri* supported by the 125th German Regiment were in the forefront. On the main road to Alexandria stood the CCCLVII Italian Artillery Group with 75/27 guns.

The central position which spanned from Bir Sultan Omar to Kidney Ridge was held by the IV *Battaglione Carri Medi* and II Battalion/15th German Panzer Division (Hill 33). XXIII *Battaglione/12° Reggimento Bersaglieri*, DLVI *Gruppo Semoventi*, CCCXXXII Italian Artillery Group with 100/17 guns, XXXIV Italian Artillery Group with 149/40 guns and the XXIX Italian Artillery Group with 88/56 guns were concentrated at Kidney Ridge. The frontline main positions were occupied by 62° *Reggimento/Trento* Division, the III Battalion/ 382nd German Grenadier Regiment and II Battalion/125th German Grenadier Regiment.

The southern front was held by the XII *Battaglione Carri Medi*, I Battalion/15th German Panzer Division, and the II Battalion/150th German Grenadier Regiment at El Wishka. XXXVI *Battaglione/120° Reggimento Bersaglieri*, DLIV *Gruppo Semoventi*, and II *Gruppo da 75/27* of the 133° *Reggimento Artiglieria/Littorio*. The frontline main positions were held by 61° *Reggimento/Trento* Division, the II Battalion/German 382nd Grenadier Regiment and II Battalion/433rd Grenadier Regiment at Sanyet. The frontline then was held on a continuous line by the *Bologna* and *Brescia* Divisions and reinforced by the *Ramcke* Parachute Brigade. These positions were backed up by *Ariete*'s XIII *Battaglione Carri Medi* and VI *Gruppo Semoventi* *(the XIII Battaglione* came from Verona, the headquarter of the 32° *Reggimento Carristi* and it replaced the *VIII Battaglione Carri Medi* that had been wiped out previously)*, while the southernmost positions were held by the *Folgore* Parachute Division and reinforced by *Ariete*'s IX and X *Battaglioni Carri Medi*, XII *Battaglione Bersaglieri*, 132° *Reggimento Artiglieria Corazzata*, and the German 33rd Reconnaissance Group. Italian divisional tank strength had been build up since the end of July as new equipment and machines along with many soldiers had been brought to the frontline.

On the eve of Operation Lightfoot at El Alamein the *Ariete*[52] Division was comprised by about 6,100 soldiers, 117 M.13/41 and M.14/41 tanks, seventeen *semoventi* self-propelled guns and fourteen command tanks, while the *Trieste* Division had 5,000 soldiers, thirty-three M.14/41 tanks and ten self-propelled guns. Meanwhile *Littorio* had 5,100 soldiers, 106 M.14/41 tanks, fifteen *semoventi*, eighteen command tanks and twenty L.6/40 light tanks. The German units had eight *Panzerkampfwagen* IV and thirty Specials, eighty-five *Panzerkampfwagen* III and eighty-eight Specials. The Commonwealth held the advantage in almost all areas and its numerical advantage with regard to tanks was considerable. It could count upon 1,029 tanks versus 500 of the Axis. Roughly a little more than half of the Axis tanks were Italian medium tanks (M.13 or 14) which by mid-1942 were obsolete especially when facing the larger and more powerful American tanks such as Grants and Shermans. It is estimated that by October 1942 the British could count upon 252 Shermans[53], a new tank that was even superior to the German more advanced *Panzerkampfwagen* IV Special, and 170 Grants.[54] According to Rommel:

> The British had a two to one superiority in tanks. This figure included on our side the 300 Italian tanks, the fighting value of which was very small. We still had only very few tanks armed with a 75m gun, whereas the British had many hundreds equipped with heavy guns. Of our 210 German tanks, only 30 or so were Panzer IVs: the majority were Panzer IIIs, half of which were of the short-barreled type and hence very out of date. As for the 300 Italian tanks – apart from their technical deficiencies which I have mentioned several times already- most of them were decrepit, and barely fit for action.[55]

The Italian medium tank was still armed with the 47mm gun, while the German *Panzerkampfwagen* IV was armed with a 75mm, the *Panzerkampfwagen* III with a 50mm and the special with a 75mm short barrel gun. In the early stages of the war both German tanks had a short barrel gun. It was only in 1942 that some German tanks were built with a long-barreled gun. As historian Liddell Hart asserts: "The greater length of the barrel gave a considerable increase in the range and penetration of the gun."[56] According to Liddell Hart, Rommel understated in 'The Rommel Papers' the strength of the Commonwealth tank forces. He maintains that the latter had a 2 ½ to 1 superiority in tanks over the Axis forces. Moreover 500 Commonwealth tanks were armed with the 75mm long-barreled gun some of which were Shermans, Lees or Grants, whereby only less than a third of Rommel's force was equipped with a 75mm gun.[57]

---

52 Ariete' units also included III *Gruppo Nizza*, XV/15 *Raggruppamento* da 105/28, XXX *Gruppo da* 88/55, CCCXXXII *Gruppo da* 100/17, plus its artillery regiment on three groups of field guns.
53 The Australian Official History provides slightly different figures: "In the first half of September 318 Sherman tanks arrived at Suez and with these General Alexander intended to equip three of his six armoured brigades. For the first time the Eighth Army had been given tanks which could match the enemy's in range and manoeuvre and outshoot all his tanks except the formidable Mark IV Specials, of which he had no more than 30." Ronald Walker, *Alam Halfa and Alamein*, p. 639.
54 Kenneth Macksey, *Rommel Battles and Campaigns* (London: Arms and Armour Press, 1979), p. 150.
55 Basil Liddell Hart, *The Rommel Papers*, pp. 296-297.
56 Ibid, p. 297.
57 Ibid., p. 296.

Both Rommel and Liddell Hart's analysis of the Italian armour totally discounted the medium tanks, while they failed to consider the approximately forty-three *semoventi* da 75 (plus another ten in the rear held as reserve), which were also equipped with a 75mm gun and provided the Italian armoured units with the only vehicle that could go head to head with the medium Allied tanks. Considering these units, the Axis had approximately 110 German tanks with a 75mm gun while the Italians had forty-three, while the Commonwealth forces had approximately 500 tanks with a 75mm gun. The other important weapon in this battle was the 88mm anti-tank gun. Rommel's *Panzerarmee* had eighty-six 88mm guns, sixty-eight 76mm captured Soviet guns and approximately thirty Italian *Cannoni* da 90/53, plus another 250-300 field guns of different sizes. The bulk of the anti-tank weapons were German Pak 50mm (250) and Italian 47mm guns (150) "that could not penetrate the armour of the Shermans, Grants, or the Valentines, except at close range."[58] In contrast, by mid-October the guns in the Eighth Army included 832 25-pdr, thirty-two 4.5-inch guns, twenty 5.5-inch, twenty-four 105mm, 735 6-pdr and 521 2-pdr anti-tank guns.[59]

The Commonwealth also enjoyed considerable air superiority. More than 1,000 aircraft were available to support the Eighth Army whereas the Axis air forces had only about 350 aircrafts based in North Africa. The Commonwealth air superiority had already played a key role in the summer battles in harassing the movements of the Axis tanks and their supply echelons. This superiority would once again play an important role in the final battle of El Alamein.

The overwhelming strength of the Commonwealth meant that they could afford to win a battle of attrition, while the Axis, short of fuel and tanks, could not survive weeks of continued fighting. As Greene and Massignani assert "The British attack plan, as elaborated by Montgomery, was a slow and methodical crumbling of the Axis field defenses, which would lead to a breakthrough and final collapse of the enemy. This was a classic battle of attrition, very different from the others fought in the desert to this point."[60]

By late October the Eighth Army was organized as follows:

> XXX Corps (Lieut-General Leese)
> 23rd Armoured Brigade Group (Brigadier Richards)
> 51st Division (Major-General Wimberley)
> 9th Australian Division (Lieut-General Morshead)
> 2nd New Zealand Division (Lieut-General Freyberg)
> 1st South African Division (Major-General Pienaar)
> 4th Indian Division (Major-General Tuker)
> XIII Corps (Lieut-General Horrocks)
> 7th Armoured Division (Major-General Harding)
> 44th Division (Major-General Hughes)
> 50th Division (Major-General Nichols)
> X Corps (Lieut-General Lumsden)
> 1st Armoured Division (Major-General Briggs)
> 10th Armoured Division (Major-General Gatehouse)[61]

---

58 Basil Liddell Hart, *History of the Second World War*, p. 298.
59 Ronald Walker, *Alam Halfa and Alamein*, pp. 639-645.
60 Greene and Massignani, *Rommel's North African Campaign*, p. 219.
61 Barton Maughan, *Australia in the War of 1939-1945 Vol. III: Tobruk and El Alamein*, p. 647.

In essence Montgomery aimed to use his infantry and combat engineers to open the way for the armour that would ultimately effectuate a breakout of the Axis defensive line. He planned two simultaneous attacks, one in the northern and one in the southern sector. In the north, the XXX Corp (9th Australian, 51st Highlander, 2nd New Zealand, 1st South African, 1st and 10th Armoured Divisions) sought a breakthrough at Kidney Ridge, while the XIII Corps (44th and 50th Infantry Divisions and the 7th Armoured Division) was to attack near the Munassib Depression. In the north, the Commonwealth forces were also expected to put pressure against two other main points: Hill 28[62], which was near the coast just north of Kidney Ridge and Hill 33 which was on the right flank of Kidney Ridge.

According to the Australian official history, "The so-called Kidney Ridge was a depression with raised lips around which the enemy had developed a powerful locality."[63] This was the area the Axis troops called Hill 33 (or Quota 33 for the Italians). It was backed up by two armoured battalions (one from *Littorio* and the other from 15th Panzer) and its frontline positions were held by one battalion from the 382nd German and an Italian artillery group (XXIX *Gruppo Liguria*) which was equipped with 88mm Flak 36 guns.

24 October

When the Commonwealth artillery opened a thundering preparatory barrage by 908 guns at 2140 on 23 October, the Axis command was taken by complete surprise. The situation of uncertainty was made even more precarious as the enemy guns greatly debilitated the Axis communication lines and isolated many of the forward frontline positions but also because General Stumme, whom Rommel while on medical leave had left in command of the *Panzerarmee*, died a few hours after the start of the battle. Following the barrage, which had already caused severe losses,[64] the Commonwealth infantry and armoured vehicles attacked on a front of about five miles. Between the railway and the coast road the attack was halted barely by the 125th Panzer Grenadier Regiment, which recovered quickly from the deadly barrage to fire their guns and rifles against the advancing enemy infantry. The greatest progress had been made by the Australian infantry units (2/48th and 2/24th Battalions supported by forty Valentines of 40th Royal Tanks) which by 0200 had crossed the minefields, overcome the enemy outposts and were pressing on the main defense line near Hill 28, a high ground position that dominated the plains and offered an excellent observation point. This main enemy thrust fell mostly on the 382nd German Panzer Grenadier Regiment and the 61st and 62nd Italian infantry Regiments of the *Trento* Division, whose battalions were positioned opposite the 9th Australian, 51st Highland and 2nd New Zealand Divisions, each division facing about one German and one Italian battalion. The II Battalion of the 382nd German Regiment, for instance, had lost most its strongpoints and had only half its original strength when its positions were overrun by the enemy infantry. *Trento*'s Division units had also suffered huge casualties from the enemy barrage

---

62 The Australians named this position Trig 29 or Point 29, while the Italians called it Quota 28. For the British Hill 28 was the same as Kidney Ridge, while the position was located north of Kidney Ridge and was a separate position.
63 Barton Maughan, *Australia in the War of 1939-1945 Vol. III: Tobruk and El Alamein*, p. 649.
64 Littorio, for instance, lost three 88/56 guns during the night between 23-24 October.

and many of their positions were also taken by the enemy infantry. In the sector facing the 6th New Zealand Brigade, for example, the attack had progressed well against two main points occupied by *Trento* Division as the 24th and the 28th (Maori) Battalions took all their objectives near Miteiriya ridge. After suffering terrible losses, for example, the remnants of the 62nd Infantry Regiment reorganized along the *Trento*'s resistance line, while to the south the *46° Reggimento Artiglieria/ Trento* Division opened fire at point blank range against enemy tanks and infantry. This unit together with the fire provided by 220th German Artillery Regiment which also fired its guns in rapid succession against the advancing enemy ranks, did enough to halt the British 2nd Armoured Brigade after the attack had initially progressed well and had overrun the battalions of *Trento* and of the 382nd German Panzer grenadier Regiment and occupied the advanced frontline positions in front of minefields L and J. Heavy losses were also sustained by the enemy especially the 2nd New Zealand Division with a loss of approximately 950 men or as Christopher Pugsley puts it: "The greatest number of killed and wounded in a 24-hour period that the Division experienced during the war."[65] Therefore, in the early hours of 24 October the Commonwealth attacking columns had pushed ahead into the Axis defenses and had penetrated in the north near the coast and Hill 28 on both flanks of Tell el Eisa as well as south at Miteiriya Ridge. They were followed by the armoured units which could only advance more slowly through the minefields while also being targeted by the Axis artillery. It was at this point that the attack was halted by a combination of artillery fire and localized counterattacks by the Axis armour. "On the Axis side, in the absence of orders from above, 15th Panzer and *Littorio* took it upon themselves to act. They launched several local armoured counterattacks against the largest Allied penetration in the north during the day."[66] Their objective was to push back the enemy infiltrations beyond the Axis resistance line mainly in the sectors held by the *Trento* and the I/382nd German Battalion.

For this purpose, the Axis mechanized troops were deployed into three mixed (German and Italian and tank and infantry units) combat groups which launched simultaneous counters against the Commonwealth troops. As *Capitano* Dino Campini of *Littorio's IV Battaglione Carri* asserts:

> The division together with German armoured troops comprised three Raum. One in the north, one in the middle and one in the south. Our Raum was in the middle near Hill 33 and it was comprised by IV *Battaglione Carri*, II Battalion of the 15th German Panzer, 8th German Armoured Company, German grenadier troops from the 115th Regiment, XXIII *Battaglione Bersaglieri*, a battery of 149mm guns, an artillery group of 88mm guns and a semoventi da 75 group.[67]

The mobile elements of the northern Raum were comprised by: LI *Battaglione Carri* and elements of the 15th Panzer Division, X and XI *Battaglioni/7° Reggimento Bersaglieri*.

---

65 Andrew Sangster and Pier Paolo Battistelli, *Myths, Amnesia and Reality in Military Conflicts, 1935-1945*, p. 98.
66 Ian Walker, *Iron Hulls, Iron Hearts*, p. 158.
67 Paolo Caccia Dominioni (ed.), *Le Trecento ore a Nord di Qattara* (Milan: Libreria Militare, 2012), p. 83.

Whereas the southern Raum was defended by the following mobile units (the so-called Stiffelmayer Group): the XII *Battaglione Carri Medi,* I Battalion of the 15th German Panzer Division, and the DLIV *Gruppo Semoventi.* The mobile combat groups were supposed to be deployed for counterattacks or to intervene once the infantry and the artillery line of their respective Raum had been breached or weakened in some way.

The combat group closest to the southern (*Stiffelmayer* Group) front was the first to launch an attack against the advancing troops of the 2nd New Zealand, 51st Highlander and several South African infantry units. The Axis tanks by machine gunning the enemy infantry halted their progress and later captured some abandoned artillery batteries. Then when faced by an enemy armoured force of 10th Armoured Division, which was headed toward El Wishka, they had to intervene to counter and push it back. The tank versus tank battle raged for more than four hours ending at 1400. The recollections of the Axis armoured crew members recall the engagement in vivid terms as they had to face large numbers of Sherman and Grant tanks and six-pdr. guns that had been brought into forward positions.

The following are the recollections of Davide Beretta of *Littorio* Division:

> For about an hour the DLIV Gruppo Semoventi had been engaged in combat counterattacking the enemy armour with great impetus. After they had submerged the infantry outposts and strongpoints, the enemy armour was attempting to overcome our feeble line of defense. Our semoventi were firing repeatedly and each frontal attack by the enemy armour was checked. In turn, the enemy would then turn around and attempt to sweep at our flanks rather than trying again to attack us frontally and pointedly concentrate fire upon the weaker medium tanks. Our job was to fend off the attacks on the medium tanks by concentrating our fire upon the Shermans and the Grants. After receiving much fire the enemy tanks stopped advancing altogether. They kept on firing against our M. 14//41 tanks from a distance and later retreated. The South African infantry troops did the same. They lined up on a ridge behind the tanks and then retreated.[68]

The battle was brought to a standstill by 1400 when both Axis and Commonwealth tanks disengaged after further penetrations into the Axis resistance line had been checked.

Meantime, the middle combat group (IV *Battaglione Carri Medi* and II Battalion of the 15th German Panzer) was initially deployed alongside the artillery of *46° Reggimento* to bolster the Axis position on Hill 33. Throughout the morning, the tanks were lined up in a defensive fashion with their hulls down and poured shell after shell against the fast moving enemy infantry and tanks preventing them from advancing any further. *IV Battaglione Carri Medi* was then moved south-east of Hill 33 to the position held by XXIX *Gruppo* which was equipped with 88mm Flak 36 guns that had been attacked by enemy forces. After a prolonged barrage by both tanks and artillery the Axis forces eliminated the dangerous breech in front of minefields J and L and continued to patrol the minefield gaps made by the enemy. Meanwhile the artillery batteries of the XXI *Gruppo* further north continued to pound both flanks of Tell el Eisa preventing the Australians from moving forward. The tanks remained on the frontline until the I Battalion/382nd Panzer Grenadier and the I *Battaglione/62° Trento* could reestablish a

---

68 Davide Beretta, *Batterie semoventi alzo zero – Quelli di El Alamein* (Milan: Mursia, 1994), p. 252.

rudimentary defensive line. Throughout the morning, they continued to be targeted by both enemy artillery shelling and the bombing forays of the RAF which prevented them from moving freely at will and further reduced their maneuverability.

By midday on the opposite end of the defensive line Commonwealth tanks of 1st Armoured Division amassed on the edge of the minefields and then suddenly in the afternoon attacked Hill 33 positions. The Central Raum had therefore to intervene to meet this dangerous threat that was set to overrun the strongpoint of 88mm guns of the XXIX *Gruppo*. The tank counter, supported by the Axis artillery, initially was made at a slow speed to entice the enemy to disperse his tank units in the battlefield. However, the Commonwealth tanks of 2nd Armoured Brigade stood still and lined up on one main line of defense and began to pour fire on the Axis tanks. This gave rise to a prolonged shooting match that went on for more than two hours and was supported on both sides by the artillery guns. The Commonwealth infantry suffered the heaviest casualties as the Axis shells fell into their exposed and advanced positions, meanwhile the Sherman tanks and the Commonwealth anti-tank guns scored direct hits against Axis armour. The fighting lasted until darkness descended when the tank crews could no longer see their targets and were forced to disengage. At the end of the day, IV *Battaglione Carri Medi* counted the loss of two medium tanks, while the German 15th Panzer Division lost five.

The following is a summary of the battle from the Australian official history which highlights the effectiveness of the new weapons introduced in large numbers at El Alamein:

> Towards sunset the enemy amour (15th Armoured and *Littorio* Divisions) attacked out of the sun, the main weight being directed more against the Highland than the Australian front. The gunfire battle furiously quickened and the Australians saw "Priests" in action for the first time. The firing continued until dark. Twenty to thirty tanks were destroyed on either side; but the Germans had to destroy British tanks in about the ratio of four to one if they were to retain a chance of avoiding armoured defeat, and that they did not do.[69]

Facing for the first time the new Priests of the 11th Royal Artillery Regiment, the Italian medium tanks had a particularly tough time while only the self-propelled guns seemed capable of engaging the new weapons in more prolonged and evenly matched duels. Even the German Panzer tanks had a tough time against the newly introduced enemy weapons and the range of their guns. The 88mm Axis gun crews also experienced difficulties when targeted at long range by the High Explosive fire of both Priests and Shermans. A first hand British account of the fighting on that day in fact reveals the effectiveness of the new Sherman tanks:

> A little later in the morning some German tanks appeared in front of us and halted about 3,000 yards away. I noted at least one of their new Mark IV Specials with its long 75mm gun amongst them. It was now that our new gunnery methods and our new Sherman tanks showed their worth. For, when the German tanks moved forward, both A and C squadron began to hit their targets and several of the German tanks went up in flames.[70]

---

69 Barton Maughan, *Australia in the War of 1939-1945 Vol. III: Tobruk and El Alamein*, p. 679.
70 Bryn Hammond, *El Alamein*, p. 195.

The first day of battle revealed the underlying dynamics of the confrontation and how a battle of attrition could ultimately only serve the Commonwealth's ultimate interests. On the 24th the Axis infantry and mechanized troops had given up some forward positions as well as suffered casualties during the massive preparatory barrage. However, they had been able during the counter thrusts to recapture some of the lost positions while inflicting casualties against the enemy. But even though the Axis troops had withstood the assault successfully, they had suffered losses especially with regard to tanks and artillery units. Since the Axis had started the battle with half the number of tanks than the Commonwealth it appeared clear from the start that they had few hopes of ultimately winning a prolonged battle. Their best chances of winning were in swiftly inflicting heavy casualties amongst the attacking forces thus undermining their morale and their willingness to come forward again. But if the Commonwealth commanders continued to pour men and equipment into the battle despite the losses, the Axis position at El Alamein was most likely doomed especially if the latter accepted a pitched and positional battle. As historian Bryn Hammond correctly asserts about 15th Panzer and *Divisione Littorio's* actions: "The three counter attacks they launched that day produced disproportionate Axis tank casualties in which the six-pounders antitank guns had their chance to shine. Tank loss rates in *Divisione Littorio* and particularly 15th Panzer Division were unsustainable. The beginnings of the real crisis for the Panzerarmee had, paradoxically been prompted by the actions of the Axis commanders."[71]

According to DAK war diary the first day of the final battle was summarized as follows: "It appears that the enemy has taken possession of the first line of defense in front of minefields J and L and that the front held by 164th Light Division and Trento Division has been split into two. The commander of 15th Panzer Division indicates that through a counterattack undertaken by 15th Panzer and Littorio the first line of defense near minefield L has been recaptured."[72]

25 October

On the 25th Rommel arrived at dusk at the command headquarters of the *Panzerarmee*. Despite being on medical leave in Europe he had been urged to return the day before by Hitler personally after the British commander had launched the operation. Although he could not direct the day's fighting Rommel quickly assessed the situation after being briefed by General von Thoma which gave him very discouraging reports about the overall military situation. He quickly surmised that he faced a very difficult situation where his troops could not count upon the element of surprise or on a highly mobile mechanized battle, in which up until then they had thrived in, due to the lack of fuel supplies. His troops indeed were called to battle in a positional and defensive battle where the deep minefields and the defensive obstacles of all kinds were to play an important part given the Axis numerical inferiority. Rommel faced a supply situation which was not very healthy and a battle of attrition against an enemy with superior forces. As Niall Barr correctly points out:

---

71 Bryn Hammond, *El Alamein*, p. 203.
72 DAK war diary cited in: Daniele Sanna, *Il caos dei comandi: L'Afrika Korps e gli italiani a El Alamein* (Milan: Mursia, 2008), p. 57.

Rommel was bitterly angry at the lack of fuel, but the truth was that he had ignored the clear warning provided by the events of late August. Alam Halfa had served notice to the British air and naval forces were now in a position to severely restrict the flow of Axis supplies to the front. If Rommel feared that he would now 'fight this battle with but small hope of success' the fault lay largely with his refusal to withdraw from the El Alamein line after Alam Halfa.[73]

By the time Rommel arrived the Commonwealth had been repelled in the south but had made some progress in the north where its overwhelming artillery fire had caused further losses to the line infantry. On the Commonwealth right flank the Australian infantry had moved forward and had achieved all its *Lightfoot* objectives in Tell el Eisa. From these positions, they again attempted to move forward but were checked by the guns of the *3° Reggimento Artiglieria/ Trento*. The British 9th Armoured Brigade overran one company of the *Trento* Division's 61° *Reggimento* but was then promptly halted by a combination of a barrage from 46° *Reggimento Artiglieria* and localized counterattacks by Axis armour which forced the enemy tanks west of Mitieirya ridge. Meanwhile the 51st Highland Division supported by an armoured brigade attempted to breach in force the thinly held line held by the 382nd Panzer grenadier Regiment on Hill 33, while the 1st Armoured Division and the 7th Motor Brigade attacked the flanks. Despite holding their positions the Axis troops in the northern section of the El Alamein line had sustained heavy losses in both men and equipment. In two days of fighting, *Trento* Division had lost almost half of its strength, while the 164th Light had suffered casualties and had lost several guns to enemy fire. This prompted again the Axis tank crews to come to their rescue and counter-attack the Commonwealth tank units that were advancing in the wake of their infantry.

The major Commonwealth thrust of the day had once again taken place in the north where 2nd Armoured Brigade supporting the Australian infantry started to advance west at dawn toward Hill 33. Later in the morning they were joined by the 7th Motor Rifle Brigade, which arrived on the position with several motor vehicles which immediately attracted considerable attention from enemy anti-tank guns.

Then, to push back the Commonwealth infiltration in the north, *Littorio* and 15th Panzer launched a series of attacks that put further pressure on the enemy armour. The first counter was made by the middle combat group and is partly described by *Capitano* Dino Campini of IV *Battaglione Carri*. The battalion was from the onset harried by the RAF and when it arrived near Hill 33 it had already lost several crew members. *Capitano* Campini picks up the story from here:

> At noon on 25 October, after a meeting with Ten. Colonnello Casamassima, and after we had chosen a direction of attack, we clashed with the enemy. The fighting lasted only a few minutes but it was extremely bloody. The enemy occupied the field and his tanks and artillery were deployed on a single line of defense in a static position. His new special piercing shells were quite an unpleasant surprise for our tank crews. These were shells comprised of phosphorus which were lethal. Despite the enemy fire our tanks ran straight at the enemy

---

73   Niall Barr, 'Rommel in the Desert' in Ian Beckett (ed.), *Rommel Reconsidered* (Mechanicsburg, Pennsylvania: Stackpole, 2013), p.104.

armour, many of which were burning and at the end of a ten-minute confrontation we had forced the enemy to retreat. We lost eighteen tanks, while the enemy lost fifteen. The attack had lasted only ten minutes. After the action, had been concluded, peace and quiet descended on the battlefield. "[74]

The combat diary of the IV *Battaglione Carri Medi* reports that the operation was intended to be a joint Axis effort, but that the German tanks arrived late at the meeting point. Thus, IV *Battaglione* medium tanks moved ahead first by itself and were later joined by the panzers. Being at the head of the column, the Italian medium tanks attracted considerable enemy fire. "Looking back at this operation," states Dino Campini, "this combat action was conducted in a very up hazard way. No prior reconnaissance was conducted. We sallied against the enemy without a preparatory barrage and without receiving a prior briefing on how the enemy was deployed. It was a cavalry charge rather than an armoured operation….The enemy fire was concentrated against our tanks. The medium tanks of the IV, weighing only 14 tons, with their 47mm gun appeared to be like little toys when deployed against the Shermans weighing 30 tons and with their 75mm gun."[75] Despite the Axis heavy losses the counter achieved its intended purpose which was to blunt the enemy progression into the German-Italian line. *Littorio*'s losses consisted of eighteen tanks, fifteen dead and nineteen wounded. Amongst the dead was *Capitano* Vittorio Piccinini, commander of the 3° *Compagnia /IV Battaglione*, who was awarded a gold medal of military valor for having led the tank attack.

This counter was followed by a second thrust conducted by the north Raum combat group which struck both elements of the 7th Motor Rifle Brigade and the 2nd Armoured Division in an area half a mile north of Hill 33. This operation conducted by German armour of 15th Panzer and by LI *Battaglione Carri* is aptly described by historian Ian Walker:

At 1400, one of these approached 2nd Armoured Brigade from north-west, led by a company of Italian M.14s from LI Armoured Battalion of Littorio, supported by five German panzers and infantry. It came within range of 2nd Armoured's Sherman tanks before turning aside into 20th Australian Brigade. They immediately came under heavy artillery fire, which isolated the Axis armour from its infantry support. Despite this, the M.14s pressed home their attack with considerable dash, some even reaching the Australian outposts. They were halted and driven back by Australian anti-tank guns, supported by fire from 7th British Motor Brigade on their left and 2nd Armoured to their south. [76]

Corporal Donald Main of 7th Motor Brigade recollected when his unit was struck by the combined German-Italian tanks:

At the same time a heavy barrage was brought down on our positions, also machine gun and mortar fire. Since we were in front with our machine guns, as the tanks drew closer we had to stop firing and take cover in the trenches. Our sixteen six-pounders engaged the

---

74 Paolo Caccia Dominioni (ed.), *Le Trecento ore*, pp. 86-87.
75 Dino Campini, *Nei giardini del diavolo. La storia inedita dei carristi della Centauro, dell'Ariete e della Littorio* (Milan: Longanesi, 1969), p. 235.
76 Ian Walker, *Iron Hulls, Iron Hearts*, p. 160.

tanks, several firings at one tank, so that the closest was knocked out fifty yards in front. The battalion were credited with fourteen tanks. As some of the enemy tanks were hit, the occupants tried to escape through the turrets. One Italian officer was hoisting himself out when a six-pounder hit him in the chest and he literally disintegrated. In front of the stationary tanks were two Italians sitting on the ground. From the right came cries of 'You rotten Pommie bastards.' The Australians strongly objected to our knocking out the tanks with six-pounders before they came within range of their two-pounders.[77]

The close quarter firing by the anti-tank screen set up by the Commonwealth forces ultimately managed to force the Axis armour to call off the attack. The 7th Motor Rifle Brigade claimed to have hit fourteen enemy tanks, while the 2nd Armoured Brigade claimed thirty-nine hits and the loss of twenty-four tanks. The German 15th Panzer Division claimed to have destroyed up to thirty tanks but it is likely that total enemy tank losses for the day were not greater than twenty-four. In addition, 20th Australian Brigade had lost eighty-five men, 7th Motor Brigade had lost forty-nine men, while 2nd Armoured Brigade had lost fifty. Several Commonwealth guns had also been destroyed. The losses sustained by LI *Battaglione Carri Medi* during their "mad dash" had been severe. *Capitano* Tito Puddu, the commander of the battalion, was severely wounded and would later die of his wounds. *Tenente* Adelmo Ferrari would also later die of his wounds, while *sottotenente* Luigi Ottaviani and several *carristi* were also wounded. It also lost seven tanks.

The southern Raum Group was also involved in the day's fighting. Throughout the morning their positions and tank concentrations were shelled by heavy field artillery largely impeding their movements. After the heavy barrage had subsided the British tanks of 8th and 9th Armoured had come forward in the wake of the infantry. These forces were checked by the Axis anti-tank screen which forced them to settle beyond the minefield beyond Miteiriya Ridge. To further push back the enemy force in the afternoon: "XII Battaglione medium tanks engaged several enemy tanks in heavy fighting south-east of El Wihska."[78] The counter against the British tanks achieved its purpose of pushing back the Commonwealth force but severe losses were sustained. *Sottotenente* Antonio De Angelis and ten *carristi* were wounded during the encounter, while *Caporal Maggiore* Guerrino Stefanoni and *sottotenente* Mario Ornano were killed. The latter, an underage volunteer, had hid on a cargo ship to reach North Africa to join *Littorio*. He would be awarded a gold medal of military valor.

Regarding the day's fighting *Littorio*'s commander reported back to Rommel's command headquarters that his troops had come under fire by a massive anti-tank screen and by up to fifty Sherman tanks. Given the disparity of resources, the commander underlined that the frontline forces were unlikely to withstand a long-winded set piece battle. He claimed that *Littorio*'s tank strength was down to seventy-five vehicles.[79]

In the southern front the DAK War Diary reports the penetration by many enemy tanks into Point 103 held by *Folgore* Division with a progression of up to forty enemy tanks toward Point 115. It was also observed that the enemy tanks had gathered at the edge of the minefield and were regrouping in anticipation of further attacks. The document goes on to say that a

---

77 Bryn Hammond, *El Alamein*, p. 201.
78 Dino Campini, *Nei giardini del diavolo*, p. 236.
79 Mario Montanari, *Le operazioni in Africa Settentrionale*, vol. III, part I, p. 431.

swift counter in the southern sector was launched by *Divisione Folgore* paratroopers and *Pavia* infantrymen and supported by the 21st Panzer and *Ariete*. The counter punched a hole in the enemy line thanks mainly to the deployment of high caliber, forward positioned anti-tank guns. After a thunderous barrage, infantry and tanks pushed back the enemy further away from the minefields.[80]

This operation would be the main initiative taken by the armour deployed initially on the southern defensive line. A few days later Rommel would move the armour to the north where the battle was raging much more furiously.

26 October

On the morning of 26 October General Montgomery requested a tally of the losses thus far sustained in the battle. The overall situation was not encouraging because the losses were considerable while the progress had been limited. Up to that point the Commonwealth had lost 250 tanks (many of which were deemed repairable) and had sustained up to 6,000 casualties, many of them in the Dominion armies such as the Australian and the New Zealand contingents. It was on this day that Montgomery began to refine his strategy and rather than continue attacks on a broad front he opted for more concentrated operations in the northern end of the line. In order not to disperse his forces he would concentrate his army near the coast and attack into two main points: Hill 28 and Kidney Ridge. He would first attack against one point, then when Rommel had transferred troops to that point to parry the blow, he would switch the attack to the second point. For several days, the attacks in the northern sector would follow this bait and switch approach. Thus, on the 26th General Montgomery continued to press infantry and armoured units forward mainly in the north in a bid to wear down his opponent and achieve the desired breakthrough in that sector. As a result, Rommel felt compelled once again to commit his armoured units to block the enemy from advancing. Moreover, Axis intelligence was convinced by this time that renewed assaults would again be concentrated in the north and therefore urged Rommel to consolidate his mobile troops there. Given the tight Axis fuel supply situation if the 21st Panzer Division and *Ariete* were moved from the south to the northern front it was unlikely that they could return to the south in case the enemy decided to attack there at some future point. Thus, Rommel was faced with a conundrum which offered no easy solution. He could move the armoured units north but then the move would risk exposing his troops in the south which were left with no armoured reserves.

In the early hours, the Commonwealth troops of the 2/48th Australian Infantry Battalion after a withering barrage followed by vicious hand to hand combat seized Hill 28, the vitally important position in the northern end of the frontline. This was a small rise, the occupation of which, allowed the Commonwealth troops to hold an advanced bridgehead into the enemy defensive line. Here the Australian infantry suffered fifty-six dead, and 256 wounded or missing, while the Germans suffered the loss of 173 soldiers of the 125th Regiment which were captured along with sixty-seven Italians from *Trento* Division. Immediately General

---

80 DAK war diary cited in: Daniele Sanna, *Il caos dei comandi: L'Afrika Korps e gli italiani a El Alamein*, p. 58.

Montgomery ordered that the position be fortified and reinforced so that it could be maintained at all costs. Thus, in the wake of the infantry's advance the tanks of 1st Armoured Division were called upon to exploit the breech to reach the rear of the Axis defense.

This is how Rommel read the battle upon his taking command of the Axis troops between 25/26 October especially in view of the enemy's success at Hill 28: "Our aim for the next few days," he later wrote, "was to throw the enemy out of our main defense line at all costs and to reoccupy our old positions, in order to avoid having a westward bulge in our front."[81]

General von Thoma read the battle similarly to Rommel believing that the Commonwealth forces were making repeated attempts to achieve a breakthrough on Kidney Ridge and in the north near the coast. In accordance with Rommel, he therefore moved the 90th Leicht Division near the coast and the battle group which was originally assigned to defend the DAK headquarters in Kidney Ridge.

On the 26th Rommel ordered several counter-attacks continuing the armoured centered strategy adopted by his subordinates on both 24 and 25 October. Upon his arrival, the day before Rommel had held a different position: "The Panzer forces must be held back for mobile operations. Enemy tanks were to be dealt with by guns in position, not armoured counterattacks…"[82] Despite the fuel shortage and the low stockpiles of tanks and ammunition the 26th and 27th would see the Axis tank formations be committed for repeated counter-attacks.

In the central sector of the northern line (Hill 33) the IV *Battaglione Carri Medi*, deployed in defense of the 88mm guns' unit, attracted considerable enemy fire from 51th Highland Division artillery. As the 7th Motor Brigade attacked Kidney Ridge, which was located southeast of Hill 33, it overran with several armoured vehicles the positions held by the battered I Battalion/382nd German unit. This prompted the Axis commander to launch a major counterthrust which began at 1500 under heavy enemy artillery and air attacks. Despite the constant interference of Commonwealth bombers and artillery guns the attack commenced promptly and involved several Italian tanks and self-propelled guns. The prompt intervention of the medium tanks of *IV Battaglione*, a few medium tanks of LI *Battaglione* and several *semoventi* from DLVI *Gruppo* successfully beat back the enemy forcing the armoured vehicles to evacuate the position. *Semoventi* shot down five enemy tanks, a few armoured vehicles and three anti-tank guns, while *Littorio*'s medium tanks damaged several armoured vehicles. The unit's war diary states that "no losses were sustained during this counter as the medium tanks maneuvered quickly forward to fire at the enemy tanks then quickly disengaged and retreated back to their positions without ever offering the enemy the opportunity to shoot them on the flanks. At least ten enemy vehicles were destroyed."[83] According to the 15th Panzer Division war diary the 7th Motor Brigade attacked with three separate waves each undertaken by units of motorized infantry and up to 100 tanks. Against this attack 15th Panzer Division "organized a defense based on German armoured units and two companies of Italian tanks and *semoventi* under Colonel Teege. The blistering fire of the armoured units repelled the attack."[84]

---

81 Basil Liddell Hart, *The Rommel Papers*, p. 306.
82 Niall Barr, 'Rommel in the Desert' in Ian Beckett (ed.), *Rommel Reconsidered* (Mechanicsburg, Pennsylvania: Stackpole, 2013), p. 104.
83 Dino Campini, *Nei giardini del diavolo*, p. 244.
84 DAK war diary cited in: Daniele Sanna, *Il caos dei comandi*, p. 59.

Carmine D'Avanzo *sergente carrista* LI *Battaglione Carri Littorio* remembers the battle that raged near Hill 33 in the following terms:

> At 1130 we received the order to get ready to oppose an enemy tank attack that aimed to infiltrate our defensive line. The LI Battaglione began to move out with its 32 tanks and drove for approximately one kilometer to position itself on the left flank of the IV Battaglione. This movement since its inception had been challenged by the enemy's artillery which kept on firing at us. At 1150 the unit went into action. Our tanks formed a semicircle. The battle, one of the fiercest we fought, lasted a long time. Our armour, despite the enemy's heavy artillery fire, threw itself against the enemy's tanks immobilizing several of them and burning others. Soon after, the fighting greatly intensified, ultimately lasting until 1500. After having suffered casualties, the enemy began to retreat. At 1540, having completed its task, the battalion returned to our lines. At the end of the operation we counted three tanks left on the field of battle while another three damaged tanks were towed back to our lines.[85]

South of Hill 33, near Kidney Ridge (El Wishka) the Commonwealth forces were also attacked from the south by the tanks of the XII *Battaglione Carri Medi*, the DLIV *Gruppo Semoventi da 75/18,* and five German Panzers. Davide Beretta, commander of the 1st Battery of the self-propelled group recalls the fierce clashes that occurred on that day:

> In front of our semoventi there were tens of M14 tanks of Littorio Division that were firing their 47/32 guns against some enemy anti-tank positions. Suddenly on the horizon there appeared overwhelming enemy formations of heavy British tanks, Shermans and Grants, aiming their 75mm guns like hunters. Sometimes they stopped their advance, and then continued forward. Our tiny M14/41s moved towards them to shorten the range, the shorter the range, the better the chances of penetrating the amour with their small guns. The British were positioned about 1,500 meters from our tanks and began to put up a rapid fire. We observed this action with dismay, because the 47mm shells of the M14s were bouncing off the heavy armour of the tanks. We were confident, however, that our own 75mm guns would have a different effect on the British. "Watch out they are advancing toward us! Tally ho!" We started to advance as well, and we reached our blazing M14s with guns ready. "Range 700, 800, 900 fire!" We managed to destroy some Shermans and Grants and the British halted their advance and tried to attack our flanks. We barely managed to stop their advance and failed to force them to withdraw; but it was a miracle indeed that we stopped them. In the evening, we counted twenty Shermans and Grants and some Valentines and Crusaders destroyed; but the price we paid in that uneven battle was far too high. We had no choice we were used to Death's presence that we did not fear it anymore; we understood that the most difficult courage lay not in dying but in continuing to live and fight in that hell.[86]

---

85 Paolo Caccia Dominioni (ed.), *Le Trecento ore*, p. 101.
86 Cited in Ian Walker, *Iron Hulls, Iron Hearts*, p. 161.

Initially the Axis tank attack gained momentum as both tanks and self-propelled guns opened fire against the enemy infantry positions. But has soon as they approached their defenses they were plastered by heavy anti-tank fire. Suddenly, they were then countered by a mixed unit of Commonwealth tanks belonging to the 2nd Armoured Brigade. In very heavy fighting the Axis force prevailed in the tank to tank battle forcing the enemy back. Thus on Miteiriya Ridge the Italian infantry units of XXI Corps could create a new defensive line almost abutted next to the Ridge, which reconstituted a new resistance line.

Meantime, on the evening of the 26th and extending into the early hours of the 27th, troops from the XI *Battaglione Bersaglieri/7° Reggimento* supported by 90th Leicht mortars and machine gun units and a few tanks from LI *Battaglione Carri Medi* and 15th Panzer launched a surprise counter-attack to retake Hill 28. After the preparatory fire, the unit with one *semovente* belonging to *1ª Batteria di semoventi* of *DLVI Gruppo* and some medium tanks charged up on the flanks and then on the top of the contested hill. The Australian defenders put down heavy blocking fire to halt their advance. While pushed back by the defenders on the pinnacle, the *Bersaglieri* managed to wrestle both flanks from the enemy at a cost of 50 dead and 150 wounded out of a total of 450. The battle diary of *Capitano* Filippo Sciortino, commander of the 1ª *Batteria DLVI Gruppo semoventi da 75* states: "On the 26th one semovente, commanded by Tenente Spera had attacked Hill 28 with the Bersaglieri Battalion. Deployed amongst the tanks of 15th Panzer, my artillerymen Apa, Marchetti and Rosa scored several direct hits and won praises from the German tankers."[87] Rommel describes the same counter-attack in the following terms:

> The British resisted desperately. Rivers of blood were poured out over miserable strips of land, which, in normal times, not even the poorest Arab would have bothered his head about. Tremendous British fire pounded the area of the attack. the *Bersaglieri* Battalion succeeded in occupying the eastern and western edges of the hill. The hill itself remained in British hands and later became the base for many enemy operations.[88]

The Australian official history also details the tough clashes that occurred on the 26th between Axis armour and infantry against the Australian defenders.

> The enemy's first effort against Trig 29 was made on the afternoon of the 26th, when 300 infantrymen moved into positions 1,500 yards to the north but were dispersed by gunfire. The 2/48th Battalion had three field regiments and one medium regiment on call at that stage and was able to defend itself with devastating fire. The western front of the 20th Brigade was also attacked on the 26th. Three attacks by infantry and tanks, the main weight of which fell on the 2/13th, were repulsed on the afternoon of the 26th.[89]

Between the first day of battle and the night of the 26th, *Littorio* Division had been at the center of all the fighting in the Northern sector. Its troops had fought effectively even through the Italian medium tanks were no match for the Sherman tanks and due to their soft skin were the easy targets of the 6-pdr guns.

---

87 Dino Campini, *Nei giardini del diavolo*, p. 247.
88 Basil Liddell Hart, *Rommel Papers*, p. 189.
89 Barton Maughan, *Australia in the War of 1939-1945 Vol. III: Tobruk and El Alamein*, p. 693.

Despite the stand at El Alamein, the continuous fighting had taken a heavy toll on *Littorio*. On the night of 26 October, it was reported that its tank strength was down to seventy operational machines and eleven *semoventi*.

The continuous Commonwealth advance, which every day was committed more troops and machines against Kidney Ridge and near the coast, had also forced Rommel on the night of 26 October to start to draw his reserves to the north. The 21st Panzer and part of the *Ariete* moved north during the night to reinforce the understrength 15th Panzer and *Littorio* Divisions and 90th Leicht Division at El Daba was ordered forward while the *Trieste* Division was ordered from Fuka to replace them. The 21st Panzer and the *Ariete* made slow progress during the night as they were heavily bombed by the RAF as the latter enjoyed air supremacy and could intervene from their nearby air bases in Egypt. This supremacy played an important role during the battle, a role that Rommel was quick to recognize in his war diary. On this occasion the planes destroyed five tanks and retarded the deployment of two divisions. Enemy aerial superiority was not the only problem that Rommel faced. His troops lacked fuel supplies and during that same day Rommel received news that the Prosperina cargo ship carrying important stocks of petrol that was enroute to Libya from Italy had been sunk by the enemy. Its destruction meant that there were even fewer stocks of fuel left for the mechanized and motorized components of Rommel's army. This further restricted their ability to maneuver against the enemy tanks.

27 October

On the night between 26/27 Montgomery gave further instructions to his commanders directing further attacks against Kidney Ridge with a focus by the 7th Motor Rifle Brigade on the capture of Hill 33 (Woodcock), while the 2nd Rifle Brigade was given the task of seizing and holding Snipe. Hill 33 lay about a mile to the north-west of Kidney Ridge, while Snipe was located a mile south. While the 7th Motor Rifle Brigade was not able to reach its objective, and its infantry and artillery ended up digging in front of Hill 33, the action conducted during the night by 2nd Rifle Brigade was particularly successful and allowed the Commonwealth to capture Snipe. Thus, on the 27th Rommel committed the Italian forces to clear out several advanced outpost and anti-tank gun positions that had been occupied during the night by the 2nd Rifle Brigade. The position, known by the British as Snipe and by the Italians as broadly Hill 33, was attacked repeatedly by *Littorio* to push back its gallant defenders.

The first armoured sally against Snipe was conducted at dawn by the German Panzers from the Stiffelmayer Group but was turned back by the artillery and anti-tank guns. The second attack went in at 0600 by *XII Battaglione Carri Medi, DLIV Gruppo Semoventi* and the 33rd *Panzerjager*. Initially two Italian medium tanks were lost to heavy enemy fire. As the remaining tanks continued to advance, *semoventi* units opened fire to cover their movements. According to the *XII Battaglione Carri* combat diary:

> The battalion goes on the attack. Despite the violent enemy fire and the resultant initial losses of tanks and men, the battalion advances firmly but keeping a certain distance from AT guns, which are extremely well dug in and camouflaged. Suddenly there is very violent fire from another eight or ten AT guns hidden on our left and scattered in depth. The battalion suffers casualties and its vehicles halt suddenly. Enemy fire becomes more and

more violent. The survivors then show incredible proof of valor: *Sottotenente* Camplani from outside his turret urges his own tanks on to the attack at the head of them, drives his own tank at full speed towards the foremost AT gun. He is stopped by a belt of mines in front of the AT positions and by a shell that damages its tracks. *Sottotenente* Stefanelli has his tank hit by an AP shell, which penetrates and explodes. At the head of his company *Tenente* Pomoni's tank is hit in the engine compartment; the crew miraculously survived. *Tenente* Bucalossi's tank is hit and set on fire. *Tenente* Zilambo is wounded in the right leg and saved by *Tenente* Luciano (the adjutant) while *Sottotenente* Delfino continues the attack and is only stopped by the minefields. At 1130 Colonel Teege orders a withdrawal back to the start line. The vehicles that have been brought back are dispersed in a wadi and the damaged ones, except the burnt-out ones, recovered. Colonel Teege's adjutant and his interpreter follow the action from their own tank and report the battalion's actions to their commander. Colonel Teege expressed his admiration for the magnificent courage shown by the battalion and for the way Capitano Preve commanded the movement of his own tanks and the SP artillery."[90]

The tanks could not proceed beyond the advanced and well entrenched screen of 6-pdr guns which continued throughout the operation to hammer with devastating effectiveness at the attackers. The losses sustained were nine tanks destroyed, three hit but later recovered, four dead and eleven wounded amongst the crews. In turn, several Commonwealth riflemen and artillerymen were either killed or wounded and some of their guns were put out of action. The British account of the fighting is as follows:

Our section was facing a north-westerly arch of fire. Dawn came and with it the thought that there might be a counterattack. Jerry didn't come in for a couple of hours and when he did it was mostly tanks and mobile guns. Our anti-tank guns did their good work with these. The six-pounders stopped them cold. Then the crews began to bail out and we opened at them. We only fired at targets we could see on our immediate front, for we had used a lot of ammunition and had to conserve what was left.[91]

Another account by Sergeant Joe Swann of 2nd Rifle Brigade recounts a similar story highlighting the effectiveness of the 6-pdr guns:

I swiveled the gun round and let him have one over open sights. It hit the tank and jammed his turret. I then put another round up the breach and put it into him, causing casualties because two or three chaps jumped out leaving one man in there badly wounded who was screaming out for help. I then got the rest of the crew up on to the gun at this stage and I went back to my own platoon.[92]

By 0800 the 24th British Armoured Brigade had reached Snipe and initially due to some confusion shelled the friendly positions of the 2nd Rifle Brigade. Once the mistake was recognized the unit began aiming against the proper targets opening fire against the concealed Axis gun batteries. Then as it inched closer against the Axis anti-tank screen it lost eight Shermans. This

---

90 Ufficio Storico: 'Relazione sul fatto d'arme della Divisione Littorio', 18 Dicembre 1942.
91 James Lucas, *The War in the Desert* (New York: Beaufort Press, 1982), pp. 221-222.
92 Bryn Hammond, *El Alamein*, p. 217.

action was followed by another Axis armoured counterattack which could not proceed beyond Snipe due to again the blistering artillery fire. The counter was resumed at 1300 after the Axis artillery effectuated a heavy barrage upon Snipe but once again it was not able to destroy all the anti-tank guns whose crews courageously continued to concentrate fire on the M.14 tanks as they rumbled forward. Another three medium tanks were lost in the confrontation, while several British anti-tank guns were destroyed along with their crews.

The fighting for the control of Snipe reached its peak at 1500 when a large-scale Axis counterthrust was ordered by von Thoma involving II/8th Panzer, *IV Battaglione Carri Medi* and a *semovente* battery. The operation opposed by a powerful British anti-tank screen could not eliminate the enemy presence on Snipe, but it did repulse the 24th Armoured Brigade which lost several tanks in the process. As Rommel states:

> Local counter-attacks were due to be launched that afternoon by the 90th Light Division on Hill 28 and by the 15th and the 21st Panzer Divisions, the Littorio and part of the Ariete, against the British positions between minefields L and I…. at 15000 hours, our dive bombers swooped down on the British lines. Every artillery and anti-aircraft gun which we had in the northern sector concentrated a violent fire on the point of the intended attack. Then the armour moved forward. A murderous fire struck into our ranks and our attack was soon brought to a halt by immensely powerful anti-tank defense, mainly from dug in anti-tank guns and many tanks.[93]

To clear Kidney Ridge sector another major attempt was made by elements of 21st Panzer and the XII *Battaglione Carri Medi* and DLIV *Gruppo Semoventi* during the late afternoon/early evening. As soon as they approached the enemy positions however, the Axis units were once again met by a flurry of fire from the anti-tank screen which impeded their movements and caused several losses. German tank losses began to mount to the point that within a short time Rommel lost a sizeable portion of his tank force. Moreover, the duel between the Italian medium tanks and the American made Grants and Shermans clearly saw the latter prevail as attested by the recollections of *Capitano* Davide Beretta of the *DLIV Gruppo Semoventi da 75*:

> The next day, we were ordered to counterattack and recover the positions lost previously, whatever the cost. It was a foolish order indeed and we were already exhausted and decimated, and it would be a desperate task even to resist another British attack. However, we were beyond caring and prepared for another counterattack. Luckily, this time we would be supported by some German III and IV tanks. As we advanced at least ten British tanks with infantry support appeared. We opened fire but did not have time to congratulate ourselves for destroying three Crusaders before a tide of enemy tanks came up in support of them. The British 25pdr guns brought hell down on us as well. Some enemy infantry was wiped out by our machine guns and I must say that, in the heat of the battle, when you killed without being killed, you were almost glad about the enemies' death. The British really did not expect our desperate counterattack. Again, the RAF came over to bomb us, destroying tanks and killing men. We counted seventy of them. Seventy deadly birds,

---

93 Basil Liddell Hart, *Rommel Papers*, p. 310.

flying in perfect formation, coming and going repeatedly. Suddenly everything was calm. It was only the calm before the storm, the next massive enemy tank attack. Since the start of the battle the 554th Gruppo had been very lucky. We still had seven semoventi with no losses at all. It was at 15.42 that we received the order: "Open formation, Tally Ho." So, started a huge and confused dogfight involving tank and artillery. We were encouraged by the fact that our 75mm gun was effective: many British tanks, even the most feared Sherman and Grants, were destroyed or immobilized by our guns. We could avenge our unlucky M14 comrades by these kills.[94]

The battle had seen the medium tanks of *Littorio* Division unable to cope and losing out most of the shooting duels against the British anti-tank screen which was comprised primarily by 6 and 25-pdr guns which had greater range and more punch. In fact, the British battalion's war diary records the estimated destruction of twenty-two German and ten Italian medium tanks.[95] However, the *semovente* units with their 75mm gun, often used to provide flanking fire to cover the medium tank counter-attacks, had once again proved their worth even against the medium sized American Grant tanks. Part of their effectiveness was due to their very low silhouette which made them good tank hunters. "The self-propelled guns could take out Shermans but in return offered a very little target to the bulky American tanks. In comparison to American tanks, the semoventi were little fleas that could bite."[96] The *DLIV Gruppo semovente* war diary reports for 27 October the destruction of eight Grant tanks and of three 6-pdr guns against no losses of self-propelled guns.[97]

On the same day, fighting also had flared up at the other point, Hill 33, which the Commonwealth troops of the 7th Motor Rifle Brigade had unsuccessfully attacked during the night between 26/27 October. "A company of the German 1st Battalion/115th came under attack and was on the verge of being overrun when two platoons from *IV Battaglione Carri* came to their aid. These platoons commanded by *sottotenenti* Colonna and Morini pushed forward beyond the positions held by the Trento Division on October 23rd and were successful in pushing back the enemy. Two tanks were lost when they stumbled into mines."[98]

The *1ª Batteria di semoventi* of *DLVI Gruppo*, commanded by Capitano Filippo Sciortino, was called upon to support *IV Battaglione* on Hill 33 and the following are the recollections of its commander:

> The enemy's VII Motor Brigade vehicles came forward, but our reaction was very violent. The first few enemy tanks were set on fire and the ones following suit began to retreat. An enemy anti-tank gun that had positioned itself at three-hundred meters of our line, was shot up within few minutes. My unit at the time was in an advanced position within range of the enemy's anti-tank screen. We raced against the British gunners who were in the process of loading their guns and showered their positions with the concentrated fire from the medium tanks and our guns with the model 32 shells. Having edged out the enemy,

---

94 Davide Beretta, *Batterie semoventi, alzo zero: quelli di El Alamein*, p. 177.
95 Bryn Hammond, *El Alamein* (Oxford: Osprey, 2012), p. 218.
96 Dino Campini, *Nei giardini del diavolo*, p. 247
97 Davide Beretta, *Batterie semoventi, alzo zero*, p. 178.
98 Paolo Caccia Dominioni (ed.), *Le trecento ore*, p. 94.

two enemy vehicles and two anti-tank guns were destroyed before the enemy's infantry began to withdraw. My batteria sustained the loss of one semovente and its pilot who died instantly and extensive damage to another self-propelled gun.[99]

The same position came under another tank attack by the 2nd Armoured Brigade later in the day but this second prong was also beaten back. "On the 27th a violent enemy attack struck the same position held by the German grenadiers, but the accurate fire of semoventi and medium tanks struck numerous armoured vehicles and lorries carrying enemy troops. This fire was enough to halt the enemy attack."[100]

The fighting subsided on both points by early evening. By then, the scene in front of Kidney Ridge was one of death and destruction. Many German and Italian armoured units were littered around the perimeter of the Axis main positions along with the dead bodies of the tank crews and the enemy infantry. Up to seven knocked out Shermans could be seen within the defensive perimeter position together with the shattered remains of sixteen Bren carriers and ten anti-tank guns. By nightfall, however, the Commonwealth troops, realizing that they had sustained severe losses during the fighting and could not properly occupy the position evacuated Snipe. Hill 33, however, remained surrounded by enemy troops.

The XX *Corpo d'Armata* diary observed that on the 27th "the fighting had been inconclusive" and admitted the following losses amongst the units of *Littorio*: sixteen tanks, four *semoventi*, five 88mm Flak 36 guns captured by the enemy and concluded by stating that the moral and physical conditions of its soldiers "were deeply shaken by the very violent enemy action."[101] The resistance line was slowly crumbling, the infantry was still holding its positions but its ranks were very thin, the armoured units could not overcome the enemy anti-tank screen and every attempt to counter the enemy infiltrations had been beaten back by fierce enemy aerial and artillery fire.

The 27th must be seen as one of the critical days of the El Alamein battle since Rommel's counter-attacks succeeded in pushing back the enemy but far too many tanks were lost in the endeavor. Because of the huge losses sustained, which were not replaceable, the Axis ranks and especially its northern tank force was much reduced.

During the evening Rommel had made a plea to Hitler's HQ to dispatch reinforcements, but the battle of Stalingrad was top of mind for the Fuhrer. His request came on the heels of a meeting that had taken place in Rome between Cavallero, Mussolini, Kesserling and Goering, who had arrived from Berlin to assess the situation. According to the Italian Official History Kesserling had raised doubts over Rommel's conduct of the battle asserting that "he had shown indecisiveness."[102] All had convened that it was imperative to dispatch more fuel and ammunition to the frontline troops, although they generally underestimated the gravity of the situation and how long it would take for the supplies to arrive.

---

99 Dino Campini, *Nei giardini del diavolo. La storia inedita dei carristi della Centauro, dell'Ariete e della Littorio*, p. 248.
100 Ibid.
101 Ibid.
102 Mario Montanari, *Le operazioni Africa settentrionale*, Vol. III, Part II, p. 767.

28 October

On the 28th a pessimistic Rommel remarked in his diary:

> Who knows whether I'll have a chance to sit down and write in peace in the next few days or ever again. Today there's still a chance. The battle is raging. Perhaps we will still manage to be able to stick it out, despite all that is against us, but it may go wrong, and that would have very grave consequences for the whole course of the war. For North Africa, would then fall to the British in a few days almost without a fight. He will do all we can to pull it off. But the enemy's superiority is terrific and our resources very small.[103]

The day's entry into the DAK diary also painted a bleak picture and even admitted that the counterattacks of the 27th had failed. The DAK diary first went on to list the heavy losses sustained by the German units including the 15th Panzer Division which had lost two thirds of its tank force since the 24th. With regard to the Italian units the DAK diary stated: "Division Littorio has lost a considerable number of tanks as well. The lack of mobility of the Italian infantry (including the clear majority of the troops of the armoured units) is clearly a debilitating factor at this stage."[104] This comment probably was related to the capture of several anti-tank guns and especially some 88mm that had been seized by the enemy on Hill 33. The lack of mobility comment specifically appears to refer to the lack of trucks to tow or transport the guns and the troops to the rear in case of a fallback to Fuka.

On the morning of the 28th Rommel communicated to his Army that: "the present battle is a life and death struggle. I therefore require that every officer and man do his utmost and thereby contribute to its success." That morning the fighting intensified even more in the Snipe position as the Commonwealth dispatched the 133rd Infantry Brigade to take up advanced positions in a bid to reoccupy it. As the British unit was dismounting from the trucks and its soldiers were in the process of placing the anti-tank guns in emplacements, it was suddenly attacked by *Littorio*'s tanks and *semoventi* units which came at them from a concealed position and infiltrated in their midst. With regard to this battle encounter historian Lucas Phillips wrote:

> At dawn, 2nd Armoured Brigade was moving round on their northern flank, as they had done the day before, but, before they could intervene, the enemy suddenly attacked with tanks and overran the Sussex, with a loss of 47 killed (including Murphy himself) and 342 missing.[105]

Since the British brigade at the time of the attack had not been able to take up proper positions and its flanks were not covered by armour, it was overrun by the enemy tanks. Its guns were destroyed along with sixty men dead and 300 captured. *Littorio* armoured battalion's war diary reports that: "a coup de grace was delivered by surprise attack against an enemy unit that was

---

103 Basil Liddell Hart, *The Rommel Papers*, p. 310.
104 DAK war diary cited in: Daniele Sanna, *Il caos dei comandi*, p. 62.
105 C.E. Lucas Phillips, *Alamein* (Boston: Little Brown and Company, 1962), p. 300.

in the process of occupying an uphill position. Our tanks burst onto the enemy position at full steam and overran it. No losses were sustained."[106]

The following is how *Capitano* Dino Campini recalled the recapture of Snipe:

> The position had been occupied by the enemy but there were still a few Italian artillery units that although encircled had not been seized. While many artillerymen were still in the field of battle since the enemy had not the infantrymen to round them up and take them to the rear. During the night, I studied a plan to infiltrate my tanks in-between the few gun battery positions that were still holding out to then sally against the enemy. At dawn my unit with great impetus sallied against the enemy anti-tank gun positions and overran them….The results were the recapture of Capitano's Giorgiole' 88mm guns, the freeing of several of our artillery men that the enemy had failed to take to the rear and the capture of 300 enemy soldiers…. Hill 33 and the nearby positions had now been recaptured. At this point the enemy action intensified. The enemy started concentrating artillery fire against us. This was not a wise move because it enabled the 21st Panzer to unleash their attack with little or no interference from the enemy guns. The enemy was struck head on and in less than a few hours vacated most of the field of battle in order to escape the encirclement."[107]

Despite this isolated Axis success, the Commonwealth forces continued to press men and equipment forward. The objective now was for 1st and 10th Armoured Divisions to reach the coast, cut off the Axis forces in the north and open a large gap in the defensive lines. At 2100 the Commonwealth artillery began to concentrate its field gun fire upon the area beyond Hill 28. For one hour the guns pounded the Axis positions with great force and a massive number of shells rained down upon the positions of the II/125th Regiment and the XI *Bersaglieri* Battalion which were holding the gap between minefields I and H. Then at 2200 the Commonwealth troops accompanied by the armour (2/13th and 2/15th Australian Battalions and 40th Royal Tank Regiment with forty Valentines) advanced against their positions. Both were stopped repeatedly multiple times, but they ultimately prevailed: "The battle raged at this point with tremendous fury for six hours, until finally II/125th Regiment and the *XI Bersaglieri* Battalion were overrun by the enemy. Their troops, surrounded and exposed to enemy fire from all sides, fought on desperately."[108]

Thus on the night between 28/29 October the Commonwealth forces (9th Australian Division accompanied by Valentine tanks) managed to wrestle the position of Hill 20 (near Hill 28) as well as several other positions near the coast in a bid to further isolate *Trieste* and the 164th Light Division strongpoints as well as to continue to degrade the Axis deployment in the northern sector.

---

106 Ufficio storico, "Relazione sul fatto d'arme della Divisione Littorio," 18 Dicembre 1942.
107 Paolo Caccia Dominioni, *Le trecento ore*, pp. 96-97.
108 Basil Liddell Hart, *Rommel Papers*, p. 312.

29 November

Axis infantry forces in the northern sectors had been decimated by the continuous days of fighting and by the bite and hold, small steps tactics applied by the Australian infantry and its heavy infantry tanks. The losses were so great that Rommel decided to deploy *Divisione Trieste*, 90th Leicht Division and 21st Panzer Division units to prop up the decimated positions held by *Trento* Division and 164th German Division. Although the move had been made necessary by the losses sustained, Rommel had in fact denuded the other sectors to check the determined Australians.

In the morning, Rommel assumed direct command of all forces in the northern sector and placed under General de Stefanis of XX *Corpo d'Armata* the command of all troops in the southern sector. The move was meant to split into two broad sectors the span of control so to provide immediate responses to enemy actions by commanders deployed near the main sectors of operation. Some elements of *Ariete* were still in the south and would be deployed for immediate counter-attacks there, whilst 21st Panzer was concentrated in the more delicate northern sector.

The day was taken up by the Axis forces to conduct a series of operations aimed at pushing back the enemy infiltrations in the northern sector. Elements from 15th Panzer and LII *Battaglione Carri Medi* made two distinct attempts to overtake the enemy positions near Hill 28. Although heavily disrupted by enemy aerial forays, the Axis armour pressed home their attack with great determination in the afternoon as stated by the Australian official history:

> Near Trig 29 all day the whole area came under tempestuous fire … Later in the morning enemy infantry and tanks formed up and two counter-attacks in which both tanks and infantry were employed were directed at Trig 29, one in the morning and another in the early afternoon. The afternoon attack, which was made with greater determination, was sustained for three-quarters of an hour. Both were repelled, but on the second occasion not before six of the Australian anti-tank guns had been knocked out.[109]

On the evening of the 29th IV *Battaglione Carri Medi* was tasked with reaching a position located two miles from Hill 28 to provide support to a *Liguria* artillery group which was equipped with batteries of 100/17 guns and the XXIII *Battaglione Bersaglieri*. During its drive toward the objective, the armoured battalion was hammered mercilessly by the RAF and the unit's war diary documents that it was subjected to thirty-four aerial bombings through the five-hour period. During the night, it eventually reached the position on the northern end of the line just in time as it was being attacked by enemy infantry. Its tanks joined the Italian infantry units already in the position in facing down the attack.

---

109 Barton Maughan, *Australia in the War of 1939-1945 Vol. III: Tobruk and El Alamein*, p. 704.

30 October

The 29th had been a decisive day of the campaign. After several days of fighting Rommel was given an inventory the following day of the tank strength of his units deployed in the northern sector that revealed a very dire situation. The data was not encouraging at all since it revealed that despite holding the enemy, the losses were very substantial. 15th Panzer had thirty-nine tanks left, *Littorio* had twenty-three M.14/41 tanks, eight *semoventi*, a single battery of 25-pdr guns (captured from the British), and one anti-tank platoon with 4,200 soldiers remaining. Although overstretched *Trieste*'s units were deployed almost exclusively in the northern sector, and the non-mechanized battalions of the 21st Panzer, which initially had helped to prop up the sector defenses, were placed on reserve. Rommel's only reserve in the North was the 21st Panzer Division which was still at full strength.

On the 29th, the other main Italian armoured forces were reputed to consist of:

- *Trieste*'s tank battalion had thirty medium tanks and 200 soldiers.
- *Ariete* had 134 armoured vehicles and 6,000 soldiers.

It was at this point, facing repeated enemy attacks, that Rommel began to think about a possible disengagement from the El Alamein line to the Fuka pocket which had a much narrower line to defend. The armour would pull back first followed by the infantry divisions as Rommel wanted to save as much of his armoured force as possible knowing full well that the Italian infantry units, being mostly non-motorized, were likely to sustain heavy losses during the pull back. His estimate was that if the pullback did go through, the clear majority of the infantry deployed in the northern sector could likely not be saved due to the lack of trucks.

On the 30th the Commonwealth forces had continued to press forward around Hill 28. "After an hour's barrage, the Australians opened their attack by pinning down the 125th Regiment at the front and assaulting its flank from the south. At the same time a strong force of British armour rolled north from the area north of Hill 28 and overran a light artillery battalion of the XXI Italian Corps, whose men, after a gallant resistance, either died or fought their way through to the neighboring sector."[110] To check the Australians Rommel ordered an immediate counter-attack by the 90th Leicht and XXIII *Battaglione Bersaglieri* to push back the enemy infiltrations north of Hill 28.

The Italian armoured units played a limited role in this operation mostly in support of the *Bersaglieri* Battalion. "The action of 90th Leicht involved at a certain stage of the operation the deployment of our armoured unit. Specifically, our semoventi were called to support the XXIII Bersaglieri infantry attack and to check enemy armoured movements directed north. Our units destroyed several enemy vehicles and tanks that were on the verge of taking position AP 411. The British armoured column that was set to attack AP 411 halted its advance and moved in a northeastern direction."[111]

During the day, the British artillery continued almost unopposed to target the enemy front-line positions as well as the rear supply echelons. Several Italian tanks were repeatedly shelled

---

110 Basil Liddell Hart, *The Rommel Papers*, p. 314.
111 Dino Campini, *Nei giardini del diavolo*, p. 349.

and one *semovente* took a direct hit and was lost. That night on the 30th Rommel ordered the 21th Panzer Division to disengage from the northern sector of El Alamein in a bid to save his armour which was to retreat to the Fuka pocket. In its place, Rommel ordered the infantrymen of *Trieste* Division to continue to take up positions between Kidney Ridge and the coast. The logic of this move, which was meant to salvage the most important armoured assets, was understood by the frontline troops even though the Italian and German infantrymen in the most advanced positions likely perceived it as highly detrimental to their survival. As the two units were in the process of executing Rommel's order, a violent artillery barrage struck the 125th German Regiment positions near the coast. With a swift offensive sally the Australians outflanked the German positions and forced the enemy to retreat to avoid capture. The Australians then consolidated their hold on these positions near Thompson's Post.

31 October

To counter Rommel ordered a further counter-attack that appears not to have involved any Italian armoured units. With regard to this operation Rommel writes that: "Our attack went in at about 1200 hours but failed to penetrate, as the enemy broke up and scattered our tanks and infantry with concentrated artillery fire and air attacks. However, contact was restored with 125th Regiment."[112]

1 November

By 1 November General Montgomery had succeeded in wearing down his opponent although he had not achieved the much-anticipated breakthrough. Operation Lightfoot's main objective, the degradation of the Axis defenses near the coast had been successful, but had not overwhelmed the Axis main resistance positions. Montgomery was under pressure from Churchill who wanted him to commit more troops forward. It was at this point that General Montgomery launched phase two of the El Alamein battle, Operation Supercharge.

2 November

This phase of the battle began at 0100 on 2 November with the preparatory barrage, and its objectives were twofold. One was to continue to launch attacks against the Axis frontline troops as well as to force the enemy armour to fight in the open, thus further degrading its few remaining mechanized reserves. The second objective was to achieve the much-anticipated breakthrough of the Axis line of defense. Montgomery was aware of Rommel's lack of fuel and tank reserves through the ULTRA intercept and sought to exploit his numerical superiority in men and machines to the fullest. To this end, Montgomery's set piece battle sought to achieve the slow but methodical destruction of the Axis defensive strongpoints through massive aerial

---

112 Basil Liddell Hart, *The Rommel Papers*, p. 315.

and artillery bombings. In fact, the intensity and the destruction of the artillery preparation behind Supercharge was to be greater than anything witnessed so far during the two weeks' battle. The ultimate objective of this operation was Tell el Aqqaqir, the logistic base of the Axis defense roughly three miles north-west of the Kidney feature and situated on the Rahman lateral track.

The reconstituted Axis line of resistance was comprised from north to south of the following units:

X B*attaglione/7th Bersaglieri* held positions near the coast, whereby next to it was deployed the III Battalion/115th German Infantry Regiment. Behind them near Sidi Abd Rahman was deployed the bulk of 90th Leicht and the Kasta battle group. The II Battalion/125th German Infantry Regiment was deployed opposite the 9th Australian Division at Bir Sultan Omar. Next on the line was the sector held by *Littorio* with the frontline positions held by the 200th/90th Leicht, XXIII *Battaglione Bersaglieri* and the I Battalion/115th German Infantry Regiment. These troops were supported by several batteries of 100/17 guns of *Liguria* Group, a group of 75/27 guns from *Littorio*, XXXVI *Battaglione Bersaglieri*, DLIV *Gruppo Semoventi*, IV, XII and LI *Battaglioni Carri Medi*, and DLVI *Gruppo Semoventi*. Behind *Littorio* stood the 15th Panzer and the 21st Panzer further behind. *Littorio's* sector faced part of the 9th Australian Division, 2nd New Zealand Division, 9th Armoured Brigade, 51st Highland Division, and the bulk of 10th Armoured Division.

On Kidney Ridge the defensive line consisted of the I and II Battalions/65th Infantry *Trieste* Division, the II Battalion/115th German Regiment, II Battalion/ 104th German Infantry Regiment, I and II Battalions/66th Infantry *Trieste* Division, which were backed up by *Trieste's* Artillery Regiment. These troops faced the troops of the 44th Infantry Division and some troops of 51st Highland.

On the El Wishka sector and facing directly the 1st South African and the 4th Indian Divisions were the II Battalion/115th German Infantry Regiment, II Battalion/382nd German Grenadier Regiment, the bulk of 61st and the entire 62nd Regiment of the *Trento* Division, the II and III Battalions/433rd German Grenadier Regiment, followed by I *Battaglione*/61st *Trento*, and finally the I Battalion/433rd German Grenadier Regiment. These largely understrength infantry forces spanning from the coast to the midway point of the line were mostly non-motorized and were probably the ones that Rommel was ready to sacrifice in a bid to save his armour. While *Littorio's* tank units were deployed near or at the frontline, the 21st Panzer units were at the back ready to make their escape to Fuka. The *Bologna*, *Ramcke* Parachute Brigade, *Brescia*, *Pavia* and *Folgore* Divisions held the southern front.

The battle opened during the night with a very intense artillery barrage that matched for its volume the first day of battle on the night between 23-24 October. German 15th Panzer diary states it suffered "the heaviest artillery fire which had so far been experienced" and "reminiscent of Great War days."[113] The record number of shells that rained down on the Axis frontline paralyzed the troops for many hours and this state of confusion allowed the troops of the Commonwealth Divisions to penetrate almost unopposed into the first line of defensive outposts in several sectors of the El Alamein line. The main attack began at 0600 on 2 November when

---

113 Cited in Jon Latimer, *Alamein* (Harvard: Harvard University Press, 2002), p. 261

up to 150 tanks of the British 9th Armoured Brigade moved forward and were soon followed by another large group of tanks from the British 1st Armoured Division. Their objective was to capture Aqaqqir Ridge from Rahman Track. As soon as the tanks crossed the line and entered contact with the Axis defenses, however, they were quickly engaged by heavy anti-tank gun fire and in some cases from guns shooting at almost point blank range. Initially it was still dark and the British tanks had the upper hand being able to maneuver at will while not being easily detected. Few casualties were sustained. But as the sun emerged, suddenly the British force found itself under heavy fire from a line of guns that was dug in and difficult to locate. Bolstered by the 88mm guns, the Axis artillery brought down considerable fire upon the enemy tanks and destroyed several of them.

The following is a British account of the close quarter fighting which occurred on that day:

> Major Eveleigh's own tank was hit and set ablaze at point blank range by a troop of Italian 47mm guns. He bailed out with his turret crew, until the amour plate became too hot to touch, desperately struggled to free the jammed hatches of his driver and co-driver, to no avail. Aware that the Italian gunners were shooting at his gunner and operator with small arms, he emptied his revolver at them. At this point, Lieutenant Charles Dorman, one of his troop leaders, seeing what was happening, attacked the Italians from a flank and wiped them out. The rest of the regiment had now come up and become heavily engaged in a series of personal close-quarter duels with the numerous gun positions … During this phase of the action the regiment accounted for fifteen anti-tank guns, four field guns and five tanks, but by 0710 it had itself been reduced to seven tanks while only four of its officers remained alive and unwounded.[114]

It is estimated that the 9th Brigade suffered losses from the combined effort of mobile and frontline Axis artillery which debilitated up to forty Sherman tanks. In turn the British unit claimed the destruction of thirty-five anti-tank guns mostly Italian 47mm units and German 50mm guns. Several Axis gun crews located in very advanced positions either died or were wounded while fighting in their gun emplacements. Some were gunned down while others were run over by enemy tanks. In the war diary of the *Littorio* Division General Bitossi would later write that: "The artillerymen of Divisione Littorio after nine days of strenuous fighting defended once again stoically their batteries to the last man. With their sacrifice, they wrote one of the most glorious pages of their unit's history."[115] Even though the 9th Brigade had lost several tanks at 0700 it linked up with the 2nd Armoured Brigade when its leading elements arrived at the Rahman Track. Thus, the latter deployed two miles north from the Track, while 8th Armoured Brigade occupied Tell el Aqqaqir, and 7th Motor Brigade deployed in between them. Having reached so far into the Axis line of deployment was an important achievement in itself even if it had been obtained at a very high cost with the destruction of one armoured brigade.

Sensing the immediate danger, Rommel dispatched the 21st Panzer Division from the north and the 15th Panzer and *Littorio* from the west to conduct counter-attacks to push the enemy

---

114 Bryan Perrett, *Iron Fist: Classic Armoured Warfare* (London: Hachette, 2012), p. 178.
115 Ufficio Storico, "Relazione sul fatto d'arme della Divisione Littorio dal giugno a novenmbre 1942," Generale Gervasio Bitossi, Novembre 1942.

back. The counter artillery fire was put down and followed by *Littorio* and 15th Panzer Division tank companies which raced to engage the enemy tanks. Upon the arrival of the Axis tanks, the Commonwealth armoured unit maneuvered to meet them with a strong force. For the next two hours, the tank battle raged with great intensity. Each charge forward by the Commonwealth was met with a counter maneuver by the Axis tanks. The first to engage the enemy were the tanks of *Divisione Littorio*, which were closer to the area of the enemy breach, while the 21st Panzer had to travel from the north and the 15th Panzer was not initially deployed.

The following is the sector by sector account of the fighting of the armoured Italian units during the Commonwealth offensive:

XII *Battaglione*, located just south of Hill 28 at AP 411, was barraged throughout the early morning hours by withering enemy fire losing two tanks. By 0200 the Commonwealth forces laid several smokescreens in front of its position. Then, "after the artillery barrage subsided," recalls *Capitano* Preve, "the enemy tank attack began on our front and flanks. This was conducted by a vastly superior armoured force."[116] Shortly thereafter Preve was severely wounded as a direct hit took out both of his legs. The remnants of the unit, led by *sottotenente* Bruno Camplani, resisted for a time but were later overpowered by Commonwealth armour. Most of its tanks were shot to pieces by the enemy armour. The *Bersaglieri* of XXIII/12th Regiment, the II *Gruppo* of *Littorio*'s artillery and the *Bersaglieri* of XXXIV *Battaglione*, which were nearby, suffered the same fate. These units, after suffering huge losses due to the intensity of the barrage, where surrounded and overwhelmed by motorized infantry as they were in transit trying to reach a position that had already been compromised by the enemy advance. Some of the units attempted to load their guns on the trucks to escape encirclement but where for the most part captured as they attempted to retreat from the battle line. North of XII *Battaglione*'s position, on both flanks of Hill 28, the Axis defensive line had also not held due to the overwhelming enemy pressure and even one armoured battalion of the 15th Panzer had been overtaken along with I and II *Battaglioni/Trieste*, and, I/200th German Regiment and the III/115th German Grenadier Battalion. The enemy had opened a large gap and had later arrived with its armour to the left and right flank beyond Hill 28 and was driving toward Rahman Track.

Aligned along the left flank of XII *Battaglione*, LI *Battaglione Carri Medi* had amongst its vehicle fleet many inoperable tanks that were dug into the defensive outposts to function as static artillery units. Together with the *2ª Batteria DLVI Gruppo Semoventi*, LI *Battaglione*'s tanks were attacked by a large enemy force. The former's war diary states that on "1 November the 2ª Batteria was deployed with LI *Battaglione Carri Medi* between AP 409 (north of Hill 33) and Hill 33. On 2 November, it was surrounded during the early morning hours by armoured vehicles and strong enemy infantry units and forced to surrender."[117]

In the middle of the Axis deployment near Hill 33 IV *Battaglione* was also surrounded by a preponderant enemy. "The enemy's artillery fire increased in intensity, and then the tanks, hundreds of them, along with the anti-tank guns closed in on us."[118] It was first subjected to a large-scale barrage then after suffering a severe pounding it was attacked by tanks followed by mobile anti-tank gun units which covered by thick smokescreens positioned themselves

---

116 Dino Campini, *Nei giardini del diavolo*, p. 271.
117 Dino Campini, *Nei giardini del diavolo*, p. 271.
118 Dino Campini, *Nei giardini del diavolo*, p. 272.

dangerously close to the Italian medium tanks. The battalion consisting at this point of only ten medium tanks and three *semoventi* faced several waves of enemy tanks and mobile anti-tank guns. In a prolonged exchange of fire "IV suffered six tanks set on fire and one semovente which took a direct hit. But facing our positions, the enemy was hemorrhaging too as *sergente* Camiciottoli's infallible aim debilitated several enemy units which were smoldering right in front of us. Several enemy tanks, however, were invulnerable as our armoured piercing shells just bounced off their armour. The only way some of them were put out of action was when we closed in on them."[119] As the shooting match raged, under the cover of the smokescreens Commonwealth sapper units were able to open up a path in the minefield for the heavy infantry tanks which closed in on the Italian positions and began to open fire at a distance of 1 and 1/2 miles against the remaining medium tanks of IV *Battaglione* which suffered additional casualties. Despite the heavy fire and the subsequent losses, the thinned out ranks of the IV *Battaglione* held on to their positions until the battle subsided. This is how the battle was described:

> At dawn on 2 November the enemy attacked again in great force deploying large numbers of tanks, artillery pieces and airplanes against our positions. After having overcome the LI Battaglione Carri, the British were soon at loggerheads against our tanks of IV Battaglione Carri which were supporting the 8th Panzer Battalion of 15th Panzer Division, which was deployed on our right. North of us, the 21st Division was repulsed by the enemy and our IV Battaglione remained, for most of the day, engaged in halting the enemy attack. The intensity of the artillery fire kept on increasing until it reached a fever pitch. The tanks and the anti-tank guns of the enemy, protected by smokescreens, were continuously coming up against us. Six of our tanks were destroyed along with a semovente. But several enemy tanks were also burning in the distance. Then the XI Battaglione Carri from Trieste was thrown into the fight to support our flank with forty medium tanks. Within less than an hour the battalion was shot to pieces. The commander, Maggiore Vetri, who was standing near my tank was hit and his legs were blown away. All my tanks by then had been hit, most of them were too inadequate to begin with to face the larger enemy tanks…. On our left a few German self-propelled guns continued to stand firm…. Despite the massive bombardment and the great disparity in forces, the enemy was not able to force us away from our positions. Perhaps fooled by several abandoned tanks on the battlefield, the enemy still believed that we still had many tanks fighting."[120]

Further south XI *Battaglione* (*Trieste*) had fielded eleven medium tanks to cover the right flank of IV *Battaglione*, but its vehicles were ambushed by a column of medium and heavy Commonwealth tanks that infiltrated its southern flank. As soon as the medium tanks deployed on the battlefield they were submerged by flanking enemy fire and had no chance to react. The unit was shot to pieces. Only a few tanks managed to escape as the unit was covering an area that was also swept with heavy fire, a deadly area that needed to be covered but that provided absolutely no cover from enemy fire. Regarding the combat engagement the commander of

---

119 Ibid.
120 Paolo Caccia Dominioni, *Le trecento ore*, p. 101.

Littorio's armoured regiment stated: "The enemy tank units were upon us without any prior warning from the infantry units deployed on the main line. The fighting soon became very confused and intense and the XII and the LI Battaglione were literally wiped out and the DLIV heavily decimated."[121]

According to Rommel's estimates the attack against the Axis defensive line had been put forth by up to 200 enemy tanks, but despite this overwhelming machine superiority the British armoured units supported by infantry units had not succeeded in breaking through. After they had overpowered the first defensive line, the German and Italian field guns and the German tanks had scored several direct hits. Rommel's twenty odd 88mm guns firing hundreds of shells broke up several forays by the enemy amour. Reports from the field of battle told of how the fighting had been fierce and the artillery duel had been fought at close quarters: "An exact indication of the harshness of the fighting was provided by 35 Axis guns of all different caliber which had been found destroyed within 100 meters of the burned out enemy tanks, some of which were almost next to the Axis guns."[122]

Despite the heavy losses, the Commonwealth infantry and armour had advanced in the Rahman Track near a small height called Tell el Aqqaqir, dangerously close to the main route leading to the Axis supply rear position. Following the first assault, had been blunted, Rommel decided to launch a large-scale counterattack that for the first time saw the full participation of the 21th Panzer Division, which up to that point had been mostly held in reserve. The latter attacked from the north while the remnants of *Littorio, Trieste* and 15th Panzer charged from the west. It must be outlined that by this time *Littorio*'s tank battalions had already lost the clear majority of its armour during the initial Commonwealth advance in the morning. At this stage its three battalions plus the remnants of *Trieste*'s tank battalion probably fielded no more than twenty or thirty tanks and self-propelled guns. The 15th Panzer was also a reduced force. The plan was to deal with the enemy armour once and for all in what appeared to be the decisive battle. It took place on the Rahman Track near Tell el Aqqaqir and it took the form of a giant wild melee involving hundreds of tanks and self-propelled guns. The battle, which pitted approximately 120 Axis versus 300 tanks mainly of the 1st Armoured Division, resulted in the decisive battle of the desert campaign. To dislodge the enemy from the Track the Axis tanks beginning at 1240 put forth repeated counter attacks that were met by both enemy tanks and artillery fire from dug in 6-pdr guns. The Commonwealth tanks had previously taken position on the Track and had their guns in a hull down position fighting in a defensive mode. Likewise, Commonwealth anti-tank guns had also been deployed waiting for the Axis tanks to come into their range. A colossal battle between Axis and Commonwealth armour raged for several hours as the former attempted to seal the gap and push the enemy tank beyond the Rahman Track.

Arthur Reddish, a Sherman tank crew member, vividly recollected the savage fighting:

> The day was hot. High temperatures, aircraft active on both sides, shelling very heavy and sniper fire also. Armour piercing shot came from right, left and center. A blazing Grant tank exploded as we passed by, its side flattening and the turret hurling some 50 meters in the air. The explosion was tremendous even when wearing earphones. Each member of

---

121 Mario Montanari, *Le operazioni in Africa settentrionale*, Vol, III, Part, III, p. 791.
122 Ian Walker, *Iron Hulls, Iron Hearts*, p. 167.

the crew had a set of earphones and a microphone. We could talk within the crew and the commander with other commanders. Everything could hear the talk on the regimental radio network, so knew the score. We in the heavies kept the battle at long range when possible to exploit our advantage in that area. The Italian tanks were hopelessly outranged and the German Mk IIIs also. But the German Mk IV and Mk III specials fought us on equal terms.[123]

The swirling and confusing huge clash of armour hung in the balance for much of the day. Ultimately, although the Axis did not lose the encounter battle, it came off worse than the Commonwealth due to its scarcity of equipment. It is estimated that half of the initial Axis tank force was lost, while the Commonwealth suffered similar, if not higher, losses.

According to the Italian official history:

> Von Thoma launched the 15th and 21st Panzer divisions along with the remnants of the Littorio and Trieste tanks against the armour of the 1st Armoured Division which had their hull down in a defensive position and were flanked by a powerful antitank screen. Moreover, over twenty bombers of the Desert Air Force launched seven consecutive bombing attacks. The Axis forces entered battle with 120 tanks while the enemy had more than double the number of tanks and could also count upon 80 Valentines from the 8th and 50th Royal Tanks. The M.13 and M.14 tanks were sacrificed one by one in attacks against Sherman and Grant tanks and the 6 pdr. guns.[124]

At the end of the day the German had only thirty-five Panzers, while the Italians had no more than twenty M.14s and fifteen *semoventi* in working order. Rommel reports in his diary that the Italian units had suffered particularly during this engagement: "The British were shooting up one after the other the *Littorio*'s and *Trieste*'s tanks. The Italian 47mm. anti-tank gun was no more effective against the British tanks than our own 50mm., and signs of disintegration were beginning to show among the Italian troops."[125]

Italian accounts of the battle do not disagree with Rommel's version of the tank battle as it regard the medium tanks, but they do differ with regard to the self-propelled guns. According to their accounts several were still standing until late afternoon and that until they held on the enemy armour could not advance for a very long time.[126]

In contrast, however, the Commonwealth still had an entire tank division, 7th Armoured, that could still be deployed into battle. Given the huge losses, which were not easily replaceable due to the naval blockade and the distance from the supply bases, Rommel was forced to call in his last armoured unit that was still available, the *Ariete* Division. "In the early afternoon, the gravity of the situation in the north forced us to the decision to bring the *Ariete* up to the north along Telegraph Track and thus denude the southern front completely."[127] The latter travelled north to be deployed along the Rahman Track. As Rommel asserts: "The Ariete set off for

---

123 Bryn Hammond, *El Alamein*, pp. 250-51.
124 Mario Montanari, *Le operazioni in Africa settentrionale*, Vol, III, Part III, p. 794.
125 Liddell Hart, *Rommel Papers*, p. 318
126 Dino Campini, *Nei giardini del diavolo*, p. 275.
127 Ibid.

the North later that afternoon, bringing with it a large part of the artillery from the southern front."[128] By nightfall Rommel began again to think about disengaging his troops from the line and retreat to Fuka, given than in his view the Axis with very few tanks and low stocks of ammunition could not emerge victorious from the battle. He writes:

> The army's strength was so exhausted after its ten days of battle that it was not now capable of offering any effective opposition to the enemy's next breakthrough attempt, which we expected to come the next day. With our great shortage of vehicles an orderly withdrawal of the non-motorized forces appeared impossible. Added to that, the mobile forces were so firmly locked in battle that we could not expect to be able to disengage all of them. In these circumstances, we had to reckon, at the least, with the gradual destruction of the army."[129]

The plan was to salvage as much equipment as possible and create a new line of defense in the Fuka pocket, approximately fifty miles west of El Alamein. At the time, both *Comando Supremo* and Field Marshall Kesserling were less pessimistic than Rommel and believed that the battle could still turn in the Axis favor. Their more positive view on the results of the final encounter battle was likely crowded by a general lack of viable information on what was happening on the ground and overly optimistic data regarding Axis strength. Some even accused Rommel of defeatism and of unnecessarily painting a very bleak picture. In their view the defensive line from the *Trento* to the north to the *Folgore* in the south was still holding despite some localized Commonwealth successes. Moreover, they argued that troops and equipment were being rushed to the front to prop up threatened areas. There was no reason thus to be overly pessimistic since the Axis forces were reputed to be able to hold the line. In contrast, realizing that his armoured reserves were few and the stocks of fuel and ammunition were dwindling Rommel issued orders on 2 November for a retreat to Fuka in a bid to preserve as much as possible of his army. *Ariete* was to be deployed on the Track to engage the enemy while the bulk of the troops retreated.

3 November

Rommel wrote that: "The battle is going very heavily against us. We're simply being crushed by the enemy weight. I've tried to salvage part of the army. I wonder if it will succeed. At night, I lie open-eyed, racking my brains for a way out of this plight for my poor troops."[130]

On the 3rd the Axis troops began their orderly withdrawal. "At nine in the morning, I drove east along the coast road as far as Forward H.Q. Large numbers of vehicles, mainly Italian, were jammed up on the road, but surprisingly there were no British fighter-bombers about."[131] But as the maneuver was in progress, Rommel received a counter order from Germany and emanating directly from Hitler instructing the Axis troops to remain and defend to the death the El Alamein line. Although Rommel was perplexed by this order he halted the withdrawal and deployed the DAK and the *XX Corpo d'Armata* along the Rahman Track. He also sent the

---

128 Ibid.
129 Ibid., p. 319.
130 Basil Liddell Hart, *The Rommel Papers*, p. 320.
131 Ibid.

following communication to the German High Command which outlined the status of the troops under his command:

> The Italian divisions and 1st Air Force Brigade in the southern sector have been ordered to shorten the line by withdrawing behind the line El Taqa-Bab el Qattara—south of Deir el Murra and defending this line to the last. The German divisions in the northern sector are very heavily engaged in the Deir el Murra-Sidi Abd el Rahman sector against a superior enemy force. All German troops that could possibly be raked up have been thrown into the fight. Casualties so far amount to fifty per cent of infantry, anti-tank and engineer units and about forty percent of artillery. Africa Corps now has 24 tanks. Of the Italian XX Corps, the Littorio Armoured Division and Trieste Motor Division are almost wiped out. The Ariete Armoured Division was brought up from the southern sector on the night of 2nd-3rd November and committed in close cooperation with the Africa Corps. We will continue to do our utmost to retain command of the battlefield."[132]

Ariete's tank regiment was deployed as follows: on the first line of defense the IX *Battaglione Carri medi* and VI *Gruppo semoventi da 75*. The X *Battaglione Carri* and the V *Gruppo semoventi da 75* were on the right flank, while XIII *Battaglione Carri* was in the rear. The first enemy probe of the new defensive line took place to the north where 2nd Armoured Brigade attempted to breakthrough but was repelled by elements from *Littorio* and DAK.

On the morning of the 4th *Ariete*'s artillery, with the help of some German 88mm guns, repelled the first attempt by the 22nd Armoured Brigade led by Brigadier 'Pip' Roberts to occupy the Track. Unable to proceed, the British unit brought up the line its own artillery and an extensive artillery duel ensued that lasted until late morning. Brigadier Roberts then issued a follow up order to: "Brush them aside, as we have bigger fish to fry!"[133] This order was followed by several long-winded skirmishes between opposing tank crews which were mainly attacks by the British amour followed up by counter-attacks by the Italian tanks. The fighting remained inconclusive for most of the day. The X *Battaglione* war diary reports that "at 0730 an order to resist indefinitely was transmitted via radio while the enemy mass reaches our positions. Approximately 250 armoured vehicles are deployed against our 111 medium tanks and 12 self-propelled guns. At around 0800, a violent artillery preparation fire ensues followed by a vigorous tank attack. Already at around 0900 the situation was unsustainable as only the fire of the self-propelled guns was effective against the Sherman tanks closing in."[134] Rommel reports that: "I was later told by Major von Luck, whose battalion I had sent to close the gap between the Italians and the Afrika Korps, that the Italians, who at that time represented our strongest motorized force, fought with exemplary courage."[135] A crew member of one of *Ariete*'s tanks, *carrista* Antonio Tomba, furnished the following account of the battle:

---

132 Barton Maughan, *Australia in the War of 1939-1945 Vol. III: Tobruk and El Alamein*, p. 737.
133 Bryn Hammond, *El Alamein*, p. 261.
134 Ufficio Storico, Diario del X Battaglione Carri Medi, "Operazioni del 1942," Il Comandante, Ottobre 1942.
135 Ibid., p. 325.

> We spotted about sixty enemy tanks that, seeing us advancing furiously, had a moment of disorientation. Our poor M13s with their 47mm guns could never be effective against them, we could only hope to hit their tracks to immobilize them at least; our shells just bounced off when we hit their armour. In addition, while they numbered sixty, we had little over half that. We did everything possible, giving our best…. We had no chance, but we proved a difficult opponent for the British. Our tactics were simple: always keep moving, never expose your flank to their guns, don't let them fire first, all the crews must act as a single unit: everyone must know what to do and when to do it, in complete harmony with each other. We managed to hold off the enemy that day, but they replaced their losses again while we could only count how many of us were left alive. We could never have resisted for another day. Everyone was good, really good, that day, everyone fought an unequal battle without complaint and without yielding, even when there was no water and no food. We were lucky when it started to rain as this slowed the English advance, and we, the last survivors of the Ariete Division, were able to escape their pursuit.[136]

Even after the last British tank attack of the day *Ariete* was still in full possession of its main frontline positions at 1600. The battle resumed when the 22nd Armoured Brigade's tanks made a frontal assault against *Ariete* which called upon its remaining tanks to parry the enemy blow.

The Italian official history observed:

> Ariete had set up an antitank gun screen and it could also count upon the field artillery of the Trieste Division. Even with these reinforcements the unit faced a very uneven fight. Many Sherman tanks came within 1500 meters of the Italian tanks and began to pigeon shoot the M13 tanks. The latter began to maneuver extensively to avoid the enemy fire. The fighting lasted a long time and it was very fierce.[137]

As the frontal assault was unfolding, the 4th Armoured Brigade was called upon to make a flanking attack to the south of *Ariete*'s main position. After initially suffering severe losses from artillery fire this last attempt was ultimately successful as it saw the British tanks shell *Ariete*'s artillery from behind. In turn, the Italian gunners responded with their own fire and has Walker asserts: "The intense Italian artillery fire only finally ceased as British tanks appeared in the rear amongst the guns themselves."[138] Some enemy tanks had even reached *Ariete*'s truck park were the unit had set up its mobile tank repair shop which led to the capture of its personnel and some tanks that were being worked on. It was at this point that General Arena reported that "enemy tanks have penetrated south of *Ariete*. *Ariete* now encircled. Location 5km north-west of Bir el Abd. *Ariete* tanks now in action." After engaging the enemy tanks for has long as they could, a sizeable portion of *Ariete*'s units disengaged and retreated in an orderly fashion, while much of its artillery was overtaken during the latter stages of the enemy tank encirclement.

A British Tommy surveying the battlefield on the night of 4 November observed:

---

136 Antonio Tomba, *Sangue e reticolati. Dal diario di un carrista dell'Ariete in Africa settentrionale* (Rome: Italia Editrice, 2008), p. 173.
137 Mario Montanari, *Le operazioni in Africa settentrionale*, Vol. III, Part. Part III, p. 812.
138 Ian Walker, *Iron Hulls, Iron Hearts*, p. 173.

As we carried on in the direction our tanks have taken, we could see, reaching up into the sky, great columns of black smoke, and enormous dust clouds. This was the funeral pyre of the Italian armoured corps (Ariete, and the remnants of Littorio and Trieste Divisions), who had been engaged for several hours by nearly one hundred tanks of 22nd Armoured Brigade. Nearly all their tanks had been knocked out, and many field guns and anti-tank guns were destroyed or abandoned. The Italians had fought with exemplary courage in this action, and although nearly surrounded, they had held their positions to the last.[139]

Capitano's Luigi Grata (commander of X *Battaglione Carri Medi*) provides an hour by hour account of *Ariete*'s tank battles on 4 November. His riveting account reveals how little by little *Ariete*'s tank strength was eroded by continuous enemy armoured attacks and artillery fire. *Ariete* repulsed several enemy attacks attempting to overrun its defenses and it finally retreated only after Rommel authorized it to do so in late afternoon.

Capitano Grata wrote:

37 Tanks
At 1500 on 2 November the battalion receives the order to deploy. At 1700 the battalion reaches the track of the XX Corpo d'armata together with the V Gruppo semoventi da 75. We lose nine tanks during the approach drive toward the front due to mechanical malfunctions.

31 tanks
On the night between 3-4 November I receive the order to deploy the battalion between point 58 and Deir el Murra. At 0545 enemy armoured units attack our left flank with the support of their artillery. The attack is repelled given the prompt intervention of 5th Compagnia. Then the enemy comes back again in greater numbers to attack our entire battalion. This second attempt is also repulsed. The enemy then remained two kilometers from our lines but then opens a tremendous artillery fire. At 0730 I am ordered to resist at all costs and enable the bulk of the Panzerarmee to retreat in an orderly manner. Once I have communicated the order to my men they all promise that they will adhere to it to the end.

At 0800 the enemy attacks again with great force again targeting our left flank and specifically 5th Compagnia, which is heavily engaged in the fighting. A few enemy tanks are put out of action. I communicate the latest developments to headquarters and I request our artillery's intervention.

I then order 5th Compagnia to pull back the armoured units that are closest to the enemy, while I request a counterattack by Ricevuti's platoon. The counter produces good results. Our tanks lunge at the enemy flanked by the fire of the semoventi. At 0900 and despite the success of Ricevuti's platoon on our right flank, the pressure against the middle and on the left flank is still overwhelming. The mass of enemy tanks can only be weakened by our semoventi while several of our medium tanks are repeatedly hit by enemy fire, two of them along with a 75/28 unit are smoldering in the distance. The battalion, despite fierce enemy attacks maintains its positions.

---

139 Bryn Hammond, *El Alamein* (Oxford: Osprey, 2012), p.262.

23 Tanks

I request permission to retreat toward a more favorable position. I receive the authorization and I move my unit approximately one kilometer southwest and deploying on the right flank of IX Battaglione (tenente colonnello Mazara). The enemy pressure subsides a bit and my battalion with 16 tanks and 3 semoventi takes up its new position.

16 tanks

At 1130 there is a renewed enemy offensive. But together with the IX Battaglione, V and VI Gruppi semoventi we take the initiative and successfully push back the enemy thrust. At 1400 there is a pause in the fighting. I use the time wisely to dispatch tenente Cereda to fetch supplies and ammunition for tomorrow. Thus, two Lancia 3 RO trucks are dispatched to our supply base at El Daba. In the meantime, I notice that our artillery is hitting with great power the enemy line in repeated and very heavy barrages. At 1400 the enemy puts forth a frontal assault with a large-scale deployment of tanks. The brunt of the attack is sustained by my battalion (X Battaglione Carri) and by two semoventi. Despite our efforts, the enemy can advance slowly and thus I ask permission for a further pull back of half a kilometer to link up with IX Battaglione. At 1600 the enemy attacks again in great force and comes at us with a frontal as well as flanking assaults. Up to 200 enemy tanks and vehicles are involved but despite the enemy's superiority we hold on to our positions. What worries me the most at this point is the lack of reinforcements and the lack of new stockpiles of equipment. The semoventi, for instance, by this time have only twenty shells per machine. I order my troops to conserve ammunition as much as possible and I reiterate to them that the order to resist at all costs has not been revoked. I also instruct them to wait for the enemy to advance and to counter and hit back at him only from a distance that enables our guns to hit the target. I communicate the situation of my unit to regimental command but I also stress that even though the troops are calm and collected, my unit will not be able to sustain the next attack. Our ranks are thinning precariously and in nine hours of continuous fighting we have lost twenty-two tanks, of which seven have caught fire, and two semoventi have been knocked out of action.

9 tanks

The enemy tanks continue to advance and are supported by a very fierce artillery barrage. They are approximately 500 meters from our position. Two more tanks are then hit and begin to burn. A third tank takes their position, but it too is hit by enemy fire.

6 tanks

I receive the order to pull back on point 78 together with IX Battaglione. Both my battalion and the IX Battaglione pull back while being shielded by the XIII Battaglione Carri. We started the battle with thirty-one tanks and now we only have six tanks in working order along with two semoventi. Ariete's tanks have delayed the enemy advance by at least ten hours and have broken up several enemy tank platoons. Point 78 is reached on the night of 5 November.[140]

---

140 Ufficio Storico, 'Relazione ufficiale del Capitano Luigi Grata', X Battaglione Carri medi, Divisione Corazzata Ariete, 7 Novembre 1942.

It was Rommel himself who had authorized the retreat by both *Ariete* and the remnants of 90th Leicht Division, after realizing that if their troops stood on the Track any longer they would have been completely obliterated. *Ariete*'s intervention had been enough to arrest the momentum of the 7th Armoured Division and its drive to encircle the Axis troops still deployed on the Track and those retreating west. At Rahman Track *Ariete* had left behind twenty-seven medium tanks, five field guns, several anti-tank guns, three *semoventi* and approximately 450 prisoners.

As Walker asserts "The Allied and German records leave us with the impression that Ariete was surrounded and destroyed in this battle, and a significant portion of the division was certainly lost. However, a remnant of Ariete nevertheless managed to escape the traps.... The dramatic day long stand by Ariete at El Alamein on 4 November, effectively stymied the Allied plans to encircle and destroy the main Axis armoured forces."[141]

The retreat was ordered on 5 November after Rommel had determined that any further resistance was untenable. The DAK, and *XX Corpo d'armata* began to travel west, while the *Bologna* Division and the VII *Bersaglieri*, deployed in advanced positions, could not be saved in time. The withdrawal was conducted for the most part in an orderly fashion with the disparate units of the *Panzerarmee* retreating together as one large column. The only troops that retreated separately where some of the Italian infantry units, most of which retreated on foot because they were largely non-motorized and especially those in the southern front that took a completely different route to reach Fuka. Although the pullback was conducted according to plan it was disrupted for the most part of the journey by RAF aerial bombings which reaped victims but did not cause the motorized or mechanized column to completely halt their movements. On the morning of 5 December XX *Corpo d'Armata* had left ten M/13/40 tanks led by *Tenente Caporale* Luigi Pascucci of *Ariete* Division in the rear guard to hold off the pursuit of the Commonwealth forces. The medium tanks were deployed near Fuka to await the arrival of the enemy mechanized forces. Once the latter spotted the position of the Italian medium tanks they opened up their guns with tremendous fire. Pascucci then decided that in order to buy more time his unit would charge against the enemy. The ten medium tanks attacked across almost three miles of desert under continuous enemy fire from mobile anti-tank guns and finally closed in against several tank units of the 8th Armoured Brigade engaging them in a prolonged shooting match. When the British tanks began to disengage, Pascucci continued to pursue them until he was killed in the last running tank battle. He would later be found dead in his knocked-out tank after the battle. In recognition of his sacrifice, he was posthumously awarded the *Medaglia d'oro al valor militare*.

After having dealt with this rear guard by midday, the 8th British Armoured Brigade, caught up with the slower moving *Panzerarmee* near the coast road between El Daba and Fuka. Here the British unit took up position along the edge of the road and with the tanks in a hull down position began to fire as soon as the Axis troops approached. Bereft of ammunition, the Axis units were targeted mercilessly for almost an hour by the enemy which was firing its guns at almost point blank range. The toll was considerable as fourteen panzers, seventeen M.14s and four guns were destroyed along with the capture of 1,000 prisoners.

---

141 Ian Walker, *Iron Hulls, Iron Hearts*, p. 174.

The overall results of the battle were clear. The Axis had sustained a major defeat and was now forced to retreat to Cyrenaica. The Commonwealth had sustained 13,500 casualties, 500 tanks disabled but only 250 were beyond repair, and had lost many field and anti-tank guns. On the other hand, the Axis suffered 5,000 dead, 8,000 wounded and 25,000 prisoners. Its German and Italian tank corps had been wiped out and the few armoured units still operating were forced to retreat west to salvage their remaining assets. Given the high Axis losses, the El Alamein battle was one of the most important battles of the Second World War, a real turning point in the fortunes of the Axis which because of its defeat was in retreat from North Africa.

Final Considerations – El Alamein III

Rommel's analysis of the battle focused upon four main elements: The first was the Commonwealth numerical superiority in almost all categories. Indeed, the Commonwealth entered the battle, for instance, with double the number of tanks with respect to the Axis, whose tank strength was almost by fifty percent comprised by the obsolete Italian medium tanks. The deployment of heavy armour such as the Sherman, Pilot and Churchill tanks ensured that the Commonwealth would emerge victorious from most shooting matches with the inferior Axis armour. The first factor has also to be considered in relation to the much-improved performance of the Commonwealth forces which by then had implemented important tactical changes. The Commonwealth did not simply win the campaign with its greater strength but also with its better use of the armoured formations and especially of its artillery arm. First and foremost, the concentrated artillery fire in the form of the heavy bombardment of the counter-attacking enemy tanks succeeded in several instances in forcing the Axis armour to confront massive and insuperable anti-tank screens. The artillery was greatly aided by "the introduction of Priest 105mm self-propelled guns improved the capability of the army to provide barrage fire further forward in support of armoured formations, whilst the Shermans and Grants of these units were also able to fire HE and, thereby standoff targets in the manner that the German PzKpfw IV Special had previously been able to do."[142] The Commonwealth by introducing new powerful weapons caused many surprises forcing the enemy tank crews on the defensive. By bringing these new weapons forward, much like the German army had done throughout the campaign, the Commonwealth vastly improved its fighting capabilities. The second factor was the lack of fuel supplies on the part of the Axis which made a tank battle of movement almost impossible. Such a battle tactic with the tanks units maneuvering between El Alamein and Fuka might have succeeded in destroying a greater number of enemy tanks by exposing them to the German combined arms procedures which had served them so well throughout the campaign. Instead, Rommel was constrained to accept battle on the static El Alamein line since he had only a few days' full petrol supplies. Third, artillery was another key factor in the battle since the Commonwealth had a greater number of guns and ammunition versus the Axis. As Rommel asserts: "In addition to the advantage given by their abundant supplies of ammunition, the British benefited greatly from the long range of their guns, which enabled them to take the Italian artillery positions under fire at a range at which the Italian guns, most of which were

---

142   Bryn Hammond, *El Alamein*, p. 270.

limited to 6,000 yards, were completely unable to hit back."[143] The fourth factor was the enemy's complete aerial superiority which enabled the Commonwealth to continuously harass and interfere with the movements of the Axis tank formations. It is estimated that up to fifteen percent of overall tank losses were the result of bombings by the RAF.

Rommel's analysis of the situation at El Alamein is correct although he does not go into in-depth analysis with regard to his own choices during the two-week battle. Nor does he recognize in his memoirs that his fuel supply situation, although precarious, was not as dire as he made it to be during the last days of battle. Two main types of criticism have been lodged against Rommel's conduct of the battle. The first criticism was made by Kesselring after the war which accused Rommel of being too offensive minded but of subsequently having accepted a set piece battle in hostile terrain. Instead, Kesselring argues the *Panzerarmee* could have been pulled back prior to El Alamein approximately fifty miles west to the Fuka pocket which was easier to defend and was also located closer to the Axis supply bases. At Fuka, Kesselring argues, given the much shorter defensive line, Rommel could have had greater possibilities to maneuver his tank forces and hit at the flanks of the Commonwealth deployment whereas such an operation could not be conducted on the more static El Alamein line. He also correctly argues that Rommel throughout the campaign paid scant attention to the supply situation and that Malta should have been neutralized in the summer of 1942 prior to Rommel's launch of his offensive. The seizure of Malta would have eased Rommel's supply problems.[144] The second criticism lodged against Rommel and primarily advanced by the Italians was the latter's recourse to frequent armoured counter-attacks in the face of the vast array of anti-tank weapons that the enemy deployed at El Alamein. This argument states that Rommel could have better preserved his armour by focusing on a more defensive minded effort by plugging holes in the resistance line and using the tanks as a more static defensive screen. Both arguments have merits although the first argument does not really deal with the political implications of a retreat in September 1942 to the Fuka pocket. Most importantly, would Hitler and Mussolini or Rommel for that matter, have accepted a tactical retreat from the El Alamein line in mid-1942? Both Kesselring and Cavallero in the summer of 1942 were on the losing end of many confrontations with Rommel who enjoyed the backing of both Hitler and Mussolini. It appears that their advice was discounted several times and that after Tobruk an exceedingly high rate of enthusiasm took hold in the Axis camp. The bigger miscalculation by Rommel, which was endorsed by both Hitler and Mussolini, was to go on the final attack in Egypt without having first conquered Malta, the key position from which the British launched countless attacks against Axis fuel and equipment supplies destined to North African ports. The destruction of Italian shipping guided by the Ultra intercept and focused on the fuel supplies especially during the final stages of the El Alamein battle, for example, greatly limited the *Panzerarmee* ability to maneuver at will during the critical stages of the fight.

Of Malta, as the critical turning point of the war in the Mediterranean, historian Heinz Magenheimer wrote:

---

143 Basil Liddell Hart, *Rommel Papers*, p. 330.
144 Albert Kesselring and Kenneth Macksey, *The Memoirs of Field-Marshal Kesselring* (New York: Skyhorse Publishing, 2016).

As many studies have shown, the British position in the Mediterranean and North Africa stood and fell with possession of the naval base of Malta…..The success or failure of Rommel's army was directly dependent upon the fall of Malta….Given Rommel's highly risky attack top priority meant a de factco renunciation of the capture of Malta, even if the operation was officially only postponed for an infinite period. This decision not only ignored the strategy of Comando Supremo but also cancelled out the plans of the Commander in Chief South, who following the original agreement, now wanted to align priority to the operation against Malta. Rommel's decision would soon prove to have been a mistake.[145]

Hailed as the best tactician of the war by British historians such as Basil Liddell Hart, Rommel's stature amongst historians of the campaign today has somewhat diminished. They argue that the failure of considering the overall implications of the supply war on the North African campaign and of not dealing with Malta first lays at Rommel's doorstep.[146]

The second argument of criticism against Rommel's command has some merit regarding exposing the Axis armour to fewer losses than the DAK's continuous counter-attacks against the mighty Commonwealth anti-tank screen. On the other hand, however, it is not easy to determine whether the Axis infantry and artillery could have held on for so long without the more dynamic support provided, albeit by a less mobile, armoured force. In addition, the lack of strong reserves of infantry and of artillery guns forced the frontline troops to defend against recurrent enemy attacks which resulted in the thinning of their ranks. Once the ranks were thinned out the armour had to be called in to counter.

For the Italians, the battle of El Alamein resulted in a terrible loss that not only destroyed their North African position but also exposed Italy, the soft underbelly of the Axis alliance, to an Allied amphibious and aerial assault from North Africa. For the Italians, the battle was lost because of the vast enemy superiority in the number of tanks and armoured vehicles. General Arena of the *Ariete* Division issued the following post battle report:

> The battle of El Alamein has shown how the enemy for the first time introduced on a mass scale heavy tanks such as the Pilot, which were already deployed in a more piecemeal fashion in the June/July battles. The *Ariete* Division entered battle on 4 November and it clashed against a mass of 200 or more enemy tanks, which was for the most part constituted by heavier medium tanks. Against these tanks, which were further reinforced by 25pdr guns which had been brought to the front through the use of smokescreens, the *Ariete* suffered huge losses. In turn, our 47mm guns mounted on the M tanks could hardly do any damage to Pilot tanks or other medium sized enemy tanks. Our tanks then attempted to fire upon the tracks of the enemy tanks to immobilize them, but they were not able to knock many of them out of action. These larger tanks could only be pierced by our Semoventi units and the few heavy artillery units. But the anti-tank screen was in turn for the most part destroyed by the enemy's overwhelming artillery power. It is estimated that *Ariete*'s

---

145 Heinz Magenheimer, *Hitler's War* (London: Arms and Armour, 1999), pp. 169-172.
146 Historian Bryn Hammond makes the argument in *El Alamein* that Rommel committed military suicide for not paying attention to the supply issue. Robert Citino makes a similar argument in Robert Citino, 'Drive to Nowhere: The Myth of the Afrika Korps', *Military History Quarterly*, summer 2012.

artillery was outgunned by an enemy force that was six or seven times bigger. Despite this overwhelming superiority, the enemy tanks refrained from confronting *Ariete* in a frontal assault but attempted to either advance where it was weakest or by making flanking attacks. Against such an overwhelming force our 47mm tanks and even the more powerful German tanks could do little to parry the blow of the British tanks. Going forward our 47mm tanks should only be deployed to conduct exploratory and reconnaissance functions given their inability to face heavy tanks. In my opinion, an armoured mass which wants to effectively parry the British should be formed with the Semovente with improved armour and armament. The artillery role of this mass should be performed by battalions of Semoventi armed with 88mm and 90mm guns. These should be accompanied by newly formed infantry battalions that should be comprised of specialists and most importantly of sappers or engineers able to lay mines in the field of battle.[147]

According to Arena by late 1942 the M tanks (whether it was the M.13 and M.14 version) could no longer be deployed effectively and no longer had any role to play in armoured warfare. The only Italian weapon that was still effective against the most powerful Allied tanks was the *semovente* either the 75mm or 90mm version that was introduced shortly thereafter. This meant that while the Allies had made critical strives in reequipping their frontline units with more durable heavy and medium tanks, the Italians had failed to keep up with advanced weapons development. From the soldiers own recollections of the battle they reiterate the point that by then the M.13/40 and M.14/41 tanks were totally powerless against the Grant and Sherman tanks, while only 75mm and 90mm weapons, which were in limited numbers, could still go properly head to head against the newer Commonwealth tanks.

General Arena's considerations are echoed by British historian Brym Hammond:

> The Germans and Italians, by comparison, also received some new equipment or already possessed better equipment for roles than their opponents. In this regard, the 88mm dual purpose anti-tank and anti-aircraft gun was especially important and Eighth Army never possessed a weapon to match it despite suggestions for using the 3.7-inch anti-aircraft guns defending Alexandria and Cairo and instillations on the Delta. However, even these dreaded German weapons had their shortcomings and numbers were deployed in the late October fighting in particular because of their high profile and attempts to use them as anti-tank weapons when occupying positions designed to support their deployment as anti-tank guns. Armoured vehicles such as the Italian Semoventi da 75/18 had a low silhouette ideal for the desert and were welcomed. Also, highly regarded were the self-propelled anti-tank guns with which some Panzerjager units were equipped and of course, the PzKpfw Mark IV Special tanks. Italian heavy artillery remained of consistently good quality throughout the campaign, a valuable contribution too infrequently recognized. However, all these weapons were available in limited numbers…..[148]

---

147 Ufficio Storico, Comando divisione Fanteria Forli'- Generale F. Arena, 'Considerazioni sull'impiego delle varie armi nella battaglia di El Alamein' in. 1664, 4 Aprile 1943, pp. 8-9.
148 Bryn Hammond, *El Alamein*, p. 271.

The Retreat

Since both *Ariete* and *Littorio* Divisions had sustained huge casualties of both men and equipment at El Alamein, the battle left the Italian Army with only one remaining fully equipped mechanized unit, which was *Divisione Centauro*. The latter was fast and furiously transferred from the Balkans to North Africa but it too was equipped mainly with M tanks and some *semovent*i. Thus, even Italy's last remaining armoured units would have to fight against better equipped Allied formations largely with obsolete and inadequate equipment.

On 7 November, the Axis troops arrived at the Egyptian/Libyan frontier. At Halfaya Pass the troops, retreating in an orderly fashion but on narrow roads, caused a huge traffic jam. The Commonwealth forces, commanded by a conservative general such as Montgomery, failed to hastily pursue their enemy and despite the huge traffic jam the troops could continue their retreat largely unmolested. At the time, Rommel, still did not know where his troops should deploy defensively and in the meantime the Italian troops in the rear were told to organize near Mersa el Brega. Rommel, unlike his superiors, later became convinced that the Axis did not have the strength to organize proper defenses on the frontier and likely aimed to retreat all the way to Tripolitania. Despite Rommel's lack of confidence that his troops could hold on at Mersa el Brega, the Italian High Command gave orders to the *La Spezia, Giovani Fascisti* and elements of *Centauro*, which had arrived in Tripoli in early November to build defensive works at Mersa el Brega. Together with Rommel's *Panzerarmee*, which consisted of 12,000 Italians and 18,000 German infantrymen, 3,000 German and 500 Italian armoured troops, fifteen German and fifteen Italian tanks, several batteries of anti-tank and field guns and five *semoventi*, these troops were to a make stand somewhere in Libya. On 12 November, as the troops continued to retreat there was another major traffic jam at Gazala and this is how Rommel described the event: "hundreds of vehicles were in tow, some with engine trouble, others out of petrol. Discipline everywhere was now good. The panic which had reigned in the German Italian column was now over, and they were all convinced that they would be able to get away."[149] Despite these serious bottlenecks, General Montgomery's prudent approach together with the Axis combat engineers laying hundreds of booby traps in the wake of the enemy induced the maximum possible caution in the enemy advance.[150] On 17 November despite pleas from the Italian command to resist at Mersa el Brega Rommel began to ponder to fall further back to Buerat, which in his view offered greater guarantees for an effective defense of Tripoli. His main point of contention against the wishes of *Comando Supremo* was that the Mersa el Brega position was vulnerable to an outflanking enemy armoured maneuver coming from the south and since the Axis did not have an armoured unit strong enough to take on this enemy thrust Rommel desired to fall back further into Libya.

On 18 November five medium tanks, a single 75mm gun, five armoured vehicles and other small units from *Centauro* had their baptism of fire in North Africa when they covered the retreat of the Axis column. The clash with elements of the 7th Armoured Division took place at Antelat. The British troops fired first but the Italian troops readily deployed in a semi-circle responded vigorously to enemy fire. The Italians had established a strong defensive position and

---

149 Basil Liddell Hart, *Rommel Papers*, p. 350.
150 Ibid.

the *Bersaglieri* had deployed their anti-tank guns and rifles. Since the British unit did not have infantry support their tanks suffered some losses. Later they were countered by the medium tanks which forced them to disengage.

Some days later the battered Axis troops finally reached Mersa el Brega. Here the positions held by the infantry were fairly developed, but Rommel feared an encirclement by enemy armoured forces. On 24 November Rommel met Cavallero and Kesserling and made the following demands, fifty German tanks with 75mm gun, fifty 75mm anti-tank guns, seventy-eight field guns, 4,000 tons of petrol, and 4,000 tons of ammunition. In Lewin's view Rommel's modest requests "reveal perhaps, a realistic pessimism about the possibility of deliveries, for by sea and by air his enemy maintained an iron grip on the Mediterranean seaways.."[151] There was now a greater attention to the issue of supply which on the heels of the capture of Tobruk had been considered by Rommel in primis, but also by Mussolini and Hitler a secondary concern to the supposed disarray in the enemy ranks that had to be exploited to the fullest. On the 28th he flew to Hitler's HQ to try to convince him to his position but the meeting was inconclusive. After the meeting Rommel recalled: "Flying back to Africa I realized that we were now completely thrown back on our resources and that to keep the army from being destroyed as the result of some crazy order or other would need all our skill."[152] Since the German High Command could not meet Rommel's demand of fifty new tanks and fifty anti-tank guns, Rommel declared that he could not make a stand at Mersa el Brega and hence after a few days he came to an agreement with the Italian High Command to fall back to Buerat. At Buerat the Italian infantry began to construct defenses while the motorized units began their journey to reach them.

On 12 December, when the Axis forces were still travelling west, Commonwealth forces attacked in a bid to cut them off and surround them. The attack took place around Bir El Merduma, between El Aghelia and Nufilia. But the timely intervention by 15th Panzer and *XX Corpo d'Armata* blocked the enemy attempt. *Ariete/Centauro* managed to destroy twenty-four enemy tanks while sustaining the loss of fourteen tanks and ninety soldiers.

The engagement unfolded as follows: On 12 December, the Axis forces were concentrated near El Aghelia and the remnants of the Italian armoured units were pooled into the joint *Ariete* and *Centauro* Combat group (*Raggruppamento Gaetano Cantaluppi*) and deployed on the southern end of the line. The total tank strength of the group was up to fifty-seven M.14 tanks, twenty-five *semoventi* and 2,000 soldiers. Some of these vehicles had been repaired at Mersa el Brega, while others were shipped from deposits in the rear. Its units were molded into one group on 9 December and it was comprised by the 66º motorized infantry regiment from *Trieste*, two armoured battalions from *Centauro* (XIV and XVII), one *Gruppo* of 90/53 guns from *Centauro (DII), Gruppo Autoblindo Monferrato,* and III/3° *Gruppo* of 75/27 guns from *Divsione Pistoia*. According to the war diary of XX *Corpo d'Armata* the units morale was low: "Everyone from troop to officers believes that it is not possible to halt the enemy advance." And then on 10 November, the following day it remarked: "The news of the Allied landing in Algeria and Morocco has made the situation even more precarious and generated further pessimism amongst the troops."[153] Enemy forces (8th Armoured Brigade) were equipped with eighty enemy tanks, many of them were Sherman. As the Axis forces continued to retreat,

---

151 Roland Lewin, *The Life and Death of the Afrika Korps*, p. 181.
152 Ibid., p. 182.
153 Mario Montanari, *Le operazioni in Africa settentrionale: Enfidaville*, vol. IV, Part. I, p. 39.

the Allies attacked the line and broke through capturing several infantry units. The Italian *Ariete/Centauro* Combat Group was at the back of the Axis column and was called to action by Rommel as they had been originally assigned in the rearguard covering the retreat of the bulk of the motorized and non-motorized troops. On the night between 12/13 December several bottlenecks were experienced as several trucks carrying cannons of all sizes slowed down the bulk of the other Axis units. As the Commonwealth reconnaissance units became aware of this traffic jam, the British commander of 8th Armoured launched his entire armoured brigade to cut them off in an envelopment attack from the Commonwealth left flank to roll over the Italians to then lay upon the 90th Leicht Division. Commanded by Brigadier Edward C. N. Custance, the 8th Armoured Brigade at the beginning of Supercharge was equipped with twenty-four Crusaders, fifty-seven Grants and thirty-one Shermans. It is not clear how many tanks it had between December 14/15, although some indicate approximately 80 tanks. The Axis rearguard troops had been positioned on a semi-circle with the motorized elements of the 90th Leicht and the *Gruppo Cantaluppi* ready to take on the enemy thrust, while the 66° *Reggimento/Trieste* backed up by several field guns from *Pistoia* Division were deployed on the defensive line on the Axis right flank. The British units initially attempted on the morning of 14 December to overrun the defensive screen but two factors halted their progress. First, the terrain between Carcura and Marada, east of El Aghelia was extremely rough and hence the British vehicles were forced to advance very slowly. Second, the artillery opened fire upon sighting the enemy further impeding it progress. The artillery fire was then followed by an initial counter push by *Gruppo Cantaluppi* that equipped with some medium tanks and a few *Semoventi* intervened every time the infantry positions were threatened with an enemy envelopment. But soon after the British unit began to prepare the main attack by barraging the Axis positions with several 25-pdr guns. This was followed by the main push by the armour at 1600 put forth by several Sherman and Grants tanks that focused their efforts upon the strongpoints held by the I/66° *Battaglione* that were attacked frontally. The latter defended itself stubbornly from the enemy forays by opening up machine gun and anti-tank fire. At 1630 *Gruppo Cantaluppi* countered and engaged the enemy tanks in a prolonged exchange of fire that lasted over two hours. While pushed back on both flanks the British tanks managed to destroy six M.14 tanks and overran seven batteries of 47mm guns in the central sector. In turn, the Italians resisted on the line and with a combination of forward positioned anti-tank gun fire and a flanking tank counter-attack managed to halt the advance destroying several tanks and two armoured vehicles. By 1730 the main battle was over, although some level of skirmishing continued throughout the night, and the bulk of both sides disengaged as darkness began to descend. Italian losses were 109 soldiers (including eight officers) either dead or wounded, eight 47mm guns, several vehicles and ten tanks destroyed or damaged.

The Italian claims of twenty-two enemy tanks damaged or destroyed are not readily verifiable as the British unit's war diary does not list the casualties but merely makes mention of a hard fight that was fought on that day.[154] It is likely that several enemy tanks were shot by the

---

154 "The 15th December saw a stiff engagement in the sand dunes South of El Agheila followed the next day by a further fight West of that place. This battle opened the road past Marble Arch to Nofilia, which was entered without opposition." 8th Armoured Brigade War Diary <http://www.warlinks.com/armour/8th_armoured/chapter_1.php> (accessed 12 December 2018).

Italian artillery and self-propelled guns, but that some of them were merely damaged and later recovered by the Commonwealth forces as they continued their advance.

The following is an eyewitness account of fighting that Rommel would later aptly describe in his war memoirs. It states how the under strength Italians with only one battery of 90/53 guns, a few *semoventi* and several obsolete medium tanks countered a sizeable enemy tank attack:

> It was up to the remnants of Ariete, the ones that had survived the battle of El Alamein, and a few reinforcements from other units, to defend the rearguard of the Axis column from a British tank attack. The Ariete combat group was positioned south west of El Aghelia and for two days it's artillery and self-propelled guns held up the enemy inflicting on him several casualties and tank losses. Then on the night between 14/15 December the Italian mediocre medium tanks counterattacked tying up a larger enemy force and allowing the bulk of the German troops to retreat in an orderly manner along the via Balbia.[155]

The defensive effort to ward off the enemy armour effort was praised by Rommel who wrote:

> Late in the morning, a superior enemy force launched an attack on Combat Group Ariete, which was located south-west of El Agheila, with its right flank resting on the Sebcha Chebira and its left linking up with 90th Light Division. Bitter fighting ensued against 80 British tanks and lasted for nearly ten hours. The Italians put up a magnificent fight, for which they deserved the uttermost credit. Finally, in the evening, the British were thrown back by a counter attack of the Centauro's armoured regiment, leaving 22 tanks and two armoured cars burnt out or damaged on the battlefield. The British intention of cutting off the 90th Light Division had been foiled.[156]

After this delaying combat action, on the 16th the retreat resumed. By nighttime the troops reached Nufilia. On the 17th the DAK stood at Nufilia, while the pursuing New Zealand troops launched an attack against the 15th Panzer Division which parried the blow with a combination of anti-tank, artillery and machine gun fire. Sirte was then reached on the 18th. On 22 December *Gruppo Cantaluppi* assumed a new name of *Gruppo Centauro* and it consisted of I/66° *Reggimento*, 131° *Reggimento Carrista* from *Centauro*, III *Gruppo Autoblindo Monferrato* and III *Gruppo da 90/53*. By 31 December the retreating Axis forces had reached Beurat and there was nothing that the tattered remnants of the *Panzerarmee* could do to halt the enemy advance and stop the rout. On that day a meeting took place between Bastico and Rommel where the latter urged a retreat to Tunisia, while the Italian wanted to make a stand at Buerat. Ultimately it was decided that the stand at Buerat was to be only temporary while the bulk of the infantry troops were to be taken further back. In fact, soon after having reached Buerat the infantry troops were transported to a position in defense of Tripoli and sections of Tunisia. Axis armour was positioned as follows in defense of the last piece of Libyan territory: a section of the *Ariete/Centauro* Combat Group was positioned at Buerat, while another held positions in the north. The 15th and the 90th Leicht were in between the Italian units holding the center.

---

155 Lucio Ceva, *Africa settentrionale, 1940-1943* (Roma: Bonacci, 1982), p. 65.
156 Basil Liddell Hart, *The Rommel Papers*, p. 373.

It was now that Rommel decided that a retreat to Tunisia was necessary where its hilly terrain landed itself well for the *Panzerarmee* on the defensive. Rommel maintained that Tripolitania could not be held because of its open terrain that could have been exploited to the fullest by the mechanized Allied army.

On 15 January 1943, what remained of the armoured component of the DAK and *Centauro* covered the retreat of the Axis infantry units that were slowly marching toward Homs and Tarhuna. The Commonwealth here attempted another major attack to box in their enemy. Lieutenant General Leese of XXX Corps plan was that the 8th Armoured Brigade was supposed to direct its effort against *Gruppo Centauro*, while the 2nd New Zealand Division was to attack 15th Panzer.

On 16 January, having reached Ben Ulid the Axis forces were assaulted by several enemy tanks battalions and further losses were sustained. The combat action then centered in a place near Sedada and it was particularly fierce. At dusk, some of the Commonwealth units had infiltrated between the meeting point of the *Centauro* and the 15th Panzer Division. This dangerous penetration had to be quickly sealed with a swift armoured counter engaging the enemy long enough to allow to bulk of the Axis troops to disengage in an orderly fashion in further retreat toward Homs-Tarhuna. As darkness descended 15th Panzer and fifteen M.14/41 tanks from *Centauro* clashed against several tanks from 8th Armoured Brigade in a pitched tank battle that lasted several hours. By late night the Axis forces had managed to complete their rearguard action that claimed four Crusader tanks at the expense of fourteen M.14/41 tanks, while German losses are not known. *Centauro* suffered heavy losses as its medium tanks went head to head against Sherman and Grant tanks but also because some of the tanks ran out of fuel in the midst of the fighting and had to be abandoned. Its total losses were 180 between dead and wounded, twelve immobilized tanks, 14 destroyed, two field guns and two anti-tank guns were lost.

Concerning the 16 January battle *Centauro*'s *Caporalmaggiore* Tomba remembers that:

> There were several charges and countercharges. In two hours of constant fighting, characterized by the smell of gunfire and the heavy swirls of sand caused by the constant maneuvers of the armoured units, many armour clashes were sustained. At the end of the day we were able to block the enemy and allow our infantry troops to make an orderly retreat. Despite the successful operation, we suffered further tank losses that we could ill afford.[157]

But even a minor success such as this at that point in the campaign could not halt in definitively the Allied advance. It likely just bought more time for the defenders to fall back even further.

On 17 January at Tarhuna the antitank screen halted another sizeable attack blocking the enemy armour from capturing or overtaking Axis tanks or trucks. Most enemy tanks were dispersed and two were knocked out of action. While the bulk of the Axis troops were making their stance at Homs-Tarhuna in the defense of the last piece of Italian Tripolitania, on 21 January Rommel decided to evacuate the Tripoli area altogether. He justified his decision by stating that Libya could not be held in definitively against overwhelming enemy pressure and the decision was made to fall back to Tunisia where already Axis troops were preparing defensive

---

157 Angelo Tomba, *La vita della sete nel deserto della sirte* (Padova: Fratelli Corradin, 2003), p. 116.

positions. After this decision was made, according to Ronald Lewin, Rommel's position as leader of the *Panzerarmee* was first challenged and then eliminated. "On the 22nd Rommel received a severe rebuke from Rome. On the 26th, the day he actually moved his headquarters across the Tunisian frontier, he was informed by Comando Supremo (to whom he was technically subordinate) that on grounds of poor health he must surrender his command, on a date of his own choosing, once his army and withdrawn as far west as the Mareth Line."[158]

During the retreat from Libya in the November and the December clashes against the pursing Commonwealth forces the Italian units that comprised Rommel's army had suffered the following losses:

2,019 soldiers
20 light machine guns
55 machine guns
6 Solothurn rifles
3 × 81mm mortars
2 × 20mm guns
10 × 47mm guns
13 artillery pieces of various sizes
3 semoventi da 75/18
Unspecified number of M.13/40 or M. 14/41 tanks

The tattered remains of the *Panzerarmee* were thus to fight another day after having reached Tunisia. Rommel's skillful retreat from El Alamein had extricated what remained of his powerful army that was now to join the newly arrived Italian and German troops that the Axis had committed to the North African theatre.

Final Considerations

Summer 1942 had been the high point of Italian troops in North Africa since not only had they successfully advanced into Egypt but would also mount a major offensive to arrive into Alexandria. The Commonwealth counter-offensive at El Alamein shattered these dreams of glory and decidedly turned the tables on the Axis forces who were then themselves forced to retreat. Despite the defeat at El Alamein substantial progress had been made by the Italian armoured units prior to the major battle, although despite this progress they were still far behind of the organizational and weapons capabilities of the German and British armoured formations. By mid-1942 the Italian Army fielded more balanced and better trained armoured units styled on the more powerful German Panzer Divisions. While the equipment remained the same, for the most part, the Italians had added additional capabilities to their armoured units as well as improved armoured tactics.

As far as the capabilities are concerned, the Italians had created a tank recovery team, a tank crew training school and a new reconnaissance unit styled against the British special operations

---

158 Ronald Lewin, *The Life and Death of the Afrika Korps*, p. 185.

units. North Africa High Command had created a recovery and repair team in support of the Italian armoured units. This unit was equipped with trucks and heavy duty tractors to recover damaged tanks on the battlefield. For the first time this specialty could fully dedicate itself to the recovery of the M tanks thus alleviating the responsibilities of the armoured units which up to that point were tasked with using their own tanks to tow away and salvage damaged tanks. Between June and September 1942 divisions such as *Littorio* suffered tremendous losses due to attrition in the battlefield and mechanical failures. These losses were partly alleviated by this special repair unit. It is estimated that the unit refit and/or repaired over twenty-five medium tanks per month during the summer of 1942.

A training school for armour personnel had also been created tasked exclusively with training new arrivals from Italy and preparing them to operate in desert like conditions. The training school was effective in training new personnel for both *Ariete* and *Littorio* Divisions.

Another specialty unit that was introduced in April 1942 was *the X Reggimento Arditi*, a highly motorized elite infantry unit that was trained to carry out similar operations of the Long-Range Desert Force or the SAS and trained to fight with the armoured units. It had been the example set by the former which forced the Italian High Command to form a similar unit capable of hitting high value targets behind the lines thus forcing the enemy to tie down many more of its units in the rear.

In May 1942, experienced and battle hardened soldiers from all three branches of the military were recruited to begin training on the outskirts of Rome.

At the time three companies were formed: *101° Arditi Paracadutisti* (a parachute company), *102° Arditi Nuotatori* (swimmer unit) and *103° Arditi Camionettisti* (jeep mounted commandos) that constituted the units' first battalion (I *Battaglione*). Another battalion (II *Battaglione*) was formed in July with the addition of three more companies 111°, 112° and 113° which had the same capabilities.

Motorized companies were equipped with special vehicles called *Camionetta Sahariana SPA Viberti AS.42* built on the same chassis of the AB-41 armoured vehicle. The vehicle was very rugged and could be used in non-paved roads in North Africa for long range missions. Soldiers of the *Reggimento Arditi* were armed with the following weapons: a *Beretta* M38A sub-machine gun or *Mannlicher-Carcano* M91 rifle, a *Beretta* M34 pistol and six hand grenades. The unit also had crew served weapons such as the *Breda Modello* 30 light machine gun and the *Brixia Modello* 35 light mortar and some flame throwers. A few soldiers within the unit were experienced with handling TNT charges, explosive bags and plastic explosives. They were also equipped to throw or stick to the enemy armour special portable anti-tank mines as each platoon was equipped with 12 anti-tank mines, 12 Molotov cocktails, and fifty hand grenades. [159]

Although not ready at the time of El Alamein, the 103° *Camionettista* was deployed first in North Africa in January 1943 where it fought in Tunisia attached to the *Trieste* Division fighting on the Mareth Line.

Overall, the most impressive change had been the gradual transformation of the armoured units into more complete all arms combat units. The improved tactics by the Italian armoured units was the result of the adoption of mixed combat groups along the lines of the German armoured formations. Armoured divisions were split into highly autonomous combat groups comprised by

---

159 Luigi Emilio Longo, *I reparti special italiani nella seconda guerra mondiale* (Milan: Mursia, 1991), p. 142.

an armoured battalion, a mobile artillery group, a reconnaissance unit and a *Bersaglieri* motorized battalion. These units then adopted some of the same tactics used by the Germans such as the carrying forward of mobile artillery and anti-tank guns, the use of self-propelled guns to support the flanks of the medium tank battalions and the greater maneuverability of these mixed combat groups in the field of battle thanks to improved training and a sounder system of command. Two factors continued to impede upon their maneuverability such as the lack of adequate radio communication systems and the general inferior performance of the engines of the Italian medium tanks. Efforts were also made to improve some of the weapons of the armoured units although there was no immediate improvement to the quality of the medium tanks as the P-40 tank continued to not be combat ready. Some of the new weapons were the *Cannoni da 90/53*, the armoured cars and especially the self-propelled guns. Despite these improvements the Italian war effort was torpedoed by the missing of the targets of the ambitious plan in mid-1942 to beef up the tank battalions with more *semoventi* and more powerful medium tanks. Each tank company was to receive two *semoventi* platoons and one M.15 tank platoon. This change would have increased the firepower of the armoured units substantially by bringing into service many 75mm guns as well as more durable medium tanks. Such a force would have possibly fared more successfully against the American Sherman and Pilot tanks at El Alamein. Unfortunately for the Italians the plan to modernize the armoured units was not an immediate plan, but one that would have taken at least six months or a year to complete the transformation. Due to low monthly production quotas, it was estimated that the modernization process would have been completed only in mid-1943. The plan, even if implemented quicker, would have run into the Malta problem and vast amounts of equipment would have been lost at sea. Unfortunately, the efforts to field more specialized and trained units and the introduction of new capabilities had been made too late in the conflict to help stem its flow. The paucity of new equipment introduced, although much improved versus the equipment fielded in 1940, was not enough to bridge the gap with the enemy and it was never introduced in great numbers. Moreover, even these specialized units and their new equipment could not overcome the overall deficiency in machinery (especially the lack of comparably strong medium and heavy tanks) that characterized the Italian war effort. Its tanks could no longer battle successfully against medium Allied tanks, while there were too few *semoventi* or mobile 90mm guns supplied to the frontline units to make a substantial difference in the campaign.

ITALIAN TANKS AND ARMOURED VEHICLES MARKINGS

Battalion markings were painted on the sides and on the rear of the vehicle. A rectangle with the following colors: red for the 1st Company, light blue for the 2nd, yellow for the 3rd, and green for the 4th was used to identify each group. The regimental number was painted in white Arabic numbers on the left side in the rear. The battalion numbers, usually of the right rear hull, were represented as high Roman numerals. The company commander's vehicle was identified by its solid rectangle. Turreted vehicles markings appeared on the front sides and turret rear. The armoured division insignia was as follows: *Centauro* used a black centaur, *Ariete* used a ram's head, while *Littorio* used a bundle die of fasces under the horsemen on a tank. The national colors of green, white, and red were also painted on some tanks.

7

Tunisia

In November 1942, American forces landed at several points along the coast of French Morocco and Algeria with the launch of Operation Torch. The amphibious landings were coordinated after an important victory obtained by the British Eighth Army, which forced Rommel's Axis troops to retreat from the El Alamein line. The aim of the Allies was to tighten the grip on North Africa, put pressure on the Axis forces from two directions of attack and eventually evict them altogether. In response to the landings, Axis forces began to move into Tunisia in a bid to maintain a foothold in North Africa and to keep Italy in the war. For a long time before the start of Operation Torch the Italians had urged the Germans to dispatch a combined force to occupy Tunisia, which given its short distance from Sicily it would have made it very difficult for Allied naval assets to intercept Italian shipping vessels, but Hitler had refused to invade Tunisia in respect of the integrity of Vichy France. Now that the French troops had failed to sternly oppose the Allied landings in Algeria, Italian and German troops explored the feasibility of taking possession of Tunisia preempting an Allied occupation of the French possession. To fill the void left by the Vichy army, the Italians dispatched to Tunisia several units such as *Superga* infantry division, XXX Army Corps, L *Brigata Speciale* and *Centauro* armoured division. *Centauro* was deployed in a piecemeal fashion and initially was split into two units with the XIV and *XVII Battaglioni Carri Medi* fighting with Rommel's army during the retreat from El Alamein and then in Tunisia along with other ad hoc armoured combat units. This unit was also at times referred to as the *Raggruppamento Cantaluppi*. On the other hand, *XV Battaglione Carri Medi* and other *Centauro* units fought from the onset together with *L Brigata* in Tunisia. Meanwhile as troops were being brought into Tunisia, the Axis continued to develop a strategy to its secure the long-term occupation. German military intelligence soon developed an assessment of Allied strength in Algeria estimated at three or four divisions. According to the Germans the defection of the French forces in Morocco and Algeria had made a major Allied attack against Tunisia more possible. The Germans expected an early Allied advance on Tunisia, and they feared that it would be executed in the areas of Sfax, or Gabes to cut off the Axis Tunisian bridgehead from Rommel's forces. Kesselring therefore, in accordance with *Comando Supremo*, ordered a further build up in Tunisia so that the Axis forces could develop a stronger presence and a more sturdy line of defense to maintain control of the Mediterranean Sea and a bridgehead in North Africa. Thus, the Germans reinforced the Tunisian bridgehead with the 5th Panzer Division, 334th Infantry Division, Division Fritz von Broich and the 10th Panzer Division.

These forces eventually were linked up with Rommel's *Panzerarmee* which arrived in Tunisia at the end of January 1943. German forces brought back by Rommel consisted of the understrength German 15th and 21st Panzer Divisions, 90th Leicht and 164th Divisions, supplemented by the 1st Luftwaffe Brigade, corps troops and reconnaissance units with a combat effective strength of almost 30,000. The Italian divisions were elements of the *Centauro* armoured division, *Pistoia* infantry division, *La Spezia* infantry division, *Trieste* which was downgraded from a motorized to a standard infantry division since it had lost most of its mechanized and motorized assets at El Alamein, Young Fascist infantry division and the *Raggruppamento Sahariano* (Saharan Group) which was comprised of mobile elements with armoured vehicles and truck mounted artillery. Italian troops numbered about 45,000. The strength of the Axis forces in Tunisia rose during January until it reached a total of approximately 150,000, of which 100,000 were Germans, and 50,000 Italian troops. Despite the buildup, the overall position of the Axis forces in Tunisia was dire as the balance of power in 1943 had significantly shifted. Not counting the strength and tremendous resources of the newly arrived American units, the Commonwealth alone in mid-January 1943 could field over 200,000 soldiers and 450 tanks versus the Axis thirty-six German tanks and fifty-seven Italian medium tanks in Tunisia plus 110 tanks (half of which were inoperable) from Rommel's *Panzerarmee*. The Commonwealth also had 360 guns, 550 anti-tank guns and 200 armoured cars, while the Axis had 170 guns, 177 anti-tank guns and 33 armoured cars.

Despite the inferiority in forces, the Tunisian campaign saw the German army deploy new weapons. Elite Panzer units, for instance, were hastily shipped from Germany to Tunisia. At the time the German army was introducing the *Panzerkampfwagen* IV tank with a long barreled 75 gun in greater numbers as well as few Tiger I heavy tanks.[1] They also introduced a high number of Pak 40 75mm guns and the most feared of all weapon the *Nebelwerfer* rocket launcher. In contrast, the Italians, apart from a few dozen *semoventi da 75*, continued to fight a rearguard battle with obsolete M.14 tanks armed with a 47mm gun and with very thin armour and the equally obsolete 47mm anti-tank gun. One can argue that during the Tunisian campaign the Italian Army was even more poorly equipped than at El Alamein because of the losses sustained in that battle and the lower output by industry at the tail end of 1941. Apart from a few modern guns, the clear majority of the Italian troops were still equipped with the 47/32 gun as the their most important anti-tank weapon, and several Skoda field guns from the First World War. By that time the 47mm was vastly outdated because it could not respond to the increases in medium tank gun protection introduced by the Allies. While other armies developed new anti-tank guns with increased caliber and penetrative power, the Italians fell behind and could not introduce a new anti-tank weapon in large numbers. Several 47mm *semoventi* mounted on the chassis of the L.6 light tank were also shipped to the front, but the weapons proved almost immediately to be worthless against medium to heavy tanks just as it been already demonstrated in Russia against the Soviet T-34. A report by the High Command had previously underlined how: "The semovente da 47/32 not only lacks firepower but was also unable to maneuver for long periods of time before breaking down or experiencing some mechanical failure."[2] But given the shortages

---

1   This was a heavy tank, 55 tons, with a 5-man crew, an 88 gun as main armament, and was built with the thickest armour ever to be fitted on a German tank by 1943 standards. The vehicle could do 15 miles per hour on roads, 5 miles per hour on non-paved roads.
2   Emilio Faldella, *L'Italia nella seconda guerra mondiale* (Bologna: Cappelli, 1967), p. 204 for the first footnote citaion and p. 205

in equipment and the lack of proper alternatives the weapon was still supplied to the Army in Tunisia because of a lack of alternatives.

The Italian Army in Tunisia, for instance, lacked large numbers of 75mm guns and of the *Cannone* da 90/53, that had performed so well in both Russia and North Africa. An inventory count of artillery weapons in Tunisia in February 1943, for example, revealed that there were only ten 90/53 guns. Production quotas were fairly modest at this point so that some divisions remained understrength throughout the campaign lacking an effective number of guns in all size ranges. Given these deficiencies the Italian troops once again improvised where they could. The AB.41 armoured vehicle, for example, was retrofitted with a heavier 47mm gun (it was initially equipped with a 20mm gun) to give it more punch. The medium tanks were again fitted with sand bags to reduce the tank overall vulnerability versus heavier medium Allied tanks. Moreover, several captured enemy tanks, guns and vehicles were pressed into service. In February 1943 between what was salvaged by Rommel and what was shipped from Italy, the Italian armoured force consisted of fifty-seven medium tanks and three *semoventi* groups (DLIII, DLVII, DLIX) with approximately twenty self-propelled guns with 75mm gun/howitzer as some of them had been lost en route to Tunisia.[3]

As Steven Zaloga asserts, "The Italian Army continued to improve due to war experiences, better training and improved tactics. Italian weaponry remained a debilitating problem, thanks to their short-sighted German allies. Instead of assisting in Italian re-equipment using the extensive arsenal captured from the Red army in 1941 or through licensed production of better German weapons design, the Wehrmacht continued to ignore Italian shortcomings to their own peril."[4]

Zaloga's point is well taken as a better equipped Italian armoured army corps would have provided more effective combat performances. Both the armour and especially the artillery, one of the most effective branches of the Italian Army, could have largely benefitted from German assistance especially to replace vintage field guns and ineffective 47mm anti-tank guns.

The Axis forces, although outnumbered, enjoyed the advantage of the terrain. Tunisia was primarily a mountainous terrain with two main ranges, the Western and Eastern Dorsals and the occupation of its key mountain passes enabled a few troops to block the passage of much greater enemy armoured and infantry troops advancing from below on the main roads. Tunisia was very different from Egypt in terms of weather and geography and this made the campaign unique for North Africa. Instead of the barren desert landscape Tunisia is very mountainous and with very thick vegetation. This landscape favored defensive tactics and like the First World War in the Alps it centered around the control of the high ground such as the mountain passes. It was not a terrain that favored armoured warfare. The real challenge for the Axis was to supply the troops in a continuous fashion from Sicily by air or by sea to ensure that the campaign could be kept going. According to early estimates made by *Comando Supremo* the Axis troops in North Africa necessitated 90,000 tons of supply per month to survive. But Italian shipping capacity was of only 70,000 to 60,000 tons per month without factoring in losses due to enemy interference. Similarly, the Axis forces necessitated at least 30,000 tons of fuel per month while Italian shipping capacity comprised of few tankers could

---

3   Pier Paolo Battistelli and Filippo Cappellano, *Italian Medium Tanks*, pp. 31-32.
4   Steven Zaloga, *Kasserine Pass 1943: Rommel's Last Victory* (Oxford: Osprey, 2005), p. 22.

guarantee only 17,000 per month. Dwindling supplies thus became the greatest challenge to the survival of the Axis Tunisian bridgehead.

The Tunisian campaign saw for the first time American infantry troops facing Axis units in combat after the United States had entered the war. As Rommel's Army was retreating in Tripolitania first and Tunisia later and being pursued by the Commonwealth forces, the Americans were coming from Algeria into Tunisia to encircle the Axis forces from the west. The American command perceived the strengths of the Axis forces to be their combat troops' experience; the superiority of certain equipment such as Tiger tanks, and the close coordination of strategic air support with ground operations. While Axis troops were well regarded by the Americans, their weaknesses were perceived to be a lack of trust between Germans and Italians, the absence of a unified and cohesive coalition that would serve the interests of both nations, and the rivalry between the major commanders especially between General Hans-Jürgen von Arnim, who had been given command of several armoured units in Tunisia, and Rommel.[5]

For Italy, the Tunisia bridgehead represented much more than another campaign in North Africa. It was vital for Italy to hold on to a piece of North African territory in a bid to salvage its campaign that had started in 1940. Also, by keeping a foothold in Tunisia, Italy aimed to preempt an assault on the peninsula. Despite these stated aims however, within the High Command and the upper military circles, many of whom were already abandoning the Duce and his war, there was plenty of skepticism as to whether Tunisia could be maintained and the first cracks within the regime had already begun to materialize after the defeat at El Alamein. Amongst high ranking generals, for instance, who had always been attached more to the monarchy than to the regime, many believed that the war was lost and that Italy should make a determined effort to make peace with the Allies.

Despite the divisions and the skepticism of top officers the Tunisian related objectives of the Italian command in January 1943 were to constitute *Centauro* Division into a full-fledged mechanized unit, the bringing up to full strength of the infantry divisions deployed in North Africa, the rearming of the same divisions, the "necessity to equip the troops with long range artillery guns and semoventi"[6] and finally the dispatch later in the year from Italy to Tunisia of a second mechanized division.

The Italian High Command was generally responsive to the demands for new troops and equipment coming from the North Africa command and where it could it attempted to satisfy them. For example, several guns were shipped fast and furiously to Tunisia as well as all the *Semoventi da 75* units that were available in the mainland, but a second armoured unit remained only an aspiration since Italy did not have any mechanized divisions nor remaining available personnel that was combat ready after El Alamein. Moreover few additional 90/53 guns were shipped due to production delays related to the absence of raw materials in February and March 1943. In fact, the Army could barely supply *Centauro* Division, led by General Giorgio Count Calvi di Bergolo, which was constituted in a piecemeal fashion and in early 1943 was still not at full strength. Its 131º *Reggimento Artiglieria Corazzata* was formed by artillery elements from the disbanded *Ariete, Littorio, Trento* and several other units that had participated to El

---

5 Kasserine Pass Battles <https://history.army.mil/books/Staff-Rides/kasserine/Vol-I-Part_2.pdf> (accessed on 23 June 2018).
6 Ufficio Storico, *Operazioni italo-tedesche in Tunisia, 11 novembre 1942-13 maggio 1943* (Rome: Ufficio Storico, 1952), p. 51.

Alamein. *Ariete* also contributed a small anti-tank unit with approximately 100 artillerymen mostly armed with 75/27 guns. In fact, the *Comando Superiore delle Forze Armate* Libya with order number 03/16728 disbanded *Ariete* Division on 1 December 1942 and its remnants were later merged into *Centauro* Division. In early 1943 the artillery regiment (131° *Reggimento Artiglieria Corazzata*) was comprised by I and II *Gruppi da 75/27*, III *Gruppo* da 105/28, DLIX *Gruppo Semoventi*, DLVII *Gruppo Semoventi* and DLIII *Gruppo Semoventi*. Its main reconnaissance unit was the *Raggruppamento Esplorante Corazzato Lodi*, which was a cavalry unit that was attached to *Centauro*. While its *XIV Battaglione Carri Medi* was initially under strength but was later reinforced with the addition of a *semovente* unit from the disbanded *Ariete* Division.[7] Its other two armoured battalions were the XV and the XVII *Battaglioni Carri Medi*. Together they comprised the 31° *Reggimento Carristi*. *Centauro*'s *Bersaglieri* Regiment (5° *Reggimento Bersaglieri*) was comprised by the XXI *Battaglione motociclisti*, XIV *Battaglione autoportato*, and XXIV *Battaglione autoportato*. Its support units included: 31° *Battaglione Genio*, 131° *Sezione Sanità* and 131° *Sezione Sussistenza*. Its strength in February 1943 was fifty-seven M.14 tanks, twenty *semoventi da 75,* twenty *semoventi* da 47, ninety-eight field guns, sixty-six anti-tank guns, and sixteen armoured cars.

Even with these limited reinforcements the division in early 1943 still had a long way to go to become a full-fledged mechanized division. It was particularly lacking in support services since it only had six trucks to transport food and supplies and it lacked fifty tanks to be brought up to the strength of a full regimental rank. Most of its infantry units also lacked trucks and only the *XVII Battaglione* had enough trucks to carry its own food provisions and supplies:

> Divisional services were still in an embryonic state lacking organic supply and transportation entities and staffed with a limited number of inexperienced personnel. All the units of the division, except for the group equipped with 67/17 towed guns and the XVII Battaglione, lacked an adequate number of trucks. According to the North Africa High Command these units were to be furnished to Centauro by the XXX Army Corps, but in January the latter did not have any additional trucks to spare. Thus, only six trucks were transferred to Centauro to provide a bare minimum supply service.[8]

Centauro was representative of other Italian units in Tunisia which were all understrength and equipped generally with inferior weapons versus the enemy. This prompted *Generale* Messe, who would take the reins of the Axis troops in Tunisia, that to win the campaign his army necessitated weapons that were "not inferior or almost equal to the enemy's guns, tanks and planes."[9]

First Tunisian Battles

As the remnants of Rommel's army were retreating to the Mareth Line, an old French fortification system in central Tunisia, the Allies attempted to capture key Tunisian positions to cut off and capture the *Panzerarmee*. The extreme southern flank of Tunisia, where the Americans

---

7   Ibid., p. 40.
8   Ibid., p. 109.
9   John Gooch, *Mussolini's War*, p. 340.

were threatening to conquer terrain, was under command of General Giovanni Imperiali of the Italian *L Brigata Speciale* (50th Special Brigade), which was also included some armoured detachments from *Centauro*.

The Americans were the first to set foot in Tunisia when on 15 November 1942 they occupied Thelepte airfield near the Algerian border. The American move prompted an immediate Axis response on 21 November when the *L Brigata* preemptively occupied Gabes, while German paras occupied Gafsa. On the same day, the Americans counterattacked the Axis forces but at Gabes they were repelled by Imperiali's men who used heavy artillery and anti-tank guns to turn back several American tanks.[10] Facing the American threat the *L Brigata* was a hurriedly put together ad hoc combat unit which was comprised by experienced fighters' who had been previously deployed in the North African campaign. The unit was comprised by: *10° bis Compagnia motorciclisti, Raggruppamento esplorante corazzato Lodi, VI Battaglione fanteria, XV Battaglione Carri Medi and DLVII gruppo semoventi da 75 (from Centauro), Gruppo di batteria motorizzate da 75/18, and 233° Compagnia mista del genio.*

The next day, near Gabes, a column of tanks from the *L Brigata Speciale* was travelling on the main road when it was suddenly ambushed by US paratroopers. The latter opened fire at close range with bazookas and guns destroying two Italian tanks and damaging three more. But an immediate counter-attack by the Italian medium tanks forced the paras to retreat. On 26 November, US paratroopers attacked Axis forces in Gafsa but were driven back by an immediate counter from the brigade's tank unit which managed to capture several enemy soldiers. On 3 December, the Americans occupied Faid Pass with a preventive raid, but the Italians responded by occupying El Guettar and Maknassy. On 9 December, further losses were sustained by the Italians when the enemy armoured units raided under cover of darkness several advanced positions at Oudref and El Haidoudi, the troops of which fell back to Metouia. *Centauro* tanks were called in to check the enemy threat which was ultimately forced to pull back after suffering several casualties. On 24 December *Lodi* reconnaissance units encountered an enemy observation point near Gafsa. *Centauro*'s tanks were called in to support while motorized infantry was deployed to pin down the enemy with artillery and mortar fire. As the medium tanks maneuvered on the enemy flanks they forced the enemy forces to scatter and retreat. Then in January 1943, an American push by General Fredendall 2nd Army Corps attempted to occupy both Gabes and Sfax but was ultimately pushed back by Axis forces.

Once it was clear that the enemy was intensifying the number of actions into Tunisia, in a bid to stop American paratroopers from occupying key posts, the Italians committed additional resources to bolster key mountain outposts of the area near Gabes in Southern Tunisia. On 14 January *Centauro* had been placed under the command of the XXX Army Corps, whose main objective was to face the Americans on the left flank of the Axis deployment blocking them from attacking the Mareth Line. In the coming days, its forces would patrol extensively the Gabes area to complete reconnaissance assignments as well as to preemptively occupy positions. Its available forces were initially deployed as follows:

---

10   Franz Kurowski, *Das Afrika Korps: Erwin Rommel and the Germans in Africa, 1941-43* (Mechanicsburg: Stackpole Books, 2010), p. 202.

- In the el Ayacha sector *Centauro*'s artillery regiment had concentrated most its guns including one battery of 75/27 guns, four batteries of 77/28 guns, and a few anti-tank units. Gabes was manned by a few small reconnaissance units of *Lodi* group and artillery units.
- El Hanna was occupied by the bulk of the *Lodi* reconnaissance unit, while Rhennouch was defended by the 5º *Reggimento Bersaglieri*. The bulk of the 31º *Reggimento Carristi* stood behind Gafsa.

On 20 January, the commander of *Centauro* ordered his troops to occupy the following locations: Dj el Ank, Bir Mabrott and O. Halfaya. Two days later Sakket and Sened were also occupied in anticipation of enemy raids and attacks.

In late January *Centauro* continuing its reconnaissance actions was involved in a series of minor skirmishes against joint French and British armoured and motorized units in which the former almost always prevailed. On 20 January, for example, a Free French raiding unit was captured almost in its entirety including its commander at Kebili. Two days later near El Hamma a clash took place against several enemy armoured vehicles and two of them were knocked out of action.

On 24 January, American forces raided Sened Station. In response, the Italians opened fire but the Americans were too quick and managed to overrun several positions and capture seventy prisoners. In response Axis troops fought back with both tanks and *semoventi* and managed to destroy two enemy tanks (the American account below states only two tanks damaged) and ultimately pushed back the American paratroopers.

> At noon, Company I, 6th Armoured Infantry, with one mortar platoon jabbed from the west while the tanks of Company I, 13th Armoured Regiment, and the remaining infantry swung around the right flank and struck Station de Sened from the south. The tanks overran some antitank guns at the southern edge and continued among the few houses and the olive trees, while infantry followed mopping up. In a little more than three hours from the opening artillery concentration to the last, the place had been overwhelmed and Combat Command C could reorganize for the return march. By 1800, it was back in bivouac near Gafsa. Two men wounded, one tank damaged by a mine and another by gunfire, were the only American casualties. Prisoners totaled ninety-six, with the killed and wounded estimated to be about the same number.[11]

On 29 January Lieutenant Colonel David Stirling and three French officers were captured while they were leading a raiding party near El Hamma by an Italian reconnaissance unit.

In late January, American infantry forces occupied the strategic Faid Pass in central Tunisia. To prevent the Allies from launching a major offensive into southern Tunisia, Rommel ordered the Axis mechanized forces to launch an attack on Faïd Pass. The operation for the capture of the pass was undertaken by the 21st Panzer Division, directly under Fifth Panzer Army control, aided by armoured and infantry elements from the Italian L *Brigata Speciale*. The objective was

---

11 George Howe, *United States Army in World War II Mediterranean Theater of Operations Northwest Africa: Seizing the Initiative In the West* (Washington DC: Office of the Chief of Military History Dept. off the Army, 1957), pp. 387-88.

not only to control the pass, but also to position a number of infantry units on the chain of mountains from north of Faïd pass to Sened village to preempt further enemy forays.

The attack, which began in earnest on 30 January, was carried out by two separate battle groups. The 21st Panzer Division, commanded by Colonel Hans Georg Hildebrandt, organized the attack into two combat units: *Kampfgruppe Pfeifer* and *Kampfgruppe Gruen*. *Kampfgruppe Pfeifer* was further subdivided into three smaller task forces. Its northern task force was to seize control of the of the north flank and it was the one that concentrated the main infantry and armoured elements of *Centauro Division*[12] together with the 2d Tunis Battalion. The former consisted of a battle group comprised of the following units: V *Battaglione Camice Nere*, DLVII *Gruppo semoventi da* 75/18, based on two batteries which six guns each commanded by *Tenente Colonnello* Baggiani, and some mobile artillery groups from *Centauro*'s artillery regiment:

> The attack began early on 30 January. The northern and southern task forces (Kampfgruppe Pfeiffer) attained their objectives readily, but the center task force and Kampfgruppe Gruen were held up for five hours. They finally forced a stubbornly intervening French force back into Sidi Bou Zid and, after another one and one-half hour's fighting, captured Faïd village. It was then midafternoon, Kampfgruppe Gruen drove off an American armoured force that approached from the northwest, after which the German tanks continued toward the pass to envelop the defenders. Mines knocked out four tanks and the effort was postponed at nightfall. By that time, they had made contact with the company of the 2d Tunis Battalion and sealed off the pass on the west. At the eastern end of the pass, Major Pfeiffer's center task force was twice stopped short; under cover of darkness, it got only 200 yards into the opening before being held up again. The French kept the area illuminated by parachute flares, forestalling night movement up the slopes by Axis troops to positions from which to aid a renewed attack in the morning.[13]

The next day the operation resumed. The objective remained clearing the positions on Faid Pass where the enemy was still resisting vigorously continuing to stifle Axis armoured maneuvers. Then on 1 February, General Hildebrandt, deployed his reserves to finally complete the capture of Faid Pass. Here the DLVII *Gruppo Semoventi da* 75/18 irrupted by force into the enemy positions from the eastern flank as German tanks attacked from the western flank. While the Italian self-propelled guns in the lead followed by the infantry reached and overcame the objective, the Germans had a more difficult time. The latter were engaged in a bitter combat against an equally numbered enemy tank force which was eventually overcome. After the position had been completely occupied, the enemy infantry began to retire in the direction of Sbeitla. As the enemy retreated, several elements of the *Lodi* Reconnaissance Group led the chase. This action led to the rounding up of several scattered groups of enemy troops which brought up the total tally of captured prisoners to over 1,000 and several hundred killed.

The operation was successful as it took the forces of the United States 1st Armoured Division by surprise. Thus, the Pass was seized and Gafsa was also occupied after the Allied troops there were dispersed. The newly captured positions were placed under the command of *Colonnello*

12
13 Ibid., p. 391.

Tommaso Lequio of the *Lodi* Reconnaissance Group, who could count upon the following units: 104° Panzer Grenadier Regiment on two battalions, DLVII *Gruppo Semoventi da* 75/18, a German battery of four 88mm Flak 36 guns, a German unit with four howitzers 152mm, two anti-aircraft German units with 20mm guns, 69th *Batteria* da 20mm, XV *Battaglione Carri Medi* and various Italian artillery groups.

The thrust on Faid Pass had partially disrupted Allied plans for an offensive drive against Maknassy. On 31 January, the American 2nd Army Corps had assaulted the Maknassy position held by elements of *Centauro* which rebuffed the attack and destroyed five tanks and captured several enemy soldiers. A renewed attack was put forth on 1 February when the Americans finally penetrated the hamlet about 1640.

In early February *Centauro* was tasked again with patrolling a very vast area of Tunisia to prevent further enemy raids. A DAK situation report of early February 1943 details that the German command viewed *Centauro* Division to be a severely under strength division for the purpose at hand:

> The O.B. leaves in the forenoon for the area southeast of Gafsa and asks the commander of the Italian Panzer Division Centauro to commit his division in the Guettar and Maknassi area. The O.B. has the impression that the forces of the division, parts of which are in line somewhere else or have not yet arrived, will not be sufficient to intercept a decisive enemy assault from the Gafsa area over Guettar to Gabes or over Maknassi on Sfax. The O.B, therefore, decides to strengthen the resistance in this sector through some mobile German forces.[14]

Despite its limited forces *Centauro* by mid-February had conducted over 120 reconnaissance patrols, 268 surveillance missions and fifteen small scale attacks against enemy forces. Its next task was to support Rommel's operation against the American II Army Corps.

Kasserine Pass

In late January 1943, after a perilous retreat for hundreds of miles and during which in several instances the Commonwealth could have captured large units of the *Panzerarmee*, Rommel's battered troops crossed the border into Tunisia.

During Rommel's retreat, *Comando Supremo* and Kesserling had at different times requested that his *Panzerarmee* make a stand in Tripolitania to safeguard some portion of the Italian Libyan colony. Rommel, short of fuel and weapons, had refused on several occasions just to stand and fight. Once Rommel reached Tunisia, however, he became more optimistic and began to plan a series of attacks against both American and Commonwealth forces. Rommel's confidence in the Mareth position, where the bulk of the Italian-German force was lined against Montgomery's Eighth Army, was not very strong. The line, he thought, could be outflanked from either the south or the west. Moreover, the line could also be attacked by the Americans

---

14 DAK War Diary <https://history.army.mil/books/staff-rides/kasserine/vol-i-part_1.pdf> (accessed 2 March 2019).

from the direction of Gafsa. His aim therefore was to push back the Americans first to then focus upon Montgomery's forces. "By combining Arnim's forces with his own, Rommel had believed for some time that the Italian-German forces could mount stiff offensives either against Eisenhower or Montgomery. He hoped in that way to buy time for the Axis and coincidentally perhaps to achieve some strategic gain. "[15]

First encounters or small scale skirmishes with the Americans had been aided by the general lack of experience of the latter in developing coherent combined arms operations. In fact, American soldiers were well armed and equipped but did not have much experience in fighting in North Africa. Because of this temporary situation, Rommel decided for a preemptive strike to debilitate American tank and infantry strength. His aim was to capture Gabes and then launch a much stronger attack to capture Tebessa in Algeria, thus cutting off a large section of American troops from its supply base. Rommel believed that if he was given command of all mechanized troops especially the 10th and 21st Panzer divisions in Tunisia he could mount such a daring counter stroke to push back the Americans and then later concentrate his forces against the Commonwealth advance.

General von Arnim, who commanded the 5th Panzer Army, which also had the heavy tanks the Tigers I at its disposal that Rommel desperately needed for his offensive, on the other hand not only did not approve Rommel's plan for a massive operation but also initially retained control of the 21st Panzer.

The two German generals could not agree to a common strategy, whilst Rommel aimed to commit the troops to major counterthrust von Arnim wanted to make a more limited tank attack against Allied troops on Sidi Bou Zid. As a result of the impasse, *Comando Aupremo* was tasked with coming up with an agreed solution but ultimately it was decided to launch two counters aimed at pushing back the Allies. In their operation, General von Arnim's tank forces easily overcame enemy resistance at Sidi Bou Zid inflicting grave losses.

The other operation, that against Gafsa, was planned and conducted by the DAK staff who assembled a composite German-Italian force in division strength. Since von Arnim's held the bulk of the German tanks, DAK recruited all available armoured forces as stated by the following entry in their war diary:

> The concentration of the units intended for the Gafsa undertaking which has received the name "Morgenluft" (morning breeze) from the army, continues as planned and will probably be completed by the evening of February 15. The attack group of the D.A.K. has been reinforced by a Panzer Battalion and an artillery battalion of the Italian Panzer Division Centauro. Moreover, it is provided that the Division Centauro, which has been instructed to cooperate in the closest way with DAK, will follow immediately after the Gafsa area has been gained and will be employed to cover the captured area.[16]

The German forces assembled were the remnants of the DAK that had followed Rommel into Tunisia, while the Italian forces were consisted mainly of the bulk of the *Centauro* Division.

---

15   Thomas E. Griess (ed.), *West Point Military Series, The Second World War: Europe and the Mediterranean* (West Point: Square One Publishers, 2002), p. 174.
16   DAK War Diary < https://history.army.mil/books/staff-rides/kasserine/vol-i-part_1.pdf> (accessed 2 March 2019).

This force was placed under the command of Colonel Freiherr Kurt von Liebenstein, formerly commanding officer of the 164th Light Africa Division. The bulk of the German forces were to move against Gafsa from the southeast, while the mobile units from *Centauro* where to drive at the objective from their station near El Guettar.

On the afternoon of 15 February, it was discovered that the Americans had evacuated Gafsa and Rommel ordered his troops into the town and thus German troops occupied the main posts while the Italian *Bersaglieri* held positions on the surrounding hills. The next day he ordered the mobile elements of his army to move toward Feriana and Thelepte. These troops reached their destinations on the 17th and also managed to capture the airfields.

Despite still not having full control of the armour, Rommel, still lured by the desire to go on the attack, sent a message to Kesselring on the afternoon of 18 February. He proposed an attack to Tebessa with the DAK, the 10th and 21st Panzer Divisions, even though some of these units were under the command of his rival commander:

> Based on the enemy situation as of today, I propose an immediate enveloping thrust from the southwest on Tebessa and the area to the north of it, provided Fifth Panzer Army's supply situation is adequate. This offensive must be executed with strong forces. I therefore request that 10th Panzer and 21st Panzer Divisions be assigned to me and move immediately to the assembly area Thelepte-Feriana.[17]

Kesselring approved of Rommel's plan whose ultimate objective was to capture the Americans' forces key logistic and supply hub. Following Kesselring's green light, *Comando Supremo* also approved it but argued for a more limited attack against Le Kef. Thus, Rommel was given control of the so-called *Dak Kampfgruppe* (DAK Combat Group), consisting only of two under-strength armoured Divisions (*Centauro* and 15th Panzer) and the *Afrika Korps*, but he was to have no authority over von Arnim's units and especially the 21st Panzer Division. This combat unit armoured strength consisted of fifty-three Panzer tanks from the 15th Panzer Division, twenty-three M.14 tanks and a *Semovente* group with ten 75mm guns from *Centauro* under the command of General Karl Bülowius.

Dak Kampfgruppe- Order of Battle 18 February 1943

> Command Staff Deutsches Afrika Korps- General Karl Robert Max Bülowius
> 8th Panzer Regiment / 15th Panzer Division (2 battalions),
> Afrika Panzer Grenadier Regiment (Menton Group),
> Panzerjäger Company,
> 1st Luftwaffe Jäger Brigade,
> Command Staff, 1st Bn/1st Afrika Artillery Regiment,
> 1st Battalion/1st Afrika Artillery Regiment,
> 71st Nebelwerfer Regiment (3 battalions),

---

17 George Howe, *United States Army in World War II Mediterranean Theater of Operations Northwest Africa: Seizing the Initiative In the West*, p. 438.

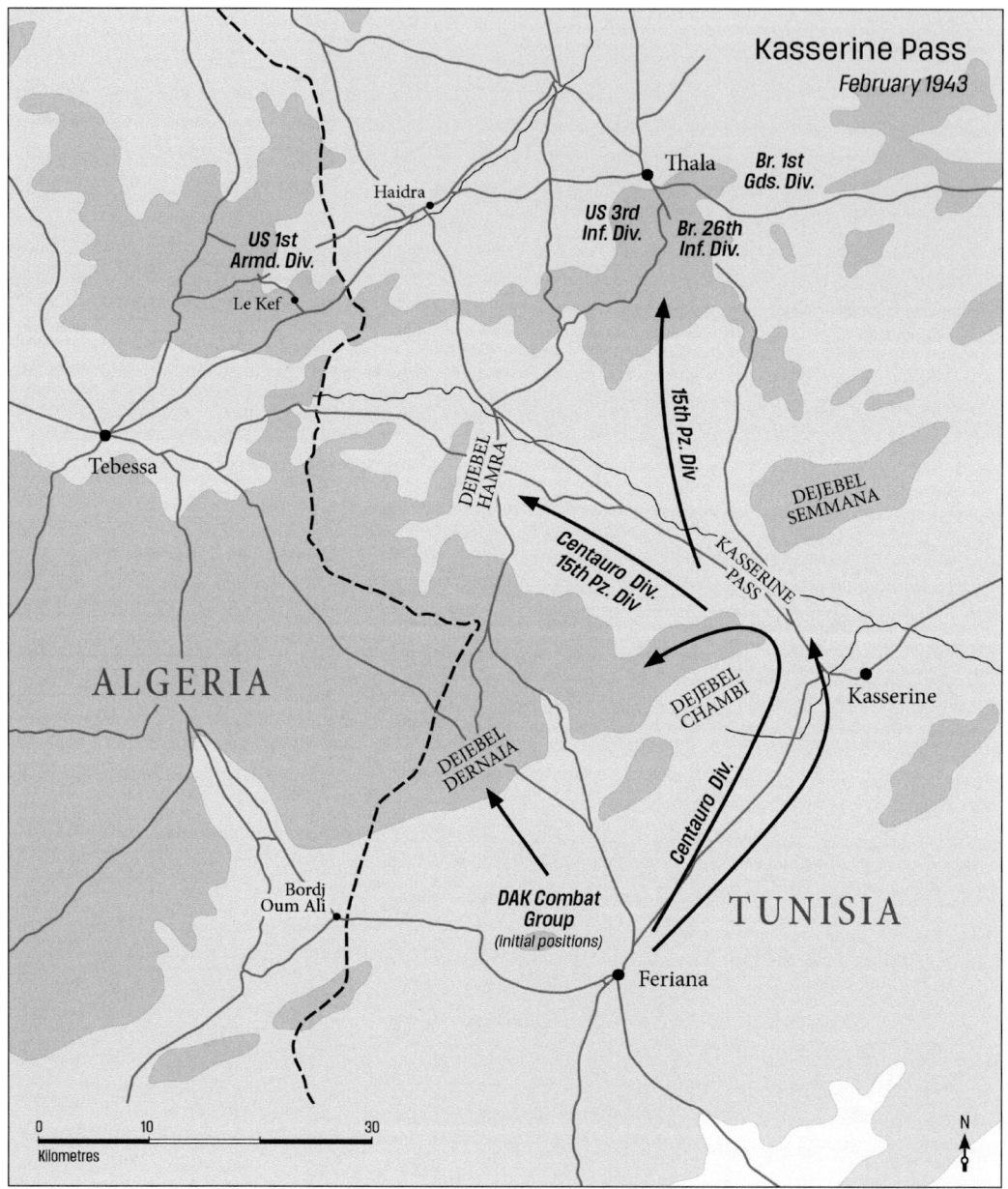

Map 3 Kasserine Pass, February 1943.

Staff/135th Flak Regiment,
33rd Reconnaissance Battalion,
200th Pioneer Battalion (1 company),
XVII/31º *Battaglione Carri Medi* (*Centauro* armoured battalion),
5º *Reggimento Bersaglieri* (XIV, XXI, XXIV *Battaglioni Bersaglieri*),
DLIX *Gruppo semoventi* da 75/18. (Italian Self Propelled Gun Battery),
III *Gruppo* da 105/28 /131º *Reggimento Artiglieria Corazzata* (Artillery Battalion).
CCIV *Gruppo* da 65/17.
(Source: Nafziger, 1999 and additions for the Italian units made by author)

The Americans established an intricate defensive positions on the Kasserine Pass in the western dorsal of the Atlas mountain range in Western Tunisia. The pass was a strategically important position being the main gateway to the American rear and their base of Tebessa in Algeria. This was Rommel's ultimate aim for the offensive to cripple enemy forces and to ultimately "protect the western shoulder of the Axis position on the Mareth Line…"[18] The DAK directive for the battle was as follows:

> Based on this enemy situation the O.B. believes through an immediate thrust of comparatively strong forces from the southwest on Tebessa and the area north a unique opportunity is offered to change the situation decisively in Tunisia. This thrust, which would be carried out by the three Panzer divisions (10th, 21st and Centauro) would penetrate in the deep flank and rear of the enemy forces facing the north Tunisian front and would likely cause the entire enemy north front to collapse.[19]

The plan entailed the Italian units to move from Feriana toward Tebessa, while the bulk of *Dak Kampfgruppe* would force the Kasserine Pass: "The combat group of D.A.K. (less one Bersaglieri Battalion. and one artillery battalion of the Division Centauro which will remain at first in the Feriana area to protect and reconnoiter to the north and northwest), starting at once, will reach Kasserine, and there will get ready to attack shortly and will then gain immediately first the mountain pass northwest of Kasserine."[20] Meanwhile the 21st Panzer Division would advance toward Le Kef, while the 10th Panzer was to be initially held in reserve and would only be deployed once Rommel had determined which of the three combat units had made the most progress. *Centauro*'s war diary reports that Rommel's orders for the attack were received only on the night between 18-19 February and the troops had to be quickly assembled and readied for the ambitious operation.

On 19 February 1943, the Axis forces began their approach march to capture Kasserine Pass, which was held by following American troops: 1st and 9th Infantry Divisions, the 19th Engineer Regiment, and the 33rd Field Artillery Battalion. On the pass, there was also a battalion of French artillerymen holding frontline positions with 75mm guns. The 1st Battalion/126th Infantry blocked the road to Thala, Colonel's Moore unit blocked the access road to Tebessa

---

18 John Gooch, *Mussolini's War*, p. 342.
19 DAK War Diary <https://history.army.mil/books/Staff-Rides/kasserine/Vol-I-Part_2.pdf> (accessed 12 January 2019).
20 Ibid

on Hill 812 and 712, while 3,000 infantry soldiers were positioned on the main defensive line behind the minefields. The American commander "planned to defend behind a triple belt of miles across the roads, by small arms and machine gun fire, and to hold the enemy's armoured vehicles at the eastern approach to the pass by the fire of two batteries of 105 howitzers of the 33d Field Artillery Battalion and one battery of towed French 75's."[21]

In addition, twenty M-3 Lee tanks from the American 13th Armoured Regiment were held in reserve to be deployed for localized counter-attacks as well as tank destroyers of the 805th Battalion.

The operation formally opened with a fierce preparatory barrage organized by batteries of German 88 guns, and Italian field guns (mainly 149 units). The barrage lasted two hours and covered the enemy positions with hundreds of shells. The first unit to attempt scaling the pass was the 33d Reconnaissance Battalion by way of a sudden, surprise attack which struck head on against the enemy defense. The latter promptly opened fire and drove out the German force, which suffered its first casualties. In the afternoon, the Germans put on repeated attacks mainly by Afrika Panzer Grenadier Regiment, supported by the tanks of 1st Battalion/8th Panzer Regiment to break into the pass. But these multiple assaults failed to make any headway into the Allied defenses, and the 8th Panzer lost five tanks that were entangled in the enemy minefields. By nightfall the only significant success that had been achieved was the capture of Hill 1191 on Djebel Semmama and approximately 100 infantry soldiers by one of the battalions of Menton Group. Meanwhile, the attack by the 21st Division toward Le Kef had also failed with the loss of ten tanks caused by American accurate artillery fire which had the benefit of good observation: "At 1230 hours, 1 kilometer south of Sbiba the division runs against comparatively strong enemy in emplaced positions with several minefields extending in front of them. After moving into position of readiness and clearing paths free of mines the Panzer Regiment resumes the attack at 1600 hours. Because of stronger resistance, new mine lines and rain making the terrain almost impassable it is impossible to break through the enemy lines."[22]

Thus, the results for the first day of operations for the Axis were dismal since no significant progress had been achieved and Rommel was particularly bitter about that outcome. During the night between 19/20 February *Dak Kampfgruppe* was reinforced by a battalion of tanks of the *Centauro* Division (XVII) and the *5° Reggimento Bersaglieri*, which came up from the Feriana-Thelepte area. In accordance with *Comando Supremo*, Rommel's decision was to attempt again to break through in the Kasserine pass area the next day. He therefore employed the 10th Panzer Division, initially kept on reserve, on the western flank of the pass rather than to commit it with the 21st Panzer Division at Sbiba.

At 0830 on 20 February the Axis forces again attempted to rush the pass following another preparatory barrage based upon a diverse set of field artillery pieces, German anti-tank guns and even *nebelwerfer*. Two battalions of Panzer Grenadier Regiment Africa, Menton Group and the *bersaglieri* supported by this fierce artillery barrage attacked the pass while the armour units (*Centauro* and 1st and 8th Battalion /8th Panzer) waited for any gaps that could be exploited. But even though the artillery preparation had been impressive, the infantry again failed to

---

21   George Howe, *United States Army in World War II Mediterranean Theater of Operations Northwest Africa: Seizing the Initiative In the West*, p. 447.
22   Fifth Panzer Army War Diary <https://history.army.mil/books/Staff-Rides/kasserine/Vol-I-Part_2.pdf> (accessed 3 March 2019).

make any headway into the Allied defensive positions, suffering a high number of casualties. Especially heavy were the casualties on the left flank were the 1st Afrika Battalion Panzer Grenadier Regiment and the *5º Bersaglieri* were operating. Here the troops found themselves fighting against an extremely difficult uphill terrain as well as accurate artillery and mortar fire. The failure to capture the pass prompted Rommel to take personal control of the operation. When he arrived on the battlefield to admonish his subordinates (Generals Bülowius and von Broich) he accused them of a cautious and prudent approach to the battle. Rommel lashed out at them and stated that he wanted to capture the pass before the Americans had had a chance to further reinforce it and desired immediate action and results.

Then Rommel immediately launched another attack against the Americans by two battalions of Afrika Panzer Grenadier Regiment, the *5º Reggimento Bersaglieri*, two armoured battalions (one from *Centauro*), together with reinforcements; mainly the motorcycle battalion of the 10th Panzer Division. But even before this attack got underway, the defenders had already lost some ground. On the left flank the troops of *5º Reggimento Bersaglieri*, which also consisted of the XIV *Battaglione*, CCIV *Gruppo* da 65 supported by the unit's mortar and small gun sections, a battery of German rocket launchers and several *semovent*i da 75, finally made some headway. Just before noon this column penetrated between the enemy's defenses and shortly afterward, observers spotted enemy tanks and infantry pulling back on the Tébessa road. By noon, Colonel Moore's command post had been overrun and his command was falling back. Progress was also being made on the right flank as the German infantry despite some losses overran a number of enemy posts. In the afternoon the reinforced Axis units provided additional manpower and equipment in the two pronged attack to finally clear the enemy positions. The two battalions of Panzer Grenadier Regiment Africa, the *5º Bersaglieri*, plus additional troops dispatched by Rommel along with the motorcycle battalion of the 10th Panzer Division, supported by the thundering fire of five battalions of artillery, began to take one position after the other and even forcing the enemy to quickly disable a number of 75mm guns and flee to the rear. Large numbers of American infantry troops were surrounded on Djebel Semmama while the Italian troops took the area of the Bahiret Foussana valley.

As American historian Citino asserts, "Over the course of the next two days German and Italian armour of the Afrika Korps launched a frontal drive against the pass. It did not break through but it did fix the defenders in place while Axis infantry methodically worked its way up the heights overlooking the pass, Dejebel Chambi in the southwest and Dejebel Semmama in the northeast."[23]

By 1600 the pass had been completely cleared by the Axis forces. Sensing that the enemy was in disarray, Rommel ordered all of General Bülowius troops forward. As the Axis infantry quickly bypassed the pass, the positions on both sides of the pass also fell in Axis hands. A last American attempt to counter the Axis forces was launched by a mixed group of eight Valentine tanks and eight Grant tanks in addition to some tank destroyers of the 894th Battalion. This forces, however, was checked with losses by 8th Battalion /8th Panzer. According to the DAK war diary:

---

23 Robert Citino, *The Wehrmacht Retreats: Fighting a Lost War, 1943* (Kansas: University Press of Kansas, 2016), p. 94.

In the left sector, the 1st battalion Panzer Grenadier regiment effectively supported on its right flank by the 5th Bersaglieri Battalion, drives the enemy out of the pass to the northwest. The enemy is still holding out at the north exit of the pass with strong forces and also tanks. The commanding general therefore decides to launch the Armoured Battalion Stotten against the enemy. In strenuous fighting the battalion succeeds in annihilating twelve enemy tanks and fifty-one armoured personnel carriers.[24]

As the Axis troops continued to stream beyond the pass the armoured units were launched to exploit the breech. Traveling on the Tebessa road these units found that some American units were confusingly retreating leaving behind several weapons and ammunition dumps. Fifteen tanks, twenty armoured vehicles and twelve tank destroyers were seized by the Axis troops as they continued to advance further. Then *Centauro*'s tanks were ordered to launch an assault before darkness to cut off enemy forces before they reached Hir Brika. "The tanks from the *Centauro* Division advanced for several miles beyond the pass but did not encounter any enemy troops. It seemed as if the road was clear and that the enemy was in considerable disarray."[25] By nightfall the Axis armoured units leaguered near the pass and waited for further instructions from Rommel's command headquarters.[26]

While the Americans were busy bringing up reinforcements to block the access to Tebessa and Thala, Rommel ordered several reconnaissance units on the early morning of 21 February on both the roads to Djebel el Hamra and Thala to determine the strength of the enemy's defenses and whether any counters were being planned. The reconnaissance units reported back that no enemy movements were observed and thus Rommel ordered the troops to continue the advance. On the Djebel el Hamra/Tebessa road the 33d Reconnaissance Battalion headed northwest from Kasserine pass. This group was charged by General Bülowius to attack and seize the mountain passes on Djebel el Hamra. The unit moved forward at 1200 with the following forces: XIV/5º *Battaglione Bersaglieri*, XVII/31º *Battaglione Carri Medi*, CCIV *Gruppo* da 65/17, the 33rd German Reconnaissance Group and three German mobile artillery pieces. The Axis troops advanced for several miles and initially faced little if no organized opposition. After travelling for several more miles it then bumped into a considerable enemy force (the Recon Company of the 13th Armoured Regiment) which opened fire against the attackers from multiple positions. Thus, the advance became intermittent conducted under a heavy enemy barrage which caused casualties and slowed down considerably the dash of the armoured units. Despite the heavy blocking fire both the armour and the infantry finally were able to organize

---

24 DAK War Diary <https://history.army.mil/books/Staff-Rides/kasserine/Vol-I-Part_2.pdf> (accessed on 12 May 2019).
25 Ufficio Storico, Divisione Corazzata Centauro, foglio operativo 2241, 20 Febbraio 1943.
26 The 5th Panzer Corps diary noted that by dawn the combat group of D.A.K. renews his attack after strong artillery preparation, the attack comes to a standstill in the violent defensive fire of the enemy stubbornly fighting in overhanging' mountain positions. Thereupon the advanced elements of the 10. Pz. Div. which have arrived in the area northwest of Kasserine are put in line on the right of the combat group of D.A.K. After hard and fluctuating fighting lasting until late afternoon the enemy is thrown out of his mountain positions. Enemy reinforcements launching an envelope movement over the mountain are caught by a counterattack, surrounded and for the most part destroyed. The panzer battalion of D.A.K. which supported the attack and forced the breakthrough on the pass road, shot down 10 enemy tanks and captured large numbers of enemy soldiers.

and put forth their attack against the objectives as the Axis artillery pinned down the defenders under counter-battery fire. The *5º Bersaglieri* managed to occupy several positions between the valley floors and the midway point on ridges at Djebel el Hamra shooting up several armoured vehicles and two tank destroyers, while they could not take the pinnacle which remained occupied by the Americans. Regarding the actions of this combat group the 5th Panzer Army War Diary reports that: "The combat group of D.A .K., after good initial progress in the attack can only make slow headway in the afternoon on account of extremely strong partly flanking defensive fire. The attack comes finally to a standstill on the plain opposite the enemy occupying overhanging mountain positions…..Its losses are considerable."[27] In the last instance the armour attempted to break through the Allied anti-tank screen but came up against heavy fire and could not proceed. The advance was finally halted by the Reconnaissance Company/13th Armoured Regiment and by numerous artillery units which opened a blistering fire barring any further movement from the Axis forces. Thus, after three hours of stiff fighting and after the occupation of several positions the operation stalled a few kilometers away from the highest mountain peak.

Meantime, another Axis unit comprised of German tanks and armoured vehicles and *Centauro*'s self-propelled guns had headed north on the road to Thala. Initially it skirmished with advanced enemy strongpoints which could not stop them until it bumped into stronger enemy defenses occupied by British armoured and infantry units (17th/21st Lancers). Here a prolonged exchange of fire took place and the Axis armour knocked out six Crusader tanks before withdrawing.

At the same time the German 10th Panzer, now under Rommel's temporary command, launched an attack along Highway 17, in the direction of Thala to the north. The German armour encountered fifty Valentine tanks of the British 26th Armoured Brigade along with a few American tank destroyers and the 2nd Battalion of the 5th Leicester Regiment. During the night, the standoff persisted as the Allied forces had slowed down the advance of the German panzers but lost several (thirty-two) tanks, several artillery batteries and 400 prisoners in the process. Because of this opposition, the Axis forces halted in front of reestablished Allied defenses at Thala, some four miles short of their objective, the fuel and ammunition supply base of Tebessa. Rommel blamed this stalemate at Thala on von Armin's refusal to send into combat fifteen Tiger I tanks, which in Rommel's view would have smashed the enemy line.

On the night between 21/22 February the Americans strongly reinforced their defense with the arrival of the heavy artillery units of the 9th Infantry Division equipped with twelve 155 guns, twenty-four 105 guns and twelve 75/16 guns. This force together with the artillery units already deployed at Thala and in front of Tebessa became the game changer that tipped the scale in favor of the Allies. In fact, the American guns were quickly deployed and at dawn on the 22nd they were hastily pressed into service.

For Rommel, the American action was a preamble for the much-anticipated enemy counterattack. His instructions to the DAK *Kampfguppe* were therefore to hold on to the occupied positions on Djbel el Hamra during the counterattack and then to resume the offensive action whenever possible. For most of the night between 21/22 February and on the morning of the 22nd the Americans had continued to target with heavy artillery fire the advanced positions

---

27 Fifth Panzer Army War Diary <https://history.army.mil/books/staff-rides/kasserine/vol-i-part_2.pdf> (accessed 12 March 2019).

held by the *bersaglieri* with great effectiveness given their exposed positions: "The 5th Bersaglieri Battalion was opposite General Robinett's line, which he had established about half a mile east of a secondary road connecting the two Djebel el Hamra passes. The line utilized the cover afforded by wadies and low ridges and benefited from superb observation points on the high hills in directing the fire of artillery batteries."[28]

On the 22nd as the reconnaissance units gleaned that an enemy counter was not imminent, the Axis troops resumed their advance against the American positions on Djebel el Hamra which were blocking the way to Tebessa. The Allied defenses were held by Combat Command B which comprised the 2d Battalion, 16th Infantry, and 2d Battalion, 6th Armoured Infantry, with the 33d Field Artillery Battalion in the rear.

The day's operation began with an armoured attack by several of *Centauro*'s tanks that aimed to take on the tanks and anti-tank units blocking the access road to Tebessa. The Italian operation was intended to tie down the Americans while the German Menton Combat Group was to overtake the enemy from infiltrating their positions from the back and flank. Given the heavy rains Menton Group lost its way during the night and ended up attacking the enemy positions far away from the meeting point with *Centauro*. As the American official history asserts: "The enemy, in a column of infantry supported by artillery and tanks, was apparently as surprised as the Allied units to find himself engaged at daylight not near Djebel el Hamra but nearly seven miles to the southeast near the Bou Chebka pass."[29] Despite being far away from the ultimate objective the two battalions of Panzer Grenadier Regiment Africa had taken possession of Hill 812 and further added to the Axis tally by capturing Battery C/33d Field Artillery Battalion with its intact five 105-mm. howitzers, three 40-mm. antiaircraft guns, and thirty vehicles. Menton Group's inability to advance toward Djebel el Hamra exposed the Italian Bersaglieri, who were strung out in front of the American troops on the opposite hills, to an Allied counterthrust. In fact, the 11/16th American Armoured Battalion counterattacked the *XIV/5° Bersaglieri* with both tanks and armoured vehicles. The *Bersaglieri* could repel a first attack at 0800 but suffered very severe casualties two hours later when the Americans put forth an even fiercer attack. Their battle diary states: "The XIV Battaglione was about to consolidate its position, when suddenly, an armoured vehicles attack took place, which was soon followed by one put forth by medium tanks. Against the latter, our 47mm projectiles, were bouncing off their armour, and could do nothing to stop them from advancing."[30] In response to the American counter, General Bülowius to aid the infantry and relive the pressure on them, ordered a concentrated tank attack by *Centauro*'s tanks and *semoventi* and I/8th Panzer battalion against the enemy on Djebel el Hamra. As the operation got underway both units came up against very heavy enemy fire from both tanks and artillery which knocked out four medium tanks and two *semoventi*. Nevertheless, the operation achieved its stated purpose of pushing back the enemy from the front held by the *Bersaglieri*, but it could not advance any further. According to the DAK diary: "In. the meantime pressure on the front of the 5th Battalion Bersaglieri has been eased by a tank attack of our own. Armoured Battalion Stotten reports that tanks and infantry are in position 2 km from its

---

28 George Howe, *United States Army in World War II Mediterranean Theater of Operations Northwest Africa: Seizing the Initiative In the West*, p. 463.
29 Ibid, p. 463.
30 Ufficio Storico, Divisione Corazzata Centauro, foglio operativo 2241, 23 Febbraio 1943.

positions (3.5 km in front of the 5th Bersaglieri). The battalion is under strong enemy fire and it is impossible to advance any further."[31]

The *bersaglieri* also attempted to advance forward but were targeted from the onset by strong Allied counter-battery fire and machine gun fire and they suffered several casualties. Later in the day a strong American counter-attack drove the Axis forces off from hill 732 and forced the *bersaglieri* to retreat after a counter-thrust by tanks and self-propelled guns.

Meanwhile on the Thala front the assault had also bogged down as the German tanks could not overtake the defensive wall of enemy artillery. During the morning, the British infantry positioned in front of Thala and supported by heavy artillery and tanks (forty British Churchill and American Sherman tanks), brought down tremendous fire against the 10th Panzer Division. During the battle ten panzers and many vehicles were destroyed. The hastily constructed but well equipped American anti-tank screen stopped the Axis advance in its tracks and has the American Official history states: "The enemy was never to get any nearer to Tebessa."[32]

On the morning of the 23rd Rommel was faced with an attack that had been bogged down by dogged enemy resistance and by the inability of the Axis to deploy additional armoured units in support of the vanguards assault detachments. Moreover, the Americans were pouring in record numbers of reinforcements comprised of both tank and infantry units and the Axis forces had by then missed their opportunity for a breakthrough. Faced by such a stalemate, Rommel decided to retreat his troops to Gafsa and halt the offensive. His aim at this point had shifted to the deployment his troops on the Mareth Line where he was expecting a British led attack against this line to take place.

As the Axis forces began to withdraw they were harried by heavy enemy forces. The *bersaglieri*, who at the time were occupying some of the most advanced Axis positions, were forced to scatter into small groups and lost most of their transport vehicles and some prisoners during the latter stages of a very disorganized retreat. The Allies also pursued the retreating Axis forces with bombing and strafing attacks by air and the toll of lost equipment and men began to mount. Nonetheless, the Axis withdrawal proceeded with considerable haste and several casualties, a clear majority managed to pull back to safety to the Axis lines in time. They also managed to destroy several Allied tanks and vehicles that they had captured during the operation but could not take with them to the new line.

Axis losses in the Kasserine Pass operation totaled 1,000 German and 400 Italian casualties with the addition of five anti-tank guns, five rocket launchers, sixty-one motor vehicles, six half-tracks, and twenty tanks. American losses were high. Of the 30,000 Americans engaged in the Kasserine Pass of the 2nd Corps, 300 were killed, 3,000 wounded, and 3,000 missing. 2nd Corps also lost 183 tanks, 194 half-tracks, 208 artillery pieces, and 512 trucks and jeeps. The 34th Division defending Sbiba had 50 men killed, 200 wounded, and 250 missing.[33]

Strong enemy resistance had prompted Rommel to call off the offensive. In a dispatch to *Comando Supremo* Rommel argued that "the continuous bolstering of the enemy positions with fresh infantry and reinforcements of all kind, the bad weather which prevented the tanks from maneuvering away from the main roads, and the numerous difficulties in operating in the

---

31   George Howe, *United States Army in World War II Mediterranean Theater of Operations Northwest Africa: Seizing the Initiative In the West*, p. 465.
32   Ibid.
33   Mario Montanari, *Le operazioni in Africa settentrionale*, Vol, IV, Part I, p. 281.

mountainous terrain"³⁴ forced his hand and induced him to call off the operation. Regarding Kasserine Pass historian Basil Liddell Hart has argued that: "Thus as a limited objective stroke it had been a brilliant success. But it had fallen short of, although coming dangerously near to, the strategic object of producing an Allied retreat from Tunisia."³⁵ The authoritative West Point History of the Second World War also underlines that the offensive had been brilliant but is more critical of Rommel's command of the overall operation. It stresses how Rommel wavered in the middle of the operation. wasting most of the morning on the 21st before ordering a resumption of the attack. "Time had run out, precious time which the Germans, including Rommel, had let slip away on February 21 and 22nd, when they had a chance for a breakthrough Allied reinforcements could consolidate defenses.³⁶ In conclusion, it can be argued that the Kasserine Pass battle resulted in a localized tactical success but it failed to succeed as a strategic victory. In the Rommel Papers, the famous German general reports that *5º Bersaglieri* was singled out by General Bülowius, commander of *Dak Kampfgruppe*, for its brilliant assault on 20 February at Djebel Semmana. Rommel himself wrote in his war diary...... "it was an exciting scene of the tank battle north of the pass....and I have special praise for the 5th Bersaglieri, who attacked fiercely and whose commander fell during the attack; they threw the American, British and French forces out of the pass, allowing the II/86 and Pz.10 to exploit the breakthrough..."³⁷

Mareth Line

After the battle ended Rommel's attention turned to the Mareth Line, where the Axis infantry and artillery unit had constructed deep trenches and anti-tank ditches, to withstand the planned offensive by the British Eighth Army. As usual, Rommel, always ready to take the initiative to the enemy, quickly put together a plan of action set to relive the pressure on the Mareth Line with a preemptive strike against the British. Despite Rommel's desire to attack right away the plan had to be postponed for several days by the need to repair as many tanks as possible. In the meantime Allied reconnaissance operations were able to gather key intelligence on the enemy's build up and this allowed Montgomery's army the opportunity to regroup. The plan, codenamed Operation Capri, was launched on 6 March 1943 to force General Montgomery's army back from his position opposite the Axis defensive line. Rommel had at his disposal 141 tanks plus the *Trieste* and *La Spezia* divisions. But the operation was met by a fierce enemy barrage which prevented the tanks from advancing. Lieutenant General Oliver Leese had at his disposal a sizeable force comprised of 350 field artillery guns, 460 anti-tank guns and 300 tanks. This supremacy in equipment together with the Allied intelligence regarding Rommel's intentions assured an Allied victory. The offensive turned out to be a failure and was called off on the first day and Rommel was then relieved of his command and would never command any Axis troops in North Africa. By then some of his troops had been incorporated in the Italian I Army. On 9 March, he handed off command of German troops to von Arnim and left Africa on sick leave for good.

---

34 Basil Liddell Hart, *The Rommel Papers*, p. 408.
35 Ibid., p. 410.
36 Thomas E. Griess (ed.), *West Point Military Series, The Second World War: Europe and the Mediterranean*, p. 174.
37 Basil Liddell Hart, *The Rommel Papers*, p. 324.

Exit Rommel

Although he had shown respect for the Italian units and the armoured ones specifically, Rommel would later heavily criticize them in the Rommel Papers and scapegoating them for being one of the factors leading to the defeat of the Axis in North Africa. In his memoirs he clearly recognized the inadequacy of their weapons but blamed them for a number of Axis defeats. Two events that have been dealt in detail in this book shed a different light on the relationship between Rommel and the Italians and offer a more critical re-examination of the Rommel Papers. First, during Operation Crusader Rommel initially failed to react to the threat of a Commonwealth preemptive strike despite mounting intelligence telling him that an offensive was imminent, but later corrected his earlier mistake by concentrating his armoured forces for his important victory on Totensonntag. His victory was greatly aided by *Ariete*'s stand at Bir el Gobi I which derailed the first part of the British counter-offensive and shielded the German Panzers from the brunt of the British tanks. When the German tanks defeated the British units on 23 November, they faced an enemy tank force that had already sustained casualties and loss of equipment as 22nd Armoured Brigade, one of the three pillars of the British tank force faced by the Germans, had sustained severe tank losses due to a combination of mechanical failure, breakdowns, and tanks being put out of action on 19 November. Rommel's subsequent 'Dash to Wire' was a brash offensive which did catch the enemy off guard but failed to achieve significant results and prevented the Axis forces from dealing a fatal blow against the Tobruk garrison. Then he came back to Tobruk with his armoured forces to deal with the British armour, but by then both the German Panzer divisions and the Italian units had sustained heavy losses of their own and could not deal with the British armoured units which had also sustained losses but in the meantime had been more readily resupplied. In the Rommel Papers, Rommel blamed the Italian mechanized unit for failing to link up with the German tank units on 5 December to deal the final blow on the British. Historians of the stature of Liddell Hart, Ronald Lewin, etc…have not only accepted Rommel's version of those events but have also been critical of the role played by the Italians during Operation Crusader. A more objective, revisionist history of the campaign would in contrast state that when 22nd Armoured blundered into Bir el Gobi the *Ariete* division's covering action undoubtedly preserved the integrity of the German tank forces while the 'Dash to the Wire' "was yet another drive to nowhere and had little impact on the operational situation."[38]

While the Rommel Papers attributed the lack of success of the Axis during Operation Crusader to the negative role played by the Italian mechanized unit, the work completely overlooked aspects of the commanders conduct of the campaign and the various defensive actions conducted by the Italians and the German infantry for that matter that helped to sustain the Axis effort during the two-month long operation.

The second aspect of the North African campaign that sheds a different light on Rommel and the Italians is the role played by the latter during the Gazala line battles and the seizure of Tobruk in mid-1942. Rommel did achieve his greatest victory by always leading his troops from the front in an offensive minded, advance at all costs operation. In such operation, the German

---

38 Robert Citino, 'Drive to Nowhere: The Myth of the Afrika Korps', *Military History Quaterly*, summer 2012.

Panzer units without doubt played the primary role in breaking through the enemy defensive boxes with flanking attacks, but the overall success of the month-long operation also depended upon the more static role played by the Italians. The latter used their infantry to maintain the siege of Tobruk, while the *Ariete* Division's artillery and self-propelled units played their part in defeating several enemy tank counter-attacks. By linking up with DAK's artillery, *Ariete*'s units dealt a series of heavy losses upon the enemy tank formations that contributed to the final victory at Ain Gazala. These two vital roles have been overlooked in key histories of the campaign and most importantly in the Rommel Papers.[39]

When Rommel arrived in North Africa he was under the command of the General Gariboldi. His relationship with Gariboldi was contentious and when he was told to halt the offensive in April 1941, Rommel rebuffed his superior and ordered his troops to continue the advance. Rommel's decision was vindicated when his bold offensive yielded the recapture of most of the territory lost during Operation Compass. With General Bastico, Rommel also had a very uneasy relationship, but Rommel was at the peak of his popularity and often appealed directly to Hitler and Mussolini to have decisions go his way.

Whilst relations between Rommel and Bastico were often tumultuous, he "got on well with all his lesser Italian commanders."[40] The post Alamein report written by *Generale di divisione* Arena of the *Ariete* revealed that his relationship with Rommel was quite good and that Italian divisional commanders such as Baldassare and Navarini generally got along well and collaborated fruitfully with Rommel and other German generals in North Africa. The troops during the Axis high tide in North Africa in mid-1942 also demonstrated a high spirit of comradeship and morale was high. After the defeat at El Alamein the morale and the relationship between Italian and German units worsened.

Martin Kitchen for instance has written that by 1942 Rommel "was gradually changing his views of his allies. In the past he had been overtly critical of them, using them as convenient scapegoats for his own mistakes. By now he had learnt to appreciate the enormous difficulties under which they were fighting and was ready to give them credit where credit was due."[41] The improvement in combat performance of the Italian troops after Beda Fomm that historians such as John Gooch, Paddy Griffiths, Jack Greene and Alessandro Massignani have widely written about sustains the argument that Rommel and his officers did change their minds. Their views, for instance, had by 1943 evolved to the point that they likely no longer shared von Thoma's dismissive view of the Italian troops in North Africa in 1940.

Two examples give us the measure of the man or how Rommel was viewed by the Italians as a soldier and as a leader of men. In the first example Rommel put the affairs of the *Panzerarmee* on the backburner to aid a wounded comrade, while the second example demonstrates that excessive and unnecessary casualties were sometimes the result of Rommel's offensive at all

---

39 Michael Carver, *Tobruk* (London: BT Batsford, 1964) and Basil Liddell Hart, *History of the Second World War* (New York: GP Putnam's Sons, 1970).
40 David Irving, Rommel: Trail of the Fox, (London: Wordsworth Editions, 1999), p.119.
41 Martin Kitchen, *Rommel's Desert War* (New York: Cambridge U. P., 2009), p. 272. John Pimlott had the following view of the relation between Rommel and the Italians: "Rommel had little or no respect for the Italian High Command, but the greatest respect for the Italian soldiery, whom he believed were perfectly good material, but badly equipped and poorly led. At Gazala, the Ariete Division had fought very well. Rommel firmly believed that if Rome had taken the war more seriously the Italian units could have acquitted themselves much better."

costs mentality. In mid-1942 while Mussolini had flown into North Africa and was headquartered at Derna and there waited for the final breakthrough against the enemy defenses to take place, he asked for a meeting with Rommel. But during his month long stay in North Africa Rommel remained at the front and could never meet Mussolini. Despite not having had time to meet with the Duce, Rommel did make time to fly to visit *Maggiore* Pardi who had sustained a heavy wound. As soon as Rommel was informed of Pardi's dire predicament, Rommel abruptly interrupted a DAK command meeting to fly on his Storch to reach the hospital at El Daba where Pardi had been interned. Once having reached the hospital he put his Storch at Pardi's disposal so that he could be taken to a bigger more endowed hospital at Mersa Matruh. But the injured soldier was so badly wounded that he could not be transported by plane. Rommel remained several hours at his side until he expired. The second example is provided by an officer of the *Ariete* Division. *Tenente* Enrico Serra of VIII *Battaglione Carri Medi/Ariete*, for instance, wrote an article in the post war that shines a different light on Rommel's command style from the Liddell Hart edited Rommel Papers. Serra recalls that on 18 April 1941 Rommel ordered a second mostly Italian-led tank attack against Tobruk despite the fact that *Ariete* had very few tanks that were still operational. He writes: "In reality the attack could not succeed given the lack of heavy field guns. The impetuous Rommel barreled into Ariete's command headquarters screaming and shouting and complaining about the failed attack. He did not listen to any explanation of why it had failed and ordered a new attack to be led by a German officer. The attack was launched and only one tank came back with several wounded on board, the others were knocked out by British fire and their crews died. The German officer was also killed in the action."[42]

Sidi Bou Zid

After the American forces, had occupied some advanced artillery positions at Sidi Bou Zid on the Western dorsal and had launched several reconnaissance teams into the area patrolled by the Italian *Lodi* Reconnaissance Group the latter was ordered by the XXX Army Corps to organize an action to push the Americans back. The objective was to sweep up the area of Sidi Bou Zid and to raid enemy positions in the direction of Sheila and Borg El Hafey. Three Axis columns began their operation at dawn on 6 March. The units undertaking this action were: *Lodi* Reconnaissance Group, XV *Battaglione Carri Medi*, and DLVII *Gruppo Semoventi da 75/18*. While from Faid Pass the Italian artillery began to pound Sidi Bou Zid and the surrounding hills occupied by enemy troops, the right-wing column secured its flank by overrunning several advanced enemy positions. Then the center column erupted into Sidi Bou Zid and occupied it. Meanwhile the left-wing column led by *Tenente Colonnello* Bottiglieri of XV *Battaglione Carri Medi* reached Borg El Hafey. On the 7th the action continued as the most advanced reconnaissance platoons were ordered to exploit the situation to the fullest to inflict casualties and destroy enemy equipment. The most relevant action of the day was when the armoured battalion was involved in combat against enemy tanks. The engagement was brief and the enemy unit was forced to pull back after losing two vehicles.

---

42   Giulio Bedeschi, *Fronte d'Africa*, p. 99.

El Guettar

In mid-March, General George Patton's 2nd Army Corps launched Operation Wop, a diversionary attack meant to tie down *Centauro* and 10th Panzer while the Mareth Line Axis positions were attacked from the south by the Commonwealth. The 2nd Army Corps was not only charged with drawing off reserves from the enemy forces facing the Eighth Army but also to recapture control of forward airfields like Thelpete and a forward maintenance center such as Gafsa from which the units of Eighth Army could draw ammunition and food supplies to maintain the momentum of their advance. At the time 10th Panzer had fifty tanks while *Centauro* had thirty-one medium tanks and were located at Gafsa. The operation that saw almost 100,000 American soldiers, manly from the 1st Armoured Division and 1st Infantry Division[43], pitted against 7,600 Axis men deployed in and around Gafsa (7,000 from *Centauro* and 600 Germans), began in earnest with a massive preparatory barrage.[44] Facing this well-equipped and effective American unit which had fought and had been bloodied at Kasserine Pass, the overstretched Axis forces based their defense on the occupation of strategic mountain passes. The positions, strategically sited to take advantage of the mountainous terrain, were centered on isolated strongpoints, each of which was supported by artillery and mortars.

The infantry and armoured units began their part of the operation on the night of 17 March after American mechanized and motorized units of 18th Infantry Regiment had converged from the north and northwest upon Gafsa which was defended by 580th German Reconnaissance Group and *Centauro*. The Americans first dispatched reconnaissance units into Gafsa which were met by heavy machine gun fire and artillery. Thus, they were quickly dispersed. As the Americans then pressed forward more troops into Gafsa and occupied hill 528 of Gebel Touinia, General Calvi of *Centauro* ordered its evacuation. In order to avoid encirclement, the Axis contingent positioned itself on the hills behind Gafsa which were more easily defensible. They dug trenches that overlooked Gumtree road and could also control the road to Gabes and Sfax. On this defensive line (made up of strongpoints numbered from 1 to 9), several counter thrusts effectuated by both armour and reconnaissance units such as the *Lodi* reconnaissance unit pushed back temporarily the enemy forces and caused them several casualties.

On 18 March, Italian forward observation posts spotted on the main road at Station de Zannouch a force of over 200 tanks and several truck mounted guns that was getting ready to advance against the Axis positions. On the 19th the enemy resumed the advance but several well positioned 90/53 guns on strongpoint n. 4 "taking full advantage of their long range are able to disable several enemy self-propelled guns while forcing the bulk of them to disperse and retreat."[45]

Concurrent with the assault against Gafsa, the 1st Infantry Division's operation east of El Guettar along the Gumtree road south of the Gafsa-Melzouna mountains encountered stiff opposition also from well sited guns. After a day of enemy surveillance, and observation, the

---

43 The American II Corps consisted of the 1st, 9th, and 34th Infantry Divisions, the 1st Armoured Division, the 13th Field Artillery Brigade and the seven battalions of the 1st Tank Destroyer Group.
44 American intelligence estimates were that the garrison at Gafsa was comprised of 7,100 Italians of the Centauro Division; and further east from Sened to Maknassy there 800 German and 750 Italian troops.
45 Ufficio Storico, *Operazioni italo-tedesche in Tunisia, 11 novembre 1942-13 maggio 1943*, p. 121.

1st Infantry Division made its first major move on the night of 20-21 March. To capture an advanced enemy position held by *Centauro* infantry on the road to Maharès, the 1st Ranger Battalion completed a difficult ten-mile hike to outflank the Italian defenders. Thanks to this audacious maneuver the Americans took hundreds of prisoners and after reached Bou Hamran. By taking control of these positions the Rangers were now able to barrage the Italian positions located south of the main road and allow the bulk of the 1st Infantry Division to advance.

Meanwhile, the 18th Infantry's attack moved southeastward along the road from El Guettar to Gabès and into the nearby hills against units of Division *Centauro*. At dawn on the 21st 1st Ranger Battalion began its the attack with an opening round which consisted of an intensive mortar barrage. As the American official history observed:

> At night, and under a hazy moon, the infantry crossed a plain where mere six-inch grass was the main cover, and where the enemy had already demonstrated that his observation in daylight was alert and accurate, and his artillery fire swift and precise. Getting through a mine field, the troops infiltrated past Hill 336 north of the road to take it at daybreak with a rush from the rear. General Patton and some of his staff visited the hill soon afterward. The first stage of the attack 'according to plan' yielded 415 prisoners.[46]

According to the *Centauro* war diary the attack took the *bersaglieri* by surprise who then pulled back leaving on the field of battle 200 prisoners.

On 22 March a large, armoured column of over 200 tanks was spotted near strongpoint n. 9 this time reinforced by truck mounted artillery units and several self-propelled gun units. The action began when 1st and 2d Battalions/18th Infantry, were engaged, in tough hand to hand combat trying to drive out Italian forces on strongpoint n. 9, the conquer of which, would have allowed them to separate several of the main strongpoints from the bulk of *Centauro*'s forces. After a heavy barrage the position was seized by an infantry attack conducted from both flanks from the American infantry battalions. Later in the day *Centauro* and the 10th Panzer Division made several attempts to counter attack and retake the lost positions but the fighting continued to be particularly bitter against a much greater American tank force. Repeated attacks by armour and infantry were made against the enemy defenses but they all slammed against the well-organized American anti-tank screen which put down very accurate fire. Ultimately, the last Axis tank attack failed under the thundering fire of heavy enemy artillery and air attacks. The American official history reports that the aerial bombings by the US Air Force played a major role in breaking up the Axis counter-attacks: "the Italians made no resolute counterattack and were driven off by artillery fire and Allied air action whenever their guns opened up or small groups of their tanks assembled."[47] As the Axis counters failed, the American infantry continued to infiltrate the El Guettar area by improving their positions along the Gumtree road, while the 16th Infantry occupied a number of positions on the valley floor near Djebel el Micheitat, and two battalions of the 18th Infantry occupied numerous heights near Gabes road, at the northeastern tip of Djebel Berda. The following is the testimony of the *Centauro* infantry commander detailing how the battle progressed:

---

46 George Howe, *United States Army in World War II Mediterranean Theater of Operations Northwest Africa: Seizing the Initiative In the West*, p. 558.
47 Ibid.

For several days, the battle had raged, the flanking strongpoints were crumbling after being subjected to massive bombings On March 22, the Americans now convinced that they would not encounter any resistance had moved to conquer the last line of resistance. A company from the battalion is sent to strongpoints 4 and 9 in the night while the fighting takes place in all its intensity. A commander of a German battalion on the left of the position in the morning no longer sees any reaction from the Italian positions. He points his binoculars and suddenly sees a sergeant going into a hole and setting off bursts of machine gun fire that target the enemy platoons that, surprised and stunned, turn back into a precipitous escape. The fighting subsided in the evening, and the enemy artillery stopped firing altogether at night. The few survivors, tattered and dazed, emerged like ghosts from the ravines and for another three days they repelled all enemy attacks heavily supported by armoured vehicles.[48]

On March 23rd, the 10th Panzer, supported by only a few tanks from *Centauro*, mounted a second counter attack. Initially the attack proceeded per plan and overran several American positions. But after the initial success the attack bogged down under the fire of a multitude of American guns which debilitated German tanks:

> German tank-infantry teams overran the American artillery and infantry positions east of Hill 336 in engagements which brought some hand-to-hand encounter, and heavy American losses. A curving belt of mines extended from Chott el Guettar across the road and along the Keddab wadi to the southeastern base of Hill 336. There the tide of battle changed. 51 American artillery and the tank destroyers of the 601st and 899th Tank Destroyer Battalions knocked out nearly thirty enemy tanks, and the mine field stopped eight more.[49]

A document dating 24 March indicated that *Centauro's XVII Battaglione Carri Medi* had only eleven tanks in working order and thanks to the support provided by 10th Panzer Division the dangerous situation at position n.9 was rectified after stiff jabs at the enemy.[50] The fighting had concentrated particularly on the strongpoint 9 that the Axis forces had initially lost to the Americans but had later partially reoccupied after several counters by *Centauro* and 10th Panzer: "The heaviest fighting which lasted several days took place on strongpoints 3 and 5 to the north, 8, 9 and 9bis to the south. Overall our defensive line held until it could be relieved by the 10th Panzer. In the sector held by infantry, which was basically isolated from the other Axis forces, three successive enemy attacks took place by both tanks and infantry. But they were all repelled."[51] Thus despite losing ground and men during the first days of the American assault, Operation Wop turned to be a phased, tactical retreat for the Axis forces that while pulling back inflicted heavy casualties upon the enemy.

---

48   Dino Campini, *Nei giardini del diavolo*, p. 360.
49   George Howe, *United States Army in World War II Mediterranean Theater of Operations Northwest Africa: Seizing the Initiative In the West*, p. 560.
50   Dino Campini, *Nei giardini del diavolo*, p. 360.
51   Ibid.

Whilst *Centauro* and the bulk of the Italian mechanized units were busy fighting in western Tunisia, the Axis troops on the Mareth line between 16-30 March fought the decisive battle of the campaign. The battle opened with a massive artillery barrage. As historian John Gooch asserts: "In the first phase of the battle, thanks to vigorous counter-attacks, effective use of their limited artillery and skillful deployment of his forces by Messe, 1st Army fought off a frontal attack and an attempt to turn his position from the western flank."[52] A second major enemy encircling operation was also successfully fought off by the Axis forces followed by a staged retreat. In both operations only German armoured units were deployed while Italian armour was concentrated in the fighting against the Americans in Tunisia's western dorsal. At the end of March 1943 Messe's Italian First Army had evacuated the Mareth Line and was reorganizing its defenses in the Chott Akarit Line. To tie down the largest number of Axis troops away from the new line of defense, General Alexander ordered General Patton to again launch another combined arms attack against the Axis forces deployed on the left flank along the El Guettar /Gabès heights. The northern flank was held by the 10th Panzer which was positioned at Djebel el Micheitat, while *Centauro* held Djebel Berda. Its forces, mainly units from the *131º Reggimento Artiglieria Corazzata, Bersaglieri*, machine gunners and a few groups of *carristi* operating artillery weapons, occupied four strongpoints on hilly terrain facing the main road to Gabès. The German troops were also dug in the hilly terrain and their positions were bolstered by artillery, anti-tank guns and even rocket launchers. The attack was to be spearheaded again by the 2nd Army Corps. Its operations at El Guettar began on 26 March with a fierce preparatory barrage which was followed by the infantry attack. The central positions occupied by *Centauro* were subjected to the fire of the 16th American Infantry Regiment mortar and small artillery units. As the barrage was pinning down the enemy, the 47th Infantry began its advance heading for Hill 369 from its jump-off position at the foot of Djebel Berda. Unfortunately, the rough terrain caused several delays. Nevertheless, with considerable elan, the 1st and 3d Battalions, 47th Infantry, captured several positions on the ridge but were unable to seize the hill top. Meanwhile the 2d Battalion/47th Infantry advancing during the night lost its way and wound up taking considerable enemy fire losing its battalion commander, intelligence officer and communication officer, its entire Company E, and the commanders of two other companies. The next day the operation resumed and the Americans obtained localized successes by overcoming several Axis positions but were not able again to take Hill 369. According to plans the 2d Battalion/39th Infantry was to seize Hill 369 with a bayonet attack, but it was repelled by heavy Axis fire. *Centauro*'s report states that: "The situation is grave. I dispatched to the frontline all available reserves including combat engineers and sappers, platoons under my immediate command, and units from various other combat groups."[53] Despite thinning Axis ranks, the Americans were once again halted mainly by machine guns' fire, mortars and heavy guns.[54] On 29 March, General Patton, to overcome the stalemate, formed Task Force Benson, a special combat unit comprised of specialized infantry, two tank battalions and an anti-tank battalion, whose role was to attack head on the enemy positions. On 30 March, this force leaped forward after a massive artillery barrage. This bombardment allowed the troops to advance

52 John Gooch, *Mussolini's War*, p. 345.
53 Ufficio Storico: Comando Divisione Centauro, 'Relazione sulla battaglia di Guettar: 16-31 Marzo, 1943', 1160/C/3/1.
54 Ibid.

upon Djebel Lettouchi, while they could not establish a footing on other hills. The 1st Infantry Division on the other hand, was more successful. After a morning attack, followed first by three hours of shelling by four artillery battalions, and then by a renewed infantry assault, its 26th Infantry could capture most but not all the southern portion of Djebel el Micheilat (Hill 482 and adjacent ridges).

Although the Americans could infiltrate the first line of defense they were later met by an intense Axis barrage which crippled several enemy tanks and vehicles:

> Task Force Benson began its attack at noon of 30 March but did not get very far. The enemy's artillery and antitank weapons, many of them mobile, were well placed and proved much too strong. A mine field barred Benson's advance through the pass between Djebel Micheilat and Hill 369. Before he could pull the column back out of range and extricate the leading vehicles, enemy fire knocked out five tanks and two tank destroyers.[55]

Therefore, the first day of battle ended with an Axis victory as the troops pushed back the American attack with losses. Even though the Axis units had held, the American penetration on Djebel Micheilat had put on alert the German 49th Battalion, which on the night between 30/31 March evacuated its positions and enabled further American advancements.

At 1300 on 31 March Task Force Benson again pushed against the Axis positions with a combined force of tanks and infantry. The American infantry again could occupy some of the advanced strongpoints but the armour initially lost three tanks and two tank destroyers due to Axis anti-tank fire and the minefield. As the Americans continued to press forward by committing more troops they managed to overrun and destroy several anti-tank weapons. Then in the proximity of the Axis resistance line the enemy tanks were met by sixteen *Centauro* medium tanks and fifteen tanks from 21st Panzer Division which engaged them in a prolonged artillery duel. The combination of Axis anti-tank fire and the flanking attack put forth by the tanks claimed nine tanks and two tank destroyers to the cost of six Axis medium tanks. The strong enemy attack, although well executed was halted by German and C*entauro's* medium tanks that ultimately restored the situation and *bersaglieri* troops retook control of the positions that initially had been overrun by the enemy. In those two days of heavy fighting Benson's force sustained heavy losses including 200 men, thirteen tanks and four tank destroyers. As the American official history states: "Clearly, the tactical situation in the valley was inappropriate for armoured exploitation. The enemy first had to be ousted from antitank positions by infantry and artillery before the armour could lunge ahead."[56] For General Calvi of *Centauro* at El Guettar the Americans had fought bravely but had adhered to a fixed plan of action that was unworkable in such hilly terrain and allowed the Axis troops to repel the attack.

American deployment at El Guettar continued between 2 and 6 April to chip away at the Axis positions on the ridges along the Gumtree and the Gabes roads. They made vast recourse to artillery preparations prior to any move forward by their infantry or the armour. This was an indication of how firm the Axis response had been and how the Americans were adapting by putting forth more cautious operations. The fighting intensified particularly around the

---

55 George Howe, *United States Army in World War II Mediterranean Theater of Operations Northwest Africa: Seizing the Initiative In the West*, p. 571.
56 Ibid. p. 572.

positions held by the *bersaglieri* on Djebel Breda. Here the 9th Infantry Division continued to attack Hill 772, but each attack was repulsed with heavy casualties. The attacks were repetitive but they did not achieve the stated purpose:

> The infantry divisions poked and jabbed at the defenders in their mountain positions without quite breaking their persistent hold. Those divisions seemed to be engaging the major part of the enemy's forces. The reinforced armoured division, on the other hand, after forfeiting its best chance of successful action early on 22 March at Maknassy, seemed to have spent itself against an enemy who was inferior in strength but had exploited skillfully his advantage of position.[57]

The following description of the battle is from the *Centauro* Division's chief of staff:

> Artillery fire and minefield defenses several times stopped the repeated attacks of hundreds of enemy tanks that were three times more numerous than our armour. On the second day of battle deploying two Semoventi and fourteen tanks we even carried out a surprise counter attack on the flank of a large, armoured formation that was pushed back ... The American infantry that followed the tanks, even when the latter were forced to retire, continued without respite to attack our lines with an impressive amount of fire ... For four consecutive days we succeeded first in holding, and then in recapturing the strong points that had fallen. One by one, successively using all the reserves that we had saved at Gafsa we were able to recapture them. It was useless to call for the support of our own aircraft; the sky above the battle was permanently dominated by the enemy aircraft, and our anti-aircraft defenses, equipped only with small-caliber weapons, succeeded only in putting off low level machine-gunning.[58]

On the 6 April, the Allied force finally broke into the main defensive line held by the Italian First Army on the main line and this spelled the end for the troops positioned on El Guettar which were now in danger of being outflanked. They withdrew to the north-east along with bulk of Messe's Army after the Battle of Wadi Akarit which lasted one day and caused again heavy casualties in the Axis ranks. According to a German historian summarizing the month long resistance at el Guettar: "The Centauro Armoured Division fought bravely at Guettar against a two-fold superiority."[59] General Giovanni Messe also exalted *Centauro*'s role during the el Guettar fighting (in Italy known as *Battaglia della Guattaria*) where a severely under-strength armoured division held on to its positions despite the enemy's numerical advantage.[60]

After suffering large losses of men and equipment on the Mareth Line and the on the Akarit Line the First Italian Army was by 10 April 1943 reduced to the following:

Young Fascists Infantry Division: 5 battalions (much depleted) and 27 guns.

---

57 Ibid., p. 575.
58 Ufficio Storico: Comando Divisione Centauro, 'Relazione sulla battaglia di Guettar: 16 Marzo-4 Aprile, 1943', 1160/C/3/1.
59 Franz Kurowski, Das *Afrika Korps: Erwin Rommel and the Germans in Africa, 1941-43* (Mechanicsburg: Stackpole Books, 2010), p. 228.
60 Giovanni Messe, *La Ia Armata Italiana in Tunisia* (Ufficio Storico: Rome, 1950).

Trieste Infantry Division: 4 battalions (much depleted) and 29 guns.

Pistoia Infantry Division: 2 battalions (being reconstituted) and 31 guns.

Centauro Armoured Division and La Spezia Infantry Division had been practically destroyed and had very few resources left.

Army Corps and army artillery: seven 105mm and ten 149mm. guns.

90th and 164th Light Africa Divisions together they had a strength that equaled one infantry division.

15th Panzer Division: its strength was equal to an armoured company.

Army artillery: a few heavy batteries.

Heavy antiaircraft: 7 batteries (approximately).

By early April *Centauro*, after the El Guettar battle, was reduced to a small combat group. with six 100/17 guns, sixteen 75/27 guns, and four 105/28 guns, eleven *semoventi* and only fifteen M.14/41 tanks.[61] These scant forces were merged with the German 15th Panzer. Equipment and manpower shortages could only in small art be compensated by reinforcements from Italy as shipping losses at sea began to mount. In March 16 percent of the supply shipped from Italy and headed to the ports of Tunis, Bizerta or Susa was lost at sea. In April 31 percent was lost, while a staggering 72 percent was lost in May.[62] As historian John Gooch argues "while it battled to the last on land, Messe's 1st Army was being steadily and inexorably throttled at sea and in the air."[63]

Whilst the final battle between the forces of General Montgomery and the First Italian Army was being waged on the Enfidaville Line starting on 19 April 1943, *Maggiore* Oderiso Piscitelli Taeggi, a senior officer who came from the artillery but had fought in North Africa in 1941-42 with *Ariete*, was tasked with leading the remains of the *Centauro* division in what became the last armoured counter-attack of the Axis in North Africa. On their new defensive line the Axis troops fought for more than a month against the Allied Eighth Army which came forward in large numbers. The defenders in several instances counterattacked to slow down the enemy operations as they sought to safeguard the small piece of Tunisian territory near the Mediterranean still in their possession. One of these defensive jabs took place on 25 April at Gebel bou Kornine mountain near Tunis and it involved the remains of the Italian armour, approximately twenty-five Axis tanks and *semoventi*, led by Maggiore Taeggi in a bid to halt the enemy's tank advance.[64]

The battle, which saw eighty Allied facing twenty-five Axis tanks, raged the whole afternoon. Facing superior numbers the Axis armour relied on their self-propelled guns to debilitate enemy tanks. As the tanks maneuvered against the enemy they forced the latter to give chase which then gave way to forward positioned howitzers which hit three enemy tanks and destroyed two. Three Italian tanks were lost.

The following is *Maggiore* Oderiso Piscitelli Taeggi's recollection of the combat experience:

---

61 Ufficio Storico, *Operazioni italo-tedesche in Tunisia, 11 novembre 1942-13 maggio 1943*, p. 439.
62 John Gooch, *Mussolini's War*, p. 348.
63 Ibid.
64 Oderisio Piscitelli Taeggi, *Diario di un combattente nell'Africa settentrionale* (Bari, G. Laterza & figli, 1946).

Our self-propelled machine bypasses a small hill and once over the top I can spot several enemy Pilot tanks that are firing against our M.14 tanks and some German Panzer from behind. These enemy tanks are not only thicker skinned than our semovente but are also equipped with a longer range 75mm gun. But our units compensate for their inferior armour and gun by the lower silhouette and greater mobility. Thanks to our agility and greater propensity to maneuver quickly and frequently we represent less of a target. As we continue to descend from the slope we advance behind fig trees that conceal our movements. At a distance of 1,000 meters from the enemy tanks I descend from my machine to give instructions to my team. The tanks on my left are to advance just beyond the trees and attract the enemy's attention while the ones behind them are to provide enfilade fire and pounce upon the enemy. As the enemy armour are still targeting the German Panzers our unit opens fire. The attack is sudden and invests the enemy with great power. The enemy tanks initially fail to react as they are still uncertain were the fire is coming from. Then soon after they begin to turn their turrets toward our direction, but since they are still searching for our positions we continue to pounce on them with impunity. Initially their shells fall mostly either behind or in front of our positions. But after a few minutes the aim of the enemy guns becomes more accurate and a heavy fight quickly develops. My gunner Fortebraccio fires his gun without respite while the smell of nafta and of gun powder together with the heat sap all my energy and it feels like I am under the influence of a heavy drug such as cocaine......meanwhile on my left the crews led by Fionda, Freccia, Strale, Picca and the German tank are fighting hard and attracting all the enemy fire. They are engaged in singular duels with enemy armour as they constantly seek and then avoid each other like in a protracted fencing duel. Each tank aims at the enemy and in turn attracts plenty of fire in return. The British tanks are heavier but less mobile than ours which are more soft-skinned but decisively better at maneuvering. Fortebraccio continues to pour fire against the enemy tanks but the latter as the battle rages on begin to fire with greater precision against us. We suffer no direct hits but a shrapnel flies into the vehicle and injures our driver. The latter bandages up his wound but then continues to fight alongside us. Our tanks continue to fire shell after shell against the enemy positions and our task is facilitated by the fact that we are firing from a concealed position behind vegetation. From 1800 meters our tanks perform very well to the point that three enemy tanks are put out of action. Then in rapid succession two more tanks are put out of action. We also receive direct hits. One tank is hit by a shell that destroys its right flank, while another is hit on the tracks and cannot continue the campaign. One tank catches fire while two of its crew members barely escape from the flames while a third member dies trapped inside the tank. We have advanced deep in the enemy line and we continue to engage them even with these high losses.[65]

After receiving some direct hits the Axis armour retreated beyond the reach of the enemy armour, while the latter did not pursue. About this combat action the bulletin n. 1068 of the Italian High Command mentioned that: "Yesterday the enemy's repeated attempts to overtake our positions were foiled despite the massive involvement of enemy tanks and artillery. The

---

65 Ibid., pp. 156-158.

Gruppo Corazzato commanded by Major Oderiso Piscicelli Taeggi particularly distinguished itself."[66]

On 6 May this unit was involved again when it laid an ambush against an Allied tank column. The results were three damaged enemy tanks against one Italian *semovente*. On 8 May the Italian self-propelled units, some German tanks and mobile artillery were committed for the last time near Port Farina. Two Italian *semoventi* were hit along with two German tanks, but the unit fought back and damaged beyond repair an American tank. This was the last armoured operation conducted by Axis troops in Tunisia. On 9 May the German 5th Army surrendered. Shortly thereafter the Axis Tunisian garrison also surrendered on 13 May and no attempt was made by the Italian or German Navy to save the combatants of the Italian First Army. Thus, the Allies captured Tunis then accepted the surrender of General Messe and his army. According to Allied estimates Italian losses in Tunisia amounted to 34,100 dead and wounded and 113,500 prisoners of war.[67] As far as the Italian armour is concerned the Tunisian campaign witnessed the destruction of Italy's only remaining armoured division as *Centauro* did not survive the North African campaign.

Special Motorized Forces in Tunisia

The motorized 103° *Compagnia Camionettisti* of the X *Arditi*, which had been raised and trained in 1942, was finally deployed in March 1943 in Tunisia. The unit's command was based at the Gabes Oasis and it used its armoured vehicles to dispatch "combat platoons"[68] to hot spots or troubled frontline areas in support of *Centauro, Giovani Fascisti, Trieste, La Spezia and Pistoia* Divisions. The only remaining document recalling the deeds of this unit is the war diary of the 1a *Pattuglia* (first platoon) commanded by *Capitano* Piero Corsini. Its first action took place on the Mareth Line in March 1943:

> A British platoon comprised by twenty soldiers moved forward to hill 46 and we were called to remove it. We moved forward under the field of fire of enemy machine guns and we responded by opening fire with our automatic machine guns. Once we reached the observation point we clashed with the enemy. The encounter ended when we launched several hand grenades in the direction of hill 46 forcing the enemy to pull back. It was forced to leave behind three dead and two wounded soldiers while we suffered two wounded, one of which had received severe wounds. The next day the enemy again attempted to seize the position. But we were waiting for him and we ambushed the platoon by attacking it suddenly and from the flank. The enemy platoon, taken completely by surprise, offered little resistance and pulled away. Two soldiers were captured during the retreat and another three (one officer and two soldiers) were captured later when we extensively patrolled hill 46. Two days later two Bren Carriers dropped off two platoons at hill 46 which placed two machine guns in position. We were alerted of the enemy's latest move by one of our artillery observation posts (sottotenente Fiaccadori) and we immediately left our positions while our movements

---

66   Ibid., p. 161.
67   John Gooch, *Mussolini's War*, p. 350.
68   Luigi Longo, *I Reparti speciali italiani nella seconda guerra mondiale*, p. 125.

were covered by a 45mm mortar squad and by a granatieri unit. Supported by covering fire we attacked the position by launching hand grenades and by firing our automatic weapons forcing the British to retreat while leaving in our hands five soldiers from the Black Watch Scottish battalion. A few days later we were called upon by the Giovani Fascisti to conduct a raid in their operating area. When we arrived, there was an operation that was already underway to recapture the so-called Binacospino strongpoint. We joined in the action by advancing on the opposite flank of the hill, while the bulk of a Giovani Fascisti battalion was operating on the right flank under heavy enemy fire. The position was recaptured after heavy fighting. The top of the hill was littered with dead British and Italian soldiers which had been killed by the artillery fire. A few days later we left the Mareth Line and retreated safely with the bulk of the Giovani Fascisti Division. During the Akarit Battle we were dispatched to the sector held by the Spezia Division where the infantry had been forced to cede several positions due to overwhelming enemy pressure. We were assigned the task by Generale Cattini to defend an artillery position which was still operating in an advanced position. While the artillery guns were firing at point blank range against the advancing enemy infantry and tank units, I deployed my troops near each gun battery so that they could protect them. We were able to resist until nighttime. Then under the cover of darkness we slipped away allowing our artillery units to be taken safely to the rear.

On the Enfidaville Line we undertook several night patrols and raids. During a patrol in the Giovani Fascisti sector we were involved in a firefight with an enemy platoon which caused the death of one of my officers killed by machine gun fire. On the Trieste Division sector during a night patrol aimed at identifying the location of an enemy position, we stumbled upon an enemy minefield which caused the death of one officer and the wounding of a soldier. During an ambush against an enemy unit positioned on a wadi near Takrouna, the 2a Pattuglia was dispatched to support Politi's Battaglione which had been ordered to resist at all costs. Once arrived at Takrouna the platoon attacked an enemy position which suffered the loss of seven dead and one wounded officer. After the enemy, had broken through after several days of fighting the 1a Pattuglia was dispatched to support Politi's Battaglione but it was unable to break through as Takrouna was surrounded by the enemy.[69]

Thus, the special reconnaissance and motorized commando units were finally deployed by the Italians after suffering the grave consequences of countless raids by enemy forces such as the LRDG throughout most of the campaign. This was another attempt to gain parity with the enemy that it also came in too late in the game to have any substantial effects.

Final Considerations

The Tunisian campaign was an experience that according to the following directive issued by the Italian High Command had shown how defensive strongholds could overcome, or at least temporarily hold, enemy armoured superiority. In fact, the directive with the potential invasion

---

69 Ibid., pp. 125-127.

of Italy in mind, stressed how few resolute defensive units could repel enemy combined arms attacks:

> The Tunisian campaign given the territory on which it was fought, its climate and the mass deployment of great weapons had the same characteristics of a European war.... The enemy based its combat operations on its great preponderance of force. Its offensive actions were predicated upon a combined arms approach which aimed to annihilate the defenses with the recourse to mass aerial and artillery bombings. These weapons aimed to neutralize the defender and even during the last stages of the infantry attack the enemy continued to support the offensive action with mass artillery operations. But the enemy's offensive units have shown themselves to be very vulnerable every time the defensive line has reacted almost immediately and very energetically to the attack. The enemy also believed that the soldiers of the Axis alliance could not fight effectively in situations of scarce visibility such as at night or while their positions were submerged by the smokescreens or gas. The proper concealment and camouflage of the defensive troops and their strongpoints is thus of primary importance during the enemy preparatory barrage. The ability to maneuver artillery weapons in the dark, the ability to launch swift and immediate counterstrokes and the autonomous actions of small defensive detachments are critical factors in repelling an enemy attack in such conditions. Even the enemy tanks should not be considered as all-powerful weapons that can't be beaten. We need to consider that the 47mm piece is not an obsolete weapon. Its shell from a short distance and fired from a flanking position can immobilize even the heaviest enemy tank. Every artillery piece light medium or heavy is an antitank weapon. The campaign has highlighted that even a few well-placed light or medium antitank guns have been able to repel armoured attacks by consistently firing their weapons from close range. Even the soldier concealed in a well dug in position is invulnerable to enemy tanks.[70]

The directive focusing upon the willingness to fight of the standard infantry soldier was evidently trying to conceal to its troops that the army lacked modern weapons which were essential in repelling an enemy combined arms attack. It also appeared more a propaganda piece to uplift morale considering a potential invasion of the peninsula than a real instruction or technical manual for the anti-tank defense.

The real lessons learned from the campaign were summarized by its numerous protagonists. It was acknowledged that the Germans throughout the campaign had been reluctant in adopting the Italian artillery tactic of the *fuoco di manovra* (maneuvered fire), which in the view of the Italian generals was reputed to be very effective. They lamented the lack of adequate numbers of Italian reconnaissance vehicles and mobile units and especially the need to support these units with heavier mobile artillery. Lastly, once again it was pointed out that the Italian tanks, armed with a 47mm gun, were no match to the much thicker armoured and heavily armed (75mm) Allied tanks. Thus domestic production had to be centered on self-propelled guns and the much promised P40 heavy tank. The Germans on the other hand argued that the Italian *effetto pronto* shells had shown to be ineffective while many Italian artillery units, which

---

70 Filippo Cappellano and Nicola Pignato, *Andare contro i carri armati*, p. 207.

comprised the majority of Axis guns deployed in North Africa, proved to be inadequate for the campaign both in range and firepower. Guns mentioned in the report were the 65/17, and 75/27 caliber guns. Instead, the 100 mm and 105 mm howitzers, which were used to reinforce the divisional artillery, were highly regarded by the Germans. But they stated that there were too few of them deployed in the field. The latter also complained that the Italian artillery at times was less effective because of the lack of mobile reconnaissance units to identify enemy positions and targets and because radio communications between artillery command and these units was often suboptimal.[71]

In 1943, after the loss of Tunisia, the Italian Army decided to focus domestic industry on the on the production of caliber 75mm guns and howitzers while decisively abandoning the 47mm gun as the main antitank weapon and on self-propelled guns and heavy tanks. The 75 mm guns were to be furnished to the newly forming armoured divisions as well as to the infantry. It was decided that there would be a 75/32 and 75/34 gun as well as two more options such as the manufacture under German license of the Pak-40 75/43 gun and of the 75/22 howitzer. An Italian Army directive of May 1943 observed:

> Our biggest problem is the lack of an effective anti-tank gun. The problem can be solved with the German 75mm M.40 which is relatively easy to manufacture with 100 percent domestic steel. It's armour piercing shell weighs 6.8 kg and can perforate a 50mm thick tank at 1,000 meters or less. The adoption of such a weapon allows for a fast and economic solution to our problem. This will be a more expeditious choice than focusing production upon the 90/53 gun and can possibly solve our lack of an effective antitank weapon.[72]

As historians Cappellano and Pignato assert with regard to the German inspired weapon:

> In 1943, the Italian Army finally decided to focus on the caliber 75mm to replace the obsolete 47/32 [...] two solutions were identified: the German gun Pak-40 75/43 which was to be allocated to the artillery arm and the 75/22 howitzer. The latter derived from the 47mm, since it was modeled on the same design and the only difference was the 75 caliber short barrel gun that fired EPS (hollow charge) ammunition. The 75/22 piece, approved in August 1943, did not even have time to enter service. It was an ingenious and simple modification to the 47/32 gun, which was inspired by a similar German gun obtained by converting the main body of the 37/45 mm gun to the caliber 75mm. This cost-effective solution allowed to avoid a complete redesign and gave the infantry a weapon that could be readily deployed against medium tanks. The weapon had a weight comparable to that of the 47mm and utilized 75mm gun and howitzers shells already in use.[73]

The weapon was supposed to be furnished to the artillery divisions that were being transferred to Sicily but due to how quickly the Sicilian campaign unfolded large numbers of guns did not arrive in time.

---

71 Ibid.
72 Ibid.
73 Circolare N.149857 del Ministero della Guerra, 'Canna da 75 da incavare su affusto da 47' cited in Filippo Caoppellano and Nicola Pignato, *Andare contro i carri armati*, p. 171.

The decision to focus on the 75mm anti-tank gun thus came too late in the conflict to have any meaningful impact upon the course of the war. In fact, few artillery groups received the weapon before the start of the Sicilian campaign. It is estimated that only two batteries of truck mounted 75/43 guns were deployed in Sicily in mid-1943 along with two more groups in Sardinia and forty-two 75mm field guns were transferred from Germany to Sicily.

Conversely, the 75/22 gun was only manufactured in the summer of 1943 and did not get to the frontline until mid-October 1943 when things had taken a decisively negative turn. In 1943 the Italian High Command had also plans to strengthen the infantry divisions with the addition of a divisional battalion of *semoventi da* 75 that were to be deployed in the anti-tank mode, an anti-aircraft unit equipped with 90mm and 20mm guns and the greater availability of trucks and armoured vehicles for each division. The plan, however, could not implemented in time for the invasion of Sicily. At the time, for instance, the *Livorno* Division was the most advanced unit from an equipment standpoint of all Italian divisions deployed but it was reinforced with only one *semovente* battalion with obsolete 47mm guns. The division lacked anti-aircraft units and only had a limited number of vehicles. At the time the only armoured unit that was combat ready and that was also well equipped was the *Ariete II* Division that had been headquartered near Rome. Although, the latter was equipped with the *semovente da 75/34* and the excellent *semovente M43 da* 105/25, it was not deployed during the campaign in the defense of Sicily for political reasons. The unit in fact in the summer of 1943 was kept by *Generale* Vittorio Ambrosio, who at the time had become the new chief of staff of the armed forces, near Rome to be deployed against the Germans after the Badoglio government changed sides. The 105/25 was a hulk and for sure the best and most effective weapon that the Italians fielded during the war. It could fire armoured piercing shells that could immobilize even the largest Soviet tank and its low silhouette made it an excellent tank hunter.

Several captured units were utilized extensively by the German Army during 1944 and 1945. The *semovente M.41M da* 90/53 was the only heavy self-propelled gun that was utilized during the battle for Sicily, but in limited numbers, and one of the few Italian armoured weapons that could still go head to head against Allied medium tanks. By May1943 the Italian Army had no longer any use for the M.13 and M.14 medium tanks and commissioned Ansaldo/Fiat to manufacture only M.15 tanks, *semoventi* and a heavy P.40 tank styled on the design of the German Panther.

Ultimately, with the end of the Tunisian campaign and the failure of the Axis to rescue its troops, the Italian Army had suffered one of its biggest losses. The battle-hardened soldiers of the Italian First Army and the German tanks captured by the Allies in Tunisia would have been of great use to the Axis cause in the defense of the southern Mediterranean and to support the repel of any potential Allied invasion. Instead, the leaders of the two countries and their respective high commands made no attempt to limit the number of troops being dispatched to Tunisia once the campaign started to turn negatively for the Axis after Kasserine Pass, nor did they attempt a Dunkirk like operation to prevent its soldiers from being captured in May 1943. Therefore, Italy now faced a potential Allied invasion from North Africa with no experienced troops to defend the peninsula and without an armoured division. By mid-1943 with *Centauro* being destroyed in Tunisia, Italy only had a few armoured battalions with obsolete tanks that were unlikely to pose any threat to the heavy Allied medium tanks.

8

Sicily

Following the defeat of Axis forces in North Africa, the Allies began planning the invasion of Europe with the ultimate aim to invade France and then concentrate on the defeat of Germany. The Allies decided to move first against Italy, hoping an invasion of the peninsula would not only remove Italy from the war but also force Germany to divert divisions from France where the Allies also subsequently planned to attack.

In preparation for the Allied invasion, the Axis was faced with a difficult conundrum as to where to locate the armoured and mobile units. First, Axis intelligence was unsure where the Allies would land and therefore urged the Italian High Command to maintain strong garrisons in Sicily, Sardinia, Corsica and in the Balkans. This caused a further dispersal of forces that ultimately did not benefit the defense of Sicily. Second, the funds and the labor for the defensive works such as anti-tank ditches and artillery bunkers were also dispersed. By the end of June 1943 *Comando Supremo* argued that according to its intelligence sources the Allied concentration of forces in North Africa pointed to a potential invasion of the peninsula, while Kesselring and the Italian Navy maintained that Sardinia was the likely target.

Meantime, *Generale* Roatta in the spring of 1943 had been given command of the Italian *6ª Armata* that garrisoned Sicily. Based on the forces available to him, Roatta had argued that at best these partly motorized infantry and disparate mechanized forces could put up an "honorable resistance" against the enemy's superiority in every field whether it was aviation, armour or artillery. Roatta maintained that the forces were inadequate but *Comando Supremo* had already warned in April 1943 that it was unlikely that additional troops and material could be made available. This prompted the Italian government (13 May 1943) to ask for German assistance requesting three German divisions, six tank battalions, 200 antiaircraft guns and fifty air force squadrons.[1] A few days later Hitler replied that he could not spare that many troops and equipment as the German army was gearing up for a major offensive against the Soviet Union. As a result only limited German forces were dispatched to Sicily by July 1943. Without further German support Roatta had to plan a defense of the island with the forces at his disposal. The Italian mechanized and motorized assets were therefore organized into tactical groups to intervene as quickly as possible where a landing had been made.

---

1   John Gooch, *Mussolini's War*, p. 362.

Preparations

Finally when in early July Axis intelligence determined that the likely invasion point was indeed Sicily one of the major conundrums became were to locate the mobile forces. One stream of thought stated that they should be dispersed throughout the island to counterattack the beachheads right away, while a second stream of thought stated that they should be concentrated and await for the enemy to make the main attack to then stage a massive counterattack. Mostly based on Kesselring's opinion (he was concerned by the slow pace of the Tiger tanks versus the other armoured and mobile units) the Axis decided on behalf of the first approach whereby the mobile divisions were dispersed and ordered to launch immediate counterattacks on any Allied landing.

According to the Axis commanders the battle was to be fought as close as possible to the landing beaches. First the coastal units were to fire their guns upon the enemy ships and the troops as soon as they attempted to land. Second, the air forces were to interfere with the landings by bombing the enemy ships and fighter planes were to engage the enemy's flying fortresses. Once the enemy had landed mobile reserves, mostly Italian mobile units were to engage and tie up the enemy. Finally, the German armoured divisions were to push back the enemy forces into the sea by making wide recourse to their tanks and heavy self-propelled guns. The plan was based on the experience of the Dieppe raid where quick and swift counters had prevented the British commandos from establishing a beachhead and from there regrouping and attacking the German defenders. The major difference between Dieppe and Sicily was the likely massive deployment that the Allies were going to throw against the island.

For this endeavor the Axis could count on two German armoured divisions, two German parachute regiments, German mortar and Flak unit, eight Italian coastal artillery divisions, four Italian infantry and partly mobile divisions and some tactical lightly armed armoured groups. The Italians had 490 field guns, and 100 tanks, while the Germans had 140 tanks. Approximately 1,000 Axis aircraft (449 combat worthy Italian planes and 563 belonging to *Luftflotte* II) would also be deployed, while it was decided that the Italian Navy could not be deployed given the enemy's vast air superiority. At the end of June, then, the *Aosta* and *Assietta* infantry Divisions and the bulk of the 15th *Panzergrenadier* Division were in the west of Sicily; the *Napoli*, *Livorno*, Hermann Göring Divisions, and one-third of the 15th *Panzergrenadier* Division were in the south and east of Sicily. The bulk of the Hermann Göring Division was assembled in and around Caltagirone and it was by far the strongest of the Axis forces deployed in Sicily. General Paul Conrath had organized the division forces into two regiments. The first consisted of a two-battalion infantry regiment mounted on trucks, an armoured artillery battalion, and an attached tank company with seventeen *Panzerkampfwagen* IV tanks. The other regiment had two tank battalions (about ninety *Panzerkampfwagen* III and *Panzerkampfwagen* III IV tanks),two armoured artillery battalions, and the bulk of the armoured reconnaissance and engineer battalions. The Tiger I company was initially to be held in reserve and in the intention of the division's commander it was to be used to unleash the coup de grace against the enemy.

The Italian forces of the *6ª Armata* in Sicily under *Generale* Alfredo Guzzoni (who in June had taken over command of the unit from Roatta who had assumed his old role of chief of staff of the Army) were organized into two battle groups; XVI Army Corps in the east and XII Army Corps in the west for a total of 192,000 officers and men.

The force was split between the coastal militia and the infantry. The most relevant and better-trained Italian unit was the *Livorno* Division with 14,000 troops and 600 vehicles. It was partly motorized, while the other Italian units were not, and it was by far the largest unit. Together with the armoured units it was considered as a tactical reserve unit to be deployed for counter-attacks. Italy had lost all its armoured strength during the North African campaign as *Ariete* and *Littorio* had been practically wiped out at El Alamein and *Centauro* had also been eliminated as a fighting force during the Tunisian campaign. Thus, in mid-1943, Italy had but two armoured units in training: *Ariete II* and the Blackshirt armoured division and some loosely organized battle groups, mainly two battalions equipped with French tanks and a *semoventi* unit. The Italian armoured force in Sicily included: the CI and CII *Battaglioni Carri*[2] with 100 French Renault R35 infantry tanks, two companies of Fiat 3000 tanks, and two companies of L.3 tanks. In addition, the Army had *semoventi* units such as three battalions of *semoventi da 47/32* built on the chassis of the L.6/40 tank belonging to the 33° *Reggimento Carristi* based in Palermo, three *semoventi da 90/53* groups (*X Raggruppamento Controcarro* with CXLI, CXLII, CXLIII *Gruppi*) with a total of twenty-six self-propelled guns, and one company of 75/18 truck mounted guns.

> **Raggruppamento semoventi (10th self-propelled Group) – Order of Battle July 1943**
>
> Comando Raggruppamento Colonnello Bedogni equipped with two command semoventi.
>   CLXI gruppo subdivided into two groups with four semoventi da 90/53 each.
>   CXLII subdivided into two groups with four semoventi da 90/53 each.
>   CXLIII subdivided into two groups with four semoventi da 90/53 each.

Based on the forces available the *X Raggruppamento Controcarro,* equipped with the 90mm guns, was the only armoured unit of the Italian army that in 1943 was equipped with modern and effective weapons that technically were on a par with German or Allied self-propelled guns and tanks. Initially, the unit was to be deployed in Russia to face the T-34 tanks but given the gravity of the situation in North Africa it was decided to initially hold it in reserve. Since after the fall of Tunisia an Allied landing was one of the main concerns of the Italian High Command, it was decided to ultimately deploy it in Sicily. Thus, the unit was moved to Sicily in late May 1943 and it was organized in three combat groups, each with two batteries with four self-propelled guns. It was led by *Colonnello* Bedogni and assigned to the XII Army Corps of *Generale* Arisio located in western Sicily, between Catalfimi, Salemi and Caltanissetta. The *semoventi* unit had at its disposal one of the heaviest self-propelled gun of its kind with a 90/53 gun mounted upon the hull of the M.14/41 tank. The hollow-shell projectiles of the 90/53 gun could pierce the 65mm of the front armour of most American tanks and in some cases also the 100mm hull of the Mk III "Churchill". It was one of the most effective weapons the Italians could field against the Allies even though it had some downsides such as a large footprint that

---

[2] These were originally part of *Centauro* but were later deployed in Sicily. The two battalions could not fight as units but were split up into multiple mobile groups.

was easily picked out by enemy reconnaissance teams and an underpowered engine. Both the Renault, the Fiat and the L.3 tanks were considered obsolete by 1943 standards and could not really stand a fighting chance against Sherman tanks, which comprised the bulk of the enemy tank forces. *Generale* Roatta in the spring of 1943 had written a brutally frank report on the conditions of the armoured forces in Sicily[3] in which he outlined the dire situation of the only armoured regiment on the southern island. The latter, according to Roatta, was one of the few combat ready armoured unit but it was equipped with antiquated French tanks that were not only poorly armed but were also very slow for 1943 standards. Moreover, the tanks had been poorly kept given the lack of original spare parts. With respect to the two companies of Fiat 3000 tanks, *Generale* Roatta stated that they were worthless. The self-propelled artillery (with the exception of the *X Raggruppamento Controcarro*) was also antiquated since at the time it could count on only three *semoventi da* 47/32 battalions (CCXXXIII, CXXXIII and IV *Battaglioni semoventi da* 47/37), which had demonstrated all of their shortcomings (thin armour and lack of firepower) experienced during the campaigns in Russia and Tunisia.

Generale Roatta had pooled these armoured units into *gruppi mobili* or mobile groups that together with special motorized infantry units were charged to organize counter attacks. Each group had a few tanks, some towed anti-tank guns, *semoventi* and AB.41 reconnaissance vehicles.

Gruppo Mobile A, B and C were attached to the XII Army Corps. The first group was in Paceco and led by *Tenente Colonnello* Perrine. It included the command company of the XII *Battaglione carri* L, 4ª *Compagnia*/CII *Battaglione carri* (Renault R35 units) and the 1ª *Compagnia*/CXXXIII *Battaglione Semoventi* with 47mm guns.

Gruppo B was based in Santa Ninfa and led by *Tenente Colonnello* Mascio. It was formed by the command company of the CXXXIII *Battaglione semoventi da* 47/32, the 6ª *Compagnia*/CII *Battaglione carri* with ten Renault R35 tanks, and the 3ª *Compagni*a of the CXXXIII *Battaglione semoventi da* 47/32. Finally, *Gruppo* C, based in Portella Misiblesi was led by *Tenente Colonnello* Mazzei. It was comprised by one Company/CIII *Battaglione carri* with ten Renault R35 and the 5ª *Compagnia*/CII *Battaglione carri*.

Gruppi D, E, F, G, belonged to the XVI Corps.

Gruppo D, which was in Misterbianco, was comprised by the 4ª *Compagnia*/CI *Battaglione carri* with two Renault 35 tanks and by the 3ª *Compagnia*/CI *Battaglione carri* with sixteen R-35 vehicles. It was led *Tenente Colonnello* D'Andretta.

Gruppo E was in Niscemi and was comprised by the following:

- 1ª *Compagnia/* CI *Battaglione Carri* with fifty Renault R35 tanks. The unit was led by *Capitano* Giuseppe Granieri which also commanded the tactical group comprised by:
- 2ª *Compagnia*/CII *Battaglione anticarri* da 47mm.
- 4ª *Compagnia Motorizzata*,
- 155ª *Compagnia Bersaglieri*,
- 9ª *Batteria Mobile*, III *Gruppo*/54° *Reggimento Artigleria Divisione Napoli* with 75/18 howitzers.
- 1ª *Sezione/* 326ª *Batteria anticarro/ Divisione Assietta* (20/65 truck-mounted machine guns)

---

3   Ufficio Storico, Generale Mario Roatta, 'Promemoria prot. n. 5300 del 10 marzo 1943'.

Gruppo F, based at Rosolini, was comprised of the 2ª *Compagnia*/CI *Battaglione carri* with ten Renault R35 vehicles.

Gruppo G, based in Comiso, was comprised of elements from 1ª *Compagnia*/CI *Battaglione carri* with seven Renault R35 tanks.

Finally, Gruppo H, headquartered in San Pietro Caltagirone, counted only one armoured company (2ª *Compagnia carri* Fiat 3000) that deployed nine obsolete Fiat 3000 and was commanded by *Tenente Colonnello* Bixi.

Aside from the lack of an adequate number of medium and heavy tank battalions the most glaring deficiencies of the Italian forces in Sicily were as follows: "There were no mobile antiaircraft guns, no proper anti-ship guns, only one soldier to defend every thirty-four kilometers and one anti-tank gun for every 2.2 kilometers and the island's fixed defenses were in a poor state."[4]

In July, the main Axis forces were deployed as follows:

> The Hermann Göring Division was headquartered at Caltagirone approximately twenty miles northeast of Gela. The 15th *Panzergrenadier* Division was split up into three main groups, one in the west, one in the middle and one in the east of Sicily. Mobile Group Schmaltz, which belonged to the Hermann Göring Division, was also headquartered in the east. The *Napoli* Division was positioned along the southern edge of the plain of Catania while the *Livorno* Division was headquartered at Licata.
>
> The Axis defense of Sicily was going to be based on three phases. "The coastal units and local reserves would provide the initial resistance; the mobile Italian divisions would then attack, followed by the Germans who would complete the task of destroying or driving the invader back into the sea."[5] The biggest concern for the Axis command was that tanks and infantry were not experienced in working together such as the troops that had taken part to the North African campaign. Moreover, the terrain, which was hilly and rocky, was not suitable for tank warfare, especially the heavy tanks such as the Tiger I and the *semoventi*. In the villages, the roads were extremely narrow and unsuitable for tanks that could be easily surrounded by tank hunters. But it was believed that a forceful rapid response was the only way to halt the landings.

Operation Husky

Operation Husky would involve 2,590 Allied ships to land 180,000 troops, 600 tanks, and 14,000 mechanized vehicles on twenty-six beaches in the southern and eastern coasts of Sicily. The Allies' Italian campaign began with the invasion of Sicily on the night of 9-10 July 1943 under the overall command of General Harold Alexander. Its plan called for the airborne and amphibious assault by two Allied armies, one landing on the south-eastern and one on the central southern coast. An Eastern Task Force was led by General Bernard Montgomery and consisted of the British Eighth Army (which also included the 1st Canadian Infantry Division) which landed on eastern Sicily along a forty-mile front stretching from the coast near Pachino to

---

4   John Gooch, *Mussolini's War*, p. 360.
5   Carlo D'Este, *Bitter Victory: The Battle for Sicily* (New York: E. P. Dutton, 1988), p. 209.

the Gulf of Noto, south of Syracuse and with the main objective being the capture of Syracuse. Once ashore and after having captured Syracuse, the Eighth Army would thrust northward toward Augusta and Catania, and then seize two airfields before the final leap toward Messina.

The Western Task Force was commanded by Lieutenant General George S. Patton and consisted of the American Seventh Army (three divisions supported by parachutists from the 505th Parachute Infantry Regimental Combat Team and the 3d Battalion/504th Parachute Infantry) that was charged with taking south-central Sicily by effectuating main landings in Gela, and Licata to then capture a number of airfields located between Licata and Comiso. General Patton organized his invasion force as follows. On the right, Major General Troy Middleton's 45th Infantry Division, would come ashore near Scoglitti and then move up to Comiso and Ragusa. In the center, Major General Terry de la Mesa Allen's 1st Infantry Division, reinforced by two battalions of Rangers under the command of Lieutenant Colonel William O. Darby, was to first seize Gela and then advance north to Niscemi. Two parachute units from the 82d Airborne Division's (505th and 504th Parachute Regiments) under the command of Colonel James Gavin would assist the troops deployed in the Gela beachhead by seizing the high ground north and blocking key road junctions leading to Niscemi and Piano Lupo. On the left flank, Major General Lucian Truscott's 3d Division, reinforced by a Ranger battalion and Combat Command A of the 2d Armoured Division, was to come ashore at Licata. The amphibious landings were to be supported by naval gunfire as well as aerial bombings which were not expected to be disrupted by Axis air forces given the Allies overwhelming mastery of the skies and the Mediterranean Sea. Ahead of the main attack paratroopers were to land in Sicily and carry out disruptive missions against enemy gun positions and fuel depots.

The landing forces were protected by the gunfire six battleships, ten cruisers, and two aircraft carriers. Allied seaborne landings were made in the early hours of 10 July. The initial phase of the landings was opposed mainly by the coastal defenses, as the bulk of the Axis forces geared for counter-attacks to be conducted a few hours after the enemy forces were onshore. Already on the morning of July 10, *Generale* Guzzoni had made a strategic assessment of the situation which given his limited forces that could not be deployed everywhere had to be concentrated. Considering the wide stretch of coast affected by the landings and finding it impossible to counter everywhere with the forces at his disposal, he decided to launch three main counterattacks against the biggest enemy concentrations at Gela, Licata and Augusta-Siracusa.

The main Italian and German divisions were to carry out these counters, but his command had trouble most of the day on the 10th in maintaining contact with the headquarters of the German divisions, which also depended more on Kesserling's HQ for their intelligence gathering efforts than upon Guzzoni's. The absence of an overall well defined command structure would limit the potential of the Axis counters against the beachheads mainly due to the lack of coordination and rapid information sharing between the troops.

Syracuse

Napoli Division was charged with organizing a counter against British forces that had landed at Syracuse and had overwhelmed the coastal defenses. The first unit to be deployed on 10 July was *Gruppo Mobile F* which made its counter at Pachino but within a few minutes lost half of its tanks due to enemy fire. The enemy had taken position on nearby hills and used its ten anti-tank guns, some of the first pieces of equipment to be disembarked, to fight off the Renault tanks. The action was just a spoiling attack that did initially slow down the unloading of more men and equipment but failed in pushing back the enemy. By mid-morning *Gruppo Mobile F* retired with only four tanks. In the afternoon *Gruppo Mobile* F had assembled again near Modica to gear up for another counter against British infantry when it came under heavy fire of British naval guns which put out of action one by one all the remaining tanks. *Napoli* Division's only other tactical Mobile Group D was then deployed together the German tactical unit led by Colonel Schmalz, which was equipped with Panzer tanks and self-propelled guns.

The plan consisted in a joint counter attack by these two forces against Floridia where the British 13th Brigade/5th Division had assembled by the evening of 10 July, while elements of the *Napoli* Division, including CIII *Battaglione Controcarri* and two 88mm guns, were to cover their flanks. The ultimate objective was the recapture of Syracuse and the overthrow of the enemy forces from the beachhead.

On 11 July at 0600 the two columns began to move from Solarino toward Floridia where the vanguard of the Axis forces began to engage the enemy. There was a protracted exchange of fire between rival artillery units that lasted until 1030. After that, the enemy launched several probing frontal and flanking attacks against the Italians and the latter responded by intensifying the artillery fire and by using the tactical group to punch holes into the enemy deployment. The Renault tank company, for instance, made several attempts to relieve the pressure upon the frontline troops at Ponte Diddino but several tanks were hit by artillery fire. Meanwhile the 105/28 and 88mm guns exacted a heavy toll upon the advancing enemy tanks by debilitating three tanks in the forefront. Unable to penetrate Solarino the British units changed course and directed their efforts to Diddino and there managed to infiltrate the Italian defenses. The Italian infantry was forced to counter but after the German Flak group evacuated their position, it was forced to retreat paving the way for a further British advance. Because of the breakthrough, the motorized *X Gruppo* and its guns were saved in the nick of time from being captured by several trucks that hastily took the equipment away.

The Italian official history asserts that the tactical group had by the afternoon "lost not only the two 88mm Flak 36 gun sections, but also numerous men and material. Meanwhile the enemy pressure on the front and flank was becoming more and more menacing and aggressive."[6] The numerical superiority of the enemy was overwhelming and by 0130 the pressure exerted against the tactical group was so strong that it was forced to retreat. It is estimated that by midday the *Gruppo Mobile* D had lost 16 percent of its initial force.

In the late afternoon, the British forces attacked again but were rebuffed.

On the same day, the German tactical unit headed by Colonel Wilhelm Schmalz counterattacked from the north to retake Syracuse. For most of the day this determined unit tied down a much larger British infantry unit but was ultimately forced to retreat. It could not put forth its counter-attack because throughout the day it was unable to link up with *Gruppo Mobile D*. When the latter retreated in the afternoon, Schmalz's combat group was no longer able to attack by itself. The following day the *Napoli* Division was tasked with reestablishing a connection

---

6   Ufficio Storico, Gruppo Mobile D, 'Relazione dei fatti d'armi dei giorni 10,11, 12, e 13 luglio 1943 nella zona di Solarino', cartella 1427, allegato 59/13.

with the Germans under Colonel Schmalz, ordered the last four remaining Renault tanks to reach Solarino, where the Germans were believed to have leaguered during the night.

After driving for 300 meters the tanks encountered an enemy checkpoint. The first tank blew up after it forced the enemy deployment and then struck a mine. Its commander *Sottotenente* Adamo Profico was awarded a silver medal of military valor posthumously. Then shortly thereafter the second tank was knocked out by an artillery shell while the third was also hit by a shell on the right flank. On impact the driver lost control and the tank was thrown off the road and it overturned. The fourth tank also forced the checkpoint but after advancing for a short distance it came face to face with a Sherman tank. The two tanks began firing at each other at close range and the Renault's shells could barely scratch the paint of the Sherman, while the latter later immobilized the Italian tank killing its crew. *Tenente* Franco Rodriguez, who refused to surrender, continued to battle until his tank was destroyed and was awarded a bronze medal of military valor.

The *Napoli* Division continued to resist on its defensive line for most of the day but by nightfall the British armoured and army units had made another breakthrough. By this time all the disparate elements of *Gruppo Mobile* D had been destroyed or captured.

On 14 July, British Commandos landed near Agnone Bagni and overcame the coastal defenses. But soon after they were countered by IV *Battaglione Semoventi* da 47/32 and three German Panzer tanks which were able to force the enemy unit to reembark on the ships and freeing up the coastal defenders. The British responded to the counter by unloading several tanks which later in the day clashed with the Italian battalion which suffered several casualties.

Gela

The biggest deployment of Italian armour and the most powerful Axis counter attack took place in the American sector at Gela. Here the *Livorno* and Herman Göring Divisions together with *Gruppo Mobile* E staged a counterattack that initially succeeded in pushing the Americans back into the beachhead.

When the American troops reached near the shoreline on the early morning of 10 July the troops of the CDXXIX *Battaglione Costiero* opened fire causing some casualties amongst the troops that were disembarking. Soon however, the Americans led by the 1/505th Parachute Infantry Regiment overwhelmed at 0530 the coastal defenses and began to advance offshore.

This forced *Generale* Mariscalco, commander of *XVIII Brigata costiera*, to call in *Gruppo Mobile* E, based in Niscemi to move on Gela and support *CDXXIX battaglione costiero* whose troops had been that was surrounded.

Artillery *Caporale* Bruno Causin, of 9ª *Batteria Mobile/54° Reggimento Artiglieria*, fighting within the mobile unit recalled the fighting:

> We arrived at the airport at Ponte Olivo in the early morning. By that time the Americans had already landed and had occupied the town. Our commander had preceded us to locate the best position for our guns. On the outskirts of Gela, the Americans had emplaced a battery of 105mm guns. When our commander came back he gave us the coordinates and on the first shot we put the enemy guns out of action. … We then continued to fire our

guns to cover the infantry as it moved forward. But the enemy's naval guns intervened and all hell broke loose.[7]

The 155ª *Compagnia Bersaglieri* and the CII *Battaglione Controcarri* were the first units of *Gruppo Mobile E* to come into contact with the Americans at 0730 near the Niscemi-Gela road (Strada Statale 117). Both units came under heavy mortar and machine gun fire and suffered casualties as they advanced to meet the enemy. It was at this point that the commander of the *Gruppo Mobile E* gave the order for the tanks to attack. The latter rushed the enemy defenses of Gela while firing their machine guns to eliminate several enemy infantry posts. As the tanks were engaging the enemy in protracted exchanges of fire they came under the fire of the American anti-tank guns of the 1st and 4th Ranger Battalions, assisted by the 1st Battalion/39th Engineer Combat Regiment, the 1st Battalion/531st Engineer Shore Regiment, mortar fire from the 83d Chemical Battalion, and naval gunfire emanating from US Navy cruiser *Boise*. The combined fire knocked out of action two Italian tanks and stripped the *Bersaglieri* from the armour as they could not advance under the barrage of fire from the enemy guns.

Despite encountering stiff opposition, ten Italian tanks managed to bypass the curtain of artillery fire and reached Gela but wound up fighting a close quarter fight against the American Rangers who enjoyed the advantage of fighting within the narrow streets of the town where the armour could not maneuver at will. All but two tanks reached the proximity of the beachhead by reaching Piazza Umberto I, where the Americans had set up their temporary headquarter:

> At 0800 on 10 July, sottotenente Angelo Navara at the head of twelve Renault tanks geared up for the counterattack. He moves towards the town of Gela, flanked only by a company of bersaglieri. The grouping is massacred by the flood of fire that comes from the sea. Only two Italian tanks remain. Sottotenente Navari advances alone. He overwhelms the American defenses outside the town, along the railway. The Rangers see him pass in front of the former Hotel Trinacria in Gela, he seems invulnerable. He forces the enemy troops to back away and gets within 300 meters from the beach. Then he loses his driver. In the end, a blow from a bazooka damages the tracks of the Renault and immobilizes it. Angelo Navari emerges from the turret armed with the pistol in his hand. Then a bullet penetrates his forehead and kills him.[8]

The second tank reached Porta Caltagirone where it came under very heavy fire. It then retreated to Priolo. While still on the outskirts of town it was hit by anti-tank gun and put out of action.

At 1100 having come under continuous heavy fire from the enemy's naval guns as 572 large caliber shells had fallen on the mobile group since 0800, *Tenente Colonnello* Conti realizing that the position could not be maintained ordered the mobile group to pull back to Ponte Olivo.

The American Official History states that Italian units at Gela were subjected to heavy bazooka, antitank and naval gunfire and suffered losses:

---

7   Ufficio Storico, *Rivista Militare*, n. 6, November 2014.
8   Andrea Augello, *Uccidi gli italiani. Gela 1943. La battaglia dimenticata* (Milan: Mursia, 2012).

Meanwhile the heterogeneous Ranger-engineer force in Gela had observed a column of thirteen Italian tanks escorted by infantry moving south along Highway 117 toward the city--the right arm of Mobile Group E's two-pronged attack. Another column, the Livorno Division's battalion of infantry, could also be seen moving toward Gela along the Butera road. While the destroyer Shubrick started firing at the tank-infantry column on Highway 117, the Ranger-manned Italian 77mm. guns opened on the Livorno battalion. The first Shubrick salvos halted the Italians in some confusion. But the tankers recovered a measure of composure; they resumed their movement, though fewer now, for several tanks were burning in the fields along the highway. Without further loss, nine or ten tanks dashed down the highway and into the city. But the same thing happened here that had happened on the Niscemi-Piano Lupo road--Italian infantrymen did not follow the tanks. And so, in the city, the Rangers and the engineers began a deadly game of hide and seek with the Italian tanks, dodging in and out of buildings, throwing hand grenades and firing rocket launchers. Colonel Darby jumped in a jeep, dashed down to the beach [and] commandeered a 37mm. antitank gun, returned with it to the city and knocked out a tank. Another burned as Rangers and engineers teamed up, first to stop it and then to destroy it. After twenty minutes of this kind of fighting, the Italians started back out of the city hotly pursued by American fire. The Italian crews suffered heavily. Almost every survivor carried with him wound. As for the Livorno Division's battalion--in almost formal, parade ground formation, the Italian infantrymen advanced against the western side of Gela. The two Ranger companies firing their captured Italian artillery pieces took heavy toll among the closely bunched enemy soldiers. Rifles, machine guns, and mortars joined in as the range closed. Not an enemy soldier reached the city. Leaving behind numerous dead and wounded, the remnants of the Italian battalion fled.[9]

Although, the counter-attack was unsuccessful, it did succeed in slowing down the unloading of more American troops and equipment. Following this attempt to counter the enemy on the beachhead, at 1400 a German force consisting of ninety German Mark III and IV medium tanks, fifteen Tiger I heavy tanks, two armoured artillery battalions, an armoured reconnaissance battalion, and an engineer battalion were sent by General Conrath into attack. The German thrust was particularly fierce fifteen German Tiger I heavy tanks, an armoured artillery battalion, and two battalions of motorized infantry from the Hermann Göring Division overran the 1st Battalion, 180th Infantry (45th Division), after a stiff fight, capturing its commander and many of its men.

The American infantry was pushed back considerably until calls for naval gunfire support were made. As the shells from the naval guns began to pour in the German tanks initially slowed down and eventually stopped advancing altogether.

The failure of the first day of operations stemmed from the inability of the Axis commanders to put forth a coordinated attack as well as the heavy American naval and field gunfire that heavily interfered with the two pronged assault. The headquarters of the Hermann Göring Division, for instance, had only heard of the landings from Kesselring's headquarter, while it was not able to contact the headquarter of *Generale* Guzzoni for most of the day.

---

9   Albert N. Garland and Howard McGaw Smyth, *Sicily and the Surrender of Italy* (Washington DC: Center for Military History, 1993), p. 152.

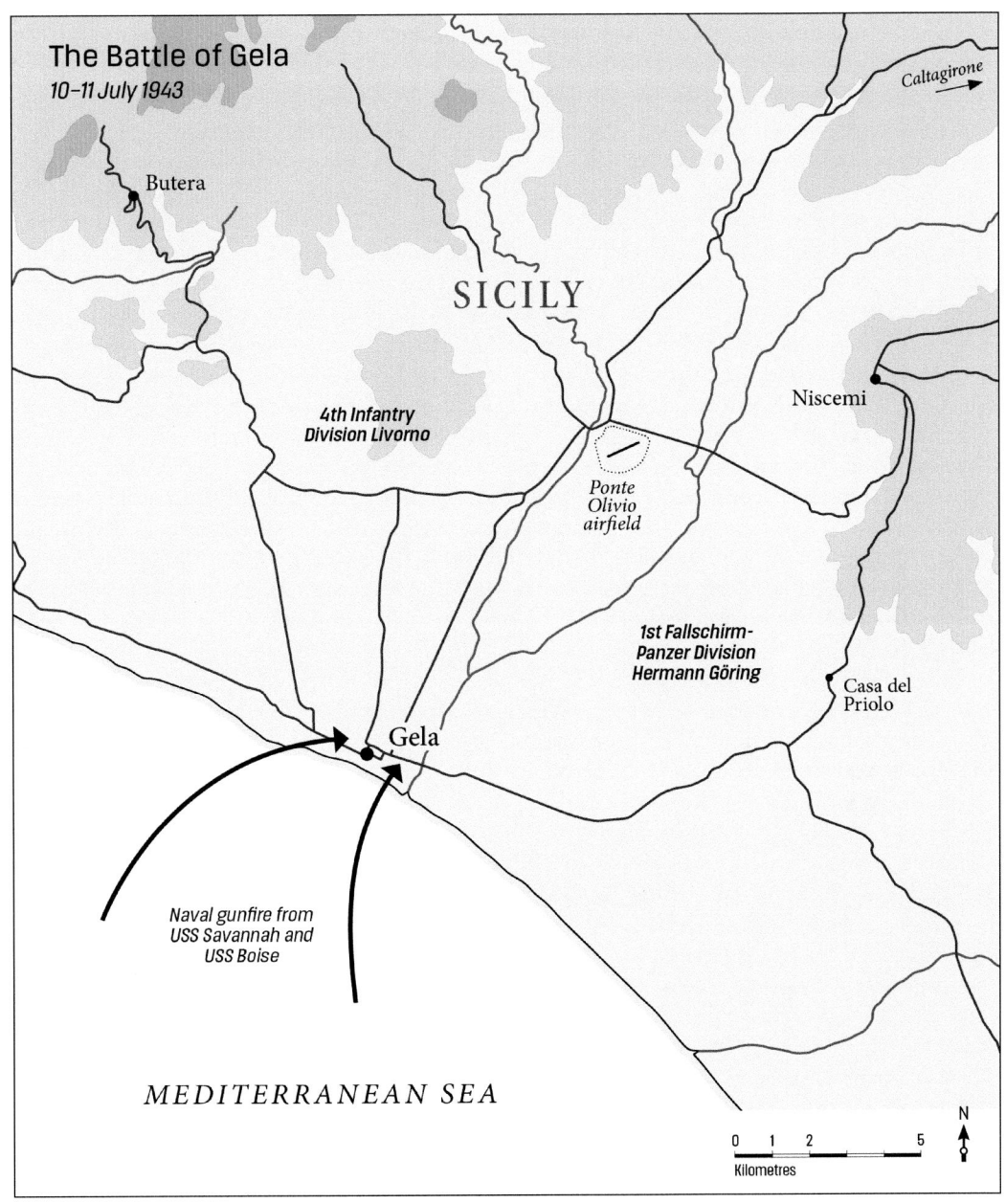

Map 4 The Battle of Gela, 10–11 July 1943.

Historian Liddell Hart, with regard to the uncoordinated Axis response on the Gela beachhead states: "A small group of Italian light tanks of obsolete type made a gallant little counterattack on the first morning, and actually penetrated into the town of Gela before they were driven off, but the main German column was delayed on the way and did not appear on the scene until the next morning."[10]

The next day the Axis forces including the bulk of *Livorno* and Hermann Göring Divisions staged the most powerful counter when they again rolled through Gela from opposite directions. The plan was to make a mad dash to essentially ram the enemy from the beachhead in conjunction with an airstrike that would have been carried out only a few minutes before the start of the counter. *Divisione Livorno*, led by *Generale di divisione* Chirieleison, which had at its disposal *Gruppo Mobile* E, was to attack from the west flank (*strada statale* 117), while the troops of Hermann Göring Division were to converge on Gela from the eastern flank. The objective of this well-designed counterattack was to isolate with a pincer movement the American troops on the beachhead. It was decided that the troops would begin their movements during the night so that they be ready in position before dawn. *Divisione Livorno* was split into three battle groups. *Livorno*'s armoured component was positioned as the column attacking from the left flank with III *Battaglione* /34° *Reggimento* which was supported by *Gruppo Mobile* E which was to advance on the Gela plain from west of *strada statale* 117. The other main columns from the *Livorno* division with the I/33° and I/34° *Battaglioni* were to attack without tank support. The middle column, comprised of one infantry battalion and one artillery group, was to advance from Butera to Gela, while the right flank column was to provide support and cover to the two attacking units from a potential enemy tank attack coming from Licata. It was comprised by I *Battaglione* / 34° *Reggimento Livorno* and an artillery group.

The brunt of the Axis attack would fall upon the 16th and 26th infantry divisions and specifically the American Rangers of X Force which were to be pushed back considerably. The Axis forces aimed to achieve tactical surprise because the Americans on day two of the operation still lacked adequate numbers of tanks and antitank tank guns which for the most part were still on the ships. At 0630 *Livorno* infantry units supported by *Gruppo Mobile* E, despite heavy enemy fire, began moving against the enemy's first line of defense and "overwhelmed the American advanced detachments at 0800 on the right flank of strada statale 117 near Poggio Frumento and Poggio Molinazzo. Approximately 100 enemy prisoners were captured and were dispatched in the direction of Monte Castellaccio and then to Niscemi."[11] Having conquered the first enemy line of defense, the troops began to advance against the second line of defense near Poggio Rosario and Case Selera. The infantry pressed the American defenses on the resistance line, which despite heavy gun fire from American ships, was also engaged. In fact, at 0830, naval artillery from the cruiser Savannah (armed with fifteen guns of 152mm and eight of 127mm) opened fire against the left-wing column forcing many soldiers to the ground to escape this avalanche of fire. Despite causing huge losses amongst the ranks of the III *Battaglione*/34° *Reggimento*, in three hours the latter reached the second enemy line and broke through its

---

10 Basil Liddell Hart, *History of the Second World War*, p. 443.
11 Alberto Santoni, *Le operazioni in Sicilia e in Calabria luglio-settembre 1943* (Rome: Ufficio Storico, 1983), p. 195.

defenses at 1100. At this point the Americans fell back to the town of Gela, while the Italians advanced all the way to the last enemy checkpoint.[12]

The attack column on the right, led by *Colonnello* Mona and comprised of I *Battaglione/ 33° Reggimento* and I *Battaglione/34° Reggimento* began to move at 0500. At the beginning there was no noticeable enemy resistance. But at 0900 the two units came under considerable field and naval artillery fire that caused the first losses amongst their ranks. At 1030 the reconnaissance units had reached the intersection of the Butera-Gela road, while the infantry companies were behind them. It was at this point that the enemy carried out a number of offensive thrusts with armoured vehicles and tanks aiming to push back the *Livorno* infantry. Supported by the mobile anti-tank guns, which dispersed with their fire the American mechanized force, the infantry advanced to the railway crossing at Casa Femmina Morta in the outskirts of Gela. As the Americans disengaged and as the Italian troops continued to thrust forward, the naval guns let loose again a very violent fire of repression aimed at stopping further progress.

General Conrath, had also deployed the Hermann Göring Division on three attack columns, subdivided as follows: The left flank column, made up of the Panzer grenadier regiment and the heavy Tiger I tanks company, was to move along the valley of the Dirillo river, then to Senia Ferrata and finally Gela. The middle column, comprised of a tank battalion and an artillery group, was to move from Case Priolo to Gela, while the third column, a tank battalion and some support units, was to attack the beaches from *strada statale* 117.

The Germans in the outskirts of Gela pressed hard against the first American defensive line by overcoming enemy resistance at Priolo. The American troops had few anti-tank guns and no armoured support, allowing the Germans to penetrate with relative ease into their defenses.

By 1100 the German tank units of the Hermann Göring had also been able to make considerable headway on the opposite flank breaking through and firing upon the troops as they were emerging from the ships:

> East of Gela, as General Conrath sent the major part of both his tank battalions toward the beaches, the Gela plain became a raging inferno of exploding shells, smoke, and fire. The lead tanks reached the highway west of Santa Spina, two thousand yards from the water. As they raked supply dumps and landing craft with fire, the division headquarters reported victory: "pressure by the Hermann Goering Division [has] forced the enemy to re-embark temporarily."[13]

This caused the American Rangers and infantry unit on the right flank to also fall back considerably into the town and then into the beachhead by 1130. *Colonnello* Emilio Faldella, the 6th Army Corps chief of staff, reported in his book published after the war *Lo sbarco e la difesa della Sicilia* (The Landing and the Defense of Sicily) of an intercepted American radio message issued at 1130 on 11 July by General Patton that ordered the U.S. 1st Division to prepare for

---

12 According to the American official history the Axis counter had been successful but costly to the point that the "dead bodies and limbs of Italian soldiers were hanging from trees and scattered all over the road."
13 Albert N. Garland and Howard McGaw Smyth, *Sicily and the Surrender of Italy*, p. 170.

re-embarkation. The order read as follows: "Bury the equipment on the beaches and be ready to re-embark. Patton."[14]

The American official history does not report any information regarding this order, nor does the war diary of the 7th American Army Corps or of 1st Division. Moreover, the order was not confirmed by any of the American generals involved, least of all by General Patton in the post war. The Italian Official History also contradicts Faldella's version of the events citing that the intercept was possibly misinterpreted. Thus, we will never know for certainty whether such a message did go out, although we do know that in the afternoon of the 11th several reinforcement units that had just landed on the beaches were reembarked.[15]

But just when the battle appeared to be at a turning point, the American Savannah and Boise ships were asked to intensify their already tremendous naval gun fire. As the naval guns tore through the Axis mobile units they halted the progress of the counter-attack on its tracks. This fire from the long range naval guns along with the arrival at 1200 of American tank units from Licata and Scoglitti and the positioning of more anti-tank artillery near the beaches combined to push the Axis forces on the defensive. The German central and right wing columns were impeded from advancing any further by the fire and with mounting losses began to retire, while the left-wing column continued to be engaged in the fighting until night.

An authoritative source argues that the lack of coordination amongst Axis troops once again limited the punch of their armour:

> Overall, this poorly coordinated attack had some effect. Properly coordinated, the forces available to attack Gela might have severely punished the landing forces. Committed piecemeal as they were and interdicted before they could reach their objectives, the Axis counterattack at Gela was a failure. In this case, much of the credit belongs to the naval gunfire support and the paratroopers who were very effective in this terrain. Much of the

---

14   Emilio Faldella, *Lo sbarco e la difesa della Sicilia* (Rome: L'Aniene, 1956), p. 148. The author conducted some research at the archive of *Ufficio Storico* but could not find the transcripts of the intercepted radio message by the Italian command post at Enna. What was located however was a document from the command of the XVIII *Brigata Costiera* that states at 1500 on 11 July: "Several American soldiers were observed as they swam back towards the ships giving the impression that some enemy elements were ready to re-embark." Ufficio Storico: "Relazione sui fatti di Gela," XVIII Brigata Costiera.

 Then there were some testimonies from soldiers of the Livorno Division such as Tenente Aldo Sampietro who testified that he observed several American tanks as they were re-embarked on the ships.

 Other items of interest are the memoirs of German General Fridolin von Senger und Etterlin, who in 1943 was German Liaison Officer to the Italian 6th Army, claims to have seen American troops reinbarking when he toured the battlefield in the afternoon of the 11 July. Carlo D'Este, *Bitter Victory: The Battle for Sicily, 1943* (New York: Dutton, 1988), p. 298. A British account suggests that it was a senior officer, but not General Patton, who issued the order for re-embarkation. Hugh Pond, *Sicily* (London, Harper, 1962), p. 99.

15   The American Official History states that as the German tanks were attacking the beachhead: "Engineer shore parties stopped unloading and established a firing line along the dunes." Thus, several units of infantry and some equipment landed on shore not according to plans but with some considerable delay in the late afternoon. While the German armoured division diary states: "pressure by the Hermann Goering Division [has] forced the enemy to re-embark temporarily." Albert N. Garland and Howard McGaw Smyth, *Sicily and the Surrender of Italy*, p. 170.

blame goes to the H.G. Div. commander, General Conrath, who could not muster his force to break through a relatively lightly armed defensive line.[16]

Along with the German tanks, the Italian troops on the opposite flank were also pushed back from their main penetration points.[17] American tanks struck I/33° and I/34° *Reggimenti* on the flanks forcing them to halt their advance. Only the column with the mobile elements, the III/34°, could continue the operation by advancing further into the town and engaging Darby's Force X. The two battalions of I/33° and I/34° were subjected to a strong energy counter but after repelling a first attempt they were ultimately overwhelmed and captured by a large energy force in the proximity of the railway crossing.

At 1300 the troops of III/34° were still in Gela when they heard that *Livorno*'s right wing column had been cut to pieces by an American armoured thrust from Licata, and that the Germans were falling back on Caltagirone. The battalion therefore remained isolated in the plain of Gela for most of the day. Some of its soldiers, the ones that had pushed on the furthest, had by then been captured by the American Rangers. *Livorno's Tenente Colonnello* Leonardi recalls that:

> The small group of prisoners proceeded slowly towards Gela... The soldiers were exhausted and some were wounded. Our squad reached Gela .... But we were entering the town not as losers but as winners! We passed through the streets of the city. Many people were moved and cried too. Quite a few offered us bread, water, cigarettes, and they would have given who knows what else if the soldiers escorting us had allowed it! A small old man, who could barely walk with the help of a walking stick, came up and shook our hands. Maybe he had seen ... maybe he knew! But the Americans immediately told him to go away. Amid so many good people, however, there were some apathetic and indifferent people. There were also those who mocked us and even insulted us because we had dared to fight....[18]

At 2400 III/34° received the order to fall back to Monte Castelluccio with the task of establishing a strong point to check any enemy advance and to cover the retreat of the other Axis units.

Several American medium tanks were ordered to harry the retreat of *Divisione Livorno*. According to the recollections of artilleryman Causin: "Seven American tanks rolled through strada statale 117. I manned the fourth gun, the closest to the road. The commander then

---

16   Jon Swanson, 'Operation Husky', US Army War College 1992 thesis.
17   Ibid. Some of the Italian units approaching from the northwest reached the outskirts of Gela before being stopped by the Rangers defending the town. Again, the defenders were well supported by naval gunfire, this time from the cruiser Savannah. The attack on the German left flank also got off to a good start where they were able to penetrate the weakened 180th RCT. The Americans along this portion of the line were driven back to a point near their own beaches..... The situation was becoming desperate for Patton and the 7th Army. The Americans were unable to get their tanks ashore and were only able to get limited anti-tank guns into action. Once again, the navy came to the rescue, providing effective fire support against the German attackers. Despite the navy's support, however, the Germans were able to get within a few hundred yards of the beach and were able to bring the supply dumps and landing craft under direct fire.
18   Nunzio Vicino, *La battaglia di Gela* (Gela: Tip. Istituto Gualandi, 1967), p, 123.

signaled to open fire when the enemy tanks were at eighty meters from our position. I could see them on the telescope as being very close to us. I remember that the first shot I fired hit the underbelly of the tank between the ground and the track and the tank stopped. Then the second tank took a direct hit and began to burn. I immediately shot another and in the end only two managed to escape."[19]

With the support of 9ª *Compagnia* equipped with 81mm mortars, the *Livorno* battalion then conducted a fighting retreat during the night. At dawn the Italian unit retreated to Castelaccio where the Americans concentrated a massive infantry preparatory fire which was followed by the infantry attack. By mid-morning the remaining troops of *Gruppo Mobile* E and *Livorno* were completely overwhelmed.

Casualties were high. Those of *Livorno* Division numbered 214 officers and 6,000 men wounded or dead and 1,300 were taken prisoner.[20] *Gruppo Mobile E* had been almost completely wiped out, while the German Division had lost over thirty-five tanks and suffered more than 600 casualties. American casualties were also considerable and just on 11 July alone the Seventh Army had suffered over 2,300 casualties. This represented the American army's greatest one day loss during the Sicilian campaign.

The American official history as well as other major works on the Sicilian Campaign have argued that the Axis counter ultimately lost steam and the latter was never able to prevail. In contrast, the West Point History of the War presents a soberer analysis. It states that the Axis counter attack produced considerable consternation even though it ultimately failed. "Kesselring's strategy of stopping the invasion at the beaches with immediate counterattacks had failed; but in the words of Wellington it was the nearest run thing you ever saw in your life."[21]

Licata

A similar counter took place in Licata on 10-11 July where several 90/53 *semoventi* took the lead. The so-called *Gruppo Venturi* with *CLXI Gruppo d'Artiglieria* equipped with eight *semoventi* attacked American forces of the 3rd Division along with *Bersaglieri* of the DXXVI *Battaglione* and other infantry units was deployed on day one of the landings. The Allies began to offload troops on shore on the early morning of 10 July. These first elements easily overcame the coastal defenses. To push them back a counter was organized by the Venturi Group: "The offensive maneuver obtained its stated aim after continuous fighting. The enemy was blocked at the strait of Favarotta and near Palma di Montechiaro."[22] The American official history also states that its forces were checked by Venturi Group but does not give any tally of the losses sustained: 'During the night of 10 July, Colonnello Venturi, who commanded the Italian 177th Bersaglieri Regiment, had arrived with one of his battalions at Favarotta, where

---

19 Ufficio Storico, Rivista Militare, n. 6, November 2014.
20 Alberto Santoni, *Le operazioni in Sicilia e in Calabria*, p. 201.
21 Thomas E. Griess (ed.), *West Point Military Series, The Second World War: Europe and the Mediterranean*, p. 230.
22 Ufficio Storico, 'Relazione sui fatti d'arme dal 10 Luglio a 2 Agosto 1943', VII Corpo d'Armata, 3 Agosto 1943.

a makeshift force of Italian artillerymen and motorcyclists had managed to halt 3d Division progress along Highway 123."[23]

On the morning of 11 July, the American advance, supported by tanks and armoured vehicles, resumed with a surprise attack in the direction of Favarotta. The *Venturi* mobile group pushed back "with an energetic response as several armoured vehicles and tanks were then put out of action by our semoventi units."[24] For four hours, Americans and Italians fought with great intensity for the control of Favarotta. Several American attacks were put forth and were rebuffed by the Italians which relied on their mobile units to halt the enemy. But the American attackers persisted in their operation bringing forward a number of anti-tank and field guns. As more troops and equipment were moved forward by the attackers three *semoventi* were put out of action. Little by little American artillery took center stage and tore through the Italian mobile and artillery units: "American artillery units firing with devastating effect on Italian artillery pieces and armoured vehicles emplaced near the small town."[25] As a result of the barrage the Italian mobile group also lost 50 percent of its automatic weapons. Heavy casualties were also sustained by the *Bersaglieri* units and *Colonnello* Venturi was also slightly injured by an enemy shell.

According to the Italian official history: "After three hours of stiff fighting that saw each enemy attack met by an Axis counter-attack for the control of Favarotta, the Venturi mobile group was forced to retreat from Casa Mustra at 0905."[26]

Retreating to Canicatti' the Axis troops were reorganized and new units were also assembled such as the CLXIII *Gruppo di semoventi* da 90/53, various artillery and infantry units and the 215th German tank Company for a counter to take place in the afternoon. That morning, the XII Corps had ordered *Generale di Brigata* Ottorino Schreiber, commander of the 207th Coastal Division, to travel to Canicatti' and assume command of the tactical group and the German forces to lead an operation aimed at retaking Licata. But the action never started. The mobile groups were targeted from the outset by intensive enemy fire which broke up and scattered the attacking forces.

This failure paved the way for an American attack by the 15th Infantry to penetrate into Campobello in the proximity of Canicatti'. According to the American Official History the troops of the 3rd Battalion ultimately entered the town at approximately 1600 after having been held up by intensive enemy fire for several hours. The Italian version of the events is slightly different. It admits the loss of Compobello but then it states that the Americans moved on Canicatti' where they initially suffered casualties: "Following the aerial bombardment several enemy tanks attempted to reach the town but their advance was stymied by the *semoventi da 90/53* which opened a blistering fire from their position on the southern outskirts of the town. At 1800 the enemy renewed the attack with greater intensity, but CLXIII *Gruppo Semoventi* was able to hit and destroy several enemy tanks and ultimately force them to retreat."[27]

---

23 Albert N. Garland and Howard McGaw Smyth, *Sicily and the Surrender of Italy*, p. 191.
24 Ufficio Storico, 'Relazioni fatti d'armi della divisione Assietta 10-21 luglio 1943', Comando Divisione Assietta, 28 July 1943.
25 Albert N. Garland and Howard McGaw Smyth, *Sicily and the Surrender of Italy*, p. 195.
26 Alberto Santoni, *Le operazioni in Sicilia e in Calabria*, p. 211.
27 Emilio Faldella, *Lo Sbarco*, p. 155.

The Americans concentrated their attack upon Canicatti the following day. Following a five-minute preparation, at 1330, on 12 July, the infantry supported by tanks and armoured vehicles advanced toward the southern outskirts of Canicattì and by 1600 the town had been occupied, while the Axis defense had already evacuated and was by then concentrated in the nearby hills. Defensive positions were manned by the German I and II Battalions of Colonel Fullriede and supported by the two *Gruppi Semoventi* from the X *Raggruppamento*. On the evening of the 12th, two more Shermans were lost outside Canicatti' as the American forces attempted to advance past the hills around the town but were shot at by the 75mm howitzers. The German artillery and the *semoventi* continued to fire on them from up above in a dug in hill position and prevented them from progressing any further:

> Scarcely pausing, the company of tanks drove out the northern exit from town and ran into Colonel Fullriede's main battle position. After expending all its ammunition and losing one tank, the company pulled back to town to await reinforcements. A tank-infantry team swung to the right and secured the eastern edge of a ridge line a mile north of town. Though the Germans fought stubbornly, they were driven off the ridge line by 2000. By darkness, CCA had Canicattì, but Group Fullriede held the bulk of the hill mass north-west of the town.[28]

In the next few days the *X Raggruppamento* fighting again within the tactical group of Italian officer Ottorino Schreiber and supported on its left flank by the German Group Fullriede held the positions mainly by performing a static artillery role.

On the 15th the Americans broke through the front in several points and all the Axis forces were ordered to pull back. The Germans took up positions at Leonforte, while the Italians at Portella Recattivo to block the main roads from Santa Caterina di Villaermosa and Villapriolo. The tactical group at this point was comprised by one Blackshirt battalion, six *semoventi* from X *Raggruppamento*, various artillery groups from *Aosta* Division and a motorized infantry battalion. On the 18th "Various enemy mechanized units are spotted as they are in the process of advancing toward our positions. Our artillery immediately opened fire. The enemy tanks headed toward Portella are forced to retreat. At 0700 the enemy artillery opens up a thunderous fire that is concentrated particularly against the positions of III/3° and in the area where the 90/53 guns are positioned. The enemy fire comes in unabated all day and heavy casualties are taken amongst the ranks of the semoventi crews. Then the enemy infantry advances against our positions and makes contact with our forward elements. Our artillery responds very effectively and restores the situation. Then several waves of enemy bombers target our positions especially our artillery strongpoints and four semoventi are put out of action. The enemy's infantry, which had come into contact with our units, are forced to retreat by our prompt response. After the enemy, had been repelled in a frontal attack various units attempt unsuccessfully to sally at our flanks."[29]

X *Raggruppamento*'s diary states that: "At 0700 the enemy artillery struck the area where the 90/53mm units were deployed. The shelling continued throughout the day and particularly

---

28 Albert N. Garland and Howard McGaw Smyth, *Sicily and the Surrender of Italy*, p. 199.
29 Ufficio Storico, "Relazione sui fatti d'arme dal 10 Luglio a 2 Agosto 1943," VII Corpo d'Armata, 3 August 1943.

bitter were the losses among the personnel of the 90/53mm semoventi. Despite the losses, the semoventi units managed to push back the Allied forces to Santa Caterina which were forced to pull back their tanks and armoured vehicles approximately 1 km from Portella."[30] However, due to the overwhelming enemy pressure the troops were forced to pull back again this time to Alimena. On this position on the 20th the Italian artillery was called to block the advance of a large group of American tanks and armoured vehicles. On the next day, the Americans breeched the Italian positions but were then pushed back by the Blackshirts, supported by *semoventi* and by the artillery. The fighting lasted for the entire day and the Italian troops, supported also by German artillery forced back the enemy who then focused his efforts upon the nearby town of Bompietro where it was checked by German forces.

Agrigento

The American 3d Infantry Division began its operation to seize Agrigento which represented the gateway to western Sicily and ultimately would lead to the capture of Palermo. On the night of 14 July to achieve the objective General Truscott selected the 7th Infantry Regiment, the 10th Field Artillery Battalion, and one battalion from the 77th Field Artillery Regiment for the task.

On the 15th the advancing enemy troops were harried all day by the three mobile groups A, B and C, which used their mobile artillery to block the progress of the Americans. On the 16th the battle for Agrigento reached its peak. The 2d Battalion/7th Infantry Regiment, advancing west from Favara, conquered two hills overlooking Agrigento, meanwhile the 1st Battalion, along *strada statale* 115, was having a hard fight trying to get into Agrigento. *Gruppo Mobile* B was called in to check the advance of the 1st Battalion. "I ordered an immediate counter by Gruppo Mobile B. The action, which was conducted by Colonnello Storti of 10th Bersaglieri, brought about after much heavy fighting to the recapture of several positions. But then our column was pushed back by enemy armour and by the medium range artillery and was forced to pull back."[31]

In Agrigento, *Colonnello* de Laurentis, commander of the Italian forces, had lost several of his soldiers due to heavy Allied naval and ground bombardments during the day. By late afternoon of 16 July all of the Italian artillery batteries had been put out of action and the town was surrounded. At night, the Americans entered the town forcing the surrender of its garrison.

On 17 July *Gruppo Mobile* B was located near the outskirts of Agrigento when several enemy units disembarked at Porto Empedocle and proceeded to advance toward the towns of Ribera and Raffadali. The tactical group was ordered to check the enemy's advance by way of a counter attack. Its action was swift and within a few minutes it gained momentum as the Renault tanks in collaboration with the *Semoventi* da 47/32 gallantly charged against the enemy forces and forced them to pull back. On the 18th *Gruppo Mobile* C held up for most of the day a much larger enemy force while the next day *Gruppo Mobile* B again engaged the enemy in a protracted battle with heavy casualties on both sides.

---

30 Ibid.
31 Ibid.

On 19 July, the Americans, determined to capture Palermo, increased the pressure in the area west of Agrigento. Near Chiusa Sclafani a motorized enemy group was challenged by *Gruppo Mobile* B which reinforced the positions held by *Bersaglieri* and held the enemy at bay for most of the day. Meanwhile *Gruppo Mobile* C led by *Tenente Colonnello* Mazzei managed to repel a much larger enemy force near Caste Termini. During the evening of the same day, *Gruppo Mobile* B of *Tenente Colonnello* Mascio had to fall back to Bivona given the overwhelming enemy pressure. Despite this pressure, it opposed a strenuous but costly resistance with mounting losses between the ranks of its tank and *semovente* companies. This action was also singled out by the American admiral and historian Samuel Eliot Morison who wrote that *Mobile Group* B put up a vigorous defense to stop the advance.[32] The next day at 0600 *Gruppo Mobile* C positioned at Cammarata faced down an enemy attack. Later, at 0900 a second attack, lasting three hours finally overcame the mobile unit. On the afternoon of 21 July, *Gruppo Mobile* B of *Tenente Colonnello* Mascio put up strong resistance at Santo Stefano Quisquina to the units of the 3rd American Division's three-pronged attack. The next day *Gruppo Mobile* A of *Tenente Colonnello* Perrone at Stazione di Villadolmo held up for several hours a much larger enemy force until it was completely overrun.

While the Axis forces began a slow and methodical retreat with the aim to withdraw from Sicily, the 7th Army finally captured Palermo on 26 July. The following day it occupied most of northern Sicily. On 26 July, the Italian monarch, sensing that the war was lost, forced Mussolini to resign and placed him under house arrest. Then he nominated Pietro Badoglio, the ex-chief of the *Comando Supremo* as the political leader of the country.

The X *Raggruppamento* ceased to exist on 6 August 1943 when at Nebrodi, in northern Sicily, its few self-propelled guns (three) remaining together with troops from *Aosta* Division and the Germans of the 15th Panzer grenadier "Sizilien" Division tried unsuccessfully to block the Allied advance toward Messina, the last slice of Sicilian territory still in Axis hands.

During the Sicilian campaign the *X Raggruppamento* had lost three out of six senior officers, four officers, fifty soldiers dead and 125 wounded. Twenty soldiers had been awarded medals of honor while the unit had been mentioned very positively in the High Command Bulletin of 24 July. The two battalions of French tanks, the semoventi da 47/32 and the other disparate groups of truck-mounted artillery were also decimated.

Primosole Bridge

The Sicilian campaign also saw the participation of the motorized battalion of the *X Reggimento Arditi* which deployed its three branches (paratroopers, navy seals and motorized commando units) to oppose the landings. Despite their limited numbers, the units of this regiment achieved some local successes thus slowing down the enemy advance.

In May 1943, the *II Battaglione/X Reggimento Arditi* was dispatched to Sicily in anticipation of an Allied landing. The motorized commando unit was deployed in anti-paratrooper operations. On 13 July, for instance, two platoons of *Camionettisti* used the AB.41 vehicles to reach an area where the enemy paratroopers had been dropped. The unit, after dismounting from their vehicles, patrolled a vast area and managed to capture twenty enemy paratroopers.

---

32 Samuel Eliot Morison, *Sicily-Salerno-Anzio* (New York: Little Brown, 1954), p. 117.

> We were deployed during the night in the area were the paratroopers had been dropped and laid in wait until dawn to begin the mop up operation. At dawn, I communicated to my troops to begin the operation. The platoons immediately met enemy paratroopers that refused to surrender by firing an 81mm mortar and several machine guns. The arditi lunged against the enemy troops that had taken up positions during the night. Even though the enemy was defending fortified strongpoints, the arditi could surround them and reduce them through the launch of several hand grenades and machine gun fire. Four enemy paratroopers were killed and twenty were captured along with an 81mm mortar, rifles, ammunition and hand grenades.[33]

The *Arditi* were then deployed in the battle of Primosole. After the landings, had been successfully completed, the Allies wanted at all costs to reach Primosole by capturing the bridge on the Simeto River a few miles south of Catania. This would have allowed them to invade the bulk of Sicily by making a breakthrough in the Axis defenses and make a quick clearance of Sicily. This strategic position was defended by a battalion of the 3rd Regiment/1. *Fallschirmjäge*r-German Division, and a unit of the 213rd Coastal Division. On the night between 14/15 July a British unit comprised of 300 paratroopers and three anti-tank guns assaulted the bridge. The German officer radioed a demand for reinforcements and thus three platoons of *Camionettisti* were driven to the position on several armoured vehicles. The *arditi* initially joined the German unit on the bridge and immediately began firing upon the advancing enemy. After repulsing the attack, the Axis forces went on the counter and the following post battle report details the role played by the motorized *arditi*:

> We charged the enemy head on using our vehicles as if they were light tanks by firing the guns while advancing against the enemy. Seeing the vehicles coming directly at them the enemy troops quickly retreated and dispersed. The platoons after having advanced with their vehicles began to dismount and advance on foot against the enemy positions. The enemy shot back with a few mortar rounds that landed on the street and caused severe damage to four armoured vehicles. The enemy, aiming to cut us off, lunged against our positions and surrounded us as we were mounting on the vehicles. The arditi, however, did not back down from the confrontation and fought off the enemy thrust. Once the enemy troops had been dispersed the arditi returned to the Axis held side of the bridge.[34]

German paratroopers and Italian *arditi* managed to hold the position at Primosole until the night of 17 July before retreating, allowing the bulk of the Axis forces to cross the Strait of Messina and avoid being captured by the Allies. This delaying action had been important because it allowed the Axis forces to bring most of its equipment to Calabria and to prevent the Allies from making a quick clearance of Sicily. The main British forces succeeded after three days of very hard fighting in capturing the bridge.

The *arditi* unit suffered the same fate of several other Italian units which were either disbanded or reorganized after suffering severe losses during the battle for Sicily. After the landings were

---

33 Ufficio Storico: 'Diario Storico del II Battaglione', documento firmato Maggiore Marciano', cartella X Reggimento Arditi.
34 Ibid.

opposed, the Allies continued to advance and eventually captured Sicily in its entirety. It was at this stage that the Italian Army collapsed under the weight of defeat in the battlefield and under the political crisis in Rome which had been precipitated by the Allied landings.

Final Considerations

Prior to the invasion, the Italian High Command had issued guidelines on how to oppose the landings. To initially shelter the troops from naval bombardments the Axis units had been positioned near but not on the coast. Thus, when the Allies landed it took, for instance, the Hermann Göring Division several hours to reach the beachhead to attack the Americans. Thus, precious time was lost since the only way that such counterattacks could succeed was by striking at the enemy as soon as its forces landed thus preventing him from bringing onshore its tanks and heavy guns. Had the action against Gela been more precipitous, the Axis forces could have more effectively countered the landings.

All Italian mobile reserve units conducted counter-attacks and suffered heavy losses by attacking repeatedly without substantial artillery support. The lack of heavy and medium tanks was keenly felt and most Renault B-35 and Italian light tanks sacrificed themselves in selfless attacks. Most of the remaining *semoventi* were also lost during the Sicilian campaign.

As Cappellano and Pignato observe "the reserve units in charge of counter attacking were too light and exiguous to properly confront head on the Sherman tanks. These tactical reserve units lacked an offensive punch given that they were totally devoid of medium tanks, large numbers of semoventi and effective antitank guns and with some of their artillery pieces which were still being pulled by horses."[35].

There is one official report on the performance of Italian troops and equipment during the Sicilian campaign that provides an overall assessment. In terms of the troops the report states that while the initial landings were properly opposed despite overwhelming enemy force, the advance into the mainland was only sporadically opposed by an army that by late July was collapsing in all sectors. The penury of equipment and especially of the armoured units, that were forced to combat the Allied units with obsolete 1930s vintage French tanks, was clearly detailed in the report. The only weapon that was singled out for being effective was the *semovente M41M da 90/53*, the only heavy anti-armoured weapon deployed in Sicily in 1943. Even though it was slow and could not easily negotiate the rocky and unpaved roads of Sicily at its top speed, its powerful 90mm gun was able to "neutralize a number Sherman tanks."[36]

In conclusion, it can be argued that by simply looking at the numbers before and after the start of the Sicilian campaign, a different perspective on the campaign emerges.

The American Official History, for example, furnishes several accounts of Italian soldiers giving themselves up to the enemy[37], a trend that was accentuated by the fact that many soldiers

---

35 Filippo Cappellano and Nicola Pignato, *Andare contro i carri armati*, p. 215.
36 Ibid., p. 269.
37 Allied intelligence reports of Italian morale in the battle for Sicily were caustic. One stated: "For the most part the Italian field formations have not shown a standard of morale and battle determination very much higher than that of the coastal units whose performance was so lamentably low … Sheer war weariness and a feeling of the hopelessness of Italy's position have, however,

were Sicilians and that many of them deserted to go back to their families and towns. But if we look at the number of casualties and specifically to those sustained by the armoured/mobile units a different view of the campaign emerges. One that demonstrates that despite the deserters and the ones that gave themselves up to the enemy, the bulk of the Royal Army and the militia along with key support provided by the German divisions fought a fairly extended campaign against overpowering enemy forces. The struggle that the Axis forces sustained in Sicily lasted 38 days. In contrast, it took Germany the same approximate number of days to subjugate Poland and France respectively. That is entire nations were conquered in the approximate same number of days it took for the Allies with their massive deployment of men and equipment to conquer Sicily. Given especially the dire condition of the Italian regime, it appears the majority soldiers fought even when all around things were falling apart politically, economically and militarily. If we then compare the campaign against other Allied operations, we can surmise that it was one of the largest seaborne offensive operations organized by the Allies during the Second World War. Only during the invasion of Normandy did the Allies deploy a larger invasion force.

obviously been more potent influences and these have moreover permeated the field army to a considerable degree, with the result that a sense of inferiority and futility has destroyed its zest and spirit." *US Army in World War II: Sicily and the Surrender of Italy* <http://www.ibiblio.org/hyperwar/USA/USA-MTO-Sicily/USA-MTO-Sicily-10.html> (accessed 10 May 2019)

9

M Armoured Division and Ariete II

Introduction

In July of 1943 Italy found itself with no combat ready armoured units as the few battalions deployed in Sicily were quickly overcome by the Allies. At the time there were two divisions in training. One was the M armoured division and the second was a reconstituted *Ariete* II division. Both essentially were much better equipped than the North African armoured divisions but they were not combat ready in the end of July 1943 when the regime collapsed.

M Division

During the war the Fascist regime deployed several Blackshirt volunteer militia units called *Legioni di Camicie Nere or Battaglioni M*, (Blackshirt legions or M battalions) that saw combat in all theatres of operation as detachments to Royal Army corps or infantry divisions. Many of these battalions such as *Tagliamento*, *Leonessa*, *Valle Scrivia* and *Montebello* had been deployed first in Ukraine and then in Russia against the Soviet Union and had fought alongside the divisions of the Italian Royal Army and of the German army since the inception of Operation Barbarossa. After the collapse of the Italian held line on the Don River, many of the volunteers that had survived the vicissitudes of the Eastern front campaign were assembled in Italy under the newly formed 1. *Divisione Corazzata Camicie Nere* M (1st Blackshirt Armoured M Division whereby M stood for Mussolini) in May 1943. This unit, the brainchild of several personalities but mainly of *luogotenente generale della Milizia Volontaria per la Sicurezza Nazionale* (the Fascist voluntary militia for national security) Enzo Galbiati, was unique amongst the Blackshirts because it was formed initially as Mussolini's personal protection unit after the defeat of the Axis forces in North Africa in May 1943. In addition, the German leadership (especially Hitler and Himmler) had also been instrumental in making the M Division possible. Hitler, fearful of a potential putsch against Mussolini and the Fascist Party after the defeat in North Africa by the Italian monarchy and the highest-ranking officers of the Royal Army, had urged its creation. He not only had advocated the constitution of an armoured division of the militia but also supplied it with weapons and equipment. The historian Renzo de Felice reports one of Hitler's statements made to the German High Command in the spring of 1943 regarding aiding and propping up the faltering Italian regime:

I could support the Duce with a conditional proposition. If he is willing to provide a unit comprised of battle hardened soldiers drawn from the militia, I would be willing to dispatch the necessary weapons and equipment. This unit would then have to be organised, equipped and trained in Germany. I am willing and ready to support the Duce by sending to Italy the most modern German equipment such as tanks, self-propelled guns, anti-tank guns, etc. to allow for the creation of an Italian panzer grenadier division. The latter should be constituted by militia soldiers and trained by German officers. It should be comprised of soldiers that are fully committed to the war effort and the Axis cause. The unit can then be used as a tactical reserve at the disposal of the Italian government.[1]

The statement is very significant, especially in the light of the events that would shortly thereafter follow in the fall of 1943, which demonstrates that one of the first proponents of the M Division was the German leadership itself. Most likely this attempt to arm the Blackshirts was seen by Germany as an attempt to keep Italy in the war by propping up its much-weakened leader and his faltering regime after the defeats in Russia and North Africa. In Russia, the Italian 8th Army had been defeated by the Soviet offensive of Operation Little Saturn which caused tremendous losses and the destruction of the entire Italian Army on the Eastern Front. The total losses included almost fifty percent of the strength of the 8th Army with 84,930 dead or captured during combat operations and 29,690 injured. Because of these tremendous losses Italian troops were transferred back to Italy and the Italian contingent to Russia was disbanded. To make matters worse for the Axis a few months later the Italian First Army was forced to surrender to the Allies in Tunisia. Thus another 200,000 Axis soldiers were taken into captivity along with artillery pieces of all kinds, tanks, trucks and hundreds of machine guns. With the loss of Tunisia, the Axis no longer had a military presence in North Africa and this defeat dangerously exposed Italy to an Allied invasion.

While Germany was clearly alarmed that the Allies could attack Italy from their bases in North Africa, the Italian proposal to initiate peace talks with the Soviet Union to then focus the Axis war effort against the British and the American forces was clearly rejected by the German leadership as a non-workable solution. But the continuation of a two-front war did not bode well for the Axis and especially for its weaker partner, Italy, which was now threatened directly. These considerations were probably the strategic underpinnings that forced Germany to expedite and facilitate the creation of the M Division as well as develop contingency plans in case Italy surrendered. Germany had provided support before but this time it was different since there was an entire Italian division that was being fully equipped with German weapons and equipment. In the past Germany, had supplied mostly captured Soviet or French Army equipment to its allies, while in some cases its military had also furnished German equipment such as batteries of 88mm Flak 36 guns to Italian troops in North Africa and 75mm artillery units supplied to the Italians in late 1942. What is striking about this new supply of weapons in mid-1943 was that the M Division was equipped with lots of modern equipment in so little time. Most likely this was the result of the precipitous situation that Italy found itself after defeat in Tunisia in May 1943. The equipment that was shipped from Germany to Italy was of

---

1   Cited in Stefano Fabei, *Tagliamento, La legione delle Camicie nere in Russia (1941-1943)* (Rome; Eribus, 2014), p. 21.

the highest quality and the most advanced from a technological standpoint. It was for sure the most advanced equipment ever placed at the disposal of an Italian unit during the war. Not only was the equipment furnished very quickly but it was also accompanied by an exceedingly high number of German officers, trainers and NCOs who had been assigned the task of training the M Division.

Originally in the winter of 1942 Enzo Galbiati, the head of the MVSN, had first broached the subject of the creation of an armoured division within the fascist Blackshirt militia. The unit was seen by Galbiati as another effort to further specialize the MVSN which a year earlier had constituted the M Battalions to deploy better trained and prepared Blackshirt assault infantry and light artillery units. In the fall of 1942 Galbiati travelled to the frontline to carry out a series of inspections to determine the state of readiness of the troops on the Eastern front in bracing for major Soviet counter-attacks. After wrapping up his visit to the front Galbiati had also conducted several interviews with members of the German High Command that had expressed negative opinions on the effectiveness of the Italian troops, including the Blackshirts on the Eastern front. Upon returning to Italy Galbiati issued a report highlighting his findings and recommending further training and specialization for the M battalions to counteract the negative perceptions.

Increased training was a way to improve the combat readiness of the troops, while more specialization was deemed to increase overall combat effectiveness. For example, an area where improvements could be made through training was in refining attack plans and raids through improved intelligence of enemy strength. Thus, newly made Blackshirt officers and NCOs were to undergo specific training on how to more fully conduct the reconnaissance and surveillance functions of enemy units with the aid of improved tools and maps. Whereas an example of specialization was the creation within the M Battalions of fully motorized command platoons. In addition, the officers and NCOs of such platoons were to be furnished with automatic weapons. This new idea of creating a Blackshirt armoured division was to address two specific needs: to provide a unit that could guarantee internal peace and order and one that also could be deployed in battle against the Allies that threatened southern Europe.

The main problem in mid-1943 was that the Army did not possess advanced modern tank units and, moreover, what little new resources were available, these were typically placed at the disposal of the Royal Army that was in also dire need of new equipment. Thus, to achieve the objective of creating a modern panzer division, securing German assistance in training the unit and equipping it with modern weapons was of uttermost importance. At the time the Royal Army had only one armoured division in training, the reconstituted *Ariete* II, which was armed with M.15/42 tanks which were clearly inferior to the German armoured units. But the Royal Army could not spare any resources or weapons.

The Blackshirts were assembled in the area near Chiesa (Siena) during the first two weeks of May 1943 and per the guidelines issued by its leadership the recruits had to be carefully selected. They had to be selected from the most experienced and battle hardened soldiers of the militia. Moreover, another pre-requisite was prior combat expertise gained in campaigns in Albania, Greece or Russia. These soldiers were to be complemented by several younger recruits, all volunteers, while the artillery crews were to be selected primarily from the units of the coastal and the anti-aircraft artillery militia. The drivers of the tanks and trucks were to be recruited, where possible, from experienced armoured or motorized units of the Royal Army. The leader of the unit was going to be designated as the *console* of the division and he had to have had extensive prior experience in leading one or more M Battalions groups in either the Balkans or Russia. Similarly, the heads of operations and of security and intelligence were to be drawn from the best and most experienced officers of the MVSN. A tank armoured specialist was also highly sought after together with a high-level officer from the artillery branch. All the officers had to have completed training at the war school in Turin for at least three years and had to have prior significant combat experience. Since most of the soldiers had little or no prior experience in operating tanks or such heavy guns, the *Divisione* M was not expected to be combat ready for many months.

The training began in earnest in mid-May. Some soldiers were sent to Germany to train on German tanks, while others began extensive training in Chiusi with the armour that had been dispatched by the Germans. German armour and artillery instructors were based in Chiusi as well to initiate an extensive training period for the units of the M Division.

The day at the divisional training camp was typically split into several sessions. The morning was dedicated to live fire exercises with the individual and crew served weapons, while the afternoon was dedicated to rehearsing maneuvers where soldiers advanced riding on or advancing behind the armoured units against makeshift enemy positions. The expenditure of ammunition was considerable during these training exercises and an incredible amount of equipment and supply was put at the disposal of the M Division. At least for Italian standards during the Second World War, the Blackshirts received above average training with unusually high numbers of weapons and ammunition. The level of training and the large availability of weapons and ammunition constituted a definite break with the past.

After almost two months of training the M Division was thus officially constituted on 25 June 1943 and had been transferred to Bracciano near Rome, but at the time it was still not deemed battle ready. According to *Generale* Galbiati, for instance, the unit could only be deemed combat ready only by the late summer or early fall of 1943. Its initial strength was comprised by 5,800 soldiers that were subdivided in the following units: an armoured battalion, four infantry battalions, two artillery battalions, a combat engineer battalion, a sapper and a signals company and several small teams of medical staff, cooks, etc. The four infantry battalions were considered as *fanteria legionaria motorizzata* (motorized legionary infantry units) since they were each comprised of three infantry companies and one machine gun company and were endowed with several trucks to transport equipment as well as soldiers. The armoured component of the M Division was comprised by the *Gruppo Carri Leonessa* (Armoured Group Leonessa) which operated the German tanks and the *Gruppo Artiglieria Valle Scrivia* which was armed primarily with twenty-four 88mm Flak 37 guns. Thus, the unit not only had approximately 5,800 soldiers but with the addition of German officers and NCOs, the drivers and armoured specialists drawn from the Royal Army, its total strength exceeded 6,000 soldiers. Its order of battle was as follows:

    1a. Divisione Corazzata Camicie Nere M: Console Generale Alessandro Lusana
        Comando e compagnia comando. (Command Company).
        Compagnia Carabinieri.
        Nucleo Movimento Stradale (Mobile Unit).
        306 ufficio Posta Militare (Postal unit).
        Autoreparto Divisionale (Mobile supply unit).

Gruppo Carri M Leonessa: *Primo Seniore* Ferdinando Tesi
    1ᵃ *Compagnia* with twelve Panzerkampfwagen Kpfw IV Ausf. H with 75mm gun.
    2ᵃ *Compagnia* with twelve Panzerkampfwagen III Ausf. N with 75mm gun.
    3ᵃ *Compagnia* with twelve StuG III Ausf. N. with 75mm gun.[2]

Gruppo Battaglioni CCNN M Tagliamento: *Console* Ermacora Zuliani
    LXIII Battaglione d'assalto M. (Udine Assault Battalion).
    LXXIX Battaglione d'assalto M. (Reggio Emilia Assault Battalion).
    XLI Battaglione d'armi d'accompagnamento M. (Trento Heavy Weapons Group)

Gruppo Battaglioni CCNN M Montebello: *Console* Roberto Gloria
    VI Battaglione d'assalto M. (Vigevano Assault Battalion).
    XXX Battaglione d'assalto M. (Novara Assault Battalion).
    XII Battaglione d'armi d'accompagnamento M. (XII Aosta Heavy Weapons Battalion).

Reggimento Artiglieria Valle Scrivia (Valle Scrivia Artillery Regiment):
Primo Seniore Franco Gallerani
    I Gruppo (First Artillery Group), 3 Batteries each with four Flak 37 88/56 guns, twenty 47mm guns, thirty-six 45mm mortars, and 81mm mortars.
    II *Gruppo* (Second Artillery Group). 3 Batteries each with four Flak 37 88/56 guns, twenty 47mm guns, thirty-six 45mm mortars, and 81mm mortars.
    Battaglione Guastatori. (Engineer Battalion)
    Reparto Misto Genio (Sappers Mixed Group):
    Compagnia artieri.
    Compagnia Telegrafisti.
    1ᵃ *Compagnia Radio Telegrafisti* (Radio Transmission Company).
    2ᵃ *Compagnia Radio Telegrafisti* (Radio Transmission Company).
    Nucleo Sanita' (Medical Services).
    Nucleo Sussistenza (Provisions unit).
    Ufficio Commissariato (Administrative unit).

On 3 July 1943, the M Division participated to a large-scale training exercise that was observed by the most senior officers of the High Command. Then on 10 July 1943 the unit carried out another full-scale rehearsal which was observed by the Duce, the head of *Comando Supremo* and several other high ranking officers of the Royal Army and the head of the MVSN. The war diary of the unit states that: "On the day the Allies landed in Sicily the unit carried out a very impressive training session with live fire exercises. The latter was exemplary demonstrating the great firepower that the M Division could unleash. Such firepower was so great with the new weapons and unprecedented and never seen before by any unit of the Italian Army."[3]

---

2   The self-propelled gun units where under the Leonessa but where tactically deployed with the artillery groups within the infantry battalions.
3   Cited in Stefano Fabei, *Tagliamento, La legione delle Camicie nere in Russia*, p. 129.

Deployment or no Deployment

On 14 July, *Comando Supremo* asked that the division be dispatched to the Salento region of southern Italy to move it away from Rome has it plotted with the Allies to switch sides, while Mussolini, who was still unaware of the plans of the King and *Comando Supremo* to seek a negotiated peace with the Allies, wanted to dispatch the unit to Sicily as fast as possible to use it to beef up Italian defenses. Both decisions, however, were opposed by the German training officers that maintained the unit was not ready and needed to train more, and by *Luogotenente Generale* Galbiati, who wanted to keep the unit near Rome. Ultimately the latter won the day and the M Division was kept near Rome, in Campagnaro to continue its training.

The military and the political situation then quickly precipitated. A few days later there was an Axis meeting in Feltre where General Ambrosio made an urgent request for military aid from Germany to help Italy against the Allies. Another request that was made was to recall all Italian troops deployed in the Balkans to Italy to be deployed against the Allies. On the day that the meeting was taking place over 400 Allied planes bombed Rome killing 3,000 civilians and injuring 10,000. It was then apparent that the Allies were determined to hit hard at the Axis forces in Italy as well as key infrastructure to force Italy to exit the war. In addition, to the bombing raids, the combined German Italian counterattack to push back the Allies from Sicily that was attempted on 11 July had failed forcing the Axis forces to give up even more terrain on the island. Even though the situation at the front was dire and called for emergency measures, the results of the Feltre meeting were inconclusive since the German High Command did not agree to dispatch additional military aid to Italy. In addition, no decision was made to seek a negotiated peace with the Soviet Union.

Facing a desperate situation at the front and with no additional aid forthcoming, the King and his advisers fast tracked a strategy to disengage Italy from the Axis alliance. The key to their plans was to overthrow the party and the regime and to disarm the militia. The attempt by the High Command to dismantle the militia in general but the M Division specifically can be gleaned from the memoirs of Marshal Badoglio which were written in 1946. In one of the passages Badoglio states:

> Generale Ambrosio had succeeded Marshal Cavallero in the position of Chief of Staff of Comando Supremo. Together we examined the situation and agreed that it was no longer possible to continue the war with Germany. We agreed that two were the goals to be achieved with extreme speed: the arrest of Mussolini and half a dozen of the most important party leaders and the neutralization of the Militia forces, especially the Armoured Division that was training near Rome.[4]

On the night of 24/25 July 1943 all the issues came to a head during the meeting of the Grand Council where Dino Grandi, a Blackshirt from the early days in the Emilia Romagna region, the birthplace of Fascism along with Milan, and the ex-foreign minister, proposed an order of the day to overthrow Mussolini. The Grand Council had not met for a few years, but Grandi, who was working closely with the King and his entourage, had asked for an emergency meeting.

---

4   Pietro Badoglio, *L'Italia nella seconda guerra mondiale* (Milan: Mondadori, 1946).

It had been granted by Mussolini and began on the early evening of 24 July. After a heated discussion, a majority (nineteen versus eight, with one abstention) voted in favor of Grandi's motion and the following day Mussolini was dismissed by the King who nominated Pietro Badoglio as the prime minister. The latter vowed publicly that Italy would continue to fight with the Axis, but behind the scenes there was an attempt almost immediately to arrive at a negotiated peace with the Allies.

Depoliticizing the M Division, the King and Badoglio took several pre-emptive measures prior to the dismissal of Mussolini. In fact, the overthrow of the regime was planned with detail and nothing was left to chance. The first initiative that was taken on 23 July was to move an armoured division (*Ariete II*) of the Royal Army near the base of the M Division and specifically stationed on the main road outside the barracks to block it inside its headquarters. This measure was taken to ensure that the M Division would not be able to leave the barracks in case it reacted to Mussolini's dismissal. A second initiative involved the moving away from Rome of some of the assault battalions such as the *Tagliamento* to break up the M Division. For instance, the plan was to move the two assault battalions of the *Tagliamento* to Puglia to guard military bases and airports from potential enemy paratrooper attacks. The third initiative involved the decapitation of the leadership of the M Division. In fact, Galbiati was arrested a few days after Mussolini was deposed and the other officers of the M Division were promoted and co-opted into the Royal Army. The fourth initiative was to rename the M Division and place it under the command of army officers loyal to the King.

The plans of the King and Badoglio to depoliticize the M Division and the MVSN were facilitated by the very cautious and prudent manner with which the heads of the MVSN reacted to the political change. When in fact they heard the news that a new government had been installed they pledged their allegiance to it vowing that the militia's charter was to serve both the regime and the monarchy.

Because of an agreement between Galbiati and Badoglio, on 26 July the commander of the M Division issued the following guidelines to his troops:

> First, all personnel of the M Division are required to stay in the barracks and at all costs should avoid clashing with civilians or with units of the Royal Army. Second, if any personnel are to leave the barracks to pick up supplies or for an emergency, it is preferable that they be accompanied by two or more soldiers. The soldiers should be armed with their rifle and well equipped with plenty of ammunition. Third, inside the barracks the soldiers are expected to behave as soldiers by keeping their composure in the face of such a grave situation and they should remain loyal to their officers. Discipline within the barracks must be maintained at all costs. Forth, the commanders, the officers and even the NCOs must persuade the soldiers to remain calm at all costs. Officers are to exert a firm degree of control over their troops.[5]

These guidelines, which essentially called on the soldiers of the M Division to stay put, were aimed to avoid any confrontation with the Royal Army or with civilians. The intent was to remain loyal to the new government and the rationale for this was that the latter had vowed

---

5   Cited in Stefano Fabei, *Tagliamento, La legione delle Camicie nere in Russia (1941-1943)*, p. 143.

to continue the war alongside the Axis partners and secondly because the militia had sworn a pledge of loyalty to both the regime and the monarchy in 1924. A secondary intent was to avoid any blood from being spilled avoiding a major confrontation between the MVSN and the Royal Army. A third motivation was that the unit had not terminated its training process. The three reasons that were given at the time to avoid a confrontation between the militia and the Royal Army were also reiterated during the post war when Galbiati published his memoirs. In this book, he reiterated that the M Division in July 1943 was not combat ready and that he had ordered it to remain in the barracks to avoid a confrontation or worse a civil war with the Royal Army.

The rank and file, however, reacted less cautiously to the news of the change of the government. Once the soldiers of the militia became aware of the latest political developments they immediately contacted the Germans of the 3rd *Panzer grenadier* Division which was also stationed near Rome. Both wowed to invade the capital and takeover key buildings and bloc main roads. The 16th Blackshirt Battalion, for instance, came out of its barracks located north of Rome and headed for city. But its attempt to alter the latest political development by way of a military intervention was short lived because it was shortly thereafter dissuaded from continuing by the intervention of the head of the MVSN.

The militia's lack of reaction after the fall of the regime has baffled military historians. Why didn't this well trained and equipped elite unit did not take up arms as the monarchy and the upper echelons of the Army and the police were attempting to overthrow the regime? Battistelli and Crociani provide the most accurate response to the question when they assert that:

> On 25 July 1943, the division had not yet reached operational status, which may explain why it did not react to these events. Nevertheless, the Italian Army staff naturally considered it completely unreliable, and took precautionary measures. Since, during the hiatus between Mussolini's downfall and the announcement of Italy's capitulation to the Allies, the units could not be disbanded without alarming the Germans, they were reorganized, with many MVSN officers being replaced by army ones.[6]

In August, the M Division unit was reorganized and renamed as the *Centauro* Division. Its MVSN officers assigned to other tasks, while a close relative of the King was placed at its head. By that time its training had also been halted. On 8 September 1943, the Badoglio government surrendered to the Allies and this precipitated major changes. Many of the Blackshirts units, including most soldiers from the old M Division, joined the German Army and took with them most of the equipment.

Ariete II

The day of the Italian surrender was also the day in which the last remaining and newly formed Italian armoured division was deployed in defense of Rome. On 1 April 1943, the last Italian armoured division (135th) was formed during the conflict and it took the name of *Ariete II*. It

---

6 Paolo Battistelli and Piero Crociani, *Italian Blackshirt* (Oxford: Ospey, 2016).

trained outside of Rome for several months before being deployed. Its core components came from the cavalry while its organization and equipment was qualitatively very different from *Ariete*.[7] First, it's tank battalions were mixed with each company being comprised of one tank and two *semoventi* companies, while *Ariete* had only one *semovente* company in 1942. This organization was first suggested in mid-1942 but it could not be implemented right away due to a lack of *semoventi da* 75/18. Second, it was comprised of much heavier artillery units such 105/25 guns instead of the 75mm units used in North Africa. Third, the tanks were the newly developed model M.15/42 which represented a slight improvement over Italian medium tanks deployed in North Africa. The division included: 8º RECO *Lancieri di Montebello* reconeisance group, DLVIII *Gruppo Semovente*, 10º *Reggimento Lancieri di Vittorio Emanuele* II, the 235º *Reggimento Artiglieria* and the CXXXV *Gruppo semovente*. In total, it could count upon 84 M.15/42 tanks, twelve command tanks, 94 *semoventi* da 75/18, twelve *semoventi* da 75/34 and twelve *semoventi M43 da* 105/25. The *semovente* da 75/34, for instance, represented an improvement over the 75/18 version having a 34-caliber long barrel gun with an effective range of 9514 yards.

Beginning on 8 September it fought against the German armour of 3rd *Panzergrandieren* and paratroopers which were approaching Rome from the north and aimed to seize government buildings and military installations. On the 8th it performed mainly reconnaissance duties at key intersections and military installations to prevent and bloc any potential enemy attempt to seize them. On the 9th an estimated German force of sixty armoured vehicles travelling on the Via Cassia was initially held up by the Italian artillery deployed at Pian delle Rose. The Germans waited for reinforcements and then resumed their offensive around 1115 but were confronted by *Ariete's II semoventi* which by opening a blistering fire forced the enemy to withdraw. At 1245 the Germans began to attack Italian positions in Bracciano provoking an extensive shooting match which was then called off when *Ariete*'s tanks counterattacked and drove the Germans back beyond the northern outskirts of Bracciano. By 1700 the Germans began taking defensive positions, while Italian tanks and *semoventi* were still deployed in Bracciano.

At night, the Italian command then ordered *Ariete* II, mainly a large column composed of tanks and motorized artillery plus other divisional units, to head towards Tivoli. The unexpected order forced unit redeployment unit away from the main area of operations. The overall losses suffered by the Germans on that day were 370 dead and wounded, 200 prisoners, 16 tanks destroyed, and 80 vehicles captured.

Final Considerations

The M and Ariete II divisions epitomize Italy's war effort during the Second World War in that they both represented an initiative that came in too little and too late. First, German equipment to arm the armoured divisions should have been secured much sooner and if this had happened the units that fought in North Africa could have accounted themselves better. Second, the M.15 tanks and the more advanced self-propelled artillery weapons should have also been deployed

---

7   Reggimento Lancieri di Vittorio Emanuele II in January 1942 was transformed into an armoured regiment to make up the core of a new armoured division (134th). A year later it was incorporated into *Divisione corazzata Ariete II*.

sooner and in greater numbers. One of the main factors that limited their production was the dispersal of Italian industry production on many obsolete vehicles in 1942 and 1943 when the *Semovente da* 47mm or light tanks or even the M.14 tanks, that by 1943 standards was already obsolete, should have been discontinued. This responsibility was primarily the result of political considerations (shielding domestic industry from foreign competition, keeping assembly lines fully employed, not pushing industry toward more effective weapon production, etc.) as well as the domestic industry's refusal to adapt to new circumstances and defending its turf at all costs.

Conclusion

How can we measure or compare military effectiveness and specifically the deployment of the Italian armoured divisions during the Second World War? As mentioned in the introduction, the benchmark to assess the performance of the armoured units is the technical term military effectiveness coined by military historians and its measure, especially in relation to the North African campaign, is the ability to wage combined arms maneuver warfare. Therefore, on the one hand we must look at the tactics themselves and whether they enabled the army to wage an all arms, mobile campaign against the Allies. On the other hand, we must also determine the capacity, measured by looking at such factors as tactical leadership, industrial prowess, technical know-how and innovation, quality of weapons and the ability of the military-industrial complex to transport supply and weapons to the front, to gauge how effective the war machine really was.

Let's start by the main critiques against military effectiveness of the Italian armoured units as summarized by MacGregor Knox:

> The Italian armoured division was similarly uncompetitive, especially considering that the Italian M14 main battle tank had half the weight and a fraction of the firepower and the off-road speed of Grant and Sherman tanks that British units in the desert received in increasing numbers in 1942.
>
> The Ariete had been even more deficient when originally deployed in North Africa in February-March 1941; initially its only tanks had been a doomed regiment of 3.5 tons L3 tankettes and it received no armoured cars until mid-1942.[1]

He then argues regarding a combined arms approach that:

> The Italian mobile units that accompanied Rommel in his desert peregrinations learned far more quickly than the British the lesson that armour, artillery and infantry must function as a team both operationally and tactically. The German example was decisive, but Italian doctrine, precisely because its authors had never heard of the work of the British all-tank theorists, was already predisposed toward integration.[2]

---

1 MacGregor Knox, *Hitler's Italian Allies*, pp. 125-126.
2 Ibid, p. 154.

Two points are worth mentioning. First, obsolete equipment, in MacGregor Knox's view, played a big part in holding the Italians back in North Africa while tactics improved over time also thanks to the German example. Some weapons over time did lag and become obsolete because of the delays by industry in innovating its models and building better weapons. While in some limited cases the equipment fielded in North Africa did improve over time but always in limited numbers. From a tactical perspective the deployment of both armoured units and infantry did improve over time and in some cases tactics improved probably more than MacGregor Knox gives the armoured units credit for. But let's examine one by one the factors that enabled or impeded military effectiveness. They include tactics, capabilities (including equipment and training/personnel), leadership, military planning, technical innovation and lastly supply.

Tactics: While the Italian armoured divisions of the Second World War had several flaws mainly in equipment and training they fought with some degree of effectiveness in North Africa after Beda Fomm and less so in the early campaigns against France and Greece due to inhospitable terrain. Their performance improved during the course of the war primarily because of three main factors such as improved training, learning and adaptation in the trial by combat experience and lastly a general increase in the number and firepower of its artillery arm.

The first campaign of the Italian armoured units in the French Alps did not prove a worthy battleground for the tank crews which found themselves advancing against narrow and uphill mountain roads that were utterly unsuited for tank warfare. The tanks in France were used sporadically and in the few instances in which they were deployed, they fought in a difficult terrain and against prepared defenses that proved to be almost insurmountable obstacles for the crews. Similarly, in Greece the few medium and the mostly light tanks deployed fought in a very rocky, uphill environment that prevented them from maneuvering at will. In addition, Italian tanks found it very difficult to advance past streams or small rivers, or to advance at all on certain days where the downpours and the mud idled the vehicles and forced them to the sidelines. Most importantly, the French and Greek campaigns demonstrated that it was almost impossible for the tanks, even for the light tanks that had been designed for that purpose, to maneuver in very difficult mountainous terrain while taking on prepared defenses equipped with heavy artillery. In contrast, in East Africa, the first Italian offensive against the British forces was more successful. The campaign saw the Italian tanks advance in a relatively fast moving operation ahead of the infantry and supported by bombers and fighter planes against the enemy defenses. This first round against the forces of the Commonwealth was a success as the Italians struck early and by surprise. But ultimately the armour there was not only scarce but it demonstrated how inadequate it was when faced by a British counterattack led by heavy Matilda II heavy tanks which led to the destruction of the Duca d'Aosta's forces. The campaign demonstrated the inadequacy of Italian tank production which could not deploy a heavy infantry tank in time to face the British counterattack, as well as the Italian artillery inability to properly stop the enemy tanks with vintage First World War guns and 47mm anti-tank guns. The Yugoslavian campaign was more successful as the tanks units made a wide sweeping maneuver that led to the encirclement and ultimate surrender of the enemy troops. It was conducted in both hilly and on paved and non-paved roads and it was a terrain that was somewhat like the Po' Valley region of Italy where the armoured troops had conducted several drills before the war. For historian John Sweet, this was by far the most successful operation conducted by Italian tanks in the Second World War and it demonstrated that when the tanks units, especially the light L tanks, were deployed in operations that were well planned and that faced primarily infantry and not tanks, as per the original design, they could succeed.

After Graziani's attack on Sidi Barrani, the North Africa campaign became the biggest and most important theatre of operations for the Italian armour. Initially in the winter of 1940-41 a hastily dispatched and trained armoured force did not perform well and could not stop the Commonwealth counteroffensive. But in the spring of 1941 things began to change. What turned the North Africa campaign around in early 1941? First and foremost, the arrival of *Generalleutnant* Rommel, a relatively unknown German senior officer until then, and his DAK. The latter in fact propped up the Italian position and then countered the Commonwealth forces with a swift and very successful operation. Although Rommel lacked a comprehensive understanding of the strategic aspects of the campaign, he distinguished himself for his tactical boldness and his intuitive feel for the battlefield.[3] Italian troops learned a lot of new things by fighting alongside the DAK. As the two faced multiple engagements with the enemy, Italian tactics improved over time. The second factor was the arrival of *Ariete*, a factor often not recognized or dismissed by many historians[4], which fought well during Rommel's major counterattacks against the Commonwealth army. In fact, although DAK was a major factor, the evolution of the Italian forces, and especially its armoured forces and its motorized artillery, in North Africa helped the Axis to achieve its successes between 1941-1942. At first *Ariete* could not fight as one division because of its piecemeal deployment and since it was necessarily weaker than the standard British or German armoured division by the lack of medium tanks and guns. During the first offensive in Cyrenaica, for example, *Ariete* was still primarily equipped with light tanks and its units were split up to form ad hoc combat groups with German units all under Rommel's operational command. But later during Operation Crusader, when *Ariete* was fully staffed and equipped with over 100 medium tanks, it fought independently of the Germans for extended periods of time. Its first real battle that it fought as an autonomous division was the clash at Bir el Gobi I against the British armour. In that battle *Ariete* accounted itself well and managed to destroy or damage up to fifty-five enemy tanks. Both the tanks crews, the mobile artillery and the motorized *Bersaglieri* units conducted a skillful tactical mobile operation that broke up the attack by the 7th Armoured Division and ultimately led to the surrounding of the enemy tank units. *Ariete*'s success at Bir el Gobi I was one of the factors that foiled the Commonwealth counter-offensive and helped to achieve the drastic reduction in enemy armoured combat power during the first phase of Operation Crusader.

Then in mid- 1942 *Ariete* had further success. By then it was deployed within the XX Army Corps which was modelled against the standard German mechanized and motorized army corps and its units comprised several all arms subunits that were highly autonomous and self-sustaining some of which were called *Raggruppamenti* and often took the name from their commander. "Another feature of Italian organization which is worthy of mention is the passion for forming "raggruppamenti," or groups. This is a method of providing, for instance, a headquarters and administrative detachment for various independent batteries of artillery which are meant to operate together. Another example is provided by such formations as the "Raggruppamento Celere Africa Settentrionale" or "RACAS" (North Africa Mobile Group)

---

3   Martin_Blumenson, *Kasserine Pass* (New York: Houghton Mifflin, 1967).
4   James J. Sadkovich, 'Of Myths and Men: Rommel and the Italians in North Africa,1940-1942', *International History Review*, vol. 13, n. 2, May 1991.

which is a force of armoured cars, mechanized infantry, portee guns and light tanks. The use of "raggruppamenti" is evidence of the Italian bent for improvisation and the desire to break the back of a rigid system of tables of organization."[5]

These units, which were the norm in the German forces under Rommel, comprised tactically self-sufficient mechanized units with mobile artillery, tanks, motorized infantry, reconnaissance and anti-aircraft and anti-tank units, while other units, primarily consisting of motorized infantry, also included a few tanks, reconnaissance vehicles, mobile artillery, and anti-tank units. The combat groups served the Italian Army well in North Africa in a highly mobile theater were mobility, unit all arms self-sufficiency and good reconnaissance to preempt enemy movements were essential factors of the campaign. These groups evolved over time and only reached a certain maturity in mid-1942 reflecting Rommel's intention that his whole force would be comprised of task oriented self-contained combat groups. It was the combination of adopting new tactics as well as the numerous reinforcements especially in the artillery arm (self-propelled guns, heavy anti-tank guns, larger numbers of 47mm and 75mm guns, and some German assistance) that led to the improved performance and to more unpredictable combat methods which has the American report above demonstrates could cause considerable trouble for the enemy troops facing them. For example, *XX Corpo' d'Armata* anti-tank guns and *semovente* assault guns faced by a sudden attack engaged on 10 June 1942 approximately forty (US-built Grant tanks and British Crusader tanks) near Bir Hacheim at close range. These weapons damaged/destroyed twenty of the British tanks and forced the remainder to retreat. This is an example of the performance of Italian armoured troops fighting more effectively and a far cry from the untrained Italian units of 1940. Such a performance would not have been possible in 1940 when the Italians were short on armoured tactics and anti-tank weapons. A few days before that battle encounter the Italian armoured corps had overrun a Commonwealth fortified position capturing a high number of enemy troops and on 5-6 June they had helped foil a major enemy counterattack beating it back with artillery and tanks, while inflicting high casualties. As Nicola Pignato correctly observes: "The Italian armoured troops' parity in equipment quality diminished as the North African campaign progressed, especially after the DAK's arrival in early 1941. Italian crews were no less aggressive than their German allies, but Italian armoured vehicles were increasingly underpowered and outgunned by their Allied counterparts

In compensation for the mediocre tanks armed with anti-tank and self-propelled guns that provided most of the hitting power of the Italian armoured corps. By mid-1942, for example, *Ariete*'s artillery strength had been significantly increased with respect to what was available in 1940. Then after the Gazala battles *Littorio* also was deployed in North Africa further reinforcing the XX *Corpo d'Armata*. Albeit *Littorio* was still equipped with the M series medium tanks, both *Littorio* and *Trieste* Divisions had been significantly reinforced with regard to mobile artillery and to anti-tank guns. Even though the Italian crews fought well at the final battle of El Alamein their units *Ariete, Trieste* and *Littorio* were literally shot to pieces by waves of heavier medium tanks such as Grant and Sherman vehicles. During that difficult and complex battle, Italian armoured units fought within the limitations of their equipment. Even at El Alamein the lionshare of the individual successes in some of the engagements against the Commonwealth

---

5   "Notes on Italian Organization," Military Intelligence Service, War Department, *Tactical and Technical Trends,* Number 26, 3 June 1943.

forces was the result of the deployment of its mobile artillery and its self-propelled guns although in the end these weapons could not compensate for the enemy superiority.

Throughout the Tunisian campaign the Italians fielded just one armoured division that for several months defended the Axis left flank. With a tank force of approximately fifty medium tanks and less than, twenty *semoventi*, *Centauro* fought first to occupy key Tunisian towns and bases from the threatening eastern movements of American troops moving from Algeria. Once these positions were secured *Centauro* then participated to several successful operations. Its highpoint was at Kasserine Pass, where *Centauro* Division tank units and *bersaglieri* executed together with the German forces Rommel's brilliant counterstroke and took part in the last Axis victory of the North African campaign. In Sicily, the armoured counter-attacks conducted by the hopelessly outmatched Italian crews equipped primarily with vintage 1940 tanks slowed down the pace of the seaborne landings but they could not stop them. Thus, despite their limitations Italian armoured units did fight effectively at times.

Personnel and Training

The change in performance over time was also the result of the introduction of elite units that were not combat ready in 1940 and that carried out in 1941-43 some of the key fighting during the campaign. This was also an evolutionary process that saw Graziani's poorly trained, infantry-based Army being gradually replaced with the arrival of the *Bersaglieri*, which were elite, mostly motorized, infantry units, the armoured elite units such as *Ariete, Littorio and Centauro* followed by specialized mobile artillery detachments and finally by the paratroops of *Folgore* Division and the motorized commando units.[6] All of these were elite units which did some of the heavy lifting during the campaign in North Africa and were responsible for some of the major Italian successes. *Ariete*'s elite status, for example, was based primarily upon two factors such as its coming together close to full strength as a combat unit before all the other armoured units and its continuous focus upon training. *Tenente* Enrico Serra in this regard states that the troops adapted to the campaign thanks to several factors one of the most important being training: "One of the great merits of our commander *Tenente Colonnello* Enrico Maretti and the battalion commanders *Capitani* Urso, Casale and Buttafuochi was that they utilized the time for the extensive training of the tank crews deployed in combat. In fact, for several reasons the initial training received in Italy was not sufficient, not organic and overall it was poor."[7]

With regard to Italian combat performance in general during the war Bastian Matteo Scianna has argued that it improved over time through a process of adaptation: "We should, therefore, understand the Italians' attempts at reform as corresponding to a general impetus operating within armies at war: battlefield lessons and new weapons constantly force them to adapt, while training 'on the job' creates new dynamics."[8] *Trieste* Division experience in North Africa is a good case of adaptation during the course of the campaign by trimming manpower, bringing

---

6   Greene and Massignani assert that: "There is a theory that most of the combat in World War II was performed by the elite units, while the regular units simply did not measure up to the same degree…. The Italian army's successes and failures in World War II reflect this theory well." Jack Greene and Alessandro Massignani, *Rommel's North Africa Campaign*, p. 19.
7   Enrico Serra, *Tempi duri* (Rome: Mondadori, 2010), p. 21.
8   Bastian Matteo Scianna, *The Italian War on the Eastern Front, 1941–1943: Operations, Myths and Memories*, p. 85.

in more heavy guns and increasing its rate of motorization. During Operation Crusader, for example, Gambara remarked that *Trieste* was still essentially a continental infantry division with not enough trucks and lacking self-propelled guns it was always vulnerable to an enemy tank attack especially when fighting autonomously.[9] Based on this assessment in early 1942 the division was reorganized. The soldiers were then trained by adopting some of the tactics used by the British Commandos while basing the subunits' reorganization upon the structural model set by the German Panzergrenadiers. Under this new organization, for example, *Trieste* fought effectively in mid-1942 displaying a tactical maturity based on a combination of flanking and frontal attacks supported by artillery and mobile forces. *Trieste*, most likely, would have fought more effectively if equipped with more tanks and self-propelled guns that could have occupied the terrain on behalf of the infantry helping it to advance at a faster pace.

This concept of adaptation can be readily illustrated with the anti-tank defense. In 1940 it was based almost exclusively on the static field guns and 47mm guns. Then, given the lack of guns and their limited caliber and mobility, the troops began to experiment with truck mounted guns such as the 100/17 howitzer which performed well during Operation Crusader. Then, finally in mid-1942, the high point of the Italian units in North Africa, the armoured units received self-propelled guns, heavier caliber anti-tank guns, and some German anti-tank guns, which were put to good use and the keys to their successes.

Equipment
During the campaign there was a considerable amount of improvement especially with regard to the weapons of the artillery arm which allowed the Italian troops to be able to deal with the significant strengthening of the enemy armoured units equipped with American and British medium and heavy tanks. The same cannot be said for the armour, especially medium tanks which was the main combat weapon of the mechanized units. In mid-1942, for example, *Ariete* had for the most part the same type of medium tanks as in early 1941 but its artillery arm had been equipped with twenty self-propelled guns (*Semoventi da 75/18*), eight *Cannoni da 90/53*, forty-two 47mm anti-tank guns, thirty-two 75mm artillery pieces and some 105mm guns. Later also some German 88mm anti-tank guns were also deployed. If we compare the anti-tank and mobile gun strength in mid-1942 with respect to what the division had at its disposal in 1940 or in the spring of 1941, we can understand how the anti-tank defense underpinned *XX Corpo d'Armata* favorable engagements at Gazala, Tobruk and beyond.

"All Italian divisions in Africa were drastically reorganized in the spring of 1942. The main features of the reorganization are increased artillery and the inclusion of support and antitank weapons within the framework of infantry units."[10] The end result of these three factors (training, trial by combat and improved artillery) led to a marked improvement at the tactical level. The armoured units by relying upon the German combined arms model, evolved and improved after Beda Fomm as they adopted mixed combat units comprised of reconnaissance teams, a tank battalion, a special motorized infantry battalion and an artillery battalion endowed with both anti-aircraft and anti-tank capabilities. All arms combat groups were not well developed during the first year of the war lacking effective training and weapons. Here the German influence was

---

9   Mario Montanari, *Le operazioni in Africa settentrionale*, vol.III, Part I, p. 431.
10 'Notes on Italian Organization', Military Intelligence Service, War Department, *Tactical and Technical Trends*, Number 26, 3 June 1943.

very pronounced especially after the spring of 1941 when divisions such as the *Ariete* began to receive better and more equipment (medium tanks, self-propelled guns, heavy guns and proper reconnaissance vehicles). Some examples of the new tactics include the use of deception by making believe that the armoured units were about to withdraw and then deploying the heavy guns forward against an expected enemy tank counter-attack, being just one of the tactics used by the Italians in their repertoire. Another one was the use of self-propelled guns, anti-tank guns and mobile artillery in forward positions and as a concerted maneuvered fire to stop an enemy attack or to support the medium tanks as they probed the flanks of the enemy lines. Another was the ability to fight at night and especially when the motorized infantry and artillery together with the armour had to deal with enemy armour. Night fighting, which was not developed at all during the early stages of the campaign, enabled the armoured corps to deal effectively with the Allied tank units. Despite the improved tactics made possible by the new weapons, two factors continued to influence in a negative way the performance of these units such as a lack of radio communications and the relatively slower moving Italian vehicles. Both were singled out by Rommel and his commanders during Operation Crusader as obstacles to becoming more mobile and agile combat units. Both would continue to plague the Italian units until the end of the conflict.

The bright spots within the mechanized forces were the self-propelled gun, the improvised ones and then the more modern mobile anti-tank guns, and the armoured vehicles. The self-propelled gun suited the Army's longtime belief that mobile artillery was the best antitank weapon. In addition, it could also be employed as mobile artillery to punch holes in enemy lines to be exploited by the infantry and tanks. Further, the self-propelled guns fit well with the Army's artillery doctrine, *fuoco di manovra*, which called for the employment of massed antitank guns and field artillery fire close to the front.

Another weapon that was highly rated by both Italian and German troops was the *Cannone da 90/53* which was used in to engage ground targets at extended distances and could also be used to engage fighter aircraft. It was one of the innovative weapons introduced by the Italians during the war which was used to bolster the armoured divisions. As Rottman asserts the *Cannone da 90/53* was overshadowed during the war by the much more famous German Flak 88mm gun, but it was equally effective. "Some of the credit given to the 'eighty-eights' as a deadly long-range tank-killer in North Africa actually goes to the superficially similar Italian cannone da 90/53. This 90mm antiaircraft gun was one of the better Italian weapons …"[11] The AB armoured vehicles series also played an important role in refining armoured corps tactics providing more speed and mobility especially to the reconnaissance function.

One of the weakest components of Italian equipment remained the armour. Whereas the Italian medium tank series remained competitive against the British tanks up until the end of 1941, these weapons became obsolete in 1942. They remained effective only when charging against enemy infantry positions up until mid-1942 as in the opening stages of Operation Venezia, when the Commonwealth troops were still primarily equipped with two-pdr guns. But once the British infantry and anti-gun units were strengthened with greater numbers of six-pdr guns and once their armoured units could field large numbers of Grant, Sherman and other heavier tanks the M series tanks were totally outclassed and could no longer go head to head

---

11   Gordon L. Rottman, *The Big Book of Gun Trivia* (New York: Bloomsbury Publishing, 2013), p. 236.

against the British units. The failure to introduce the P-40 tank in time, or of not producing enough anti-tank weapons and *semoventi* to compensate for the medium tank weaknesses and the protectionist industrial policy that denied the purchase or the manufacture of German or other tanks, were all factors that forced the tanks crews to fight with obsolete vehicles well into mid-1943.

> **The Rommel Myth and the Italians: Rival Interpretations**
>
> During the immediate post war period two historians such as Desmond Young and Basil Liddell Hart constructed the 'Rommel Myth.' In their view, Rommel was a masterful armoured warfare tactician as well as a first-rate army corps commander. Basil Liddell Hart for example writes: "In Rommel's case they were combined. While the theory of blitzkrieg, the new super mobile style of warfare with armoured and motorized forces, had been conceived in England, long before he came on the stage, the quickness with which he grasped it and the way he developed it showed his fresh mindedness and innate conceptive power. He became next to Guderian, the leading exponent of the new idea. That was the more remarkable because he had no experience of tanks until given command of the 7th Panzer Division in February 1940 and then had less than three months to study the theory and master the problem handling such forces before he was launched into action."
>
> In constructing the 'Rommel myth' both historians used the 'Rommel Papers' as a basis for studying the campaign in North Africa, often without challenging it critically. In their view, Rommel was a great general producing relevant outcomes while struggling to overcome the weaknesses of his Italian allies and the lack of support from Berlin. This view, which still permeates several contemporary historical accounts of the campaign not only is factually incorrect regarding aspects of the conflict, but also has largely ignored the role that the Italians played in Axis victories in North Africa. Historian James J. Sadkovich provides a very different interpretation of the North African campaign to rebalance the respective roles of German and Italian forces:
>
>> I consider Rommel's impact on the Axis war effort in the Mediterranean to have been problematic. His drive on Egypt in 1942 certainly made the loss of North Africa inevitable by overloading Italian logistical systems and frittering away the forces assembled for Operation C/3. The wastage of Axis units on the Eastern front also played a part; a half million Italian, Hungarian, Romanian, and Slovak troops were lost at Stalingrad, depriving Germany of the support of its "minor" allies on the Eastern front. Both the war in the East and the failure to take Malta, of course, can be laid at Germany's door, as can the failure to secure use of Tunisia's ports, a failure that made the occupation of Malta all but mandatory if the Axis were to secure their seaborne supply routes to North Africa. The importance of occupying Malta and the folly of advancing on Egypt with exhausted troops whose air cover and logistical support dwindled the farther they advanced were apparent to the Italians, but not to the Germans. By late June, Rommel's six Italian divisions – Ariete, Littorio, Brescia, Pavia, Trento, and Sabratha – had only 8,100 men, thirty-four tanks, and 240 guns; his German units a few thousand infantry and ninety tanks. On 20 June, Mussolini and Ugo Cavallero urged Hitler to support

> the seizure of Malta rather than approve another offensive in Cyrenaica. They argued that the time was right to do so because earlier that month Italian and German air and naval forces had interdicted a convoy bound for the island and had sunk a cruiser, five destroyers, a minesweeper, and six merchantmen, and damaged a number of other British vessels. Rommel's offensive had already delayed the landings, and Mussolini and Cavallero were worried that if the island was not taken in August, the Italian navy would be unable to oppose future British convoys, owing to a lack of fuel oil.
>
> Source: James J. Sadkovich, "Rebuttal to Bagnasco Q&A," Global War Studies.

Leadership, Industrial Capability, Technical Innovation and Supply

Leadership

Examination of other factors such as leadership, industrial capacity, technical innovation, and the ability to transport supply to the front to gauge how well the war machine supported the combined arms tactics at the front.

Leadership of the armoured forces was ineffectual during Graziani's tenure in North Africa as the mechanized forces did not coordinate their attacks and committed the armour in a piecemeal fashion. While it is said that Graziani suffered from a crisis during the British counteroffensive, both Babini and Maletti were experienced armoured commanders, who had not only commanded armoured units prior to the North African campaign, but also had a long career within the armoured units. At the time of Operation Compass both had assumed important command positions in North Africa but did not enjoy the kind of organizational support that was made available to the commanders of the *Ariete* and the CAM in 1941. Leadership was improved with the arrival of the *Ariete* Division and with the formation of the armoured corps, because divisional and regimental commanders, who had experience leading mechanized units, now could rely on a trained officer staff under their command. The various commanders of the Italian armoured corps such as Baldassarre, De Stefanis etc..came to North Africa with more and better trained HQ and regimental staff. Better trained officers and NCOs led both the CAM and the XX *Corpo d'Armata*, to operate more effectively helped by the focus that senior officers at the regimental and battalion level placed upon training and adopting new tactics. The decision-making process was also streamlined when the army corps was formed placing one commander and his staff at the head of all the armoured and motorized units deployed in the theatre. Then later there was a further reorganization with the formation of the combined German and Italian *Panzerarmee* that placed under one commander the entire Axis mechanized and motorized force. Ultimately, by further streamlining the decision-making process under one Axis commander further improvement was made to the combat performance of the armoured and mechanized units, while certain limitations within the Italian formations persisted.

Industrial Planning and innovation

Another factor to consider is industry's contribution to the war whereby the latter supported by the government and the military establishment produced the weapons the Army requested and also improved the efficacy of its equipment over time. Not meeting production targets remained a limiting factor for Italian industry for the duration of the war and most part due to a host of factors such as lack of raw materials and energy feedstocks, outdated assembly lines, work stoppages, Allied bombardments of factories and uneven technical development. In addition, Italian purchasing practices and a strong and perhaps too close relationship between industry and the military and especially the ministry shielded the national industry from competition and stifled technical innovation.

For example, in contrast to Finland or Hungary, the Italian Army failed to use significant numbers of superior German armoured vehicles during the war while favoring the domestic production of Italian designed tanks and self-propelled guns. While the Italian Royal Army use and adoption of German tanks was extremely limited, other German allies relied much more heavily on equipment made for the German Army. The Hungarian army, for instance, made widespread use of large numbers of *Panzerkampfwagen* III, while the Finnish army deployed many German self-propelled guns. German support was offered to the Italians but in a more indirect way granting to domestic manufacturers the license to produce German tanks. These offers that were made between 1941-43 came with several caveats such as the purchase of raw materials from Germany which limited their appeals to the Italian authorities which feared that Germany would in essence control large swaths of Italian industry. Apart from governmental fears of undo German influence on Italian affairs, the domestic monopolies of Fiat and Ansaldo also played their part in ensuring that German tanks would not be produced in Italy. Fearing the potential loss of their hold on military commissions both Fiat and Ansaldo lobbied government not to approve the opening up of factories to produce German tanks and instead relaunched the P-40 heavy tank as an alternative. For both political and economic reasons the German offer of assistance was thus refused and the domestic industry retained its hold on tank and engine production.[12] This decision led to the production of an obsolete 15 tons medium tank in 1943 when the Allies were fielding medium tanks weighing 30 tons or more. If the Italian armoured units had been equipped with a combination of German medium tanks and self-propelled guns made in Italy, for example, it is likely that they would have performed better in North Africa making a greater contribution to the Axis war effort overall. This outcome would also have freed up Fiat and Ansaldo to produce more self-propelled guns and anti-tank guns per month which would have aided the war effort. The gap in mid-1942 between the M tanks and the Grants and Shermans would have been considerably narrowed by the adoption of the *Panzerkampfwagen III* or even the IV. Even though German tanks would have allowed the Italian units to increase their firepower, the limited amount of production coming out of the Italian plants, along with Germany's weakened economic base, would have still relegated Italy to one of the most modest armoured forces of the war. Its sheer production output would have still limited the armoured unit's potential to at best replace destroyed or damaged vehicles. Of all the major combatants in fact, the Italian Army was behind most other combatants in the volume assembly of new tanks and self-propelled guns. For example, the 1942 production quotas are very telling. While the Italians in 1942 produced 667 tanks, the British produced 8,611 and the Americans 14,000. This enormous gap within Allied monthly quota production was never narrowed at any stage during the war for a host of reasons but mainly because of the weaker economic base.

---

12   As Knox asserts: "Ultimately this course was not chosen, possibly due to the monopoly (duopoly) that Fiat and Ansaldo had on tank construction." MacGregor Knox, *Hitler Italian Allies*, p. 126.

Production quotas alone do not relate the entire story. Technical innovation during the war was another key factor that is well illustrated by a comparison between the Italian and the British industrial base. For example, Beale states that in 1941 British tanks were not suitable for blitzkrieg armoured warfare that was necessary to conduct the campaign in North Africa.[13]

The British official history states that General Wavell, in spring of 1941, had misgivings about launching a major offensive because he maintained that British armour was inferior both from a technological and armament point of view to German armour. The lack a of successful outcome of Operation Battleaxe would then become one of the factors to force improvement in British tank production. "The British armoured cars had proved very vulnerable to air attack and were out-gunned and out-paced by the heavy German cars; this was a great handicap in the fight for information. The 'I' tanks were too slow for the armoured battle in the desert and yet were vulnerable to the larger German antitank guns. The cruisers, a little faster than the German mediums, were too liable to breakdowns."[14] Unlike the Italians that did not have the quantities of raw materials and the mass production capabilities of the Allies as well their higher quality engines, the British were quick upon to seize on the fact that in the heat of war, it was paramount to produce new, more powerful armoured weapons quickly.

As a result of this transformation British industry and its government would then introduce the Crusader tanks, upgraded Valentine tanks, a series of self-propelled guns and most importantly purchase American tanks such as large quantities of Grant and Sherman tanks. In essence, the British brought about technological innovation by producing better tanks domestically and by relying upon American support as the war progressed.[15] The Italians in contrast, suffered tremendously from their original sin and refused to look abroad for help (Skoda or Germany). The relative lack of firepower and durability of Italian armour stemmed from the initiation of hostilities long before the planned expansion of the *Regio Esercito* was complete. A crisis that was accentuated by the limitations of the Italian economy and by desultory planning during the war. These factors led to a failure to introduce a combat medium tank that represented a vast improvement from the M.13/40 or M.14/41 tanks (which were comparable to the Cruiser tank of 1940-41 or the Crusader series) and also, given the lethargy of its domestic industry which failed to introduce the P-40 tank in a timely manner. Therefore, while the domestic industry could not keep up with developments in tank design after mid-1941, its armoured forces found themselves outgunned and outranged by the British/Commonwealth armoured units. The P-40 heavy tank, for instance, which was built with very thick armour based on the design of the Russian T-34 tank, was fielded far too late to affect the outcome of the conflict. It's likely that if it had arrived sooner, the P-40 tank could have given the Italian tank crews more leverage in the tank to tank engagements with British crews.

It was not only new tanks that were rushed into service but the British also rushed into combat the self-propelled Bishop howitzer when they were in dire need of mobile artillery. This was basically a Valentine tank with a new, much larger turret sporting a 25-pdr cannon. The weapon was not as effective as originally thought to be leading British industry then to turn to a quick fix solution. By October/November 1942 it introduced an improved self-propelled gun,

---

13　Paul Beale, *Death by Design* (London: Stroud, 1988).
14　*The Mediterranean & Middle East: The Germans Come to the Aid of Their Ally, 1941* <http://www.ibiblio.org/hyperwar/UN/UK/UK-Med-II/UK-Med-2-8.html> (accessed on 12 December 2021).
15　James Buckley, *British Armour in the Normandy Campaign* (London: Routledge, 2006).

the U.S.-made 105 M7, dubbed the Priest. This proved to be an excellent weapon and the British government requested the FDR administration to supply 5,500 of these weapons. The order was never completed in full by the end of 1943, but the British figure of actual guns received was several times greater to the less than 700 self-propelled guns manufactured by the Italians between 1941 to mid-1943. That number alone shows why the Italian armoured formations, without greater German support, were never in a condition to succeed in North Africa.

Text Box 11: British Versus Italian key Tanks

Matilda I and II 2,908 units produced during the war.	No Comparable Italian tank 1940-1943
Maximum weight 26.7 tons	
Maximum armour 78mm	
Gun 2 pounder	
Maximum range 160 miles	
Crusader 4,917 built	M.13/40 (M.14/41), 1,405 built
Maximum weight 20	Maximum weight 14.5 tons
Gun 2 and 6 pounders	Gun 47/32
Maximum armour 66	Maximum armour 42mm
Maximum range 100 miles	Maximum range 200 km
Cruiser Mark IV 890 produced	M.11/39 100 units produced
Maximum weight 14.75	Maximum weight 11 tons
Gun 2 pounder	Gun 37/40
Maximum armour 30 mm	Maximum armour 30mm
Maximum range 90 miles	Maximum range 210 km

Thus, sheer numbers also point to the fact that Italy could never have played a greater role during the war given its lack of a comparable industrial base of production to the Allies. As John Sweet asserts by mid-1942 only a modest improvement in the number of armoured divisions was achieved: "The Italians only made a small increase in the total number of divisions capable of being used in modern war."[16]

Sadkovich makes the opposite argument by stating that armour would not have been effective in Italy's campaigns against France or Greece. "Even had Italy created an elite mechanized force of fifteen divisions, they would have been of little use in Albania, Yugoslavia, the French Alps, or Ethiopia, where the bulk of the Italian army operated in 1940 and early 1941."[17] But ultimately more and improved armoured vehicles could have been critical during the early stages

---

16   John Timothy Sweet, *Iron Arm*, p. 159.
17   James J. Sadkovich, 'Some Considerations Regarding Italian Armoured Doctrine Prior to June 1940', p. 63.

of the North African campaign where an early invasion of Egypt by Balbo or by Graziani supported by medium tanks and *semoventi* could have produced better results. This was ultimately Italy's main theater of operations and where some of its major forces were concentrated. In fact, Italy's best chances in North Africa where primarily tied to an early, swift and sudden invasion of Egypt and the concurrent neutralization of Malta as argued by Christie in Fallen Eagles: "The operational plan Marshal Graziani and his staff should have developed was for a two-phase invasion, utilizing Italian mechanized doctrine, based on the forces available to him. This plan would have called for the stripping of all trucks from the Italian V Army and using just arriving M.11 medium tanks as the main mechanized striking force."[18] For this to happen successfully Graziani's Army would have also needed tank transporters, self-propelled guns and mobile artillery which were necessary for a large scale offensive.

In North Africa, once the Commonwealth began to build up its forces with Operation Compass and then Crusader and then following the arrival of American troops in North Africa in 1943, Italy's chances to succeed became slimmer and slimmer. Italy's limited armoured force along with opposition in Germany to substantially strengthening Rommel's DAK at critical junctures of the campaign meant that at best the Axis forces had the combat strength to retain control of Tripolitania and recapture parts of Cyrenaica.

Technical Innovation

As historian David French asserts, "The story of tank development during the Second World War illustrated a large truth. Armies in combat developed a dialectical relationship. Improvements in design by one side served only to encourage the other to redouble its own efforts to produce something better or to find other ways to nullify the enemy's advantage. In general and measured in terms of weapons, German mortars, machine guns, artillery and anti-tank guns were probably more destructive than their American and British counterparts, although in the T-34 the Soviets undoubtedly possessed the war's best medium tank."[19]

The Italian effort demonstrates the validity of the dialectical relationship, but only with regard to some of the equipment furnished to the troops. After being on the losing end of confrontations in the winter of 1940 when the Italians faced the heavier infantry tanks and in November 1941 the Crusader tanks during Operation Crusader they had to improvise with makeshift self-propelled artillery. This produced a number of mobile guns and howitzers that gave the armoured and motorized units a greater punch and made possible certain successful battlefield victories while facing much improved enemy equipment and vehicles. The successful utilization of such weapons and the feedback received from the field allowed industry to introduce more long term solutions to the anti-tank defense. Beginning in the spring of 1942 the self-propelled 75mm gun was introduced to better serve the troops. Similarly, the 90mm self-propelled gun was developed and introduced fairly quickly to face the T-34 tank in the Eastern front and the heavier British tanks in North Africa. Both examples point to some innovative solutions to address specific needs of the frontline units. While these solutions were viable with existing Italian engines, for the self-propelled guns because they had a low profile and

---

18   Major Howard Christie, *Fallen Eagles: The Italian 10th Army in the Opening Campaign in the Western Desert*, p. 210.
19   David French, 'Fighting Power' in Richard Overy, *The Oxford Illustrated History of World War II* (Oxford: Oxford University Press, 2015), pp. 208-209.

maximum hitting power, the same did not apply to the medium tanks which were in dire need of new and improved engines enabling them to carry a larger caliber gun. As far the medium tanks go, the main weapon of an armoured division, the dialectical relationship failed miserably. The M 15/42 tank, for example, boasted a new 12 litre Fiat 190hp engine. It was introduced fairly late in the campaign and it was the most advanced medium tank the Italians fielded in the war. Meanwhile by that time the Allies had secured large quantities of the M4 Sherman tank which was equipped with the air-cooled Continental-produced Wright R-975 Whirlwind 9 cylinder radial gasoline engine which produced 350hp.

Technical innovation was also missing when it came to communications with the lack of radios sets in the tanks produced before mid-1941, while the commanders also lacked adequate radio sets to communicate with their subordinates. "During the winter of 1941-42 the corps command of the Ariete and Trieste Divisions had only three radio sets available, all with inadequate range. This was a problem that not even the availability of the radio and command tanks made good, for at El Alamein the Ariete division commander remarked how his own HQ had neither of them, and not even any kind of AFVs to protect itself."[20] The war diary of the *Trieste* division, for example, with regard to radio sets states: "In mid-1942 we paid attention to the dramatic problem of communicating orders from the top to the battalion heads, given the insufficiency of the equipment available. Despite the effort in this area we were not able to achieve significant improvements."[21] These were probably the two biggest obstacles to the implementation of German combined arms tactics since they were based on speed and the availability of instant two-way communication. Not surprisingly, some of Rommel's biggest complaints against the Italian tank forces were their lack of speed and their delays in receiving and executing orders.

Supply

The last factor to be considered was the supply of the Army in North Africa, a task that was almost exclusively handled by the Italian Navy and Bastico's administrative staff in Libya. Many historical works on the North African campaign have accepted without any critical re-examination Rommel's account which while giving a very accurate description of the supply needs of his army discusses the lack of sufficient supplies of all kinds and largely blames the Italians for the predicament of his troops. The transportation of supplies from Italy to North Africa was conducted in three steps: transport ships carrying equipment, provisions and soldiers would begin their journey from Italian ports, they were then unloaded in the Libyan ports and finally brought to the front by trucks. All phases were subject to potential British attacks in the form of aerial and naval (including submarine) attacks which were facilitated by the ULTRA intercept. Rommel makes several charges in 'The Rommel Papers' against treacherous officers within the Italian Navy that supposedly did all they could to sabotage the supply convoys. These charges have been in many cases accepted uncritically as true by several historians of the conflict which have overlooked both the impact of ULTRA and Rommel's own attempts to protect his legacy and furnish the most favorable interpretation of his command of the Axis forces. According to the *Regia Marina* estimates the Axis forces in North Africa necessitated 75,000 tons of supplies

---

20 Paolo Battistelli and Filippo Cappellano, *Italian Medium Tanks*, p. 39.
21 Dattilo Ciampini, 'La fanteria motorizzata tra modello ed esperienze: la Trieste in Africa settentrionale 1941-1942', *Rivista della Societa' Italiana di storia militare*, 2009, p. 163.

per month to operate in Libya/Egypt. During the campaign 896 convoys were dispatched to Libya that comprised a total of 206,402 men (of which 92% arrived) and 2,245,381 tons of supply of various kind (of which 86% arrived). Tunisia received 72,269 men while 5,468 died at sea to enemy attacks, while it received 433,601 tons of material out of a total shipped of 560,601 tons. Even in October of 1942 205,599 tons of supply arrived in North Africa during the most troubled time for the Axis troops.[22] While the British Navy and the RAF were unable to block the vast amount of supplies from reaching North Africa because the major convoys were accompanied by the battlefleet, their deliberate strategy of focusing upon sinking the petrol tankers at critical times such as in September/October 1942 was successful and became a key factor hampering the *Panzerarmee* during the Battle of El Alamein. In late 1942 losses increased because the Italian Navy had to abandon its long convoy strategy which used the battlefleet to escort the transports. During the Tunisian campaign, the Navy went back to an earlier strategy to ship piecemeal convoys to avoid detection. Despite the successes of the Royal Navy and Malta's pivotal role in the campaign, it can be argued that the *Regia Marina* shipped vast amounts of supplies and men to North Africa and through the duration of the conflict it continuously carried out its main role of keeping the sea lanes open between Italy and North Africa despite Malta and the British Navy. This was done also by using the battlefleet as escort of large scale operations which in the long run proved unsustainable because of the large amounts of fuel oil that was consumed. The war in Western Desert absorbed the vast majority of Italian armour produced during the war and 1,582 vehicles were shipped to North Africa between June 1940 and October 1942, with a further seventy vehicles shipped into Tunisia in the winter of 1942-43. After Operation Crusader, for example, *Ariete* had less than twenty-five tanks in running order, but by mid-January its tank force was back up to ninety-three medium tanks. By March 1942 *Ariete* had 101 tanks and *Littorio* had sixty-four. In May 1942 *Ariete*'s strength was further enhanced with a total of 193 tanks (123 M.13/40 and 70 M.14/41), while *Littorio* had 157 tanks (39 M.13/40, 117 M.14.41 and one M.15/42). *Trieste* had fifty-two M. 14/41 and 17 M.13/40 tanks. All units had a modicum number of self-propelled artillery units. After the capture of Tobruk, but especially after Alam Halfa the number of tanks in running order decreased markedly, but once again the Navy stepped up to deliver additional vehicles prior to El Alamein. On the eve of El Alamein *Ariete* had 117 medium tanks, seventeen *Semoventi* and fourteen command tanks, while *Littorio* had 106 medium tanks, fifteen *Semoventi* and eighteen command tanks. *Trieste* had 33 tanks and ten *semoventi*. Thus, it can be argued that whereas Italian tank production could not keep pace with the output of British tank and self-propelled factories, the Navy did readily re-supply the armoured troops at the front with the vehicles and the equipment that came out of the factories, even during high pressure times such as during the month that preceded El Alamein. The situation would have been further improved if Malta had been neutralized in mid-1942. Thus the combined arms capabilities of the armoured units was maintained for the duration of the campaign and for some specific types of equipment the volumes increased over time. The quantity of most equipment types was always an issue since the armoured divisions were never at full strength throughout the campaign and some of the most valuable weapons such as the 90mm anti-tank guns were dispatched in limited numbers because of the limitations of the war economy.

22 Jack Greene and Alessandro Massignani, *Rommel's North Africa Campaign*, p. 181.

Therefore, it can be argued that the *Regia Marina* and the North African High Command enabled a progressive evolution of the armoured forces by continually supplying with both men and equipment while the other three factors (leadership, industrial capacity and innovation) had a more uneven influence. Leadership evolved in a positive way with the consolidation under Rommel of all Axis armoured forces while industrial output and capacity and technical innovation lagged. Technological innovation saw some improvement on the margins with the introduction of self-propelled artillery, armoured cars and more anti-tank guns, but not enough equipment was produced to turn the tide. Heavy tanks remained an inspiration while medium tank production did not significantly improve upon the existing models fielded in 1940 and this aspect remained a major weakness of the Italian forces in North Africa.

Ultimately, the Italian armoured units like their counterparts in the infantry divisions faced a long and highly attritional conflict. The armoured units fought at times effectively throughout the conflict and sustained very high casualty rates. By 1943, the armoured battalions of *Littorio*, *Ariete* and *Centauro* each approximately 300 to 500 men strong – suffered the following losses: 9,542 total casualties, including 4,382 killed, 3,875 wounded, and 1,285 missing.[23] The other components of the armoured units such as the motorized *Bersaglieri* battalions, the mechanized artillery, the reconnaissance and *semoventi* units also suffered high losses. Their high contribution to the war can also be demonstrated by the high number of medals of military valor awarded to the armoured personnel.

The book can conclude with the fair and unbiased assessment of the capabilities of Italian armoured forces made by Major General F. W. von Mellenthin – a *Panzerarmee Afrika* staff officer:

> I have no sympathy with those who talk contemptuously about the Italian soldier, without pausing to consider the disadvantages under which he laboured. The armament of the Italian army was below modem requirements: the tanks were too light and very unreliable from the technical point of view and the Italian wireless [radio] sets were quite unsuited to mobile warfare and could not function on the move. During the North African campaign, Italian troops gave many proof of dash and courage; this applies particularly to those who came from the cavalry regiments.[24]

Von Mellenthin was correct in that Italian industry took far too long to improve the quality of issue equipment. In the few areas in which they succeeded, the new weapons appeared too late and in too few numbers to make a more substantial contribution. Thus, the regime, the upper echelons of the Army and industry were the primary culprits failing to prepare the Army for a major conflagration that lasted for so long. This ultimately calls into question the leadership's gamble of entering a major war with an Army that was not ready in 1940 and whose procurement plans estimated that it would only be ready by 1943.

---

23   Nicola Pignato, *Italian Armoured Vehicles of World War Two*, p. 121.
24   Ibid.

Appendix I

Rommel Communication to Axis Troops after the Tobruk Battle of Early May 1941

CORPO TEDESCO D'AFRICA

Il Comandante
Zona di Guerra, 6 Maggio 1941

E' per me un grande dovere trasmettere a tutti gli appartenenti alle Unita' italiane dipendenti dal Corpo Tedesco d'Africa il mio particolare elogio per il buon comportamento mostrato durante l'attacco alla cintura fortificata di Tobruk.

Fianco a fianco con i loro camerati tedeschi per i quali e' un onore aiutarLi nella riconquista della Cirenaica, essi hanno compiuto cose straordinarie nelle ore piu' difficili.

In combattimenti duri ed accaniti, che non hanno precedenti, sui terreni piu' difficili, si e' potuto irrompere nella cintura fortificata e tenere la posizione conquistata nonostante i ripetuti, quotidiani attacchi inglesi.

Il mio ringraziamento e il mio elogio va particolarmente ai valorosi reparti della Divisione Corazzata Ariete che, in inaudito combattimento difensivo, nella notte dal 3/5 al 4/5 hanno reso impossibile ogni avanzata al nemico ed hanno saldamente tenuto in mano i fortini conquistati il giorno precedente. E' per me' un onore ed una gioia esprimere questo riconoscimento.

E con me' saranno dello stesso parere e con la stessa volonta', tutti i camerati italiani per non lasciare nulla di intentetato nella lotta pur di battere il nemico fino al suo definitivo annientamento. Noi batteremo il nemico ovunque lo troveremo!

Prego far conoscere questo elogio a tutti i reparti della Divisione
F. TO Rommel

GERMAN AFRIKA KORPS

The Commander
Warzone, May 6, 1941

It is for me important to convey to all the members of the Italian Units fighting under the DAK my praise for the good behavior shown during the attack on the Tobruk fortified defensive belt.

Side by side with their German comrades for which it is an honor to help you in the reconquest of Cyrenaica, you have done extraordinary things in the most difficult hours. In hard and fierce fighting, which has no precedents, on the most difficult terrain, it was possible to break into the fortified belt and keep the conquered positions despite repeated, daily British attacks.

My thanks and my praise goes especially to the valiant units of the Ariete Armored Division which, in unprecedented defensive combat, on the nights from 3/5 to 4/5 have made impossible any advance to the enemy and have firmly held the fortresses conquered the previous day.

It is an honor and a joy for me to express this recognition. And with me and with the same will, all Italian comrades will be asked to leave nothing of intent in the struggle to beat the enemy until his definitive annihilation. We will beat the enemy wherever we find him! Please let this document be known to all units of the Division.

F. TO Rommel

Appendix II

Rommel Communication to Axis Troops on 21 January 1942

Il Comando del Gruppo Corazzato d'Africa
Ordine del Giorno dell'Armata
Soldati Tedeschi e Italiani!

Avete appena sostenuto duri combattimenti contro un nemico di gran lunga superiore, ma io sono certo che il Vostro spirito combattivo non e' vento meno.
    Al presente noi siamo numericamente piu' forti del nemico schierato dinanzi a noi. Per l'annientamento di questo nemico, l'Armata sferra l'attacco.
    Io, in questi giorni decisivi, mi aspetto che ogni soldato compia uno sforzo supremo. Viva l'Italia! Viva il Grande Reich Tedesco!
    Viva il nostro Führer!
    Il Comandante Rommel, Generale delle Truppe Corazzate.

* * **

Commander Panzerarmee Afrika
German and Italian Soldiers,

You have already engaged in very hard combat against a far superior enemy force, but I am sure that your combative spirit has not abated one bit.
    Right now, we are numerically stronger than the enemy deployed before us. For the annihilation of this enemy, the Army will now launch the attack.
    In these decisive days, I expect every soldier to make a supreme effort.
    Long live Italy!
    Long live the Great German Reich!
    Long live our Führer!
    Commander Rommel, General of the Armored Troops.

Appendix III

Italian Armoured Vehicle Production 1940-1945

Italian tank and armoured vehicle production was steady throughout the war but could never match up with the quantities produced by the Allies or Germany. Tank production was primarily based at Fiat's plants in Turin, while *semovente* production was based in Genoa at the Ansaldo plant.

FIAT Production:
1320 L tanks and,
100 M.11-39 tanks,
400 L.6-40 light tanks,
300 Semoventi da 47/32 and,
665 Armoured Personnel Carriers.

Ansaldo production:
710 M.13-40s plus 30 command tanks
695 M 14-40s plus 34 command tanks
220 M.15-42s plus 45 command tanks (plus 28 and 41 respectively after the Armistice, 3 September 1943)
30 90/53 self-propelled guns plus 15 command vehicles
60 M.13-40 Semoventi da 75/18
162 M.14-41 Semoventi da 75/18
103 M.15-42 Semoventi da 75/18
190 M.15-42 Semoventi da 75/18 (plus 55 after the Armistice)
61 M.15-42 Semoventi da 75/34 (plus 49 after the Armistice)
30 M 43 Semoventi da 105/23 (plus 91 produced after the Armistice)
11 M 43 Semoventi da 75/46 (all produced after the Armistice)
1 M 43 Semovente da 75/34 (plus 29 produced after the Armistice)
1 P.40 tank (plus 100 produced after the Armistice)
624 AB 40-4 1 armoured cars
200 modified L 35s (known in the Italian Army as the L 35 modified or L 38)
1 AB 43 armoured car (plus 102, including some AB 41s produced after the Armistice)
Source: Nicola Pignato, *Italian Armoured Vehicles of World War II*.

Appendix IV

Medaglia d'oro Awarded to Armoured Officers and Men

Sottotenente *Carrista* BRUNO PIETRO Died at Bir El Abd (North Africa), 3-4 November 1942: "Involved in heavy combat against preponderant enemy forces and despite being wounded, he led his crews in a fierce flanking attack."

Capitano *Carrista* CALZECCHI ONESTI ICILIO died at Got el Ualeb, Libya, 29 May 1942: "Was able to penetrate deeply into the enemy's position leading a tank attack against strong and prepared anti-tank defenses."

Maresciallo *Carrista* CHIAMENTI CARLO died at Prroni i That (Albanian-Yugoslav front), 15 April 1941: "At the head of the tank platoon and fighting with an open hatch to better identify the objectives to pursue, he was the first to move against the enemy positions with his tank sowing panic and inflicting serious losses."

Caporale *Carrista* CRACCO GIOVANNI died at Bordy (Tunisia), 11 April 1943: "During a combat action against a much larger enemy force he continued to fight in an exposed position with half of his body protruding from the turret. When his tank was hit killing the driver and injuring him severely he fired three more rounds before dying."

Additional information: Medium tank M.14/41 RE 3625 8. Compagnia/ XV Battaglione Carri/31° Reggimento Carristi – Divisione Corazzata CENTAURO

Colonnello Carrista- D'AVANZO LORENZO died at Gabz – Gdeif – Ghirba (Libya) 1 June 1940: "Commander of a celere column which sternly opposed an attack by heavy armoured forces, he improvised a defensive position comprised of infantrymen and artillerymen while under fire. Then decidedly went on the counterattack with the few remaining light tanks."

Sergente Carrista- DIANDA UMBERTO died at Alam Abu Hileiuat (North Africa) 19 November 1940: "As driver of an M.11/39 tank during a heavy combat action against a five-fold superior enemy tank force, he maneuvered his tank with great initiative and courage moving from one hot spot to another as the enemy action intensified. Led a counter that inflicted heavy enemy losses."

Capitano -DE MARTINI FRANCESCO captured in the Red Sea 1 August 1942: "A tank crew officer that evaded capture during the East Africa campaign and was able to torch an enemy supply dump prior to being captured at sea."

Sergente Tenente Carrista- FIORITTO VINCENZO died in Rome 10 September 1943: "Commander of a medium tank platoon, after having received the order to attack a powerful armoured German tank unit supported by heavy artillery, he continued to advance despite facing superior forces."

Tenente Carrista-FLORIANI MARCELLO, North Africa 1941: "Armed with the last remaining anti-tank gun while running out of ammunition and despite being surrounded and under heavy enemy fire, he refused to surrender. Rather than give up he continued to fight with hand grenades. Wounded again he continued to fight to the end."

Sergente Carrista GALAS BRUNO died in Bardia, 3 January 1941: "During an enemy assault his tank malfunctioned. He dismounted from the tank and went to try to get the engine to start again, while bullets and shells were flying all around. Back in the tank he faced a renewed enemy attack that perforated and immobilized his tank. Despite being unable to maneuver the tank he continued to fire the gun until one last shot destroyed his vehicle."

Sottotenente Carrista JERO FULVIO died in Bardia 3 January 1941: "After his unit had all of its tanks immobilized from enemy fire, he gathered a small group of carristi and led them into hand to hand combat against the enemy infantry. After being wounded several times he was killed by a burst of machine gun fire consecrating with his sacrifice the heroic traditions of the carristi d'Italia."

Tenente Carrista LOCATELLI GIUSEPPE died Alam Abu Hileiuat, 19 novembre 1940: "Led thirteen tanks against an enemy force comprised of fifty tanks supported by several artillery guns in a battle lasting over three hours. When his tank was the last one standing, he stood his ground while other troops could retreat until his death."

Sergente Maggiore Carrista MITTICA PIETRO died January 1941 in North Africa: "After the unit's tanks had been knocked out of action he led a group of carristi in a bloody hand to hand combat against the enemy. Fighting to the death he shielded the unit's Colonnello and was hit by enemy fire. His last words were "I just did my duty. My thoughts go out to our flag and our fatherland."

Tenente Carrista PASCUCCI LUIGI died Bir el Abd-Fuka, 4-5 november 1942. "Tasked with covering the retreat of the Axis units he launched his tank platoon in a violent clash against a much larger enemy tank force. His tank was the last to be destroyed after a prolonged fight." Divisione Ariete

Tenente Carrista PASSALACQUA UGO died Klisura (Greece), 26-27 January 1941: "Commander of a tank company he led it into a bitter fight against the enemy. He then drove with his tank on a risky operation into the enemy lines to salvage the crews of disabled tanks.

His tank was struck and perforated by an enemy shell that injured his crew members and took out both his legs. He returned to safety with his tank still in operating conditions and while he was being carried to the hospital he urged his carristi to stand firm and continue the fight." Divisione Centauro

Sottotenente Carrista cpl. PENTIMALLI LIVIO died Got el Ualeb, 26 May 1942 – Tobruk 21 June 1942: "Led his tank unit against the defenses of the fortress of Tobruk where on three separate operations his unit destroyed a number of enemy tanks. In the final battle he engaged a number of enemy tanks until his tank was destroyed and his crew was burned to death." Divisione Ariete.

Capitano Carrista PICCININI VITTORIO died El Alamein 25 October 1942: "He led with great courage a tank unit against overwhelming enemy force after all the senior officers had fallen. Badly burned, wounded in the neck and in the chest, he continued to lead his tank unit against the enemy until he died. Divisione Littorio.

Tenente Colonnello Carrista PRESTISIMONE PASQUALE Bir Hacheim 27 May 1942: "Commander of a battalion of M.13/40 tanks he led it in an attack against a fortified enemy position surrounded by a minefield. Once inside the enemy's defenses he urged his tanks on despite strong enemy artillery fire. After being wounded several times he finally succumbed to the enemy fire." Divisione Ariete.

Tenente Carrista SCAPUZZI LUIGI died Sicily, 10-22 July 1943 "He volunteered to be sent to the frontline with a unit of semovonti da 47/32 which he led in a bitter night fight against an overwhelming enemy force. Once all of the self-propelled guns had been destroyed or had run out of ammunition he continued to fight with a machine gun until he was gunned down by the enemy."

Capitano Carrista SECCHIAROLI GIOVANNI, died Bir Hacheim, 27 May 1942 "Machine gunner of a M.13 tank after having been wounded he continued to fire against the enemy positions. After having been hit by an anti-tank projectile he died shortly thereafter. A few minutes before he expired he had told his commander that he was glad to die for his fatherland."

Sottotenente Carrista TODESCHINI LEO died Alam Abu Hileiuat, 19 November 1940: "Fought courageously leading two tanks against at least twenty enemy tanks to cover the retreat of an Italian infantry motorized column. While attempting to bring to safety the command tank of his unit, he was hit by enemy fire while trying to tow it back."

Tenente Colonnello Carrista ZAPPALA' SALVATORE died El Duda 30 June 1942: "Commander of an M.13 battalion he led it into a very heavy clash against the enemy mechanized forces. Despite the much lighter Italian tanks he engaged the enemy long enough so that his Division could retreat to safety. He fell in battle along with eleven tanks and their crews." Divisione Littorio

Appendix V

American Assessments of Italian Weapons

Italian Self-propelled Fun-Howitzer 75/18

It has been reported that the 75/18 (caliber 75 mm., length of bore 18 calibers) gun-howitzer is mounted on a turretless M.13/40 tank chassis. The equipment is known as "Semovente" artillery. The report does not state whether it is the model 1934 or model 1935 of the 75/18 that is employed. However, the two models have identical performances, the only difference being in the carriage. Particulars of the gun are as follows:

Length of bore	18 cals.
Muzzle velocity	1,430 f.s.
Weight of shell	13.9 lbs.
Maximum range	10,300 yards
Maximum elevation	65° (model 34) 45° (model 35)
Maximum depression	10°
Maximum traverse	50°
Weight in action	1,760 lbs. (model 34) 1.1 tons (model 35)

The M.13/40 tank has so far proved to be the best of the Italian tanks and it seems more probable that the less satisfactory M.11/39 would be converted. The chassis of the two tanks are very similar.

Source: *Tactical and Technical Trends*, No. 6, 27 August 1942.

Italian 90/53 Self-propelled Gun

There has been a previous reference in *Tactical and Technical Trends* (No. 25, p. 48) to the Semovente (self-propelled) 90/53* gun. Further information on this Semovente 90/53 (3.54-inch) self-propelled AA/AT gun has been received.

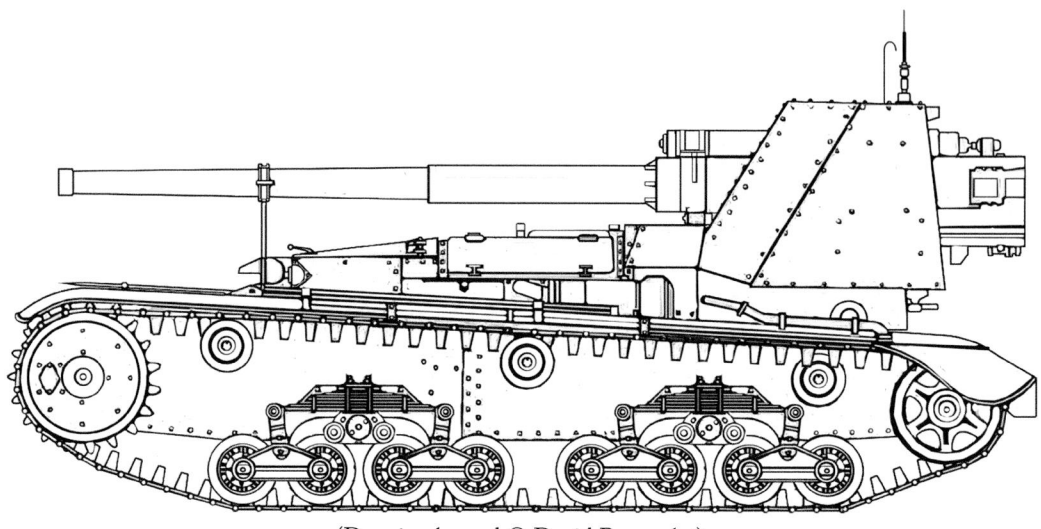

(Drawing by and © David Bocquelet)

On the basis of the present report, it appears that this gun is mounted on the rear of a turretless 14-ton, Model 14/41 tank chassis. In order to accommodate the gun, it would appear that the normal positions of the engine and transmission in the hull have been rearranged. The engine, normally in the rear, seems to have been moved forward to the center of the hull, access being provided by two doors in the superstructure roof. There is probably room for one member of the crew besides the driver in front of the engine. It would seem that the engine is overloaded, so that the vehicle is slower and less maneuverable than the M 14/41 tank. The speed probably does not exceed 12 mph. Presumably the 125-hp Diesel engine of the M 14/41 tank is retained.
*Caliber 90 mm, length of bore 53 calibers.

Source: *Tactical and Technical Trends*, No. 26, 3 June 1943.

Enemy Self-propelled Guns – A Summary of Known Equipment

f. Italian Self-Propelled Guns
(1) 75/18 Gun-Howitzer
This seemingly effective, self-propelled equipment is the chassis of the M13, mounting a 75/18 gun-howitzer (see figure 9). The turret and part of the superstructure of the tank are removed, and a new vertical front plate is fitted, as well as new side plates without the hull entrance-doors. The fighting compartment is roofed with .39-inch plate. Ready for action, the gun weighs about 11 tons. It is 16 ft. 2 in. long, 7 ft. 3 in. wide, and only 5 ft. 10 in. high, presenting a rather squat

appearance. The unusual engine is a 105-hp Gasolio, burning a mixture of gasoline and fuel oil. On the roads, the radius is about 120 miles. The cross-country radius is not stated. The armour is substantial: 1.69 inches on the gun mantlet, and two plates, 1.46 and .91 inches, forming the front vertical plate. Sides and tail plates are .98 inch. The crew is three.

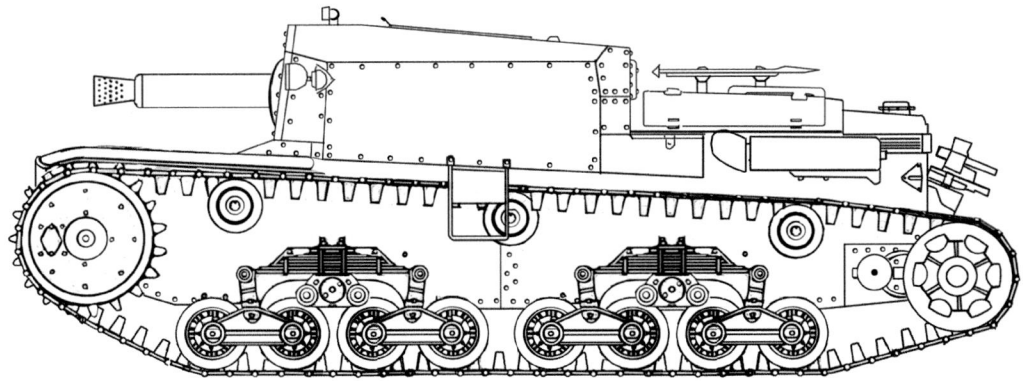

(Drawing by and © David Bocquelet)

The gun has a traverse of 45 degrees and an elevation of from 15 degrees minus to 25 degrees plus. It is an 18 caliber weapon with a maximum range of 8,350 yards. The ammunition consists of 13.9-pound HE shell, 14.1-pound AP and a 14.5-pound shrapnel. Storage for only 29 rounds is provided, but many more will certainly be carried.

(2) The 75/27 Gun, Truck-Mounted

It has been reported that there is in service a somewhat clumsy self-propelled mount comprising a 75/27 gun on the back of an unarmoured "S.P.A." truck. The standard small shield is retained and a second small shield mounted in front of it; the trail legs are shortened and clamped to the chassis. The gun fires forward over the hood of the truck.

The gun is rather better than the 75/18, with a muzzle velocity of 1,675 f/s. The elevation is from minus 15 to plus 65 degrees; the traverse is practically 60 degrees. In addition to the HE, shrapnel, and AP shell already noted, the gun fires a 13.79-pound streamlined HE, a 15.9-pound case-shot,* and a hollow-charge shell.

(3) 75/27 Antiaircraft Gun, Truck-Mounted

This is an obsolete 75/27 Krupp antiaircraft gun mounted on a Ceirano 50 C.M.A. 53-hp truck, or a Fiat 18 BL 40-hp truck. Both are four wheeled. The Ceirano truck has a radius of 150 miles on the road; the Fiat, 112. The gun has a muzzle velocity of only 1,675 f/s, with a horizontal range of 6,600 yards and vertical range of 15,200 feet. The elevation is 70 degrees, the traverse 160. A 14.5-pound, time-fuzed, HE shell is fired.

(4) 90/53 AA/AT Gun, Truck-Mounted

This is a 90/53 AA/AT gun mounted on a four-wheeled 60-hp Lancia Ro truck. It is probable that the gun can be used only against ground targets. The radius of action is about 150 miles.

A muzzle velocity of 2,756 f/s gives the 22.2-pound HE shell a range of 19,100 yards. The practical rate of fire is from 15 to 20 rpm. The elevation is from slightly below horizontal to 85 degrees, and the traverse, 360. An AP shell of unknown weight is reported to penetrate 4.41 inches of plate on a 30-degree slope at 500 yards, and 5.63 inches of plate at the vertical. At 2,000 yards, the respective penetrations are 3.15 and 4.13 inches.

(5) 90/53 AA/AT Gun on a Tank Chassis
It has been reported that the 90/53 gun is now found on a mount of entirely new design in the center of what appears to be a tank chassis, firing forward, with a 40-degree traverse. The muzzle is said to slightly overhang the front of the chassis. The chassis itself is stated to be identical with that of the earlier M 13/40 medium tank as regards suspension, armour, and appearance, but the engine is more powerful. In order to fire the gun, the tracks, apparently, have to be locked by the steering levers. Only a limited number of rounds can be carried. The crew is probably six. Whether the chassis is used for the 90/53 self-propelled gun only, or is that of an M15 tank, is at present obscure.
Source: *Tactical and Technical Trends*, No. 25, 20 May 1943.

Fiat-Ansaldo Carro Armato
P 40 Heavy Tank Specifications
Length: 5.8 m (19 feet 0.4 inch)
Width: > 2.8 m (9 feet 2.2 inches)
Height: 2.5 m (8 feet 2.4 inches)
Combat Weight: 26,430 kg (58,267 pounds)
Armour Thickness: 14 mm to 50 mm
Engine: One 330 hp SPA eight-cylinder, liquid-cooled, inline engine
Armament: One 75mm Ansaldo L/34 gun with 65 rounds and one 8mm Breda Model 38 machine gun with 576 rounds in turret.
Maximum Speed: 42 kmh (26 mph)
Maximum Range: 275 km (171 miles)
Crew: Four

Bibliography

Archival Sources

The National Archives (TNA), Kew
WO 169/1399: 3rd County of Yeomanry War Diary
WO 169/1399: 4th County of Yeomanry War Diary
WO 169/1397: 2nd Royal Gloucestershire Hussars War Diary

Bundesarchiv, Freiburg
Oberkommando des Heeres, en St D H, abt, Fremde Here West Nr. 960/39, das Italienische Krigsheer, Januar 1940, Militararchiv RHD 18/169.

Ufficio Storico dell'Esercito (Rome)
Ufficio Storico, 'Commento alle grandi manovre pronunziato da S.E. il Generale Grazioli al gran rapporto finale', Agosto 1934, Rep. L-13, Fondo Grazioli.
Ufficio Storico: 'Relazione del Comando del Corpo d'Armato Corazzato', Ufficio Stato Maggiore sulle grandi esercitazioni anno XVII.
Ufficio Storico: Diario storico della Divisione Centauro, 'Relazione dei fatti d'armi dell'offensiva dell'Epiro', 20 Novembre 1940.
Ufficio Storico: Diario storico della Divisione Centauro, 'Relazione dei fatti d'armi di Klisura', 27 Gennaio 1941.
Ufficio Storico, Carte Graziani, b. 59. Comando 10a Armata – Uff. Operazioni, 'Operazioni per la presa di Sidi Barrarni' – Relazione n. 01/8769 prot., Bardia, 20.10.1940 XVIII.
Ufficio Storico, Generale Miele, Promemoria per il Comandante Superiore, 2 Dicembre 1940, A.C.S., Carte Graziani, b. 60.
Ufficio Storico, Stato Maggiore Regio Esercito, Ufficio Addestramento, 'L'impiego delle unita' corazzate', circolare n. 18000, 1941.
Ufficio Storico, Stato Maggiore Regio Esercito, Ufficio Addestramento, 'Impiego del raggruppamento esplorante corazzato RECO', 1941.
Ufficio Storico, Diario Storico 132° Reggimento fanteria carrista, Comando VII Battaglione Carri Medi, 'Relazione sull'avvistamento, inseguimento e tiro contro camionette autoblindo', 18 Novembre 1941.
Ufficio Storico, 'Relazione Enrico Maretti sul comportamento del 132° Ariete in A.S., ' Cartella 1160, prot.1809, Novembre 1942.
Ufficio Storico, 'Fatto d'arme di Sghifet en Naama', V.E. Borsi, cartella 906 allegato 5.

Ufficio Storico, 'Relazione sui fatti d'arme dei giorni 12, 13, 14, 15 e 16 dicembre 1941 redatta dal colonnello Umberto Bordoni', 5 Gennaio 1942.
Ufficio Storico, Comando XX Corpo d'armata- Stato Maggiore 'materiale da 90/53', foglio n.2475, 2 Giugno 1942.
Ufficio Storico, 'Relazione sul fatto d'arme della Divisione Littorio dal giugno a novembre 1942', Generale Gervasio Bitossi, Novembre 1942.
Ufficio Storico, Comando divisione Fanteria Forli- Generale F. Arena, 'Considerazioni sull'impiego delle varie armi nella battaglia di El Alamein', n. 1664, 4 Aprile 1943.
Ufficio Storico, 'Relazione ufficiale del Capitano Luigi Grata', X Battaglione Carri medi, Divisione Corazzata Ariete, 7 Novembre 1942.
Ufficio Storico: Comando Divisione Centauro, 'Relazione sulla battaglia di Guettar: 16-31 Marzo, 1943', 1160/C/3/1.
Ufficio Storico, Gruppo Mobile D, 'Relazione dei fatti d'armi dei giorni 10,11, 12, e 13 luglio 1943 nella zona di Solarino', cartella 1427, allegato 59/13.
Ufficio Storico, 'Diario Storico del II Battaglione', documento firmato Maggiore Marciano', cartella X Reggimento Arditi.
Ufficio Storico, 'Relazione sui fatti d'arme dal 10 Luglio a 2 Agosto 1943', VII Corpo d'Armata, 3 Agosto 1943.
Ufficio Storico, 'Relazioni fatti d'armi della divisione Assietta 10-21 luglio 1943', Comando Divisione Assietta, 28 Luglio 1943.

Printed Sources

Massimiliano Afiero and Ralph Riccio, *The Italian Army in North Africa* (Warwick: Helion and Co., 2022).
Pietro Badoglio, *L'Italia nella seconda guerra mondiale* (Milan: Mondadori, 1946).
Correlli Barnett, *The Battle of El Alamein* (London: Macmillan, 1964).
Niall Barr, *The Pendulum of War* (London: Random House, 2010).
Pier Paolo Battistelli and Filippo Cappellano, *Italian Light Tanks: 1919-45* (Oxford: Osprey, 2017).
Pier Paolo Battistelli and Filippo Cappellano, *Italian Medium Tanks* (Oxford: Osprey, 2012).
Pier Paolo Battistelli and Piero Crociani, *Italian Soldier in North Africa: 1940-43* (Oxford: Osprey, 2013).
Pier Paolo Battistelli and Piero Crociani, *Italian Blackshirt* (Oxford: Osprey, 2016).
Paul Beale, *Death by Design* (London: Stroud, 1988).
Ian Beckett (ed.), *Rommel Reconsidered* (Mechanicsburg, Pennsylvania: Stackpole, 2013).
Giulio Bedeschi, *Fronte d'Africa: c'ero anch'io* (Milan: Mursia, 1979).
Davide Beretta, *Batterie semoventi alzo zero – Quelli di El Alamein* (Milan: Mursia, 1994).
Brian Bond, *Liddell Hart: A Study of his Military Thought* (London: Cassell, 1977).
Oreste Bovio, *In alto la bandiera. Storia del Regio Esercito* (Foggia: Bastogi Editrice Italiana, 1999).
William F. Buckingham, *Tobruk: The Great Siege* (London: Random House, 2010).
James Buckley, *British Armor in the Normandy Campaign* (London: Routledge, 2006).

Hermann Büschleb, *Operation Crusader: Tank Warfare in the Desert, Tobruk 1941* (Philadelphia: Casemate, 2019).
Daniel Allen Butler, *Field Marshal: The Life and Death of Erwin Rommel* (New York: Casemate, 2015).
Dino Campini, *Nei giardini del diavolo. La storia inedita dei carristi della Centauro, dell'Ariete e della Littorio* (Milan: Longanesi, 1969).
Emilio Canevari, *La guerra italiana, vol. I* (Rome: Studi Politici, 1948).
Filippo Cappellano and Nicola Pignato, *Andare contro i carri armati* (Gorizia, LEG, 2007).
Filippo Cappellano and Basilio Di Martino, *Un esercito forgiato nelle trincee. L'evoluzione tattica dell'esercito Italiano nella grande guerra* (Gorizia: LEG, 2008).
Michael Carver, *Tobruk* (London: B. T. Batsford LTD, 1964).
Ugo Cavallero, *Diario 1940-1943* (Rome: Ciarrapico Editore, 1984).
Lucio Ceva, *La condotta Italiana della guerra* (Milan: Feltrinelli, 1975).
Lucio Ceva, *Africa settentrionale, 1940-1943* (Roma: Bonacci, 1982).
Lucio Ceva and Andrea Curami, *La meccanizzazione dell'esercito Italiano dalle origini al 1943*, vol. I (Rome: Ufficio Storico, 1994).
Major Howard Christie, *Fallen Eagles: The Italian 10th Army in the Opening Campaign in the Western Desert* (New York: Pickle Partners, 2012).
Galeazzo Ciano, *Diary, 1937-1943 (New York: Enigma, 2002).*
Santi Corvaja, *Hitler & Mussolini: The Secret Meetings* (New York: Enigma, 2002).
Neal Dando, *From Tobruk to Tunis* (Solihull, Helion and Co., 2016).
Carlo D'Este, *Bitter Victory: The Battle for Sicily* (New York: E. P. Dutton, 1988).
Frederick Deakin, *The Brutal Friendship: Musssolini, Hitler and the Fall of Italian Fascism* (New York: Weidenfeld and Nicolson, 1962).
Paolo Caccia Dominioni (ed.), *Le Trecento ore a Nord di Qattara* (Milan: Libreria Militare, 2012).
Paolo Caccia Dominioni, *El Alamein* (London: Allen and Urwin, 1962).
Paolo Caccia Dominioni, Takfir (Milan: Mursia, 2007).
John Connell, *Auchinleck* (London: Cassell, 1957).
J. F. Cody, *21st Battalion* (Wellington: Historical Publications Branch, 1953).
Renzo De Felice, *Mussolini, il Duce, vol. III* (Turin: Einaudi, 1999).
Stefano Fabei, *Tagliamento, La legione delle camicie nere in Russia (1941-1943)* (Rome: Eribus, 2014).
Emilio Faldella, *Lo sbarco e la difesa della Sicilia* (Rome: L'Aniene, 1956).
Emilio Faldella, *L'Italia nella seconda guerra mondiale* (Bologna: Cappelli, 1967).
Albert N. Garland and Howard McGaw Smyth, *Sicily and the Surrender of Italy* (Washington DC: Center for Military History, 1993).
Oscar E. Gilbert and Romain Cansiere, *Tanks: A Century of Tank Warfare* (London: Casemate, 2017).
John Gooch (ed.), *Decisive Campaigns of the Second World War* (London: Frank Cass, 2004).
John Gooch, *Mussolini and His Generals: The Armed Forces and Fascist Foreign Policy* (Cambridge: Cambridge University Press, 2002).
John Gooch, *Mussolini's War* (New York: Pegasus, 2020).
Paddy Griffith, *World War Two Desert Tactics* (Oxford: Osprey, 2008)
Agar-Hamilton, J.A.I. & Turner, L.F.C, *The Sidi Rezegh Battles: 1941* (Cape Town: Oxford University Press, 1957).

Bryn Hammond, *El Alamein* (Oxford: Osprey, 2012).
Glyn Harper, *The Battle for North Africa: El Alamein and the Turning Point for World War II* (Bloomington: Indiana University Press, 2017).
Basil Liddell Hart, *The Tanks: The History of the Royal Tank Regiment and its Predecessors, Heavy Branch, Machine-Gun Corps, Tank Corps, and Royal Tank Corps, 1914-1945*, vol. II (New York: Praeger, 1959).
Basil Liddell Hart, *The Rommel Papers* (New York: Harcourt, Brace and Co., 1972).
Basil Liddell Hart, *History of the Second World War* (New York: GP Putnam's sons, 1970).
George Howe, *United States Army in World War II Mediterranean Theater of Operations Northwest Africa: Seizing the Initiative In the West* (Washington DC: Office of the Chief of Military History Dept. of the Army, 1957).
David Irving, *Rommel: Trail of the Fox* (London: Wordsworth Editions, 1999).
William Jackson, *The North African Campaign* (London: Batsford, 1975).
Howard Kappenberg, *Infantry Brigadier* (Oxford: Oxford University Press, 1949).
Kaufmann, Kaufmann, Potocnik, Lang, *The Maginot Line* (Barnsley: Pen & Sword Military, 2017).
Martin Kitchen, *Rommel's Desert War* (New York: Cambridge U. P., 2009).
Macgregor Knox, *Hitler's Italian Allies* (Cambridge: Cambridge University Press, 2009).
Macgregor Knox, *Mussolini Unleashed* (Cambridge; Cambridge University Press, 1999).
Franz Kurowski, *Das Afrika Korps: Erwin Rommel and the Germans in Africa, 1941-43* (Mechanicsburg, Pennsylvania: Stackpole Books, 2010).
John Latimer, *Operation Compass 1940* (Oxford: Osprey, 2000).
Jon Latimer, *Alamein* (Harvard: Harvard University Press, 2002).
Ronald Lewin, *The Life and Death of the Afrika Korps* (Barnsley: Pen and Sword, 2003).
Armando Luciano, *Guerra dei corazzati in Africa Settentrionale: Battaglie e ricordi* (Modena: Mucchi, 1982).
Salvatore Loi, *Aggredisci e vincerai. Storia della divisione motorizzata Trieste* (Milan: Mursia, 2008).
Luigi Emilio Longo, *I reparti speciali italiani nella seconda guerra mondiale* (Milan: Mursia, 1991).
Umberto De Lorenzis, *Dal primo all'ultimo giorno, ricordi di guerra 1939-45* (Milan: Longanesi, 1971).
James Lucas, *The War in the Desert* (New York: Beaufort Press, 1982).
Kenneth Macksey, *Beda Fomm: The Classic Victory* (New York: Ballantine Books, 1972).
Kenneth Macksey, *Rommel Battles and Campaigns* (London: Arms and Armour Press, 1979).
Kenneth Macksey, *Tank Versus Tank* (London: Grub Street, 1999).
Heinz Magenheimer, *Hitler's War* (London: Arms and Armor, 1999).
Giuseppe Mancinelli, *Dal fronte dell'Africa settentrionale* (Milan: Rizzoli, 1970).
Barton Maughan, *Australia in the War of 1939-1945 Vol. III: Tobruk and El Alamein* (Canberra: Australian War Memorial, 1987).
Allan R. Millet and Williamson Murray (eds.) *Military Effectiveness*, vol. 2 (Cambridge: Cambridge Univ. Press, 2020).
Samuel Mitcham, *Triumphant Fox: Erwin Rommel and the Rise of the Afrika Corps* (New York: Stein and Day, 1984).
Samuel Mitcham Jr., *Rommel's Desert War: The Life and Death of the Afrika Korps* (Mechanicsburg, Pennsylvania: Stackpole, 2007).

Mario Montanari, *L'esercito italiano nella campagna di Grecia* (Rome: Ufficio Storico, 1999.
Mario Montanari, *Le operazioni in Africa settentrionale* (Rome: Ufficio Storico, 1985), vol. I, II, III and IV.
Mario Montanari, *The Three Battles of El Alamein* (Rome: Ufficio Storico, 1991).
Philip Morgan, *The Fall of Mussolini: Italy, the Italians, and the Second World War* (Oxford: Oxford University Press, 2008).
W.E. Murphy, *The Relief of Tobruk* (Wellington: Historical Publications Branch, 1961).
George F. Nafziger, *The German Order of Battle: Panzers and Artillery in World War* II (New York: Greenhill Books, 1999).
David French, 'Fighting Power', in Richard Overy, *The Oxford Illustrated History of World War II* (Oxford: Oxford University Press, 2015).
Alpheo Pagin, *I ragazzi di Mussolini* (Milan: Mursia, 1999).
Rolando Panetta, *Il ponte di Klisura* (Milan: Mursia 1974).
C.E. Lucas Phillips, *Alamein* (Boston: Little Brown and Company, 1962).
Brian Perrett, *The Matilda* (London: Allen, 1973).
Bryan Perrett, *Iron Fist: Classic Armoured Warfare* (London: Hachette, 2012).
John Pimlott, *Rommel in His Own Words* (Oxford: Amber Books, 2018).
Nicola Pignato, *Italian Armored Vehicles World War Two* (Carrollton: Signal, 2004).
Nicola Pignato, *I mezzi blindo-corazzati italiani 1923-1943 (*Parma: Albertelli, 2007).
Nicola Pignato, *Gli Autoveicoli da combattimento dell'Esercito Italiano*, vol. 2 (Rome: Ufficio Storico, 2002).
Brian Pitt, *The Crucible of War* (London: Cassell, 2001).
I.S.O. Playfair, *The Mediterranean and the Middle East Volume 1: The early Successes Against Italy* (London: Her Majesty's Stationary Office, 1966).
I.S.O. Playfair, *The Mediterranean and the Middle East Volume 2: The Germans Come to the Help of their Ally (1941)* (London: Her Majesty's Stationary Office, 1966).
I.S.O. Playfair, *Mediterranean and Middle East, Volume 3: British Fortunes Reach Their Lowest Ebb* (London: Her Majesty's Stationary Office, 1966),
Hugh Pond, *Sicily* (London, Harper, 1962).
Andrea Rebora, *Carri Ariete combattono. Le vicende della divisione corazzata Ariete nelle lettere del tenente Pietro Ostellino. Africa settentrionale 1941-1943* (Milan: Prospettiva, 2016),
Ralph Riccio, *Italian Tanks and Fighting Vehicles of World War 2* (Aberdeen: Roadrunner, 2011).
Mario Roatta, *Otto milioni di baionette* (Rome: Mondadori, 1971).
Alberto Rovighi and Filippo Stefani, *La partecipazione italiana alla guerra civile spagnola*, vol. I (Rome: Ufficio Storico, 1993).
Andrew Sangster and Pier Paolo Battistelli, *Myths, Amnesia and Reality in Military Conflicts, 1935-1945* (Cambridge: Scholars Publishing, 2017).
Daniele Sanna, *Il caos dei comandi: L'Afrika Korps e gli italiani a El Alamein* (Milan: Mursia, 2008).
Bastian Matteo Scianna, *The Italian War on the Eastern Front 1941-1943* (London: Palgrave, 2019).
J.L. Scoullar, *Battle for Egypt: The Summer of 1942* (Wellington: Historical Publications Branch, 1967).
Emanuele Sica, *Mussolini's Army in the French Riviera* (Chicago: Univ. of Illinois Press, 2016).

Enrico Scala, *Storia delle fanterie italiane*, vol. VII (Rome: SME Ispettorato dell'Arma di Fanteria, 1954).
Enrico Serra, *Tempi duri* (Rome: Mondadori, 2010).
Andrew Stewart, *The First Victory* (New Haven: Yale University Press, 2017).
John Timothy Sweet, *Iron Arm: The Mechanization of Mussolini's Army, 1920-40* (Mechanicsburg, Pennsylvania: Stackpole, 2016).
Antonio Tomba, *Sangue e reticolati. Dal diario di un carrista dell'Ariete in Africa settentrionale* (Rome: Italia Editrice, 2008).
Oderisio Piscitelli Taeggi, *Diario di un combattente nell'Africa settentrionale* (Bari, G. Laterza & figli, 1946).
Ufficio Storico, *I bollettini del Comando supremo* (Rome: Ufficio Storico, 1984).
Ufficio Storico, *Le Operazioni del Giugno 1940 sulle alpi occidentali* (Rome: Ufficio Storico, 1994).
Ufficio Storico, *Operazioni italo-tedesche in Tunisia, 11 novembre 1942-13 maggio 1943* (Rome: Ufficio Storico, 1952).
Ufficio Storico, *Seconda offensiva brittanica in Africa settentrionale e ripiegamento italo-tedesco* (Rome: Ufficio Storico, 1949).
Ian Walker, *Iron Hulls, Iron Hearts* (Ramsbury: Crowood Press, 2003).
Roland Walker, *Alam Halfa and Alamein* (Wellington: Historical Publications Branch, 1967).
The West Point History of World War II, vol. I (New York: Simon and Schuster, 2016).
Steven Zaloga, *Kasserine Pass 1943: Rommel's last victory* (Oxford: Osprey, 2005).

Journals and Periodicals

Bruno Benvenuti, 'Regio Esercito carro armato FIAT 2000', *Storia Militare*, n.12, 1994.
Bruno Benvenuti, 'La chimera del Regio Esercito: Carro P40', *Storia Militare*, n.6, 1994.
Basilio Di Martino, 'Giulio Douhet and the Doctrine of Air Power in Italy', *Nacelles*, No. 9, Fall 2020.
Dattilo Ciampini, 'La fanteria motorizzata tra modello ed esperienze: la Trieste in Africa settentrionale 1941-1942', *Rivista della Societa' Italiana di storia* militare, 2009, pp. 151-181.
Richard Carrier, 'Some Reflections on the Fighting Power of the Italian Army in North Africa, 1940–1943', *War in History*, 2015, vol. 22, n.4, pp. 503–528.
Lucio Ceva, 'The North African Campaign 1940-43: A Reconsideration', *Journal of Strategic Studies*, vol. 13, n. 1, 1990, pp. 84-104.
Robert Citino, 'Drive to Nowhere: The Myth of the Afrika Korps', *Military History Quarterly*, summer 2012.
Ward A. Miller, 'The 9th Australian Division versus the Africa Corps: an infantry division against tanks-Tobruk, Libya, 1941', (Fort Leavenworth, Kansas: U.S. Army Command and General Staff College, 1985).
Domenico Petracarro, 'The Italian Army in Africa: An Attempt at Historical Perspective', *War and Society*, vol. 9, n. 2 (1991), pp. 103-27.
Nicola Pignato, 'La Colonna D'Avanzo', *Storia Militare*, n. 55, April, 1998.
Nicola Pignato, 'Prime esperienze italiane di guerra corazzata in Africa Settentrionale', Quaderno 1999, *Societa' Italiana di Storia Militare*.

M. Rubertini, 'La Divisione di Fanterìa Catanzaro nel secondo conflitto mondiale', *Studi storico-militari-1990*, USSME, 1993.

James J. Sadkovich, 'Some Considerations Regarding Italian Armored Doctrine Prior to June 1940', *Global War Studies*, vol. 9, n.1, 2012, pp. 40-74.

James J. Sadkovich, 'Anglo-American Bias and the Italo-Greek War of 1940-41', *The Journal of Military History*, vol. 58, n. 4, 1994, pp. 617-42.

James J. Sadkovich, 'Rebuttal to Bagnasco Q&A', *Global War Studies*, vol. 7, issue 1, 2010.

James J. Sadkovich, 'Understanding Defeat: Reappraising Italy's Role in World War II', *Journal of Contemporary History*, vol. 24, n.1, 1989, pp. 27-61.

James J. Sadkovich, Military Incompetence through Italian Eyes', *War in History*, vol. 1 no. 1, 1994, pp. 39-62.

James J. Sadkovich, 'Of Myths and Men: Rommel and the Italians in North Africa, 1940-1942', *International History Review*, vol. 13 n. 2, May 1991, pp. 286-287.

Bastian Matteo Scianna, 'Rommel Almighty? Italian Assessments of the ' Desert Fox ' during and after the Second World War', *The Journal of Military History*, vol. 82, 2018, pp. 125-146.

Brian R. Sullivan, 'The Consequences of Italian Intervention in the Spanish Civil War', Conference Paper, 2009.

'Ricordi del conduttore artigliere Tritto', *Italia Giovane*, Novara, Maggio 1943.